Intelligence Science

Intelligence Science
Leading the Age of Intelligence

ZHONGZHI SHI

Institute of Computing Technology, Chinese Academy
of Sciences, Beijing, China

Elsevier
Radarweg 29, PO Box 211, 1000 AE Amsterdam, Netherlands
The Boulevard, Langford Lane, Kidlington, Oxford OX5 1GB, United Kingdom
50 Hampshire Street, 5th Floor, Cambridge, MA 02139, United States

Notices
Knowledge and best practice in this field are constantly changing. As new research and
experience broaden our understanding, changes in research methods, professional practices,
or medical treatment may become necessary.

Practitioners and researchers must always rely on their own experience and knowledge in
evaluating and using any information, methods, compounds, or experiments described
herein. In using such information or methods they should be mindful of their own safety
and the safety of others, including parties for whom they have a professional responsibility.

To the fullest extent of the law, neither the Publisher nor the authors, contributors, or
editors, assume any liability for any injury and/or damage to persons or property as a matter
of products liability, negligence or otherwise, or from any use or operation of any methods,
products, instructions, or ideas contained in the material herein.

British Library Cataloguing-in-Publication Data
A catalogue record for this book is available from the British Library

Library of Congress Cataloging-in-Publication Data
A catalog record for this book is available from the Library of Congress

ISBN: 978-0-323-85380-4

For Information on all Elsevier publications
visit our website at https://www.elsevier.com/books-and-journals

Publisher: Glyn Jones
Editorial Project Manager: Naomi Robertson
Production Project Manager: Swapna Srinivasan
Cover Designer: Mark Rogers

Typeset by MPS Limited, Chennai, India

Working together
to grow libraries in
developing countries

www.elsevier.com • www.bookaid.org

Contents

About the author

Zhongzhi Shi, Professor at the Institute of Computing Technology, Chinese Academy of Sciences. Fellow of China Computer Federation (CCF), China Association of Artificial Intelligence (CAAI), Institute of Electrical and Electronics Engineers' senior members, Association for the Advance of Artificial Intelligence (AAAI), Association for Computing Machinery (ACM) members. His research interests mainly include intelligence science, artificial intelligence, cognitive  science, multiagent systems, machine learning, and neural computing. He has been responsible for 973, 863, key projects of National Natural Science Foundation of China (NSFC). He has been awarded various honors, such as the National Science and Technology Progress Award (2002), the Beijing Municipal Science and Technology Award (2006), the Achievement Award of Wu Wenjun Artificial Intelligence Science and Technology by CAAI (2013), the Achievement Award of Multi-Agent Systems by China Multi-Agent Systems Technical Group of Artificial Intelligence and Pattern Recognition (AIPR), CCF (2016). He has published 20 books, including *Mind Computation, Intelligent Science (in Chinese), Advanced Artificial Intelligence, Principles of Machine Learning*, and *Neural Networks,*" in addition to more than 500 academic papers. He presently serves as Editor in Chief of the *International Journal of Intelligence Science*. He served as Secretary General of the CCF, Vice Chair of the CAAI, Chair of the Machine Learning and Data Mining Group WG12.2, IFIP TC12.

Preface

Intelligence science studies the essence and realization technology of intelligence, which is a frontier interdisciplinary subject created by brain science, cognitive science, and artificial intelligence. Brain science studies the mechanism of natural intelligence at the molecular level, cell level, and behavioral level, establishes a brain model, and reveals the essence of the human brain. Cognitive science is the science that studies human perception, learning, memory, thinking, consciousness, and other brain mental activity processes. Artificial intelligence research uses artificial methods and technology to imitate, extend, and expand human intelligence and to realize machine intelligence. Intelligence science should not only carry out functional simulation but also study and explore new concepts, theories, and methods of intelligence. Intelligence research should not only use reasoning, top-down, but also learning, from the bottom to the top. Intelligence science studies the intelligent properties and behaviors of open systems by using the method of comprehensive integration.

Intelligence science is the quintessence of life science and the core of information science and technology. The forefront and commanding point of modern science and technology involve the deep mystery of natural science and touch on the basic proposition of philosophy. Therefore once a breakthrough is made in intelligence science, it will have a profound and huge impact on the national economy, social progress, and national security. At present, intelligence science is in a transformation period of methodology, the climax of theoretical innovation and the pioneering period of large-scale application, full of original opportunities.

The rise and development of intelligence science indicate that the research on human centered cognition and intelligent activities has entered a new stage. The research of intelligence science will give humans self-understanding and self-control, and increase human knowledge and intelligence to an unprecedented height. The phenomenon of life is complex, many problems have not been well explained, and the content that can be learned from it also has a great number of aspects. How to extract the most important and key problems and corresponding technologies from them is a long-term goal pursued by many scientists. In order to solve the many difficulties faced by human beings in the 21st century, such as the great demand for energy, the pollution of environment, the exhaustion of resources, and the expansion of population, it is not enough to rely on the existing scientific achievements alone. We must learn from biology and find a new way to develop science and technology. The research of intelligence science will establish the theoretical basis for the intelligent revolution, knowledge revolution, and information revolution and provide new concepts, new ideas, and new methods for the development of intelligent systems.

Since the beginning of the 21st century, great attention has been paid to intelligence science and its related disciplines, such as brain science, neuroscience, cognitive science, and artificial intelligence. On January 28, 2013, the European Union launched its flagship Human Brain Project. On April 2, 2013, the United States launched the Brain Program. In September 2014, Japanese scientists announced the Brain/MINDS (Brain Mapping by Integrated Neurotechnologies for Disease Studies) program. On July 8, 2017, the China State Council officially released the development plan for the new generation of artificial intelligence. On March 22, 2018, China established Beijing Brain Science and Brain-like Research Center. On August 7, 2018, the Shanghai Brain Science and Brain-like Research Center was established. Countries all over the world are fighting for the commanding heights of high technology, trying to hold the leading position in the new round of international scientific and technological competition.

This book systematically introduces the concepts and methods of intelligence science; absorbs the research results of brain science, cognitive science, artificial intelligence, information science, formal system, and philosophy; and comprehensively explores the nature and law of human intelligence and machine intelligence. The book consists of 14 chapters. Chapter 1, Introduction, is an introduction of the scientific background of the rise of intelligence science and research content. Chapter 2, Foundation of Neurophysiology, introduces the physiological basis of intelligence science. Chapter 3, Neural Computing, discusses the progress of neural computing. Chapter 4, Mind Model, introduces important mind models. Chapter 5, Perceptual Intelligence, discusses the theory of perception intelligence. Chapter 6, Language Cognition, explores language cognition. Chapter 7, Learning, focuses on important learning theories and methods. In as much as memory is the basis of thinking, Chapter 8, Memory, discusses the memory mechanism. Chapter 9, Thought, focuses on the form and type of thought. Chapter 10, Intelligence Development, studies the development of intelligence and cognitive structure. Chapter 11, Emotion Intelligence, discusses the theory of emotional intelligence. Chapter 12, Consciousness, explores the problems of consciousness. Chapter 13, Brain Computer Integration, discusses brain computer integration. The final chapter, Brain–Like Intelligence, summarizes research progress and the basic principles of major brain-like intelligence projects in the world and looks forward to the development of a roadmap of intelligence science.

The book can serve as a textbook for senior and graduate students in the area of intelligence science, cognitive science, cognitive informatics, and artificial intelligence in university. The book also has important reference value for scientists and researchers engaged in intelligence science, brain science, cognitive science, neuroscience, artificial intelligence, psychology, philosophy, and other fields.

Intelligence science is at the forefront of research and development in the disciplines; many of the concepts and theories are waiting to be explored.

Combined with the author's limited knowledge, the book may contain some errors. I look forward to reader's feedback.

Zhongzhi Shi

Acknowledgment

I would like to take this opportunity to thank my family, particularly my wife Zhihua Yu and my children, Jing Shi and Jun Shi, for their support in the course of writing this book. I would also like to thank my organization, Institute of Computing Technology, Chinese Academy of Sciences, for providing supportive conditions to do research on intelligence science.

In the process of writing this book, the author collaborated with Professor Marvin Minsky of MIT, Professor L.A. Zadeh of the University of California, Berkeley, Professor J.L. McClelland, Stanford University Center for Mental and Brain Computing, Professor David van Essen, University of Washington at St. Louis, Professor M. Blum at Carnegie Mellon University, and Professor J.E. Laird, P.S. Rosenbloom, T.M. Mitchell, C. Eliasmith, K. Meier, F. Baader, B. Goertzel, B. Zhang, R.Q. Lu, J.Y. Weng, and Y.X. Zhong, and others. They all played an important role in the establishment and development of the book's academic ideas. I would like to express my heartfelt thanks to these scholars and professors.

I thank my colleagues and students, including 10 postdoctors, 52 doctors, and 128 masters, for their valuable work. The book contains our research efforts granted by National Key Basic Research and Development Programs (973) "Cognitive Computing Model of Brain Computer Cooperation" (no. 2013cb329502), "Content Understanding and Semantic Representation of Unstructured Information (image)" (no. 2007cb311004); and "Big Data Mining Based on Cloud Computing" as a key project of National Natural Science Foundation of China (NSFC) (no. 61035003), "Research on Intelligent Computing Model Based on Perceptual Learning and Language Cognition" (no. 60435010); "New Theory and Method of Web Search and Mining" (no. 60933004); National High-Tech Projects (863), "Content Management, Analysis and Mining Technology and Large-Scale Demonstration Application of Massive Web Data" (no. 2012aa0011003); "Software Self-healing and Self-recovery Technology" (no. 2007aa01z132); the Knowledge Innovation Program of Chinese Academy of Sciences; and other funding and projects. The book would not possible without these financial supports.

My special thanks to Tsinghua University Press for publishing the book in Chinese over three editions since 2006. I am most grateful to the editorial staff and artists from Elsevier and Tsinghua University Press who provided all the support and help needed in the course of my writing the book.

CHAPTER 1

Introduction

Intelligence science studies the basic theory and implementation technology of intelligence, which is a frontier interdisciplinary subject created by brain science, cognitive science, artificial intelligence (AI), etc. [1]. Intelligence science is an important means to realize human level AI [2].

1.1 The Intelligence Revolution

There are three revolutions with impact in human history, the tool-making revolution, the agricultural revolution, and the industrial revolution. Accompanying these revolutions are transformations in the situation of society, the economy, and civilization. What is the next revolution? The answer is the intelligence revolution with the goal of replacing work performed by the human brain to work performed by a machine brain, which is the dream of mankind.

The Industrial Revolution was a period from the 18th to the 19th centuries where major changes in agriculture, manufacturing, mining, and transport had a profound effect on socioeconomic and cultural conditions in the United Kingdom. The changes subsequently spread throughout Europe, North America, and eventually the world. The Industrial Revolution was one of the most important events in history, extending the reach and physical power of human hands.

The history of human development is an endless pursuit. The Industrial Revolution has replaced manual human labor with machines and brought about economic and social progress. Human beings have been making unremitting efforts to make machines replace human intellectual labor.

Aristotle (384−322 BCE) proposed the first formal deductive reasoning system, syllogistic logic, in *Organon*. Francis Bacon (1561−1626) established the inductive method in *Novum Organum* (or "New Organon"). Gottfried Leibniz (1646−1716) constructed the first mechanical calculator capable of multiplication and division. He also presented the concepts of "universal symbol" and "reasoning calculation" to treat the operations of

Intelligence Science
DOI: https://doi.org/10.1016/B978-0-323-85380-4.00001-4
1

formal logic in a symbolic way, which is the germination of "machine thinking."

Since the 19th century, the advancement of sciences and technologies such as mathematical logic, automata theory, cybernetics, information theory, computer science, and psychology laid the ideological, theoretical, and material foundation for the development of AI research. In the book *An Investigation of the Laws of Thought*, George Boole (1815–1864) developed Boolean algebra, a form of symbolic logic to represent some basic rules for reasoning in thinking activities. Kurt Gödel (1906–1978) proved the incompleteness theorems. Alan Turing (1912–1954) introduced the Turing machine, a model of the ideal intelligent computer, and initiated the automata theory [3]. In 1943 Warren McCulloch (1899–1969) and Walter Pitts (1923–1969) developed the MP neuron, a pioneer work of artificial neural networks research. In 1946 John Mauchly (1907–1980) and John Eckert (1919–1995) invented the ENIAC (Electronic Numerical Integrator and Computer), the first electronic computer. In 1948 Norbert Wiener (1894–1964) published a popular book on *Cybernetics*, and Claude Shannon (1916–2001) proposed the information theory.

China has invented many intelligent tools and machines. For example, the abacus is a widely used classical computer; the hydrologic observatory is an instrument for astronomical observation and star image analysis; and the wind waiting seismograph is an instrument for earthquake prediction and display. The Yin-Yang theory put forward by Chinese ancestors contains rich philosophy and has a great influence on the development of modern logic.

In the summer of 1956, John McCarthy, a young assistant professor at Dartmouth University, Minsky at Harvard University, Shannon at Bell Labs and Rochester, the information research center of IBM, initiated a conference. They invited Newell and Simon from Carnegie Mellon University, Selfridge and Solomon from MIT, and Samuel and More from IBM. Their research majors include mathematics, psychology, neurophysiology, information theory, and computer science. They were interdisciplinary and discussed the possibility of AI from different perspectives. McCarthy first introduced the term "artificial intelligence" (AI) in the proposal for the Dartmouth summer research project on AI. He defined AI as "making a machine's response way like the intelligence on which a person acts." The Dartmouth conference marks the official birth of AI.

For more than 60 years, the heuristic search and nonmonotonic reasoning put forward by AI scholars have enriched the methods of problem solving. The research of big data, deep learning, knowledge discovery, and so on has promoted the development of the intelligent system and has achieved practical benefits. The progress of pattern recognition has enabled the computer to listen, speak, read, and see to a certain extent.

On February 14−16, 2011 Watson, the IBM AI system, defeated two "Ever Victorious generals" Jennings and Rutter in the famous American quiz show jeopardy. From March 9 to 15, 2016 AlphaGo of Google adopted deep reinforcement learning and a Monte Carlo search algorithm to beat the Korean go champion Li Shisha 4:1 [4]. These major events mark the arrival of the era of the intelligence revolution.

1.2 The rise of intelligence science

The goal of AI research is to make a computer have human-like behaviors, such as listening, talking, reading, writing, thinking, learning, and adapting to ever changing environments etc. In 1977 E. Feigenbaum, a young scholar of Stanford University and graduate student of Simon put forward the concept of knowledge engineering in the 5th International Joint Conference on Artificial Intelligence (IJCAI1977), which marked the transition from traditional reasoning to knowledge-centered research in AI research [5].

Knowledge is a nation's wealth, and the information industry is vital for a country's development. The fifth-generation computer—intelligent computer symposium was held in Tokyo Japan in October of 1981. Professor Moto-Oka Tohru from Tokyo University proposed "the Fifth-Generation Computer System: FGCS" [6]. After that, Japan made an ambitious plan to develop fifth-generation computers in 10 years. In the summer of 1982, Japan established "the new generation of computer technology institute" (ICOT) headed by Fuchi Kazuhiro. The Japan Ministry of International Trade and Industry fully supported the plan, and the total investment budget reached $430 million. Eight large enterprises, including Fujitsu, NEC, Hitachi, Toshiba, Panasonic, and Sharp, were invited to this project.

It took almost 10 years on the project for ICOT colleagues, who had no time for normal lives and spent all their time shuttling between the lab and their apartments. However, the outcome of the FGCS was somehow tragic. Its failure in 1992 might come from the bottleneck of key technologies such as human-machine dialog and program automatic proving. After that, Professor Fuchi Kazuhiro had to return to his university.

Also, it is said that the FGCS is not a total failure, in that it achieved some expected goals in the first two phases. In June 1992, ICOT demonstrated the prototype of FGCS with 64 processors for parallel processing, which had similar functions of the human left brain and could perform advanced precision analysis on proteins.

The failure of FGCS pushed people to find a new avenues for research on intelligence. Intelligence requires not only function simulation but also mechanism simulation. Intelligence requires not only top–down reasoning also bottom–up learning as well, which may be finally combined to achieve human level Intelligence. The perceiving components of the brain, including visual and auditory, movement, and language cortex regions, not only play the role of input/output channels but also contribute to thinking activities directly.

In 1991 a special issue on the foundation of AI was published in *Journal of Artificial Intelligence* (Vol. 47) to point out some trends in AI research. D. Kirsh proposed five foundational problems in AI [7]:

1. *Preeminence of knowledge and conceptualization*: Intelligence that transcends insect-level intelligence requires declarative knowledge and some form of reasoning-like computation—called cognition. Core Al is the study of the conceptualizations of the world presupposed and used by intelligent systems during cognition.
2. *Disembodiment*: Cognition and the knowledge it presupposes can be studied largely in abstraction from the details of perception and motor control.
3. *Kinematics of cognition are language-like*: It is possible to describe the trajectory of knowledge states or informational states created during cognition using a vocabulary very much like English or some regimented logic-mathematical version of English.
4. *Learning can be added later*: The kinematics of cognition and the domain knowledge needed for cognition can be studied separately from the study of concept learning, psychological development, and evolutionary change.
5. *Uniform architecture*: There is a single architecture underlying virtually all cognition.

All these questions are cognitive problems critical to AI research, which should be discussed from the perspective of fundamental theories of cognitive science. These questions have become the watershed for different academic schools of AI research, as these schools usually have different answers to them.

In December 2001, the National Science Foundation and the Department of Commerce of the United States in Washington organized experts and scholars from government departments, scientific research institutions, universities, and industry to discuss the issue of converging technologies to improve human performance. Based on the papers and conclusions submitted by the conference, in June 2002, the National Science Foundation and the U.S. Department of Commerce jointly put forward a meeting technical report. According to the report, nanotechnology, biology, informatics, and cognitive science (NBIC) are developing rapidly at present. The organic combination and integration of these four sciences and related technologies form convergence technology, abbreviated as NBIC.

In the 21st century, with the development of convergence technology, the combination of life science and information technology has given birth to interdisciplinary intelligent science. In 2002 the Intelligence Science Laboratory of Institute of Computing Technology, Chinese Academy of Sciences established the world's first Intelligence Science Website: http://www.intsci.ac.cn/.

In 2003 Zhongzhi Shi published the paper entitled "Perspectives on Intelligence Science" [1]. This article proposed *intelligence science* as the study of the fundamental theory and technology of intelligence, creating the interdisciplinary subject of brain science, cognitive science, and AI. Brain science studies the intelligence mechanism of the brain, establishes the model of the brain, and reveals the essence of the human brain from the molecular level, cell level, and behavioral level. Cognitive science studies perception, learning, memory, thinking, and awareness of humans. AI studies simulations, extensions, and expansions of human intelligence using artificial methods and techniques to realize machine intelligence. The three disciplines work together to study and explore new conceptions, new methods, and new theories of intelligence science, ultimately to create a brilliant future in the 21st century.

1.2.1 Brain science

The human brain is the most complicated system in the known universe. It is formed by a huge quantity of neurons and synapses. Both the neurons and synapses are highly complicated, highly multifarious, and highly complete electronic-chemical apparatuses. The beauty of thinking resides in the complexity of the brain. The research in neural science has revealed that a simple nervous system may have amazing complexity, which reflects its function, evolution history, structure, and encoding scheme. The human brain is a complex system that is able to perform study and work on itself.

Brain science is a large area in science consisting of various brain-researching disciplines. It studies the structure and functions of the brain, as well as the relations between the brain and human behavior and thinking. Brain science also explores brain evolution, its biological components, neural networks, and corresponding mechanisms. Human recognition on the brain has taken a long time and has progressed from the superficial to the profound. This history can be divided into three phases according to research levels.

The first phase may be called the precursor period. In this period, humans gradually realized that the brain is the organ for thinking and had a superficial understanding of its structures. During the 5th to 7th centuries BCE, people in China had realized the association between the brain and thinking.

The brain was deeply studied in Ancient Greece. Pythagoras and Plato both held that the brain produces senses and wisdom. Democritus thought that the brain produces atoms, which in turn produces activities of the soul. Hippocrates affirmed that the brain was the thinking organ with an anatomical approach. Erasistratus from the Alexander school studied structures of brains using the same approach. Herophilus distinguished the cerebellums and cortexes. Galen, an ancient Greek doctor, further discovered the internal structures of brains, such as the corpus callosum and pineal gland, and he put forward the theory that the left brain is responsible for feeling and the right brain for movement.

The second phase is the mechanical period. Major progress came with the establishment of reflexology and positioning theories. The Middle Ages witnessed little progress in research on the anatomical brain. With the development of modern sciences, research on brain developed rapidly. In the 18th century, Hubble, a Swiss physiologist, found that brains transmit stimulation using nerves. René Descartes put forward the brain's reflexology theory and the dualism theory in which spirit and brains interacted with each other. Russian scholar N. M. Pavlov perfected the brain's reflexology theory. In the 19th century, Austrian physician F. J. Gall established the positioning theory initially, which later became cranioscopy science. French doctor Paul Broca discovered the Broca's area by dissecting the brains of aphasia patients, which marked the scientific foundation of positioning theory. The study of the brain in this period has some traits of Mechanism.

The third phase is the modern period. In this period, the brain was studied from multilevels, multilayers, and multiviews, including not only global study but also partial study; not only systemic study but also study at the neuron, cell, and molecular levels; not only study on from the physical, chemical, psychological perspectives but also comprehensive research.

Computational neuroscience is the stimulation and study of nervous systems using mathematical analysis and computer simulation methods from the real creature physical models of neurons at the different levels, their dynamic interactions, and the structural learning of neural networks in order to develop a quantitative computational theory of brain tissue and nervous tissue from studying the nonprogrammatic, adaptive, and brain-like nature and potentials of information processing, to explore new information processing mechanisms, finally to create artificial brains.

The study of computational neuroscience has a long history. In 1875 Italian anatomist C. Golgi first identified individual nerve cells using a dyeing method. In 1889 R. Cajal founded the neuron theory, according to which nervous systems are built with independent nerve cells. Based on this theory, in 1906, C. S. Sherrington put forward the notion of synapses between neurons [8]. In the 1920s, E. D. Adrian proposed nerve action potentials. In 1943 W. S. McCulloch and W. Pitts put forward the M-P neural network model [9]. In 1949 D. O. Hebb put forward the rules for neural network learning [10]. In 1952 the Hodgkin-Huxley model was proposed by A. L. Hodgkin and A. F. Huxley, which describes the changes in the current and voltage of cells [11]. In the 1950s, F. Rosenblatt proposed a perception machine model [12].

Neural computation has made great progress since the 1980s. J. J. Hopfield introduced the Lyapunov function (also called calculated energy function) and proposed the criterion of network stability for associative memory and optimization calculation [13]. Amari did various works on the mathematical theory of neuron networks including statistical neural dynamics, dynamics theory of the neuron field, associative memory, and particularly fundamental works in information geometry [14]. Research on computational neuroscience involves the following characteristics of the brain: (1) The cerebral cortex is a grand and complex system with extensive connections. (2) The computation in the brain is based on large-scale parallel simulation processing. (3) The brain is strongly "error tolerant" and is skilled in association, generalization, and analogy. (4) The function of the brain is restricted not only by an innate factor but by acquired dispositions as well, such as experience, learning, and training. This shows that the brain is self-organized and adaptive to environments. Many human intelligence activities are controlled not by logical reasoning but by training.

The Blue Brain Project initiated by H. Markram of the Federal University of technology in Lausanne, Switzerland, has been implemented since 2005 [15]. After 10 years of effort, the computation and simulation of cortical functional columns in specific brain regions were completed. But overall, there is a big gap to be crossed in order to simulate cognitive function. In 2013 H. Markram conceived and led the planning of the Human Brain Project (HBP) of the European Union, which was selected as the flagship technology project in the future of the European Union and which won the financial support of €1 billion, becoming the most important human brain research project in the world. The goal of this project is to use supercomputers to simulate human brain, to study the working mechanism of human brain and the treatment of brain diseases in the future, and to promote the development of brain-like AI. The scientists involved come from 87 research institutions in EU Member States.

The United States proposed "Brain Research Through Advancing Innovative Neurologies (BRAIN)," The U.S. brain program focuses on the research and development of new brain research technologies in order to reveal the working principles of the brain and the mechanism of major brain diseases. Its goal is not only to lead the frontier scientific development but also to promote the development of related high-tech industries, like the human genome program. An additional $4.5 billion will be invested over the next 10 years. The brain program puts forward nine priority areas and goals: identifying neural cell types and reaching consensus; mapping brain structure; developing new large-scale neural network electrical activity recording technology; developing a set of tools for regulating neural circuit electrical activity; establishing the relationship between neural electrical activity and behavior; integrating theory, model, and statistical method; solving the basic mechanism of human brain imaging technology; establishes the mechanism of human brain data collection; the dissemination of brain science knowledge and personnel training.

The China Brain Project takes the neural basis of understanding the cognitive function of the brain as the research subject, treats brain-like intelligence technology and the diagnosis and treatment methods for major brain diseases as two wings, as shown in Fig. 1.1 [16].

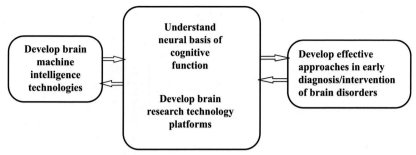

Figure 1.1 Schematic diagram of China Brain Project.

1.2.2 Cognitive science

Cognition is the process and activity of the brain and nervous system to produce mind. Cognitive science is a science that takes the cognitive process and its laws as the research object to explore how human intelligence is generated by matter and how human brain processes information [17]. Specifically, cognitive science is the frontier science to study the essence and law of human cognition and intelligence. The scope of cognitive science research includes cognitive activities at all levels, including perception, attention, memory, behavior, language, reasoning, thinking, consciousness, and emotion. Integrating philosophy, psychology, linguistics, anthropology, computer science, and neuroscience and studying how information is transmitted in the process of cognition constitute the basis of cognitive science.

In recent decades, the theory of complex behavior has three main schools: new behaviorism, Gestalt psychology, and cognitive psychology. All schools of psychology want to better understand how the human body works. They study behavior from different aspects and emphasize different points in their methodologies. New behaviorism emphasizes objective experimental methods and requires the strict control of experiments. Gestalt psychology believes that all forms and attributes are not equal to the sum of all parts. Cognitive, which incorporates the beneficial results of behaviorism and Gestalt psychology, psychology uses information processing to explain people's complex behaviors. Cognitive psychology also believes that complex phenomena can be studied only by breaking them down into the most basic parts.

In the 1990s, cognitive science ushered in a new era of prosperity and development. With the emergence of brain imaging technology, cognitive scientists could observe the activities of different brain regions as people complete various cognitive tasks. Cognitive neuroscience has become one of the most active fields in cognitive science. Emotions, feelings, and consciousness, which were regarded as taboo in the past, have become the hot topics of cognitive science research. The research object of cognitive science is no longer limited to cognitive activities in the narrow sense, such as perception, memory, language, reasoning, and learning, but tries to cover all aspects of the mind. Not only is the mind closely related to the structure and activity of the brain, but also the body is its important physical basis. Embodiment (involving the body) has become one of the key factors in understanding the mystery of the mind. Not only that, the boundary of mind is extended beyond the body, and the material environment and social environment become its inseparable components, which is the basic proposition of extending cognition and extending mind. The theory of a dynamic system strongly questions the theoretical basis of mainstream cognitive science, namely psychological representation and calculation, and advocates the use of differential equations and concepts such as phase change, attractor, and chaos to depict and understand the nature of mind. From the perspective of evolution and adaptation, the formation and development of human cognitive ability, as well as the study of the cognitive ability of other animal species, has become an important subject of cognitive science research in this period.

The development of cognitive science is highly valued and supported within international scientific and technological circles, especially the governments of developed countries. Cognitive science research is the focus of the International Human Frontier Science program. Cognitive science and its information processing research are listed as one of the three major parts of the supporting technology (the other two parts are material and energy conversion). Perception and cognition, movement and behavior, memory and learning, and language and thinking are listed as four of the 12 major focus issues of Human Frontier Science. In recent years, the United States and the European Union have launched the Ten-Year Plan of Brain and the Human Brain Project (HBP) comes up for EU respectively. Japan has launched an ambitious Brain Science Era plan with a total budget of US$20 billion. In the plan of Brain Science Era, research on cognitive function and information processing by the brain is the most important. All levels and aspects of human cognitive and intelligent activities, including perception, attention, memory, behaviors, language, reasoning and thinking, consciousness, and even emotion, have been included in the focus of the study; the combination of cognitive science and information science to study new computers and intelligent systems has also been listed as one of the three aspects of the plan.

A. M. Turing Award winner A. Newell explores cognitive architecture with cognitive psychology as the core. So far, the cognitive models State, Operator And Result (SOAR) and Adaptive Control of Thought—Rational (ACT-R), which are widely used in the field of cognitive psychology and AI, have been developed under the direct leadership of A. Newell or inspired by him, and they have enabled the modeling of various cognitive functions of human beings. D. Marr not only is a pioneer of computer vision but has also laid the computational foundation for memory, processing, and transmission of information among neuron groups, making an especially important contribution to the neural computational modeling of learning and memory, visual neural circles.

1.2.3 Artificial intelligence

AI is intended to make machines recognize, think, and learn like human beings, to imitate, extend, and expand human intelligence, and to realize machine intelligence through artificial methods and technologies [2]. Since the birth of AI in 1956, it has experienced hardships and frustrations and has made remarkable achievements. In the past 60 years or more, the development of AI has experienced periods of formation, symbolic intelligence, and data intelligence.

1.2.3.1 The formation period of artificial intelligence (1956–1976)
The formation period of AI runs from about 1956 to 1976. The main contributions of this period are:
1. In 1956 A. Newell and H. A. Simon's "logic theorist" program simulated the thinking law of people when they use mathematical logic to prove theorems.
2. In 1958 J. McCarthy put forward the table processing language LISP, which can process not only data but also symbols conveniently. It has become an important milestone of AI programming language. At present, LISP is still an important programming language and development tool of AI system.
3. In 1965 J. A. Robinson proposed the resolution method, which is a breakthrough, and brought about another climax to the study of theorem proving.
4. In 1968 E. A. Feigenbaum and chemist J. Lederberg successfully developed the expert system of chemical analysis, DENDRAL. From 1972 to 1976, Buchanan and Feigenbaum successfully developed the medical expert system MYCIN.

1.2.3.2 Symbolic intelligence period (1976–2006)

In 1975 H. A. Simon and A. Newell won the Turing Award, the highest award in computer science. In 1976 they put forward the physical symbol system hypothesis in his award-winning lecture and became the founder and representative of the most influential semiotics in AI [18].

In 1977 E. A. Feigenbaum, a computer scientist at Stanford University, proposed a new concept of knowledge engineering at the Fifth International AI Joint Conference [5]. In the 1980s, the development of expert systems tends to be commercialized, creating huge economic benefits. Knowledge engineering is a subject that takes knowledge as the research object. It converts research on AI from theory to application, from a reasoning model to a knowledge model, making AI research practical.

In 1981 Japan announced the development plan of the fifth generation of electronic computers. The main characteristics of the developed computer were intelligent interface, knowledge base management, automatic problem-solving ability, and human intelligent behavior in other aspects.

In 1984 L. Valiant put forward the theory of learnability after combining foresight in the field of computational science and mathematics and cognitive theory with other technologies, which ushered in a new era of machine learning and communication [19].

In 2000 J. Pearl put forward the probability and causality reasoning algorithm, which completely changed the direction of AI based on rules and logic [20]. In 2011 J. Pearl won the Turing Award for his basic contribution to AI. In 2018 Pearl and D. Mackenzie published *The Book of Why: The New Science of Cause and Effect* [21]. In this book, Pearl argues that the exact causal relationship between all variables should be explicitly symbolized in graphical form and that only then can mathematical operations tease out the precise causal effect.

1.2.3.3 Data intelligence period (2006-present)

Data is an important resource of intelligence. Scientific discovery is very creative work. From 1978 to 1983, six versions of BACON were published successively by the Simon team, and more than 10 important laws of physics and chemistry in the history of science, such as Kepler's third law of planetary motion, Boyle's law, Galileo's law of simple pendulum, ideal gas law, etc. have been rediscovered [22].

In 2006 G. Hinton and others published the deep belief network, creating a new stage of deep learning [23]. An article "The Era of Big Data Has

Come," published on the website of *The New York Times* on February 21, 2012, affected every area of AI study.

In 2016 AlphaGo adopted deep reinforcement learning to beat Li Shisha, one of the best human go players, to promote the development and popularization of AI.

In 2018 the Turing Award was given to G. Hinton, Yann Lecun, and Y. Bengio, for creating a deep neural network and laying a foundation for the development and applications of deep learning.

We should learn from the human brain and study the methods and algorithms of the brain's information processing. No longer is the human brain's information processing based only on guesswork, but the working mechanism of the brain is obtained through interdisciplinary and experimental research. Thus inspired by the brain's information processing mechanism, learning from the brain's neural mechanism and cognitive behavior mechanism in order to develop intelligence science has become a research hotspot in the field of AI and information science in recent years. Intelligence science is in the ascendancy, leading to the rapid development of AI and intelligent technology.

1.3 Ten big issues of intelligence science

In July 2005 coinciding with the 125th anniversary of its founding, the famous international journal *Science* put forward 125 natural questions in the field of science in this century. Among them, the 25 most important questions are as follows: What is the biological basis of consciousness? How is memory stored and extracted? How can skin cells become nerve cells? How does cooperative behavior evolve? What are the limits of computers? Among the remaining questions raised are: Why does language learning have a critical period? What causes schizophrenia? To what extent can we overcome Alzheimer's disease? What is the biological basis of addiction? Is it ethical to implant hardware into the human brain? What is the limit of machine learning? These problems are related to key scientific problems in the field of intelligence science, and the exploration and solution of each problem call for the intersection of multiple disciplines.

A. Turing was a rare genius with extraordinary insight in the history of science in the world. The Turing machine theory model proposed in 1936 took the brain as the prototype system and mental model. It is of great interest that later cognitive science took the computer as the prototype of brain and that the two drew lessons from each other and developed independently. June 23, 2012, marked the 100th anniversary of the birth of British mathematician Turing. To pay homage to Turing, *Nature* suggested that the year of Turing's centenary, 2012, be named the Year of Intelligence in memory of the scientific prophet.

At present, the research of intelligence science is not enough. What we are facing is a new field full of unknowns. We must make a deep exploration of the fundamental principles and computational theory. The following 10 big issues of intelligence science are now viewed as main research themes [17].

1.3.1 Working mechanism of brain neural network

The brain is a collection of about 10 billion interconnected neurons. Neurons are electrically excitable cells in the nervous system that process and transmit information. A neuron's dendritic tree is connected to a thousand neighboring neurons. When one of those neurons fire, a positive or negative charge is received by one of the dendrites. The strengths of all the received charges are added together through the processes of spatial and temporal summation. The aggregate input is then passed to the soma (cell body). The soma and the enclosed nucleus do not play a significant role in the processing of incoming and outgoing data. Their primary function is to perform the continuous maintenance required to keep the neuron functional. The output strength is unaffected by the many divisions in the axon; it reaches each terminal button with the same intensity it had at the axon hillock.

Each terminal button is connected to other neurons across a small gap called a synapse. The physical and neurochemical characteristics of each synapse determine the strength and polarity of the new input signal. This is where the brain is the most flexible—and the most vulnerable. At the molecular level, neuron signal generation and transmission and neurotransmitters are the basic problems attracting research scientists to engage in brain science investigation.

One of the greatest challenges in neuroscience is to determine how synaptic plasticity and learning and memory are linked. Two broad classes of models of synaptic plasticity are phenomenological models and biophysical models. Phenomenological models are characterized by treating the process governing synaptic plasticity as a black box. The black box takes in as input a set of variables and produces as output a change in synaptic efficacy. No explicit modeling of the biochemistry and physiology leading to synaptic plasticity is implemented. Two different classes of phenomenological models, rate based and spike based, have been proposed.

Biophysical models, in contrast to phenomenological models, concentrate on modeling the biochemical and physiological processes that lead to the induction and expression of synaptic plasticity. However, since it is not possible to implement precisely every portion of the physiological and biochemical networks leading to synaptic plasticity, even biophysical models rely on many simplifications and abstractions. Different cortical regions, such as the hippocampus and visual cortex, have somewhat different forms of synaptic plasticity.

1.3.2 Mind modeling

Mind is a very important issue and a tough problem in intelligence science. Mind can be defined, as it is on the Medical Dictionary website, as "that which thinks, reasons, perceives, wills, and feels. The mind now appears in no way separate from the brain. In neuroscience, there is no duality between the mind and body. They are one." A mind model is intended to be an explanation of how some aspect of cognition is accomplished by a set of primitive computational processes. A model performs a specific cognitive task or class of tasks and produces behavior that constitutes a set of predictions that can be compared to data from human performance. Task domains that have received considerable attention include problem solving, language comprehension, memory tasks, and human–device interaction.

Researchers try to construct mind models to illustrate how brains work. In the early 1980s, SOAR was developed to be a system that could support multiple problem-solving methods for many different problems [24]. In the mid-1980s, Newell and many of his students began working on SOAR as a candidate of unified theories of cognition. SOAR is a learning architecture that has been applied to domains ranging from rapid, immediate tasks such as typing and video game interaction to long stretches of problem-solving behavior. SOAR has also served as the foundation for a detailed theory of sentence processing, which models both the rapid online effects of semantics and context, as well as subtle effects of syntactic structure on processing difficulty across several typologically distinct languages.

Anderson and colleagues have demonstrated that a production rule analysis of cognitive skill, along with the learning mechanisms posited in the ACT model, provides detailed and explanatory accounts of a range of regularities in cognitive skill acquisition in complex domains such as learning to program LISP [25]. ACT also provides accounts of many phenomena surrounding the recognition and recall of verbal material and regularities in problem-solving strategies.

Such mind models are constructed in terms of production systems. The author proposes a novel mind model called Consciousness And Memory (CAM), which is cast in terms of CAM functions [26].

1.3.3 Perceptual representation and intelligence

The perceptual system contains primarily visual, auditory, and kinesthetic input, that is, pictures, sounds, and feelings. There is also olfactorial and gustatorial input, that is, smells and tastes. Perceptual representation is a modeling approach that highlights the constructive, or generative, function of perception, or how perceptual processes construct a complete volumetric spatial world, complete with a copy of our own body at the center of that world. The representational strategy used by the brain is an analogical one; that is, objects and surfaces are represented in the brain not by an abstract symbolic code or in the activation of individual cells or groups of cells representing features detected in the visual field. Instead, objects are represented in the brain by constructing full spatial effigies of them that appear to us for all the world like the objects themselves, or at least so it seems to us only because we have never seen those objects in their raw form but only through our perceptual representations of them.

Perceptual intelligence refers to the ability to interact with the environment through various sensory organs, such as vision, hearing, touch, etc. The visual system gives the organism the ability of visual perception. The auditory system gives the organism the ability of auditory perception. Using the research results of big data and deep learning, the machine has gotten closer and closer to the human level in perception intelligence.

1.3.4 Linguistic cognition

Language is fundamentally a means for social communication. Language is also often held to be the mirror of the mind. Chomsky developed transformational grammar by which cognitivism replaced behaviorism in linguistics [27].

Through language we organize our sensory experience and express our thoughts, feelings, and expectations. Language is interesting from a cognitive informatics point of view because its specific and localized organization enables exploration of the functional architecture of the dominant hemisphere of the brain.

Recent studies of the human brain show that the written word is transferred from the retina to the lateral geniculate nucleus and from there to the primary visual cortex. The information then travels to a higher-order center, where it is conveyed first to the angular gyrus of the parietal-temporal-occipital association cortex, and then to Wernicke's area, where the visual information is transformed into a phonetic representation of the word. For the spoken word, the auditory information is processed by the primary auditory cortex. Then the information is input to the higher-order auditory cortex before it is conveyed to a specific region of the parietal-temporal-occipital association cortex, the angular gyrus, which is concerned with the association of incoming auditory, visual, and tactile information. From here the information is projected to Wernicke's area and Broca's area. In Broca's area, the perception of language is translated into the grammatical structure of a phrase, and the memory for word articulation is stored [28].

1.3.5 Learning ability

Learning is the basic cognitive activity and the accumulation procedure of experience and knowledge. Through learning, system performance is improved. The basic mechanism of learning is to try to transfer successful performance behavior to another similar new situation. People's cognitive ability and intelligent ability are gradually formed, developed, and improved in their lifelong learning. Any intelligent system must have the ability to learn. Learning ability is the method and skill of learning and the basic characteristic of human intelligence.

Over the past 100 years, psychologists have naturally formed various theoretical views and schools, including the behavioral school, cognitive school, and humanistic school, due to their different philosophical bases, theoretical backgrounds, and research methods.

In March 2016, Google's AlphaGo combined the deep neural network with the Monte Carlo tree search and beat the go world champion Lee Shisha of South Korea 4−1.

The computer may have defeated the world go champion and AI has made great progress, but there is a big difference in machine intelligence compared with the human level. It is necessary to combine machine learning with brain cognition to develop cognitive machine learning so that machines can have human-level intelligence [17].

1.3.6 Encoding and retrieval of memory

Memory is the encoding, consolidation, and retrieval process of information. Understanding memory is the key to understanding human cognition and behavior. A brain has a distributed memory system; that is, each part of brain has several types of memories that work in somewhat different ways, to suit various purposes. According to the stored time of the contents, memory can be divided into long-term memory, short-term memory, and working memory. Current working memory attracts more researchersmore than the other two types.

Working memory provides temporal space and enough information for complex tasks, such as understanding speech, learning, reasoning, and attention. There are memory and reasoning functions in the working memory. In 1974 Baddeley and Hatch proposed a model of working memory based on an experiment consisting of three components: central nervous performance system, video space primary processing, and phonetic circuit [29]. Many behavioral studies and much neuropsychological evidence show that working memory is closely related to language comprehension, attention, and reasoning. Working memory contains the mystery of intelligence.

Eric Kandel first clarified the changes of synaptic function related to memory and the molecular mechanism involved in short-term and long-term memory through the phosphorylation of second messengers and proteins. In 2000 Eric Kandel shared the Nobel Prize in physiology or medicine together with his good friends, Paul Greengard and Alvey De Carlson.

The neocortex plays an important role in the mammalian brain for intelligent thinking. In 2004 Hawkins proposed hierarchical temporal memory, which provides a theoretical framework for understanding neocortex and its function [30].

1.3.7 Thought

Thinking is the conscious, indirect, and general reflection of the nature and internal regularity of objective reality by the human brain's consciousness, which is manifested by implicit or explicit language or action [31]. In recent years, there has been a noteworthy shift of interest in cognitive science. The cognitive process raises a human's sense perceptions and impressions to logical knowledge. According to the abstraction degree of the cognitive process, human thought can be divided into three levels:

perception thought, image thought, and abstraction thought. A hierarchical model of thought that illustrates the characteristics and correlations of thought levels has been proposed [32].

In 2011 the Turing Award was given to Pearl for his "foundational contribution to AI through probability of development and causal reasoning—a breakthrough echoed in his 2018 book, coauthored with D. Mackenzie [21]. According to Pearl, existing machine learning models had made great progress; unfortunately, all models are only accurate at the curve fitting of data. Pearl argued that we needed a "cause and effect revolution." Researchers should consider using the causal inference model to study from the perspective of causality rather than simple data.

1.3.8 Intelligence development

Intelligence development refers to the regular change of individual intelligence with aging under the influence of social living conditions and education. Intelligence development is an important part of overall psychological development. From birth to maturity, the development of children's intelligence is a continuous process that occurs in a certain order. The order of development is certain, but the development speed of each development stage is not the same. J. Piaget believes that intelligence has a structural basis, and the schema is a particularly important concept used to describe the cognitive structure.

Piaget's new intelligence development theory basically gave up the theory of operation structure and replaced it with the theory of morphism category. The development series of traditional preoperation, concrete operation, and formal operation has become the development series of intramorphic, intermorphic, extramorphic.

In intelligence science, cognitive structure refers to the organizational form and operation mode of cognitive activities, including a series of operation processes such as the components in cognitive activities and the interaction between components, namely the mechanism of psychological activities. Cognitive structure theory takes cognitive structure as the research core, emphasizing the nature of cognitive structure construction and the interaction between cognitive structure and learning. Throughout the theoretical development of cognitive structure, there are mainly Piaget's schema theory, Gestalt's insight theory, Tolman's cognitive map theory, Bruner's classification theory, Ausubel's cognitive assimilation theory, and so on.

1.3.9 Emotion

Emotion is a complex psychophysical process that arises spontaneously, rather than through conscious effort, and evokes either a positive or negative psychological response and physical expression. Research on emotion is conducted at varying levels of abstraction, using different computational methods, addressing different emotional phenomena, and basing their models on different theories of affect.

Since the early 1990s, emotional intelligence has been systematically studied [33]. Scientific articles have suggested that there exists an unrecognized but important human mental ability to reason about emotions and to use emotions to enhance thought. Emotional intelligence refers to an ability to recognize the meanings of emotion and their relationships and to reason and problem-solve based on them. Emotional intelligence involves in the capacity to perceive emotions, assimilate emotion–related feelings, understand the information of those emotions, and manage them.

In the book *Emotion Machine*, M. Minsky points out that emotion is a special way of thinking for human beings and proposes six dimensions of building future machines [34].

1.3.10 Nature of consciousness

The most important scientific discovery of the present era will the answer to how exactly do neurobiological processes in the brain cause consciousness? The question, "What is the biological basis of consciousness?" is selected as one of 125 questions, a fitting number for Science's 125th anniversary. There have been recent scientifically oriented accounts of consciousness emerging from the properties and organization of neurons in the brain. Consciousness is the notions of mind and soul.

The physical basis of consciousness appears to be the most singular challenge to the scientific, reductionist worldview. The book *The Astonishing Hypothesis* written by F. Crick is an effort to chart the way forward in the investigation of consciousness [35].

D. J. Chalmers suggests that the problem of consciousness can be broken down into several separate questions [36]. The major question is the neuronal correlate of consciousness (NCC), which focuses on specific processes that correlate with the current content of consciousness. The NCC is the minimal set of neurons, most likely distributed throughout certain cortical and subcortical areas, whose firing directly correlates with the perception of the subject of the moment.

B. Baars combines psychology with brain science and cognitive neuroscience and transforms a theater metaphor that has been used to understand consciousness since Plato and Aristotle into a theater model of consciousness. Based on the model, Baars proposed the global workspace theory [37].

G. Tononi published a series of papers to clarify the integrated information theory of consciousness [38]. Tononi proposed two measures of integrated information for integrated information theory.

In 2017 Z. Z. Shi has proposed the Machine Consciousness of Mind Model CAM, which presents an architecture of machine consciousness containing awareness, global workspace, attention, motivation, metacognition, and introspective learning modules [26].

1.4 Research contents

The research contents of intelligence science include computational neural theory, cognitive computing, knowledge engineering, natural language processing, intelligent robots, and so on.

1.4.1 Computational neural theory

The brain is a neural network. The relationship between neurons depends on synapses. These interconnected neurons form a certain neural network to play the role of the brain. These interactions play a key role in the balance, complexity, and information processing of neural circuits. At the same time, the receptors and ion channels on the membrane of neurons are very important for controlling the excitability of neurons, for regulating synaptic function, and for the dynamic balance of various neurotransmitters and ions in neurons. Understanding the neural network structure of the brain and the mechanism of forming complex cognitive function are the basis of understanding, developing, and utilizing the brain.

Computational neural theory studies the expression, coding, processing, and decoding of knowledge and external things in the brain from the molecular level, cell level, and behavior level; reveals the mechanism of human brain intelligence; and establishes a brain model. The problem to be studied is how to form a neural network? How is the central nervous system constructed? In the process of neural network formation, there are the differentiation of nerve cells, the migration of neurons, the plasticity of synapses, the activity of neurons and neurotransmitters and ion channels, the formation of neural circuits, and the integration of information. The study of these problems will provide a strong brain science basis for the mechanism of intelligence.

1.4.2 Cognitive mechanism

Cognitive mechanism studies how the human brain realizes the mental activities of perception, learning, memory, thinking, emotion, and consciousness from the micro, meso, and macro scales. Perception is the process of people's perception and the perception of objective things. Sensation is the reflection of the human brain on the individual attributes of objective things directly acting on the sensory organs. Perception is the overall reflection of the human brain to the objective things directly acting on the sensory organs. The expression, integrity, organization, and integration of perceptual information are the basic problems of perceptual research, which are the basis of other cognitive levels. So far, four kinds of perceptual theories have been established: the constructionist's discussion has exerted great influence on the factors of learning and memory, believing that all perception is influenced by people's experience and expectation; Gibson's ecology focuses on the information of the whole environment inherent in the stimulus pattern and believes that perception is direct without any reasoning steps, mediating variables, or associations. Gestalt theory emphasizes the congenital factors of perceptual organization and proposes that the whole is greater than the sum of parts; the action theory focuses on the feedback effect of perceptual detection in his environment. Pattern recognition is a basic human intelligence. The research of pattern recognition mainly focuses on two aspects: one is how organisms (including people) perceive objects; the other is how to use computers to realize pattern recognition under given tasks.

Learning is a basic cognitive activity, a process of accumulating experience and knowledge and a process of grasping and understanding external things in order to improve the performance of system behavior. Learning theory refers to the theoretical discussion and explanation of the essence of learning, the process of learning, the law of learning, and the various conditions restricting learning. In the process of exploring learning theory, due to the different philosophical bases, theoretical backgrounds, and research methods, various theoretical views have naturally formed, and various theoretical schools have been formed, including behavioral school, cognitive school, humanistic school, and so on.

The neurobiological basis of learning is the synaptic plasticity of the connection structure between nerve cells, which has become a very active research field in contemporary neuroscience. The synaptic plasticity condition is that when the presynaptic fibers and the associated postsynaptic cells are excited at the same time, the synaptic connection is strengthened. In 1949 D. O. Hebb, a Canadian psychologist, proposed the Hebb learning rules [10]. He assumed that during the learning process, the relevant synapses changed, leading to the enhancement of synaptic connections and the improvement of transmission efficiency. Hebb's learning rules become the basis of connective learning.

Memory is past experience or experience in the brain and the production of an accurate internal representation that can be correctly and efficiently extracted and used. Memory involves the acquisition, storage, and retrieval of information, which means that memory needs different brain regions to cooperate. In the initial stage of memory formation, the brain needs to integrate multiple scattered features or to combine multiple knowledge blocks to form a unified representation. In terms of space, memory with different characteristics may be stored in different brain regions and neuron groups. In terms of time, memory can be divided into working memory, short-term memory, and long-term memory. Studying the structure and function of working memory is of great significance in understanding the essence of human intelligence. As previously mentioned, working memory contains the mystery of intelligence.

Thinking is the conscious human brain's self-conscious, indirect, and general reflection of the essential attribute and internal regularity of the objective reality, and it is manifested by implicit or explicit language or action. Thinking is enabled by the complex brain mechanism. It processes the objective relationship and connection in multiple layers and reveals the intrinsic and essential characteristics of things. It is an advanced form of cognition. The main forms of human thinking are abstract (logical) thinking, image (direct sense) thinking, perception thinking, and inspiration (epiphany) thinking. The study of thinking has important scientific significance and application value in understanding the nature of human cognition and intelligence and in the development of AI. Through the study of the different levels of the thinking model, the study the law and the method of thinking provides the principle and model for the new intelligent information processing system.

Minsky thinks that emotion is a special way of thinking in human beings. How can a machine without emotion be intelligent? Therefore, let the computer have emotion to make it more intelligent. In addition to providing a new way for the development of AI, the research of emotional computing has important value for understanding human emotions and even human thinking. Research on emotion itself and the interaction between emotion and other cognitive processes has become a research hotspot in intelligent science.

Consciousness is the awareness of the external world and the brain's own psychological and physiological activities. Consciousness is the core problem of intelligence science research. To reveal the scientific law of consciousness and to construct the brain model of consciousness, it is necessary to study not only the conscious cognitive process but also the unconscious cognitive process, namely the automatic information processing process of the brain and the mutual transformation of the two processes in the brain. The cognitive principle of consciousness, the neurobiological basis of consciousness, and the information processing of consciousness and unconsciousness are the key problems to be studied.

Mind is all human spiritual activities, including emotion, will, feeling, perception, representation, learning, memory, thinking, intuition, etc. The technology of building a mind model is often called mind modeling. Its purpose is to explore and study the human thinking mechanism, especially the human information processing mechanism, and provide new architecture and technical methods for designing a corresponding AI system. The mind problem is a very complex nonlinear problem. We must study the mental world with the help of modern scientific methods.

1.4.3 Knowledge engineering

Knowledge engineering studies the representation, acquisition, reasoning, decision-making, and application of knowledge [8], including big data, machine learning, data mining and knowledge discovery, uncertain reasoning, knowledge mapping, machine theorem proving, expert system, machine game, digital library, etc.

Big data refers to data collection that cannot be captured, managed, and processed by conventional software tools within a certain time range. It is a massive, high-growth rate, and diversified information asset that requires a new processing mode to have stronger decision-making power, insight, and discovery ability and process optimization ability [13]. IBM puts forward the 5-V characteristics of big data: volume (large amount), velocity (high speed), variety (diversity), value (low value density), and veracity (authenticity).

Machine learning studies how computers simulate or implement human learning behaviors in order to acquire new knowledge or skills and to reorganize existing knowledge structure to improve its performance [32]. Machine learning methods include induction learning, analogy learning, analytical learning, reinforcement learning, genetic algorithm, link learning, and deep learning [34].

1.4.4 Natural language processing

In the process of human evolution, the use of language has caused the functional differentiation of the two hemispheres of the brain. The emergence of the language hemisphere distinguishes humans from other primates. Some studies have shown that the left hemisphere of human brain is related to serial, sequential, and logical information processing, while the right hemisphere is related to parallel, visual, and nontemporal information processing.

Language is a system that takes phonetics as its shell, vocabulary as its material, and grammar as its rules. Languages are usually divided into spoken and written languages. The form of spoken language is sound, while the form of writing is image. Spoken language is much older than written language; personal language learning also entails learning spoken language first, then learning words. Language is the most complex, systematic, and widely used symbol system. Studying Chinese from the three levels of nerve, cognition, and computation gives us an excellent opportunity to open the door of intelligence.

Natural language understanding implements various theories and methods to communicate effectively with natural language between human and computer. It studies the context, semantics, pragmatics, and language structure of natural language, including computer input of speech and text, intelligent retrieval of large vocabulary, corpus and text, generation, and synthesis and recognition of machine speech, machine translation, and simultaneous interpreting among different languages.

1.4.5 Intelligent robot

Intelligent robot has a well developed "artificial brain," which can arrange actions according to the purpose and also has sensors and effectors. The research of the intelligent robot can be divided into four levels: basic frontier technology, common technology, key technology and equipment, and demonstration application [39]. Among them, the basic frontier technology mainly involves the design of new robot mechanism, the theory and technology of intelligent development, and the research of new-generation robot verification platform such as mutual cooperation and human behavior enhancement [40]. Common technologies mainly include core components, robot-specific sensors, robot software, test/safety and reliability, and other key common technologies. Key technologies and equipment mainly include industrial robots, service robots, special environment service robots, and medical/rehabilitation robots. Demonstration applications are oriented to industrial robots, medical/rehabilitation robots, and other fields. At the end of the 20th century, the computer culture has been deeply rooted in the hearts of the people. In the 21st century, robot culture will have an immeasurable impact on the development of social productivity, the way of human life, work, thinking, and social development.

1.5 Research methods

Many different methodologies are used to study intelligence science. As the field is highly interdisciplinary, research often cuts across multiple areas of study, drawing on research methods from psychology, neuroscience, cognitive science, AI, and systems theory.

1.5.1 Behavioral experiments

In order to have a description of what constitutes intelligent behavior, one must study behavior itself. This type of research is closely tied to that in cognitive psychology and psychophysics. By measuring behavioral responses to different stimuli, one can understand something about how those stimuli are processed.

1. *Reaction time*: The time between the presentation of a stimulus and an appropriate response can indicate differences between two cognitive processes as well as some things about their nature. For example, if in a search task the reaction times vary proportionally with the number of elements, then it is evident that this cognitive process of searching involves serial instead of parallel processing.

2. *Psychophysical responses*: Psychophysical experiments are an old psychological technique, which has been adopted by cognitive psychology. They typically involve making judgments of some physical property, such as the loudness of a sound. Correlation of subjective scales between individuals can show cognitive or sensory biases as compared to actual physical measurements.

1.5.2 Brain imaging

Brain imaging involves analyzing activity within the brain while performing various cognitive tasks. This allows us to link behavior and brain function to help understand how information is processed. Different types of imaging techniques vary in their temporal (time-based) and spatial (location-based) resolution. Brain imaging is often used in cognitive neuroscience.

1. *Single photon emission computed tomography (SPECT) and positron emission tomography (PET)*: SPECT and PET use radioactive isotopes, which are injected into the subject's bloodstream and taken up by the brain. By observing which areas of the brain take up the radioactive isotope, we can see which areas of the brain are more active than others. PET has similar spatial resolution to fMRI, but it has extremely poor temporal resolution.

2. *Electroencephalography (EEG)*: EEG measures the electrical fields generated by large populations of neurons in the cortex by placing a series of electrodes on the scalp of the subject. This technique has an extremely high temporal resolution but a relatively poor spatial resolution.

3. *Functional magnetic resonance imaging (fMRI)*: fMRI measures the relative amount of oxygenated blood flowing to different parts of the brain. More oxygenated blood in a particular region is assumed to correlate with an increase in neural activity in that part of the brain. This allows us to localize particular functions within different brain regions. fMRI has moderate spatial and temporal resolution.

4. *Optical imaging*: This technique uses infrared transmitters and receivers to measure the amount of light reflectance by blood near different areas of the brain. Since oxygenated and deoxygenated blood reflects light by different amounts, we can study which areas are more active (i.e., those that have more oxygenated blood). Optical imaging has moderate temporal resolution but poor spatial resolution. It also has the advantage that it is extremely safe and can be used to study infants' brains.

5. *Magnetoencephalography (MEG)*: MEG measures magnetic fields resulting from cortical activity. It is similar to EEG, except that it has improved spatial resolution since the magnetic fields it measures are not as blurred or attenuated by the scalp, meninges, and so forth as the electrical activity measured in EEG is. MEG uses SQUID (superconducting quantum interference device) sensors to detect tiny magnetic fields.

1.5.3 Computational modeling

Computational models require a mathematically and logically formal representation of a problem. Computer models are used in the simulation and experimental verification of different specific and general properties of intelligence. Computational modeling can help us to understand the functional organization of a particular cognitive phenomenon.

There are two basic approaches to cognitive modeling. The first is focused on abstract mental functions of an intelligent mind and operates using symbols; the second follows the neural and associative properties of the human brain and is called subsymbolic.

1. *Symbolic modeling*: evolved from the computer science paradigms using the technologies of knowledge-based systems, as well as a philosophical perspective. They are developed by the first cognitive researchers and were later used in knowledge engineering for expert systems. Since the early 1990s, symbolic modeling was generalized in systemics for the investigation of functional human-like intelligence models, such as personoids, and, in parallel, developed as the SOAR environment. Recently, especially in the context of cognitive decision-making, symbolic cognitive modeling is extended to a sociocognitive approach including social and organization cognition interrelated with a subsymbolic, not conscious layer.

2. *Subsymbolic modeling*: includes connectionist/neural network models. Connectionism relies on the idea that the mind/brain is composed of simple nodes and that the power of the system comes primarily from the existence and manner of connections among the simple nodes.

1.5.4 Neurobiological methods

Research methods borrowed directly from neuroscience and neuropsychology can also help us to understand aspects of intelligence. These methods allow us to understand how intelligent behavior is implemented in a physical system. There are several approaches: single-cell recording, direct brain stimulation, animal models, postmortem studies, and so on.

1.5.5 Simulation

Simulation is the virtualization of real things or processes. The simulation should show the key characteristics of the selected physical system or abstract system. The key problems of simulation include the acquisition of effective information, the selection of key characteristics and performance, the application of approximate simplification and assumptions, and the reproducibility and effectiveness of simulation. The difference from experimental or practical systems is that the simulation is not based on the actual environment but on the actual system image of the system model and on the corresponding "artificial" environment carried out under that image. Simulation can truly describe the system operation, evolution, and the development processes.

1.6 Prospects

The scientific goal of intelligence science is to explore the essence of intelligence, establish the computational theory of intelligence science and new intelligent system, and solve the fundamental theory and key technical problems of intelligent systems that are of great significance to intelligence science. It will be widely used in brain-like intelligent machines, intelligent robots, brain computer integration, intelligent systems, etc.

Since the development of human civilization, there have been five scientific and technological revolutions. The influence of previous scientific and technological revolutions can be evaluated from the following three points of view:

1. *A series of revolutions*: The first scientific and technological revolution mainly includes the birth of new physics and the all-round development of modern science. The second is the emergence of the steam engine and textile machine, with machines replacing human resources. The third is mainly the emergence of the generator, internal combustion engine, and telecommunication technology (at the same time, our living space has been greatly expanded). The fourth scientific and technological revolution is the beginning of modern science, mainly the great expansion of cognitive space. The fifth scientific and technological revolution is the information revolution, which greatly expands the ways of social communication and information acquisition.

2. *Major theoretical breakthroughs*: The first scientific and technological revolution mainly produced the Copernicus theory, Galileo theory, and Newtonian mechanics. The second scientific and technological revolution was the establishment of thermodynamics' Carnot theory and the law of conservation of energy. The third scientific and technological revolution was mainly the establishment of electromagnetic wave theory. The fourth was mainly the theory of evolution, relativity, quantum theory, and DNA double helix structure The fifth scientific and technological revolution is the information revolution, which produced von Neumann theory and Turing theory.

3. *The impact on economy and society*: The Enlightenment of science in the first scientific and technological revolution laid a theoretical foundation for the future mechanical revolution. The second technological revolution started the Industrial Revolution characterized by factory mass production. The third scientific and technological revolution expanded the emerging market and opened up the modern industrial era.

The fourth scientific and technological revolution promoted the vast majority of science and technology in the 20th century The fifth scientific and technological revolution promoted economic globalization and the era of big data has come.

Today's world science and technology are at the dawn of a new round of revolutionary change. The sixth scientific and technological revolution will be an intelligence revolution, replacing or enhancing human intellectual labor with machines. In the sixth scientific and technological revolution, intelligence science will play a leading role, explore the essence of intelligence, and promote development of new-generation AI, such as cognitive machine learning, integrated intelligence, meaningful interaction, and self-aware learning.

References

[1] Z.Z. Shi, Perspectives on intelligence science, Sci. Chin. 8 (2003) 47−49.
[2] Z.Z. Shi, Progress in research on intelligence science. Keynotes Speaker, AGI-19, (2019), August 7, Shenzhen.
[3] A.M. Turingi, On computable numbers with an application to the Entscheidungsproblem, Proc. London Maths. Soc., Ser. s2−42 (1936) 230−265.
[4] Z.Z. Shi, Advanced Artificial Intelligence, second ed., World Scientific, New Jersey, 2019.
[5] E.A. Feigenbaum, The art of artificial intelligence, themes and case studies in knowledge engineering, IJCAI 5 (1977) 1014−1029.
[6] Moto-oka, T. (Ed.), Fifth generation computer systems, North Holland, (1982).
[7] D. Kirsh, Foundations of AI: the big issues, Artif. Intell 47 (1991) 3−30.
[8] C.S. Sherrington, The Integrative Action of the Nervous System, 1961 ed., Yale University Press, New Haven, CT, 1906.
[9] W.S. McCulloch, G.W. Pitts, A logic calculus of the ideas immanent in nervous activity, Bull. Math. biophysics 5 (1943) 115−133.
[10] D.O. Hebb, The Organization of Behavior: A Neuropsychological Theory, Wiley, New York, 1949.
[11] A.L. Hodgkin, A.F. Huxley, A quantitative description of ion currents and its applications to conduction and excitation in nerve membranes, J. Physiol. (Lond.) 117 (1952) 500−544.
[12] F. Rosenblatt, Principles of Neurodynamics, Spartan Books, 1962.
[13] J.J. Hopfield, Neural networks and physical systems with emergent collective computational abilities, Proc. Natl Acad. Sci. USA 9 (2554) (1982).
[14] S. Amari, Differential geometrical methods in statistics, Springer Lecture Notes in Statistic, 28, Springer, 1985.
[15] H. Markram, The blue brain project, Nat. Rev. Neurosci. 7 (2006) 153−160.
[16] M.M. Poo, J.L. Du, Y. Nancy, et al., China Brain project: basic neuroscience, brain diseases, and brain-inspired computing, Neuron 92 (3) (2016) 591−596.
[17] Z.Z. Shi, On intelligence science, Int. J. Adv. Intell. 1 (1) (2009) 39−57.
[18] A. Newell, H.A. Simon, Computer science as empirical inquiry: symbols and search, Commun. Assoc. Comput. Machinery 19 (3) (1976) 113−126. ACM Turing Award Lecture.

[19] L.G. Valiant, A theory of the learnable, Commun. ACM 27 (11) (1984) 1134−1142.

[20] J. Pearl, Causality: Models, Reasoning, and Inference, Cambridge University Press, New York, NY, 2000.

[21] J. Pearl, D. Mackenzie, The Book of Why: The New Science of Causal and Effect, Basic Books, 2018.

[22] H.A. Simon, Machine discovery, Found. Sci. 1 (2) (1995/1996) 171−200.

[23] G.E. Hinton, R. Salakhutdinov, Reducing the dimensionality of data with neural networks, Science 313 (5786) (2006) 504−507.

[24] A. Newell, Unified Theories of Cognition, Harvard University Press, Cambridge, MA, 1990.

[25] J.R. Anderson, The Adaptive Character of Thought, Erlbaum, Hillsdale, NJ, 1993.

[26] Z.Z. Shi, Mind Computation, World Scientific, New Jersey, 2017.

[27] N. Chomsky, Syntactic Structures, Mouton, The Hague, 1957.

[28] R. Mayeux, E.R. Kandel, Disorders of language: the aphasias, in: E.R. Kandel, J.H. Schwartz, T.M. Jessell (Eds.), Principles of Neural Science, third ed., Elsevier, 1991, pp. 840−851.

[29] A.D. Baddeley, G.J. Hitch, Working memory, in: G.A. Bower (Ed.), The Psychology of Learning and Motivation [M], Academic Press, New York, 1974, pp. 47−89.

[30] J. Hawkins, S. Blakeslee, On Intelligence. Times Books, Henry Holt and Company, New York, 2004.

[31] Z.Z. Shi, Cognitive Science (In Chinese), University of Science and Technology of China Press, 2008.

[32] Z.Z. Shi, Hierarchical model of mind. Invited Speaker. Chinese Joint Conference on Artificial Intelligence, (1990).

[33] D.A. Norman, Emotion and design: attractive things work better. Interactions Magazine, (2002).

[34] M. Minsky, The Emotion Machine, Simon & Schuster, New York, 2006.

[35] F. Crick, The Astonishing Hypothesis, Scribner, 1994.

[36] D.J. Chalmers, What is a neural correlate of consciousness? in: T. Metzinger (Ed.), Neural Correlates of Consciousness: Empirical and Conceptual Issues, MIT Press, 2000.

[37] B. Baars, In the Theater of Consciousness: The Workspace of the Mind, Oxford University Press, NY, 1997.

[38] G. Tononi, Consciousness as integrated information: a provisional manifesto, Biol. Bull. 251 (2008) 216−242.

[39] I. Asimov, Run Around. I, Robot, Doubleday, Garden City, New York, 1950.

[40] Z.Z. Shi, Principles of Machine Learning, International Academic Publishers, 1992.

CHAPTER 2

Foundation of neurophysiology

The human brain is the most complex substance in the world and the physiological basis of human intelligence and advanced mental activities. The brain is the organ for understanding the world. To study the cognitive process and intelligence mechanism of human beings, we must understand the physiological mechanism of this extraordinarily complex and orderly material. Brain science and neuroscience study the mechanism of natural intelligence from the molecular level, cell level, and behavior level; they establish the brain model, reveal the essence of the human brain, and greatly promote the development of intelligence science. Neurophysiology and neuroanatomy are the two cornerstones of neuroscience. Neuroanatomy introduces the structure of the nervous system, while neurophysiology introduces the function of the nervous system. This chapter mainly introduces the neurophysiological basis of intelligence science.

2.1 The human brain

The human brain is composed of four parts: cerebrum, diencephalon, mesencephalon, and metencephalon (hindbrain) (Fig. 2.1) [1]. Each part of the brain undertakes different functions and has a connection with the cerebral cortex such that information from all over the body is assembled and processed in the cerebral cortex. Forebrain includes cerebral hemispheres and diencephalons.

1. The *cerebrum* comprises a right and a left cerebral hemisphere. There is a longitudinal crack between them, at the bottom of which some laterigrade fibers (called the corpus callosum) connect with the two hemispheres. There are spaces (called lateral ventricles) inside the hemispheres that locate symmetrically on both sides. Each cerebral hemisphere is covered by the gray matter, the cortex. Many sulci and gyri on the surface increase the surface area. The medulla is beneath the cerebral cortex, and some gray nucleus groups, including basal ganglia, hippocampus, and amygdala, are

Intelligence Science
DOI: https://doi.org/10.1016/B978-0-323-85380-4.00002-6

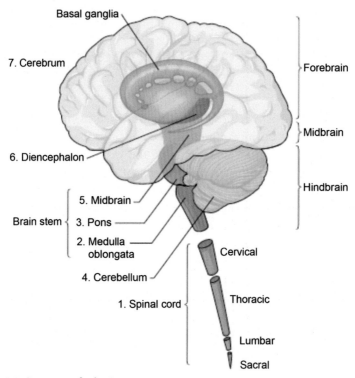

Basal ganglia

7. Cerebrum

Forebrain

Midbrain

6. Diencephalon

Hindbrain

Brain stem
5. Midbrain
3. Pons
2. Medulla oblongata
4. Cerebellum

1. Spinal cord

Cervical

Thoracic

Lumbar

Sacral

Figure 2.1 Structure of a brain.

hidden in the medulla. The cerebral cortex can be divided into frontal, temporal, parietal, and occipital lobes.

2. The *diencephalon* is the encephalic region surrounding the third ventricle. The very thin superior wall of the ventricle is composed of the choroids plexus. Gray matter within the superior of both lateral walls is called the thalamus. Its dorsal is covered by the stratum zonale, a thin layer of fibers. The internal medullary lamina is consecutive to the stratum zonale, which splits the thalamus into anterior, medial, and lateral nuclear groups in a "Y"-shaped manner. The epithalamus is located in the superior wall of the third ventricle, while hypothalamus locates in the anterior-inferior of the thalamus, which includes some nuclear groups within the inferior part of the lateral walls of the third ventricles. The thalamus extends backward to form the metathalamus, which consists of lateral geniculate body (related with vision) and medial geniculate body (related with audition). In addition, subthalamus is a transitional zone between diencephalons and caudal

mesencenphalon. Thalamus is responsible for encoding and transferring information to the cerebral cortex and coordinating functions of vegetality, endocrine, and internal organs.

3. The *mesencephalon* comprises of the cerebral peduncle and corpora quadrigemina. It takes charge of coordinating the functions of sensation and movement.

4. The *metencephalon* is composed of the pons varolii, cerebellum, and medulla oblongata. The cerebellum has two cerebellar hemispheres joined by a sagittal, transversely narrow median vermis. It coordinates the functions of movement. Pons varolii is so named in that it is like a bridge connecting bilateral cerebellar hemispheres that mainly transfers information from the cerebral hemispheres to the cerebellar hemispheres. The medulla oblongata is located between the pons varolii and spinal cord, which is the autonomic nervous center controlling heartbeat, respiration, and digestion. The pavimentum ventriculi of the fourth ventricle (fossa rhomboidea) is formed by the dorsal of pons varolii and medulla oblongata, while its cupula is covered by the cerebellum. It communicates upward with the third ventricle through the cerebral aqueduct and downward via the spinal canal.

Human brain is a system of complicated structures with complete functions. As a whole, two cerebral hemispheres can be divided into several regions with different functions. Among them, the occipital lobe in the posterior part of the cerebral hemisphere is the visual area for analyzing and synthesizing visual stimulation. The parietal lobe is anterior to the occipital lobe. Its anterior part is in charge of the analysis and synthesis of tactile stimulations and stimulations from muscles and joints. The temporal lobe is inferior-anterior to the occipital lobe. Its superior part takes responsibility for the analysis and synthesis of stimulations from the auditory organ. The frontal lobe is located in the anterior part of the cerebral hemispheres, and its area is the largest of all lobes. Its posterior part reports signals about body's movements and their space allocations. Respective researches on cerebral hemispheres show that they have two systems for information processing and that their neural nets reflect the world with different modes. For the majority of people, the left cerebral hemisphere plays a main role in languages, logical thinking, mathematical computing, and analyzing, while the right cerebral hemisphere does well in space problem solving and is in charge of intuitional creative activities, such as music or art. These two modes serve as good partners, and coshape the unified and complete cognition of the integral human brain to the objective world.

Modern neurophysiologists hold that the emergence of sophisticated brain functions is linked closely with neural-net activities. For instance, Sperry, a famous American neurophysiologist and Nobel Prize laureate, said very clearly in his view that the subjective consciousness and thinking depending on the neural network and relevant physiological characteristics was one component of the brain course and the result of the high-level activities of the brain. Sanger, a French neurophysiologist, also said that all kinds of behaviors—thinking, emotion and so on—stem from physical and chemical phenomena produced in that brain and that they result from the assemblage of concerned neurons.

Real neuroscience originated at the end of the last century. C. Golgi, an Italian anatomist first discerned the single nerve cell by staining in 1875. R. Cajal founded neuron doctrine in 1889, which held that the whole nervous system was formed by relatively independent nerve cells in the structure. In recent decades, research on neuroscience and brain function has made extremely fast progress. It is estimated that the total quantity of the neurons in the human brain is about 10^{11}. Each neuron comprises two parts: the neural cell body and the processes (dendrites and axons). The size of the cell body ranges in diameter from 5 to 100 μm. The quantities of processes arising from each nerve cell, their lengths, and their branches are all different. Some processes are more than 1 m long while others are no longer than 1/1000 of the long process. Neurons communicate with one another by synapses. The quantity of synapses is tremendous. According to one measurement, the number of synapses of one neuron in the cerebral cortex is more than 30,000, while the synapse count for the whole brain ranges from 10^{14} to 10^{15}. There are various communication models among the synapses. The most common type of synapse occurs between the terminal of an axonal branch of a neuron and the dendrite or the soma of another. In addition, there are other types, such as axo-axonal synapses and soma-somatic synapses. Different types of synapses have different physiological functions.

Combinations among neurons are also of diverse types. One neuron can form synapses with many neurons by its fiber branches, which enables information from one neuron to transfer to other neurons. Whereas the nervous fiber terminals from those neurons located in different regions can also aggregate in one neuron, information from different sources can be centralized in the same area. In addition, there are ring-shaped and catenuliform combinations. Therefore, communications among the neurons are very reticular.

The complexity and diversity of the neural net lie not only in the great quantity of neurons and synapses, complicated combining types, and extensive communications but also in the complicated mechanisms of synaptic transmission. The elucidated mechanisms of synaptic transmission at present include postsynaptic excitation, postsynaptic inhibition, presynaptic inhibition, presynaptic excitation, long-term depression, and so on. Among these, the release of neurotransmitters is the central step of realizing synaptic transmission, and different neurotransmitters have different effects and characteristics.

The human brain is a product of the long evolution of living beings. It took the animal kingdom about 1 billion years to evolve. Unicellular organisms had nothing like a nervous system. Neurons began to concentrate on the head to form the ganglia until living beings evolved to flatworms. The primary differentiation of the animal cerebrum was related to smell; amphibians and animals inferior to fish had only an olfactory lobe related to smell. Vertebrates began to have central nervous system (CNS). A fish's brain had five parts: telencephalon, diencephalon, mesencephalon, metencephalon, and medulla oblongata. The cerebral neocortex first occurred in reptiles, while a real brain—the neocortex—was seen in mammals. Primates' cerebral cortex, with sufficient development, took control of the overall and subtle regulation of various bodily functions. At the end of the evolving process, the extremely complicated neural net formed, which constituted the thinking organ of a huge system—the human brain.

Research on the human brain has already become the advanced front of scientific research. Some experts estimate brain science will be the next tide following the tide of molecular biological research in biology set up by J. D. Watson and F. Crick, the winners of the Nobel in physiology—medicine because they proposed the double-coiled spiral structure of DNA in the 1950s and successfully resolved questions about hereditary knowledge. Many first-class Western scientists engaging in biological or physical research shift their research field to human brain research, one after another, after they have obtained the Nobel Prize.

The following books summarize the worldwide progress and results of brain research. The book *Principles of Neural Science* (5th edition) introduces a large of amount knowledge about the nerve system, including the following key inquiries: (1) How does the brain develop? (2) How do nerve cells communicate? (3) How do various patterns of interconnections give rise to different perceptions and motor acts? (4) How is communication between neurons modified by experience? Last, (5) How is neural communication modified by disease? [1]

The book *Neuroscience: Exploring the Brain* (4th edition) takes a fresh, contemporary approach to the study of neuroscience, emphasizing the biological basis of behavior [2].

The book *Cognitive Neuroscience* (3rd edition) is on the field of study focusing on the neural substrates of mental processes. It is at the intersection of psychology and neuroscience but also overlaps with physiological psychology, cognitive psychology, and neuropsychology. It combines the theories of cognitive psychology and computational modeling with experimental data about the brain [3].

2.2 Nervous tissues

The nervous system is composed of two principal cellular constituents: the nerve cells (or neurons) and neuroglial cells (or glia). The characteristics exhibited by nervous systems include excitation, conduction, integration and so on, all of which are the functions of neurons. Although glia account for more than half the volume of the brain and their quantity greatly exceeds that of neurons, they just play an assistance role.

2.2.1 Basal composition of neuron

The nerve cell is the most elemental unit constituting the nervous system, and it is usually called a neuron. Each neuron has three specialized regions: cell body (soma), axon, and dendrites. The general structure of a neuron is shown in Fig. 2.2.

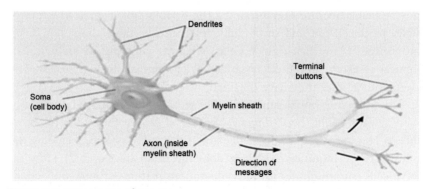

Figure 2.2 Appearance of neuron.

2.2.1.1 Soma or cell body

The cell bodies are the main part of neurons and are located in gray matter of the brain and spinal cord and ganglia. They are of different shapes; star-shaped, pyramid-shaped, pear-shaped, and ball-shaped neurons are commonly observed. The sizes of cell bodies are not uniform, and their diameters range from 5 to 150 μm. The cell body is the metabolic and nutrient center of the neuron. Its structure is similar to that of common cell, including nucleolus, cell membrane, cytoplasm, and nucleus. The cytoplasm of the living neuron takes a granular shape, and appropriate staining shows it contains neurofibrils, chromophil substance (Nissl bodies), Golgi apparatus, endoplasmic reticulum, mitochondria, and so on. Neurofibrils are the unique characteristic of neurons.

2.2.1.2 Cell membrane

The cell membrane covering the cell body and the processes is continuous and intact. Except for the process membrane with its specialized structure, the majority of cell membraned are unit membranes. The cell membrane of the neuron has sensitive and excitable characteristics. Various receptors and ionic channels in the cell membrane are composed of distinct membrane proteins. The membrane of process thickens. The receptors in the membrane can bind with relative neurotransmitters. When the receptors bind with acetylcholine or gamma-aminobutyric acid (GABA), the ion permeability of the membrane and the potential difference between the two sides of membrane change, causing related physiological activity of membrane: excitation or inhibition.

2.2.1.3 Nucleus

The nucleus is located usually in the center of cell body of the neuron, big and round. It has a few heterochromatin usually located inside the nuclear membrane with many euchromatin dispersed in the center of the nucleus. Therefore the nucleus has superficial staining. It has one or two big and obvious nucleoli. The nucleus migrates usually to the periphery when the cell degenerates.

2.2.1.4 Cytoplasm

The cytoplasm surrounds the nucleus, so it is called the perikaryon. It contains developed Golgi bodies, smooth endoplasmic reticulum (SER), abundant mitochondria, Nissl bodies, neurofibrils, lysosomes, lipofuscin, etc. For the neuron with a secretion function, its cytoplasm has secretory granules, such as the neurons located in the hypothalamus.

2.2.1.5 Process
Process is the extension of the cell body of the neuron. It can be divided into dendrite and axon according to its structure and functions.

2.2.1.6 Dendrite
One cell body can give rise to one to multiple dendrites, arranged in a radiated pattern. Their proximal trunks near the cell body are thick, and their branches become thinner and thinner, like an arborization. The structure of the dendrite is similar to that of the cell body. It has Nissl bodies, mitochondria, and paralleling neurofibrils but no Golgi complex. In the specimen with special silver staining, many spine-like processes, which are about 0.5-1.0 μm long and 0.5-2.0 μm thick, are visualized; and these are called dendritic spines and are the sites of forming synapses. The dendritic spine contains several flat uesicae (spine apparatus) under a general electronic microscope. The dendrite's branches and dendritic spines can increase the neuron's surface area for receiving stimulation. The dendrite has the functions of receiving stimulation and transferring impulses to the cell body.

2.2.1.7 Axon
Each neuron has only one axon. The initial segment of the axon is cone-shaped, called the axon hillock, which contains mainly neurofibrils but no Nissl bodies. The initial segment of the axon is about 15-25 μm long and is thinner than the dendrite, with the uniform thickness. Its smooth surface has few branches and no myelin sheath surrounding it. The portion of axon far from the cell body is wrapped by a myelin sheath, and that is the myelinated nerve fiber. Fine branches at the end of axon are called as axon terminals, which can make contact with other neurons or effector cells. The membrane covering the axon is axolemma, while the plasma in the axon is axoplasm, in which there are many neurofibils paralleling the long axis of the axon and slender mitochondria, but no Nissle bodies and Glogi complex. Thus there is no protein synthesis in the axon. The metabolic turnover of the axon's components and the synthesis of neurotransmitters in the synaptic vesicles occurs in the cell body and then flow to

axon terminal through the microtubules and neurofilaments in the axon. The main role of the axon is conducting nerve impulses from the cell body to other neurons or effector cells. Impulse conduction begins at the axon's initial segment and then continues along the axolemma. Axon terminals formed by continuous branching constitute synapses with other neurons or effector cells.

During the long evolving process, neurons morph and form their own specialized functions. The neurons associated directly with receptors and conducting information to the center are called sensory neurons or afferent neurons. The neurons associated directly with effectors and conducting impulses from the center to the effector are called motor neurons or efferent neurons. Besides these neurons, all other neurons are interneurons forming neural networks.

The total number of efferent neurons in the human nervous system is several hundreds of thousands. The number of afferent neurons is more one to three times that of efferent neurons. The number of interneurons is the greatest; the number of interneurons just in the cerebral cortex is known as 14–15 billion.

2.2.2 Classification of neurons

There are many kinds of classifications for neurons, but they are usually classified according to the number and functions of neural processes.

1. Neurons can be divided into three classes according to the number of neural processes:

   Pseudounipolar neuron: One process arises from the cell body and then splits into a T shape with two branches at a site not far from the cell body. Thus it is called as pseudounipolar neuron. One branch with the structure similar to the axon is long and thin and extends to the periphery, which is called peripheral process, and its function is same as that of the dendrite. The peripheral process senses stimulation and conducts impulses to the cell body. The other branch, called the central process, extends to the center, and its function is equal to that of the axon, conducting impulses to another neuron, like the sensory neuron in the spinal ganglia.

   Bipolar neuron: The bipolar neuron erupts into two processes. One is the dendrite and the other is the axon, for example the sensory neurons in the cochlear ganglion

Multipolar neuron: The multipolar neuron has one axon and multiple dendrites. Multipolar neurons are the most numerous, such as the motor neurons in cornu anterius medullae spinalis, the pyramidal cells in the cerebral cortex, and so on. Based on the length of the axons, multipolar neurons are also classified into two types: Golgi type I neuron and Golgi type II neuron. Golgi type I neurons have big cell bodies and long axons, which can extend collateral branches on their way, such as the motor neurons in cornu anterius medullae spinalis. Golgi type I neurons have small cell bodies and short axons, which extend collateral branches near the cell bodies, for example the small neurons in the cornu posterius medullae spinalis and association neurons in the cerebrum and cerebellum.

2. Based on their functions, neurons fall into three types,

Sensory neurons (afferent neurons): These receive stimuli and transmit afferent impulses to the CNS, and their cell bodies are located in the cerebrum and spinal ganglia. Most of them are pseudounipolar neurons, and their processes constitute the afferent nerves of peripheral nerves. The terminals of nerve fibers form sensors (receptors) in the skin or muscles.

Motor neurons (efferent neurons): These transmit efferent impulses. Most of them are multipolar neurons. Their cell bodies are located in the gray matter of the CNS or vegetative ganglia, and their processes constitute efferent nerve fibers. The terminals of the nerve fibers are located in the muscle tissues and glands to form effectors.

Interneurons (association neurons): These play a role of communication between the neurons. They are multipolar neurons, and they are the most numerous in the human nervous system. Interneurons construct the complicated network of the CNS. Their cell bodies are located in the gray matter of the CNS, and their processes are generally located in the gray matter too.

2.2.3 Neuroglial cells

Neuroglial cells (abbreviated as glial cells) are distributed extensively in the central and peripheral nervous systems (PNSs). They are far more numerous than neurons, with a ratio of glial cell to neuron about 10:1 to 50:1. Like the neurons, glial cells also have processes, but the processes are no different from the neurons' dendrites and axons, and they can't transmit impulses. In the CNS, there are mainly astrocytes, oligodendrocytes (together with the former called macroglia), and microglia. Traditionally, glial cells belong to connective tissue, and their function is only to connect and support various nerve components. In fact, glia also plays the role of distributing nutrients, participating in repair, and phagocytosis, which is different from ordinary connective tissue in morphology, chemical characteristics, and embryonic origin.

1. *Astrocyte*: The astrocyte is one kind of glial cell with the biggest volume. Astrocytes and oligodendrocytes are also called macroglia. The cell appears star-shaped, and its comparatively large nucleus is round or oval and has light staining.

   Astrocytes can be divided into two kinds: (1) The fibrous astrocyte is distributed mainly in white matter. It has thin, long processes with fewer branches and cytoplasm containing a mass of glial filaments. Glial filaments are composed of glial fibrillary acidic protein. This kind of astrocyte can be observed by immunocytochemical staining. (2) Protoplasmic astrocyte is distributed mainly in gray matter. It has short and thick processes with many branches and cytoplasm containing fewer glial filaments. The processes of astrocytes extend and fill between the cell bodies and processes of neurons, which play their roles of supporting and separating neurons. The terminals of some processes form end feet, attaching to the capillary wall or the surfaces of brain and spinal cord to form the glial limiting membrane.

   Intracellular spaces between astrocytes are narrow and tortuous, about 15-20 nm wide, and they contain tissue fluid, by which neurons carry out substance exchanging. The astrocyte can absorb $K+$ from intracellular spaces to maintain a stable $K+$ concentration for neurons. It can also uptake and metabolize some neurotransmitters, such as γ-aminobutyric acid, to regulate the concentration of neurotransmitters, which is favorable to the activities of the neurons. During the developing period of the nerve system, some astrocytes can introduce neurons migrating to presumptive areas and cause the neurons to set up synaptic linkage with other neurons. When the CNS is damaged, astrocytes will proliferate, become hypertrophic to fill defective space, and form glial scar.

2. *Oligodendrocyte*: The oligodendrocyte has few processes in specimens with silver staining but not so in specimens with specific immunocytochemical staining, when many branches can be observed. The oligodendrocyte has a smaller cell body compared with the astrocyte. Its nucleus is round, with dark staining. Its cytoplasm seldom has glial filaments but does have many microtubules and other organelles.

The oligodendrocyte is distributed near the cell bodies of neurons or around nerve fiber, and its process terminals extend to form a flat and thin pellicle, which wraps neuron's axon to form myelin sheath. Thus it is the cell of myelination in the CNS. Recent researches believe that the oligodendrocyte also has the function inhibiting the growth of regenerated neurite.

3. *Microglia*: Microglia is the smallest glial cell. It has a slim, long or oval cell body, a flat or triangular small nucleus, dark staining. Its process is long and slim and has branches. Its surface has many small spinous processes. Microglias account for only 5% of the total glial cells. When the CNS is damaged, microglia can convert to macrophages, which swallow cell debris and degenerated myelin sheath. And circulating monocytes also intrude into the damage zone and convert to microphages to take part in phagocytosis. Some think microglias originate from monocytes in the blood and belong to mononuclear phagocyte system due to its phagocytosis.

4. *Ependymal cell*: Cube or cylinder-shaped ependymal cells are distributed in the cavosurfaces of the cerebral ventricles and spinal canal to form simple epithelium, called ependyma. The surfaces of ependyma cells have many microvilli. The ependyna cells in some regions are called tanycytes because their basal surfaces have slender processes extending to the deep part.

2.3 Synaptic transmission

A special kind of cell junction between neurons or between neuron and non-neural cells (muscle cell, glandular cell) is called a synapse, which is a connection of neurons and the critical structures for undertaking physiological activities [4]. Intercellular communication is realized through synapses. The most common type of synapse occurs between a terminal of an axonal branch of one neuron and a dendrite or dendritic spine or a soma of another neuron to form axon—dendritic synapses, axon—dendritic spinal synapses, or axosomatic synapses. In addition, there are axo-axonal synapses and dendrodendritic synapses, and so on. Synapses can be classified into two major types: chemical synapses and electronic synapses. The former utilizes a chemical substance (a neurotransmitter) as communicating media, while the latter, also called gap junctions, transfer information by electric current (electronic signal). For the mammalian nervous system, chemical synapses in the majority, so the synapses mentioned usually refer to the chemical synapses.

Synaptic structure can be divided into presynaptic element, synaptic space, and postsynaptic element. Cell membranes in the presynaptic element and postsynaptic element are called presynaptic membranes and postsynaptic membranes, respectively, between which is a 15—30 nm narrow gap, called the synaptic cleft, containing glycoproteins and some filament. The presynaptic element is usually an axonal terminal of a neuron, appearing globular intumescentia and attaching to the soma or the dendrite of another neuron, called the synaptic button.

2.3.1 Chemical synapse

Under the electronic microscope, the synaptic button contains many synaptic vesicles and small amounts of mitochondria, SER, microtubules and microfilaments, and so on (shown as Fig. 2.3). Synaptic vesicles have different sizes and shapes and are mainly round, with diameters of 40—60 nm, but some vesicles are thin and flat. Some synaptic vesicles are clear and bright, and some contain pyknotic nuclei (granular vesicles). The diameter of the big granular vesicle is about 200 nm. Synaptic vesicles contain neurotransmitters or neuromodulators. Both presynaptic membranes and postsynaptic membranes are thicker than the common cell membrane, which is caused by some densic materials attaching to the membrane (in Fig. 2.3). The presynaptic membrane has electron-dense, coned-dense projections that intrude into the cytoplasm; the spaces between these dense projections hold synaptic vesicles. Synaptic vesicle—related protein attaching to the surface of the synaptic vesicle is called

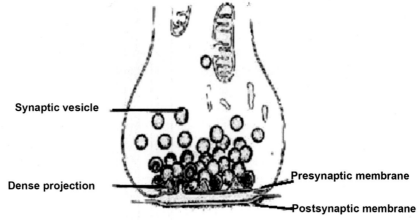

Synaptic vesicle

Dense projection

Presynaptic membrane

Postsynaptic membrane

Figure 2.3 Chemical synapse.

synapsin I, which makes synaptic vesicles gather and attach to the cytoskeleton. The presynaptic membrane contains abundant voltage-gated channels, while the postsynaptic membrane contains rich receptors and chemically gated channels. When nerve impulse is transferred along the axolemma to the synaptic terminal, voltage-gated channels in the presynaptic membrane are triggered and open. This causes extracellular Ca^{2+} to flow into the presynaptic element and make synapsin I; phosphorylate with adenosine triphosphate (ATP), triggering synaptic vesicles moving and attaching to the presynaptic membrane, and then the neurotransmitters in the synaptic vesicles are released into the synaptic cleft by exocytosis. One part of the neurotransmitters combine the concerned receptors in the postsynaptic membrane and induce receptor-coupled chemically gated channels to open. This makes related ions go in or out to change the distribution of ions on both sides of postsynaptic membrane, showing excited or inhibited effects and thus affecting the activities of the postsynaptic neuron and/or nonnervous cells. The synapse exciting postsynaptic membrane is the excitatory synapse, while the synapse inhibiting postsynaptic membrane is the inhibitory synapse

2.3.1.1 Presynaptic element

The axon terminals of the neurons appeared globular enlargement, and the axolemma thickens to form the presynaptic membrane, about 6 to 7 nm thick. Within the cytoplasm of the presynaptic part, there are many synaptic vesicles, some microfilaments, microtubules, mitochondria, SER, and so on. The synaptic vesicle is the characteristic structure of the presynaptic element and contains chemical substances called neurotransmitters. The shapes and sizes of the synaptic vesicles in various synapses vary because they contain different neurotransmitters. The common types of synaptic vesicles are as follows: (1) The globose vesicle, with a diameter of 20−60 nm, is clear and bright and contains excitatory neurotransmitters like acetylcholine. (2) The granulated vesicle with electron−dense granules can be divided into two subtypes according to its size: (a) The small granulated vesicle with a diameter of 30−60 nm contains usually amines-neurotransmitters like epinephrine and norepinephrine (NE) and so on. (b) The big granulated vesicle, with a diameter of 80−200 nm contains some peptides-neurotransmitters such as 5-hydroxytryptamine (5-HT) or enkephalin and so on. (3) Flat synaptic vesicles, with a long diameter of 50 nm or so, are flat and round and contain inhibitory neurotransmitters like γ-aminobutyric acid and so on.

Various kinds of neurotransmitters are synthesized in the soma and transported rapidly toward the axon terminal by forming vesicles. New research discovers that two or more neurotransmitters coexist in one neuron of the central and PNS; thus there are two or more synaptic vesicles in the synaptosome. For instance, acetylcholine and vasoactive intestinal peptide coexist in the sympathetic ganglia. The former controls secretion of sweat glands, while the latter acts on vessels' smooth muscles around glands to relax them, which can increase regional blood flow. Coexistence of neurotransmitters can coordinate neurophysiological activities and make nervous regulation more precise and concordant. At present, many findings indicate that coexistence is not an individual phenomenon but a universal law, and many novel coexisting transmitters and their location have been confirmed. The majority of them are the coexistence of nonpeptide (choline, monoamine, and amine) and peptide transmitters.

It is known that synaptophysin, synapsin, and vesicle-associated membrane protein are associated with the packaging and storage of synaptic vesicles and with the release of the transmitter. Synaptophysin is a Ca^{2+} binding protein in a synaptic vesicle. When excitation arrives at the synapse, Ca^{2+} entry increases abruptly, as it is probably important to the exocytosis of synaptic vesicles. Synapsin is phosphorylated protein with the function of regulating the release of neurotransmitters. Vesicle-associated membrane protein is a structural protein of the membrane of synaptic vesicles, which is probably important to the metabolism of synaptic vesicles.

2.3.1.2 Postsynaptic element

The postsynaptic element is usually the membrane of soma or dendrite of postsynaptic neuron. The portion opposite the presynaptic membrane thickens to form postsynaptic membrane. It is thicker than presynaptic membrane, about 20-50 nm. There are receptors and chemically gated ion channels in postsynaptic membrane. Based on the thickness of the dense materials in the cytoplasm surface of presynaptic and postsynaptic membrane, synapses can be divided into type I and type I: (1) In a type I synapse, dense materials in the cytoplasm surface of the postsynaptic membrane are thicker than that of presynaptic membrane. It is called an asymmetrical synapse due to the asymmetrical thickness of its membrane, and it has round synaptic vesicles and 20−50 nm wide synaptic cleft. Type I synapses are usually considered excitatory synapses, which are mainly axon—dendritic synapses distributed in the trunk of dendrite. (2) A type I synapse has few dense materials in the cytoplasm surface of the presynaptic and postsynaptic membrane, and its thickness is similar in presynaptic and postsynaptic membrane, so it is called a symmetrical synapse. The symmetrical synapse has flat synaptic vesicles and a narrow 10—20 nm synaptic cleft. Type I synapses are usually considered inhibitory synapses, which are mainly axon—somatic synapses distributed in the soma.

2.3.1.3 Synaptic cleft

About 20—30 nm wide, the synaptic cleft is an extracellular space between presynaptic and postsynaptic membranes that contains glycosaminoglycan such as sialic acid and glucoprotein and on the like. These chemical components can bind to neurotransmitters and promote transmitters moving from the presynaptic membrane toward the postsynaptic membrane, which limits external diffusion of transmitters or eliminates redundant transmitters.

When nerve impulses propagate along the axolemma to the presynaptic membrane, voltage-gated Ca^{2+} channels are triggered to open, and extracellular Ca^{2+} enters the presynaptic element. Inflow Ca^{2+} cooperates with ATP, microfilaments, and microtubules to make synaptic vesicles move toward the presynaptic membrane and release neurotransmitters into the synaptic cleft by exocytosis. One part of the neurotransmitters binds to related receptors on the postsynaptic membrane and cause receptor-coupled, chemically gated channels to open, which causes the corresponding ions to enter the postsynaptic element and changes the bilateral ion distribution of the membrane, showing excitatory (the depolarization of the membrane) or inhibitory (the hyperpolarization of the membrane) alteration, thereby affecting the activity of the postsynaptic neuron (or effector cell). The synapse exciting or inhibiting postsynaptic membrane is called the excitatory or inhibitory synapse, respectively. Synaptic excitation or inhibition is decided by the species of neurotransmitters and their receptors. It is a series of physiological activities of the organelles of the neurons including synthesis, transportation, storage, release, and effects of neurotransmitters and their inactivation by the action of the related enzyme. A neuron usually has many synapses, among which some are excitatory and others are inhibitory. If the summation of the excitatory synaptic activities surpasses that of the inhibitory synaptic activities, which makes the initial segment of the axon of the neuron produce action potentials and nerve impulses to occur, the neuron appears excitatory; conversely, it appears inhibitory.

The characters of the chemical synapse include two species: The neuron of its one side releases neurotransmitters of vesicles by exocytosis to the synaptic cleft, and the postsynaptic membrane of the neuron (or effector cell) of its other side has related receptors. The cell with the related receptor is called the effector cell or target cell of the neurotransmitter. Its characteristics ensure unilateral chemical synaptic transmission. The two specialized neurolemma portions—the presynaptic and postsynaptic membranes—maintain the structures and functions of two neurons and realize unification and balance of the organism. Therefore, the synapse is sensitive to the changes of the internal and external environments. For instance, anoxia, acidosis, fatigue, anesthesia, and so on all decrease its excitability, whereas theophylline, alkalosis, and so on all increase its excitability.

2.3.2 Electrical synapse

Electrical synapse, the simplest style of information transmission between the neurons, is located in the touching site of two neurons, in which there is a gap junction; the diameter of the touching point is more than $0.1-10 \mu m$. An electrical synapse also has presynaptic and postsynaptic membranes and a synaptic cleft with only $1-1.5 nm$ width. Membrane protein particles of the presynaptic and postsynaptic membranes span the full thickness of the membranes and exhibit a hexagonal structural unit. Their top is exposed to the surface of the membrane, and their center forms a micro passage with about a $2.5 nm$ diameter, which is vertical to the surface of the membrane and permits a substance with a diameter smaller than $1 nm$ to pass through, like amino acid. Bilateral membranes of the gap junction are symmetric. The tops of the membrane protein particles of the neighboring two synaptolemmas get in touch with each other, and the central tubules communicate with each other. The axonal terminal has no synaptic vesicles, and conduction does not require neurotransmitters. The electrical synapse conducts information by electric current, and the transmission of nerve impulse is usually bidirectional. Local current passes easily through it due to the low intercellular electric resistance and the high permeability of the neurons. The bidirectional transmission of the electric synapse decreases the space for the transmission, which makes the transmission more effective. Under the electronic microscope, the synaptic button contains many synaptic vesicles and small amounts of mitochon.

It has been identified now that electric synapses are dispersed in mammal corticocerebral astrocytes, basket cells, and astrocytes of the cerebellar cortex; horizontal cells and bipolar cells of the retina and some nuclei like the motor nuclei of oculomotor nerve; and vestibular nuclei and spinal nuclei of the trigeminal nerve. The electric synapse has various styles such as dendrodendritic synapse, axo-axonal synapse, soma-somatic synapse, axosomatic synapse, axon−dendritic synapse, and so on.

Electric synapse is sensitive to the changes of the internal and external environments. Its excitability decreases under the conditions of fatigue, anoxia, anesthesia, or acidosis, whereas its excitability increases under the condition of alkalosis.

2.3.3 Mechanism of synaptic transmission

During synaptic transmission, where the action potential is conducted to the axonal terminal and causes depolarization of the soma portion and increases Ca^{2+} permeability of the membrane, extracellular Ca^{2+} influx promotes synaptic vesicles to move forward and fuse with the presynaptic membrane. Then laceration occurs in the fusion site, and transmitters are released into the synaptic cleft and bind to special receptors in the postsynaptic membrane by diffusion. Then chemically gated channels open, which increases the permeability of some ions of the postsynaptic membrane. The postsynaptic membrane potential changes (depolarization or hyperpolarization of postsynaptic potential) produce a summation effect, which makes the postsynaptic neuron excitatory or inhibitory. Fig. 2.4 shows the basic process of the synaptic transmission.

The effects of Ca^{2+} in the process of synaptic transmission are:

1. *to lower the viscosity of axoplasm*, which favors the migration of synaptic vesicles by reducing the combination of actin binding protein on the vesicae with actin;
2. to eliminate interior negative potential of the presynaptic membrane, which promotes synaptic vesicle contact and fusion with the presynaptic membrane and then membrane splits and releases neurotransmitters.

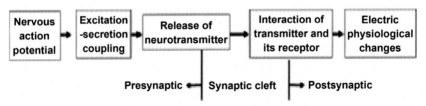

Figure 2.4 Basic process of synaptic transmission.

Presynaptic electric activity of the nervous system of higher animals never directly causes the activity of the postsynaptic component, and no electric coupling exists. Synaptic transmission acts uniformly by the medium with a special chemical substance called neuromediator or neurotransmitter. Synaptic transmission is carried out only from the presynaptic membrane toward the postsynaptic membrane, and it is unidirectional. It takes 0.5 to 1 ms to finish the excitation-secretion coupling from the release of the mediator and diffusing of the mediator in the cleft until depolarization of the postsynaptic membrane, as a synaptic delay. Synaptic transmission has the following characteristics: (1) unidirectional transmission; (2) synaptic delay; (3) summation, including temporal summation and spatial summation; (4) sensitive to internal environment and fatiguability; (5) excitatory rhythmicity modification (impulse frequency firing from the afferent nerve and efferent nerve is inconsistent in the same reflex); (6) after discharge (the efferent nerve still fires impulses for some time even after stimulation stops).

2.4 Neurotransmitter

Neurotransmitter is a special chemical substance that is released by the presynaptic nerve terminals and acts on the receptors located in the postsynaptic membrane. It is a special chemical substance that transmits information between neurons or between neurons and effector cells. After signal transmission, neurotransmitters inactivate them by enzymes or other means on the postsynaptic membrane.

There are five standards to identify whether endogenous nervous active material is a transmitter or not:

1. *Existence*: It should exist especially in the neurons; the terminals of the neurons have an enzymatic system used to synthesize the transmitter.
2. *Location*: After the transmitter is synthesized in the terminals of the neurons, it is usually stored in the vesicles, which can prevent it from being destroyed by other enzymes.
3. *Release*: The presynaptic terminal can release enough substance to cause a certain response of the postsynaptic cell or effector cell.
4. *Effect*: The transmitter passes through the synaptic cleft to act on the special site of the postsynaptic membrane, called the receptor, in order to cause the changes of ion permeability and potential of the postsynaptic membrane.

5. *Mechanism of inactivation*: The transmitter's function must end rapidly once it has produced the preceding effects to ensure swift synaptic transmission highly. There are several pathways for ending the effect of transmitter: (1) being hydrolyzed by enzyme and losing its activity; (2) being uptaken by the presynaptic membrane or partly by the postsynaptic membrane; (3) one part of transmitter enters the blood circulation and others are degraded by enzyme.

Many neurotransmitters have been discovered to date. Some of the best known are Ach, catecholamines (NE and DA), 5-HT, GABA, some amino acids, oligopeptides, among others.

2.4.1 Acetylcholine

Acetylcholine(Ach) is an excitatory neurotransmitter secreted by neurons in many areas of the brain but especially by the terminals of the large pyramidal cells of the motor cortex, by the motor neurons that innervate the skeletal muscles, by the preganglionic neurons of the autonomic nervous system, and by the postganglionic neurons of the parasympathetic nervous system.

Ach is synthesized in the presynaptic terminal from choline and acetyl coenzyme A in the presence of the enzyme *choline acetylase*:

$$(CH_3)_3N^+\text{---}CH_2\text{---}CH_2\text{---}OH \ + \ CH_3\text{---}CO \sim CoA \xrightarrow{\text{Choline acetylase}}$$
$$\underset{\text{Choline}}{} \qquad \underset{\text{Acetyl CoA}}{}$$

$$(CH_3)_3N^+\text{---}CH_2\text{---}CH_2\text{---}O\text{---}CO\text{---}CH_3 \ + \ CoA$$
$$\underset{\text{Acetyl choline}}{}$$

Choline acetylase is located in the cytoplasm, so it is conceived that Ach is first synthesized in the cytoplasm and then transported into its specific vesicles. Normally, Ach in vesicles and Ach in cytoplasm account for half each of the total quantity, and they are probably in balance. Ach stored in the vesicles binds with proteins, whereas it becomes free when it is released.

When a nerve impulse is conducted to the terminals along the axon, vesicles move toward the synaptic membrane, fuse with it, and then break. At this time, bound Ach converts to free Ach, and it is released into the synaptic cleft. At the same time, some freshly synthesized Ach in the cytoplasm is also released to join the response.

Ach has a physiological effect by acting on the receptor on the surface of the postsynaptic membrane. It has been identified that the

Ach-receptor is a lipoprotein present in the membrane, with a weight of 42,000 molecular weight.

Ach separates from its receptor after transferring information and dissociates in the synaptic cleft. Very little Ach is uptaken to the presynaptic neuron by its carrier system. The majority of Ach is hydrolyzed into choline and acetic acid in the presence of acetylcholine esterase and loses its activity. One part of Ach departs from the synaptic cleft by diffusion.

2.4.2 Catecholamines

Catecholamines are the amines containing basal structure of catechol. Catecholamines with biological activity in vivo include DA, NE, and E. Their structures are as follows:

NE and E are both hormones secreted by the adrenal medulla and the neurotransmitters secreted by the noradrenergic fibers of the sympathetic nerve and the CNS. NE is dispersed extensively in the center with great content. E has little content. Thus we mainly introduce the metabolism of NE. DA is also a kind of neurotransmitter mainly present in the extrapyramidal system.

2.4.2.1 Biological synthesis of catecholamines

Raw material used to synthesize catecholamines in the nervous tissues comes from tyrosine in blood.

During this process, tyrosine hydroxylase, tetrahydrobiopterin, O_2, and Fe^{2+} are involved in the first step. Among them, tyrosine hydroxylase locates in the cytoplasm of the noradrenergic fibers. It is a rate-limiting enzyme of NE synthesis due to its low content and low activity, while tetrahydrobiopterin is its coenzyme, and O_2 and Fe^{2+} are also the indispensable factors for NE synthesis. The reaction in the second step is catalyzed by the aromatic amino acid decarboxylase with not high specifity in the cytoplasm. Like the general amino acid decarboxylase, the aromatic amino acid decarboxylase requires pyridoxal phosphate as a coenzyme. The oxidizing reaction in the third step is catalyzed by DA hydroxylase, with the oxidation site being in the β carbon atom. DA hydroxylase is not in the cytoplasm but is attached to the inner wall of vesicles, and it belongs to the protein family containing Cu^{2+} and needs vitamin C as its cofactor.

In the view of the subcellular level distribution of these enzymes, the last step of NE synthesis is undertaken only within the vesicles, and the synthetic quantity of NE is not regulated by tyrosine hydroxylase. Furthermore, free NE with a high concentration in the nerve terminal may inhibit activity of tyrosine hydroxylase by negative feedback to decrease the synthesis of NE.

Phenylethanolamine-N-methyltransferase is found mainly in the adrenal medullary cells, and it can methylate NE to produce E. The quantity of this enzyme in the brain is low; thus it is believed that the normal mammalian brain contains very little E. Some people consider that if the content of phenylethanolamine-N-methyltransferase is too high, it can convert DA to N-methydopamin directly and cause a metabolic disorder of these neurotransmitters, which is probably the reason of schizophrenia.

2.4.2.2 Norepinephrine
1. *Storage and release*: NE is stored inside its specific vesicles after its synthesis. It binds loosely with ATP and chromogranin, which makes it hard for to penetrate into the cytoplasm and avoid being destroyed by monoamine oxidase (MAO). When the nerve impulse is conducted to the terminals, the vesicles nearby the presynaptic membrane fuse with it and break into pores. At this time, the NE inside the vesicles is released into the synaptic cleft together with chromogranin.
2. *NE's removal in the synaptic cleft*: NE released into the synaptic cleft can bind with NE receptor in the postsynaptic membrane to produce physiological effects. Then about three-quarters of NE is reuptaken by the presynaptic membrane and transported into the vesicles again. Reuptaking is a process of energy consumption that is related to Na^+, K^+-ATPase in the presynaptic membrane, and Mg^{2+}-ATPase in the vesicle membrane. One part of NE can be uptaken by the postsynaptic membrane and degraded and loses its activation there. Other parts are either destroyed in the synaptic cleft or diffused into blood. Except for the NE reuptaken by the presynaptic membrane that can be reused,

the rest suffers generally from enzymatic degradation and loses its activation. MAO and Catechol-O-Transmethylase (COMT) are two main enzymes catalyzing catecholamine to degrade, which are not only in the nervous tissues but also distributed widely in nonnervous tissues and in the mitochondrial membrane of neurons. In the presence of MAO, NE is oxidated first to aldehyde by oxidative deamination, and then the latter is converted into ethanol or acid. 3-methoxy-4-hydroxyphenylglycol is the main degradation product of NE in the center, while vanillylmandelic acid (VMA) is the main degradation product of NE in the peripheral. In the presence of COMT, circulating NE (mainly as hormone) is converted into methoxyl metabolic products in the livers and kidneys to be excreted. Nowadays, VMA content in urine has been a clinical index for the function of the sympathetic nerves. For the patient suffering from pheochromocytoma or neuroblastoma, VMA, the metabolic product of NE or E, increases accordingly because the tumor tissue also produces NE or E. Therefore it is very significant to measure VMA content in urine for diagnosis.

The somas of adrenergic neurons in the CNS concentrate upon the medulla oblongata and pons varolii, and their pathways have been identified. However, it is not certain that NE in the center is an inhibitory or excitatory neurotransmitter, which may be related to position. It is difficult to express the physiological effect of NE with simple terms like excite or inhibit. Some animal experiments show that NE can cause animal drowsiness, hypothermy, and feeding behavior. Some people believe that a fall of NE in the brain can induce ademosyne; conversely, an overdose of NE can induce mania. In short, NE in the brain is probably associated closely with body temperature, feeding behavior, analgesia, regulation of the cardiovascular system, and mental status.

2.4.2.3 Dopamine

In the process of the biological synthesis of catecholamines transmitters, DA is the precursor of NE. DA exists in any tissue of the body where NE exists. Because there is a high concentration of DA in some portions of the center and its distribution is not parallel to that of NE, it is also considered as an independent neurotransmitter generally.

DA in the brain has various functions including enhancing body movement, enhancing the endocrine of pituitary gland and regulating psychoactivity.

$$CH_3O-\!\!\!\!\overset{\displaystyle\bigcirc}{\underset{HO-}{}}\!\!\!\!-CH_2-COOH$$

3-methoxyl-4-hydroxyphenylacetic acid

The vesicles of the dopaminergic nerve terminal are the storage sites of DA, and they are different from those vesicles storing NE. The former have no DA-β-hydroxylase; therefore they cannot convert DA to NE. In addition, only if the substance has the β-hydroxyl structure can it be stored in vesicles of the noradrenergic fibers, but no β-hydroxyl exists in the structure of DA. The storage, release, and degradation of DA are all very similar to those of NE, but its renewal velocity is faster than that of NE. 3-methoxyl-4-hydroxyphenylacetic acid (homovanillic acid), the main metabolic product of DA in the brain.

2.4.3 5-hydroxytryptamine

5-HT is also referred to as serotonin, which was discovered initially in serum. There are 5-hydroxytryptaminergic neurons in the CNS. However, no 5-hydroxytryptaminergic neuron has been discovered in the PNS to date.

5-HT cannot permeate the blood—brain barrier, so 5-HT in the center is synthesized in the brain, and it has a different source from peripheral 5-HT. It has been identified by histochemical method that 5-hydroxytryptaminergic neural somas are mainly distributed in the rapheal nuclei group of the midbrain stem and that their terminals are distributed widely in the brain and spinal cord. The precursor of 5-HT is tryptophane that is converted to 5-HT by two enzymatic reactions: hydroxylation and decarboxylation. The process is similar in some degree to that of synthesis of catecholamines.

Similar to tyrosine hydroxylase, tryptophan hydroxylase also needs O_2, Fe^{2+}, and tetrahydrobiopterin as a coenzyme. But it has a lower concentration in the brain and lower activity, so it is a rate-limiting enzyme for the biological synthesis of 5-HT. In addition, the concentration of 5-HT in the brain may affect the activity of tryptophan hydorxylase and serves its own self-regulation by feedback. Free tryptophane concentration in serum can also affect the synthesis of 5-HT in the brain. When free tryptophane in serum increases (for example, by injecting tryptophame into a rat's abdominal cavity), tryptophane entering the brain increases, which can accelerate the synthesis of 5-HT.

Similar to catecholamines, 5-HT released into the synaptic cleft is reuptaken predominantly by the presynaptic nerve terminal, and then one part is restored in the vesicles and one part is oxidized by MAO in the mitochondrial membrane.

5-hydroxytryptamine   5-hydroxyindolacetic acid

This is the main mode of degradation of 5-HT. 5-hydroxyindolacetic acid is inactive.

By detecting the functions of 5-HT to various neurons, it is discovered that 5-HT can excite the majority of sympathetic preganglionic neurons while it can inhibit parasympathetic preganglionic neurons. 5-HT content in the brain decreases apparently when animal rapheal nuclei are destroyed and the synthesis of 5-HT is blocked with drugs, which can make animals suffer sleep disorders and their pain threshold to decrease, at the same time that the analgesic effect of morphine decreases or disappears. Stimulating a rat's rapheal nuclei with electricity can cause its temperature to rise and then accelerate renewal of 5-HT. These phenomena reveal that sleeping, analgesia, and temperature regulation are all related to 5-HT in the brain. Furthermore, it is reported that 5-HT can alter the hypophyseal endocrine function. In addition, some suggest that hallucinations of the patient suffering psychosis result from the destruction of the 5-hydroxytryptaminergic neuron. It is thus clear that psychoactivity is also related to 5-HT in some degree.

2.4.4 Amine acid and oligopeptide

Amine acids are present everywhere in the brain. It was thought previously that they were only the materials of the synthesis of proteins or the metabolic products of proteins. For the past few years, researchers have noticed that some amine acids play a role of transmitter in the synaptic transmission of the center. Furthermore, neutral amine acids such as γ-aminobutyric acid, glycine, β-alamine and the like, all appear inhibitory to the central neurons while acidic amino acids like glutamic acid and aspartic acid appear excitatory.

Some micromolecular peptides also function as neurotransmitters. Enkephalin, discovered in 1975, is an oligopeptide composed of five amino acid residues. Enkephalin separated from pig brain can be divided into two types—(1) Met-enkephalin: H-Tyr-Gly-Gly-Phe-Met-OH and (2) Leu-enkephalin: H-Tyr-Gly-Gly-Phe-Leu-OH—both of which are the peptides synthesized by brain cells. They have similar functions to morphine and hence are called enkephalin. It is well-known that morphine must be bound to the morphine receptor first before it plays its role of analgesia and euphoria. Morphine is exogenous while enkephalin is endogenous. In addition, there is another peptide called endorphine in the brain, which can bind to the morphine receptor and produce morphine-like effects. It is still not certain whether these peptides are real neurotransmitters, but it is significant for elucidating the brain's function, especially algesia principle, to study their effects.

2.4.5 Nitric oxide

A breakthrough in the field of intracellular information transmission has been initiated from important experimental results obtained from rabbit aorta specimens by Furchgott et al. in 1980. They observed, with the endothelium of the specimen being moved, Ach lost its role of relaxing the smooth muscle of the specimen. However, its relaxation of smooth muscle could be recovered if the specimen without endothelium makes contact with arterial stripe specimen with endothelium. Their conclusion was that Ach played its role of relaxation by inducing vascular endothelial cells to release a substance called the relaxing factor from the vascular endothelium by them. The substance was very easy to be decomposed, thus it took several years to identify it as nitric oxide for three research teams led by Furchgott, Ignarro, and Murad, respectively. The three leaders were endowed with the Nobel Prize in 1998 for their work.

Nitric oxide is a kind of gas, only slightly soluble in water. Academic circles were shocked by the discovery of the gas messenger. Nitric oxide is converted from L-arginine in the presence of nitric oxide synthetase and affects target material not by the transduction of receptor but by diffusing directly through the cell membrane. It has many target materials. Among them, guanosin monophospate cyclase is the representative one that can foster guanosine triphosphate (GTP) to form cGMP. Once guanosin monophospate cyclase is activated by nitric oxide, it can decrease the concentration of intracellular Ca^{2+} by signal transduction to cause the relaxation of smooth muscle.

As a messenger, nitric oxide produced under the neurologic type of nitric oxide synthetase is involved in many functions of the CNS, such as synaptic plasticity, memory, vision, smell, and so on. It is the main messenger of nonadrenergic and noncholinergic neurons in the PNS.

2.4.6 Receptor

The concept of receptor (R) was proposed first in 1905 by J. N. Langley, an English pharmacologist. He observed that curare could not directly repress muscle contraction by electric stimulation but could antagonize muscle contraction caused by nicotine. Hence, he imagined that both of the agents just bond to intracellular definite nonnervous and nonmuscular substances. The difference between the combinations among nicotine and the definite substance produced further biological effect, muscle contraction, while the combination between curare and the definite substance produced antagonism of muscle contraction. He named the definite substance as a receptive substance. As a matter of fact, the concept of the receptive substance (receptor) proposed by J. N. Langrey at that time is still in use now, in that he pointed out two important functions of a receptor: recognizing special substance and producing biological effect.

Nicotine and curare can affect selectively specific molecules in the body and produce biological effects. They are called bioactive substances that can be divided into two types according their sources: endogenous bioactive substances, inherent in vivo, such as transmitters, hormones, nutrition factors, and so on; exogenous bioactive substances, present in vitro, for example, some drugs like nicotine, curare, and poisons. Receptors are the biological macromolecules in the membrane and cytoplasm or nuclei that can recognize and bind with the special bioactive substances to produce biological effects. The bioactive substances with the character of binding selectively to receptors are called ligands. Among them, those substances that can bind to receptors to produce biological effects are called agonists, while those substances that can bind to receptors to antagonize the biological effects produced by agonists are called antagonists. Those substances that have agonism and antagonism are called partial agonists. The receptors in the neuron are called neuroceptors.

Since Numa and his colleagues purified and determined successfully the primary structure of AchR in 1983 and established the first line of studying the structure and functions of receptor molecules, the primary structures of many receptors and their subunits have been identified, which makes it possible for us to classify the receptors according to their molecular structure characters and analyze their activity mechanisms.

Generally, receptor should have the following four characteristics according to biochemical identification: (1) *Saturability*: The quantity of receptor molecules is limited, so the dose effect curve of binding ligand with receptor is also limited, and their specific bindings appear as high affinity and low capacity. There are nonspecific bindings between cell and ligand, and they appear as low affinity, high capacity, and no saturability. (2) *Specificity*: A specified receptor only binds to specific ligand to produce biological effect. Therefore, people often study the characteristics of receptors by comparisons of a series of biological effects of ligands and then classify them according to their functions. (3) *Reversibility*: The combination of ligand and receptor should be reversible in physiological activities. The dissociation constant of the ligand—receptor complex is different; however, the dissociated ligand should be not its metabolic product but primal ligand.

Receptors have two main functions: selectively recognizing the transmitter and activating the effector. Thus, on the one hand, according to their transmitters, receptors can be classified into Ach-receptor, Glu-receptor, GABA-receptor, Gly-receptor, 5-HT-receptor, Histamine-receptor, Ad-receptor recognizing NA and A, and receptors recognizing various neuropeptides. On the other hand, the primary structures of many receptors have been elucidated, so according to their molecular mechanisms of acting on effectors, they can be also divided into ionic channel type and metabolic regulating type, which regulate the activities of ionic channels directly or indirectly. Receptor molecules of ionic channel type have both receptor sites of recognizing transmitter and ionic channels, so their activity speed is very fast. This type of receptor includes nAch-receptor, $GABA_A$-receptor, $5-HT_3$-receptor, and iGlu-receptor. Receptor molecules of the metabolic regulating type contain only receptor sites for recognizing transmitters but no micropores permitting ions pass through. Their function coupling with effectors is realized by a guanine–nucleotide-binding protein, G-protein. This type contains two gene families: mAch-receptor, $GABA_B$-receptor, mGlu-receptor, $5-HT_{1,2,4}$-receptor, and various receptors of neuropeptides, and so on. In addition, some receptors, with C-terminal containing kinase or not, are activated by nutrition factors, hormones, and some neuropeptides.

2.5 Transmembrane signal transduction

Briefly speaking, signal transduction is the stimulating factor of external environment, or the intercellular signaling molecules in vivo. The first messengers such as hormones, neurotransmitters, or ligands bind to receptors on the surface of cells or intracellular receptors, and intracellular second messengers form through transmembrane signal conversion. Then information is transferred by a cascade of responses to the specified sites of effectors to produce physiological effects or to induce gene expression. The classical transduction pathway is briefly as follows:

External or internal stimulators → ligands → receptors → transmembrane → the second messengers → a cascade of phosphorylation signaling transmission → functional regulation of the body

Hydrophilic neurotransmitters can not only pass generally into cells but can bind to receptors in the membrane and transfer information to receptors. The ionic channel type of receptors receives signals and responses directly by the effectors themselves. The metabolic regulating type of receptors must transfer information to the inside of the cell by a series of transmissions and then transfer it to ionic channels or effectors of metabolic pattern. The process of information transferring from receptors to ionic channels or intracellular effectors of metabolic pattern is called signal transmembrane transduction. In the last 20 years, the research in this field has developed rapidly since the second messenger hypothesis about hormone action was proposed and G-protein was discovered. The hypothesis proposed in the research on the action mechanism of hormones and the novel discovery further push the research of the action mechanisms of neurotransmitters and other bioactive substances.

2.5.1 Transducin

In 1958, Sutherland discovered that glycogenolysis of the hepatocytes spurred by glucagons and adrenalin is realized by cyclic adenosine monophosphate (cAMP), a novel substance that he discovered. Both hormones bond to their own receptors to activate adenylate cyclase (ACase), and the latter catalyzes ATP to produce cAMP. He also discovered that cAMP was essential for the activation of cAMP-dependent protein kinase (PAK) and then activated PAK activated phosphoesterase to further catalyze decomposition of liver glycogen. Sutherland proposed the second messenger theory about hormone action in 1965 based on the results that were not entering the cell. Hormones brought information to specified receptors on the membrane as the first messengers; then receptors activated ACase in the membrane to convert intracellular ATP to cAMP. After that, cAMP as the second messenger transferred information to effectors to respond. This hypothesis led to the discovery of guanosine nucleotide binding protein (G-protein).

In the experiment of preparation of lipocyte debris, Rodbell demonstrated that several hormones like glucagons, adrenalin, ACTH, and others all catalyzed ATP by ACase to produce cAMP, the common second messenger. In 1970, he also discovered that GTP was essential in the conversion of ATP to cAMP by means of a system of hormone, receptor, and ACase. The experiment still showed that GTP was neither decomposed nor bound to the receptor and ACase in the reaction. In 1987, Gilman successfully isolated and purified the transduction from a membrane specimen, which could both bind to GTP and connect with receptor and ACase, called GTP-binding protein. This is the signal transmembrane transduction pathway first proposed. For it, Sutherland obtained the Nobel Prize in 1971, and Gilman and Rodbell received the Prize in 1994.

G-protein is a group of soluble intramembrane proteins with molecular weight of 100,000 that are involved in the signal transmembrane transduction of neuron. According to its function, it can be divided into four species: Gs, Gi, Go, and Gt. Gs can activate ACase, and it can be activated by cholera toxin directly and open some Ca^{2+} channels. Gi can inhibit the activity of ACase, and it is sensitive to pertussis toxin (PTX). In the presence of PTX, Gs cannot be activated by a receptor. It can open some K^+ channels to produce an inhibitory response. In the beginning, Go indicated those G-proteins that didn't affect ACase, but now they only represent those G-proteins that are sensitive to PTX and can activate PKC, while those G-proteins that are not sensitive to PTX but can activate PKC are called Gpc. Go and Gpc are abundant in brain tissues. They can open some K^+ channels and also inhibit T-type and N-type voltage-gated Ca^{2+} channels. Gt is a kind of G-protein coupling rhodophane in photoreceptor with the enzyme cGMP-PDE in primary effectors, which can close Na^+ channels.

At the resting statement, receptor is in activated state and has high affinity with ligand, while G-GDP is inactivated. When the ligands

(A) bind to receptors (R) to form A-R complex, the latter has high affinity with G-GDP to form an A-R-G-GDP complex. Following the formation of the complex, GDP is replaced by GTP in cytoplasm to form activated G-GTP. During this process, G-protein converts from inactivation to activation. Once GTP substitution is finished, the complex is decomposed into three components: A-R, α-GTP, and $\beta\gamma$. Among them, α-GTP can hydrolyze GTP to form GDP; thus at the same time as activating effectors, α-GTP loses its phosphoric acid molecules to become α-GDP. α-GDP has high affinity with the $\beta\gamma$ subunit, and they combine to form G-GDP again, which indicates that it returns to the inactivated form at the resting statement. On the other hand, the combination of A-R and G-GDP lowers the affinity of receptor with ligand, which makes R separate itself from A-R, so R also returns to the activated form at the resting statement. At the same time, effectors activated by G-protein become inactivated.

2.5.2 The second messenger

There are nearly 100 kinds of transmitters and endogenous bioactive substances as the first messenger, while their receptors are twice or three times that number. The majority of them are the metabolic regulating receptors, which depend on G-protein's coupling with the effector in some fashion.

The second messengers produced by the hydrolysis of membrane phospholipids include inositol triphosphate(IP_3), diacyl glycerol (DG), aracidonic acid, among others. Transmembrane signal transduction is divided accordingly into cAMP system, IP_3 system, and aracidonic acid system. In the recent years, NO produced by the action of the enzyme nitric oxide synthetase has also been discovered as a second messenger. Maybe CO is another one.

The common transduction pathway of the second messenger is shown in Fig. 2.5 [1]. The activities of the three systems can be divided into three steps: (1) the first messenger outside the cell; (2) the receptor in the membrane, transducin binding to the inner wall of the membrane and primary effector (enzyme) in the membrane; (3) the intracellular second messenger and secondary effector. Different transmitters act on their own receptors respectively to activate their own primary effectors by the transduction of some G-protein and conduct information to the second messenger to activate the secondary effector.

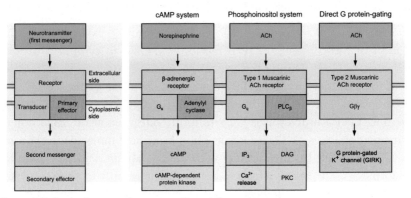

Figure 2.5 Synaptic second message G-protein sequence.

Most secondary effectors are kinases. One kind of kinase, phosphorylates often different target proteins, which can cause the signals to be magnified and cross each other, finally make ions channels open or close, or induce relevant metabolic changes. The quantity of G-proteins is far larger than that of receptors, thus one receptor binding with the transmitter can activate multiple molecules of G-protein, causing signals to be magnified.

A cAMP-dependent PAK that is the secondary effector in a cAMP system is composed of two regulatory subunits (R-subunits) and two catalytic subunits (C-subunits). The two identical R-subunits have four regions: (1) The N terminal region is the binding site of companion subunits; (2) the next region, combining with C-subunit, inhibits its enzymatic activity; (3) two identical regions bind with cAMP. The molecule of PKA can be written as R_2C_2. ATP is converted into cAMP by the action of the enzyme ACase: $R_2C_2 + 4 \text{ cAMP} = 2 (R \cdot 2\text{cAMP}) + 2C$, and then C can further phosphorylate effector protein.

As shown in Fig. 2.5 [1], in phosphoinositide system, phosphoinositide is first hydrolyzed by PLC into IP_3 and DG. Hydrophobic DG is kept in the membrane. PKC is inactive in the cytoplasm. When DG is produced, PKC is activated due to binding with DG in the membrane, and then activated PKC phosphorylates its substrates in the membrane or in the cytoplasm. IP_3 is another second messenger. Some receptors can cause IP_3 to be produced. It can open Ca^{2+} channels in sarcoplasmic reticulum Ca^{2+} storage to increase intracellular Ca^{2+} concentration and then arouse various cell responses.

In the arachidonic acid system, arachidonic acid is released from the membrane by the action of the enzyme of PLA_2, and then is converted immediately into several bioactive metabolic products by three kinds of enzymes, as shown in Fig. 2.5.

Besides these three kinds of the second messenger systems, there is also a cGMP system first discovered in rod and cone cells. With the effect of light, rhodopsin produces the second messenger cGMP by the transduction of Gt, and the latter can regulate Na^+ channels directly. The dark, higher concentration of cGMP can open cGMP-gated Na^+ channels to cause the relative depolarization of visual cells. Rhodopsin activated by the light stimulates cGMP phosphodiesterase to lower the cGMP concentration and close channels to induce hyperpolarization of visual cells.

From the preceding viewpoint, there are several styles about the regulation of G-protein on ionic channels: (1) α subunit or $\beta\gamma$ subunits in G-protein acts/act directly on the ionic channels, such as K^+ channel and Ca^{2+} channel; (2) G-protein acts first on the enzyme of the effector and the second messenger, and then the latter acts as ionic channel; (3) G-protein acts first on the enzymes of the effector and the second messenger, and then the latter acts as ionic channel through the actions of kinases.

As indicated by some data recently, with the effects of exogenous factors such as transmitters, modulators, nutrition factors, and hormones, membrane receptors and nuclear receptors of neurons transfer signals to nuclei by the transduction of G-proteins and the phosphorylation of intracellular effectors to induce the changes of gene expression that are closely associated with the mechanisms of synaptic plasticity, learning, and memory. Among them, there is much research on direct early genes and delayed early genes.

Zhuan Zhou, an investigator of Shanghai Institutes for Biological Sciences of the Chinese Academy of Sciences, discovered with his student, Chen Zhang, in an experiment with rat sense dorsal root ganglia in which neurotransmitter was released to the next neuron not only by the command of Ca^{2+} but also by voltage impulse [5]. The neural signal conduction mechanism induced only by the neural impulse was an unexpected novel discovery, causing a series of new projects in the neural science research to be proposed.

How is the neural signal transferred from one neuron to another? It is a focus of neural science research. Currently, the dominant view in the academic field is as follows: The first neuron in an excitatory state produces an electric impulse (action potential); then extracellular Ca^{2+} flow into the cell and induce the cell to secrete some bioactive molecules (neurotransmitters). The latter diffuse to the surface (membrane) of the next neuron. When membrane receptors bind with neurotransmitters, the second neuron produces an electric impulse. In a similar way, neural signals pass on as a cascade until the brain's senior functions like learning and memory occur finally. This is the neurotransmitter releasing and neural signal transduction mechanism commanded by Ca^{2+}. Another neural signal transduction is mediated merely by neural electric impulse, not by Ca^{2+}; that is, the discovery of Zhuan Zhou and Chen Zhang may take on importance in neural signal transduction and information integration. Zhuan Zhou revealed that there was only one neurotransmitter secretion pathway in some neural cells, for example the adrenal chromaffin cells. In addition, the signal transduction mechanism of non-Ca^{2+} voltage-secretion coupling had also been an important project to be further pursued in neural science research.

2.6 Resting membrane potential

Bioelectricity was discovered first in the research of neural and muscular activities. The so-called balcony experiment undertaken at the end of the 18th century by Galvani, an Italian doctor and physiologist, is the beginning of bioelectricity research. When he hung the specimen of frog lower limb with a cuprum hook to the iron baluster on the balcony to observe the effects of lightening on nerves and muscles, he discovered unexpectedly that muscles contracted when the frog limb touched iron baluster when blown by the wind. Galvani thought it was a proof of bioelectricity.

I. Nobeli, a physicist, improved the current meter in 1827 and used it to record the current flow between muscular transection and intact longitudinal surface, with a negative charge in the trauma site and positive charge in the intact portion. This was the first direct measurement of bioelectricity (injury potential). Du Bois Reymond, a German physiologist, on the one hand, improved and designed the equipment used to study bioelectric phenomena such as the key set, nonpolarizable electrode, induction coil, and more sensitive current meters. On the other hand, he carried out extensive and in-depth research on bioelectricity. For example, he found bioelectricity in the cerebral cortex, glands, skin, and eyeball. And especially in 1849, he recorded injury potential in the nerve trunk and its negative electricity changes in activities, which were neural resting potential and action potential. Based on this, he first proposed his hypothesis about a bioelectricity-generating mechanism, the polarized molecule hypothesis. He conceived that the surface of the nerve or muscle was composed of magnet-like polarized molecules lining up in order. There was a positive charge zone in the center of each molecule and negative charge zones in its two sides. A positive charge was assembled in the longitudinal surface of the nerve and muscle, while a negative charge was assembled in their transactions; thus a potential difference occurred between them. When the nerve and muscle are excited, their polarized molecules, lined up in order, became disordered, and the potential difference between the surface and the inside disappeared.

With the progress of electrochemistry, Bernstein, a student of Du Bois Reymond, developed a bioelectric existence hypothesis that is still considered fairly correct now and pushed the membrane theory of bioelectric research. The theory presumed that electric potential existed in the two sides of the neural and muscular membrane. In a resting state, the cell membrane permitted K^+ but not multivalent cations or anions to penetrate. The resting potential occurred due to the selective permeability of the membrane to K^+ and the K^+ concentration difference between the outside and inside of the membrane. When the nerve was excited, the selective permeability of the membrane to K^+ disappeared, causing electricity difference between two sides of membrane to disappear transiently, so action potential formed.

In the 1920s, Gasser and Erlanger introduced modern electronic equipment like the cathode ray oscilloscope to neurophysiological research, which spurred bioelectric research to develop rapidly. They obtained the Nobel Prize in 1944 together because of their analysis of electric activities of nerve fibers. Young had reported that inkfish nerve trunk had a giant axon with a 500 μm diameter. British physiologists A. L. Hodgkin and Huxley realized the intracellular record of resting potential and action potential first by inserting a glass capillary electrode longitudinally from the cut into the giant axon. They proposed the sodium theory about action potential based on exact quantitative analysis of the two kinds of potential and confirmed and developed Bernstein's membrane theory about resting potential. Thereafter, they further utilized voltage-clamp techniques to record action current in the inkfish giant axon and confirmed the current could be divided into two components: Na^+ current and K^+ current. Based on that, they proposed a double-ion channels pattern again and encouraged others to study molecular biology of ion channels.

With the push of microelectrode recording techniques, neural cellular physiological research stepped into a new developing period. Eccles began his electrophysiologic study on spinal neurons in vivo and their axons by utilizing glass microelectrodes and discovered the excitatory and inhibitory postsynaptic potentials. Because of their dedication to neural physiology, A. L. Hodgkin, Huxley, and Eccles shared the physiology or medicine Nobel Prize in 1963. Meanwhile Katz began to study the neuromuscular junction synapse using microelectrode techniques and obtained the Nobel Prize in 1970 for it. Based on the explosion of nervous system research, a comprehensive subject, neurobiology and neuroscience formed in the 1960s.

Various transient electric changes occurring in activities like receptor potential, synaptic potential, and action potential are all based on resting potential, so it is the most fundamental electric phenomenon in excitable cells such as neurons and muscle cells [6]. For convenience of description, the state of potential difference between the two sides of the membrane is usually referred to as polarization, the rise of absolute value of resting potential is referred to as hyperpolarization, and the falling of absolute value of resting potential is referred to as depolarization (see Fig. 2.6).

The potential difference between two sides of the membrane of excitable cells like neurons and muscle cells is about 70 mV, which

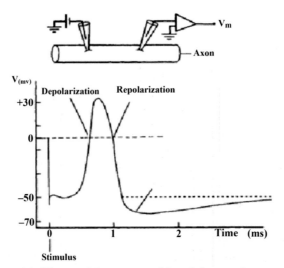

Figure 2.6 Potential difference between two sides of the membrane.

indicates that negative and positive ion clouds are dispersed respectively on the inside and the outside of the membrane surface. No ion has equal concentration in neural cytoplasm to that in the extracellular fluid, especially K^+, Na^+, and Cl^-, with the concentration reaching the level of mmol/L in external or internal fluid and the transmembrane concentration difference of one order of magnitude, called constant ions. Na^+ and Cl^- gather outside while K^+ gathers inside. Some big organic anions (A^-) occur only in the cells, and their concentrations also reach about the level of mmol/L.

Ion channels are some big protein molecules inlaid dispersedly in the membrane composed of continuous lipid bilayer. They cross the membrane and contain hydrophilic micropores permitting selectively specific ions to pass through the membrane. According to the permeable ion species, they can be classified to K^+ channels, Na^+ channels, Cl^- channels, and Ca^{2+} channels. Ion channels have at least two states: opening state and closing state. When the channels open, specific ions cross the membrane along the concentration gradient. Resting potential forms just because specific ions pass through the so-called resting ion channels, which are continuously open in the resting state along the concentration gradient.

The cell membrane of the neuron plays the role of electric resistance on electric current. This electric resistance is called membrane resistance. Besides as electric resistance, cell membrane has also the function of capacitor, which is called membrane capacitance. Fig. 2.7 shows how to detect the changes of membrane potential [1]. Whether switched on or off, the current toward the cell membrane must go first through the charging or discharging of the capacitor respectively and then make the electrotonic potential rise or fall exponentially. When $t = 0$, current is injected into firstly cell membrane, and the potential at any time is recorded as V_t, then:

$$V_t = V_\infty(1 - e^{-t/\tau}) \tag{2.1}$$

V_∞ in the formula is a constant value after the charging to the capacitor is finished. When $t = \tau$, the formula (2.1) can be written briefly as:

$$V_t = V_\infty\left(1 - \frac{1}{e}\right) = 0.63 V_\infty \tag{2.2}$$

That is, τ is the duration time of electronic voltage rising to $0.63\ V_\infty$. Thus τ is the time constant value representing the changing velocity of

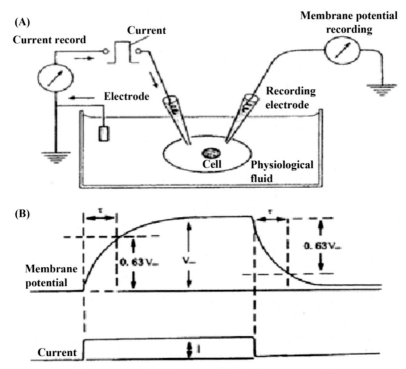

Figure 2.7 Membrane potential of neuron. (A) Membrane potential measurements; (B) Membrane potential changes.

the membrane's electronic potential, and it is equal to the product of the multiplication of membrane capacitance (C) and membrane resistance (R):

$$\tau = RC.$$

Among them, R can be figured out by the electric current value in the experiment, dividing V_∞. In this way, membrane resistance and membrane capacitance can be measured respectively. In order to compare the electric characteristics of various excitable cells, it is necessary to further figure out specific membrane resistance and specific membrane capacity per membrane unit area. Membrane capacitance originates from the lipid bilayer in the membrane while membrane resistance comes from ion channels in the membrane.

2.7 Action potential

Excitability and conductivity are two characteristics of the neuron. When some portion of the neuron receives stimulation, excitation will occur in this part and propagate along the neuron. If the conditions are right, it can transfer to the related neurons or other cells by synaptic transmission and make the activities or states of the target organs change finally.

When the cell is stimulated, based on the resting potential, the potentials in two sides of membrane perform once rapid retroversion and recovery, which is called action potential (as shown in Fig. 2.6). For the stimuli with subthreshold intensity, local current rises with the increase of the stimulus intensity. However, different from it, action potential never occurs with subthreshold stimulus. Once stimulus intensity reaches the threshold or greater, action potential will occur on the basis of local current and reach the fixed maximum quickly by self-regeneration, and then recover the initial resting potential level quickly. This responsive style is called the *all-or-nothing* response.

Another characteristic of action potential is nondecremental conduction. As electric impulse, once the action potential is set off on one site of neuron, membrane potential on this site becomes negative outside and positive inside explosively, so the site becomes a battery, which forms the stimulus for the adjacent site in resting potential state and its intensity apparently exceeds the threshold. The adjacent site enters the excitable state due to receiving suprathreshold stimulus and produces action potential according to all-or-nothing principles. In this way, the action potential on one site of the neuron induces the adjacent site to produce orderly action potential, and it can conduct toward the distal sites with no decrement because of its all-or-nothing response. However, the amplitude of action potential in the axon terminal becomes lower because its diameter becomes thinner.

Once action potential is set off on some sites of the neuron's membrane, the excitability on this site will produce a series of changes. In the overshooting phase of action potential, any stimulus with any intensity cannot elicit action potential on the site again. This phase is called the absolute refractory period. In the following period, only the superthreshold stimulus is strong enough to elicit action potential on the site, but its amplitude is lower. This phase is called the relative refractory period. For example, if the duration of the action potential is 1 ms, then the summation of the two phases should be shorter than 1 ms; otherwise the next action potential will overlap the former.

The main functions of action potential are:
1. conducting electric signals rapidly and over a long distance;
2. regulating the release of neurotransmitters, contraction of muscles, secretion of glands, and so on.

Action potentials of several excitable cells have common characteristics, but there are differences in their amplitudes, shapes, and ionic bases to a certain extent.

The discovery of the overshooting phase of action potential contradicted the explanation about action potential with classical membrane theory proposed by Bernstein; that is, the view of action potential contributing to the transient disappearance of selective ion permeability of the membrane is unacceptable. In the 1950s, A. L. Hodgkin et al. carried out precise experiments on the axons of inkfish, which showed that K^+, Na^+, and Cl^- permeability coefficients of axolemma in the rest state were $P_K: P_{Na}: P_{Cl} = 1: 0.04: 0.45$, while in the peak of action potential, they were $P_K: P_{Na}: P_{Cl} = 1: 20: 0.45$. Apparently, the ratio of P_K to P_{Cl} didn't change, but the ratio of P_K to P_{Na} increased notably by three orders of magnitude [7]. According to the data of these experiments and others, they proposed the sodium ion theory; that is to say, the occurrence of action potential was up to the transient rise of Na^+ permeability of cell membrane because the cell membrane changes abruptly from the resting state based mainly on K^+ equilibrium potential to the active state based mainly on Na^+ equilibrium potential.

The changes of sodium conductance and potassium conductance in the action potential process are shown in Fig. 2.8. Increased Na^+ permeability causes membrane potential to approach the Na^+ equilibrium

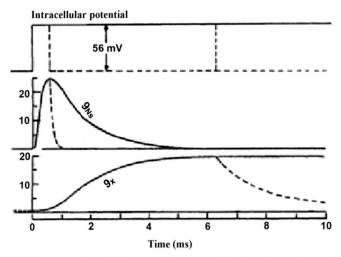

Figure 2.8 Sodium and potassium conductance changes when depolarization of giant axon of inkfish reaches 56 mV.

potential, and soon it falls rapidly. Following it, K^+ permeability rises continuously, which makes the membrane potential recover to the proximal level of K^+ equilibrium potential in the resting state. Sodium conductance decreases in two different ways: fixing the membrane potential level to -9 mV, sodium conductance occurs, and then the membrane potential recovers to the resting level in a short time (0.63 ms in this example), as shown in Fig. 2.8 (left dashed line), and sodium conductance disappears rapidly (as shown by the dashed line). At this time, if the membrane potential depolarizes again, sodium conductance may still occur. The other way is, if the membrane potential jumps to -9 mV and lasts at that level, sodium conductance will gradually become smaller until it disappears. At this time if membrane potential depolarizes again, no sodium conductance occurs. This phenomenon is called deactivation of sodium current. Only if the membrane potential recovers for several milliseconds does the second stimulus become effective. The process from the deactivation to recovery of activation is called reactivation. Different from sodium conductance, potassium conductance can still maintain the highest level after depolarization for above 6 ms (Fig. 2.8, right dashed line). It disappears in the curve opposite to that of emergence when the membrane potential recovers the primary level. The potassium current deactivates very slowly; thus it has been considered that it has no process of deactivation.

The action current of the giant axon of inkfish is composed of Na^+ inward flow and delayed K^+ outward flow. The two ion currents are produced when two kinds of ions pass through their own voltage-gated channels to cross the membrane. After progress was obtained in the research on the giant axon of inkfish, the research of action current analyzed by the voltage-clamp technique expanded quickly to other excitable cell membranes. Results indicated that two voltage-gated channels existed in all excitable cell membranes that had been studied. In addition, a voltage-gated Ca^{2+} channel was also discovered, and a voltage-gated Cl^- channel was discovered in some neurons. Four voltage-gated channels have different subtypes. Na^+ channel has at least two subtypes: the neurological type discovered in neurons and the muscular type discovered in muscles. The Ca^{2+} channel has four subtypes (T, N, L, and P types); the K^+ channel has four types (delayed rectifier K^+ channel, fast transient K^+ channel or A channel, anomalous rectification K^+ channel, and Ca^{2+} activated K^+ channel). Cells producing action potential are called excitable cells, but the amplitudes and duration of action potential produced by different types of excitable cells vary because the type and the quantity of ion channels involved in the formation of action potential are different.

The formation mechanism of action potential in the axolemma and multiple kinds of neuron membrane is simple. Its ascending phase is formed by Na^+ current, and it is called Na^+-dependent action potential. This kind of action potential has a relatively big amplitude, short duration, and rapid conduction velocity. Whether or not the K^+ current is involved in the descending phase of axon action potential depends on the kinds of animals. For example, the action potential of the nodal membrane of myelinated nerve fibers in rabbits is different from that of giant axon in inkfish. The former has no component of K^+ current. As for the axolemma of the Ranvier node of frog, and especially the axolemma of the excitable node of invertebral prawn, the action potential has the component of K^+ current, but it is not only very small, its threshold of activation is relatively high; thus it has no apparent effect on the shortening duration of action potential.

Different types of neurons and even the different sites of a single neuron have different excitability. For example, there are differences of excitability among axon hillock, axon terminals, and dendrites. Differences of excitability are determined by the kinds of voltage-gated channels in the excitation membrane and their density. The action potentials of the cell body and axon terminals in some neurons are coformed by Na^+ current and Ca^{2+} current, and their durations are relatively long. It is also discovered in some neurons' dendrites that action potential with low amplitude and long duration is formed by Ca^{2+} current.

Once action potential (nerve impulse) is elicited at one point in the membrane of a neuron (except in the thin dendrites), it travels over the remaining portion with constant velocity and amplitude. When action potential occurs explosively, membrane potential at one point that can make local current develop to action potential is called threshold potential. Depolarization from the resting membrane potential to threshold potential is usually called critical depolarization. The critical depolarization value is about 32 mV. Generally speaking, the threshold value is the difference between the resting membrane and threshold potential; that is, the threshold value is in direct proportion to the critical depolarization, and it will change with relative changes of the two potentials. Threshold potential is the membrane potential at the point where Na^+ permeability

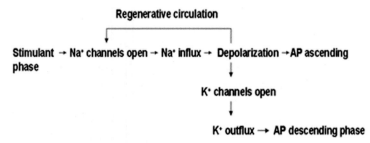

Figure 2.9 Formation of action potential.

caused by depolarization increases to make Na^+ inward flow volume just equal to the K^+ outward flow volume. Local current occurs because sodium conductance (g_{Na}) begins to rise, but potassium conductance (g_K) is still bigger than g_{Na} before depolarization reaches threshold potential level. Because g_K is the factor causing membrane change toward hyperpolarization, the membrane potential change ends in local current. When depolarization reaches the threshold potential level, g_{Na} is equal to or greater than g_K, so g_{Na} is the factor causing depolarization. With depolarization, developing, g_{Na} will further rise, while a rise of g_{Na} will promote depolarization all the more. This self-regeneration develops until Na^+ equilibrium potential occurs. This process is called the activation of Na^+ current. When Na^+ current reaches its peak, even though the membrane potential is clamped at a stable level, it rapidly becomes small until reaching the resting level. This process is called the deactivation of Na^+ current. As Fig. 2.9 shows, it seems to be undergoing mutation from local current to action potential, but the changes of membrane sodium conductance and potassium conductance are continuous. If $g_{Na} = g_K$ is taken as a border, one side is negative local current, and the other side is self-regenerative action potential.

Local current is the weak electric change (smaller depolarization or hyperpolarization) produced between two sides of membrane when the cell receives a subthreshold stimulus. That is to say, local current is the potential change before depolarization reaches the threshold potential when the cell is stimulated. Subthreshold stimulus makes one part of the membrane channels open to produce a little depolarization or hyperpolarization, so local current may be depolarization potential or hyperpolarization potential. Local currents in different cells are formed by different ion flows, and ions flow along concentration gradient without energy consumption. Local current has the following characteristics:

1. *Ranking*: The amplitude of local current is in positive correlation with stimulus intensity but is not related to ion the concentration difference between the two sides. It is not all-or-nothing because just parts of the ion channels open, and the ion equilibrium potential cannot occur.

2. *Summation*: Local current has no refractory period. One subthreshold stimulus cannot elicit any action potential but one local reaction; however, multiple local reactions elicited by multiple subthreshold stimuli may cause the membrane to depolarize to the threshold potential by temporal summation or spatial summation, and then action potential breaks out.

3. *Electronic spread*: Local current does not propagate to distal sites as action potential does, but it can affect adjacent membrane potential in the manner of electronic spread. It attenuates as propagation distance increases.

Fig. 2.9 shows the formation of action potential. When the membrane potential surpasses threshold potential, a great quantity of Na^+ channels open, which makes membrane potential reach critical membrane potential level to elicit action potential. The effective stimulus itself can make the membrane to depolarize partly. When depolarization reaches threshold potential level, its regenerative circulation mechanism opens a great quantity of Na^+ channels through positive feedback.

There is potential difference between the excited area and adjacent unexcited areas, so local current occurs. Local current intensity is several times that of threshold intensity, and it can make unexcited areas depolarize. Thus it is an effective stimulus that makes unexcited areas depolarize to threshold potential to produce action potential and that effects the conduction of action potential. Conduction of excitation in the same cell is a gradual excitation process elicited by local current.

Nerve impulse is the excitation conducted along nerve fibers, and its essence is that the depolarization process of the membrane propagates quickly along nerve fibers, that is, the conduction of action potential. Conduction of the receptive impulse is of two kinds: impulse conduction along nonmyelinated fiber; the other is impulse conduction in myelinated nerve fibers, whose transmission is saltatory. When some area of nonmyelinated fiber is excited by a stimulant, a spike potential occurs immediately; that is to say, the membrane potential at that area inverts temporarily to depolarize (positive charge inside and negative charge outside). Thus the potential difference between the excited area and adjacent unexcited area occurs and causes the electric charge to move; this is called local current.

The local current stimulates adjacent rest portion one by one, making the spike potential conduct along the entire never fiber; impulse conduction of myelinated never fiber [8]. It is salutatory conduction.

In 1871, Ranvier discovered that the myelin sheath did not wrap continuously around the axon of peripheral myelinated fiber but regularly broke off every $1 \sim 2$ mm. The breaks came to be known as Ranvier's node after Ranvier. Its physiological function was not elucidated for a long time. In 1925, Lillie proposed a hypothesis based on experiments of simulating nerve fiber conduction with wire: Nerve excitation probably jumped down the fiber from node to node. The myelin sheath on myelinated nerve fiber has electrical insulating property, so local current can only occur between two Ranvier's nodes, which is called salutary conduction [8].

The myelin sheath of myelinated nerve fiber does not permit ions to pass effectively. However, the axon at Ranvier's node is naked, and the membrane permeability at the site is about 500-fold of unmyelinated nerve membrane permeability, so it is easy for ions to pass. When one Ranvier's node is excited, depolarization occurs in the area, and local current only flows within the axon until the next Ranvier's node. With the stimulant of local current, excitation jumps forward from node to node; thus the conduction velocity of myelinated fiber is faster than that of unmyelinated fiber. The conduction of nerve impulse has the following characteristics: *Integrity* indicates that nerve fiber must keep integrality both in anatomy and in physiology; *insulation*, that is, nerve impulse cannot conduct to adjacent nerve fibers in the same nerve trunk; *bidirectional conduction*, that is, an impulse produced by stimulating any site of nerve fiber can conduct simultaneously toward two terminals with relative indefatigability and no decrement.

2.8 Ion channels

On October 7, 1991, in a conference for presenting the Nobel Prize, Erwin Neher and Bert Sakman were endowed with the Nobel Prize in physiology because of their important achievements—the discovery of a single ion channel in the cell membrane. The cell membrane isolates the cell from outside; however, the cell undertakes material exchanges with the outside via many channels in the membrane. The channels are composed of a single molecule or of multiple molecules, and they permit some ions to pass through. Regulation of the channels influences the life and function of the cell. In 1976, Erwin Neher and Bert Sakman cooperated to record successfully the current of a single channel in nAc subdivision by a newly established patch clamp technique and initiated the first line of studying ion channel function directly. The results showed that a very slender current occurred when ions passed through ion channels in the membrane. Because their diameters were proximate to those of ion channels, Erwin Neher and Bert Sakman selected Na^+ and Cl^- to do experiments, and finally they got consensus in the existence of ion channels and how the ion channels exerted their functions [1]. And they even discovered the inductors in some ion channels and their location in channel molecules (as shown in Fig. 2.10).

In 1981, the British Miledi laboratory injected cRNA of nAchR by biosynthesis into the egg cells of the Africa clawed frog in developing phase (phase V) and succeeded in the expression of the ion channel receptor in the membrane. During 1983 and 1984, the Japanese Numa laboratory first determined the entire primary structure of nAchR and Na^+ channel of electric fish organ with over 200,000 molecular weight. More than three works not only confirmed directly the existence of ion channels from the function and structure but also provided efficient research methods for the analysis of the function and structure of ion channels.

The preceding basic types of ion channels have been discovered in the membrane of neurons, and each of them has some similar isomers. Ion channels can adopt multiple conformations, but, based on the phenomenon of permitting ions to pass through or not, it has only two states: open state and close state. The conversion of ion channels between the open and close states is controlled by the gate of micropore. This mechanism is

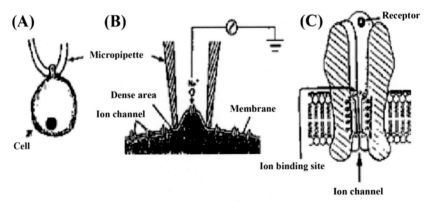

Figure 2.10 Schematic diagram of ion channel. (A) Neuronal cell; (B) Membrane ion channel currents; (C) Ion channel.

called gated control. In fact, many ion channels still have a shutoff state called inactivation, in addition to the open and close states, such as the Na^+ channel.

The gated control mechanism is still not very clear. Three styles have been visualized: (1) One site of the porous channel is gated (like the voltage-gated Na^+ channel and K^+ channel); (2) the structure change of the whole porous channel envelops the porous channel (like the gap junction channel); (3) specific inhibitory particles stop up the channel entrance (like the voltage-gated K^+ channel) [1]. It is known that three motivators, including voltage, mecho-stretch, and chemical ligandin, can regulate the activities of channel gates. The ion channels are called voltage-gated ion channel, mechanically gated ion channel, and ligand-gated ion channel, respectively.

Ion channels are a kind of constitutive protein in the cell membrane. They penetrate the cell membrane dispersedly. Since the Numa laboratory first determined the total amino acid sequence of nAchR and Na^+ channel in the electric organ of electric fish by DNA cloning technology, the primary structure of multiple ion channels has been elucidated. It is possible to judge their second-level structures, functional groups in molecules, and their evolution and heredity through the analysis of data from X light diffraction, electron diffraction, and electron microscopy.

According the data about the primary structure of ion channels, genes coding ion channels can be divided into three families. Each member of a family has a very similar amino acid sequence, so these members are thought to have evolved from a common progenitor gene: (1) gene family coding voltage-gated Na^+ channel, K^+ channel and Ca^{2+} channel; (2) gene family coding ligand-gated ion channels, its members including the ion channels activated by Ach, GABA, glycine and glutamic acid; and (3) gene family coding gap junction channels.

2.9 The nervous system

The nervous system is the organization of all kinds of activities in the body. It receives literally millions of bits of information from the different sensory organs and neurons and then integrates all these to determine the responses to be made by the body.

A nervous system can be divided into the CNS and PNS according its morphology and location. CNS comprises the brain and spinal cord. The former lies in the cranial cavity, while the latter is located in the vertebral canal. It can also be divided into the somatic nervous system and autonomic nervous system according to its quality. The nerve center of somatic nervous system is located in the brain and the spinal cord while its peripheral part constitutes the brain nerves and the spinal nerves. Somatic sensory nerves receive the stimulants from the skin, muscles, junctions, bones and so on via the receptors in their terminals and conduct the impulses to the nervous center while somatic motor nerves transfer the impulses from the center to the effectors, controlling the contraction and relaxation of skeletal muscles. The nerve center of autonomic nervous system also is located in the brain and the spinal cord, whereas its peripheral portion has two parts: (1) the brain nerves and the spinal nerves; (2) the self-governed autonomic nerve. The autonomic motor nerves include the sympathetic nerves and parasympathetic nerves, controlling the activities of the cardiac muscles, the smooth muscles, and glands.

2.9.1 Central nervous system

The CNS is composed of two parts, the brain and the spinal cord. The brain is the most important part of the whole CNS. For individual behaviors, almost all complex activities, such as learning, thinking, perception, and so on, have a close relationship with brain nerves. The brain includes the hindbrain (epencephalon), midbrain (diencephalons), and forebrain. Each of them includes multiple kinds of nervous tissues.

The spinal cord is located in the spinal column, which connects with the brain and the 31 pairs of peripheral nerves distributed along both sides of spinal column for individual behaviors. The functions of the spinal cord are:

1. to conduct nerve impulses from the sensory receptors to the superior center of the brain, then to transmit them from the brain to the motor organs via efferent nerves. Thus the spinal cord is the pathway connecting the peripheral nerve with the superior center of the brain.
2. to accept the impulse transferred via afferent nerve and cause reflex activity directly as the reflex center.

A butterfly-shaped internal mass of gray matter encompasses the central canal, which opens upward into the fourth ventricle. Bilateral gray matters extend anteriorly and posteriorly to the anterior horn and posterior horn, respectively. The former connects the anterior root and relates to movements, while the latter connects the posterior root and relates to sensation. Gray matter between the anterior horn and the posterior horn of the thoracic and upper two or three lumbar spinal segments are referred to as lateral horns, which make up the preganglionic nueron of the autonomic nerves.

White matter around the gray matter has anterior, lateral, and posterior funiculi, which consist largely of longitudinal nerve fibers and are the pathway connecting the brain with the spinal cord. Propriospinal tracts adjacent to the gray matter are linked with each of the segments.

2.9.2 Peripheral nervous system

PNS includes the somatic nervous system and the autonomic nervous system. The somatic nervous system innervates in the striated muscles spreading all over the head, face, trunk, and four limbs. Based on its functions, the somatic nervous system can be classified into two species: afferent nerve and efferent nerve. The afferent nerves connect with receptors of sense organs and are responsible for transferring nerve impulses induced by external stimulants to the central nerve, so this species of nerves is called sensory nerves, which construct the basal unit of sensory nerves, that is, sensory neuron.

After receiving an external nerve impulse, the central nerve gives a response. The response is also a type of nerve impulse that is transferred by efferent nerve to motor organs to cause muscle movements. Thus this species of nerves is called motor nerves. The basal unit of the motor nerve is the motor neuron, which transfers impulses from the center to the motor organ to produce the related action and response.

The somatic nervous system manages the behaviors of striated muscles, while the management of the functions of internal organs such as the inner smooth muscles, cardiac muscles, and glands is controlled by the autonomic nervous system. The activities of internal organs have some automaticity, which is different from the somatic muscular system. Humans cannot control the activities of their internal organs by will. Afferent impulses from the internal organs are different from that of the skin or other specific sensory organs; it cannot produce clear sense on consciousness. According to the originated sites and their functions, the autonomic nervous system can be divided into the sympathetic nerve system and the parasympathetic nerve system.

The sympathetic nerve system originating in the thoracic spinal cord. The lumbar spinal cord receives impulse from the centers of the spinal cord, medulla oblongata, and midbrain, and it is controlled by the CNS.

Strictly speaking, these cannot be called autonomic nerves and cannot be controlled by individual will. Sympathetic nerves mainly innervate internal organs including the heart, lung, liver, kidneys, spleen, gastrointestinal system, reproduction organs, and adrenal glands. Another part of them innervates the vessels of the head and neck, body wall, arrector muscle, and iris of eyes. The main function of the sympathetic nervous system is to excite internal organs, glands, and other related organs. For example, excitation of the sympathetic nerves can increase heart rate, blood pressure, respiratory volume, blood glucose, expand pupils, promote secretion of E, but only inhibit secretion of saliva.

The parasympathetic nervous system is composed of a set of cranial nerves (III-oculomotor nerve, III-facial nerve, III-pharyngeal nerve, III-vagus nerve) and pelvic nerves originating in the pelvic portion of the spinal cord. Parasympathetic nerves locate near or within the effectors, so their postganglionic fibers are very short and usually only their preganglionic fibers can be observed. Their main function is contrary to that of sympathetic nerve, so it produces antagonism to sympathetic nerve. For example, the parasympathetic nerve inhibits the function of heart while sympathetic enhances its function. In contrast, parasympathetic nerve enhances the movement of the small intestine while the sympathetic nerve inhibits its movement.

2.10 Cerebral cortex

In 1860, P. Broca, a French surgeon, observed the following case: The patient could not speak but could understand language. His larynx, tongue, lip, vocal cords and so on had no disability to prevent routine movements. He could give off individual words and sing a tune, but he could neither speak a complete sentence nor express his thoughts by writing. The autopsy discovered there was an egg-sized damaged zone in the posterior frontal lobe of the left hemisphere of the patient's cerebrum, degenerated brain tissue adhered to meninges, but the right hemisphere was normal. Afterward, P. Broca studied eight similar patients with the same damage zone in the left hemisphere of the cerebrum. Based on these discoveries, in 1864, P. Broca announced a famous principle about the brain's function—"We speak in the left hemisphere" —which was the first direct proof about functional localization in the human cerebral cortex. This zone (Brodmann 44, 45 areas) is now called Broca's expressive aphasia area or Broca's area, which exists only in the cerebral cortex of left hemisphere. This is also the first proof that the left hemisphere is the predominant cerebral cortex.

In 1870, G. Fritsch and E. Hitzig, two German physiologists, discovered that stimulating a certain region of the cerebral cortex with electric current could regularly elicit a certain movement of the limbs of the opposite side, which confirmed by experiments that there were different functional localization in the cerebral cortex. Later, Carl Wernicke discovered another cortex area related to linguistic capacity, which is now called Carl Wernicke area and is located in the junctions among temporal posterior part, parietal lobe, and occipital lobe. When this area is damaged, the patient can speak but cannot understand language, that is, he can hear the sound but can't understand its meaning. This area is also well developed in the left hemisphere.

Since the 19th century, a great deal of knowledge about the functional localization of the cerebral cortex has been achieved through all-round experimental researches and clinical observation of physiologists and doctors, as well as the combination of clinical observation, surgical treatment and science research. In the 1930s, Wild Penfield et al. undertook a great quantity of research about the functional localization of human cerebral cortex. In the process of neurosurgical procedures, under the condition of local anesthesia, they stimulated the patients' cerebral cortex with electric current, observed the patients' movement response, and asked their subject feeling. According to cytoarchitectural difference, Brodmann divided the human cerebral cortex into 52 areas (Fig. 2.11) [1]. From the angle of

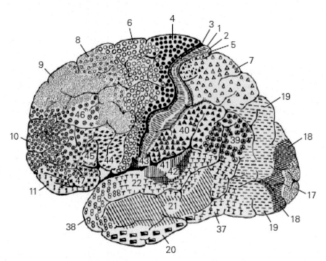

Figure 2.11 Brodmann's division of the human cerebral cortex.

function, the cerebral cortex is composed of sensory cortex, motor cortex, and associated cortex. The sensory cortex includes visual cortex (area 17), auditory cortex (areas 41, 42), somatosensory cortex (areas 1, 2, 3), gustatory cortex (area 43), and olfactory cortex (area 28); the motor cortex includes primary motor cortex (area 4), premotor area and supplementary motor area (area 6); the associated cortex includes parietal association cortex, temporal association cortex, and prefrontal association cortex. The associated cortex is not involved in pure feeling or motor function but accepts and integrates information from the sensory cortex, then transfers information to the motor cortex, thereby regulating the activities of behavior. The associated cortex plays a role of association between sense input and motor output, which is the origin of its name.

The human parietal association cortex includes the Brodmann 5, 7, 39, 40 areas. Area 5 mainly receives the projections from the primary somatosensory cortex (areas 1, 2, 3), and nucleus lateralis posterior thalami while area 7 mainly receives the projections from the anterior of the striate visual area, tuberculum posterior thalami, superior temporal gyrus, prefrontal lobe cortex, and cingulated gyri (areas 23, 24). Areas 5 and 7 have different input sources, but they have the common target areas of projections, which consist of the premotor area, cortex of prefrontal lobe, cortex of temporal lobe, cingulate gyri, insular gyri, and basal ganglia. The more projections from area 5 are in the premotor area and motor area, while the projections from area 7 are in the subarea of the temporal lobe related to border structure. In addition, area 7 projects directly toward parahippocampal gyres and receives the projections from the locus ceruleus and raphe nucleus. Therefore, area 5 is mainly involved in somatosensory information and movement information processing, while area 7 is probably mainly involved in visual information processing and movements, attention, regulation of emotions, and so on.

The human association cortex of the prefrontal lobe is composed of Brodmann's areas 9−14 and areas 45−47. The general name of areas 11−14 and area 47 is the orbital gyri of the prefrontal lobe. The general name of areas 9, 10, 45, and 46 is the dorsolateral of the prefrontal lobe, and some authors also induce areas 8 and 4 to the cortex of prefrontal lobe. The association cortex of the prefrontal lobe has several notable anatomic characteristics: (1) It is located in the anterior aspects of the neopallium of the brain; (2) it has a significantly advanced granular layer (IV layer); (3) it receives direct projections from the mediodorsal thalamic nucleus; (4) it has wide association with afferent and efferent fibers. During the evolutionary process from lesser to higher development, the area of the association cortex of the prefrontal lobe becomes bigger and bigger. The primates, including humans, have the most advanced association cortex of the prefrontal lobe. The area of the human association cortex of the prefrontal lobe accounts for about 29% of the entire cerebral cortex.

The association cortex of the prefrontal lobe has fiber associations in the cortex and beneath it. The interactive fiber associations exist among the cortex of the prefrontal lobe, striate visual anterior area, temporal association cortex, and parietal association cortex. The cortex of the prefrontal lobe is the only neopallium that has interactive fibers with a mediodorsal thalamic nucleus and also has direct projection toward the hypothalamus. The cortex of the prefrontal lobe has direct or indirect fiber associations with the basal forebrain, cingulated gyri, and gyrus hippocampi. It projects fibers out to the basal ganglia (caudate nucleus and putamen) and so on. The functional complexity of the cortex of the prefrontal lobe is attributed to the complicated fiber associations.

Human cerebral cortex is a very subtile controlling system. The layer of gray matter covering the cerebral cortex has an average thickness of 2−3 mm. The surface of the cortex contains many upfolds called gyri and downfolds referred to as sulci, which increase the surface area of the cerebral cortex, reaching 2200 cm^2. It contains about 14 billion neurons, which are mainly pyramidal cells, stellate cells, and spindle cells. Complicated associations exist among the neurons, but the distribution of several of neurons in the cortex is not disordered but strictly hierarchical. The archaeocortex located inside the cerebral hemisphere only has three layers: (1) molecular layer, (2) pyramidal layer, (3) polymorphic layer. The neopallium located outside the cerebral hemisphere has six layers:

1. The molecular layer contains a very small quantity of cells but has a great number of nerve fibers paralleling its surface.
2. The external granular layer is mainly composed of many small pyramidal cells and stellate cells.
3. The pyramidal layer consists mainly of medium-sized and mini-sized pyramidal cells.
4. The internal granular layer is composed of dense stellate cells.
5. The ganglionic layer consists mainly of medium-sized and large pyramidal cells. Pyramidal cells in the anterior central gyrus are especially big, their dendrite tops extend to the first layer, and their long and

thick axons travel to the brain stem and the spinal cord, which are the
main components of pyramidal tracts.

6. The polymorphic layer mainly contains spindle cells. One part of the
axons of spindle cells and the axons of the cells of the fifth layer
together compose the efferent nerve fibers down the brain stem and
the spinal cord, the other part of them running to the homolateral or
contralateral hemisphere compose the association fibers associating all
areas of the cortex.

In the view of their functions, the first, second, third, and fourth layers
of the cerebral cortex mainly receive nerve impulses, and associated
related nerves, especially specific sensory fibers from the thalamus, go into
the fourth layer directly. The axons of pyramidal cells and spindle cells in
the fifth layer and the sixth layer consist of efferent fibers that run downward to the brain stem and spinal cord, and the cranial nerves or spinal
nerves conduct impulses to related domains in the body to regulate the
activities of a variety of organs and systems. In this way, the cerebral cortex has not only the characteristic of a reflex path but also a complicated
chain system among various neurons. Complexity and catholicity give the
cortex the abilities of analysis and synthesis, which constitutes the material
basis of human conceptual work.

The study on the structure and function of the cerebral somatosensory
area indicates that the longitudinal columnar-arranged cortical cells consist
of the most fundamental functional electric potential, which is called the
function column. The column structure has a 200–500 μm diameter,
running toward the brain surface through the six layers. Neurons within
the same column structure all have the same function, for instance
responding to the same type of stimulation of senses from the same receptive field. After receiving the same stimulation, the discharging latency
of the neurons is very similar, only with difference of 2–4 ms, which
illustrates that only several successive neurons lie between the first activated neuron and the last activated neuron, and only several successive
neurons can finish the contact loop of the neurons in the same column
structure. One column structure is the integration processing unit of
input–output information. The afferent impulses first go into the fourth
layer and are propagated vertically by the cells of the fourth and second
layers; finally, the cells of the third, fifth, and sixth layers send out the
efferent impulses from the cerebral cortex. The horizontal fibers of the
third layer cells also have the function of inhibiting the adjacent cell column, thus once one column elicits excitation, its adjacent cell column

will be inhibited, which form the excitation—inhibition mode. The morphological and functional characteristics of the columnar structure also exist in the second sensory area, visual area, auditory area, and motor area.

References

[1] E.R. Kandel, J.H. Schwatz, T.M. Jessell, Principles of Neural Science, fifth ed., McGraw-Hill Education, 2013. ISBN 9787111430810, 9780071390118.

[2] M.F. Bear, B. Connors, M.A. Paradiso, Neuroscience: Exploring the Brain, fourth ed., Lippincott Williams & Wilkins, 2015.

[3] M.S. Gazzaniga, R.B. Ivry, G.R. Mangun (Eds.), The Cognitive Neurosciences: The Biology of the Mind, third ed., W. W. Norton & Company, 2009.

[4] C.S. Sherrington, The Integrative Action of the Nervous System, 1961 ed., Yale University Press, New Haven, CT, 1906.

[5] C. Zhang, Z. Zhou, Ca^{2+}-independent but voltage-dependent secretion in mammalian dorsal root ganglion neurons, Nat. Neurosci. 5 (5) (2002) 425—430.

[6] A.L. Hodgkin, A.F. Huxley, A quantitative description of ion currents and its applications to conduction and excitation in nerve membranes, J. Physiol. (Lond.) 117 (1952) 500—544.

[7] A.L. Hodgkin, The Conduction of the Nervous Impulse, Liverpool University Press, Liverpool, 1965.

[8] D. Debanne, E. Campanac, A. Bialowas, E. Carlier, G. Alcaraz, Axon physiology, Physiol. Rev. 91 (2011) 555—602.

CHAPTER 3

Neural computing

Neural computing studies the nature and ability of nonprogramming, as well as adaptive and brain-style information processing. Based on the neural network, the computing model is established to solve problems in science and engineering. Connectionism regards human intelligence as the result of high-level activities of the human brain and emphasizes that intelligent activities are the result of a large number of simple units running in parallel through complex interconnections.

3.1 Introduction

Neural computing studies the nature and ability of information processing of artificial neural networks, specifically nonprogramming, adaptive, and brain-style [1]. An artificial neural network, which is composed of a large number of processing units, is a large-scale adaptive nonlinear dynamical system with learning ability, memory capacity, computing power, and intelligent processing functions. In varying degrees and levels, it imitates the information processing, storage, and retrieval functions of the human brain. It is based on the results of modern neuroscience researches in an attempt to design a new machine with the information processing capacity of the human brain by simulating brain network processing, and memorizing information. At the same time, such research on the artificial neural network will further deepen the understanding of thinking and intelligence. To simulate the mechanism of brain information processing, the artificial neural network is nonlinear, nonlocal, unsteady, nonconvex, and so on. The artificial neural network's unified algorithm has a structure is a mixture of hardware and software.

Modern neural computation started with the pioneering work of W. S. McCulloch and W. Pitts [2]. In 1943 McCulloch and Pitts published their papers in a neurons modeling group. The paper affected Von Neumann, who used McCulloch and Pitts' neurons to derive idealized switching delay elements in his Electronic Discrete Variable Automatic Computer, thus improving EDVIC (Electronic Numerical Integrator and Computer). EDVIC is the first

Intelligence Science
DOI: https://doi.org/10.1016/B978-0-323-85380-4.00003-8

general-purpose electronic computer, which was made from 1943 to 1946 at the University of Pennsylvania Moore School of Electrical Engineering. The formal neural network theory of McCulloch and Pitts distinguished in his second of four reports in 1949 by von Neumann at Illinois University.

In 1948 N. Wiener's famous *Control Theory* described a number of important concepts for control, communications, and statistical signal processing [3]. In 1961 the second edition of the book published, and new materials on the learning and self-organization were added. In the second chapter of the second version, N. Wiener seemed to have grasped the physical meaning of the statistics mechanism in the main context, but the fruitful results on the joint statistics mechanism and learning system were left to J. J. Hopfield. The second important development happened in 1949. In D. O. Hebb's book *Behavior Histology* [4], he clearly explained the amendment to the physiological synaptic learning rules for the first time. Hebb argued that the brain's connection continuously changes with the brain learning different tasks and that nerve tissue is created by this change. Hebb inherited Ramony and Cajal's early assumption and introduced his now famous learning hypothesis: Variable synapses between two neurons are increased by repeated activation of the neurons at both ends of the synapses. Hebb's book has widely affected psychologists but unfortunately has little impact on engineers.

Hebb's book is a source of inspiration for learning and the development of a computation model of a self-adaptive system. In 1956 Rochester, Holland, Habt, and Duba's thesis might be the first attempt to use the computer to simulate a test of Hebb's learning hypothesis of the neural theory. Simulation results of the paper show that inhibition must be added for it to work. In the same year, Uttley demonstrated that a neural network with a modifiable synapse can learn to classify a simple binary model set. Uttley introduced the so-called quadrature leakage and fire neurons (leaky integrate-and-fire neuron), and then Caianiello conducted a formal analysis of it. In later work, Uttley assumed that the effects of variable synapses in the nervous system depend on the statistical relationship of the fluctuation states of both ends of synapses, and so it was associated with Shannon's theory.

In 1952 Ashby's book *Design of the Brain: The Origin of Adaptive Behavior* was published [5]. Today, it is as interesting as it was in the past. This book is eye-catching because its basic view is that adaptive behavior is not innate but learned, and, through learning, animals' (system) behavior changes for the better. The book stressed the dynamic view that eye-catching living body is like a machine, as well as the concept of stability. In 1954 Minsky at Princeton University wrote a doctoral thesis on the neural network, entitled "Enhanced Neural Systems Theory and Its Application in Modeling the Brain." In 1961 Minsky published an early paper on AI, "Progress in Artificial Intelligence." This article included a large chapter on the neural network. In 1967 Minsky published a book entitled *Calculation: Finite and Infinite Machines*. It is the first to expand the results of McCulloch and Pitts in the form of a book and put them in the context of automatic theory and computing theory. Also, in 1954, one of the earliest pioneers of communication theory and the inventor of holography, Gabor put forward the idea of nonlinear adaptive filter, and together with his partners they established such a machine. Samples generated by random process, as well as a machine-generated objective function, together completed the online learning. In the 1950s Taylor began to study associative memory, followed by Steinbuch introducing the learning matrix; this matrix was composed by switching the plane network that was interpolated between the "feel" receiver and the "motor" effect pose. In 1969 Willshaw, Buneman, and Longuet-Higgins issued an outstanding paper on nonholographic associative memory. This article gives two types of the network model: the simple optical system of correlation matrix realization and the associated neural network made by the optical memory. An important contribution to the early development of associative memory was Andelson, Kohonen, and Nakano's article of 1972, in which they independently introduced the idea of a correlation matrix memory on the basis of learning rules.

Von Neumann was the master of science in the first half of the 20th century. To commemorate him, people named the basis for the design of the digital computer the Von Neumann structure. Yale University in 1956, invited him to make a Silliman report. He died in 1957, and later his unfinished Silliman report was published in 1958 as a book, *Computers and the Brain*. This book is very meaningful because it prompted what Von Neumann would do. He began to realize the great differences between the brain and the computer.

A concern to be considered about the neural network is the use of an unreliable neuron component to build a reliable neural network. In 1956 Von Neumann solved this important issue by using the idea of redundancy. Such thinking made Winograd and Cowan propose, in 1963, using the distribution of redundancy in neural networks, reflecting the individual concept of the robustness and parallelism of many elements in the collective.

McCulloch and Pitts's classic paper was published 15 years after Rosenblatt's works about perceptron, a new method of pattern recognition, a new method of supervised learning [6]. The perceptron convergence theorem made Rosenblatt's work a complete success. In 1960, he raised the first proof of the perceptron convergence theorem. Proof of the theorem also appeared in Novikoff (1963) and in other people's work. Widrow and Hoff introduced the least mean squares algorithm and used it to constitute the Adaline (adaptive linear element). The difference between Adaline and perceptron lies in the training process. One of the first trainable hierarchical neural networks with multiple adaptive elements was the Madaline (multiple-adaline) structure put forward by B. Widrow and his students [7]. In 1967 S. Amari used statistical gradient method for pattern classification. N. Nilsson published *Learning Machine* in 1965 and to date it is still the best work on differentiating linearly separable patterns with hyperplane. In the 1960s, perceptron neural networks seemed to be able to do anything. In 1969, Minsky and Papert cowrote the book *Perception*. Mathematical theory was used to prove the natural limitations of the calculation done by the single-layer perceptron [8]. In the section about the multilayer perceptron, they believed that there is no reason to suppose that any limitation of the single-layer perceptron can be overcome in the multilayer perceptron. An important issue to face in the design of the multilayer perceptron is the issue of confidence level (that is, the confidence level issues of hidden neurons in the network). In 1961 Minsky, in his book *Strengthen the Issue of Confidence Level in the Learning System*, first used the terminology "confidence level." In the 1960s most of the ideas and basic concepts necessary for solving the problem of confidence level had been formulated, and so had been many inherent ideas of the recursive (attractor) network now known as the Hopfield network. However, it was not until the last century, in 1980, that solutions to these very basic questions appeared. In the late 1970s these factors in one way or another hindered further study of the neural network. In addition to several psychological and neurological experts, many researchers had changed their research field. Indeed, only a handful of early pioneers continued to study the neural network. From the engineering point of view, we can trace back the late 1970s as the incubation period for the neural network.

In 1970 an important activity was that self-organization theory using competitive learning emerged. In 1973 von der Malsburg's work of computer simulation might be the first demonstration of self-organization. Inspired by topology order in human brain mapping, in 1976, Willshaw and von der Malsburg produced their first paper on the formation of self-organization mapping.

In the late 1980s several achievements were made in neural network theory and design, and then neural network research entered a recovery phase. Based on early work in competitive learning theory [9], Grossberg established a new principle of self-organization, which is the now well-known adaptive resonance theory (ART). Basically, this theory includes a bottom-up recognition layer and a top-down production layer. If the input forms and learning feedback forms match, a state of uncertainty called adaptive resonance (i.e., the extension and enlargement of neural activity) happens. This forward or reverse mapping originally had been rediscovered by other researchers under different conditions.

In 1982 J. Hopfield formed a new method that proposes calculation with the idea of energy function implemented by the recursive network with a symmetric connection. And he established isomorphism between the Ising models used in such a recursive network and statistical physics. The analogy paved the way for a series of physical theories entering the neural model, and the field of the neural network changed. Such a special neural network with feedback caused a great deal of concern in the 1980s. At that time, the well-known Hopfield network appeared. Although the Hopfield network cannot be a true model of a neural biological system, such a system is covered in principle, that is, the principle of storing information in a dynamic stable network, which is extremely profound.

Another major development in 1982 was T. Kohonen's work on the use of the self-organization mapping of one-dimensional or two-dimensional structures [10]. In the literature, Kohonen's work has attracted increasing attention and has become the assessment criterion of other innovations in this area.

In 1983 S. Kirkpatrick, C. D. Gelatt, and M. P. Vecchi described a new method of solving the problem of combination optimization, which was called simulated annealing [11]. Simulated annealing, rooted in statistical mechanics was based on a simple technique that was used for the first time in computer simulation by N. Metropolis [12]. D. H. Ackley, G. E. Hinton, and T. J. Sejnowski used the idea of simulated annealing to develop a random machine called the Boltzmann machine [13], which was the first successful resolution of multilayer neural network. Although demonstrating that the learning algorithm of the Boltzmann machine is not computationally efficient as the back-propagation (BP) algorithm, it demonstrates that the ideas of Minsky and Papert are not tenable and break psychological barriers. It also foreshadowed the work of the subsequent sigmoid belief network by R. M. Neal [14]. Sigmoid belief network achieved two things: (1) significantly improved learning; (2) connecting the neural network and belief network.

In 1986 D. E. Rumelhart, G. E. Hinton, and R. J. Williams reported the development of the BP algorithm. The same year, the famous book *Parallel Distributed Processing: Exploration of the Microstructure of Cognition*, edited by D. E. Rumelhart, and J. L. McClelland, was published [15]. This book had a significant impact on the use of the BP algorithm. It has become the most common multilayer perceptron training algorithm. In fact, BP learning was found independently at the same time in two other places. In the mid-1980s, after the BP algorithm was found, we found that as early as August 1974 in Harvard University, P. J. Werbos in his PhD thesis had described it [16]. P. J. Werbos's doctoral thesis is the first documentation of effective the BP model to describe the gradient calculation, and it can be applied to the general network model, including neural networks as its special case. The basic idea of BP can be further traced back to the book *Applied Optimal Control* by A. E. Bryson and Y. C. Ho. In a section of the book entitled "Multi-stage System," using a Lagrange form to derive BP is described. However, the final analysis concluded that a few BP algorithm honors should be given to D. E. Rumelhart, G. E. Hinton, and R. J. Williams because they brought it to the machine learning application and demonstrated how it worked.

In 1988 D. S. Broomhead and D. Lowe described the process of using RBF (radial basis function) to design a multilayer feed-forward network. RBF provided an alternative for the multilayer network. The basic idea of the RBF dated back at least to O. A. Bashkirov, E. M. Braverman, and I. B. Muchnik, who first proposed the potential function method, and to M. A. Aizerman, E. M. Braverman, and L. I. Rozonnoer, who developed the potential function theory. In 1990 T. Poggio and F. Girosi used the Tikhonov regularization theory to further enrich the RBF network theory [17].

In 1989 C. A. Mead's book *Analog VLSI and Neural System* was published. This book provided unusual hybrid concepts from neurobiology and VLSI technology. In short, it included sections written by Mead and his collaborators on silicon retina and silicon, which were living examples of Mead's creative thinking.

In the early 1990s V. N. Vapnik and his collaborators put forward a supervised learning network, which was strong in computing and was called SVM (support vector machines). It was used to solve pattern recognition, regression, and density estimation problems [18]. The new method was based on limited samples of the learning theory. A novel feature of SVM was that the Vapnik-Chervonenkis (VC) dimension was included in the design in a natural way. VC dimension provided neural networks with a measure of capacity of learning from a sample set.

In 2006 Jeffrey Hinton and his student Ruslan Salakhutdinov formally put forward the concept of deep learning [19]. They gave a detailed solution to the problem of gradient disappearance—training the algorithm layer by layer through unsupervised learning methods and then using the supervised BP algorithm for optimization. The proposal of this deep learning method immediately had great repercussions in academic circles. Many world-famous universities, represented by Stanford University and Toronto University, have invested huge human and financial resources in the field of deep learning, after which it spread rapidly to industry.

A neural network is a large-scale parallel distribution processor consisting of a simple processing unit. It is born with the characteristics of storing knowledge and experience so that they can be used. The neural network simulates the brain in two ways:

1. The knowledge neural network obtains is learned from the outside environment.
2. The intensity of the internal neuronal connection, or synaptic weight, is used for the storage of the knowledge acquired.

The procedure for the completion of learning process is known as the learning algorithm, and its function is to obtain the desired design objects by changing the system weight values in an orderly manner.

From the features and functionality of neurons, we can know that neuron is a multiinput single-output information processing unit, and its information processing is nonlinear. According to the characteristics and function of neurons, they can be abstracted as a simple mathematical model. The artificial neural model used in engineering is shown in Fig. 3.1.

In Fig. 3.1, $X_1, X_2, \ldots, X_n$ is the input of n neurons, that is, the information of the axons from n neurons of the former level of. A is the threshold of neuron i; $W_1, W_2 \ldots, W_n$ are the neurons weights to X_1, $X_2, \ldots, X_n$, also known as the transmission efficiency of synaptic; Y is the output of neurons; f is activation function, which determines the manner of the output when neurons reach a threshold at the common stimulation by input $X_1, X_2, \ldots, X_n$.

From Fig. 3.1, the model of neurons, the expression of the mathematical model can be given:

$$f(u_i) = \begin{cases} 1 & u_j > 0 \\ 0 & u_j \leq 0 \end{cases}$$

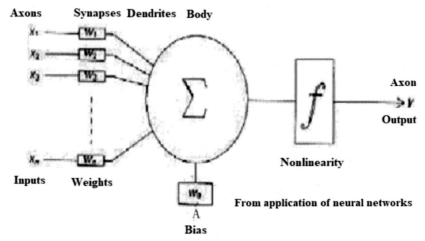

Figure 3.1 The mathematical model of neurons.

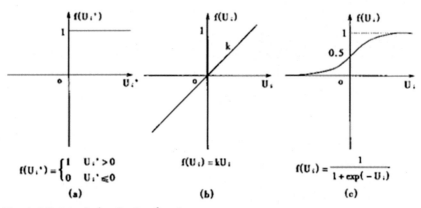

Figure 3.2 A typical activation function.

For activation function f, there is a variety of forms, the most common of which include the step, linear, and S-type forms, as shown in Fig. 3.2.

The mathematical model of neurons just described is the most widely used and the most familiar. In 2020 Zhang and Zhou proposed a new neuron model, the flexible transmitter (FT), which has flexible plasticity and supports complex data processing [20]. The FT model uses the transmission transmitter parameter pair (W, V), rather than the real weight W in the MP model, to represent synaptic plasticity.

3.2 Back-propagation learning algorithm

The BP network was proposed by a group of scientists led by Rumelhart and McCelland in 1986. It is a multilayer feed-forward network trained by an error BP algorithm. The generalized feed-forward multilayer network structure is shown in Fig. 3.3. It contains the input layer, output layer, and the hidden layer between the input and output layers. Neurons in the hidden layer are also known as hidden units.

The BP algorithm is a supervised learning algorithm. Its main idea is that input learning samples use a BP algorithm to repeatedly adjust the weight and deviation of the network, so that the output vector and the expected vector are as close as possible. When the error sum of the output layer of the network is less than the specified error, the training is completed, and the weight and deviation of the network are saved.

In the application of the BP algorithm to feed-forward multilayer network, when Sigmoid is used as the activation function, the following steps can be used on the network for weights W_{ij} recursive. Note if there are n neurons in each layer, that is, $i = 1, 2, \ldots, n; j = 1, 2, \ldots, n$. For neuron i of layer k, there are n weights $W_{i1}, W_{i2}, \ldots, W_{in}$ $_{+1}$ is taken for the threshold θ_i; and when inputting sample X, let $X = (X_1, X_2, \ldots, X_n, 1)$. The algorithm steps are as follows:

1. Set the initial of weight W_{ij}. Set a smaller random nonzero number as coefficient W_{ij} of each layer, but $W_{i,n+1} = -\theta$.

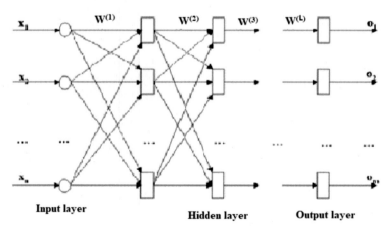

Figure 3.3 Feed-forward multilayer network structure.

2. Enter a sample $\boldsymbol{X} = (X_1, X_2, \ldots, X_n, 1)$, as well as the corresponding desired output $\boldsymbol{Y} = (Y_1, Y_2, \ldots, Y_n)$.

3. Calculate output at all layers. For output X_i^k of neuron i in layer k, there is:

$$U_i^k = \sum_{j=1}^{n+1} W_{ij} X_j^{k-1}$$
$$X_{n+1}^{k-1} = 1, \quad W_{i,n+1} = -\theta \tag{3.1}$$
$$X_i^k = f(U_i^k)$$

4. Find the learning error d_i^k for all layers. For the output layer, $k = m$:

$$d_i^m = X_i^m (1 - X_i^m)(X_i^m - Y_i) \tag{3.2}$$

For other layers:

$$d_i^k = X_i^k (1 - X_i^k) \cdot \sum_l W_{li} \cdot d_i^{k+l} \tag{3.3}$$

5. To modify weights W_{ij} and threshold θ:

$$\Delta W_{ij}(t + 1) = \Delta W_{ij}(t) - \eta \cdot d_i^k \cdot X_j^{k-1} \tag{3.4}$$

We can get:

$$\Delta W_{ij}(t + 1) = \Delta W_{ij}(t) - \eta \cdot d_i^k \cdot X_j^{k-1} + \alpha \Delta W_{ij}(t) \tag{3.5}$$

where

$$\Delta W_{ij}(t) = -\eta \cdot d_i^k \cdot X_j^{k-1} + \alpha \Delta W_{ij}(t - l) = W_{ij}(t) - W_{ij}(t - l) \tag{3.6}$$

6. When the weights of different layers are calculated, the quality indicators can be set to determine whether the requirements are met or not. If the requirements are met, the algorithm ends; if not, return to step 3. The learning process, for any given sample $\boldsymbol{X}_p = (X_{p1}, X_{p2}, \ldots X_{pn}, 1)$ and the desired output $Y_p = (Y_{p1}, Y_{p2}, \ldots, Y_{pn})$, should be implemented, until all the input and output requirements are met.

The multilayer feed-forward BP network is currently the most widely used model of neural network, but it is not perfect. In order to better understand and apply the neural network to problem solving, its advantages and disadvantages are now discussed. Here are the advantages of multilayer BP network:

1. It is able to adapt and learn independently. This is the basis and advantage of the BP algorithm. According to the preset parameter updating

rules, the BP algorithm constantly adjusts the parameters of the neural network to achieve the most desired output.

2. It has strong nonlinear mapping ability.
3. It has a rigorous derivation process. The BP process error is measured by a very mature chain method, and its derivation process is rigorous and scientific.
4. It has strong generalization ability; that is, after BP algorithm training, the BP algorithm can use the knowledge learned from the original knowledge to solve new problems.

The disadvantages of the multilayer BP network are as follows:

1. Because there are many parameters in the BP neural network, it needs to update many thresholds and weights every time, so the convergence speed is too slow.
2. From the mathematical point of view, the BP algorithm is a fast gradient descent algorithm, making it easy to fall into the problem of local minimum.
3. There is no clear formula for the number of hidden layer nodes in the network.

3.3 Adaptive resonance theory model

ART was proposed by S. Grossberg of Boston University in 1976 [21,22]. ART is a kind of self-organizing neural network structure, which is a learning network without teachers. S. Grossberg and G. A. Carpenter proposed the so-called ART to solve the stability/plasticity dilemma of neural network learning by imitating the interaction between human vision and memory. Here, the so-called stability refers to when new things are input, the characteristics of old things should be properly preserved; plasticity refers to when new things are input, the network should learn quickly. Unlike other artificial neural network models, ART is divided into the learning stage and the testing stage. It needs to prepare a training mode set and a testing mode set in advance. ART is always in the learning state and testing state, it does not need training.

There are many versions of ART. ART1, the earliest version, contains a master—slave algorithm with parallel architecture [23]. It uses a set operation in the activation and matching functions of the algorithm. It mainly deals with the problem of image recognition (i.e., black and white) with only 0 and 1. ART2 can process gray scale

(i.e., analog value) input [23]. ART3 has a multilevel search architecture, which integrates the functions of the first two structures and
expands the two-layer neural network to any multilayer neural network [24]. Since ART3 incorporated the bioelectrochemical reaction
mechanism of neurons into the operation model of neurons, its function
and ability were further expanded.

The basic architecture of ART1 is shown in Fig. 3.4. It consists of
three parts: attention subsystem, adjustment subsystem, and gain
control. The attention subsystem and the adjustment subsystem are
complementary. The ART model deals with familiar or unfamiliar
events through the interaction between these two subsystems and a
control mechanism. In the attention subsystem, F_1 and F_2 are composed of short-term memory units, namely STM-F_1 and STM-F_2. The
connecting channel between F_1 and F_2 is long-term memory LTM.
Gain control has two functions: One is used to distinguish bottom–up
and top–down signals in F_1; the other is that F_2 can play a threshold
role for signals from F_1 when input signals enter the system. The
adjustment subsystem consists of A and STM reset wave channels.

In the ART model, its working process adopts the two-thirds rule.
The so-called two-thirds rule is that in the ART network, two of the
three input signals must work to make neurons produce output signals.
When double input comes from the bottom–up, among the three

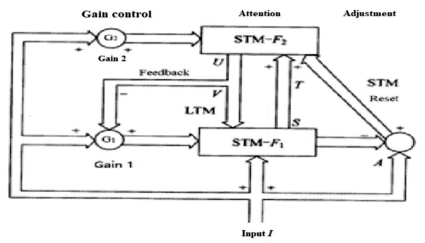

Figure 3.4 Adaptive resonance theory basic architecture.

input signal sources of F_1, there is the input signal I for input, and input to F_1 is generated after I passes gain control 1. Because these two input signals work, neurons in F_1 are activated, and F_1 can generate signal output.

3.4 Bayesian linking field model

In recent years, with the research and development of biological neuroscience, R. Eckhorn et al. proposed a new network model, the pulse-coupled neural network (PCNN), by studying the working mechanism of the visual cortex nervous system in small mammals. PCNN is derived from the research results of mammalian cat visual cortex neurons. It has the characteristics of synchronous pulse excitation, threshold attenuation, and parameter controllability. Because of its biological background, spatial proximity, and similar brightness cluster, it has wide application prospects in digital image processing and other fields. Combining the latest theoretical research results of PCNN with other new technologies to develop a new algorithm with practical application value is one of the main directions of neural network research.

3.4.1 Elkhorn model

In 1952 A. L. Hodgkin and A. F. Huxley began to study the electrochemical properties of neurons. In 1987 C. M. Gray et al. found that there were neural excitation—related oscillations in the primary visual cortex of cats [9]. In 1989 R. Elkhorn and Gray studied the visual cortex of cats and proposed a network model with the characteristics of a pulse synchronous release [25]. In 1994 J. L. Johnson published a paper on the periodic fluctuation of PCNN and its rotation, scalability, distortion, and intensity invariance in image processing [26]. The PCNN model is formed by improving the model proposed by Elkhorn. In 1999 IEEE Transactions on Neural Networks published a special album of PCNNs.

In 1990 based on the synchronous oscillation phenomenon of a cat's visual cortex, R. Elkhorn proposed a pulse neural network model [27], as shown in Fig. 3.5. This model consists of many interconnected neurons, each of which consists of two functionally distinct input parts: the conventional feeding input and the modulating linking input. However, the relationship between the two parts is not that of adding coupling but that of multiplying coupling.

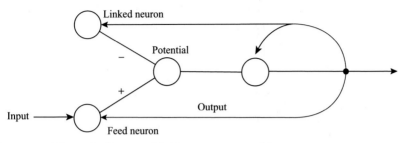

Figure 3.5 Schematic diagram of Eckhorn neuron model.

The Elkhorn model can be described by the following equations:

$$U_{m,k} = F_k(t)[1 + L_k(t)] \tag{3.7}$$

$$F_k(t) = \sum_{i=1}^{N} \left[w_{ki}^f Y_i(t) + S_k(t) + N_k(t) \right] \otimes I(V^a, \tau^a, t) \tag{3.8}$$

$$L_k(t) = \sum_{i=1}^{N} \left[w_{ki}^l Y_i(t) + N_k(t) \right] \otimes I(V^l, \tau^l, t) \tag{3.9}$$

$$Y_k(t) = \begin{cases} 1 & U_{m,k}(t) \geq \theta_k(t) \\ 0 & else \end{cases} \tag{3.10}$$

Here, it is generally expressed as:

$$X(t) = Z(t) \otimes I(v, \tau, t) \tag{3.11}$$

and

$$X[n] = X[n-1]e^{-t/\tau} + VZ[n], \quad n = 1, 2, \cdots N \tag{3.12}$$

where N is the number of neurons and w is the synaptic weighting coefficient. When the external excitation is S-type, Y is binary output.

Fig. 3.6 illustrates the structure of a neuron, which has only one dendrite, in the linking field network. Let the feeding inputs of the dendrite be $f_1(t), f_2(t), \ldots, f_n(t)$, and the linking inputs be $l_1(t), l_2(t), \ldots, l_m(t)$. Then the output of the neuron is calculated:

$$\begin{cases} U(t) = (\sum_{i=1}^{n} f_i(t)) \cdot (1 + \beta \sum_{j=1}^{m} l_j(t)) \\ Y(t) = \begin{cases} 1 & if \ U(t) > \theta(t) \\ 0 & else \end{cases} \end{cases} \tag{3.13}$$

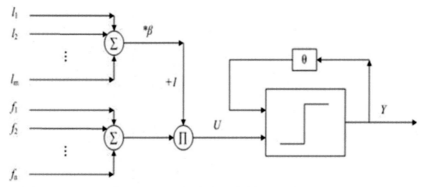

Figure 3.6 Structure of a neuron in the linking field network.

where $U(t)$ is the membrane potential of the neuron, β is the coupling parameter indicating the coupling strength, $Y(t)$ represents the output of the neuron, and $\theta(t)$ is an adaptive threshold, which is determined by the values of Y and t.

3.4.2 Noisy neuron firing strategy

The Bayesian linking field model (BLFM) is also a network model composed of interconnected neurons. Neurons in our model contain two types of inputs, namely feeding inputs and linking inputs, and they are coupled via multiplication. The difference is that we also impose a noisy neural model, the Bayesian method, and a competition mechanism to tackle the problem of feature binding.

According to the detailed neuron model, the change of neural membrane potential exhibits a threshold-like property. When the input stimuli exceed some threshold, neuron will generate an action potential. For simplicity, many formal neuron models import the threshold concept directly. When the nonlinear transformation of inputs exceeds some predefined value, neurons will fire. The spike response model, integrate–and–fire model, and Elkhorn model all utilize this strategy. In vivo recordings of neuronal activity are characterized by a high degree of irregularity, which is caused by various noises in the neural system. On the one hand, the existence of noise makes the modeling of neurons more complicated; on the other hand, it improves the coding capability of neuron models, for it allows noisy models to code subthreshold inputs. One of the popular noisy neuron models is the escape noise model [28]. In this model, the firing of neurons is not controlled by a threshold but is described by a firing probability. Different input will change the firing probability of a neuron. In our BLFM, we adopt the noisy firing strategy from the escape noise model; that is, the outputs of neurons in our model are probabilities but not pulses. As a result, in our model, the coding sphere of input stimuli is largely enlarged, and the proposed model carries more neurobiological properties.

3.4.3 Bayesian coupling of inputs

The coupling of inputs of a neuron needs to be coupled with firing probabilities. In cognitive research, if we use a neuron to represent a perceptual object, its feeding presynaptic neurons usually denote its composing features or compartments, and its linking presynaptic neurons indicate other objects, which have more or less of a relationship with the neuron. Thus if we leave linking inputs out of consideration, based on the relationship of parts and whole, we get:

$$P(X) = \sum_i w_i P(f_i) \qquad (3.14)$$

where X is the neuron, f_i is its feeding presynaptic neuron, and w_i is weight for the synaptic connection, which indicates the importance of f_i as a part in the whole entity X.

Now we examine the influence from linking inputs. Suppose that all the linking inputs are conditionally independent. Based on the Bayesian theorem:

$$P(l_i | l_1, \ldots, l_{i-1}, l_{i+1}, \ldots, l_n) = P(l_i) \quad i = 1, \ldots, n \qquad (3.15)$$

where X is the neuron, l_j is its linking presynaptic neuron, and $w_j = P(l_j | X)/P(l_j)$ is the weight for the synaptic connection, which represents the importance of l_j to X. $P(X)$ is the prior probability calculated from feeding information; $P(X | l_1, l_2, l_3, \ldots)$ is the postprobability after getting information from linking inputs; $P(l_j)$ is the firing probability of l_j. Fig. 3.7 illustrates the structure of a sample neuron in our model. From Eqs. (3.14) and (3.15), we can see that in our model, coupling among feeding inputs is additive, while coupling among integrated feeding inputs and all the linking inputs is multiplicative. These coupling rules are deduced based on the Bayesian theorem. From the analysis of J. L. Johnson et al. [29], we learn that the coupling of inputs from presynaptic neurons is quite complicated. It contains many high-order multiplicative coupling factors. So our coupling strategy fits the neurobiological properties of neurons.

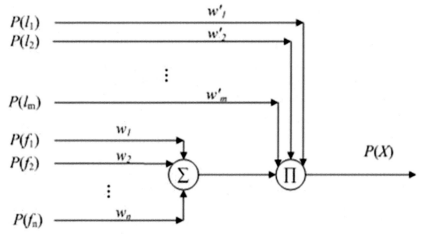

Figure 3.7 The structure of Bayesian linking field model.

3.4.4 Competition among neurons

Sufficient biological evidence shows that there are numerous competition phenomena in the neural activities of brain. Perry and Linden's work demonstrated that there are competitive relations among the cells in the retina Poldrack and Packard's research proved that, for both human beings and animals, there are broad competitive phenomena in various regions of brain cortex [30]. Accordingly, we import competitive mechanism into our model.

Let X_1 and X_2 be two different neurons; let F_1 and F_2 be the set of their feeding presynaptic neurons, respectively. Then there exists a competitive relationship between X_1 and X_2 if and only if at least one of the two following conditions holds.

1. $F_1 \cap F_2 \neq \emptyset$
2. Existing $f_1 \in F_1$ and $f_2 \in F_2$, f_1 and f_2 are competitive.

To implement competitive relations, we normalize the firing probabilities of the neurons that are competitive each other.

Let $X_1, X_2, \ldots, X_n$ be n neurons that are competitive with each other; $P_{before}(Xi)$ is the firing probability of Xi before competition. Then the firing probability of Xi after competition is:

$$P_{after}(X_i) = \frac{P_{before}(X_i)}{\sum\limits_{j=1}^{n} P_{before}(X_j)} \tag{3.16}$$

Based on this discussion, the complete BLFM is shown in Fig. 3.7. The model is also a network model composed of many neurons, and the neurons in the model contain two types of inputs: One is the feeding input, the other is the linking input, and the coupling relationship between the two types of inputs is multiplication. Different from the Elkhorn model, in order to solve the problem of feature binding, we also introduce the idea of a noise neuron model, the Bayesian method, and a competition mechanism.

BLFM model is a network composed of neurons, which has the following characteristics:

1. It uses the noise neuron model, that is, the input and output of each neuron is the probability of release, not the pulse value.
2. Each neuron can contain two parts of input: feeding input and linking input.
3. The connection weight between neurons reflects the statistical correlation between them, which is obtained through learning.
4. The output of neurons is not only affected by input but also restricted by competition.

3.5 Recurrent neural networks

A recurrent neural network (RNN) is a class of artificial neural network where connections between nodes form a directed graph along a sequence. This allows it to exhibit temporal dynamic behavior for a time sequence. Unlike feed-forward neural networks, RNNs can use their internal state (memory) to process sequences of inputs [31]. This makes them applicable to tasks such as unsegmented, connected handwriting recognition or speech recognition. A typical RNN is shown in Fig. 3.8 [32].

RNNs contain input units, and the input set is labeled $\{x_0, x_1, \ldots, x_t, x_{t+1}, \ldots\}$, and the output set of the output units is marked as $\{y_0, y_1, \ldots, y_t, y_{t+1}, \ldots\}$. RNNs also contain hidden units, and we mark their output

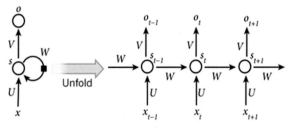

Figure 3.8 A typical recurrent neural network structure.

sets as $\{s_0, s_1, \ldots, s_t, s_{t+1}, \ldots\}$; these hidden units have done the most important work. You will find that in the Fig. 3.8, there is a one-way flow of information from the input unit to the hidden unit, along with another one-way flow of information from the hidden unit to the output unit. In some cases, RNNs break the latter's limitations, and the boot information is returned to the hidden unit from the output unit. These are called back-projections, and the input to the hidden layer also includes the state of the last hidden layer, that is, within the hidden layer. Nodes can be self-connected or interconnected.

For example, for a statement containing five words, the expanded network is a five-layer neural network, with each layer representing a word. The calculation process for this network is:

1. x_t is the input at time step t. For example, x_1 could be a one-hot vector corresponding to the second word of a sentence.

2. s_t is the hidden state at time step t. It's the "memory" of the network. s_t is calculated based on the previous hidden state and the input at the current step: $s_t = f(Ux_t + Ws_{t-1})$. The function f usually is a nonlinearity such as tanh (hyperbolic tangent) or ReLU (rectified linear unit). s_{-1}, which is required to calculate the first hidden state, is typically initialized to all zeroes.

3. o_t is the output at step t. For example, if we wanted to predict the next word in a sentence, it would be a vector of probabilities across our vocabulary. $o_t = \text{softmax}(Vs_t)$.

You can think of the hidden state s_t as the memory of the network. s_t captures information about what happened in all the previous time steps. The output at step o_t is calculated solely based on the memory at time t. As previously mentioned, it is a bit more complicated in practice because s_t typically cannot capture information from too many time steps ago.

Unlike a traditional deep neural network, which uses different parameters at each layer, an RNN shares the same parameters (U, V, W) across all steps. This reflects the fact that we are performing the same task at each step, just with different inputs. This greatly reduces the total number of parameters we need to learn. Fig. 3.8 has outputs at each time step, but depending on the task, this may not be necessary [32]. For example, when predicting the sentiment of a sentence, we may only care about the final output, not the sentiment after each word. Similarly, we may not need inputs at each time step. The main feature of an RNN is its hidden state, which captures some information about a sequence.

RNNs can be used to map input sequences to output sequences, such as for recognition, production, or prediction problems. However, practical difficulties have been reported in training RNNs to perform tasks. Bengio et al. pointed out that learning long-term dependencies with gradient descent is difficult [33]. Based on an understanding of this problem, alternatives to the standard gradient descent are considered.

3.6 Long short-term memory

RNNs have shown great success in many NLP tasks. At this point we should mention that the most commonly used type of RNNs are long short-term memories (LSTMs), which are much better at capturing long-term dependencies than vanilla RNNs are. LSTMs are essentially the same thing as the RNN; they just have a different way of computing the hidden state.

LSTM is a deep learning system that avoids the vanishing gradient problem. LSTM is normally augmented by recurrent gates called forget gates [34]. LSTM prevents back-propagated errors from vanishing or exploding. Instead, errors can flow backward through unlimited numbers of virtual layers unfolded in space. That is, LSTM can learn tasks [35] that require memories of events that happened thousands or even millions of discrete time steps earlier. Problem-specific LSTM-like topologies can be evolved. LSTM works even given long delays between significant events and can handle signals that mix low- and high-frequency components.

LSTMs are explicitly designed to avoid the long-term dependency problem [33]. Remembering information for long periods of time is practically their default behavior, not something they struggle to learn! All RNNs have the form of a chain of repeating modules of the neural network. In standard RNNs, this repeating module has a very simple structure, such as a single tanh layer.

LSTMs also have this chain-like structure, but the repeating module has a different structure. Instead of having a single neural network layer, there are four, interacting in a very special way shown in Fig. 3.9 [34]. The key to LSTMs is the cell state, the horizontal line running through the top of the diagram. The cell state is like a conveyor belt. It runs straight down the entire chain, with only some minor linear interactions. It is very easy for information to just flow along it unchanged. The LSTM does have the ability to remove or add information to the cell state, carefully regulated by structures called gates. Gates are a way to optionally let information through. They are

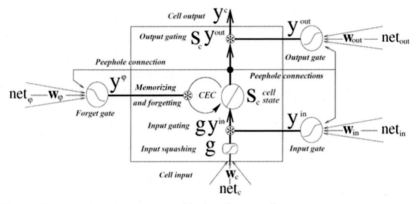

Figure 3.9 Long short-term memory block with one cell.

composed of a sigmoid neural net layer and a pointwise multiplication operation. The sigmoid layer outputs numbers between zero and one, describing how much of each component should be let through. A value of zero means "let nothing through," while a value of one means "let everything through!" An LSTM has three of these gates to protect and control the cell state.

Fig. 3.9 shows an LSTM block with one cell. The three gates are nonlinear summation units that collect activations from inside and outside the block and control the activation of the cell via multiplications (small black circles). The input and output gates multiply the input and output of the call, while the forget gate multiplies the cell's previous state. No activation function is applied within the cell. The gate activation function f is usually the logistic sigmoid, so that the gate activation functions are between 0 (gate closed) and 1 (gate open). The cell input and output activation functions (g and h) are usually tanh or logistic sigmoid, though in some cases h is the identity function. The weighted "peephole" connections from the cell to the gates are shown with dashed lines. All other connections within the block are unweighted. The only output from the block to the rest of the network emanate from the output gate multiplication.

Many applications use stacks of LSTM RNNs [36] and train them by Connectionist Temporal Classification (CTC) [37] to find an RNN weight matrix that maximizes the probability of the label sequences in a training set, given the corresponding input sequences. CTC achieves both alignment and recognition. LSTM can learn to recognize context-sensitive languages unlike previous models based on hidden Markov models and similar concepts.

3.7 Neural field model

Artificial neural network is considered a learning machine with a broad nonlinear relationship approximation mechanism and a nonlinear data relationship classifier. It is essential in that it provides a nonlinear function relationship approximation theory. In 1985 S. Amari proposed an information geometric and used it in the study of the theory of neural computation [38]. The basic idea is to regard the space making up of all the neural network transformation as a manifold space. The manifold space is an extension of general Euclidean space and Hilbert space, which enables us to establish approximation theory and topology correction theory in a more generalized nonlinear space and non-Euclidean space in order to better understand the neural network model transformation mechanism and learning problems through geometry and topology structural analysis. Zhongzhi Shi and Jian Zhang analyzed the expression of neural network architecture, system identification, the mechanism of transformation from the perspective of the microshape and topological transform in order to understand the organizational structure and the positioning mechanism of the neural network in more general information processing system space. We consider the overall structure of neural computation, propose the overall structure coupling of the field organization transformation and field response transformation as the new method of information processing, the mechanism of transformation of the artificial neural network model; we also introduce the modular, hierarchical, scalability of models, use manifold dual geometry to explain it, and raise the corresponding learning algorithm [39].

The neural network includes input units, hidden units, and output units. The hidden units are regarded as nonmeasurable and are values that need to be estimated in the information processing. We understand the information processing of neural network as noncomplete data information processing. We give a new description of the neural network transformation mechanism. The transformation mechanism of the neural network consists of two processes: The organization process of neural field realizes expression from the input mode through the hidden units, and the neural field reaction process realizes the transformation from expression to the output (see Fig. 3.10). Here, X is the input space; $X \times Z$ is the space, called neural field expression; Y is the output space. The field organization transform model is expressed as $T: X \to X \times Z$, in which Z is measurable space, or the space for auxiliary information. The field organization model realizes the characteristics of input patterns that may be

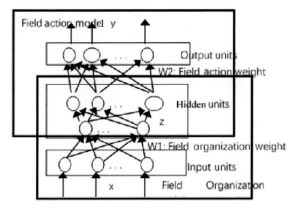

Figure 3.10 Neural field model.

achieved by the algorithm or mapping. Its purpose is to extract the characteristics of the structure of input mode, so that the desired output mode is much easier; in the neural network, the connection weights contained in the field organization model, are known as field organization weights value or cognitive weights.

3.8 Neural column model

Since 1957 V. B. Mountcastle discovered column structure, many research results have shown that in visual cortex, auditory cortex, somatosensory cortex, motor cortex, as well as other coexisting cortexes of different species (rat, cat, rabbit, monkey, human, etc.), there is a functional column structure. These results suggest that the functional column is a common structure and the basic unit of structure and physiology; the activities of these columns constitute a basis for the activities of the entire cerebral cortex [40].

In order to deeply understand the biological significance of columns and their roles in information processing, researchers carried out a number of mathematical modeling studies. Wilson-Cowan equations are the most common method to describe the function column in model study. For example, H. G. Shuster and others simulated synchronous oscillation found in the visual cortex [41]; B. H. Jansen et al. proposed a coupling function column model produced an EEG-type waveform and evoked potential [42]; T. Fukai designed a functional column network model to simulate the access of visual design and so on [43]. Some other feature column modes describing functional oscillation activities of the column are phase column models. Only a small number of models are based on the single neuron. For instance, E. Fransén and others replaced the single cell in the traditional network with multicell functional columns to build an attractor network in order to simulate the working memory; D. Hansel et al. built a super column model under the structure of the direction column of visual cortex column, studied synchronization and chaotic characteristics, and explained the mechanism of the function column with direction selection.

Su Li used modeling neurons as the basic unit, organized the function column model in accordance with the cortical function structure, explored the relationship between these models and the outside input and network structure, and researched the network model formed by a number of functional column links and what new characteristics it has in patterns of activity [44].

The Rose-Hindmarsh equations are selected to describe the single neuron:

$$\dot{x} = y + ax^3 - bx^2 - z + I_{syn} + I_{stim}$$
$$\dot{y} = c - dx^2 - y \qquad (3.17)$$
$$\dot{z} = r[s(s - x_0) - z]$$

where x represents membrane potential; y is the rapid return current; z describes the slow change in the adjustment of current; I_{syn} is the synaptic current; I_{stim}, external input; a, b, c, d, r, s, x_0 are constants. Here $a = 1$, $b = 3$, $c = 1$, $d = 5$, $s = 2$ and $x_0 = -1.6$. The time scale in Rose-Hindmarsh model is 5 units, equivalent to 1 ms.

According to the results of physiological tests, neurons' cortical functional columns, in accordance with their physiological characteristics, fall into two categories: RS (regular-spiking) cells and FS (fast-spiking) cells. RS cells are excited, in the form of pyramidal cells, and are characterized by a clear and rapid dissemination frequency of adaptation for continuous current stimulation over time to rapidly reduce the dissemination frequency. FS cells are suppressed in the usual form of nonpyramidal cells, with physiological characteristics of low adaptability to continuous input current frequency. We use different parameters r to represent the characteristics of these two cells: $rRS = 0.015$, $rFS = 0.001$.

The model takes a synaptic model based on currents. Before the synaptic action potential in each cell will trigger the postsynaptic cell input I_{syn}, synaptic current I_{syn} is expressed as:

$$I_{syn} = g_{syn} V_{syn} \left(e^{-t/\tau_1} - e^{-t/\tau_2} \right) \qquad (3.18)$$

where g_{syn} is the membrane conductance, τ_1 and τ_2 are time constants, and V_{syn} is the postsynaptic potential. V_{syn} is used to regulate the strength of synaptic coupling. Use V_{RR} to express the excitement connection V_{syn} between RS cells. Similarly, V_{syn} projected from RS cells onto FS cells and from FS cells onto RS cells are expressed, respectively, as VRF and V_{FR}. The parameter is set to $g_{RR} = 4$, $\tau_1(RR) = 3$, $\tau_2(RR) = 2$, $g_{RF} = 8$, $\tau_1(RF) = 1$, $\tau_2(RF) = 0.7$, $g_{FR} = 4$, $\tau_1(FR) = 3$, $\tau_2(FR) = 2. V_{FR}$ is always set to -1. V_{RR} and V_{RF} in the process of the simulation vary between 0.1 and 1.

References

[1] Z.Z. Shi, Neural Computing (In Chinese), Electronic Industry Press, 1993.
[2] W.S. McCulloch, G.W. Pitts, A logic calculus of the ideas immanent in nervous activity, Bull. Math. Biophys 5 (1943) 115−133.
[3] N. Wiener, Cybernetics, or Control and Communication in the Animal and the Machine, The Technology Press, Cambridge, MA, 1948. New York: John Wiley & Sons, Inc.
[4] D.O. Hebb, The Organization of Behavior: A Neuropsychological Theory, Wiley, New York, 1949.
[5] W.R. Ashby, Design for a Brain, Wiley, New York, 1952.
[6] F. Rosenblatt, Principles of Neurodynamics, Spartan Books, 1962.
[7] B. Widrow, Generalization and information storage in networks of adaline 'neurons', in: M.C. Yovitz, G.T. Jacobi, G. Goldstein (Eds.), Self-Organizing Systems 1962, Spartan Books, Washington, DC, 1962, pp. 435−461.
[8] M. Minsky, S. Papert, Perceptrons, MIT Press, 1969.
[9] S. Grossberg, Neural expectation: cerebellar and retinal analogs of cells fired by learnable or unlearned pattern classes, Kybernetik 10 (1972) 49−57.
[10] T. Kohonen, Self-organized formation of topologically correct feature maps, Biol. Cybern. 43 (1982) 59−69.
[11] S. Kirkpatrick, C.D. Gelatt, M.P. Vecchi, Optimization by simulated annealing, Science 220 (1983) 671−680.
[12] N. Metropolis, A. Rosenbluth, M. Rosenbluth, A. Teller, E. Teller, Equations of state calculations by fast computing machines, J. Chem. Phys. 21 (1953) 1087−1092.
[13] G.E. Hinton, T.J. Sejnowski, Learning and relearning in Boltzmann machines, in: D.E. Rumelhart, J.L. McClelland (Eds.), Parallel Distributed Processing: Explorations in the Microstructure of Cognition. Volume 1: Foundations, MIT Press, Cambridge, MA, 1986.
[14] R.M. Neal, Bayesian Learning for Neural Networks, Springer, Berlin, 1996.
[15] D.E. Rumelhart, J.L. McClelland (Eds.), Parallel Distributed Processing: Explorations in the Microstructure of Cognition, vol. 1, MIT Press, Cambridge, MA, 1986.
[16] P.J. Werbos, Beyond regression: new tools for prediction and analysis in the behavioral sciences. Ph.D. Thesis, Harvard University, Cambridge, MA (1974).
[17] T. Poggio, F. Girosi, Reguiarization algorithms for learning that are equivalent to multilayer networks, Science 247 (1990) 978−982.
[18] V.N. Vapnik, The Nature of Statistical Learning Theory, Springer-Verlag, New York, 1995.

[19] G.E. Hinton, R. Salakhutdinov, Reducing the dimensionality of data with neural networks, Science 313 (5786) (2006) 504−507.

[20] S.Q. Zhang, Z.H. Zhou, Flexible transmitter network. arXiv:2004.03839 [cs.NE] (2020).

[21] S. Grossberg, Adaptive pattern classification and universal recoding: I. Parallel development and coding of neural detectors, Biol. Cybern. 23 (1976) 121−134.

[22] S. Grossberg, Adaptive pattern classification and universal recoding: II. Feedback, expectation, olfaction, illusions, Biol. Cybern. 23 (1976) 187−202.

[23] G.A. Carpenter, S. Grossberg, ART2: self-organization of stable category recognition codes for analog input pattern, Appl. Opt. 26 (23) (1987) 4919−4930.

[24] G.A. Carpenter, S. Grossberg, ART3: hierarchical search using chemical transmitters in self-organizing pattern recognition architectures, Neural Netw. 3 (1990) 129−152.

[25] R. Eckhorn, H.J. Reiboeck, M. Arndt, et al., A neural networks for feature linking via synchronous activity: results from cat visual cortex and from simulations, in: R.M.J. Cotterill (Ed.), Models of Brain Function, Cambridge Univ. Press, Cambridge, 1989.

[26] J.L. Johnson, Pulse-coupled neural nets: translation, rotation, scale, distortion, and intensity signal invariance for images, Appl. Opt. 33 (1994) 6239−6253.

[27] R. Eckhorn, H.J. Reitboeck, M. Arndt, et al., Feature linking via synchronization among distributed assemblies: simulations of results from cat visual cortex, Neural Comput. 2 (1990) 293−307.

[28] V.H. Perry, R. Linden, Evidence for dendritic competition in the developing retina, Nature 297 (1982) 683−685.

[29] J.L. Johnson, M.L. Padgett, PCNN models and applications, IEEE Trans. Neural Netw. 10 (3) (1999) 480−498.

[30] R.A. Poldrack, M.G. Packard, Competition among multiple memory systems: converging evidence from animal and human brain studies, Neuropsychologia 41 (3) (2003) 241−244.

[31] J.L. Elman, Finding structure in time, Cognit. Sci. 14 (2) (1990) 179−211.

[32] Y. LeCun, Y. Bengio, G. Hinton, Deep learning, Nature 521 (7553) (2015) 436−444.

[33] Y. Bengio, P. Simard, P. Frasconi, Learning long-term dependencies with gradient descent is difficult, IEEE Trans. Neural Netw. 5 (1994) 157−166.

[34] F.A. Gers, E. Schmidhuber, LSTM recurrent networks learn simple context-free and context-sensitive languages, IEEE Trans. Neural Netw. 12 (6) (2001) 1333−1340.

[35] J. Schmidhuber, Deep learning in neural networks: an overview, Neural Netw. 61 (2015) 85−117.

[36] S. Fernandez, A. Graves, J. Schmidhuber, Sequence labelling in structured domains with hierarchical recurrent neural networks, in: Proceedings of the 20th International Joint Conference on Artificial Intelligence, IJCAI2007, (2007) 774−779.

[37] A. Graves, S. Fernández, F. Gomez, Connectionist temporal classification: Labelling unsegmented sequence data with recurrent neural networks, in: Proceedings of the International Conference on Machine Learning, ICML (2006) 369−376.

[38] S. Amari, Differential geometrical methods in statistics, Springer Lecture Notes in Statistic, 28, Springer, 1985.

[39] J. Zhang, Z.Z. Shi, An adaptive theoretical foundation toward neural information processing NFT, in: Proceedings of ICONOP'95, (1995) 217−220.

[40] V.B. Mountcastle, The columnar organization of the neocortex, Brain 120 (1997) 701−722.

[41] H.G. Shuster, P. Wagner, A model for neuronal oscillations in the visual cortex. I: mean-field theory and derivation of phase equations, Biol. Cybern. 64 (1990) 77−82.

[42] B.H. Jansen, G. Zouridakis, M.E. Brandt, A neurophysiologically-based mathematical model of flash visual evoked potentials, Biol. Cybern. 68 (1993) 275–283.

[43] T. Fukai, A model of cortical memory processing based on columnar organization, Biol. Cybern. 70 (1994) 427–434.

[44] S. Li, X.L. Xi, H. Hu, Y.J. Wang, The synchronous oscillation in neural networks model of function column structure, China Sci. C, Life Sci. 34 (4) (2004) 385–394.

CHAPTER 4

Mind model

The mind means all the spiritual activities of human beings, including emotion, will, sensibility, perception, representation, learning, memory, thought, intuition, etc. The mind issue is one of the most fundamental and significant issues of intelligence science [1]. People use modern scientific methods to study the form, process, and law of the integration of human irrational psychology and rational cognition. The technology of building a mind model is often called mind modeling, which aims to explore and study the human thinking mechanism, especially the human information processing mechanism, and provide new architecture and technical methods for designing a corresponding artificial intelligence system.

4.1 Mind

In intelligence science, "mind" means a series of cognitive abilities, which enable individuals to have consciousness, sense the outside world, think, make judgments, and remember things [2]. The mind is a human characteristic; however, other living creatures may also have mind.

The phenomenon and psychological aspects of the mind have long been intertwined. The phenomenal concept of mind is a consciously experienced mental state. This is the most confusing aspect of the mind. Another is the psychological concept of mind, which is a causal or an explanatory basis of behavior. In this sense, a state is mental if it plays an appropriate causal role in terms of behavior formation, or it at least plays a proper role in terms of behavior interpretation.

In accordance with the concept of phenomenology, mind is depicted by way of sensing, while in accordance with the concept of psychology, the mind is depicted by its behavior. There is no competition problem between these two mind concepts. Either of them may be a correct analysis of the mind. They involve different fields of phenomenon, both of which are quite real.

A particular mind concept can often be analyzed as a phenomenal concept, a psychological concept, or as a combination of both. For example, sensing is best seen as a phenomenal concept in its core meaning:

Intelligence Science
DOI: https://doi.org/10.1016/B978-0-323-85380-4.00004-X

a sensing of a certain sensing status. On the other hand, learning and memory are best viewed as a psychological concept. Roughly speaking, something is to be learned, since it is appropriate to adjust the capacity to respond to certain environmental stimuli. In general, the phenomenal characteristics of the mind are depicted by those subjects with the appropriate characteristics. Psychological characteristics of the mind are represented by those roles, which are associated with the causal relation or explanation of behavior.

The states of mind mean psychological states, including belief, ability, intentions, expectations, motivation, commitment, and so on. They are important factors in determining intelligent social behavior and individual behavior. The concept of the human mind is related to thoughts and consciousness. It is the product of human consciousness development at a certain stage. Anthropologists believe that all creatures have some kind of mind, mind development went through four stages: (1) *Simple reflection stage*: For example, the pupil shrinks when eyes are stimulated by strong light, which cannot be controlled by consciousness. (2) *Reflex stage*: Pavlov's famous experiment showed that stimuli can make dog saliva outflow. (3) *Tool stage*: Chimpanzees can get fruits from the tree using sticks. (4) *Symbol stage*: It is the ability to use language symbol to communicate with the outside world, which only humans can do. Therefore, in comparison with the animal mind at a relatively early stage, the human mind is the product of mind development at the highest stage. The generation and development of human intelligence cannot be separated from the symbolic language of mankind.

4.1.1 Philosophy issues of mind

In a long time, people are trying to understand what the mind is from the perspective of philosophy, religion, psychology, and cognitive science and to explore the unique nature of the mind. Many famous philosophers studied in this domain, including Plato, Aristotle, R. Descartes, G. W. Leibniz, I. Kant, M. Heidegger, J. R. Searle, D. Dennett, et al. Some psychologists, including S. Freud and W. James, also set up a series of influential theories about the nature of the human mind from the perspective of psychology in order to represent and define the mind. In the late 20th and early 21st centuries, scientists have established and developed a variety of ways and methods to describe the mind and its phenomenon in the field of cognitive science. In another field, artificial intelligence began to explore the possibility of the existence of the nonhuman mind by combining the control theory and information theory. They also looked for a method of realizing the human spirit's influence on the machine.

In recent years, mental philosophy developed rapidly, which has become a fundamental and pivotal subject in the field of philosophy. If we said the movement from modern philosophy to contemporary philosophy has gone through a kind of Copernicus revolution, in which linguistic philosophy replaced epistemology and became a symbol of contemporary philosophy, then mental philosophy has become the foundation of contemporary genres. If we said that the solution to the problem of ontology and epistemology cannot be separated from linguistic philosophy, then that of linguistic philosophy depends on the exploration and development of mental philosophy. For example, to explain the meaning, reference, nature, and characteristics of language, we must resort to the intention of mental state (but not as the only factor). What is amazing are the large number of works, the depth and vastness of the problems, the novel and unique insight, the fierce debates, the rapid progress in this domain.

The study of mind philosophy is mainly about the form, scope, nature, characteristics, relationship between mind and body, psychological content and its source, and the philosophical reflection [3] on the explanatory model of folk psychology. With the deepening of cognition, mental philosophy has changed or is changing the traditional psychology. Because the psychological phenomenon is an important part of the cosmic structure, the newest exploration has touched the fundamental cosmic view, such as collateral, dependence, decision, covariance, reduction, rule, and so on. There are indications that the development of mental philosophy will be one of the most important sources and forces of future philosophy. From this point of view, philosophy of mind is not a narrow mental knowledge but a profound domain with stable core, fuzzy boundary, open character, and the broad future. At present, the focus is as discussed next.

4.1.1.1 Mind—body problem

The mind—body problem involves the nature of psychological phenomenon and the relationship between the mind and body. The current debate is mainly concentrated on reductionism, functionalism, and the dilemma of realizationism and physicalism.

The nature of the problem is the relationship between the brain and the nervous system. The discussion is about the mind—body dichotomy, whether the mind is independent of human flesh to some extent (dualism), and whether the flesh is independent from physical phenomena can be regarded as physical phenomena including neural activity (physicalism). The discussion is also about whether the mind is consistent with our brains and its activity. The other question is whether only humans have mind or whether all or some of animals and creatures have mind, or even whether a human-made machine could have mind.

Regardless of the relationship between the mind and the body, it is generally believed that the mind makes individual subjective and intentional judgments about the environment. Accordingly, individual can perceive and respond to stimulation via a certain medium. At the same time, the individual can think and feel.

4.1.1.2 Consciousness

Consciousness here is used in a limited sense, meaning the common awareness that runs through humans' various psychological phenomena. Scientists have formed a special and independent research field around consciousness, some of which also puts forward the particular concept of "consciousness." There are numerous problems with consciousness, which can be classified in two kinds: difficult problems and easy problems. The former refers to the problem of experience, which attracts the lion's share of attention.

4.1.1.3 Sensitibility

Sensitibility is the subjective characteristic or phenomenological nature of people experiencing the psychological state of feeling. Nonphysicalists argue that physicalism has been able to assimilate all kinds of counterexamples except the qualia. Sensitibility is the new world of the psychological world, a nonphysical thing that cannot be explained by physical principle. However, physicalists will counter that, in the effort to move physicalism forward.

4.1.1.4 Supervenience

Supervenience is a new problem and a new paradigm in mental philosophy, referring to the characteristic that the psychological phenomenon is interdependent with the physical phenomenon. Definitely, it can also be generalized to other relations or attributes, so as to become a universal philosophical category. Throughout the study, people are trying to further grasp the essence and characteristics of mental phenomena and its status in the cosmic structure. They also want to look for the product of a middle path between reductionism and dualism. All these relate to the crucial problem of decision, reduction, inevitability, and psychophysical law in mental philosophy and cosmology.

4.1.1.5 The language of thought
The language of thought refers to machine language, which is different from natural language and which is the real medium of the human brain. It seems to many people that natural language has echoism, so it cannot be processed by the brain.

4.1.1.6 Intentionality and content theory
This is an old but new problem, which is the intersection of linguistic philosophy and mental philosophy. Many people think that the meaning of natural language is related to mental state and that the latter is rooted in the semantic of both the language of thought and mental representation. But what is the semantic of the language of thought? What is the relationship between it and the function of mental state? What is the relationship between it and the syntactic of psychological statement? All these are the focuses of debate.

4.1.1.7 Mental representation
Mental representation is the expression of information, which is stored and processed by people. The information is attained when they acquaint themselves with the world and their own. These studies reach deeply into the internal structure, operation, and mechanism of the mental world.

4.1.1.8 Machine mind
The machine mind is the problem of "other mind," that is, is there any other mind except the human mind? If it exists, how can we recognize and prove that it exists? What is its basis, reason, and process? What is the foundation to judge whether the object like a robot is intelligent? The debate focuses on the skepticism and analogous argumentation of "other mind."

The mental philosopher has been arguing about the relationship between the phenomenal consciousness and the brain and mind. Recently, neural scientists and philosophers have discussed the problem of neural activity in the brain that constitutes a phenomenal consciousness and how to distinguish between the neural correlates of consciousness and nervous tissue? What levels of neural activity in the brain constitute a consciousness? What might be a good phenomenon for study, such as binocular rivalry, attention, memory, emotion, pain, dreams, and coma? What should consciousness know and explain in this field? How to apply tissue relationship to the brain, mind, and other relationships like identity, nature, understanding, generation, and causal preference? The literature [4] brings together the interdisciplinary discussion of the problems by neural scientists and philosophers.

Experimental philosophy [5] is a new thing in the 21st century. In just over a decade, like a powerful cyclone, it shook the philosophers' dream about the rationality of traditional research methods and sparked a reflection on philosophical methodology. With the heated debate, its influence is spread rapidly around the world.

4.1.2 Mind modeling

Research on the brain, like intelligence in intelligence science, is closely related to the computational theory of mind. Generally, models are used to express how the mind works and to understand the working mechanism of the mind. In 1980, Newell first proposed the standard of mind modeling [6]. In 1990, Newell described the human mind as a set of functional constraints and proposed 13 criteria for mind [7]. In 2003, on the basis of Newell's 13 criteria, Anderson et al. put forward the Newell test [8] to judge the criteria to be met by the human mental model and the conditions needed for better work. In 2013, the literature [9] analyzed the standards of mind models. In order to construct a better mind model, the paper proposed the criteria for mind modeling.

4.1.2.1 To behave flexibly

The first criterion is to behave flexibly as a function of the environment, and it was clear that it should have computational universality and that it was the most important criterion for human mind. Newell recognized the true flexibility in the human mind that made it deserving of this identification with computational universality, even as the modern computer is characterized as a Turing-equivalent device despite its physical limitations and occasional errors.

When universality of computation is the factor of human cognition, even if computers have specialized processors, they should not be regarded as only performing various specific cognitive functions. Moreover, it shows that it is much easier for people to learn some things than other devices. In the field of language, "natural language" is emphasized, and the learning of natural language is much easier than that of non-natural language. Commonly used artifacts are only a small part of an unnatural system. When people may approach the universality of computation, they only obtain a small part of computable function and execute it.

4.1.2.2 Adaptive behavior

Adaptive behavior means it must be in the service of goals and rationally related to things. Humans don't just do fantastic intelligence computation but choose the ones that meet their needs. In 1991 Anderson proposed two levels of self-adaptability: One is the basic process and related forms of the system structure, providing useful functions; the other is whether the system is regarded as a whole and whether its whole computation meets people's needs.

4.1.2.3 Real time

For a cognitive theory, just flexibility is not enough. The theory must explain how people can compete in real time. Here "real time" represents the time of human execution. For people who understand neural networks, cognition has its limitations. Real time is a restriction on learning and execution. If it takes a lifetime to learn something, in principle, this kind of learning is not useful.

4.1.2.4 Large-scale knowledge base

One of the key points of human's adaptability is that we can access a lot of knowledge. Perhaps the biggest difference between human cognition and various "expert systems" is that in most cases people have the necessary knowledge to take appropriate action. However, a large-scale knowledge base can cause problems. Not all knowledge is equally reliable or relevant. For the current situation, relevant knowledge can quickly become irrelevant. There may be serious problems in successfully storing all knowledge and retrieving relevant knowledge in a reasonable time.

4.1.2.5 Dynamic behavior

In the real world, it is not as simple as solving maze and Hanoi Tower problems. Change in the world is beyond our expectation and control. Even if people's actions are aimed to control the world, they will have unexpected effects. Dealing with a dynamic and unpredictable environment is the premise of the survival of all organisms. Given that people have built complexity analysis for their own environment, the need for dynamic response is mainly faced with cognitive problems. To deal with dynamic behavior, we need a theory of perception and action as well as a theory of cognition. The work of situational cognition emphasizes how the structural cognition of the external world appears. Supporters of this position argue that all cognition reflects the outside world. This is in sharp contrast to the earlier view that cognition can ignore the external world [10].

4.1.2.6 Knowledge integration
Newell called this standard "symbols and abstraction." Newell's comments on this standard appear in his book *Unified Theories of Cognition*: The mind can use symbols and abstractions [7]. We know that just from observing ourselves. He never seemed to admit that there was any debate on the issue. Newell thinks that the existence of external symbols such as symbols and equations is rarely disputed. He believes that symbols are concrete examples of table processing languages. Many symbols have no direct meaning, which is different from the effect of philosophical discussion or calculation. In Newell's sense, as a classification standard, symbols cannot be installed. However, if we pay attention to the definition of his physical symbols, we will understand the rationality of this standard.

4.1.2.7 Use language
The seventh criterion is to use language, both natural and artificial. Newell claimed that language is a central feature of human mind—like activity, and he believes that language depends on symbol manipulation.

4.1.2.8 Consciousness
Newell acknowledged the importance of consciousness to human cognition as a whole. Newell asked us to consider all the criteria, not just one of them. Consciousness includes subconscious perception, implicit learning, memory, and metacognition.

4.1.2.9 Learning
Learning is another uncontrollable standard of human cognitive theory. A satisfactory cognitive theory must explain the ability of human beings to acquire their competitiveness. People must be able to have many

different kinds of learning abilities, including semantic memory, situational memory, skills, priming, and conditions. There may be more than one way to learn.

4.1.2.10 Development

Development is the first of three constraints in Newell's initial list of the cognitive system structures. Although the functions associated with imagination and new cognitive theories are fully mature in the imaginary world, human cognition is constrained in the real world by the growth of the organism and the corresponding experience. Human development is not an ability but a constraint.

4.1.2.11 Evolution

Human cognitive ability must be improved through evolution. Various elements have been proposed—specific capabilities, such as the ability to detect cheaters or the constraints of natural language, which evolved at specific times in the history of human evolution. The change of evolutionary constraint is comparative constraint. How is the architecture of human cognition different from that of other mammals? We have taken cognitive plasticity as one of the characteristics of human cognition, and language is also a certain characteristic. What is the basis and unique cognitive attribute of the human cognitive system?

4.1.2.12 Brain

The last constraint is the neural realization of cognition. Recent research has greatly increased the functional data on specific brain regions that can be used to study cognitive constraint theory.

The world of the mind is much more complex than the possible world described with mathematics and logic. How might we move from the finite, noncontradictory use of the deductive method to construct relatively simple possible worlds into the infinite, contradictory use of a variety of logic and cognitive methods in a more complex mind world?

The goal of intelligence science is to uncover the mysteries of the human mind. Its research can not only promote the development of artificial intelligence and reveal the essence and significance of life but also have extraordinary significance in promoting the development of modern science, especially psychology, physiology, linguistics, logic, cognitive science, brain science, mathematics, computer science, and even philosophy.

4.2 Turing machine

In 1936 British scientist Turing submitted his famous paper "On Computable Numbers, with an Application to the Entscheidungsproblem" [11]. He put forward an abstract computation model, which can accurately define the computable function. In this pioneering paper, Turing gave "computable" a strict mathematical definition and put forward the famous Turing machine. The Turing machine is an abstract model rather than a material machine. It can produce a very easy but powerful computing device, which can compute all the computable functions ever imagined. Its physical structure is similar to the finite state machine.

Fig. 4.1 shows that the Turing machine has a finite state controller (FSC) and an external storage device that is an infinite tape that can randomly extend rightward. (The top left is the tape head, identified as "⊢.") A tape is divided into cells. Each cell can be blank or can contain a symbol from some finite alphabet. For convenience, we use a special symbol B, which is not in the alphabet, to represent the blank symbol. FSC interconnects with the tape by using a head that can read and write. Generally, the symbol B will be marked at the right.

At any given moment, FSC is in a certain state. The read/write head will scan every cell. According to the state and the symbol, the Turing Machine will have an action for changing the state of FSC. It will erase the symbol on cells that have been scanned and write a new symbol for it. (The new symbol might be the same as the previous one, which makes the cell content stay the same.) The read/write head will move left or right by one cell. Or the head is stationary.

The Turing machine can be defined as a 5-tuple

$$TM = (Q, \Sigma, q_0, q_a, \delta) \tag{4.1}$$

where

Q is a finite set of states;

Σ is a finite set of alphabet symbols on the tape, with the augmented set $\Sigma' = \Sigma \cup \{B\}$;

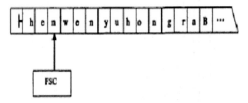

Figure 4.1 Turing machine's physical model.

$q_0 \in Q$ is the initial state;

$q_a \in Q$ is an accept state;

δ is the state transition function of $Q \times \Sigma' \to Q \times \Sigma' \times \{L, R, N\}$, which is $\delta(q, x) = (q', w, \{L, R, N\})$.

Generally, the transition function (or rules of Turing machine) will be marked as:

$$< q, x, q', w, \{L, R, N\} > \qquad (4.2)$$

where x, $w \in \Sigma \cup \{B\}$ means that if symbol x is scanned, the state will transform from q to q'. And a new symbol w will be written. The read/write head will move to the left (L), right (R), or not move (N).

4.3 Physical symbol system

Simon has defined that a physical symbol system (SS) is a machine that, as it moves through time, produces an evolving collection of symbol structures. Symbol structures can and commonly do serve as internal representations (e.g., "mental images") of the environment to which the SS is seeking to adapt [12]. A SS possesses a number of simple processes that operate upon symbol structures—processes that create, modify, copy, and destroy symbols. It must have a means for acquiring information from the external environment that can be encoded into internal symbols, as well as a means for producing symbols that initiate action upon the environment. Thus it must use symbols to designate objects and relations and actions in the world external to the system.

Symbol systems are called "physical" to remind the reader that they exist in real-world devices, fabricated of glass and metal (computers) or flesh and blood (brains). In the past, we have been more accustomed to thinking of the SSs of mathematics and logic as abstract and disembodied, leaving out of account the paper and pencil and human minds that were required to actually bring them to life. Computers have transported SSs from the platonic heaven of ideas to the empirical world of actual processes carried out by machines or brains or by the two of them working together.

A SS consists of a memory, a set of operators, a control, an input, and an output. Its inputs are the objects in certain locations; its outputs are the modification or creation of the objects in certain (usually different) locations. Its external behavior, then, consists of the outputs it produces as a function of its inputs. The larger system of environment plus SS forms a closed system, since the output objects either become or affect later input objects. SS's internal state consists of the state of its memory and the state of the control; and its internal behavior consists of the variation in this internal state over time. Fig. 4.2 shows you a framework of a SS [6].

Two notions are central to this structure of expressions, symbols, and objects: designation and interpretation. Designation means that an expression designates an object if, given the expression, the system can either affect the object itself or behave in ways dependent on the object. Interpretation has been defined such that the system can interpret an expression if the expression designates a process and if, given the expression, the system can carry out the process. Interpretation implies a special form of dependent action: Given an expression, the system can perform the indicated process, which is to say it can evoke and execute its own processes from expressions that designate them.

The 1975 Association for Computing Machinery (ACM) Turing Award was presented jointly to Allen Newell and Herbert A. Simon at the ACM Annual Conference in Minneapolis on October 20. They gave a Turing lecture entitled "Computer Science as Empirical Inquiry: Symbols and Search." At this lecture, they presented a general scientific

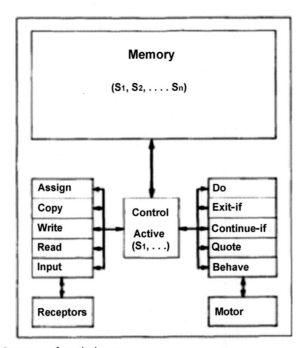

Figure 4.2 Structure of symbol system.

hypothesis—a law of qualitative structure for SS's: the Physical Symbol System Hypothesis [13]. A physical SS has the necessary and sufficient means for general intelligent action. By "necessary" we mean that any system that exhibits general intelligence will prove upon analysis to be a physical SS. By "sufficient" we mean that any physical SS of sufficient size can be organized further to exhibit general intelligence. By "general intelligent action" we wish to indicate the same scope of intelligence as we see in human action: that in any real situation, behavior appropriate to the ends of the system and adaptive to the demands of the environment can occur, within some limits of speed and complexity. The Physical Symbol System Hypothesis clearly is a law of qualitative structure. It specifies a general class of systems within which one will find those capable of intelligent action. Its main points of the hypothesis are as follows:

1. The hypothesis of a physical SS is the necessary and sufficient condition of representing intelligent actions through a physical system.
2. Necessary means that any physical system of representing intelligence is one example of a physical SS.
3. Sufficiency means that any physical SS could represent the intelligent actions through further organizing.
4. Intelligent behaviors are those that human owns: Under some physical limitations, they are the actually occurring behaviors that fit the system purpose and meet the requirement of circumstance.

Given these points, since the human being has intelligence, it is a physical SS. A human being can observe and recognize outside objects, receive the intellectual tests, and pass the examinations. All these are a human being's representation. The reason humans can represent their intelligence is based on their procedure of information processing. This is the first deduction from the hypothesis of the physical SS. The second inference is that, since the computer is a physical SS, it must show its intelligence, which is the basic condition of artificial intelligence. The third inference is that since the human being is a physical SS and the computer is also a physical SS, we can simulate the human being's actions through the computer. We can describe the procedure of human action or establish a theory to describe the whole activity procedure of the human being.

4.4 SOAR

SOAR is the abbreviation of State, Operator And Result, which represents the state, operand, and result. It reflects the basic principle of applying the weak method to continuously use the operands in the state and obtain new results. SOAR is a theoretical cognitive model. It carries out the modeling of human cognition from the aspect of psychology and proposes a general problem-solving structure.

By the end of 1950s, a model of storage structure was invented by using one kind of signals to mark other signals in neuron simulation. This is the earlier concept of chunks. The chess master keeps in mind memory chunks about experiences of playing chess under different circumstances. In the early of 1980s, Newell and Rosenbloom proposed that system performance can be improved by acquiring knowledge of a model problem in a task environment and that memory chunks can be regarded as the simulation foundation of human action. By means of observing problem solving and acquiring experience memory chunks, the complex process of each subgoal is substituted and thus ameliorates the speed of the problem solving of the system, thereafter laying a solid foundation for empirical learning.

4.4.1 Basic State, Operator And Result architecture

In 1987 J. E. Laird from the University of Michigan, Paul S. Rosenbloom from the University of Stanford, and A. Newell from Carnegie Mellon University developed the SOAR system [14], whose learning mechanism is to learn general control knowledge under the guidance of an outside expert. The outer guidance can be direct or an intuitionistic simple question. The system converts the high-level information from the outer expert into inner presentations and learns to search the memory chunk [15]. Fig. 4.3 presents the architecture of SOAR.

The processing configuration is composed of production memory and decision process. The production memory contains production rule, which can be used for searching the control decision. The first step is detailed refinement; all the rules are referred to working memory in order to decide the priorities and which context should be changed and how to change it. The second step is to decide the segment and goal that needs to be revised in the context stack.

Problem solving can be roughly described as a search through a problem space for a goal state. This is implemented by searching for the states that bring the system gradually closer to its goal. Each move consists of a decision cycle, which has an elaboration phase and a decision procedure.

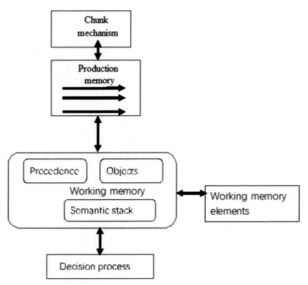

Figure 4.3 Architecture of SOAR.

SOAR originally stood for State, Operator And Result, reflecting this representation of problem solving as the application of an operator to a state in order to get a result. According to the project FAQ, the Soar development community no longer regards SOAR as an acronym, so it is no longer spelled in all caps, though it is still representative of the core of the implementation.

If the decision procedure just described is not able to determine a unique course of action, Soar may use different strategies, known as *weak methods* to solve the impasse. These methods are appropriate to situations in which knowledge is not abundant. When a solution is found by one of these methods, Soar uses a learning technique called chunking to transform the course of action taken into a new rule. The new rule can then be applied whenever Soar encounters the situation again.

In the process of SOAR problem solving, it is especially important to use the knowledge space. It is basically the trilogy about the analysis, decision, and action when using the knowledge to control the action of SOAR.

1. **Analyzing phrase**

   Input: the object in library.

   Task: put the object into the current environment from library.

   Increase the information role of object in the current environment.

   Control: repeat this process until it is finished.

2. The phrase of decision

Input: the object in library.

Task: agreement, opposing or denying the objects in library. Select a new object to replace the congeneric objects.

Control: agree and oppose simultaneously.

3. The phrase of execution

Input: current state and operands

Task: put the current operand into the current state. If a new state appears then put it into the library and use it to replace the original current state.

Control: this is a basic action which cannot be divided.

The memory chunk, which uses working–memory–elements (w–m–e) to collect conditions and constructs memory chunks in the Soar system, is the key for learning. When a subgoal is created for solving a simple problem or assessing the advice from experts, the current statuses are stored into w–m–e. System gets initial statuses of the subgoal from w–m–e and deletes solution operators as the conclusion action after the subgoal is solved. This generative production rule is the memory chunk. If the subgoal is similar to the subgoal of the initial problem, the memory chunk can be applied to the initial problem, and the learning strategy can apply what has already learned from one problem to another.

The formation of a memory chunk depends on the explanation of subgoal. The imparted learning is applied when converting the instructions of experts or simple problems into machine-executable format. Lastly, experiences obtained from solving simple and intuitionistic problems can be applied to initial problems, which involve analogy learning. Therefore, the manner of learning in the Soar system is a comprehensive combination of several learning methods.

4.4.2 Extended version of SOAR

Through the years, there have been substantial evolution and refinement of the Soar architecture. During this evolution, the basic approach of pure symbolic processing, with all long-term knowledge being represented as production rules, was maintained, and Soar proved to be a general and flexible architecture for research in cognitive modeling across a wide variety of behavioral and learning phenomena. Soar also proved to be useful for creating knowledge-rich agents that could generate diverse, intelligent behavior in complex, dynamic environments.

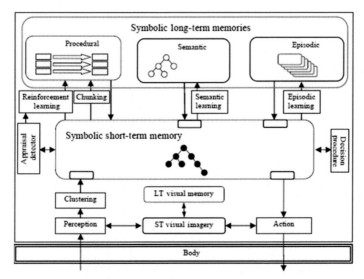

Figure 4.4 Block diagram of SOAR 9.

Fig. 4.4 shows the block diagram of SOAR 9 [16]. SOAR's processing cycle is still driven by procedural knowledge encoded as production rules. The new components influence decision making indirectly by retrieving or creating structures in symbolic working memory that cause rules to match and fire. In the remainder of this section, we will give descriptions of these new components and discuss briefly their value and why their functionality would be very difficult to achieve by existing mechanisms.

4.4.2.1 Working memory activation

SOAR 9 added activation to Soar's working memory. Activation provides meta-information in terms of the recency of a working memory element and its relevance, which is computed based depending on when the element matched rules that fired. This information is not used to determine which rules to fire, as Soar fires all rules that match, but it is stored as part of episodic memories, biasing their retrieval so that the episode retrieved is the most relevant to the current situation. Empirical results verify that working memory activation significantly improves episodic memory retrieval. Working memory activation will be used in semantic memory retrieval and emotion.

4.4.2.2 Reinforcement learning

Reinforcement learning (RL) involves adjusting the selection of actions in an attempt to maximize reward. In early versions of Soar, all preferences for selecting operators were symbolic, so there was no way to represent or adjust such knowledge; however, they added numeric preferences, which specify the expected value of an operator for the current state. During operator selection, all numeric preferences for an operator are combined, and an epsilon-greedy algorithm is used to select the next operator. This makes RL in Soar straightforward — it adjusts the actions of rules that create numeric preferences for selected operators. Thus, after an operator applies, all of the rules that created numeric preferences for that operator are updated based on any new reward and the expected future reward, which is simply the summed numeric value of the numeric preferences for the next selected operator. RL in Soar applies across all goals, including impasse-generated subgoals.

4.4.2.3 Semantic memory

In addition to procedural knowledge, which is encoded as rules in Soar, there is declarative knowledge, which can be split into things that are known, such as facts, and things that are remembered, such as episodic experiences. Semantic learning and memory provides the ability to store and retrieve declarative facts about the world, such as tables have legs, dogs are animals, and Ann Arbor is in Michigan. This capability has been central to ACT-R's ability to model a wide variety of human data, and adding it to Soar should enhance the ability to create agents that reason and use general knowledge about the world. In Soar, semantic memory is built up from structures that occur in working memory. A structure from semantic memory is retrieved by creating a cue in a special buffer in working memory. The cue is then used to search for the best partial match in semantic memory, which is then retrieved from working memory.

Because the knowledge is encoded in rules, retrieval requires an exact match of the cue, limiting the generality of what is learned. These factors made it difficult to use data chunking in new domains, begging the question as to how it would naturally arise in a generally intelligent agent.

4.4.2.4 Episodic memory

In Soar, episodic memory includes specific instances of the structures that occur in working memory at the same time, providing the ability to remember the context of past experiences as well as the temporal relationships between experiences [17]. An episode is retrieved by the deliberate creation of a cue, which is a partial specification of working memory in a special buffer. Once a cue is created, the best partial match is found (biased by recency and working memory activation) and retrieved into a separate working memory buffer. The next episode can also be retrieved, providing the ability to replay an experience as a sequence of retrieved episodes.

Although similar mechanisms have been studied in case-based reasoning, episodic memory is distinguished by the fact that it is task-independent and thus available for every problem, providing a memory of experience not available from other mechanisms. Episodic learning is so simple that it is often dismissed in AI as not worthy of study. Although simple, one has only to imagine what life is like for amnesiacs to appreciate its importance for general intelligence.

Episodic memory would be even more difficult to implement using chunking than semantic memory because it requires capturing a snapshot of working memory and using working memory activation to bias partial matching for retrieval.

4.4.2.5 Visual imagery

All of the previous extensions depend on Soar's existing symbolic short-term memory to represent the agent's understanding of the current situation and with good reason. The generality and power of symbolic representations and processing are unmatched, and the ability to compose symbolic structures is a hallmark of human-level intelligence. However, for some constrained forms of processing, other representations can be much more efficient. One compelling example is visual imagery, which is useful for visual-feature and visual-spatial reasoning. They have added a set of modules to Soar that support visual imagery, including a short-term memory where images are constructed and manipulated; a long-term memory that contains images that can be retrieved into the short-term memory; processes that manipulate images in short-term memory; and processes that create symbolic structures from the visual images. Although not shown, these extensions support both a depictive representation in which space is inherent to the representation, as well as an intermediate, quantitative representation that combines symbolic and numeric representations. Visual imagery is controlled by the symbolic system, which issues commands to construct, manipulate, and examine visual images.

With the addition of visual imagery, it is possible to solve spatial reasoning problems orders of magnitude faster than without it and using significantly less procedural knowledge.

4.5 ACT-R model

ACT-R (Adaptive Control of Thought—Rational) is a cognitive architecture mainly developed by John Robert Anderson at Carnegie Mellon University. Like any cognitive architecture, ACT-R aims to define the basic and irreducible cognitive and perceptual operations that enable the human mind. In theory, each task that humans can perform should consist of a series of these discrete operations.

The roots of ACT-R can be backtracked to the original HAM (human associative memory) model of memory, described by John R. Anderson and Gordon Bower in 1973. The HAM model was later expanded into the first version of the ACT theory. This was the first time the procedural memory was added to the original declarative memory system, introducing a computational dichotomy that was later proved to hold in the human brain. The theory was then further extended into the ACT* model of human cognition.

In the late eighties, Anderson devoted himself to exploring and outlining a mathematical approach to cognition that he named rational analysis. The basic assumption of Rational Analysis is that cognition is optimally adaptive and that precise estimates of cognitive functions mirror statistical properties of the environment. Later, he came back to the development of the ACT theory, using national analysis as a unifying framework for the underlying calculations. To highlight the importance of the new approach in the shaping of the architecture, its name was modified to ACT-R, with the "R" standing for rational.

In 1993 Anderson met with Christian Lebiere, a researcher in connectionist models mostly famous for developing, with Scott Fahlman, the cascade correlation learning algorithm. Their joint work culminated in the release of ACT-R 4.0. which included optional perceptual and motor capabilities, mostly inspired from the EPIC architecture, which greatly expanded the possible applications of the theory.

After the release of ACT-R 4.0, John Anderson became more and more interested in the underlying neural plausibility of his lifetime theory and began to use brain imaging techniques pursuing his own goal of understanding the computational underpinnings of the human mind. The necessity of accounting for brain localization pushed for a major revision of the theory. ACT-R 5.0 introduced the concept of modules, specialized sets of procedural and declarative representations that could be mapped to known brain systems. In addition, the interaction between procedural and declarative knowledge was mediated by newly introduced buffers, special-ized structures for holding temporarily active information (see the preceding section). Buffers were thought to reflect cortical activity, and a subsequent series of studies later confirmed that activations in cortical regions could be successfully related to computational operations over buffers.

A new version of the code, completely rewritten, was presented in 2005 as ACT-R 6.0. It also included significant improvements in the ACT-R coding language.

Fig. 4.5 illustrates the basic architecture of ACT-R 5.0 which contains some of the modules in the system: a visual module for identifying objects in the visual field, a manual module for controlling the hands, a declara-tive module for retrieving information from memory, and a goal module for keeping track of current goals and intentions [18]. Coordination of the behavior of these modules is achieved through a central production system. This central production system is not sensitive to most of the activities of these modules but rather can only respond to a limited amount of information that is deposited in the buffers of these modules. The core production system can recognize patterns in these buffers and make changes to them. The information in these modules is largely

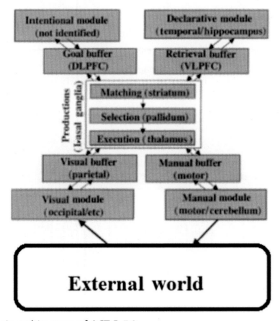

Figure 4.5 Basic architecture of ACT-R 5.0.

encapsulated, and the modules communicate only through the information they make available in their buffers.

The architecture assumes a mixture of parallel and serial processing. Within each module, there is a great deal of parallelism. For instance, the visual system is simultaneously processing the whole visual field, and the declarative system is executing a parallel search through many memories in response to a retrieval request. Also, the processes within different modules can go on in parallel and asynchronously.

ACT-R contains main components modules, buffers, and pattern matcher. The workflow of ACT-R is shown in Fig. 4.6.

1. *Modules*: There are two types of modules: (a) Perceptual–motor modules, which take care of the interface with the real world (i.e., with a simulation of the real world). The most well developed perceptual–motor modules in ACT-R are the visual and the manual modules. (b) Memory modules. There are two kinds of memory modules in ACT-R: declarative memory, consisting of facts such as *Washington, D.C. is the capital of United States*, or *2 + 3 = 5*, and procedural memory, made of productions. Productions represent knowledge about how we do things: for instance, knowledge about how to type the letter "Q" on a keyboard, about how to drive, or about how to perform addition.

2. *Buffers*: ACT-R accesses its modules through buffers. For each module, a dedicated buffer serves as the interface with that module. The contents of the buffers at a given moment in time represents the state of ACT-R at that moment.

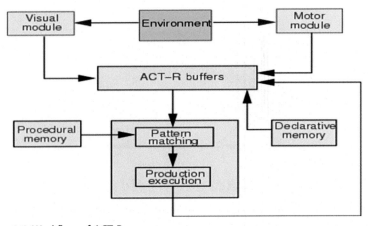

Figure 4.6 Workflow of ACT-R.

3. *Pattern matcher.* The pattern matcher searches for a production that matches the current state of the buffers. Only one such production can be executed at a given moment. That production, when executed, can modify the buffers and thus change the state of the system. Thus, in ACT-R cognition unfolds as a succession of production firings.

ACT-R is a hybrid cognitive architecture. Its symbolic structure is a production system; the subsymbolic structure is represented by a set of massively parallel processes that can be summarized by several mathematical equations. The subsymbolic equations control many of the symbolic processes. For instance, if several productions match the state of the buffers, a subsymbolic utility equation estimates the relative cost and benefit associated with each production and decides to select for execution the production with the highest utility. Similarly, whether (or how fast) a fact can be retrieved from declarative memory depends on subsymbolic retrieval equations, which consider the context and the history of usage of that fact. Subsymbolic mechanisms are also responsible for most learning processes in ACT-R.

ACT-R has been used successfully to create models in domains such as learning and memory, problem solving and decision making, language and communication, perception and attention, cognitive development, or individual differences.

Beside its applications in cognitive psychology, ACT-R has been used in human—computer interaction to produce user models that can assess different computer interfaces; education (cognitive tutoring systems) to "guess" the difficulties that students may have and provide focused help; computer-generated forces to provide cognitive agents that inhabit training environments; neuropsychology to interpret fMRI data.

4.6 CAM model

In mind activities, memory and consciousness play the most important role. Memory stores various important information and knowledge; consciousness gives humans the concept of self, according to the needs, preferences-based goals, and the ability to do all kinds of cognitive activity according to memory information. Therefore, the main emphasis on the mind model Consciousness And Memory (CAM) is on memory functions and consciousness functions [19]. Fig. 4.7 shows the architecture of the mind model CAM, which includes 10 main modules, briefly introduced as follows.

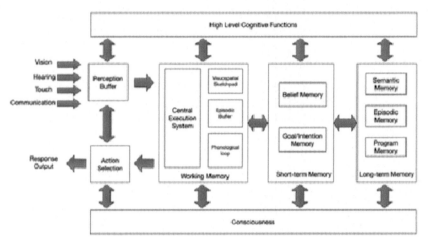

Figure 4.7 Architecture of mind model CAM.

4.6.1 Vision

Human sensory organs including vision, hearing, touch, smell, taste. In the CAM model, visual and auditory are focused on. The visual system of the organism gives visual perception ability. It uses visible light to build the perception of the world. According to the image, the process of discovering what objects are in the surrounding scenery and where the objects are located is a process of discovering the useful symbolic description for image. Visual system has the ability to reconstruct a three-dimensional world from a two-dimensional projection of the outside world. It should be noted that the various objects in the visible light spectrum can be perceived in a different location.

In the processing of outside objects' images in the retina, actually the light stimulus is transformed by retinal photoreceptor cells (rods and cones) into electrical signals, which, by means of retinal ganglion cells within the bipolar cells, form nerve impulses that is visual information. Visual information is transmitted to the brain via the optic nerve. Bipolar cells can be regarded as the Level 1 neurons of the visual transduction pathway neurons; ganglion cells are Level 2 neurons. Many ganglion cells send out nerve fibers composed of coarse optic nerve, optic nerve at the back end of the eye leaving the eye back into the cranial cavity. At this point, the left and right sides of the optic nerve cross. The crossing is called the optic chiasm. The optic tract at the bottom of brain is connected to the lateral geniculate body, which is an important intermediate visual information transmission station containing Level 3 neurons. They emit a large number of fibers that are composed of so-called radiation. Fiber optic radiation is projected to the visual center of the occipital lobe—the visual cortex. Visual information finally reaches the visual cortex of the brain and is processed, analyzed, and then finally formed into the subjective visual experience.

The visual cortex refers to the part of cerebral cortex that is responsible for processing visual information. It is located in the rear of the occipital lobe of the brain. The human visual cortex includes the primary visual cortex (V1, also known as the striate cortex) and extrastriate cortex (V2, V3, V4, V5, etc.). The primary visual cortex is located in the 17th area. The extrastriate cortex comprises areas 18 and 19.

The output of the primary visual cortex (V1) forward takes two pathways to become the dorsal and ventral stream flows. The dorsal stream begins with V1, through V2, into the dorsal medial area and the temporal area (MT, also known as V5), then arrives at the inferior parietal lobule. The dorsal stream is often referred to as the space path. It is involved in spatial location and related motion control of objects, such as saccades and stretch to take. The ventral stream begins with V1, followed by V2 and V4, into the inferior temporal lobe. This passage is often called a content access, participating in object recognition, such as face recognition. The path is also related to long-term memory.

4.6.2 Hearing

Why humans can hear sound and understand speech is dependent on the integrity of the entire auditory pathway, which includes the external ear, middle ear, inner ear, auditory nerve, and central auditory. Auditory pathways outside the central nervous system is called the auditory outer periphery. The auditory pathway that is inside the central nervous system is called the auditory center or central auditory system. The central auditory, spanning the brainstem, midbrain, thalamus of the cerebral cortex, is one of the longest central pathways of the sensory system.

Sound information is conducted from the surrounding auditory system to the central auditory system. The central auditory system performs processing and analysis functions for sound, such as functions to feel the tone, pitch, intensity, and determine the orientation of sound. Specialized cells are able to respond to where the sound begins and ends. Auditory information spreading to the cerebral cortex has connections with the language center of the brain that manages reading, writing, and speaking.

4.6.3 Perception buffer

The perception buffer, also known as the sensory memory or instantaneous memory, is the first direct impression of sensory information on the sensory organ. The perception buffer can cache information from all the sensory organs in ranges from tens to hundreds of milliseconds. In the perception buffer, the information may be noticed and become significant after the encoding process. It may proceed to the next phase of processing, and, if unnoticed or not encoded, the sensory information will automatically subside.

A variety of sensory information is stored in the perception buffer in its unique form for a time period and continues to work. These sensory information forms are visual representations and sound representations, called video images and sound images. Imagery can be said to be directly and primitively memorized. Imagery can exist for only a short period of time; even the most distinctive visual image can be kept for only tens of seconds. Perception memory has the following characteristics:

1. The memory is very transient.
2. It can handle the same amount of energy as receptors in anatomy and physiology.
3. It encodes information in a straightforward way, transiently saving all kinds of signals coming from the sensory organs.

4.6.4 Working memory

Working memory consists of a central executive system, visuospatial sketchpad, phonological loop, and episodic buffer. The central executive system is the core of working memory, which is responsible for associating various subsystems and long-term memory, paying attention to resource coordination, strategy selection and planning, and so on. The visuospatial sketchpad is mainly responsible for the storage and processing of visual-spatial information. It contains visual and spatial subsystems. The phonological loop is responsible for the sound-based storage and control of information, including sound storage and pronunciation control. In silent reading, the characterization of faded voice can be reactivated in order to prevent a recession and also can transfer words in a book into speech. The episodic buffer store connects information across the region, in order to form a visual, spatial, and verbal integrated unit in chronological order, such as for a story or a movie scene memory. The episodic buffer also associates long-term memory and semantic memory.

4.6.5 Short-term memory

Short-term memory stores beliefs, goals, and intentions. It responds to a rapidly changing environment and operations of agents. In short-term memory, the perceptual coding scheme and experience coding scheme for related objects are prior knowledge.

4.6.6 Long-term memory

Long-term memory is a container with large capacity. In long-term memory, information is maintained for a long time. According to the stored contents, long-term memory can be divided into semantic memory, episodic memory, and procedural memory.

1. Semantic memory stores the words, the concepts, general rules in reference to the general knowledge system. It has generality and does not depend on time, place, and conditions. It is relatively stable and is not easily interfered with by external factors.
2. Episodic memory stores personal experience. It is the memory about events that are taking place in a certain time and place. It is easily interfered with by a variety of factors.
3. Procedural memory refers to technology, process, or how-to memories. Procedural memory is generally less likely to change but can be automatically exercised unconsciously. It can be a simple reflex action or a combination of a more complex series of acts. Examples of procedural memory include learning to ride a bicycle, typing, using an instrument, or swimming. Once internalized, the procedure memory can be very persistent.

4.6.7 Consciousness

Consciousness is a complex biological phenomenon. A philosopher, physician, or psychologist may have different understandings of the concept of consciousness. From a scientific point of view of intelligence, consciousness is a subjective experience. It is an integration of the outside world, physical experience, and psychological experience. Consciousness is a brain-possessed "instinct" or "function"; it is a "state," a combination of a number of brain structures for a variety of organisms. In CAM, consciousness is concerned with automatic control, motivation, metacognition, attention, and other issues.

4.6.8 High-level cognition function

High-level cognitive brain functions include learning, memory, language, thinking, decision making, and emotion. Learning is the process of continually receiving stimulus via the nervous system, accessing new behaviors and habits, and accumulating experience. Memory refers to keeping up and reproducing behavior and knowledge by learning. It is made up of the intelligent activities that we do every day. Language and higher-order thinking are the most important factors that differentiate humans from other animals. Decision making is the process of finding an optimal solution through analysis and comparison of several alternatives; it can be a decision made under uncertain conditions to deal with the occasional incident. Emotion is an attitudinal experience arising in humans when objective events of things meet or do not meet their needs.

4.6.9 Action selection

Action selection means building a complex combination of actions by the atomic action, in order to achieve a particular task in the process. Action selection can be divided into two steps. The first step is atomic action selection, which is choosing the relevant atomic actions from the action library. Then, using planning strategies, the selected atomic actions is composed of complex actions. The action selection mechanism is implemented by the spike basal ganglia model.

4.6.10 Response output

Response output is classified from overall objective. It can be influenced by surrounding emotion or motivation input. Based on the control signal, the primary motor cortex directly generates muscle movements in order to achieve some kind of internal given motion command.

If you want to understand the CAM model in detail, please refer to the book *Mind Computation* [20].

4.7 Cognitive cycle

The cognitive cycle is a basic procedure of mental activities in cognitive level, it consists of the basic steps of the cognitive-level mind activity. Human cognition recurs as brain events in the cascade cycle. In CAM, each current situation is perceived in the cognitive cycle according to the intended goal. Then an internal or external flow of actions is constituted in order to respond to the desired goal [21], as shown in Fig. 4.8. The CAM cognitive cycle is divided into three phases: perception, motivation, and action planning. In the

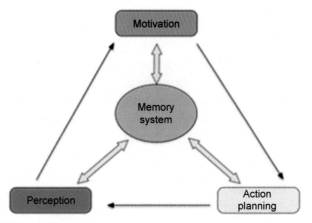

Figure 4.8 CAM cognitive cycle.

perception phase, the process of environmental awareness is realized by sensory input. Sensory input and information in working memory are taken as clues, and then a local association is created with the automatic retrieval of episodic memory and declarative memory. The motivation phase is focused on the learner's needs in terms of belief, expectations, sorting, and understanding. According to the motivation factors, such as activation, opportunities, continuity of actions, persistence, interruptions, and preferential combination,the motivation system is built. An action plan is achieved through action selection and action planning.

4.7.1 Perception phase

The perceptual phase achieves environmental awareness or understanding and organizes and interprets sensory information processing. The sensory organ receives an external or internal stimulus. This is the beginning of meaning creation in the perception phase. Awareness is the event feeling, perception, consciousness state, or ability. At this level of consciousness, sensory data can be confirmed by the observer but does not necessarily mean understanding. In biological psychology, awareness is defined as a human's or animal's perception and cognitive response to external conditions or events.

4.7.2 Motivation phase

The motivation phase in CAM determines the explicit goals according to the need. A target includes a set of subgoals, which can be formally described as:

$$G_t = \{G_1^t, G_2^t, \ldots, G_n^t\} \quad \text{At time } t$$

4.7.3 Action planning phase

Action planning is the process of building a complex action composed of atomic actions to achieve a task. Action planning can be divided into two steps: The first is action selection, which is the selection of the relevant action from the action library; second is the use of planning strategies to integrate the selected actions. Action selection is instantiating the action flow or selecting an action from a previous action flow. There are many action selection methods, most of them based on similarity matching between goals and behaviors. Planning provides an extensible and effective method for action composition. It allows an action request to be expressed as a combination of objective conditions and regulates a set of restrictions and preferences, under which a set of constraints and preferences exists. In CAM, we use dynamic logic to formally describe the action and design action planning algorithms.

4.8 Perception, memory, and judgment model

The research results of cognitive psychology and cognitive neuroscience provide much experimental evidence and theoretical viewpoints for clarifying the human cognitive mechanism and the main stages and pathways of the cognitive process, that is, the stages of perception, memory, and judgment (PMJ), as well as the fast processing pathway, fine processing pathway, and feedback processing pathway. Fu et al. constructed the PMJ mind model [22], as shown in Fig. 4.9. The dotted box in the figure is the mental model, which summarizes the main cognitive processes, including the three stages of PMJ (represented by the gear circle) and three types of channels (represented by arrow lines with numbers) of rapid

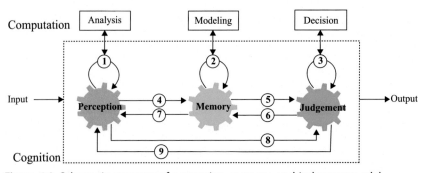

Figure 4.9 Schematic structure of perception, memory, and judgment model.

processing, fine processing, and feedback processing. In each stage, under the constraints of various cognitive mechanisms, the cognitive system receives information input from other stages, completes specific information processing tasks, and outputs processed information to other stages. Each stage cooperates with the other to realize a complete information processing process. Each kind of processing path represents the transmission of processing information. In the model, the corresponding relationship between cognition and calculation is also given, that is, the perception stage corresponds to the analysis in the calculation process, the memory stage corresponds to the modeling in the calculation process, and the judgment stage corresponds to the decision making in the computation process.

According to existing research results, the PMJ model classifies the main pathways of cognitive processing into the fast processing pathway (analogous to large cell pathway and its related cortical pathway), fine processing pathway (analogous to small cell pathway and its related cortical pathway), and feedback pathway (top-down feedback).

4.8.1 Fast processing path

The fast processing path refers to the processing from the perception stage to the judgment stage (as shown in ⑧ in Fig. 4.9) to realize perception-based judgment. This process does not need too much knowledge and experience to participate. It mainly processes the whole characteristics, contour, and low spatial frequency information of stimulus input. On this basis, it carries out primary rough processing of the input information and makes rapid classifications and judgments. Visual saliency features can be classified and judged by the rapid processing pathway.

4.8.2 Fine processing pathway

The fine processing pathway refers to the processing from the perception stage to the memory stage and then from the memory stage to the perception and judgment stages (as shown in ④, ⑤, and ⑦ in Fig. 4.9), to realize memory-based perception and judgment. This process relies on existing knowledge and experience, and mainly processes the local characteristics, details, and high spatial frequency information of stimulus input. It matches the knowledge stored in long-term memory precisely and then makes a classification and judgment. People's perception of the outside world is usually inseparable from attention. We need to filter the useful information from a great deal of other information through attention screening, store it in the memory system, and then form a representation. The information stored in the memory space of the memory representation adaptive dynamic memory system is constructed and changed dynamically with cognitive processing activities.

4.8.3 Feedback processing pathway

The feedback processing pathway refers to the processing from the judgment stage to the memory stage, or from the judgment stage to the perception stage (such as ⑥ or ⑨ in Fig. 4.9) in order to realize judgment-based perception and memory. The cognitive system corrects the knowledge stored in the short-term or long-term memory according to the output results of the judgment stage; the output results of the judgment stage also provide clues to the perception stage, making information processing in the perception stage more accurate and efficient.

References

[1] Z.Z. Shi, Perspectives on intelligence science, Sci. Chin. 8 (2003) 47−49.
[2] Z.Z. Shi, On intelligence science, Int. J. Adv. Intell. 1 (1) (2009) 39−57.
[3] X. Gao, Z. Chu, The Philosophy of Mind (in Chinese), Commercial Press, Beijing, 2002.
[4] G. Miller, What is the biological basis of consciousness? Science 309 (2005) 79.
[5] J. Knobe, S. Nichols, Experimental Philosophy, Oxford University Press, UK, 2008.
[6] A. Newell, Physical symbol systems, Cognit. Sci. 4 (1980) 135−183.
[7] A. Newell, Unified Theories of Cognition, Harvard University Press, Cambridge, MA, 1990.
[8] J.R. Anderson, C.L. Lebiere, The Newell test for a theory of cognition, Behavioral and Brain Science 26 (2003) 587−637.
[9] Z.Z. Shi, J.P. Yue, J.H. Zhang, Mind modeling in intelligence science. IJCAI2013 Workshop Proceedings of Intelligence Science, Beijing, (2013) pp. 30−36.
[10] A. Clark, The dynamic challenge, Cognit. Sci. 21 (4) (1998) 461−481.
[11] A.M. Turing, On computable numbers with an application to the Entscheidungsproblem, Proc. Lond. Maths. Soc., Ser. s2-42 (1936) 230−265.
[12] H.A. Simon, The Sciences of the Artificial, second ed, The MIT Press, 1982.
[13] A. Newell, H.A. Simon, Computer science as empirical inquiry: symbols and search, Commun. Assoc. Comput. Machinery 19 (3) (1976) 113−126. ACM Turing Award Lecture.
[14] J. Laird, A. Newell, P. Rosenbloom, SOAR: an architecture for general intelligence, Artif. Intell. 33 (1987) 1−64.
[15] A.R. Golding, P.S. Rosenbloom, J.E. Laird, Learning general search control from outside guidance, in: Proceedings of IJCAT'87, (1987) pp. 334−337.
[16] J.E. Laird, Extending the soar cognitive architecture, in: Proceedings of the First Conference on Artificial General Intelligence (AGI-08) (2008).
[17] A. Nuxoll, J.E. Larid, Extending cognitive architecture with episodic memory, in: Proceedings of the 22nd AAAI Conference on Artificial Intelligence (2007) pp. 1560−1564.

[18] J.R. Anderson, D. Bothell, M.D. Byrne, S. Douglass, C. Lebiere, Y. Qin, An integrated theory of the mind, Psychol Rev. 111 (4) (2004) 1036–1060.

[19] Z.Z. Shi, Research on brain-like computer. Keynote Speaker, BI-AMT 2009, Beijing (2009b).

[20] Z.Z. Shi, Mind Computation, World Scientific, New Jersey, 2017.

[21] Z.Z. Shi, X.F. Wang, J.P. Yue, Cognitive cycle in mind model CAM, Int. J. Intell. Sci. 1 (2) (2011) 25–34.

[22] X.L. Fu, L.H. Cai, Y. Liu, et al., A computational cognition model of perception, memory, and judgment, Sci. China, Ser. F: Inf. Sci. 57 (2014) 1–15.

CHAPTER 5

Perceptual intelligence

Perceptual intelligence refers to the ability to interact with the environment through various sensory organs, such as vision, hearing, touch, etc. The visual system gives the organism the ability of visual perception. The auditory system gives the organism the ability of auditory perception. Using the research results of big data and deep learning, the machine has gotten closer and closer to the human level in perceptual intelligence.

5.1 Introduction

Perception is produced by the external world acting directly on human sensory organs. In social practice, people can contact objective things through the eyes, ears, nose, tongue, and body. Under the stimulation of external phenomena, the human sense organs generate an information flow that is transmitted to the brain along specific neural channels, forming a sensation and impression of the color, shape, voice, heat and cold, smell, pain, etc. of the objective things.

Perceptual knowledge is produced by the external world acting directly on humans' sense organs. Perceptual knowledge experiences three basic forms in its development: sensation, perception, and representation. Sensation is the reflection of individual attributes and characteristics of objective things in the human brain. Perception is the synthesis of all the kinds of sensation and the reflection of the whole objective thing in the human brain. It is more comprehensive and complex than sensation. Perception has the characteristics of selectivity, significance, constancy, and integrity. On the basis of perception, appearance is produced. Appearance is impression, which reappears through recollection and association. Different from sensation and perception, it is formed on the basis of multiple perceptions of the same thing or the same kinds of thing in the past, with certain indirectness and generality. But appearance is only the simplest form of generalized perceptual materials, and it cannot reveal the essence and law of things.

Vision plays an important role in the human sense world. Most of our responses to environmental information are transmitted to the brain

Intelligence Science
DOI: https://doi.org/10.1016/B978-0-323-85380-4.00005-1
151

through vision, which dominates the human sensory system. If people use vision to receive a message, and another message is received through another sensory organ, and if the two messages contradict each other, people must respond to visual information.

In the 1980s according to the visual computing theory of Marr, computer vision is divided into three levels:

1. Low-level vision processing, such as edge detection and image segmentation, is carried out.
2. The main methods to obtain 2.5-dimensional description of depth information and surface orientation are to restore the three-dimensional shape by shading, contour, and texture, to restore the depth information of the scene by means of stereo vision, to determine the three-dimensional shape and motion parameters of the object by image sequence analysis, and to obtain and analyze the distance image and structural light method.
3. The method based on a generalized cylinder can be used to model, represent, and recognize objects according to three-dimensional information. Another common method is to express the shape of an object as a set of planes or surface blocks (referred to as surface primitives). The parameters of each surface primitives and the relationships between them are expressed by attribute relation structure, so that the problem of object recognition can be transformed into the matching problem of attribute relation structure.

In 1990 J. Aloimonos proposed qualitative vision, active vision, etc. The core of the qualitative vision method is to regard the vision system as a subsystem of a larger system to perform a certain task. The information that the vision system needs to acquire is only the information necessary to complete the task of the large system. The active vision method is a combination of perception, planning, and control. Through the dynamic call of these modules and the interaction of the information acquisition and processing processes, it can complete the visual task more effectively. The core of this method is the establishment of the active sensing mechanism, which is to plan and control the sensor types and their pose for the next step according to the current tasks, environmental conditions, stage processing results, and relevant knowledge. It is also the key technology to realize multiview or multisensor data fusion.

The auditory process includes mechanical → electrical → chemical → nerve impulse → central information processing and so on. The movement from the outer ear to the inner ear basement membrane is a mechanical movement.

The stimulation of hair cells causes electrical changes, the release of chemical media, the generation of nerve impulses, and other activities. The transmission of impulses to the center is a series of complex information processing processes.

In the 1980s the research on speech recognition and language understanding was greatly strengthened and developed. The DARPA strategic computing project, which had been running for 10 years since 1983, included speech recognition and language understanding, general corpus, etc. Participants included MIT, CMU, Bell Lab, and IBM.

IBM uses a discrete parameter hidden Markov model (HMM) to form some basic acoustic models and then uses fixed finite basic acoustic models to form a word model. This method needs less training data to get better statistical results. At the same time, this method can make the training complete automatic.

In the 1990s the neural network became a new way of speech recognition. The artificial neural network (ANN) has the characteristics of adaptability, parallelism, nonlinearity, robustness, fault tolerance, and learning. It shows its strength in structure and algorithm. It can associate pattern pairs, map complex acoustic signals to different levels of phonetics and phonology and train comprehensive input patterns without being constrained to select special speech parameters, and recognition can integrate the auditory model into the network model.

In 2006 G. E. Hinton and others proposed deep learning [1]. In 2010 Hinton used in-depth learning with GPU computing to improve the computing speed of speech recognition by more than 70 times. In 2012 deep learning came to a new climax. In that year's ImageNet competition (there were 1.2 million photos as the training group, 50,000 as the test group, 1000 categories to be grouped), deep learning was adopted for the first time, reducing the error rate of only slight changes in the past few years from 26% to 15%. In the same year, a Microsoft team published a paper showing that they reduced the error rate of the ImageNet 2012 data set to 4.94% through in-depth learning, which is lower than the error rate of human 5.1%. In 2015 Microsoft won the ImageNet 2015 championship again, and this time, the error rate dropped to an ultra-low level of 3.57%. Microsoft uses a 152-layer-deep learning network.

5.2 Perception

Cognitive psychology regards perception as the organization and explanation of sensory information, that is, the course of getting the meaning of sensory information. Objective things act on people's sense organs directly, producing the whole reflection of each part and attributes of these things in the human brain. This kind of reflection is called perception. Both perception and feeling are the reflection of present things in the brain. Their difference lies in feeling as a reflection of the specific attributes (such as color, smell, temperature) of external things, while perception is the reflection of each part and attributes of things and comprehensive reflection of their interrelation. In perception, what is generated by the brain is not an isolated reflection of the specific attribute or part of things but the reflection of the concrete things combined by various feeling—for instance, people, computer, house, etc. Anything is a complex that is composed of a lot of attributes and parts. The whole thing and its specific attribute and part are inseparable. Seeing a house, one should be aware that this is an institute, factory, residential block, etc. Meanwhile, knowledge must regard feeling as a foundation. One must see a bedroom, kitchen, etc. to be aware of the residential block. The more abundant the specific attributes and parts of the things, the more intact and correct the perception of things will be. All people directly reflect things in actual life in the form of perception; that is to say, the objective reality is reflected in the brain as concrete things. People seldom have isolated feelings. Only when doing scientific analysis in psychology do people isolate feelings for study.

The perception is the subjective reflection of objective reality in the human brain; therefore the perception is limited by people's various characteristics. One's knowledge, interest, mood, etc. all influence the perception course directly. People have accumulated the experience and knowledge of certain targets in practice; then they recognize current stimulus as the definite things of the realistic world with the aid of that knowledge and experience. If current things have no relation with past experience and knowledge, one can't confirm it as a certain object.

Experience plays an important role in perception because the perception is a result of the brain activities of complicated analysis and integration. It is the reflection activity of stimulating things and the relation of stimulating things. The temporary relation formed in the past will influence the content and property of the perception.

In general, the perception is produced by the united activities of many kinds of analyzers. The common participation of many analyzers can reflect the target's various attributes and produce the comprehensive and intact perception. For example, when people watch TV, in fact it is the result of the united activities of the visual analyzer and audio analyzer, but the visual analyzer plays a leading role.

While compound stimulant things act, the intensity and interrelation of each component are significant. The strong components of compound stimulant things cover the weak components. The weak components seem to lose their own effect. The same components in different relation become different perception unity; that is, they have formed different relational reflex, such as a different melody in the music. The overall perception has great meaning for life. Things and phenomena in the objective world are all constantly changeable. Due to the overall perception, people can adapt to the changing environment. When people encounter the object in a new environment, they can recognize it by various relationships between objects, for example the recognition of relative and script. The overall perception makes people's understanding of objective things become more and more complete and thus guarantees the effective execution of the activities.

When the condition of the perception has changed within a certain range, the reflection of the perception has still kept relatively unchanging. This is the constancy of consciousness. In visual perception, the constancy is very obvious. The reflection of objects, such as color, shape, size, etc., is not always governed by the laws of physics. Whether in the daytime or at night, the perception of coal is always black. This kind of perception constancy has very great effect on life. It guarantees to reflect things in terms of the real appearances of the things in different cases, thus it can adapt the environment in terms of the actual meaning of objects.

5.3 Representation

Representation is the repeated course that the images of the objective targets maintained in the notion appear in the notion when objective targets do not appear in front of the subject. Representation has the following characteristics.

5.3.1 Intuitivity

Representation is generated on the basis of perception. The materials that construct representation all come from the content perceived past. So the representation is the perceptual reflection of intuition. However, representation is different from perception. It is the general repeated appearance of perception. Compared with perception, representation has the following characteristics: (1) Representation is not as intact as the perception. It cannot reflect the exhaustive characteristic of the object, and it is even an incomplete one and a partial one. (2) Representation is not as stable as the perception. It is varying and flowing. (3) Representation is not as vivid as the perception. It is fuzzier and dimmer, and it reflects only the outline and some main characteristics of the object. But under some conditions, representation can present the details of the perception. Its essential feature is intuitivity. For example, the phenomenon "eidetic image" can happen among children. Show a picture with complicated content to children, remove the picture dozens of seconds later, and turn their gaze to one gray screen, then they can "see" the same clear picture. These children can describe the detail in the picture accurately according to the image produced at that time, even though they do not think the picture is before their eyes any longer.

As for the classification of representation, it reflects certain images of a concrete object, which is called a specific representation or single representation. The phenomenon of eidetic image previously described is a kind of specific representation. Representation that reflects a kind of common characteristic of a target is called general representation. General representation has those characteristics that distinguish the perception previously described even more.

5.3.2 Generality

Generally speaking, representation is the result summarized from perception repeated many times. It has a perceived prototype but is not limited to a certain prototype. So representation has generality; it is the generality reflection of the perceptual image of the surface to a kind of target. This kind of generality is often denoted as the target's outline instead of the details.

The generality of representation has certain limits. As for complexity and relation, the representation is difficult to include. For example, if the aforementioned pictures produced by eidetic image present one part of story, then the cause and effect of the whole story, a person's ins and outs with interactive relation, cannot appear in the representation completely. Each representation about the story is only the illustration to express the story part. If we want to express story plot and meaning, concept and proposition in language description should be used. Understanding a picture-story book depends on the language to make pages consistent. The deep meaning of the book is revealed by the generalization of the word too.

Therefore, representation is a transitive reflection form and intermediary phase between perception and thinking. As a reflection form, representation is not only close to the perception but also higher than the perception because it can be produced without the concrete target; representation has generality, and it is lower than the generalization level of the word. It offers the perceptual material for thinking of the word. From the development of individual psychology, the emergence of representation is between perception and thinking.

5.3.3 Representation happens on paths of many kinds of feelings

Representation can be various images of feeling, including representation of visual, hearing, smell, taste, touching, etc. Representation will happen in general among people, but it can also vary with each individual. Because of the visual importance, most people have more vivid and visual representations that often happened. Many examples prove that a scientist or artist can finish a creative work through visual thinking in image. It is even quite valid in mathematics or physics research.

Visual representation brings creativity to the artist or writer too. An intact fine piece of writing appears in visual representation from Coleridge's masterpiece poem "King Khan." The artist often has the advantage of visual representation. Sound representation plays an important role in forming the intelligence of language hearing and music hearing. Movement representation is extremely important in forming various movements and their skill; for the operation of some musical instruments, such as the string instruments of piano and violin, the advantages of both hearing representation and visual representation are needed.

5.3.4 Role of representation in thinking

Representation is not only a person's image but also a kind of operation; that is, psychological operation can go on in the form of representation. This is the thinking of image activity. In this sense, the psychological operation, image thinking, and concept thinking of representation are in different interactions.

Representation thinking (image thinking) is the thinking operation that depends on representation. Research on psychological rotation offers convincing evidence. In an experiment involving psychological rotation, a letter "R" appears with a different rotation angle, sometimes as "R" positive and sometimes as "R" negative. The test was to judge whether the letters were positive written or negative written. The results indicate that the greater the rotated angle in the vertical direction, the longer the time was for making a judgment. The result can be explained as follows: The letter must rotate in the head at first, until it is in the vertical position, then the judgment can be made. The time difference, when reflecting on psychological rotation and representation operation, proved the existence of image thinking and representation operation. In fact, attempting to use other methods, such as through examples, to describe the position of the letter is difficult.

In more cases, information can be encoded in the brain and can be encoded with pictures. Representation and word can be double encoded in the psychological operation. Under certain conditions, picture and word can be mutually translated. The concrete picture can be drawn, described, and organized by language. For example, authors of a screenplay usually carry on the picture encoding, then store it through the language; eventually, this is a screenplay. Meanwhile, the director regenerates the pictures according to the screenplay; this is performance—that is to say, the pictures are played out through the language.

Participation and the support of necessary representation in the thinking operation of the word, even whether the representation operation is needed in the thinking operation, are different because the thinking task is different. For example, in computation, geometry depends on the support of image operation to a great extent. Graphical operation is the essential backbone of geometric computation. However, algebra and equations make mathematical calculations according to the formula with only the symbol concept. They are totally free of the image to operate.

It can be seen that representation and perception are all perceptual knowledge and vivid intuition. But representation is different from sensation in that things act on sense organs directly. It is formed based on perceiving the same thing many times or same kinds of things in the past. It has certain indirectness and generality. Under the adjustment and control of people and the word, these representations with certain generality probably grow from perceptual knowledge relying mainly on perceiving rational knowledge and on concept and thinking progressively; this is a qualitative leap. Therefore, representation is a necessary intermediate link of transition from perceiving directly to abstract thinking. However, representation is the most arbitrary form of general materials. It can't reveal the essence and law of things yet.

Representation has more generality than feeling and perception. This is a key psychological question. But because the representation is an internal psychological process, it is not as apparent outside feeling and perception. Therefore, the research of representation has been in a lagging and confused state for some time. Behaviorism psychology denies the existence of perception, acknowledging only the so-called objective stimulus reaction. Thus it eliminates representation with other perception phenomena from psychology. Although Gestalt psychology acknowledges the existence of representation, it uses viewpoints with the same type of dualistic theory to explain things. Modern cognitive psychology uses information processing theory, emphasizes the operation order of the mental process, and therefore has made certain progress in this respect, proposing theories such as antithesis encoding, mutual encoding, etc.

Modern cognitive psychology thinks that studying representation is studying internal courses that people use to process visual information and space information without any outside stimuli. Through objective conditions and effects that can be observed objectively, such as reaction speed and success rate, we can explore the same effect generated by representation and corresponding perception under the same objective conditions. At this moment, representation is regarded as the analog of the true object, but the processing of representation is similar to information processing in feeling the real object. Through experiment and studying, it can be proved that representation is not limited by the visual passway or other feeling passway, and it is not the primitive image without processing stored in the brain; that is, it is not a mechanical duplication of things. This enables people to see more objectively and concretely; representation is the same as feeling, perception, and other psychological phenomena. It is the initial reflection of objective things.

Representation can reflect both the specific characteristics and general characteristics of things. It has both intuitivity and generality. Looked at from the intuitivity perspective, it is close to perception; from a generality perspective, it is close to thinking. The general representation is accumulated and fused by specific representation progressively. Specific representation develops into general representation in people's activity. Without the general representation that reflects objective things leaving concrete things, people's understanding will be confined to the perception of the present things forever and will forever be confined to real, intuitive, and perceptual understanding. Therefore, the general reaction function of representation, not limited by concrete things, makes it possible to become a transition and bridge from perceiving to thinking.

From the physiological mechanism, the representation is reproduced (resumed) in the human brain due to the stimulant trace. This kind of trace is analyzed and synthesized constantly in people's reflecting the course of external things; thus it has produced general representation and has prepared the conditions for the transition to thinking. From the viewpoint of the information theory, modern cognitive psychology has proved the storage of this kind of trace, that is, the storage of information. This kind of trace of representation can not only store but also process and encode various stored traces (information).

To summarize the forming of representation, it can generally be divided into two modes: combination and fusion. The combination of representation is the course in which the representation is accumulated continuously, such as the representation of the same thing or the same kind of things is combined continuously, making the representation more abundant and broad. On the day that an undergraduate enters the university for the first time, her representation regarding the university is simple and poor. But in university life afterward, the representation about the classroom, auditorium, and classmates is accumulated and combined. This gives the perceptual knowledge more generality. Here, association law (close, similarity, comparison) plays an important role. The combination of representation is the main characteristic of memory representation.

The fusion of representation is a form of creative transformation of a kind of representation that is more complicated than association. All the representations taking part in this kind of fusion change their own quality more or less and fuse a new image. The mermaid in mythology or the typical character that the writer creates is the new representation after being fused. This is the main characteristic of creative representation.

General representation is the direct foundation that the feeling and perception transit to the concept. Continuously generalizing the representation makes it continuously leave the direct perceptual foundation, thus it may transit to concept and thinking.

Generality of representation and the transition to concept and thinking cannot be separated from the function of people's language and word. The participation of language and word is not only the essential condition of transition from concrete representation to abstraction but also can cause, restrict, and transform representation. Therefore, modern cognitive psychology mostly thinks that representation is encoded by the antithesis. It can be either an image code or a language code. Image and language can be mutually translated under certain conditions because the mutual restraints of the abstract concept can lead to the concrete image: red, round, hard, ball, three, inch, diameter, what these words refer to are all abstract concepts. In the phrase "the hard-red ball of three inches in diameter," because these abstract concepts limit one another, it expresses a concrete thing. So the images can be stored in the form of language through coding; language can be restored to images through decoding, such as reconstructing imagination. What kind of coding is completely subject-oriented. However, it should be pointed out that representation is an important link that transits from perception to concept and thinking, but there exist essential differences in representation and thinking. No matter what great generality the representation has, it always has the characteristic of iconicity, and it belongs to perceptual knowledge. Therefore, representation and thinking have relations and differences. It is incorrect to see the connection only and not see the difference. As Lenin said, "Representation can't hold the whole sport, for example, it can't hold sport of 300,000 km/s, but thinking can hold and should hold."

In the transformation from the generality of representation to concept and thinking, there are generally two routes. Although these two routes are close and integral in the understanding of average people, they have different advantages for people engaged in different work or activities. For example, scientists and philosophers are generally good at abstract thinking, and writers and engineers are better at image thinking. We can't say one type of thinking is good and the other is not. In children's thinking development, children at first have more image thinking, and this kind of image thinking develops toward abstract thinking. In this sense, we can say that image thinking is of a lower grade than abstract thinking. But in an adult's thinking just described, making a certain kind of thinking more advantageous due to the need of the work at hand is neither advanced nor low grade. For scientists and philosophers or for writers and engineers, they all need not only abstract thinking ability but also image thinking ability. Neither can be lacking; they need to develop one kind of thinking more than others due to their different working requirements.

Representation has various forms or kinds. This was divided according to different angles or standards. According to its generality, representation can be divided into specific representation and general representation (or generalization representation).

When we perceive a certain thing, the perception that reflects this specific thing is produced. For example, perception about a certain desk is not the perception of another desk. The corresponding representation is the image about a certain desk, not the image of another desk; this is specific representation. In people's understanding, they usually not only perceive a certain desk but also perceive a lot of different desks. Then it exceeds the representation of the specific thing at this moment and reflects the representation of a kind of things briefly (such as various desks). This is general representation or generalization representation. Specific representation reflects the characteristics of the specific thing, and general representation reflects general characteristics that a lot of similar things own in common.

General representation is produced based on specific representation. It is generalized by specific representation. The characteristics of specific representation that generalization representation reflects do not remain untouched, stiff reflection but change, to some extent, to selective reflection. What general representation reflects are often those similar (or common) and relatively fixed characteristics of specific representation. Language and words play an important role in the course of forming general representation.

Because of people's activity, generally speaking, representation is always developed from the specific to the general, and general representation is always developed in a more general direction and developed more widely and deeply.

However, no matter what big generality the representation has, it always has certain intuitivity, materiality, and iconicity. It is always the reflection of the intuitive characteristics of things. Compared with concept, there is an essential difference. Since concept is formed in the abstract activity of thinking, when people form concept, they always leave general representation and dispense with the concrete characteristics that some objects have, reflecting only on the most general connection and regularity of things.

Certainly, during the process of studying children's thinking, we often discuss intuitive action thinking, concrete image thinking based on the source, and the process of concept and thinking. We absolutely do not want to confuse the boundaries of perception, representation, and logical thinking.

The functions of representation can be divided into remembering representation, which mainly includes memory, and imagining representation, which mainly includes innovation.

5.3.4.1 Remembering representation

Remembering representation is the image trace of things reproduced in the brain based on past perceived things, when things are not in the front of the mind. Remembering representation has the following characteristics:

1. It is different from eidetic representation. Eidetic representation can be very distinct, confirming, and complete as perception, while remembering representation is often relatively dim, unstable, and partial.

2. These characteristics of remembering representation are its shortcomings (not as good as perception) and its advantages too. Because of these characteristics, remembering representation is not restricted and constrained by present perception. Therefore, on the basis of people's continuous activities, the representation in the brain can continuously go from specific to general by perceiving a kind of thing repeatedly. General representation is no more than the simple reproducing of the image of things. It achieves the standard more abundantly and deeply than specific representation through compounding and merging. Thus it makes representation the supreme form of perceptual knowledge. Abundant and deep general representation is the crucial link that transits from people's direct and concrete perception of the objective world and to indirect and abstract thinking.

3. The generality of remembering representation is the result that people continuously perceive the things in the activity. It is the result that language and word take part in this reflection course too. The language and word can not only cause representation; more importantly, it can also strengthen the generality of representation, in a qualitative leap that achieves the level of concept and thinking.

4. The forming and development of memory are determined by the memory law. In order to make children and teenagers have abundant and deep remembering representation, they should be trained according to the memory law.

5.3.4.2 Imagining representation

Imagining representation is a new image that is processed and reconstructed by the brain based on original representation.

1. Both imagining representation and remembering representation have certain generality, but imagining representation is different from remembering representation. It is the new image that is processed and reconstructed by the brain based on original representation. For example, the infant acts as mother in the "playing house" game. This combines representation about mother and representation about children together in the brain. The creativity here is very low. When the writer

molds a typical role, it is an extremely complicated creation course. Here exists abstract thinking and image thinking too, but imagining representation plays an important role.

2. Like remembering representation, imagining representation stems from both specific perception and the help of language and words.

3. Imagination can be divided into accidental imagination and intentional imagination according to different intentions. Accidental imagination is without specific intention, unconscious and inferior. It is common in the imagination of the infant. Dream is the extreme form of accidental imagination. Intentional imagination has some intention and is conscious. Intentional imagination plays an important role in people's positive and creative thinking.

4. Imagination can be divided into reconstituted imagination and creative imagination because of differences in independence, novelty, and creativity. Reconstituted imagination is the image that is imagined in terms of things never perceived on the basis of present and others' description, such as images of students' thinking about ancient slaves, faraway geographical images, etc. Reconstituted imagination plays an important role in the course of student study and the thinking activity in the work of scientific and technical personnel. Creative imagination is the image of new things created independently and does not depend on existing descriptions. It plays a key role in a student's creative study, in the thinking activities that people create new technology, new products, and new works.

Remembering representation is different from imagining representation, not mainly because the representation materials that they use are different but because the goals and the needs of people's activity are different; therefore the processing and the use mode of representation are different too. In people's activity, some need more remembering representation, while others need more imagining representation. For example, when a music player plays a particular melody, he needs certain creative factors (display of his specific understanding and special attitude toward the melody played) but not reproducing the content of the melody briefly without any emotion. Otherwise he is not a good player. However, it is the memory representation that occupies the main position in the playing course after all. He must play following the representation because what he plays is a melody with specific characteristics, instead of other melodies. However, in the creative works of writers, poets, composers, and design engineers, the case is different. They work mainly based on imagining representation. Certainly, abundant and deep remembering representation is also very important in the course of their working. In this sense, remembering representation is often a foundation of imagining representation.

To classify the representation from people's feeling passway (or the analyzer), there can be representation in conformity with every kind of feeling passway, such as visual representation, hearing representation, tasting representation, smelling representation, touching representation, movement representation, etc.

This kind of representation classified by the feeling passway has a relative meaning. For most people (including musicians, painters), feeling representation has mixed properties. In people's activity, generally speaking, we do not have a single visual representation and a single hearing or movement representation but often the mixing of different representation because people should always use various sense organs when they perceive things. Only in a relative sense can we say that some people's visual representation is a bit more developed, while others' hearing representation is a bit more developed.

The form is a mental process with particular characteristics. It is noticeable in the early development of modern psychology. But as behaviorism psychology dominated, representation had begun to go quiet in the 1920s. After the rise of cognitive psychology, the research of representation gained attention and developed rapidly again, and the achievement is abundant. Research on cognitive psychology on "psychological rotation" and "psychological scanning" also attracted attention. In psychological consultation and psychotherapy, the function of representation also plays an important role.

5.4 Perceptual theory
5.4.1 Constructing theory

In the past, knowledge and experience mainly played a role in perception in the form of hypothesis, expectation, or factor. When perceiving, people receive sensory input and, based on existing experience, form expectations about what the current stimulus is or activate certain knowledge units to form a certain object. Perception is guided and planned by these assumptions and expectations. According to J. S. Bruner and other development construction theorists, all perceptions are influenced by people's experience and expectations. The basic assumptions of construction theory are as follows:

1. Perception is a process of activity and construction, which to some extent is more than the direct registration of feelings. Other events cut into stimulation and experience.
2. Perception is not directly caused by the stimulus input but by the ultimate product of the interaction between stimulus and internal assumptions, expectations, knowledge, motivation and emotional factors.
3. Perception can sometimes be influenced by incorrect assumptions and expectations. As a result, perception can make mistakes.

The view of constructivism on perception is that memory plays an important role. They think that memory traces of previous experience are added to the sensation induced by stimulation at this time and in this place, so a perceptual image is constructed. Moreover, constructivists claim that the organized perceptual basis is the process of selecting, analyzing, and adding stimulus information from a person's memory rather than the natural operation caused by the natural law of brain organization advocated by Gestalt theorists.

The hypothesis test theory of perception is a kind of perception theory based on past experience. Other important arguments support this theory. For example, there is no one-to-one relationship between external stimuli and perceptual experience. The same stimulus can cause different perceptions, while different stimuli can cause the same perception. Perception is directional, extracting features, which are compared with the knowledge in memory, and then directional, extracting features and comparing them again, so it circulates until the meaning of gestalt stimulus is determined, which has many similarities with hypothesis testing theory.

5.4.2 Gestalt theory

Gestalt psychology was born in 1912. Gestalt psychologists found that perceptual organization is a very powerful additional constraint on pixel integrity, which provides a basis for visual reasoning. Gestalt is a translation of the German word, which is often translated into "form" or "shape" in English. The starting point of Gestalt psychologists' research is "form," which refers to the whole experience organized from perceptual activities. In other words, Gestalt psychologists believe that any "form" is the result or function of the positive organization or construction of perception rather than the object itself. It emphasizes the integrity of experience and behavior and opposes the popular constructivism element theory and behaviorism "stimulus response" formula at that time. It holds that the whole is not equal to the sum of parts, the consciousness is not equal to the set of sensory elements, and the behavior is not equal to the circle of reflection arc. Although the Gestalt principle is more than a theory of perception, it is derived from the study of perception, and some important Gestalt principles are mostly provided by perception research.

Gestalt scholars believe in the inherent and innate laws of brain tissue. They argue that these laws explain important phenomena: the differentiation, contrast, contour, convergence, the principle of perceptual combination, and other organizational facts of the background. Gestalt scholars believe that there is a "simplicity" principle behind the various perceptual factors they put forward. They assert that any pattern that contains larger symmetries, convergences, closely intertwined units, and similar units appears "relatively simple" to the observer. If a structure can be seen in more than one way, for example, a picture composed of lines can be seen as flat or as a square, the "simpler" way will be more common. Gestalt scholars do not ignore the effect of potential experience on perception, but their primary focus is on the role of the intrinsic mechanism that is inseparable from the nervous system. So they hypothesized that kinesthetic or Φ-like phenomena are the result of the brain's innate tendency to organize.

In general, there are few patterns of single graphic background, and the typical pattern is that several graphics have a common background. Some individual figures also tend to be grouped together by different combinations of perception. Wittheim, one of the founders of Gestalt psychology, systematically expounds the following "combination principles":

1. *Proximity principle*: The stimuli close to each other tend to combine more than those far away from each other. Proximity can be spatial or temporal. In a series of taps that occur at irregular intervals, sounds close in time tend to be combined. For example, when it rains in summer and thunder and electricity are added, we perceive them as a whole, that is, perception is a part of the same event.

2. *Similarity principle*: Similar stimuli have a greater tendency of combination than different stimuli. Similarity means similarity in some physical properties such as intensity, color, size, shape, etc. As the saying goes, "Birds of a feather flock together and people flock together." That saying contains this principle.

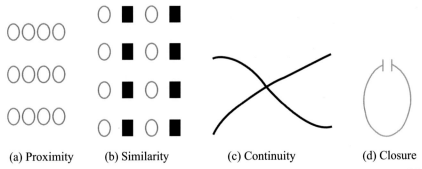

(a) Proximity   (b) Similarity   (c) Continuity   (d) Closure

Figure 5.1 Example of Gestalt perceptual organization principle. (a) Proximity (b) Similarity (c) Continuity (d) Closure.

3. *Principle of continuity*: People tend to perceive the form of coherent or continuous flow, that is, some components are connected with other components, so that it is possible to make a straight line, a curve, or an action continue in the established direction.
4. *Closure principle*: People's perception tends to form a closed or more complete figure.
5. *Symmetry principle*: People tend to perceive an object as a symmetrical figure on both sides of the center, resulting in a symmetrical or balanced whole rather than an asymmetrical one.
6. *Principle of common direction*: this is also known as the principle of common destiny. If a part of an object moves in the same direction, the moving parts are easy to be perceived as a whole. This combination principle is essentially the application of similar combination in moving objects, and it is an important means in dance design. In each stimulus pattern, some components have some degree of the proximity shown in Fig. 5.1(a), some degree of the similarity shown in Fig. 5.1(b), and some degree of the fitness for "good graphics" by continuity shown in Fig. 5.1(c), or the closure shown in Fig. 5.1(d). Sometimes some of the combined tendencies work in the same direction, and sometimes they conflict with one another.

Gestalt theory reflects some aspects of the essence of human vision, but it is only an axiomatic description of the basic principles of perceptual organization rather than an organic description. Therefore, since it was put forward in the 1920s, it has not been able to play a fundamental guiding role in visual research, but research on the principle of perceptual organization has not stopped. Especially after the 1980s, Wittkin, Tenenbaum, Lowe, Pentland, and others have made new and important research achievements in the principle of perceptual organization and the application in visual processing.

5.4.3 Gibson's ecology theory

American psychologist J. J. Gibson is well-known in academia because of his study on perception. He proposed the ecological perception theory in 1950. He thinks the perception is direct and does not have any inference step, intermediary's variable, or association. Ecology theory (theory of stimuli) stands in contrast with constructing theory (theory of hypotheses testing). It maintains that the perception has direct properties and denies the function of past knowledge and experience. J. J. Gibson thinks that the stimulus of the nature is intact, and it can offer abundant information. People can utilize the information completely, generating the perception experience corresponding to the stimulus produced and acting on the sense organ directly, without the need of forming hypotheses and testing on the basis of past experience. According to his ecological perception theory, the perception is the course kept in touch with the external world and the direct action of stimuli. He interprets such direct stimulant function as the types and variables of physical energy in reaction to the sense organs. The view that perception is the result of the direct action of environment deviates from the traditional perception theory. Gibson uses a formula to denote the concept of "stimulant ecology," which expresses the surroundings of a person, including the relation of slope and reflected surface, and the gravitation that people all experience while walking, sitting down, and lying down. He firmly believes that perception does not change, so when the environment provides a continuous and stable information flow for the active organism, the organism can react to this. These views are reflected in the work the "Perception of Visual World" published in 1950 and "The Senses Considered as Perceptual Systems" published in 1966.

Gibson's perception theory is presented in "The Ecological Perception Theory" [2]. The article puts emphasis on the environmental facts that have the greatest relationship with living beings. For Gibson, feeling is the adaptation of the environment for evolution. Furthermore, some important phenomena in the environment—for instance gravity, diurnal circulation, and comparison of sky with ground—do not change in the history of evolution. An unchanged environment brings stability and offers the reference frame for individual life. So the success of species evolution depends on the sensory system that reflects the environment correctly. From the point of view of ecology, the perception is the course that the environment shows to the perceiving person. The nervous system does not build the perception but extracts it. In Gibson's opinion, the rich information of sensory stimulation has been excluded under laboratory conditions, such as using tachycardia to show stimuli quickly. But people usually have enough time to observe in daily life, and people can walk around and change the angle of observation. With the change of viewpoint, some characteristics of the light stream change, while others stay unchanged. As previously pointed out, there exists a light distribution in any point in the space. The change of the viewpoint must cause the change of light distribution, but the light distribution always contains certain structures. Gibson believes that the perception system extracts invariance from the flowing series. His theory is called the ecology theory of perception and forms a school.

Gibson refers to superficial perception with structure as normal or the ecological perception. He thinks, compared with his own view, the Gestalt theory is mainly based on the analysis of the perception in special circumstances. In this kind of circumstance, construction is reduced or not relevant, just as the structure of this chapter is irrelevant to the content printed above it.

In the constructing theory, perception often utilizes information from memory. And Gibson thinks that the world that has structure and is highly structured has supplied abundant and accurate information. The observer can choose from it and needn't choose from the information that was stored in the past. Gibson believes that usually perception guides our movements. This is different from movement theories of perception, which assumes the signal that our muscles get is turned into the impact on the perception. The developing athletic skill guides the developing perception skill. The ecology theory firmly believes that people all treat the world by a similar means. It places emphasis on the importance of the overall complex of the information that can be had in the natural environment.

Gibson's ecology perception theory has a certain scientific basis. He assumes that the perception reaction is an innate view and is in accordance with the deep perception of the newborn animal. At the same time, it conforms to the research conclusion in neural psychology that the single cells of the visual cortex can react to specific visual stimuli. However, his theory excessively emphasizes that individual perception response is biological and ignores the function in the perception reaction of factors such as individual experience, knowledge, personality characteristic, etc. Thus it is also criticized by some researchers.

5.4.4 Topological vision theory

Visual perception research for more than 200 years has been running through the dispute between atomism and holism. According to *atomism*, the process of perception starts from the analysis of the characteristic properties or simple components of an object, from local properties to large-scale properties. However, *holism* holds that the process of perception starts from the perception of the whole object, from a large-scale nature to a local nature.

In 1982, Lin Chen creatively put forward the hypothesis of "initial perception of topological nature" on the fundamental issue of where the perception process starts [3]. This is his original contribution in the field of visual perception, which challenges the theory of characteristic analysis and which has dominated for half a century. In order to understand the basic expression of perceptual information, to understand the relationship between perception and the part and the whole of cognitive process, and to understand the relationship between cognition and computation, the theoretical basis of cognitive science, a theory framework is proposed.

A series of visual perception experiments show that there is a functional level in visual perception. The visual system not only is able to detect a wide range of topological properties but is also more sensitive to a wide range of topological properties than the local geometric visual system. The detection of a wide range of topological properties determined by spatial proximity occurs at the initial stage of the visual time process.

In 2005 Lin Chen published a "major theme paper" in the fourth issue of "Visual Cognition" [4], summarizing the topological vision theory: "The topological research of perceptual organization is based on one core idea and includes two aspects. The core idea is that perceptual organization should be understood from the perspective of transformation and invariance perception. Two aspects are: on the one hand, it emphasizes the topological structure in shape perception, that is, the large-scale nature of perceptual organization can be described by topological invariance; on the other hand, it further emphasizes the early topological nature perception, that is, the topological nature perception takes precedence over the local characteristic quality perception. "Priority" has two strict meanings: first, the whole organization determined by topological properties is the basis of perception of local geometric properties; second, the perception of topological properties based on physical connectivity is prior to the perception of local geometric properties.

5.5 Vision

The visual system gives the organism the ability of visual perception. It uses visible light information to construct the perception of the body in the surrounding world. It is the process of finding out what objects are in the surrounding scenery and where they are according to the image, that is to say, the process of getting a useful symbol description for the observer from the image. The vision system has the ability to reconstruct the two-dimensional projection of the external world into a three-dimensional world. It should be noted that the visible light that different objects can perceive is in different positions in the spectrum.

5.5.1 Visual pathway

Light enters the eye and reaches the retina, which is a part of the brain. It is composed of several types of neurons that process visual information. It clings to the posterior wall of the eyeball and is only about 0.5 mm thick. It includes three levels of neurons: The first level is photoreceptor, which is composed of numerous rod cells and cone cells; the second level is bipolar cells; the third level is ganglion cells. Axons from ganglion cells form the optic nerve. These three neurons constitute the direct channel of visual information transmission in the retina.

There are four photo-receptors in the human retina: rod cell and three kinds of cone cells. There is a special pigment in each receptor. When such a pigment molecule absorbs a quantum of light, it triggers a series of chemical changes in the cell; at the same time, it releases energy, leading to the generation of electrical signals and the secretion of synaptic chemical transmitters. The pigment of rod cells is called rhodopsin, and the peak wavelength of its spectral absorption curve is 500 nm. The absorption peaks of the three kinds of cone cytochromes are 430, 530, and 560 nm, which are most sensitive to blue, green, and red, respectively.

The optic nerves cross in a special way before entering the brain center. The fibers from the nasal retina of both eyes crossed to the contralateral cerebral hemisphere; the fibers from the temporal retina do not cross and are projected to the ipsilateral cerebral hemisphere. The results are as follows: The fibers from the temporal retina of the left eye and the fibers from the nasal side of the right eye converge into the left optic disk and project to the left lateral geniculate body, and then the left lateral geniculate body projects to the left cerebral hemisphere; the corresponding brain area is the right half visual field. On the contrary, the fibers from the nasal retina of the left eye and the temporal retina of the right eye converge into the right optic tract and project to the right lateral geniculate body, and then the right lateral geniculate body projects to the right hemisphere, the brain area corresponding to the left half visual field. The visual cortex of the two hemispheres of the brain is connected to each other through the fibers of the corpus callosum. This mutual connection mixes the information from both sides of the field of vision.

The visual cortex has two main kinds of nerve cells: stellate cells and cone cells. The axons of stellated cells make contact with the projecting fibers. A cone cell is triangular, with the tip toward surface layer emitting upward a long dendrite, the fundus issuing several dendrites to contact breadthwise.

The visual cortex, like other cortex areas, includes six cells layers, denoted by I—VI from surface to inner. The trunks of the cortex cell's tubers (dendrites and axons) all distribute in direction vertical to the cortex surface; the branches of dendrites and axons distribute breadthwise in different layers. The different cortex areas make contact with one another by axons through deep white matter, while the inner cortexes make contact through transverse branches of dendrites and axons in cortexes.

In recent years, the scope of the visual cortex has already extended to many new cortex areas, including the parietal lobe, occipital lobe, and part of the frontal lobe [5], amounting to 25. In addition, it has seven visual association areas, which has both visual and other sense or movement functions. All visual areas account for 55% of new brain cortex area. Thus the importance can be seen of visual information processing in overall brain function.

A present edge-cutting issue of visual research is to research function division, grade relationship, and reciprocity of the visual areas. The evidence confirming an independent visual cortex area is (1) the area has an independent visual field projecting map, (2) the area has the same input and output nerve connection as other cortex areas, (3) the area has a similar cellular structure, (4) the area has different function characters from other visual cortex areas.

Wernicke and Geschwind believe that the pathway of visual recognition is as shown in Fig. 5.2. According to their model, visual information is transmitted from the retinas to the lateral geniculate body, passing from the lateral geniculate body to the primary visual cortex (V17), then reaching a more advanced visual nerve center (V18), from here traveling to the angular gyrus, then arriving at the Wernicke area [6]. Visual information is translated to speech (hearing) idea. After the sound patterns are formed, they pass on to the Broca area.

The 17th area in the visual cortex is called the first visual area (V1) or stripe cortex. It receives the direct input of the lateral geniculate body,

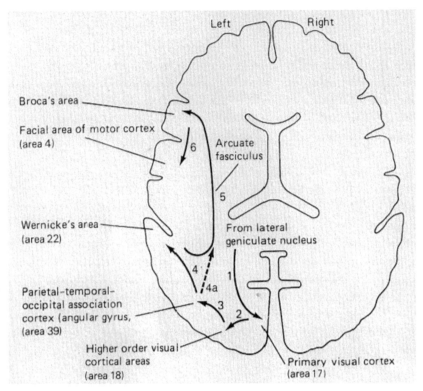

Figure 5.2 Visual pathway.

which is also known as the primary visual cortex. The functional studies for the visual cortex mostly are conducted on the level cortex. Except for the 17th area receiving direct projection from lateral geniculate body, the vision-related cortex has also a stripe proparea (the 18th area) and stripe outskirt (the 19th area). According to morphological and physiological research, the 17th area does not project to the lateral cortex but to 18th area, and the 18th area projects forward to the 19th area, and again feeds back to the 17th area. The 18th area includes three visual areas, called V2, V3, and V3A, respectively, and their main input is from V1. Vl and V2 are the biggest visual areas. The 19th area, buried deeply in the posterior paries of the superior temporal sulcus, includes the fourth (V4) and the fifth visual areas (V5). V5 also called as the middle temporal area has entered the scope of the temporal lobe. The other vision-related cortex areas in the temporal lobe are the inner upper frontal area and the inferior temporal area. There is the top occipital area, the ventral interparietal, the postabdominal area, and the 7a area in the parietal lobe. The cerebral cortex area outside the occipital lobe possibly belongs to a higher level. Why are there so many representative areas? Do different representative areas detect different graphical characteristics (such as color, shape, brightness, movement, depth, etc.)? Or do the different representative areas deal with information at different levels? Does a higher-level representative area integrate the separate graphical characteristics, thereby giving the biological meaning of graphics? Is there a special representative area that is responsible for the storage of images (visual learning and memory) or in charge of visual attention? These are the issues to be resolved in visual research in the future.

5.5.2 Marr's visual computing

Visual information processing is a process by which one find what objects there are in surrounding scene and where they are based on images, that is, a process that provides the observer with a useful symbol description from the image. There is a huge gap between an input image to the scene description, so it is necessary to go through a series of information processing and understanding processes. Understanding the nature of this process is the key to discovering the visual mystery, but we are still far from thorough understanding of these.

The visual recognition of objects is to constitute the correspondent relationship between image elements and the descriptions of the known landscape objects. Elements of images are point pixels; the value of a pixel is the pixel's gray value, which is point data. An object is described through its shape, size, geometry, color, and other features. These features represent the overall character of the object. To constitute the corresponding relationship between the input point data and the overall character of objects, a process of grouping point data is required. This grouping process occurs not only in vision but also in hearing and the other senses.

The issue relative to how to generate overall characters is the issue of constancy. As we all know, the gray of each point of images is the integrated result of many factors. These factors include light, the reflective properties of the object surface, the distance and position of the observer relative to the object, and the object's shape. Any changes in these factors will lead to changes in the gray images, also in the images we see. However, the shape, size, and color of the object we sense through vision are unrelated to the situation of the observers, as well as lighting conditions. More specifically, when lighting conditions and distance from the observer's position relative to the object change, even though the images produced in the retinal change, people always see a certain shape and size of the object. People perceive in the brain constant characteristics of the objects behind their variable appearances. Therefore, the brains not only organize point sensor information into a whole but also through a factoring process separate from the conditions affecting sensor information—that is, lighting conditions, distance and position of the observer—to acquire pure information of the objects. This information is not changed with the previously mentioned conditions and is therefore known as constancies. In short, rather than directly imaging from the retinal projection of the outside world, the brain recognizes objects by means of the information from the grouping and factoring process.

A very important issue related to analysis of these two processes is the relationship between the grouping process, which converts point information of the image into the overall description, and the factoring process, which parses a variety of factors affecting the results of imaging. Can we proceed with the gathering process before finishing the decomposition process? Some scientists like D. Marr believe that before acquiring pure information of the objects, such as depth, surface orientation, reflectance etc., any grouping processing is vain [7]. They call this kind of pure information intrinsic images, so they adopted the visual information processing methods based on reconstruction, namely through the reconstruction of these intrinsic images, to identify the objects. Other scientists believe that some preorganizing process not only provides the necessary foundation for the factoring process but also form the image relationship responding to the object's spatial structure, in accordance with the relationship between these images generating the image content assumption. Therefore, they adopted reasoning and identification-based visual information processing methods. The former point of view is represented by Marr's computational theory of human vision; the latter point of view is represented by the Gestalt school, and its follow-up, such as Lowe, Pentland, and other perception organization theorists. The two theories reflect the basic contradictions in the visual process, but neither has interpreted the visual process satisfactorily. Arguments for the two theories fuel the research on vision (see Fig. 5.3).

The professor of the MIT Artificial Intelligence Laboratory, D. Marr, from the end of 1970 to early 1980, created the visual computing theory,

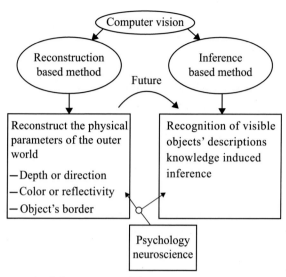

Figure 5.3 Two methods in computer vision.

advancing visual research a major step forward [7]. Marr's visual computing theory, based on computer science, systematically summed up the all-
important results of psychological physics, neurophysiology, and clinical
neuropathology and is by far the most systematic theory of vision. The
emergence of Marr's theory has had a profound impact on the development of neuroscience and artificial intelligence research.

Marr believed that vision is an information processing process. This
process generates descriptions useful to observers in accordance with outside world images. The descriptions are composed in turn of many different but fixed representations, each of which records certain characteristics
of the outside world. Representation is improved by this step because it
expresses certain information, and this information will facilitate further
explanation of the information. According to this logic, we can conclude
that, before interpreting the data further, we need some information of
the observed objects, the so-called intrinsic images. However, the data's
entering our eyes needs light be media. Gray-scale images contain at least
the information on the lighting situation and the observer position relative
to the objects. Therefore, according to Marr's method, the first problem
to be solved is how to decompose these factors. He believes that
low-level vision (that is, the first stage of visual processing) is to distinguish
which changes are caused by which of the various factors. Generally
speaking, this process goes through two steps: The first step is to obtain

representations representing changes and structures of images. This includes such processing as the detection of grayscale changes, representation, and analysis of local geometry, as well as detection of lighting effects. The results of the first step is known as the primal sketch appearance; the second step is a series of operations to the initial sketch to obtain representation that reflects the geometric features of the surface appearance; such a representation is known as a 2.5-D sketch or intrinsic image. These operations include extracting the depth information from three-dimensional visual computing, restoring the surface direction in accordance with gray shadow, texture, and other information, obtaining surface shape and space relationship from movement visual computing. The results of these operations are integrated into intrinsic images, at the level of intermediate representation. The intermediate representation is derived by removing the many different meanings of the original image, representing purely the object's surface characteristics, including illumination, reflectance, direction, distance, and so on. This information, represented by intrinsic images, can reliably divide images into clear-meaning regions (known as segmentation), obtaining a more high-level description than lines, regions, shapes, etc. The processing level is known as intermediate processing. The next representative level in Marr's theory is the three-dimensional model, which applies to object recognition. This level of processing involves objects and relies on and applies a priori field knowledge to constitute a description of scenes, called high-level visual processing.

Marr's theory of visual computing is the first visual system theory, promoting research on computer vision significantly, but it is still far from resolving the issue of human visual theory and in practice has encountered serious difficulties. Many scholars have already made improvements.

Marr first researched strategies addressing the issue of visual understanding. He believed that vision is an information processing process. It requires three levels to understand and address:

1. *Computing theory level*: Researching what information should be computed and why.
2. *Representation and algorithm level*: The actual computation according to the computing theory—how to represent input and output?—and the algorithm transforming input to output.
3. *Hardware implementation*: The implementation represented by the representation and algorithm, implementing and executing algorithms, and researching to complete a specific algorithm and specific institutions.

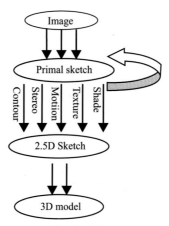

Figure 5.4 Visual system representation levels.

For example, the Fourier transform belongs to the first level of the theory, while the algorithms of the Fourier transform, such as the fast Fourier transform algorithm, belong to the second level. As for the array processors, realizing the fast Fourier algorithms belongs to the hardware implementation level.

We think that vision is a process that generates descriptions useful to observers in accordance with outside world images. The descriptions are composed in turn of many different but fixed representations, each of which records certain characteristics of the outside world. Therefore choosing the representation method is of utmost importance to visual understanding. According to the assumption made by Marr, the visual information processing process includes three main levels: the primal sketch, a 2.5-dimensional model, and a three-dimensional model [7]. According to some evidence of psychology, the human visual system representation is as shown in Fig. 5.4.

5.5.2.1 The primal sketch

Grayscale images include two important pieces of information: the grayscale change and the local geometric characteristics in images. The primal sketch is a primitive expression method, which can fully and clearly express information.

The most of the information in primal sketches focused on the gray scale rapid changes relative to the actual edges and the termination points of edges. Each grayscale change arising from the edges has a corresponding description, which includes the grayscale change rate of edges, a total change of grayscale, the edge length, curvature, and direction. Roughly speaking, the primal sketches represent changes in grayscale image in draft form.

5.5.2.2 2.5-D sketch

The 2.5-D sketch contains the information of the scene surface, which can be regarded as the mixed information of some internal characteristics. Grayscale images are influenced by many factors, which mainly include the lighting conditions, object geometry, surface reflectivity, etc., as well as the perspective of the observer. Therefore we must distinguish the effects of these factors, that is, first describe more fully surfaces of objects in the scene in order to proceed with the establishment of a three-dimensional model of objects. So it is needed to build an intermediate representative level, 2.5-D sketch. Local surface characteristics can be described by the so-called intrinsic properties. Typical intrinsic characteristics include surface orientations, distances from observers to the surfaces, reflecting and incident light, and surface texture and material properties. Intrinsic images comprise single intrinsic property values of image points, as well as where the intrinsic properties generate the discrete information. The 2.5-D sketch can be seen as a mixture of some intrinsic images. In short, the 2.5D sketch represents fully and clearly the information on the object's surface through following parameters:

- γ: relative depth (according to vertical projections), that is, the distance from observers to surface points
- $\delta\gamma$: γ's continuous or small changes
- $\Delta\gamma$: γ's discontinuous points
- S: the direction of the local surface
- δS: S's continuous or small changes
- ΔS: S's nonconsecutive points

In primal sketches and 2.5-D sketches, the information is often represented in terms of the coordinates linked to observers; this representation is referred to as an observer-centered one.

5.5.2.3 Three-dimensional model

In the representation of 3D model, the decomposition based on the standard axis of a shape is the easiest to get. Each of these axes is associated with a rough spatial relationship; this relationship provides a natural combination of the main shape element axis in the scope of the spatial relationship. We call the module defined in this way the three-dimensional model. Therefore every three-dimensional model represents the following [7]:

1. A model axis refers to a single axis determining the scope of the spatial relationship of the model. It is an element of representation that can tell us roughly several characteristics of the overall shape described, for example, the size and direction information of the overall shape.

2. There are the relative spatial position and size of the main element axis for choosing the spatial relationship determined by the model axis. The number of element axes should not be too great, and they should also be roughly the same size.

3. Once the three-dimensional model of the spatial elements associated with the element axis is constructed, then these element names (internal relations) can be determined. The model axis of spatial elements corresponds to the element axes of the three-dimensional model.

In Fig. 5.5, each box represents a three-dimensional model, with the model axis painted on the left side of the box and the element axis painted on the right side of the box. The model axis of the three-dimensional model of the human body is an element, which describes clearly the general characteristics (size and direction) of the whole shape of the human body. The six element axes corresponding to the human body, head, and limbs can connected with a three-dimensional model, which contains the additional configuration information further parsing these element axes into smaller elements. Although the structure of a single three-dimensional model is very simple, in accordance with this hierarchical structure to combine several models, we can constitute to any degree of precision the description of the geometric nature of the shape. We call the hierarchical structure of the three-dimensional model the three-dimensional model description of a shape.

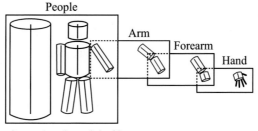

Figure 5.5 Three-dimensional model of human.

The three-dimensional representation represents fully and clearly the object shape information. It is important to adopt the concept of generalized cylinders, but it is very simple. An ordinary cylinder is generated by a circle moving along its center line. More generally, a generalized cylinder is generated by a two-dimensional cross-section moving along the axis. During the moving process, the angle between the cross-section and axis remains fixed. The cross-section can be any shape; during the moving process, its size may be changing, and the axis may not necessarily be a straight line.

Complex objects are often composed by connecting several generalized cylinders. Considering mutual impacts at different levels, one probability is that information flows to each representation in bottom–up way and that the computation of each layer only depends on the description of the front adjacent layer. For example, the computation of 2.5-D sketches needs only the information of the primal sketches, neither to need direct information from the images nor to use any clues to what can be seen from the image. Each of the processes used in computation is carried on in an independent or quasi-independent manner.

Another possibility is that a wide variety of computing in the primary and 2.5-D sketches is conducted by a mixed constraint spread. For example, the information from the three-dimensional processing can be used to improve computing from the grayscale shadow to the direction of the surface, and vice versa. Information can flow in all directions. It is also possible that information flows top down, so understanding the image depends on a controlled imagination to a large extent. In that case, the early vision is guided by the fixed forecast of what should be seen.

5.5.3 Image understanding

For a digital image or a moving image sequence that is represented in the form of a dot matrix (raster) and made up of all sorts of light–dark or colored pixel sets, we think that computers have already understood this image or image sequence if the computers know the semantics expressed by the image and answer the question about semantic contents proposed by human beings (for example, are there any people in the image? How many? What are they doing?) by means of analyzing and recognizing images. Image understanding is in general the integration of such low-level processes as denoising processing, edge extraction, region segmentation, feature extraction, target extraction, and high-level inference analysis. It can also starts from the high-level prior knowledge or model assumptions and make hypotheses testing on low-level gradual processing. This process is the research direction set by us in the hope of further replacing advanced human vision and inference abilities through machine simulation. It is also regarded as more advanced image processing than general image analysis and recognition because recognition is basically equivalent to classification and identification in pattern recognition while understanding demands the abstraction of deeper meanings after thorough and repeated inferring and comparing. However, for the same image, it is not absolutely true that different persons will obtain the same understanding results. If we are interested in different problems, the focus on the same image will be different. In addition, different people have different levels and views of understanding the same objects or even have contradictory conclusions. Thus the so-called image understanding currently is an intentional proposition, which lacks strict definitions or theory models. In practical applications, the expected results can be obtained only if we constrain the objects and the problems in a fairly small but definite range.

Image segmentation is the process of dividing an image into several different parts or regions. It is an important step in digital image processing, image analysis, and image understanding. Its purpose is to segment the image into useful or meaningful regions so as to make image analysis and understanding easier. There exist two common ways of segmenting images into several areas with definite meanings (all sorts of objects or background): One is to make segmentation based on the different gray values or color components among the image pixels, which is called pixel-based image segmentation; the other is to make segmentation based on the discontinuity of different types of areas in the images, which is called area-based image segmentation. For example, we can make segmentation based on the fact that different regions have different textures (organized structure features). In addition, the discontinuity of images may lead to the boundary, and we can segment the image by use of the boundary. A pixel-based segmentation method can be used to segment the images having white characters with white paper background or yellow walls with brown doors. However, if the image to be segmented contains two kinds of figured cloth, we have to resort to an area-based segmentation method. The pixel-based segmentation method can be further divided into the threshold- and histogram-based approach, while the area-based segmentation method can also be divided into edge-based, region-based, and edge-and—region-based methods.

The edges in the images are the boundaries of two regions that have fairly large differences on the intensities (or colors). It is generally assumed that the intensities of the boundaries have rather sudden variation. From a mathematical point of view, the derivatives of the intensities on the boundaries to the space (two-dimensional image plane coordinates) will have relatively large absolute values. Therefore most of the edge detection techniques are based on the derivation method. The computers represent the images by use of some discrete values rather than the continuous functions, which makes it a must to utilize a discrete difference algorithm to calculate the derivatives. (In image processing, the difference is represented by some feature extraction operators). In edge detection, the concept of intensity gradient is frequently used. The image's intensity gradient is a vector whose components are partial derivatives calculated by the image intensity from two coordinate directions. When the image is represented by a continuous function $f(x, y)$:

$$G = \begin{bmatrix} G_x \\ G_y \end{bmatrix}, \quad G_x = \frac{\partial f(x, y)}{\partial x}, \quad G_y = \frac{\partial f(x, y)}{\partial y} \tag{5.1}$$

In the actual image, the two components of gradients can be calculated by using the following template operators:

$$\begin{bmatrix} -1 & 1 \\ -1 & 1 \end{bmatrix} \text{ and } \begin{bmatrix} 1 & 1 \\ -1 & -1 \end{bmatrix}$$

The magnitude of the gradient is:

$$\sqrt{G_x^2 + G_y^2} \tag{5.2}$$

The direction of the gradient is:

$$\tan^{-1}\left(\frac{G_y}{G_x}\right) \tag{5.3}$$

This algorithm and the feature extraction algorithms all work on the isolated points by use of the information contained in a small neighborhood. Usually after using these algorithms, the jobs of further detection and connection are required to obtain meaningful object boundaries or the boundary lines of the surfaces. For the purpose of determining and connecting boundaries, there generally exist two methods: the local analysis method and the global analysis method.

1. Local analysis method is the simplest method of determining connections. Taking a small neighborhood into consideration, for example 3*3 or 5*5, we connect the similar points in this neighborhood to form a boundary of some common properties. In general, two aspects are considered with regard to the similarity: One is the intensity (the magnitude of the gradient) obtained after the calculation with edge detection operators; the other is the ratio of the two derivatives that are calculated along two different coordinate directions (the direction of the gradient). In some image regions, if the differences of the magnitude and the direction of the gradient of the detected two points are both below some given values, we think they belong to the same boundary and will be marked in the image. This process can be repeatedly made on the whole image in the block.

2. Global analysis method studies the interrelationship of the possible detected boundary pixels on the whole image plane. Hough transformation can be used to make the global analysis and determination.

The edge detection method can determine whether one pixel is on the edge or not by making local operations on the subwindow surrounding the pixel. In general, the operations are differentiation or correlation on the ideal edge. After that, a threshold operation is made on the obtained images to generate binary images. The detected edge points will be connected as one meaningful line. This can be implemented by tracking the edge points according to some kind of rule. Many special situations will be encountered, such as the gap between edges, the sudden change of curves, and the false edge points caused by noises in the tracking. It demands more complicated tracking rules.

The region-based segmentation method accomplishes segmentation by finding the regions in which the pixels have similar gray values (or properties). The two approaches are complementary and will get the same results in ideal cases. Image region-based segmentation is an image segmentation technique based on the differences of the properties of image regions. The basic idea of region-based segmentation is to identify all the regions of similar features in the image. The similar features can be shape, pixel value, or texture. In pattern recognition, clustering techniques are also used in region-based image segmentation.

1. Template matching is to match the image region with a group of given templates so as to segment the objects satisfying the templates from the other parts of the image. The other methods are required in

analysis of the left image. For example, template matching can be used to segment the graph-text manuscripts. Once the texts are found out by the template matching method, the graphics are analyzed by other methods. The procedure of template matching is always depending on correlation and convolution operations.

2. In texture segmentation, when the object is in the background of apparent textures or has strong texture features in itself, texture-based region segmentation method is needed. Since the texture is some kind of pattern or alternately the repetition of patterns, designs, and structures, it is hardly possible to describe by the use of single pixel. Naturally it is impossible to employ the pixel-based classification methods. There exist large amounts of edges in the textures. Therefore, we can hardly obtain desirable segmentation results on the images with abundant textures by use of the edge tracking method unless the textures are filtered.

3. The descriptions of textures are the foundations of classification and segmentation. When we know that there exists some kind of texture in the image, it can be found by utilizing the known texture features (i.e., the descriptions of this texture in the frequency domain or spatial gray relation matrix). If no prior knowledge is had in advance, we can use region-based clustering methods to segment the texture regions. One solution that can be easily thought of is to first divide the image into several small blocks, then to calculate the texture features of each block, and lastly to decide to combine the blocks or not based on the features' differences.

4. The region-based clustering method in general can be divided into the region growing method and the splitting-merging method. Its basic idea is to grow the object in all directions starting from the points or regions that satisfy the detection criteria. The growth is based on the assumption that region features of the same type, such as gray values, colors, and texture features, have only a few differences. The neighborhoods that satisfy some merging conditions can enter this region. In the growing process, the merging conditions can also be adjusted. The growth stops when no more regions are available for merging. The basic idea of the splitting-merging method is to first divide the images into several "initial" regions and to split or merge these regions, then improve the criteria of region segmentation gradually until the image is segmented into the minimum approximately consistent regions (satisfying some requirement). In general, the criterion of

consistency can be measured by use of the property's mean square error. Compared with the edge-based image segmentation method, the region growing method and splitting-merging method are not very sensitive to noises but have high computational complexity.

5.5.4 Face recognition

Face recognition technology refers to the use of analysis and comparison of computer technology for face recognition. Face recognition technology is based on human face features. For the input face image or video stream, first judge whether there is a face. If there is a face, the location and size of each face and the location information of each main facial organ are further given. Based on these information, the identity features contained in each face are further extracted and compared with the known face to identify each face.

The process of face recognition is generally divided into three steps:

1. First, the face image file of human face is established. Use a camera to collect face image files of unit personnel or take their photos to form face image files, and encode and store these face image files to generate face prints.
2. Get the current human face. Use the camera to capture the face image of the current person in and out, or take the photo to input, and generate the face image file to generate the face pattern code.
3. Compare the current face texture code with the file inventory. The current face image's face code is retrieved and compared with the face code in the file inventory. The previously mentioned "face coding" method works according to the essential features and the beginning of the face. This kind of facial pattern coding can resist the changes of light, skin tone, facial hair, hairstyle, glasses, expression, and posture, and it has strong reliability, so that it can accurately identify someone from millions of people. The process of face recognition can be completed automatically, continuously, and in real time by using common image processing equipment.

The face recognition system mainly consists of four parts: face image acquisition and detection, face image preprocessing, face image feature extraction, matching, and recognition (see Fig. 5.6).

5.5.4.1 Face image acquisition and detection

Face image collection: Different face images can be collected by the camera lens, such as static images, dynamic images, different positions, different expressions, and so on. When the user is in the shooting range of the

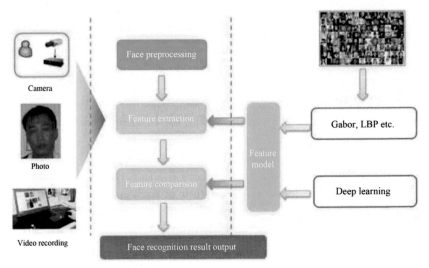

Figure 5.6 Face recognition system.

acquisition device, the device will automatically search and take the user's face image.

Face detection: Face detection is mainly used in the preprocessing of face recognition in practice, that is, accurately demarcate the position and size of the face in the image. There are many pattern features in face image, such as histogram, color, template, structure, and hair. In face detection, the useful information is picked out and used to achieve face detection.

The mainstream face detection methods use the AdaBoost learning algorithm based on the preceding features. The AdaBoost algorithm is a method for classification. It combines some weaker classification methods to form a new and strong classification method.

In the face detection process, the AdaBoost algorithm is used to select some rectangular features (weak classifiers) that can best represent the face. According to the method of weighted voting, the weak classifier is constructed into a strong classifier, and then the trained strong classifiers are connected in series to form a cascade structure of cascade classifiers, which can effectively improve the detection speed of the classifier.

5.5.4.2 Face image preprocessing

The image preprocessing of the human face is based on the result of human face detection, which processes the image and ultimately serves the process of feature extraction. Because of the limitation of various conditions and random interference, the original image acquired by the system cannot be used directly. It must be preprocessed in the early stage of image processing, such as gray correction, noise filtering, and so on. For the face image, the preprocessing process mainly includes light compensation, grayscale transformation, histogram equalization, normalization, geometric correction, filtering, and sharpening.

5.5.4.3 Face image feature extraction

The features that the face recognition system can use are usually divided into visual features, pixel statistical features, face image transformation coefficient features, face image algebraic features, and on the like. Face feature extraction is based on some of the features of the face. Face feature extraction, also known as face representation, is the process of face feature modeling. The methods of facial feature extraction can be divided into two categories: One is knowledge-based representation; the other is algebra-based representation or statistical learning representation.

The knowledge-based representation method is mainly based on the shape description of facial organs and the distance between them to obtain the feature data that is helpful for face classification. Its feature components usually include Euclidean distance, curvature, and angle between feature points. The face is composed of eyes, nose, mouth, chin, and other parts. The geometric description of these parts and their structural relationship can be regarded as the important features of face recognition, which are called geometric features. Knowledge-based face representation mainly includes the geometric feature-based method and template matching method.

5.5.4.4 Face image matching and recognition

The feature data of the extracted face image is searched and matched with the feature template stored in the database. By setting a threshold, when the similarity exceeds this threshold, the matching result is output. Face recognition is to compare the face features to be recognized with the obtained face feature template and to judge the identity information of the face according to the similarity degree of the extracted features. This process is divided into two categories: One is confirmation, which is a one-to-one image comparison process; the other is recognition, which is a one-to-many image matching and comparison process.

Face recognition technology is widely used in the government, military, bank, Social Security, e-commerce, security, and defense fields. E-passports and ID cards, for example, are the largest applications. The International Civil Aviation Organization has determined that face recognition technology is the first recognition mode in 118 member countries and regions since April 1, 2010. This regulation has become an international standard. The United States required countries with visa-free agreements to use e-passport systems that combine biometrics such as face fingerprints before October 26, 2006. By the end of 2006, more than 50 countries had implemented such systems.

5.6 Audition

Auditory process includes the stages of mechanical, electrical, chemical, central information processing, etc. Mechanical movement ranges from sound receiving by the external ear to the basilar membrane movement of the inner ear. Stimulating the hair cells leads to a change of electricity, the release of a chemical mediator, the generation of nerve impulse, etc. After the impulses are transmitted to the nerve center, complicated information processing takes place.

5.6.1 Auditory pathway

The ear is composed of three parts: the external ear, the middle ear, and the inner ear. The external ear collects sound stimulus, while the middle ear transfers the sound vibration to the inner ear. The inner ear is the location of sound receptor cells, which transform the mechanical sound energy into neural energy.

The pathway from the cochlea to the auditory cortex is the most complicated one of all the sensory pathways. The information process and activity happening at every level of the auditory system have a certain effect on the activities of relatively higher and lower levels. The auditory pathway is extensively intersected from one side of the brain to the other side.

The fibers bifurcated from the eighth cranial nerves terminate at the dorsal and ventral parts of the cochlea nucleus. The fibers initiate from the dorsal cochlea, pass through the central line and rise to the cortex via lateral lemniscuses. The lateral lemniscus ends at the inferior colliculi of the midbrain. The fiber initiating from the ventral cochlea nucleus first establishes a connection with the homonymous and contralateral superior olivary complex by synapse. As the first stop in the hearing pathway, the superior olivary complex is the site where the interaction of the two ears occurs.

The superior olivary complex is a part of the auditory system that attracts a lot of attention. It is composed of several nucleuses, of which the biggest are the inner superior oliva and the lateral superior oliva. Research on several kinds of mammals has found that the size of these two nucleuses is related to the sensory ability of the animal. Harrison and Irving suggest that these two nucleuses are capable of different functions. They maintain that the inner superior oliva is related to the sound orientation of eye movement. For all the animals that are equipped with advanced visual system as well as the ability of tracing sounds and making responses, the inner superior oliva has a conspicuous appearance. On the other hand, they infer that the lateral superior oliva is associated with the sound orientation that is independent of the visual system.

Animals with acute hearing but limited visual ability often have quite distinct lateral superior oliva. Bats and dolphins have quite limited visual ability but they are blessed with a sophisticated hearing system; as a result, they are completely lacking an inner superior oliva.

Fibers initiating from the superior oliva complex rise to the inferior colliculus via the lateral lemniscus. The inferior lemniscus then transmits the impulse to the medial geniculatum body of the thalamus. The fiber bundle linking these two areas is called brachium colliculi inferioris. The hearing-reflecting fibers conduct the impulse to the superior temporal gyrus (area 41 and area 42), which is also referred to as the auditory cortex.

5.6.2 Speech coding

The technique of speech digitalization can be generally classified into two kinds: the first is to model the waveform and code it digitally on the prerequisite that the waveform is strictly abided. The second is to process the modeled waveform but code only speech that can be heard during the course of speech perception. Three frequently used methods of speech coding are PCM, difference PCM (DPCM), and delta modulation (DM). Normally, the digital telephones in the public switch telephone network adopt these three techniques. The second speech digitalization method is mainly related to the speech coder that is used in a narrowband transmission system or capacity-limited digital facility. Equipment adopting this digitalization technique is generally referred to as vocoder. Currently the vocoder is widely used, particularly in speech of frame-relay or internet protocol (IP) address.

Besides the technique of compressed coding, people also use many other bandwidth-saving techniques to minimize the bandwidth occupied by speech and to optimize the network resource. The silence speech inhibition technique that people use in asynchronous transfer mode (ATM) and the frame-relay network could eliminate the silent speech data in a connection while not influencing the transmission of other information data. The voice activity detection technique speech activity detection can be used to trace the noise power watt level and set up a sharing voice detection threshold for it. In this way, speech/silent speech detector can dynamically match the user's background noise environment and minimize the audibility of the silent speech suppressed. To replace the audio signal in the network, these signals do not pass through the network. The comfortable background noise is integrated into a signal path on either side of the network so as to ensure the speech quality and natural speech connection on both ends of the speech channel. The speech coding method can be grouped into the following three kinds: waveform coding, source coding, and hybrid coding.

5.6.2.1 Waveform coding

Waveform coding is a relatively simple process. Before coding, the sampling theorem quantifies the modeled speech signal and then quantifies the amplitude; finally binary coding is performed. After the decoder makes the digital/ analog conversion, the low-pass filter restores the original modeled speech waveform, which is the simplest impulse code modulation (PCM), also called linear PCM. Data compression could also be realized by means of nonlinear quantification, difference between prior and post sample values and adaptive prediction. The goal of waveform coding is that the modeled signal restored by the decoder should be identical as much as possible to the original waveform before coding, that is to say, distortion should be the minimum. The waveform coding method is quite simple, and the digital ratio is relatively high. From 64 to 32 kbit/s, the sound quality is quite good. Nevertheless, when the digital ratio is lower than 32 kbit/s, the sound quality would degrade remarkably, and when the digital ratio is16 kbit/s, the sound quality is extremely poor.

5.6.2.2 Source coding

Source coding is also referred to as vocoder. Based on the human articulation mechanism, the vocoder analyzes the speech signal at the coding end and decomposes it into sounds and nonsounds. The vocoder analyzes the speech at regular intervals and transmits the corresponding analytic coding of sound/nonsound and filter parameters. The decoding end resynthesizes the speech based on the parameters received. The code rate generated by vocoder coding can be extremely low—1.2 kbit/s, 2.4 kbit/s. However, it has shortcomings too. Firstly, the quality of the synthetic speech is rather poor, with high intelligibility but low naturalness. Therefore, it is quite difficult to distinguish the speaker. Secondly, it is of high complexity.

5.6.2.3 Hybrid coding

Hybrid coding combines the principle of waveform coding and vocoder, with a digital ratio ranging from 4 to 16 kbit/s. It generates sounds of high quality. Lately there is a certain algorithm that can produce sound quality equivalent to that of waveform coding and yield complexity between waveform coding and vocoder.

The three methods of speech coding can be grouped into many coding methods. The attributes of speech coding can be classified into four kinds: bit rate, time delay, complexity, and quality. Bit rate is a very important factor of speech coding, ranging from 2.4 kbit/s of a confidential telephone communication to 64 kbit/s of G.711PCM coding and G.722 wideband 7 kHz speech coder.

5.7 Speech recognition and synthesis

Automatic speech recognition (ASR) is a key technology to realize human—computer interaction. It enables the computer to "understand" human speech and convert it into text. After decades of development, ASR technology has achieved remarkable results. In recent years, more and more speech recognition intelligent software and applications have been popular in our daily life. Apple's Siri, Microsoft's Cortana, Baidu's Duer, and the voice input method of USTC's IFLYTEK are typical examples. With the continuous progress of recognition technology and computer performance, speech recognition technology will have a broader prospect in future society.

5.7.1 Speech recognition

Since the beginning of the 21st century, speech recognition technology based on deep learning has become the mainstream. The context sensitive deep neural network hidden Markov framework proposed in 2011 is considered the start of the change. Based on connection temporal classification (CTC), the construction process is simple, and the performance is better in some cases. In 2016 Google proposed CD-CTC-SMBR-LSTM-RNNS, marking the complete replacement of the traditional GMM-HMM framework. Acoustic modeling changed from the traditional segmented modeling method based on the short-term stationary hypothesis to the modeling based on the direct discriminant discrimination of indefinite length sequence. As a result, the performance of speech recognition is gradually approaching the practical level, while the development of the mobile Internet brings a huge demand for speech recognition technology, each of which promotes the other. Parameter learning algorithms, model structures, and parallel training platforms related to deep learning have become the research hotspot at this stage. And this stage can be regarded as the stage of rapid development and large-scale application of deep learning speech recognition technology. Speech recognition is gradually becoming the key technology of the human—computer interface in information technology, and the research level is gradually moving from laboratory to practical.

A speech recognition system consists of four main modules: front-end signal processing and feature extraction, the acoustic model, the language model, and the decoder (see Fig. 5.7)

The input of the signal processing module is the speech signal, and the output is the feature vector. With the increasing demand of far-field

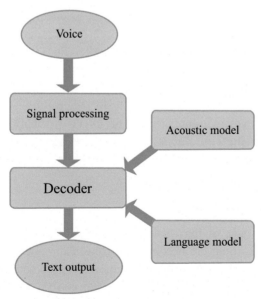

Figure 5.7 Speech recognition system framework.

speech interaction, front-end signal processing and feature extraction are more and more important in speech recognition. Generally speaking, the main process is to locate the sound source through a microphone array and then eliminate the noise. The sound collected by the radio is adjusted to the normal amplitude through the automatic gain control. The speech is enhanced by denoising and other methods, then the signal is converted from the time domain to the frequency domain, and finally the feature vector suitable for amplitude modulation (AM) modeling is extracted.

The acoustic model module models the knowledge of acoustics and phonics. Its input is the feature vector generated by the feature extraction module, and the output is the acoustic model score of the given speech. The acoustic model is a knowledge representation of the variables of acoustics, phonetics, and environment, as well as the differences of speaker's gender and accent. The acoustic model directly determines the performance of the whole speech recognition system.

The language model module is a knowledge representation of a set of words, which is used to estimate the probability of a text statement, called the score of language model. The model stores the co-occurrence probability of different words, which is usually estimated from the corpus of text format. The language model is closely related to the application fields and tasks. When the information is known, the score of the language model is more accurate.

According to the acoustic model and language model, the decoder transforms the input speech feature vector sequence into character sequence. The decoder combines the acoustic model score and language model score of all candidate sentences and outputs the sentence with the highest score as the final recognition result.

IFLYTEK has developed a speech recognition framework of a deep full convolutional neural network (DFCNN), which uses a large number of convolution layers to directly model the whole speech signal and better express the long-term correlation of speech. DFCNN directly converts a sentence of speech into an image as input, that is, first Fourier transforms each frame of speech and then time and frequency as two dimensions of the image. Then, through the combination of many convolution layers and pooling layers, the whole sentence of speech is modeled, and the output unit is directly connected with the final recognition result, such as corresponding syllables or Chinese characters.

In China, IFLYTEK is the leader in the field of speech recognition, whether in terms of market share or technological innovation.

IFLYTEK's first dialect recognition engine supports 15 dialects with more than 250 million users.

5.7.2 Speech synthesis

Speech synthesis is the technology that makes the computer generate speech. Its goal is to make the computer output clear, natural, and fluent speech. According to different levels of human speech function, speech synthesis can also be divided into three levels: from text to speech (TTS) synthesis, from concept to speech synthesis, from intention to speech synthesis. These three levels reflect the different processes of forming speech content in the human brain and involve the high-level neural activities of the human brain. At present, the mature speech synthesis technology can only complete TTS synthesis, which is also often called TTS technology.

The methods of speech synthesis have gone through a series of stages: from parameter synthesis to splicing synthesis and finally to the combination of the two methods. The continuous stimulus for this development is the improvement of people's cognition and demands. At present, the common speech synthesis technique includes the following: formant synthesis, LPC synthesis, pitch synchronous overlap add (PSOLA) splicing synthesis, and the log magnitude approximate (LMA) soundtrack modeling technique. All of them have both advantages and disadvantages; therefore, it is necessary that people integrate these techniques or import the strength of one technique onto the other so as to overcome the shortcomings of the other technique.

5.7.2.1 Formant synthesis

The mathematical model of speech generation is the theoretical foundation for speech synthesis. The speech generation process can be described as follows: spurred by the stimulation signal, the sound wave goes through the resonator and radiates the sound waves through the mouth or nose. Therefore the sound track's parameters and its resonance characteristics have been the kernel of the research. Fig. 5.8 displays the frequency response of certain speech. In the figure, Fp1, Fp2, Fp3... mark the peaks of the frequency response, which suggests the time when the transmitted frequency response of the sound track reaches its utmost. Normally, these peaks of the frequency response in sound track transmission are referred to as formants. The distribution characteristics of the formant frequency (peak frequency) play a decisive role in the tone quality of the speech.

Speeches of different tone qualities differ in formant pattern; hence, the formant filter can be constructed by taking the formant frequency and

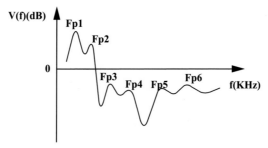

Figure 5.8 Frequency response of certain speech.

bandwidth as parameters. Next, several combinations of these filters can be used to simulate the transmission characteristics of the sound track (the frequency response) and to adjust the stimulated signal. Then by applying the radiation model, synthetic speech can be obtained. This is the basic principle of formant synthesis technique. Three practicable models are based on formant theories.

1. *Series formant model*: In this model, the sound track is regarded as a set of sequential second-order resonators. This model is mainly used for the synthesis of most vowels.
2. *Parallel formant model*: Many researchers argue that the aforementioned series formant model cannot adequately describe and simulate special vowels (such as nasalized vowels) and most consonants, which leads to the birth of the parallel formant model.
3. *Hybrid formant model*: In the series formant model, the formant filters are connected end to end. In the parallel formant model, the input signals have to go through amplitude adjustment first and then be added to every formant filter; after that, the outputs of all the circuits are added up. Comparing these two models, we can see that for those speeches whose synthesized sound source locates at the end of the sound track (including most vowels), the serial formant model is more tallied with acoustic theories and, moreover, is free from the burden of making an amplitude adjustment for every formant filter. However, for those speeches whose synthesized sound source are located in the middle of the sound track (including most tenuis and stops), the parallel model is more suitable. Nevertheless, it is very complicated to adjust the amplitudes in the parallel model. Taking all this into consideration, people combined these two models and created the hybrid formant model.

In fact, all three models have successful applications. For instance, the OVE system of Fant adopts the series formant model, and the synthesizer of Holmes employs the parallel formant model. The most representative and successful model is the Klatt synthesizer, which is established on the foundation of the hybrid formant model. As for the speech synthesis of Mandarin Chinese, researchers have developed some application system based on formant models.

Formant models simulate the sound track accurately, which can be used to yield speech of high naturalness. Additionally, as the formant parameters have definite physical meanings that correspond directly to the sound tract parameter, it is easy to use the formant models to describe the various phenomena in natural speech and summarize the acoustic rules, which ultimately leads to its application in the formant synthesis system.

However, people have also discovered that this technique has conspicuous shortcomings. First, as it relies on the simulation of the sound track, the inaccurate simulation of the sound track will definitely affect the synthetic quality. Second, practical applications have demonstrated that although the formant model describes the most important and basic part of the speech, it cannot represent other delicate speech signals that influence the naturalness of speech. Finally, it is very complicated to manipulate the formant synthesis model. For a refined synthesizer, manipulation parameters can be in the dozens, making it difficult for realization.

As a result, researchers went on to find and develop other, new synthesis techniques. Inspired by direct recording and the playing of waveform, some came up with the synthesis technique of waveform splicing, which can be represented by the linear prediction coding (LPC) and PSOLA synthesis technique. Different from the formant synthesis technique, waveform splicing synthesis relies on splicing the recorded waveform of the synthesized element rather than on the simulation of the articulation.

5.7.2.2 Linear prediction coding parameter syntheses

The development of the speech coding and decoding technique has a close relationship to the development of waveform splicing, of which the development of LPC technique had an enormous impact on the development of the waveform technique. The LPC synthesis technique is in essence a coding technique of the time waveform, and its purpose is to slow down the transmission rate of the time signals.

The Institute of Acoustic, Chinese Academic of Science has done a lot of work applying the LPC synthesis technique to research on speech synthesis and TTS of Mandarin Chinese. They introduced the multiple-pulse excitation the LPC technique in 1987, the technique of vector quantization in 1989, and the technique of coding excitation in 1993. They have made significant contributions to the application of the LPC synthesis technique in the synthesis of Mandarin Chinese.

LPC synthesis technique has the advantage of being simple and straightforward. Its synthesis process is in essence a simple process of decoding and splicing. Additionally, as the synthetic unit of the LPC splicing technique is the waveform data of the speech and all the speech information is preserved intact, it is possible to obtain a signal synthetic unit of high naturalness.

However, natural speech flow differs greatly from speech in isolation. If it were as simple as splicing all the isolated speech together bluntly, then the quality of the overall speech is bound to be unsatisfactory. On the other hand, the LPC technique is essentially the process of recoding and replaying; therefore the LPC technique is inadequate for yielding satisfactory continuous speech. Hence the LPC technique has to be integrated with other techniques for the sake of improving the quality of the synthesized speech.

The PSOLA synthesis technique (pitch synchronous overlap add) put forward in 1980s has infused new life into the waveform splicing synthesis technique. PSOLA concentrates on the manipulation of suprasegmental features of the speech signal such as F0, syllable duration, and intensity, which are of crucial importance to the manipulation and modification of speech. Therefore the PSOLA technique has the advantage of being more revisable over the LPC technique, which makes it possible to yield speech of high naturalness.

The main features of the PSOLA technique are as follows: Before splicing the speech waveform segments, it is necessary to adjust the prosodic features of the spliced segment to the context using the PSOLA algorithm, which preserves the primary suprasegmental features of the original speech while at the same time enabling the spliced segments to be in line with the context so as to produce speech of high naturalness and intelligibility.

Universities and institutions in China have done extensive research on how to apply the PSOLA technique to the TTS system of Mandarin Chinese. Based on research on the PSOLA technique, the Mandarin TTS system has been developed, and measures to improve this technique and the naturalness of the synthetic speech have been proposed.

The PSOLA technique inherits the strengths of the traditional waveform splicing technique, being simple, straightforward, and fast. Furthermore, PSOLA can control the prosodic parameters of the speech signals conveniently and is ready for synthesizing continuous speech. All these characteristics have made it widely applicable.

However, the PSOLA technique also bears disadvantages. First, PSOLA is based on the fundamental tone synchronous speech analysis/synthesis technique, which requires accurate identification of the fundamental tone cycles and their starting points. Any erroneous identification of the cycle and its starting point will affect the outcome of the PSOLA technique. Moreover, PSOLA is in essence a simple mapping and splicing of the waveform. It is not yet settled as to whether this splicing can achieve a smooth transition and how it affects the frequency parameter. Therefore it is likely to yield unfavorable outcomes in the course of the synthetic process.

5.7.2.3 LMA vocal tract model

As people are becoming more and more stringent about the naturalness and quality of the synthetic speech, the PSOLA algorithm has been found with shortcomings; namely, it is weak at adjusting prosodic parameters, and it cannot handle coarticulation. Therefore, another speech synthesis method has been proposed that is based on the LMA vocal track model. Similar to the traditional parameter synthesis, this method can agilely adjust the prosodic parameter, and moreover it can produce better synthetic qualities than the PSOLA algorithm.

At present, the main speech synthesis techniques are the formant synthesis technique and the waveform splicing synthesis technique based on the PSOLA algorithm. Both techniques have their advantages. The formant technique is more mature and has a lot of research behind it, while the PSOLA technique is relatively new and has a bright prospect for development.

In the past, these two methods were basically developed independently. Nowadays many scholars are starting to investigate the relationship between them and trying to combine the two techniques efficiently for the sake of generating more natural speech. For example, researchers in Tsinghua University have done research on applying the formant revision technique to the PSOLA algorithm and the improvement of the sonic system. They have yielded a Mandarin TTS system of higher naturalness.

The TTS system that is based on waveform splicing has to meet at least the following four requirements during the course of splicing and prosodic manipulation so as to ensure quality outcomes:

1. The frequency spectrum has to be smooth in the boundary of the synthetic units.
2. Frequency should be kept constant during time scale modification.
3. Time should not be changed during pitch scale modification.
4. Modification on the amplitude of the synthetic unit should be linear.

5.7.3 Concept to speech system

Speech synthesis is the technology that makes the computer generate speech. Its goal is to make the computer output clear, natural, and fluent. According to different levels of human speech function, speech synthesis can also be divided into three levels: from TTS synthesis, from concept to speech synthesis, from intention to speech synthesis. These three levels reflect the different processes of forming speech content in the human brain and involve the high-level neural activities of the human brain. At present, mature speech synthesis technology can only complete TTS synthesis (or TTS technology).

A typical TTS synthesis system is shown in Fig. 5.9. The system can be divided into the text analysis module, prosody prediction module, and acoustic model. The following three modules are briefly introduced.

5.7.3.1 Text analysis module

Text analysis module is the front end of the speech synthesis system. Its function is to analyze the input natural language text, output as many language-related features and information as possible, and provide the necessary information for the follow-up system. Its processing flow is as follows: text preprocessing, text normalization, automatic word segmentation, part of speech tagging, word sound conversion, polyphonic disambiguation, grapheme to phoneme (G2P), phrase analysis, etc. Text preprocessing includes deleting

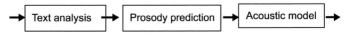

Figure 5.9 Typical structure of speech synthesis system.

invalid symbols, breaking sentences, etc. The task of text normalization is to recognize the nonordinary characters (such as mathematical symbols, physical symbols, etc.) in the text and transform them into a standardized expression. The task of character sound conversion is to convert the text sequence to be synthesized into the corresponding pinyin sequence. Multi tone word disambiguation is to solve the problem of multi tone word. G2P deals with words of unknown pronunciation that may appear in the text, which often appear in English or other alphabetic languages.

5.7.3.2 Prosody prediction module

Prosody is the cadence and priority in actual speech flow, such as the location distribution and grade differences of stress, the location distribution and grade difference of the prosody boundary, the basic framework of intonation and its relationship with tone, rhythm, stress, etc. Because these features need to be realized by the change of features on more than one segment, they are also called ultrasonic segment features. Prosody performance is a very complex phenomenon. The study of prosody involves many fields, such as phonetics, linguistics, acoustics, psychology, and so on. The prosody prediction module receives the processing results of the text analysis module and predicts the corresponding prosody features, including the suprasegmental features such as pause and sentence stress. The main function of the prosody module is to ensure the natural cadence of synthesized speech and to improve the naturalness of it.

5.7.3.3 Acoustic model module

The input of the acoustic model re the text-related features provided by the text analysis module and the prosody features provided by the prosody prediction module, and the output is the natural speech waveform. At present, the mainstream methods of the acoustic model can be summarized into two kinds: one is the splicing synthesis method based on time-domain waveform. The acoustic model module first models the information of fundamental frequency, time length, energy, and rhythm, then selects the most appropriate speech unit in a large-scale corpus according to the information, and then generates the natural speech waveform through the splicing algorithm. The other kind is the synthesis method based on speech parameters. The acoustic model module obtains the acoustic parameters of speech, such as spectral parameters, fundamental frequency, etc., according to the guidance of the prosody and text information, and then generates the natural speech waveform through the speech parameter synthesizer.

The acoustic model of a speech synthesis system can be divided into two categories: the voice organ—based model and the signal-based model. The former attempts to directly model the whole human speech organ, through which speech synthesis is carried out. This method is also known as speech synthesis based on physiological parameters. The latter is based on the speech signal itself to model or directly to select and splice the primitives. In comparison, the method based on the signal model has a stronger application value, so it has attracted more attention from researchers and industry. Many methods are based on the signal model, including primitive splicing synthesis and statistical parameter speech synthesis.

5.8 Attention

Attention, as a subject for research, is both old and new. More than 100 years ago, attention was the subject for experimental psychologists as the control center of human behavior and psychological activity. Subsequently its dominant position was gradually lost due to the behaviorism and psychological school of Gestalt, which caused the study of attention to fall to a low point. The behaviorism school denies the initiative of human behavior, but Gestalt regards notice and consciousness as integrated. Until the middle period of the 50th, with the rise of cognitive psychology, the importance of attention in information processing by the human brain was recognized again. In the past 10 years or somewhat longer, with the rapid development of brain imaging technology, cranial nerve physiology, and theory brain model theory, attention is not only a psychological concept but also a visible neural network whose cognitive and neural physiological effects can be measured. Now, attention studies have become a branch that can potentially uncover the secrets of the brain—a hot subject for neural scientific research.

Attention involves many kinds of sensory systems, such as the senses of vision, hearing, and touch. Here we only discuss the functional network, anatomic localization and synergetic mechanism of visual attention mechanism.

5.8.1 Attention network

Though the studies on the attention mechanism have a history of more than 100 years, it has been an undecided problem as to whether an independent attention system exists in the brain. This is because the attention mechanism cannot cause a unique and qualitative feeling experience like touch can; at the same time, neither can it generate muscle action responses automatically like the system of action muscles. We have some choice with respect to feeling stimulation, memory information, or muscle action response, but all these do not mean that there is an independent attention system in the brain because the whole brain has participated in the course of choice.

Recent years, with the rapid development of the technology of brain imaging and nerve physiological research, it has become possible to isolate the attention network from other information processing systems. Take, for example, the advantages of the positive electronic fault (PET) scan and function magnetic resonance imaging technology, which can more accurately measure the change of brain blood flow regionally during the specific attention task and then confirm each function structure's dissect location in the attention subnetwork. At present, though knowledge about attention network dissection still incomplete, brain imaging of existing brain and neural physiology has proved that the attention mechanism is not characteristic of a single brain district and that it is also not a function of the whole brain. There is really an independent attention network [8] in the human brain for three reasons: First, an attention system and a data handling system are separate in dissecting; though they interact with the other parts of the brain, they keep their own characteristics. Second, attention composed of a network of several dissection areas is not a characteristic of a single center, and it is also not the general function of overall operation of the brain. Third, there are different functions among the attention network dissect areas, and they can be described in the academic language of cognition.

According to the existing study results, Posner divides the attention network into three subsystems: anterior attention system, posterior attention system, and vigilance attention system [8]. The anterior attention system involves frontal cortex, anterior cingulate gyrus, and basal ganglion. The posterior attention system includes frontal-parietal cortex, pulvinar, and superior colliculus. The vigilance attention system then mainly involves the input from the locus coeruleus norepinephrine in the right hemisphere to the cerebral cortex. The functions of these three subsystems can be summarized as orientation control, guiding search, and keeping vigilance, respectively.

5.8.2 Attention function

5.8.2.1 Orientation control

Orientation control means that the brain leads the focus-of-attention to the place of interest and then exercises the ability of space choosing. There are two kind methods of choosing space information: First, the attention mechanism involves the eyes. Urged by the outstanding goal in the visual field or personal will, the observer's eyes move to the place of interest and watch the corresponding goal. The eyes enable the goal representation in the retina central concave through the watching mechanism, thus obtaining more detailed goal information. This kind of orientation control and attention shift system that relies on eye movement to be realized is called explicit attention shift system. The second kind of attention transfer mechanism does not involve any eye movement or head movement. It occurs between two large beating eye movements and turns attention to a position outside the fixation point in a covert way. This kind of attention transfer is called implicit attention transfer. Posner holds that implicit attention may involve three kinds attention: removal of attention from the present focus-of-attention (involving the brain terminal leaf); moving the attention pointer to the area where the goal is (in the charge of the midbrain district); reading the data in the place of the attention point (the function of the thalamus's pillow). Humans have the ability of the implicit attention shift system. In an experiment when the attention was turned to a certain place outside the watched point implicitly by an attention clue, the person tested not only improved the simulating response speed to this place and reduced the threshold value of measuring but also strengthened the corresponding electric activity of scalp. The directivity of attention explains that we can't pay attention to many goals in the visual field at the same time. Rather, we move our attention point sequentially one by one; that is to say, we can only adopt a serial way of moving. But we can choose a corresponding input processing yardstick with the vision. The attention point can focus finely and scatter in a wider space range. In the attention cognitive model, regarding the attention point as the spotlight of the variable focus reflects this kind of characteristic vividly.

The directional alternative of attention is related to the limited information handling capacity of the attention system. The enhancement of place information processing efficiency comes with the cost of inhibiting the nonattention information place.

In a clinical observation showed that for the patients with right parietal lobe injury, when the attention cues were presented in the right visual field and the targets were presented in the left visual field, the directional control ability was seriously damaged; But in other situations, the harm is little, indicating that when the ability is damaged, attention is removed from the inducing clue place. From PET data obtained from a normal tested person, when attention moves from one place to another, whether the movement is driven by the will or stimulated by the external world, the area affected is mainly on the terminal leaf on left and right sides, where the blood flow obviously increases. This is the unique area activated by attention shift. The record from a sober terminal leaf cell from a monkey proves that the terminal leaf neuron is involved in attention orientation control. P-study reveals that the dissection network modulating the exodermis of other lines selectively crosses thalamus's pillow core; strain, loss, interference with, or strengthening of the goal causes the obvious effect in the thalamus pillow core too.

PET measures and clinical observation indicate that the attention functions of the two hemispheres of brain are asymmetric. Attention moves in the two visual fields of the left and right sides can enhance blood flow in the terminal leaf on the right side, and the enhancement of blood flow in the left terminal leaf only relates to the attention move of right visual field. This find could explain why damage of the right brain hemisphere causes more attention damage than damage to the left. But a normal brain, with an equal number of disturbance targets distributed in the left and right visual fields, cannot accomplish the mask quickly enough to concentrate on single vision. But to the patient with a resected callosum, when disturbance targets are distributed in double visual fields, the speed of searching for the targets is two times faster than when disturbance targets are concentrated in single vision. This means that after the injury of corpus callosum, the attention mechanisms of the left and right hemispheres are disconnected.

5.8.2.2 Guiding search

In the task of vision searching, the guidance function of attention, is obvious. The time that the tested subject takes to find the goal increases linearly with increase in the disturbance targets' number. However, finding a certain goal does not require searching through all goals. There is conclusive evidence that the search can go on under the guidance of the characteristic of position in the goal. These characteristics include color, form, sport, etc.

The experiment proves that when attention is paid to color, form, or sport, the neural activity of the brain frontal lobe district is obviously strengthened, but there was no enlarged effect in the brain terminal leaf district. This shows that guiding the search is the responsibility of the pre attention system.

In the preceding attention system, the anterior cingulate gyrus's function is called the execution function. Execution has two meaning. First, the organizing brain interior must notify the "executor" of the process course—what is taking place; then the "executor" implements attention control to the whole system. The experiment found that the neural activity number in this area increases with the increase of target number and the reduction of the training number. This is identical to attention's cognitive theory. In dissecting, the anterior cingulate gyrus has pathway between the after parietal and prefrontal cortex. The prefrontal cortex plays a key role in keeping the representation of the past things. And the anterior cingulate gyrus involves the clear feel and control of the target. These finds indicates that before-attention system is the neural basis of willed attention and the central of issuing orders by brain [9]. This kind of conjecture may be reasonable because the frontal lobe district of the human brain's cortex area is exactly the cortex that is related to make plans; it is a psychological supreme control center.

The experiment also found that choosing according to position or according to characteristics such as color, form, etc. interferes with each other less. So some might speculate that the before-attention system and the after-attention system may the measure of time share or time division.

5.8.2.3 Keeps vigilance

The function of the vigilance system is to make the brain ready and vigilant, in order to deal with signals with supreme priority fast. Keeping vigilance is closely related to attention and involves a subnetwork of attention.

The positive electron fault scans reveal that when trying to keep the vigilant state, the blood flow of the right frontal lobe district strengthened; and when this area is damaged, brain loses the ability to stay vigilant. It means that keeping the vigilance state involves an attention subsystem lying in the right side of brain.

5.8.3 Selective attention

If you are at a cocktail party or in a noisy hotel, there are three ways to help you pay attention to the speech information of the person you want to hear (i.e., pay attention to the target): First, the distinctive sensory characteristics of the target speech (for example, high and low pitch, step, rhythm); second, sound intensity (loudness); third, the location of the sound source. After paying attention to the physical characteristics of the target speaker's voice, you can avoid being disturbed by the semantic content of the nontarget speaker's speech information. Obviously, the sound intensity of the target also helps. In addition, you may intuitively use a certain strategy to locate the voice, so that the task of dual ear simultaneous listening becomes the task of dual ear separate listening: You turn one ear to the target speaker, while the other ear avoids the target speaker.

The mechanisms of selective attention include the filter model, attenuation model, reaction selection model, energy allocation model, etc.

5.8.3.1 Filter model

This model was initially proposed by the famous British psychologist D. Broadbent in 1958. It is an earlier theory model about attention. The model is called the single-channel model by Welford. The filter model thinks that a large amount of information comes from the external world, but the processing ability of people's advanced center of the nervous system is extremely limited. Thus the bottleneck appears. In order to prevent the system from overloading, a filter is needed to regulate information and to choose some of it to enter the advanced analysis stage. Other information may be stored in a certain memory temporarily and then decline rapidly.

The function of attention is just like the filter. Through its filtration, it enables some information of the input channel to enter the advanced center through the limited passing of internal capacity, while other information is filtered. So the work of attention is done in an all or nothing way.

At a cocktail party or other kind of party, you are talking with several people absorbedly. At this moment, you cannot discern the conversation of other people, but if someone outside mentions your name, you may notice, while other people talking with you might not. When we put sound on both earpieces of the headset at the same time, the stimulant message that each ear accepts is different. We investigate the relationship between the tested reaction information and the accepted information of both ears through the experiment; thus we can understand the characteristics of tested attention. The experimental result finds that the test can reproduce the stimulant information according to the characteristics of the material in such an experiment, such as 6, 2, 9; DEAR AUNT JANE.

Regarding this kind of experimental results, there are two views:
1. The filter channel can be shifted quickly.
2. The working mechanism of attention does not work with the single-channel model and in all-or-nothing way, the filter model is incorrect.

5.8.3.2 Decay model

The decay model is proposed based on the revised filter model by American psychologist A. M. Treisman in 1960 [10]. This theory does not think the filter works in a whole-or-nothing way. The channel that accepts information is not single channel but multichannel. This model is the result of Treisman improving the filter model based on the experimental results of processing the nonfollow information in the following experiment.

The decay model asserts that the working way of attention is not by the single-channel way of the whole-or-nothing but the multichannel way. However, the information processing of the multichannel is different in the degree of information processing of each channel, as shown in Fig. 5.10.

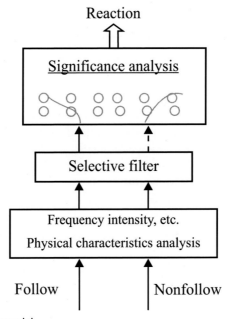

Figure 5.10 Decay model.

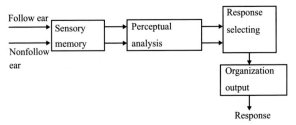

Figure 5.11 Response selection model of attention.

The information processing way of the follow ear is shown in the filter model, while the information of the nonfollow ear is also probably processed through the filter. Nevertheless, the signal of the nonfollow ear is processed when it passes the filter, so it is denoted with the dotted line. In the course of significance analysis, it is probably filtered or probably strengthened because of some other factors too (such as one's own name).

The decay model introduces an important concept for the information that enters the advanced analysis level threshold. It states that the excitement threshold with which information stored in the brain is at the advanced analysis level is different from one another, thus influencing the selection of the filter.

5.8.3.3 Response selection model
In 1963 J. Deutsch proposed the response selection model [11]. This model (see Fig. 5.11) holds that attention lies not in selecting the perception stimuli but in selecting the response to the stimulus. This theory thinks that all the stimuli felt by the sense organ should enter the senior analytic process. The center is processed according to certain rules; thus it can react to important information, while the unimportant information may be soon washed out by new content.

5.8.3.4 Energy distribution model
In 1973 D. Kahneman proposed the energy distribution model [12]. The energy distribution model states that attention is an energy or resource that is limited in quantity for people to use for executing the task. The resources and arousal are linked in people's activity, and its arousal level is influenced by many factors, such as mood, medicine, and tension of muscle, etc. The energy produced is assigned to different possible activities through a distribution scheme and finally forms various responses. Fig. 5.12 shows the sketch map of the energy distribution model.

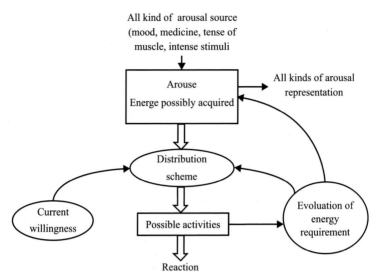

Figure 5.12 Energy distribution model.

5.8.4 Attention in deep learning

Deep learning based on attention has recently become a hot spot in neural network research. The attention mechanism was first proposed in the field of visual images. It was going to be proposed in the 1990s, but in 2014, the Google mind team published the paper [13]. The motivation of their research is also inspired by the mechanism of human attention. When people observe images, in fact, they don't see every pixel in the whole image all at one time. Most of them focus on specific parts of the image according to their needs. Moreover, humans will learn from the previous images where they should focus their attention in the future.

Fig. 5.13 shows the recurrent neural network (RNN) attention model proposed by V. Mnih et al. [13]. Through the attention to learn the part of an image to be processed, it processes the attention part of the pixel for each current state rather than all the pixels of the image. The advantage is that fewer pixels need to be processed, which reduces the complexity of the task. Here, the attention problem is regarded as a goal-directed sequential decision-making process, which can interact with the visual environment. At each point in time, the agent can observe only the part of the global situation according to the perceptron with limited bandwidth. We can see that the application of attention in images is very similar to the mechanism of human attention.

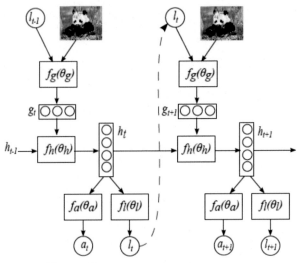

Figure 5.13 Recurrent attention model.

Y. Bengio et al. used the mechanism similar to attention to carry out translation and alignment simultaneously in machine translation tasks [14]. Their work was the first to propose the application of the attention mechanism to natural language processing (NLP). Then, a similar RNN model extension based on attention mechanism was applied to various NLP tasks.

In September 2016 Google announced the development of a Google neural machine translation system (GNMT) [15]. Google's neural machine translation system uses a large ANN of deep learning to infer the most relevant translation by using millions of more extensive sources to improve the quality of translation. The results are then rearranged to form a grammatical translation based on human language.

The GNMT system improves the previous Google translation system. The GNMT system can handle zero point translation, that is, directly translating one language into another, such as Chinese to Japanese. Google Translate used to translate the source language into English and then English into the target language rather than going directly from one language to another. The development of a neural machine translation, represented by the GNMT system, provides a necessary guarantee for the future human—computer integrated translation.

References

[1] G.E. Hinton, R. Salakhutdinov, Reducing the dimensionality of data with neural networks, Science 313 (5786) (2006) 504−507.

[2] J.J. Gibson, The Ecological Approach to Visual Perception, Houghton Mifflin, Boston, 1979.

[3] L. Chen, Topological structure in visual perception, Science 218 (1982) 699−700.

[4] L. Chen, The topological approach to perceptual organization (invited lead paper) Vis. Cognition 12 (2005) 553−637.

[5] D.C. van Essen, Functional organization of primate visual cortex, in: A. Peters, E.G. Jones (Eds.), Cerebral Cortex, vol. 3, Plenum, New York, 1985, pp. 259−329.

[6] R. Mayeux, E.R. Kandel, Disorders of language: the aphasias, in: E.R. Kandel, J.H. Schwartz, T.M. Jessell (Eds.), Principles of Neural Science, third ed., Elsevier, 1991, pp. 840−851.

[7] D. Marr, Vision: A Computational Investigation into the Human Representation and Processing of Visual Information, W. H. Freeman, San Francisco, 1982.

[8] M.I. Posner, Attention: the mechanism of consciousness, Proc. Natl Acad. Sci. U.S.A. 91 (16) (1994) 7398−7402.

[9] F. Crick, C. Koch, The problem of consciousness, Sci. Am. (1992) 152−159.

[10] A. Treisman, Perceptual grouping and attention in visual search for features and for objects, J. Exp. Psychol Hum. Percept. Perform. 8 (1982) 194−214.

[11] J. Deutsch, D. Deutsch, Attention: some theoretical considerations, Psychol. Rev. 70 (1963) 80−90.

[12] D. Kahneman, Attention and Effort, Ru, Englewood Cliffs, NJ, 1973.

[13] V. Mnih, N. Heess, A. Graves, Recurrent models of visual attention. Advances in neural information processing systems. (2014) 2204−2212.

[14] D. Bahdanau, K. Cho, Y. Bengio, Neural machine translation by jointly learning to align and translate. (2015) ICLR 2015 1−15.

[15] Y.H. Wu, M. Schuster, Z.F. Chen, et al., Google's neural machine translation system: bridging the gap. (2016) arXiv:1609.08144v2.

CHAPTER 6

Language cognition

Language is the "material shell" of thinking, which is the main driving force of human thought. Language cognition combines the psychological language model and neural science to explain how the brain gets semantics through oral and written words and to understand the neural model of human language.

6.1 Introduction

Cognitive intelligence is an advanced stage of intelligence science. It aims to conduct in-depth mechanism research and computer simulation on human natural language, knowledge expression, logical reasoning, autonomous learning, and other abilities, so as to promote machines to have similar human intelligence and even have the knowledge accumulation and application ability of human experts in various fields.

As the most basic tool for humans to express and exchange ideas, natural language exists everywhere in human social activities. Natural language processing (NLP) is the theory and technology of processing human language by computer. As an important high-level research direction of language information processing technology, NLP has always been the core topic in the field of artificial intelligence. NLP is also one of the most difficult problems due to its polysemy, being context related, fuzziness, nonsystematicness, close correlation with the environment, and wide range of knowledge involved.

Generally speaking, NLP mainly includes three parts: cognition, understanding, and generation. Natural language cognition and understanding mean letting the computer turn the input language into symbols and relations with specific meanings and then do the corresponding processing according to the user's purpose. Natural language generation system is a system that transforms computer data into natural language.

If the computer can understand and process natural language, and the information communication between human and computer can be carried out in the native language, it will be a major breakthrough in computer technology. The creation and use of natural language is the expression of

Intelligence Science
DOI: https://doi.org/10.1016/B978-0-323-85380-4.00006-3
215

the human's high intelligence. Therefore, the study of NLP will help to uncover the mystery of human high intelligence and deepen the understanding of language ability and thinking essence.

The rapid development of computer technology and artificial intelligence technology promotes the continuous progress of the NLP research. NLP can be divided into three stages:

1. *Budding and rule-based period (1960s—1980s)*: The first computer came out in 1946 and shocked the whole world. Almost at the same time, A. D. Booth of the United Kingdom and W. Weaver of the United States began to study machine translation. In 1966, the Natural Language Processing Advisory Committee of the United States submitted a report to the American Academy of Sciences, saying that "although great efforts have been made in machine translation, the development of this technology will not succeed in the foreseeable future." This has led to a low level of research on machine translation.

In this period, N. Chomsky put forward the concepts of formal language and formal grammar [1]. He put natural language and programming language on the same level and used unified mathematical methods to explain and define. Chomsky's Transformation Generation grammar (TG) has caused a great sensation in the field of linguistics, enabling the study of linguistics to enter into quantitative research.

Since the 1970s, the research of natural language has made great progress in syntactic—semantic analysis. Based on rules to establish lexical and syntactic—semantic analysis, there have been a number of influential natural language understanding systems. Representative systems of this period include LUNAR designed by W. Woods, which is the first man—machine interface to allow dialog with the database in common English [2]. The SHEDLU system designed by T. Winograd is a natural language understanding system for English dialog in the "building block world." It combines syntax, reasoning, context, and background knowledge flexibly [3]. Syntax, semantics, and pragmatics are three important factors in natural language understanding, which lead to different methods of NLP [4,5].

2. *Based on statistics and corpus period (since 1990s)*: In corpus linguistics, statistical processing technology is the main means to acquire all kinds of knowledge from the corpus [6]. Its basic idea is using corpus as the only information source. All knowledge (except the construction method of the statistical model) is obtained from the corpus. Knowledge is acquired by statistical methods, and knowledge is explained in a statistical sense. All parameters are automatically obtained from the corpus through statistical learning [7].

3. *Deep learning period (since 2008)*: Deep learning plays an important role in speech and image processing. NLP researchers begin to turn their attention to deep learning and enter a new stage of development, which is mainly reflected in the following aspects: (a) Neural word bag model, which simply averages the embedding of each word in a text sequence as the representation of the whole sequence. The disadvantage of this method is the loss of word order information. For long text, the neural bag model is more effective. However, for short text, the neural bag model is difficult to capture semantic combination information. (b) Recurrent neural networks (RNN, LSTM, GRU) can encode an indefinite-length sentence and describe the information of the sentence. (c) Convolution neural network, through multiple convolution layers and subsampling layers, finally get a fixed-length vector. (d) Encode—decode technology can realize the transformation from one sentence to another. These technologies are the core technologies of machine translation, dialog generation, and question answering systems.

There are two basic forms of natural language: spoken (oral) language and written language. Written language is more structured than spoken language, and the noise is relatively small. Oral information includes many semantic incomplete clauses. For example, if the audience does not have a good understanding of the objective and subjective knowledge of the topic of a speech, sometimes the audience may not understand the speaker's oral information. Written language understanding includes lexical analysis, grammar analysis, and semantic analysis, while oral language understanding needs to add phonetic analysis on this basis.

6.2 Oral language

6.2.1 Perceptual analysis of language input

The input signals of spoken language and of written language are quite different. For readers, the letters on the page are important physical signals; however, they will encounter a variety of sounds under different environment. So they need to identify and distinguish other "noise" related to the voice signal.

The important element of spoken language is the phoneme, which is the smallest unit to express a meaning. The brain of the listener should have the ability to deal with the difficulties caused by the speech signal, and some of the difficulties are associated with signal variability. The phoneme is usually not in the form of a separate piece of information, which causes additional difficulties for the listener. In other words, they lack segmentation. In written language, however, physical boundaries separate words and sentence. When you read an English article, you will find the spaces between words and each sentence ended with a full point. These physical tips help you distinguish between words and sentences. On the other hand, the boundaries of the spoken word are ambiguous. In addition to a pause, an oral sentence always lacks a clear gap.

There are a lot of changes in the listener's auditory input. In spoken language, it is impossible to get a one-to-one contact for physical signal and the memory representation, so the human perception of the auditory transmission should be considered. In the face of such variability of the physical signals, how is the meaning of the speech extracted for the brain, and what is the abstract unit of speech input representation?

Some researchers propose that these statements are based on the spectral characteristics of the input signal. These spectral features vary with the sounds. These features may form a speech representation, while the speech representation may be encodings extracted from the phoneme. But other researchers present different representations of the unit, such as the phoneme, syllable, and the way the speaker has planned. Other theorists refuse to accept that sound signal can be represented by discrete units.

Sound information from a speech rhythm and a speaker's voice can help us break down the speech stream into meaningful parts. The rhythm of speech comes from the duration of the word and the change of the position of the pause. Rhyme is obvious in all the spoken languages, and it can be detected when the narrator puts forward a question or emphasizes something. The narrator may increase the frequency of the sound at the end of a story or raise the volume of the sound and add a pause for emphasis.

6.2.2 Rhythm perception

Rhythm is a common feature of all natural languages. It plays a very important role in verbal communication. By comparing the combination of voice information, rhythm can show the better speaker's intention and understanding. The perfection of rhythm control model determines the natural property of synthetic language. Rhythm perception has attracted increasing attention in the field of linguistics and language engineering. It is vital to understand the rhythm of natural language for research on speech coding and the increase of speech synthetics. Speech stream information is composed of speech information and rhythm information. The former is revealed by timbre while the latter is revealed by prosodic features.

Earlier research focused on the processing of grammar and semantics, leaving rhythm aside. Until the 1960s of the last century, researchers began to systematically study rhythm.

6.2.2.1 Prosodic features

Prosodic features are comprised of three aspects: stress, intonation, and prosodic structure (boundary structure of prosodic components). Because they can cover two or more sound segments, they are also called supra segmental features. Prosodic structure is a hierarchical structure, which owns a variety of classification methods. Three levels are generally recognized: rhythm of the word, prosodic phrase, and intonation phrase [8].

1. *Chinese stress*:
   a. Word stress and sentence stress
   b. The type of sentence stress
   c. The location and level of stress of the sentence

   Chinese prosodic stress is complex. In the announcer language, a large number of contrast methods, including the contrast of the distance and the time of contrast, are adopted.

2. *Chinese intonation*: The intonation structure is composed of a combination of linguistic accents. It is a language form, which shows the function semantics of grammar by information focus. Rhythm can be obtained from the tree type relations. Multihierarchy rhythm units are constructed via finite decomposition of acoustic form. The language stress and rhythm stress can regulate the high and low audio lines of pitch. The combination of all audio range features can distinguish different tone types. Therefore the tone is the important element for readjustment for pitch, while pitch range forms the basis of function pitch and intonation.

   The basic elements of Chinese pitch are composed of prehead, head, nucleus, and tail. The typical construction of pitch is as the follows [9]:
   a. The head and nucleus is accented with strong stress, while prehead has only tone syllables; there is no accented stress in tail.
   b. A distinct gap is formed after the high line is down in the nucleus.
   c. In the nucleus of the voice, a syllable is obviously lighter. After a syllable and a significant rise, the high line appears to fall in nucleus pitch.

Many facts demonstrate that in the light of the syllable combination, the level of high and the low pitch is changed with the language itself. In the former strong and weak group, after a syllable of the high point goes down, with the potential difference, the latter may be lightened. When there is strong language at the back, the high notes can be restored to a certain distance.

In a statement, the falling of a high pitch line is soon finished. Therefore, at the beginning of the tail or after one or two syllables, the high pitch line has already been to the lowest level; this is the falling type of high pitch. Depending on question type, the falling of high pitch can be achieved gradually. That is to say, the first few syllables in the tail will show a slowly declining curve, and this is the gradually falling type. The high and low pitch lines are two independent factors, so the statement tone is the combination of sudden falling and low pitch falling and is not the adjustment type of range factor of a single degree of freedom. Similarly, the question tone is the combination of the gradual falling of high pitch and low pitch folding, which is composed of two freedoms, forming four basic combinations. The fact of voice shows that the sudden falling and low pitch folding are the normal imperative tone besides the statement and questions. The gradual falling of high pitch and the delay of low pitch are very important exclamation intonations. These four function tones have different variations. Different intonations and other pitches have a lot to do with the whole or part of the adjustment of voice range.

3. *Intonation marking*:
   a. High note without marks—a sudden drop of tone. High pitch line suddenly drops after the nuclear; the light syllable will show up.
   b. High note with marks—a gradual drop of tone. High pitch line gradually drops after the nuclear, and the light syllable will show up. Some research shows that the sudden raise and falling will appear after the four tones in Chinese pronunciation.
   c. Low note without marks denotes decurrence tone. The low note has a large rise and fall.
   d. Low note with marks denotes the folding of intonation. The low note is getting smaller and smaller, and the convergence is the most obvious in the nuclear and tail.

   The intonation of the interrogative sentence is strongly convergent, and the imperative tone is of weak convergence. There may be other unknown features. The classification of function tone and intonation are consistent, including similar acoustic characteristics and the increase of the bandwidth characteristics. They are minimum adjustments of the high and low pitch lines. The meaning of "intonation" is related to the basic function of the functional intonation (semantic).

4. *Prosodic structure*:
   a. Prosodic word: Chinese rhythm is reflected by a double syllable or three syllables. The inner rhythm cannot be stopped, while a pause can appear at the boundary of the prosodic word.
   b. Prosodic word group: It is generally composed of two or three more closely linked prosodic words. There is usually no obvious pause between the prosodic words in one prosodic word group, and there is a pause at the end of the prosodic word group that cannot necessarily be observed—a clear silence segment from the language point of view.
   c. Prosodic phrase: A prosodic phrase consists of one or several prosodic word groups. There is usually a distinct pause between word groups that can be observed clearly as a silence segment. The important feature of the prosodic phrase is the gradual decline of the low voice line.
   d. Intonation phrase: This is composed of one or several prosodic phrases. Intonation phrases can be simple sentences, complex sentences, or clauses, isolated by punctuation marks. After the intonation phrase, there is usually a long pause.

As can be seen from this definition, there is an inclusion relation among four prosodic units: The boundary of the intonation phrase must be the boundary of the prosodic phrase, while the boundary of the prosodic phrase must be the boundary of the prosodic word group. But the boundary of the prosodic word group is not necessarily the boundary of dictionary, and vice versa.

6.2.2.2 Prosodic modeling

The characteristics of context and rhythm have a strong correlation under different contexts. The distribution of prosodic features is influenced by contextual information, and this distribution satisfies a certain probability rather than a simple function. From a probabilistic point of view, given a sentence as a parameter, the corresponding rhythm features as a parameter, which is the largest of all prosodic features:

$$Y = \underset{n}{\operatorname{argmax}} P(Y_n|A) \tag{6.1}$$

Based on the Bayesian formula:

$$Y = \underset{n}{\arg\max}\, P(Y_n|A) = \underset{n}{\arg\max}\, \frac{P(A|Y_n)P(Y_n)}{P(A)} \tag{6.2}$$

The statistical distribution of the context information can be considered a constant, and then Eq. (6.2) will be further converted to:

$$Y = \underset{n}{\arg\max}\, P(Y_n|A) = \underset{n}{\arg\max}\, P(A|Y_n)P(Y_n) \tag{6.3}$$

Eq. (6.3) shows that the $P(Y_n|A)$ can be converted to $P(A|Y_n)$, and that $P(Y_n)$ is the distribution of prosodic features, which is reflected by the occurrence probability and interaction between the prosodic features. $P(A|Y_n)$ is a priori probability. In theory, it can be used as the basis for its implementation.

6.2.2.3 Prosodic labeling

Prosodic labeling is a qualitative description of the prosodic features with language function in speech signals. The labeling sentence has the functional linguistics, like intonation patterns, stress patterns, and tonal changes in prosodic structure. The changes of the pitch under the influence of different tones are of prosodic labeling, while the inherent variations of tones for vowel and collaborative pronunciation for different syllables do not belong to prosodic labeling. Prosodic labeling is often of hierarchy, the segment of sound becomes the basis for prosodic labeling, therefore becoming an essential hierarchy. The labeling for different levels is based on the practical application and characteristics of speech. Chinese prosodic labeling system should have the following characteristics:

1. *Reliability*: Different labeling should be consistent with human annotation.
2. *Comprehensiveness*: The most important prosodic phenomena should be revealed.
3. *Learnability*: Labeling can be learned in a short period of time.
4. *Compatibility*: The labeling system should be combined with the latest methods of speech synthesis, speech recognition, and the current syntax, semantics, and pragmatics.
5. *Operability*: The labeling symbol should be simple.
6. *Open*: The uncertainty of the label item is allowed to exist.
7. *Readability*: The labeled symbol can be identified by machines.

From the viewpoint of engineering applications, the prosodic labeling is a description of the phonological system, which is related to linguistics and speech. It is easy to model the correlation between linguistics and speech information based on the labeled information. Therefore, prosodic labeling plays a more and more important role in oral speech recognition and the speech synthesis system.

Prosodic labeling has a hierarchy, and each level marks a different prosodic or related phenomenon. Users can choose a certain labeling level based on individual needs. The system is divided into two levels in the Chinese Tone and Break Index (C-TOBI's) prosodic labeling system:

1. *Syllable level*: Mark the phonetic form of Putonghua syllables, such as Putonghua with 1, 2, 3, 4 respectively for four tones, light tone with 0. The tone is marked after Pinyin.

2. *Actual pronunciation level*: Labeling the actual pronunciation of consonants, vowels, and tones. The International Phonogram Symbol system labeling convention for standard chinese (SAMPA-C) is adopted.

3. *Tone level*: The construction of tone is determined by prosodic structure and stress. Namely, if the stress structure and the prosodic structure are decided, the tone curve can be decided as well. The research shows that the change of the tone is mainly demonstrated in tone range and order, which is based on the change of the tone. The tone range will change based on the psychological status, mood, and prosodic structure, etc. Therefore, the label for tones should reflect the expansion and narrowing of tone range. Besides, it should reveal the trend of the whole curve of the tone.

The segmentation is performed on each speech unit (including a syllable, tone, or even smaller voice unit) and then gives a detailed description of the characteristics of sound. The Chinese audio segment labeling should be performed on different levels. The label expansion for the speech segment is mainly focused on labeling the actual pronunciation based on regular pronunciation and labeling the phenomenon of sound change on segments and supra segments. Therefore, the Chinese phonetic system corresponding to the use of SAMPA-C is adopted. For the spoken language corpus, we should also label the language and nonlanguage phenomena.

SAMPA is a universal and internationally recognized reading and speech keyboard symbol system, which is widely used in segment labeling systems. A practical SAMPA-C symbol system is already formulated in Mandarin pronunciation. We hope that this system can be extended, including Chinese dialects. Therefore we must first determine the establishment of the SAMPA-C principle:

1. The Chinese language symbol is formulated based on the symbol system of SAMPA (http://www.phon.ucl.ac.uk/home/sampa/).
2. An additional symbol should be appended for the special speech phenomenon of Chinese.
3. In an open system, a new symbol can be added, and those not applicable can be amended.

SAMPA-C mainly focuses on labeling the Chinese audio segment, that is, designing a Chinese label system for consonants, vowels, and tones and the symbol system of Mandarin. Besides the specific voice symbol, systems designed for the Guangzhou dialect, Shanghai dialect, Fuzhou dialect, and other dialects can be expanded based on this mode.

6.2.2.4 Prosodic generation

Prosodic generation has attracted attention as the word can be considered part of phonological encoding from the beginning. With the development of research methods, prosodic generation for phrases and sentences is also studied. These studies are mainly conducted from the perspective of information processing. Some representative prosodic generation models are the Shattuck-Hufnagel scanned copy model and Dell connectionism model. These two models do not specifically discuss prosodic generation. So far, the most comprehensive prosodic encoding and processing model is presented by W. J. M. Levelt. [10].

Levelt believes that during the generation of spoken sentences, all the sentence processing stages are parallel and gradual. There are different prosodic encoding processes (i.e., some on the word level and others on the sentence level). During the expansion of a sentence based on grammatical structure, the audio plan for vocabulary occurs at the same time. The vocabulary is generally divided into two parts: characters (including semantic and syntactic features) and morpheme extraction (including morphology and phonology). The latter is performed at the morpheme prosody stage, which needs characters as input to extract corresponding term and prosodic structure. Thus the generated prosodic features do not need to know the audio segment information. This morphological and prosodic information is used to extract the audio segments of the word (including the location of the phoneme and syllable) during the extraction phase, and the prosody and sound segments are combined.

At the final stage, the prosody generator executes the language planning, resulting in the sentence prosody and intonation patterns. There are two main steps for the generation of prosody: First, prosody units, such as prosodic words, prosodic phrases, and intonation phrase are generated; then a rhythm grid of prosody structure is generated (rhythm can denote stress and time pattern). Specifically, the generation for prosody units is as follows: The results of morphology-prosody extraction are combined with connection components to form prosodic words. A prosodic phrase can be constructed based on the grammatical structure of the sentence and other information. Intonation phrase is obtained via the pause at some point during the audio stream. The generation of the rhythm grid is based on the prosody structure of the sentence and rhythm grid for the single word.

Levelt presented a new point of prosody generation for word generation in 1999 [11], claiming there is word prosody pattern in a stress language such as in Holland, England, and Germany. Namely, the stress is on the first syllable. Therefore, the stress of a regular word is not extracted but is automatically generated based on this rule. The stress of an irregular word cannot be generated automatically. Thus only irregular words of the prosodic structure are stored as a part of the speech code. The prosodic structure of irregular words is used to guide the prosody of irregular words. The prosody of the result is the generation and a larger prosodic unit.

These models are constructed based on the study of English, Dutch, and German. Compared with these languages, Chinese pronunciation owns two significant features: The number of syllables is small, only one-tenth of the English language; Chinese is a tonal language, while English and other languages are stress languages without tone. Thus the mechanism of the prosody generation in Chinese is different from these models [8]. However, there are few studies of Chinese prosody generation.

6.2.2.5 Cognitive neuroscience of prosody generation

Levelt et al. analyzed research results of 58 brain function images using the meta-analysis method [11], coming to the conclusion that during the generation of vocabulary, the left part of brain is easily activated, including the frontal gyrus (Broca's area), middle temporal gyrus, superior temporal gyrus, superior temporal gyrus, temporal back (Wernicke area), and left thalamus. The introduction of visual concept involves the occipital and ventral temporal lobe and frontal zone; and the activation comes to the Wernicke area, where the phonological code is stored. This information will spread to the Broca area, with postphonological coding (275−400 ms), followed by speech encoding. It has a lot to do with the sensory motor area and cerebellum, activating the sensory motor area to pronounce.

In 2002 Mayer et al. took advantage of fMRI to study normal prosody produced by brain activity [12], finding that the front cover at the bottom of the left and right hemispheres of the skull is relatively small and the nonoverlapping region has a correlation with prosody. The prosody of the language is activated only in the left hemisphere, while the prosody of the emotion is activated only in the right hemisphere.

6.2.3 Speech production

Language production refers to the psychological process in which people use language to express their thoughts, including the conversion from thought code to language code, and then to physiological and moving code, that is to say, the use of speech organs to produce sounds referring to a certain meaning [13]. Language production includes speech production and writing production.

Speech production (spoken language) is the process of organizing the communication intention, activating the concept, extracting the word meaning, syntax and pronunciation information, and controlling the sound of the vocal organs. It is an important part of the human language ability, and it is an important means for the expression of human consciousness.

The speech production process can be divided into three levels [14,15]: The highest level is conceptualization, which is the process of establishing the concept of intention and expression. The intermediate process is language organization, which is converting the concepts to the form of language. The last level is articulation, involving more specific pronunciation and pronunciation program, that is, converting the voice encoding into a vocal muscle exercise program, and the execution of the program. Speech organization includes vocabulary generation and grammar encoding. The latter is how to choose words and how to sort these words, namely, a syntactic framework of a sentence is produced via the meaning of words and the grammatical nature of the correct words. The former is one of the core issues in the study of speech generation. This process can be divided into five parts [11]: concept preparation, vocabulary selection, voice encoding, encoding, and articulation.

Concept preparation refers to the process of conceptualized thoughts and ideas in the brain, which is the initial stage of speech generation. Lexicalization and lexical selection are performed after concept preparation. The prepared concept will activate semantic representation corresponding to the mental lexicon, and the activated semantic representation will be converted into a lexical representation of a word. It is generally believed that there is an abstract representation between the semantic and phonological representations: lemma, which covers the grammatical features of the word. Lexicalization consists of two stages: The first stage is transferring the activation of semantic representations into the specific lemmas of the input level; that is, lemmas re activated by the concept. After a period of time, the lemma with the highest ratio of activation is activated, and the lemma is used to provide the syntax of the sentence for grammar encoding. The second stage is the phonological form. To be more specific, the activation of the intermediate layer is further transmitted to a phonetic representation for a specific lemma, thus allowing the speaker to extract the pronunciation of the lemma. The activated or extracted phonetic representation performs the so-called morphophonological encoding. In this stage, the structure of the word, the prosodic feature, and the phoneme segment are expanded, and the phonological information of the morpheme unit is combined to conform to the actual pronunciation of the syllable. It is generally believed that this syllabification is performed from left to right and that the phoneme segment and prosodic structure are extracted, respectively. The phoneme segment will be inserted into the prosodic structures from left to right to form a syllable of a word. There may be the extraction of a syllable pronunciation between speech encoding and phonate. The abstract pronunciation program that is frequently used is stored in a "warehouse," which is extracted from left to right. Activation of these procedures is also attributed to the activation of the spread of the speech encoding. Once the syllable pronunciation program is extracted, the pronunciation of a word starts immediately. The pronunciation system calculates the best scheme for performing the abstract pronunciation program, thus guiding the respiratory system and throat system to produce sound.

At present, the theoretical model of language production is symbolic and concrete but not distributed and abstract. Two important models need noticing: a two-stage interactive activation model presented by Dell [14] and a two-stage independent model (or serial processing model) by Levitt [11] and Roelofs [16]. The two-stage interactive activation model can be divided into three levels in terms of the extraction process from semantic representation to speech. Each level owns a large number of nodes. The top layer is the semantic layer, whose nodes represent semantic features; the middle layer is the lemma layer, while the bottom layer is the morpheme layer, which is composed of the onset phoneme, nucleus phoneme, and coda phoneme. The main contribution of this model is to propose the idea of interactive activation in language generation. The activation of the transmission mode is the waterfall, that is, the activation can be transmitted between any nodes in the network. The "interaction" means that all nodes are connected in a way that they can only promote the connection between them and the connections cannot be inhibited, while the activation of the transmission is also bidirectional, with transmission from the top level to the bottom and vice versa. Words and lemma nodes with the highest activation ratio will be chosen, which is determined by the structure of the external syntax. The selected word nodes will transfer to activation for corresponding speech encoding. In this model, the high-frequency words with bidirectional coupling and feedback structures are more easily activated, suggesting that it can explain the word frequency effect and syllable frequency effect.

The two-stage interactive activation model can also be divided into three levels. Nodes in the top layer represents the entire lexicon concept, which denotes the semantic features; the middle layer is syntactic layer representing grammar and features, including grammar structure, change features, and parts of speech. The bottom layer is the phonological or lexeme level, containing a large number of lemma nodes, or phonological and phoneme nodes. In the whole model, there is no inhibition relationship between the nodes. Leavitt et al. assumed that the concept layer and lemma layer are shared by language production and recognition, while the lexeme level only exists in the language production system [11]. The connection between the concept layer and the lemma layer is bidirectional, where the activated information can be transmitted. The lemma level and lexeme level are independent of each other, which means there is one-way transmission information without any feedback. Thus it is called the two-stage interactive activation model. In 1997, Roelofs et al. summarized the research and proposed Word-form Encoding by Activation and Verification [16].

Almost all language production theories admit the five stages process for lemma production, but there are serious differences in the specific details of each stage and the real-time processing at different stages. In the concept selection and word semantic activation stage, a controversial question is how the meaning of a word is stored in the mental lexicon. Another important issue in the process of speech information conversion is how to deal with the prosodic structure of a word, such as the combination of light and stress, vowel and consonant.

6.3 Written language

6.3.1 Letter recognition

In writing, there are three different ways to symbolize text: letters, syllables, and knowing. Many Western languages (such as English) use the alphabet system, and the symbol is like the phoneme. However, some languages using the alphabet system differ from each other in terms of close correspondence of letter and pronunciation. Some languages, such as in Finland and Spain, have a close relationship, that is, the simple text. Relatively speaking, English often lacks correspondence between letters and pronunciation, which means that English has a deep orthography.

Japanese has a different writing system. The Japanese writing system uses the Katakana syllable system; each symbol represents a syllable. There are only 100 different syllables in Japanese, thus the syllable system is possible for Japanese. Chinese is an ideographic system; each word or morpheme refers to unique symbols, and Chinese characters can represent morphemes. However, the Chinese character also corresponds to the phoneme, so Chinese is not a pure understanding system. The reason for this representing system is that Chinese is a tonal language. The same word can express different meanings depending on the pitch or tone. It is difficult to represent this pitch change in a system that only represents a sound or a phoneme.

Three writing systems reflect different perspectives of language (phoneme, syllable morpheme, or word), but they all use the mandatory symbol. Regardless of the writing system, the reader must be able to analyze the original function or shape of the symbol. For the pinyin text system, the processing is visual analysis for horizontal, vertical, and closed curves, open curves, and other basic shapes.

In 1959 Selfridge proposed the Pandemonium model [17]. Based on feature analysis, the model is divided into four levels for pattern recognition. Each level has a number of "demons" to perform specific tasks, and these levels work in a certain sequence, the ultimate realization is for pattern recognition. The structure of the model is shown in Fig. 6.1.

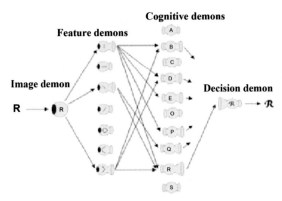

Figure 6.1 Structure of the Pandemonium mode.

As can be seen from Fig. 6.1, the first level is the image demon, which encodes the external stimulus to the form a stimulating image. Then the second-level feature demon mainly focuses on analyzing the image and decomposing it into various features. In the process of analysis, each function demon is specific, seeking only the feature it is responsible for, such as the letter of the vertical line, horizontal line, right angle, etc. In addition, a clear report should be given on the number of features and whether there is specific feature. The third level is that of the cognitive demons who are always monitoring the responses of the feature demon. Each of the cognitive demons is responsible for one pattern (letter); they are looking for some of the features related to the specific pattern from the response of the feature demon. When the relevant functions are found, they shout. The more features they find, the louder they shout. Finally, decision demon (fourth level) selects the pattern to be recognized from the loudest cognition demon. For example, in letter recognition, the image demon will first report there are altogether a vertical line, two horizontal lines, a diagonal, a discontinuous curve, and three right angles. These cognitive demons monitoring the feature demons are looking for features related to them, therefore, P, D, and R shout loudly. Among them, R is chosen as its feature is totally in accordance with all the feature demons, while P and D have some unfit features. Thus the decision demon decides that R is the pattern to be recognized.

In 1981 McClelland and Rumelhart proposed an important model for the recognition of visual letters [18]. The model assumes three levels of characterization: word alphabet feature layer, letter layer, and word representation layer. The model has a very important feature: It allows for advanced cognitive top-down word information. The impact occurs at the early stage for lower-lever letters and feature representation. This model is in contrast with the Pandemonium model, which follows a strict bottom-up information flow: from the image demon to feature demon, to the cognitive demon, and finally the decision demon. The difference between these models is actually a significant difference between the modular and the interaction theories.

In 1983 Fodor published *The Modularity of Mind* [19], formally proposing the module theory. He believes that the modular structure of the input system should have the following characteristics:

1. *Specific areas*: The input system receives different information from different sensory systems, and a specific encoding system is adopted to deal with this information. For example, the language input system converts the visual input to a voice or oral speech representation.

2. *Information encapsulation*: The process follows a strict direction; incomplete information cannot be sent. There is no top-down effect in language processing.

3. *Functional positioning*: Each module is implemented in a specific area of the brain.

The interactive view challenges all of these assumptions. However, the most important objection to the modular structure theory is that higher levels of cognitive processing can be influenced by the feedback of the system. The module theory claims that different subsystems can only communicate with each other in a bottom-up mechanism.

Another important distinction between these two models is that in the McClelland and Rumelhart model, processing can be parallel, so a few letters can be processed simultaneously. However, in the Pandemonium model, only one letter can be processed in a sequence each time. Three different levels of nodes are represented by features of letters, letters, and words. Each layer node can be connected to each other by the external display (arrow) or implicit (line), which affects the level of activation of other nodes. The McClelland and Rumelhart model allows excitement and inhibited contact between two layers [18]. For example, if you read the word "tip," and then all the letters and functions matching the word "tip," together with the trip itself, will be activated. But when the word node "tip" is activated, it sends an inhibitory signal to the lower layer, namely nodes with the letters and features not matching the word node "tip." The McClelland and Rumelhart model shows its superior performance when it is applied to the simulation word. When three kinds of visual stimuli are briefly presented to the subjects, we observed this effect in experiments. The stimulation can be a word (trip), nonword (Pirt), or a letter (T). The task to be tested is to decide what they saw contains letter "t" or "k." When this letter appears in a real word, the subjects can do a better job. Interestingly, the letters in a certain word seem to be better than they are as single letters. This result suggests that the word is not perceived on the basis of the alphabet. The McClelland and Rumelhart model can explain "best word effect." Based on their model, top-down information can be activated and inhibited, which is helpful for letter recognition.

6.3.2 Word recognition

The process for lexical processing is composed of lexical choice and lexical integration. Lexical access refers to such a process that the output of visual analysis activates orthographic representation in the mental lexicon, including the semantic and syntactic properties. In most cases, the process of lexical access is different from the visual and auditory form. For people who understand the language, unique challenges exist under two circumstances as the encoding signal connected to the mental lexicon has different morphological characteristics. In writing, there is a question of how we can read the words that cannot be converted directly into sounds and also read "false words" that do not match the real words. Reading the false words cannot be mapped directly to the form of the text output because there is no such mapping. Therefore, in order to read the false word "lonocel," we need to convert it to its corresponding phoneme letters. On the other hand, if we want to read the word "colonel," if we convert it to the corresponding phoneme, we'll read a wrong word. In order to prevent such mistakes, a direct orthogonal representation should be used for orthographic units. This observation makes researchers present the dual pathway reading model: a direct pathway from the morphology to the orthography and an indirect pathway or synthesis pathway that will convert the text input speech to form a mapping.

In 1993 Coltheart presented a direct path from reading the character to word representation. However, going from the input of the Chinese character to word representation in the mental lexicon can be accomplished in two ways: morphological pattern to speech, that is, the so-called indirect path, and the direct write input to mental lexicon, that is, a direct access [20].

In 1989 Seidenberg proposed a single-access computer model that uses only speech information [21]. In this model, the written unit and the speech unit continue to interact with each other, and the information feedback is allowed to learn the correct pronunciation. This model is very successful for real words, but it is not very good at reading false words, which is not very difficult for the ordinary people.

6.4 Chomsky's formal grammar

In computer science, a formal language is a set of strings of symbols that may be constrained by rules that are specific to it, while formal grammar is a method to depict the set. The reason for naming formal grammar is that it is similar to the grammar in the natural language of human beings. The most common grammatical classification systems are presented by Chomsky in 1950, and all of the grammatical categories are classified into four types: phrase structure grammar, context-sensitive grammars, context-free grammars (CFGs), and regular grammars. Any language can be expressed by unrestricted grammar, the remaining three categories of grammar and the corresponding language classes are enumerate language, context-free language (CFL), and formal language [1]. According to this arrangement, these four types of grammar have stricter and stricter rules, and the language they can express becomes severe. Although the expression ability is weaker than that of phrase structure grammar and context-sensitive grammar, CFGs and regular grammar are the most important types of grammar.

6.4.1 Phrase structure grammar

Phrase structure grammar is a kind of nonrestricted grammar, also known as 0-type grammar, which is an important kind of grammar in formal language theory. A four tuple $G = (\Sigma, V, S, P)$, where Σ is the terminal symbols over a finite alphabet, V is the nonterminal symbols over a finite alphabet, $S \in V$ is the start symbol, P is a finite nonempty set of generation rules, where the generation rules are defined as $\alpha \to \beta$, where $\alpha \in (\Sigma \cup V)^* V (\Sigma \cup V)^*$ and $\beta \in (\Sigma \cup V)^*$. Phrase structure grammar is also called the 0-type grammar as there are no restrictions on α and β; it is also called unrestricted grammar. 0-type grammar can generate exactly the same language that the Turing machine accepts; it is called L_0 language or recursive enumerable language (commonly LRE for short).

For example, let $G = G = (\{a\}, \{[,], A, D, S\}, S, P)$, where $P = \{S \rightarrow [A]$, $[\rightarrow [D, D] \rightarrow], DA \rightarrow AAD, [\rightarrow \wedge,] \rightarrow \wedge, A \rightarrow a\}$. Apparently, G is a phrase structure grammar, which can generate a 0-type language $L(G) = \{a^{2^n} | n \geq 0\}$.

The standard form of phrase structure grammar is $A \rightarrow \xi$, $A \rightarrow BC$, $A \rightarrow \wedge$, $AB \rightarrow CD$, where $\xi \in (\Sigma \cup V)$, A, B, C, $D \in V$, $\wedge$ is empty words.

Context-sensitive grammar, CFG, and regular grammar can be obtained when some restrictions are applied for generation rules in phrase structure grammar.

6.4.2 Context-sensitive grammar

Context-sensitive grammar is an important grammar in formal language theory, in which the left-hand sides and right-hand sides of any production rules may be surrounded by a context of terminal and nonterminal symbols.

A formal grammar $G = (\Sigma, V, S, P)$, where V is a set of nonterminal symbols, Σ is a set of terminal symbols, P is a set of production rules, and S is the start symbol, is context-sensitive if all rules in P are of the form $\alpha A \beta \rightarrow \alpha \gamma \beta$, where $A \in V$, α, $\beta \in (\Sigma \cup V)^*$, $\gamma \in (\Sigma \cup V)^+$. Context-sensitive grammar is also called 1-type grammar, with an intuitive meaning that A can be replaced by γ under the context of α in the left and β in the right. The language generated by 1-type grammar is called context-sensitive language or 1-type language. L_1 is used for denoting the 1-type language class.

Monotonous grammar. If all the production rules of grammar $G = (\Sigma, V, S, P)$ is of the form $\alpha \rightarrow \beta$ and $|\alpha| \leq |\beta|$, where $\alpha \in (\Sigma \cup V)^* V (\Sigma \cup V)^*$, $\beta \in (\Sigma \cup V)^+$, then G is called a monotonous grammar. Monotonous grammar can be simplified where the length of the right-hand side of all production rules is 2 at most, namely, if $\alpha \rightarrow \beta \in P$, then $|\beta| \leq 2$. It is already proved that the language class generated by monotonous grammar is the same as 1-type language class. Therefore the definition of monotonous grammar can also be used for context-sensitive grammar.

For example: $G = (\{a, b, c\}, \{S, A, B\}, S, P)$, where $P = \{S \rightarrow aSAB/aAB$, $BA \rightarrow AB, aA \rightarrow ab, bA \rightarrow bb, bB \rightarrow bc, CB \rightarrow cc\}$, Obviously, G is a monotonous grammar, which is also the context-sensitive grammar. The language that it generates is $L(G) = \{a^n b^n c^n | n \geq 1\}$, which is context-sensitive language.

The standard form of context-sensitive grammar is as follows: $A \to \xi$, $A \to BC$, $AB \to CD$, where $\xi \in (\Sigma \cup V)$, A, B, C, $D \in V$. Context-sensitive language classes have the same language class as what a linear bounded automaton can accept. For the closeness and the decision problem of type 1 language operations refer to phrase structure grammar. In particular, it is pointed out that these 1-type languages are a problem that is not closed to the latest of the operation.

6.4.3 Context-free grammar

CFG is an important kind of transformational grammar in formal language theory. In formal language theory, a CFG is a formal grammar in which every production rule is of the form $V \to w$, where V is a single nonterminal symbol, and w is a string of terminals and/or nonterminals (w can be empty). A formal grammar is considered context-free when its production rules can be applied regardless of the context of a nonterminal.

CFGs can be simplified as one of the two simple paradigms, that is, any CFL can be generated by two kinds of standard CFG: One is the Chomsky model, whose production rules are of the form $A \to BC$ or $A \to a$; the other is the Grey Bach paradigm, which is of the form generative $A \to aBC$ or $A \to a$, where A, B, $C \in V$(nonterminal); $a \in \Sigma$ or terminator; $\alpha \in \Sigma^*$.

There are many methods of inference to generate language via grammar. For instance, there are two inferences for grammar $\{S \to AB, A \to a, B \to b\}$: $S \Rightarrow AB \Rightarrow aB \Rightarrow ab$ and $S \Rightarrow AB \Rightarrow Ab \Rightarrow ab$. If the nonterminal on the left-hand side of the left is taken from the rule each time for inference; as in the former example, it is called left inference. If there are two different left inferences for the same result, this grammar is ambiguous and is called ambiguous grammar; otherwise it is called an unambiguous grammar. For some ambiguous grammars, there is an equivalent unambiguous grammar to generate the same language. Language without ambiguous grammar is called essence ambiguous language. For instance, $\{S \to A, S \to a, A \to a\}$ is an ambiguous grammar. $L = \{a^m b^n c^n \mid m, n \geq 1\} \cup \{a^m b^m c^n \mid m, n \geq 1\}$ is essence ambiguous language. A pushdown automaton can accept CFL. Determined pushdown automaton and undetermined pushdown automaton can accept determined CFL and undetermined CFL, respectively. The former is the proper subset of the latter. For example, $L = \{a^n b^n \mid n \geq 1\} \cup \{a^n b^{2n} \mid n \geq 1\}$ is a undetermined CFL.

For any positive integer n, let $\sum_n = \{a_1, \ldots, a_n\}$, $\sum_n' = \{a_1', \ldots, a_n'\}$ $G = (\Sigma, V, S, P)$ is defined for $(\sum_n \cup \sum_n', \{S\}, S, \{S \rightarrow, Sa_i \ Sa_i'$ $S | 1 \le i \le n\})$. The generated grammar is called a Dyck set. If a_i is considered an open bracket, and a_i' is considered a closed bracket, then the n-dimension Dyck set is a matched sequence composed of n kinds of different brackets. For example, $a_1 a_2 a_2 a_2' a_2' a_1'$ and $a_1 a_1' a_2 a_2' a_1 a_1'$ all belong to D_2.

The Dyck set is a tool to expand regular language to CFL. For any CFL L, there are two homomorphic mapping $H1$ and $H2$, and a regular language R, making $L = h_2[h_1^{-1}(D_2) \cap R]$, where $D2$ is two-dimensional Dyck set and vice versa.

In addition, the family of CFLs is a minimal language family, which contains D_2, and is closed under three kinds of algebraic operations: homomorphism, inverse homomorphism, and the intersection of regular language.

As CFGs are widely applied to depict the grammar of programming language; thus it is vital to obtain the subgrammar of CFG that automatically performs grammar decomposition. The most important one is unambiguous CFG, as unambiguity is very important in computer language for grammar analysis. A subclass of unambiguous CFG is LR (k) grammar, which only needs to look ahead for k symbols to perform grammar decomposition correctly from left to right. LR(k) grammar can describe all of the deterministic CFLs. For arbitrary $k > 1$, the language generated by LR(k) grammars can be generated by an equivalent LR(1) grammar. Language generated by LR(0) grammar is the subclass of language generated by LR(1) grammar.

6.4.4 Regular grammar

Regular grammars come from the study of the natural language in the middle 50, the 3-type grammar in Chomsky grammar structure. Regular grammar is a proper subclass of CFGs (2-type) and has been applied to the lexical analysis of the computer programming language compiler, switch circuit design, syntactic pattern recognition, and so on. It is one of the topics for information science, physics, chemistry, biology, medicine, applied mathematics, and so on.

Of the variety of equivalent definitions for regular grammar, we can use the "left linear grammar" or "right linear grammar" to define regular grammar. The production rule of "left linear grammar" can only contain one nonterminal symbol, while the right-hand side of the rule can be an empty string, a terminal symbol, or a nonterminal symbol followed by a terminal symbol. While the "right linear grammar" requires that the left-hand side of the production rule can contain only one nonterminal symbol, while the right-hand side can be an empty string, a terminal symbol, or a terminal symbol followed by a nonterminal symbol.

A "left linear grammar" is defined as $G = (V, \Sigma, P, S)$, where V is a set of nonterminal symbols, Σ is a set of terminal symbols, P is a set of production rules, and S is the start symbol, $w \in \Sigma^*$. It is a regular grammar if all rules in P are of the form $A \rightarrow w$ and $A \rightarrow wB (A \rightarrow Bw)$. The "right linear grammar" is equivalent to "left linear grammar"; namely, they can generate the same language.

The structure and complexity of a regular grammar are determined by the number of variables, the number of production rules, the height of the directed graph of the grammar, and the number of nodes of each layer. $S|\overset{*}{\underset{G}{}}w$ denotes inference of w with a finite number of production rules used in P. The regular grammar G can be used for the generator to produce and depict regular language $L(G) = \{w \in \sum\nolimits^* |S|\overset{*}{\underset{G}{}}w\}$. For instance, $G = (\{S, A, B\}, \{0,1\}P, S)$, $P = \{S \rightarrow 0\,A|0, A \rightarrow 1B, B \rightarrow 0\,A|0\}$, G is a regular (right linear) grammar (G) containing terminal 0, $(S \rightarrow 0)$, $01010(S \rightarrow 0\,A \rightarrow 01B \rightarrow 010\,A \rightarrow 0101B \rightarrow 01010)$. The regular language is also called a regular set, which can be expressed as a regular expression. For any regular expressions, nondeterministic finite automata (NFA) with ε actions can be constructed to accept it in linear time, a deterministic finite automata (DFA) without ε actions also can be constructed to accept it in the time square. The regular language can also be accepted by two-way deterministic finite automaton (2DFA); NFA, DFA, and a2DFA are equivalent, that is, the class of languages that can be accepted are the same.

Regular expressions are recursively defined as follows. Let Σ be an finite set:

1. $\varnothing$, ε, and $a(\forall a \in \Sigma)$ are a regular expressions on Σ respectively, they denote empty set, empty word set $\{\varepsilon\}$, and set $\{a\}$;
2. if α and β are regular expressions on Σ, then $\alpha \cup \beta$, $\alpha \bullet \beta = \alpha\beta$, and α^* are regular expressions on Σ. They represent the $\{\alpha\}$, $\{\beta\}$, $\{\alpha\} \cup \{\beta\}$, $\{\alpha\}\,\{\beta\}$, and $\{\alpha\}^*$, (operator $\cup$, $\bullet$, *) denote the union, connection, and the star (the power of closure $\{\alpha\}^* = \{\bigcup_{i=0}^{\infty} \alpha^i\}$), and the priority orders are *, $\bullet$, $\cup$, respectively;

3. The expression obtained by limited use of (1) and (2) are regular expressions on Σ. And the regular set is defined as the regular expression on Σ.

To simplify the regular expression, the following formulas are typically used:

1. $\alpha \cup \alpha = \alpha$(Idempotent law)
2. $\alpha \cup \beta = \beta \cup \alpha$(Exchange law)
3. $(\alpha \cup \beta) \cup \gamma = \alpha \cup (\beta \cup \gamma)$(Binding law)
4. $\alpha \cup \varnothing = \alpha$, $\alpha\varnothing = \varnothing\alpha = \varnothing$, $\alpha\varepsilon = \varepsilon\alpha = \alpha$(Zero or one law)
5. $(\alpha\beta)\gamma = \alpha(\beta\gamma)$(Binding law)
6. $(\alpha \cup \beta)\gamma = \alpha\gamma \cup \beta\gamma$(Distributive law)
7. $(g)\varepsilon \cup \alpha^* = \alpha^*$
8. $(\varepsilon \cup \alpha)^* = \alpha^*$

When α is changed to β using 1 and 2, α is said to be similar with β.

It is convenient to use the regular expression equation $X_i = a_{i0} + a_{i1}X_1 + \ldots + a_{in}X_n$ to deal with language, as in such equations, the union of $\Delta = \{X_1, \ldots, X_n\}$ with Σ is $\varnothing$. α_{ij} is the regular expression on Σ. If α_{ij} is $\varnothing$ or ε, it is the same as the coefficients of the ordinary linear differential equation are 0 and 1, respectively, which can be solved based on Gauss elimination method. Of course, the solution is a set, which suggests the solution is not unique, but the algorithm can correctly determine a minimal fixed point solution. Suppose R is a regular language, there is a constant n, so that all words w whose lengths are not less than n can be written as $xyz (y \neq \varepsilon$ and $|xy| \leq n)$ and for all nonnegative integers i, $xy^iz \in R$, which is called the pumping lemma. It is a powerful tool to prove that certain languages are not regular, and it helps to establish an algorithm to determine whether a given language is a finite or infinite generated by a certain regular grammar. We can use arithmetic operations of language to determine whether a certain language is regular or not. It is known that regular language is closed on Boolean operations (and, union, complementary), connection, * (Krini closure), left and right business, replacement, inverse INIT (prefix), FIN (), MAX, CYCLE, Reversal, MIN, etc. And when $p(x)$ is a non-negative integer coefficient polynomial, R is a regular language, $L_1 = \{w|$ for some $|y| = p(|w|)$, $wy \in R\}$, $L_2 = \{w|$ for some $|y| = p(|w|)$, $wy \in R\}$ is also a regular language. When R, R_1, and R_2 are regular languages, the following problems are determinable: $w \in R$? $R = \varnothing$? $R = \Sigma^*$? $R_1 = R_2$? $R_1 \subseteq R_2$? $R_1 \cap R_2 = \varnothing$?

6.5 Augmented transition networks

In 1970 the artificial intelligence expert Woods presented an automatic language analysis method, known as augmented transition networks (ATN) [2]. ATN is an extension of finite state grammar. A finite state grammar can be represented by a state graph, but the function of this grammar is generation. If we start from the point of view of sentence analysis, we can also use the state graph to express the analysis of a sentence; such a state graph is called a finite state transition diagram (FSTD). An FSTD consists of many finite states and arcs from one state to another, The arc can be marked with a terminal symbol (that is, the specific word) and lexical category symbols, such as <Verb>, <Adj>, <Noun>, etc., The analysis starts at the beginning state, and, following the direction of the arrow in a finite state transition graph, the input word is scanned one by one, the input is checked to see if it matches the label on the arc. If the end of an input statement is scanned, the FSTD enters the final state, which suggests that the FSTD accepts an input sentence, and the analysis is successfully finished (see Fig. 6.2).

ATNs can only recognize limited state language. We know that the rewrite rules of finite state grammars are $A \rightarrow aQ$ or $A \rightarrow a$, which is relatively simple, and that FSTD is sufficient to identify the languages generated by finite state grammars.

For example, we can put forward a noun phrase, which is analyzed by FSTD. It starts with a <Noun> at the beginning and ending, and there is an arbitrary <Adj> at the beginning and ending:

the pretty picture(Beautiful picture)
the old man(The elderly)
the good idea(Good idea)

The ATN is shown in Fig. 6.2. If the noun phrase entered is "the pretty picture," the analysis starts from the state q and follow the arc that is marked with "the." As "the" is the leftmost word for the input string, these two are matched and then entered into the state q_1. The rest of the

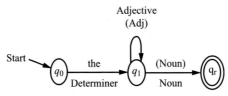

Figure 6.2 Augmented transition networks.

input string to be dealt with is "pretty picture." Following the arc of the circle marked with <Adj>, we enter the state q_1 again, and the rest of the input string is "picture." Since the word is a noun, and the arc of the label <Noun> is therefore matched, the final state q_f is reached. At this time, the input string of all the words are checked, the results of the analysis are done, and FSTD accepts this symbol string.

Finite state grammars are not suitable for dealing with complex natural languages. Therefore, it is necessary to extend the FSTD to provide a recursive mechanism to increase the recognition ability, so as to deal with the CFL. For this purpose, recursive transition networks (RTN) are proposed. RTN is also a finite state transition graph; however, the marking on the arc not only contains a terminal symbol (i.e., the specific word) and lexical category symbol but also can be the phrase-type symbols (such as NP, S, PP, etc.). Since each phrase-type symbol can be represented by a finite state transfer graph, the RTN is capable of recursion. When it scan phrase-type, RTN can temporarily transfer to another finite state transition graph corresponding to the phrase-type, so that the analysis process can be temporarily controlled. In this way, RTN can recognize not only the finite state language but also the CFL, which expands the FSTD recognition ability (see Fig. 6.3).

The operation mode of RTN is similar to the operation mode of FSTD. If the mark on the arc is terminal symbol or lexical category symbol, then you can deal with this arc like FSTD. For example, the word "ball" can be matched with the arc of <Noun> but not with <Adj> as a marker. If the symbol on the mark is of phrase-type, and this phrase-type corresponds to a finite state transition graph, then the current state is placed into a stack, and control is transferred to the finite state transition

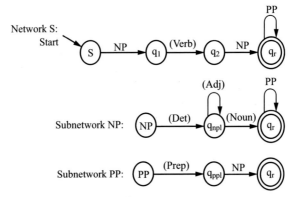

Figure 6.3 Recursive transition networks.

graph. When the performance is successfully over or fails, control goes back, returning to the original state to continue operating.

For example, an RTN is made up of a network named S, and two subnetworks NP and PP. Here, NP stands for noun phrases, PP represents a prepositional phrase, <Det> is a "determiner," <Prep> is a preposition, <Adj> is an adjective, <Noun> is a noun, and q_f represents not only final state. If the input string is "the little boy in the swimsuit kicked the red ball," the RTN is analyzed in the following order:

NP: the little boy in the swimsuit

PP: in the swimsuit

NP: the swimsuit

Verb: kicked

NP: the red ball

In the network S, the scanning process starts from S. When it scans to the subnetwork NP, "the little boy in the swimsuit" is dealt with; when "the little boy" is scanned, the PP "in the swimsuit" can be scanned, and the control comes into the subnetwork pp, continuing processing. In this subnetwork, after scanning the <Prep>, that is, "in," the NP "the swimsuit" should be scanned. Therefore control enters the subnetwork NP, deals with "the swimsuit," and enters the final state of the NP. Thus "the little boy in the swimsuit" has been successfully dealt with, and control goes back to network S. Entered into q_1, "kicked" is scanned, entered into q_2; scanning NP, "the red ball" is finally dealt with, and the sentence analysis is finished.

RTN can handle CFL. However, we know that CFGs, which can generate CFLs, are still not perfect in processing natural languages. Therefore, the further expansion of RTN is necessary to have a stronger recognition ability. In this way, Woods has proposed ATNs [22]. The ATN consists of the following three aspects in order to expand RTN:

1. Add a register for storing information. For example, in different subnetworks, a number of derivation trees may be formed locally, such that the derivation tree can be temporarily stored in these registers.

2. The arc in the network can also be checked out of the condition of the entry besides marking the symbols as the terminal symbol, the lexical category symbol, and the phrase-type symbol.

3. Certain actions can be performed in the arc, and the structure of a sentence can be reorganized

In addition, as the register, condition, and operation are expanded, the function of ATN can be increased to the level of the Turing machine.

In theory, the ATN can recognize any language that a computer can recognize.

The operation mode of ATN is similar to RTN. The difference lies in the following. If the arc is marked with a check, you must first perform this check, and only when the check is successful can you continue to scan the arc. In addition, if the arc is to perform the action associated with it, then, after the scan is done, these actions must be performed. At present, the research on ATN has been successfully applied to the man—machine conversation and the generation of articles.

ATN also has some limitations. It is excessively dependent on grammar parsing, which limits its ability to deal with some of the sentences that are semantically correct but that do not completely conform to grammar.

6.6 Concept dependency theory

In 1972 R. C. Schank proposed the concept of dependency theory [23], serving as a representation of the meaning of phrases and sentences. The theory also provides a common reasoning knowledge for the computer, and thus the automatic understanding of language can be realized. The basic principles of concept dependence theory are as follows:

1. For any two sentences with identical meaning, regardless of language, there is only one concept dependence representation.
2. The meaning of this concept dependence representation is composed of a very small semantic meaning, which includes the meta-motion and the original state (the value of the property).
3. Any information in the implicit sentence must be represented by an explicit representation of the meaning of the sentence.
   The concept dependence theory has three aspects:
1. The concept dependence → action elements, including:
   a. The basic action physical world = {GRASP, MOVE, TRANS, GO, PROPEL, INGEST, HIT}.
   b. The basic movement of the spirit world = {MTRANS, CONCEPTUALIZE, MBUILD}.
   c. Basic movements of means or tools = {SMELL, LOOK-AT, LISTEN-TO, SPEAK}.
2. The script → description of common scenes in a number of basic fixed set of movements (by the action of the basic elements)
3. Plan → each step is composed by the script.

Here, we introduce the concept dependence theory, and it is divided into the following categories:

1. *PP*: A concept term that is used only for physical objects and is also called the image generator. For example, people, objects, etc. are PP, it also includes the natural wind and rain, lightning, and thinking of the human brain (the brain as a generative system).
2. *PA*: Physical objects' properties, together with its values can be used to describe the physical objects.
3. *ACT*: The action performed from a physical object to another physical object, it may be a physical object of its own actions, including physical action and mental action (such as criticism).
4. *LOC*: An absolute position (determined by the cosmic coordinates) or a relative position (relative to a physical object).
5. TIME: A time point or time slice, also divided into two kinds of absolute or relative time.
6. AA: An action (ACT) attribute.
7. VAL: Value of various attributes.

R. C. Schank formed a new concept by the following method (conceptualization):

1. An actor (active physical object), plus an action (ACT).
2. The following modification of the preceding concept:
   a. An object (if ACT is a physical action, then it is a physical object; if ACT is a mental action, then it is another concept).
   b. A place or a receiver (if ACT occurs between two physical objects, it indicates that a physical object or concept is passed to another physical object. If ACT occurs between two sites, it denotes the new location of the object).
   c. A means (which in itself is a concept).
3. An object with a value of a property that is added to the object.
4. A combination of concepts in some way, forming new concepts, for example, in combination with a causal relationship.

Originally, R. C. Schank's goal was to atomize all concepts, but in fact, he only atomized action (ACT). He divided ACT into 11 kinds:

1. *PROPEL*: Application of physical forces for an object, including push, pull, play, kick, etc.
2. *GRASP*: An actor grabs a physical object.
3. *MOVE*: The body part of the actor transforms a space position, such as lifting, kicking, standing up, sitting down, etc.

4. *PTRANS*: Transformation of the physical objects, such as entering, leaving, going upstairs, diving, and so on.

5. *ATRANS*: Changes in abstract relationships, such as (holding relationship changes), to give up (all of the relationship changes), the revolution (rule of change), etc.

6. *ATTEND*: Use a sense organ to obtain information, such as the use of an eye search, use of ears to hear, and so on.

7. *INGEST*: The actor wants to bring a thing into it, such as eating, drinking, taking medicine, and so on.

8. *EXPEL*: The actor puts something out, such as vomiting, tears, urine, spitting, and so on.

9. *SPEAK*: A voice, including singing, music, screaming, wailing, crying, and so on.

10. *MTRANS*: The transfer of information, such as conversation, discussion, calls, etc.

11. *MBUILD*: The formation of new information from old information, such as anger from the heart.

Based on these 11 definitions of atomic action, R. C. Schank had a basic idea that these atomic concepts are designed not mainly for representing the action itself but that the result of the action is of the essence. Therefore, it can be considered concept reasoning. For example, "X transfer Y from W go to Z by ATRANS" indicates the conclusions of the following reasoning:

1. Y in the W at first.
2. Y is now in the Z (no longer in the W).
3. A certain purpose of X is achieved by ATRANS.
4. If Y is a good thing, it means that things are going to be in favor of Z, which is not conducive to the direction of W; otherwise it is not.

If Y is a good thing, it means that X does this action for the benefit of Z; otherwise it is the opposite.

One important sentence is the causal chain. R. C. Schank and some of his colleagues have designed a set of rules on the concept dependency theory. The following are five important rules:

1. The action may cause a change in the state.
2. The state can start actions.
3. The state can eliminate actions.
4. State (or action) can activate the mental event.
5. Mental events may be the cause of action.

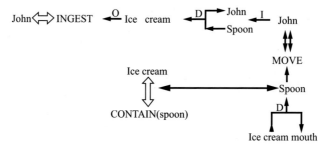

Figure 6.4 Concept of dependence of implicit information.

This is the basic part of world knowledge. Concept dependency includes each (as well as combinations) shorthand for causal connection. In the concept dependency theory, any information in the implicit sentence must be a clear representation of its explicit meaning. For example, the concept dependency of the sentence "John eats the ice cream with a spoon" is explained in Fig. 6.4. Vectors D and I are expressed to explain direction and the dependence, respectively. Note that in this case, the mouth is part of the concept, even though it does not appear in the original sentence. This is the basic difference between concept dependency and parse tree.

6.7 Language understanding

Language understanding refers to an active and positive process in which people construct meaning in their minds with the help of auditory or visual language materials. It can reveal the meaning of language materials.

6.7.1 Overview

Research on natural language information processing began with the advent of electronic computers, and in the beginning of the 1950s, machine translation tests were conducted. At that time, the research method could not be called "intelligent." Chomsky's transformational generative grammar is widely recognized. The core of generative grammar consists of the phrase structure rules. The process of the analysis of sentence structure is the process of using rules from top to bottom or from bottom to top.

Realizing that grammar generation always lacks semantic knowledge. In the 1970s, with the development of cognition science, semantic representation methods such as the semantic web, the concept dependency theory, the framework, etc. were presented. These grammatical and semantic theories were developed quickly and gradually began to become integrated with one another. In the 1980s, several new grammar theories were presented, including the lexical functional grammar (LFG), functional grammar (FUG), generalized phrase structure grammar, etc. These rules-based analysis methods can be regarded as "rationalism" in NLP. The basic starting point of rationalism is the pursuit of perfection, that is, to solve the problem one hundred percent perfectly. Chomsky proposed the standard theory in the 1960s, and in the 1970s, the extension of standard theory was presented. Government and binding theory was proposed in the 1980s, and the minimalist program was introduced in the 1990s. The goal of rationalism is abstract. On the basis of the study of language cognition or pure language theory, it seeks a kind of cross-language similarity element periodic table. Although existing analysis methods can understand a single sentence, it is difficult to cover the comprehensive phenomenon of language, especially for the whole paragraph or text.

Research on "empiricism" as the main research direction is based on a large corpus of many texts. After the emergence of the computer, data could be easily stored, and it became easy for computers to retrieve relevant information. With the emergence of electronic publications, data collection was no longer difficult. Brown and LOB were two computer corpora, which were compiled in the 1960s, with a 1,000,000-word vocabulary size. By the 1990s, it was easy to list a number of corpora, such as DCI, ICAME, ECI, BNC, LDC, CLR, and so on, whose scale was up to 10^9.

There are three aspects of the study of the corpus: development of tool software, the corpus label, and the corpus-based analysis method. The raw material collected can provide knowledge based on lexical, syntactic, and semantic analysis. The method of processing this information is to label all kinds of marks in the corpus, which include parts of speech, semantics, phrase structures, sentence patterns, and relations between sentences. With corpus annotation gradually maturing, it become a distributional and statistical source of knowledge. This knowledge source can be used for many linguistic analyses; for example, the frequency of new text can be annotated by the frequency of the data from the annotated corpus.

The knowledge provided by the corpus is represented by statistical intensity rather than certainty. With the expansion of the corpus scale, it is designed to cover the full linguistic phenomenon. However, the basic rule of language is still used to judge the size of statistical strength, which is contrary to people's common sense. The problem in empiricism can be made up by the rationalism method. The fusion of the two kinds of methods is also the trend of the development of NLP.

G. M. Olson, an American cognitive psychologist, proposed the standard of language comprehension:

1. The ability to answer questions about language materials, that is to say, the ability to answer questions is a standard in understanding language.
2. Given a large amount of material, the ability of summary.
3. Ability to use their own language, that is, to use different words to repeat the material.
4. Ability to translate from one language to another.

Given these four abilities, language comprehension can be used in the following ways:

1. *Machine translation*: Multilingual translation with 10,000-word vocabulary; 90% accuracy of machine translation, 10% artificial intervention. In the comprehensive system, the computer serves as a translator for participation from editing to print at all levels; the total spending of machine translation is 30% or less than human translation.
2. *Understanding of the document*: Machine reading, digesting the contents of the document to make a summary of the document, or answering specific questions on this basis.
3. *File generation*: The machine can be stored in the computer in the form of information, generating a natural language.
4. *Other applications*: As a natural language interface in big systems. For example, a large database using natural language retrieval (the LADDiR system), with the support of the United States Department of Defense naval research, stores more than 100 bodies of water and 40,000 ships in a considerable number of computers. The system can be used to talk to the staff or decision makers and ask questions.

The development of a natural language understanding system can be divided into two stages: the first-generation system and the second-generation system. The first-generation system is established on the basis of the analysis part of the speech and word order, frequently by means of statistical methods; the second-generation system introduced semantics and even pragmatic and contextual factors, and statistical techniques are rarely used.

The first generation of the natural language understanding system can be divided into four types: special format system, text-based systems, finite logic system, general deduction system.

Since 1970, there have been a number of second-generation natural language understanding systems. These systems are mostly procedural deduction systems, using semantics, context, and pragmatics for analysis. These more famous systems are the LUNAR system, SHRDLU system, MARGIE system, script applier mechanism (SAM) system, and pluggable authentication modules (PAM) system. These systems are all used for question answer and natural language understanding by written input and output sentences. The oral natural language understanding system, which involves complex techniques such as speech recognition, speech synthesis, and so on, is clearly more difficult. In recent years, the research of oral natural language understanding system is also in progress.

6.7.2 Rule-based analysis method

From the perspective of linguistics and cognition, a set of linguistic rules is set up so that the machine can understand natural language. The rule-based approach is a theoretical approach. Under ideal conditions, the rules can form a complete system, covering all language phenomena. Then the rule-based method can be used to explain and understand all language problems.

The natural language understanding system involves syntax, semantics, and pragmatics to some extent. Syntax is the rule that links words to phrases, clauses, and sentences, while syntactic parsing is one of the best for the three areas. Most natural language understanding systems contain a syntactic parsing program that generates syntactic trees to reflect the syntactic structure of an input sentence, in order to prepare for further analysis.

Considering the existence of multiple syntactic ambiguities, many different words can be considered different lexical categories in different contexts, so that the correct syntactic structure information can only be obtained by syntactic parsing. So it is necessary to rely on some form of semantic analysis. Semantics involves the meanings of words, phrases, clauses, and sentences.

For the sake of correct analysis, certain semantic information is often needed, and even the intervention of external world knowledge is needed. There are two different approaches for the analysis of syntax and semantics.

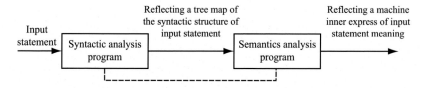

(A) Analyze separation process scheme of syntactic and semantics

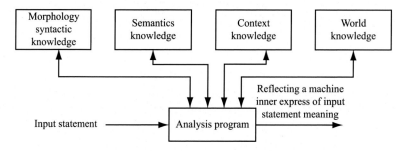

(B) An integration process method of syntactic and semantics

Figure 6.5 Solutions to the natural language analysis system.

1. *Serial processing of syntactic parsing and semantic analysis separately*, as shown in Fig. 6.5A: Traditional linguists claim that the analysis of syntactic parsing and the semantic analysis should be completely separated. But many famous natural language understanding systems, such as SHRDLU systems, allows calling on the functions of semantic interpretation of the input statements in the course of processing to assist in analysis. Even so, these two methods generate some form of syntax tree as a result of syntactic parsing.

2. *Integration of syntax and semantics*, as shown in Fig. 6.5B. This kind of treatment can be considered the mode represented by R. C. Schank. The feature of this scheme is to cancel the relative independence of the syntactic parsing module and thus no longer produce the intermediate results of the syntactic structure of the input sentence. Their guiding ideology is to make comprehensive references in the analysis as early as possible. They are not completely devoid of syntactic knowledge in the analysis, but they do not rely on the syntactic parsing excessively. Many psychologists have argued that this integrated approach is closer to the understanding of language. English analysis systems CA and ELI are representative of this scheme.

Semantic knowledge engineering, part of NLP, has been studied since the 1980s. The semantic knowledge base has mainly focused on the semantic relationship with the characteristics of relativity. Semantic knowledge is mainly used as the constraint condition, and it plays an important role for the computer to transform languages. Emphasis is attached to the semantic category, and the semantic constraint condition can be extracted. The resulting semantic knowledge can better and more directly serve for NLP.

One of the tasks of pragmatics is considering factors such as who writes the sentence and where (place) and when (time) this happens in order to make a more comprehensive interpretation of the sentence. This analysis clearly requires that the system has a wider range of contextual information and knowledge of the world. In 1972 T. Winograd combined linguistics method and reasoning method to properly handle the interaction of syntax, semantics, and pragmatics. He even successfully developed the NLP system SHRDLU On PDP10. It is a theoretical model of human language understanding that has aroused the interest of many researchers [3].

This system includes an analytical procedure, an English grammar, a semantic analysis program, and a problem solver. The system is written in list processing (LISP) language and MICRO-PLANNER language, which is based on LISP. The design of the system is based on the belief that, in order to understand the language, the program must deal with the overall view of syntax, semantics, and reasoning. Only when the computer system understands its subject can it study the language and system reasonably. And there is a simple model of its own intelligence; for example, it can recall and discuss its plans and actions. Knowledge is represented as the process in the system, not by a rule table or pattern. Knowledge is exhibited by syntax, semantics, and reasoning, as each knowledge can be a process. It will be able to directly call any other knowledge in the system, and therefore the SHRDLU system has the ability to achieve unprecedented levels of performance.

Yixin Zhong put forward the concept of full information. The information expressed in natural language is a variety of information, which, of course, belongs to the category of epistemology. The main body of knowledge, generally speaking, is a person and can be a variety of creatures or even a human-made machine system. However, the most meaningful subject is the selfsame person. From the perspective of epistemology, there are three basic characteristics of the normal subjects for cognition: observation, understanding, and purpose. Therefore, the main body of the perception or the expression of the "things movement state and its mode of change" must include:

1. the grammatical information of things, concerned with the form of the movement of things and the way of its change;

2. the semantic information of the object, concerned with the meaning of the movement of things and the way of its change.

The pragmatic information of things is concerned with the movement of things and its change so as to understand the purpose of the subject. Organic whole information is formed by the combination of grammatical information, semantic information, and pragmatic information, which is called full information [24].

The movement of things and state changes make up the grammatical information of things. They are the form of performance of the movement of things and how it is changing. Once the form of this state and its change is associated with its corresponding real object, it has a concrete practical meaning (the central and the left part of the diagram), which is the semantic information. And it is no longer an abstract thing but a very concrete thing. Furthermore, if the form of the state, its changing way, and its meaning are associated with a particular subject, it will show the effectiveness as the main purpose for the subject, which is the pragmatic information.

Thus grammatical information is an abstract information level, while semantic information is the result of the correlation between grammatical information and its corresponding objects. Pragmatic information is the result of the mutual relationship between grammatical information, semantic information, and the subject; therefore it is the most concrete level. Grammatical information and semantic information are related only to objects, and pragmatic information has the relationship with the subject. The concept of the full information is an organic system.

6.7.3 Statistical model based on corpus

Research on corpus linguistics focuses on the acquisition, storage, labeling, retrieval, and statistics of natural language. The aim is to quantitatively analyze the linguistic facts of large-scale real texts and to support the development of the NLP system. Its application areas include the measurement and analysis of language, language knowledge acquisition, work style analysis, dictionary compilation, full-text retrieval, natural language understanding system and machine translation system.

The origin of modern corpus linguistics can be traced back to the structural linguistics era of the late 1950s in the United States. At that time, linguists thought that the corpus was large enough to serve as language database. This linguistic data is naturally occurring and thus is necessary and sufficient for the task of linguistic research, and the intuitive evidence is, at best, in a poor second place. In late 1950s, Chomsky created a conversion to generate the grammar. He advocated that intuition is reasonable and that any natural corpus is distorted. The rationalism of his point of view constitutes the orthodox ideas of contemporary theoretical linguists, resulting in curbing early corpus linguistics to a great extent. But practice has proved that it is impossible to cover all kinds of linguistic facts that appear in the large-scale real texts. With the rapid development of computer and computing technology, the size of the corpus extends from 100,000 words in the 1960s to 1−10 billion times in the 1990s, expanding some thousands of times in 30 years. This was not foreseen by the experts who rejected the intuition method in the 1950s and the corpus-based methods in 1960s. This fact makes it possible for a language's lexical and syntactic phenomena to be investigated with the help of corpora.

In 1959, some scholars put forward the idea of establishing a corpus of modern English Usage Survey. In the beginning of the 1960s, the Brown corpus of modern American English was established in the United States, marking the beginning of the second period of corpus linguistics. Brown corpus and LOB corpus of modern British English, both of which are input by keyboard and created in 1970s with a capacity of 1 million words are called the first generation of corpus. In the 1980s, optical character recognition technology replaced the corpus's artificial keyboard entry mode, so that the corpus size is growing rapidly. During this period, the establishment of the corpus includes COBUILD corpus, with 200 million words and the Longman/Lancaster English corpus with 300 million words. They belong to the second-generation corpus. Since the 1990s, due to the popularity of word processing, editing software, and desktop publishing, a huge amount of machine-readable text has entered the corpus from inexhaustible resources, leading to some 1−10 billion words in the corpus, that is, the third-generation corpus, such as the American Institute for Computational Linguistics ACL/DCI corpus, the Oxford text archive in the United Kingdom, and so on. Based on the growth of the corpus in the past 30 years, Leech has predicted there will be a super large-scale corpus with 1 trillion words by 2021.

The size of the corpus and the principle of material selection are important, as they directly affect the reliability and applicability of the statistical data. However, as the supporting environment of corpus linguistics, processing depth is more important for the corpus. Taking Chinese for example, the original "raw" data can only be used for word frequency (including several adjacent word co-occurrence frequency) and sentence length statistics, providing a simple keyword search (KWIC). In order to achieve the word level count and retrieval, we must segment the original corpus using a marking sign. In the process of subsequent processing, it is also able to label the corpus with parts of speech, syntactic relations, and semantic items, so that the inventory data is gradually changed from "raw" to "mature." When all the kinds of information carried by the data is saturated, the corpus will eventually become the corpus of a language knowledge base [28].

The main contents of corpus linguistics include:

1. the construction of the basic corpus;
2. corpus processing tools, including automatic word segmentation, a parts of speech tagging system, a syntactic analysis system, a meaning tagging system, a discourse analysis system, etc.;
3. a "mature" corpus with labeled information, based on data processing;
4. technology and methods acquired from linguistics knowledge in the corpus.

At present, the world has already established hundreds of corpora, including a variety of languages, which constitute an important resource for researchers in linguistic research and the development of NLP systems. At the same time, the construction and use of the corpus have become an important part of international academic journals and conferences. At the Fourth Machine Translation High-level Conference in Britain, held in July 1993, scholars made a special report pointing out that since 1989, the world had entered the third generation of machine translation system research. The main sign was that the corpus-based method was introduced to the classical rules-based method, including statistical methods, instance-based methods, and linguistic knowledge base obtained from the data processing of the corpus.

In order to make the Chinese corpus universal, practical, and popular, as well as to enable it to become the basic provider of the important resources of NLP, we need to build a multilevel Chinese corpus composed of the fine processed corpus, the basic corpus, and the Web corpus. Then the research focus on the construction of the corpus can turn to how to get the resources of the three levels of corpus and to use them effectively. The fine processing corpus can provide a large amount of excellent language processing specifications and examples for various language studies. The basic corpus is a broad and large-scale raw corpus, which can provide more accurate data for language analysis. The Web corpus is a language resource that can realize dynamic updating, including many new words, new collocation, and new usage. It can be used to track the Web language, new words, and popular words and can also be used to observe changes in time. It can overcome the problem of data sparseness and corpus updating in the traditional corpus-based on the multilevel Chinese corpus. The corpus scale is gradually reduced, but the quality of the processing depth is gradually improved. Fine corpus is maintained on the scale of 10 million words, and it is more reasonable to maintain more than 1 billion words for the basic corpus. The underlying Web corpus reflects the opening of online resources.

6.7.4 Machine learning method

Machine learning is based on the understanding of the mechanisms of human learning, such as physiology or cognitive science, in order to develop various learning theories and methods. The general learning algorithm can be studied and subjected to theoretical analysis. Finally, a learning system based on a task-oriented learning system needs to be established. These studies' targets will be promoted with the mutual influence. At present, machine learning methods are widely used in language information.

6.7.4.1 Text classification

The purpose of classification is to learn a classification function or classification model (also often referred to as the classifier). The model can map the data in the database to a given class. Classification and regression can be used for prediction. The purpose of the prediction is to automatically derive from the use of historical data records for the promotion of a given data description, so as to predict future data. Unlike the regression method, the output of the classification is a discrete category value, and the output of the regression is a continuous value. Here we will not discuss the regression method.

To construct a classifier, a training sample data set is required as input. The training set consists of a set of database records, or a tuple, and each tuple is a feature vector, which is composed of the value of the field (also called the attribute or feature). The form of a specific sample can be $(v_1, v_2, \ldots, v_n; c)$, where v_i represents a field value, and c represents a class.

The construction method of the classifier includes the statistical method, machine learning method, neural network method, etc. Statistical methods include the Bayesian method and the nonparametric method (nearest neighbor learning or case-based learning), and the corresponding knowledge representation is the discriminant function and the prototype case. Machine learning methods include decision tree and rule induction; the former corresponds to the decision tree, while the latter is generally production rules. The representative neural network method is the BP algorithm, which is a forward feedback neural network model (composed of the nodes of the neural network and the edge of the connection weight). BP algorithm is in fact a nonlinear discriminant function. In addition, a new method of rough set has recently emerged, whose knowledge representation is of production rules.

6.7.4.2 Text clustering

According to its different characteristics, the data can be divided into different data clusters. The purpose is to make the distance between individuals belonging to the same category as small as possible, while the distance between individuals in different categories is as large as possible. Clustering methods include the statistical method, machine learning method, neural network method, and database-oriented method.

In statistical methods, cluster analysis is one of the three methods of multivariate data analysis (the other two are regression analysis and discriminant analysis). It is mainly focused on clustering based on geometric distance, such as Euclidean distance, the Ming Kowski distance, etc. Traditional statistical clustering analysis methods include the system clustering method, the decomposition method, the adding method, the dynamic clustering method, the ordered sample clustering, overlapping clustering, and fuzzy clustering. The clustering method is based on global comparison; it needs to investigate all the individuals to decide the final cluster. Therefore it requires that all the data must be given in advance, and that new data objects cannot be dynamically added. The clustering analysis method does not have linear complexity; it is difficult to apply to the database when it is very large.

In machine learning, clustering is called unsupervised or nonteacher induction as compared to classification, in which examples or data objects are labeled, while clustering data is unlabeled and needs to be determined by the clustering algorithm. In much artificial intelligence literature, clustering is also called concept clustering. Because the distance is no longer the geometric distance in the statistical method, it is determined by the description of the concept. When clustering objects can be dynamically added, the concept cluster is called the concept formation.

In neural networks, there is a kind of unsupervised learning method, a self-organizing neural network method, such as the Kohonen self-organizing feature map network, competitive learning network, etc. In the field of data mining, the neural network clustering method, which is reported in the field of data mining, is a self-organizing feature mapping method, and IBM takes advantage of it to cluster its database.

6.7.4.3 Case-based machine translation

Case-based machine translation was first proposed in the 1990s by Japanese scholars. This method is based on case-based reasoning (CBR). In CBR, the problem or situation is referred to as the target case, while the memory of the problem or situation is called the source case. In simple terms, CBR is a solving strategy based on the hint of the target case to acquire the source case and solving the problem under the guidance of the source case. Therefore, the general idea of translation is as follows: A corpus consisting of a bilingual translation unit is created in advance. Then the search unit chooses a searching and matching algorithm, and the optimal matching unit is searched in the corpus.

If we want to translate the source language text "S," the translation examples of S that need to be found in the bilingual corpus is similar to S. According to S', T is the translation case. And the translation result T is finally acquired. In general, the case-based machine translation system includes several steps, such as the pattern retrieval of candidate instances, sentence similarity computation, bilingual word alignment, and analogical translation. How to find the most similar translation examples from the source language text is the key problem of the case-based translation method. So far, researchers have not found a simple way to calculate the similarity between sentences. In addition, the evaluation of the sentence similarity problem still requires a lot of human engineering, language psychology, and other knowledge.

Case-based machine translation method is almost not needed to analyze and understand the source language. It only needs a relatively large sentence-aligned bilingual corpus, so it is easy to get the knowledge acquisition. If there are similar sentences in the corpus, the case-based method can get a good translation, and the more similar the sentences are, the better the translation effect is, and the higher the quality of the translation will be.

There is one more advantage for the case-based translation method. The knowledge representation of an instance pattern can be expressed in a concise and convenient way to express a large amount of human language.

However, the shortcomings of case-based machine translation are obvious. When a similar sentence is not found, the translation declares a failure. This requires that the corpus must cover a wide range of linguistic phenomena, for example, like the PanEBMT system of Carnegie Mellon University [25], which contains about 2,800,000 English and French bilingual sentence pairs. Although researchers use the PanEBMT system in a number of ways, for open text test, the coverage of translation of PanEBMT is only 70%. In addition, it is not easy to establish a high-quality, large bilingual sentence-aligned corpus, especially for minority languages.

Trados is desktop computer auxiliary translation software, which is based on a translation memory (TM) base and term base, which provides a complete set of tools for creating, editing, and checking high-quality translation [26]. The company of Trados GmbH was founded in 1984 by Hummel and Knyphausen in Germany. The company began to develop translation software in the late 1980s and released the first batch of Windows software in the early 1990s; they developed MultiTerm and Workbench Translators in 1992 and 1994, respectively. In 1997, thanks to Microsoft using Trados software for localization translation, the company became the desktop TM software industry leader in the late 1990s. Trados was acquired by SDL in June 2005.

SDL Trados Studio 2014 can work in the team to collect their translation in order to establish a language database (TM). In this database, the software is determined to be reused. When translators translate new content and meet with the translated sentences that are similar to or in the same sentence, the software automatically puts forward suggestions of reusable content. The features of SDL Trados Studio are as follows:

1. Based on the principle of TM, it is currently the world's most famous professional translation software and has become the standard of professional translation.
2. It supports 57 languages two-way translation.
3. It greatly improves work efficiency, reduces costs, improves quality.
4. Its background is a powerful neural network database to ensure the security of the system and information.
5. It supports all popular document formats; users do not need to do layout (DOC, RTF, HTML, SGML, XML, FrameMaker, RC, AutoCAD DXF, etc.).

6. It improves the auxiliary functions, such as time, measurement, form, automatic replacement, and other fixed format, helping customers greatly improve work efficiency.
7. The interface is clear. Both the original and the translation are clearly displayed on both sides. It is able to customize the environment in a variety of ways: Keyboard shortcuts, layout, color, and text size can be customized, so as to maximize the comfort and work efficiency.
8. It provides the most extensive file format support, from the Office2013 Microsoft file to the complex XML file.

The study of cased-based machine translation, one of the main aspects of research, is to focus on how to improve the translation of the translation system under the relatively small number of the cases or on how to reduce the size of the case model to maintain the effectiveness of the translation. To achieve this goal, we need to extract as much linguistic knowledge as possible from the database of case patterns, including syntax, lexical knowledge, and semantic knowledge.

6.8 Neural model of language understanding

6.8.1 Aphasia

Brain injury may lead to the language barrier of aphasia. Broca made a conclusion that the generation of the oral speech is located in the left hemisphere based on the study of the aphasia; this region is called the Broca area. In the 1870s, Wernicke treated two patients speaking fluently but uttering meaningless sounds, words, and sentences and having serious difficulties in the interpretation of utterances. Wernicke examination revealed damage was found in the superior temporal gyrus region. As auditory processing occurs in the vicinity, which is in front of the temporal back on the transverse temporal gyrus, Wernicke speculated that more regions from the back involved word auditory memory. The area was later known as the Wernicke area. Wernick believes that since this region has lost the memory associated with words, the damage of the region leads to the difficulty of language understanding. He pointed out that the meaningless discourse of the patient is due to their inability to monitor their own word output. It has established a mainstream view that has affected the relationship between the brain and language for 100 years. Damage to Broca's area of the left hemisphere frontal side causes language difficulties, that is, aphasia. Injury to the left hemisphere parietal lobe posterior and lateral temporal cortex, including the supramarginal gyrus, angular gyrus, and superior temporal gyrus region, hinders language understanding, that is, the acceptance of aphasia. Fig. 6.6 shows the human brain area of language processing.

Fig. 6.6 shows the major groove of the left hemisphere and the area associated with the language function. The Wernicke area is located near the posterior superior temporal cortex, auditory cortex. The Broca language area is near the motor cortex of the facial representation area.

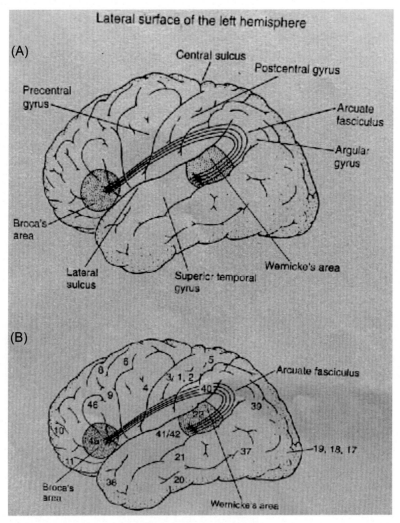

Figure 6.6 Human brain area of language processing.

The linking region between Wemicke and Broca region is called the arcuate fasciculus. In model B, The Brodmann partition of the left hemisphere is given. Area 41 is the primary auditory cortex, area 22 is the Wernicke language area, the area 45 region is the Broca language area, and area 4 is the primary motor cortex. In accordance with the original model, people hear a word via the nerve of the medial geniculate body information from the basilar membrane of the cochlea, which is then transmitted to the primary auditory cortex (Brodmann area 41), to higher cortical areas (42), behind the angle (39). The angular gyrus is a specific area of the parietal, temporal, and occipital cortex, which is believed to be related to the integration of afferent auditory, visual, and tactile information. Therefore, the information is sent to the Wernicke district (district 22) and the Broca area of the arcuate fasciculus (zone 45). In the area of Broca, the perception of language is translated into phrases of grammatical structure, and the sounds of memory are stored. Then the information of the phrase's sound pattern is transmitted to the facial motor cortex to control the area of pronunciation, so that the word can be uttered clearly.

In the Broca area, most of the studies focus on word-level analysis, almost without considering the sentence-level processing loss. This view believes that the memory of the word is the key. The Broca area is the position of the action memory of the word. The Wernicke area is a region associated with the feeling of the word. These ideas have led to the concept of three brain centers: the production area, the interaction between domains, and the concept of language function.

6.8.2 Classical localization model

Wernick, Broca, and their contemporary researchers promoted a view that language was positioned on a structure of anatomy and further constructed the formation of the brain. Sometimes this is called a classical localization model or a linguistic model of language. In the 1960s, the idea developed after the thinking of the American psychologist Geschwind [27] and, in the 1970s, became the dominant position. Note that the Geschwind connectionist model and the model developed by McClelland and Rumelhart are different from the computer simulation realization of interaction or a connectionist model. In the latter model, the interaction process plays the important role. Unlike the Geschwind connectionist model, it is distributed and not local. To avoid confusion, we call the Geschwind model the classic localization model.

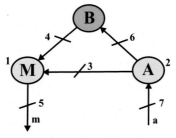

Figure 6.7 Geschwind model for language processing.

Fig. 6.7 shows a classical localization model proposed by Geschwind in the 1880s. In this model, three major centers for the processing of auditory or spoken language are labeled as A, B, and M in Fig. 6.7. The Wernicke area (that is, are A) is the home of the speech dictionary, which memorizes the word sounds permanently. The Broca area (M) is the area of planning and organizing spoken language. Concept memory is located in are B. The concept is widely distributed in the brain of the language model in the 19th century, but the new Wernicke-Lichtheim-Geschwind model is more discrete. For example, in this model, the supramarginal gyrus, angular back is considered as the site for the processing of sensory input characteristics (auditory, visual, tactile) and regional characteristics.

The classic localization model of this language suggests that linguistic information is local, in which individual brain regions are interconnected by the white matter area. Language processing is considered to be active in these language representations and to involve transmission of these representation of the language. The idea is very simple. According to the classic localization model, the information flow of the auditory language is as follows: Auditory input is converted in the auditory system, and the information is transmitted to the center of the occipital cortex and then transmitted to the Wernicke area, which can be extracted from the speech information. Information flow is transferred from the Wernicke area to the Broca area, the place where grammar features are stored and in which phrase structure can be arranged. Then the concept representation activates the center relevant concept. In this way, auditory comprehension occurs. As for oral language, in addition to the activation of the concept area to generate the concept pronunciation in the Wernicke area and to be transmitted to the Broca's area to organize oral English pronunciation, the other processes are similar.

In Fig. 6.7, there is a cross-link between A, B, and M. These connections represent the white matter fibers between the Wernicke area, the

Broca area, and the concept center, which are connected to one another in the brain. These fibers are considered to be separated from these regions. Damage to the A, B, and M center itself causes specific language barriers. Therefore, if the Wernicke-Lichtheim-Geschwind model is correct, we can predict the form of the language defect from the form of brain damage. In fact, all kinds of aphasia are in line with the prediction model, so this model is quite nice. Fig. 6.8 is an ideal model for the linguistic processing pathway [28].

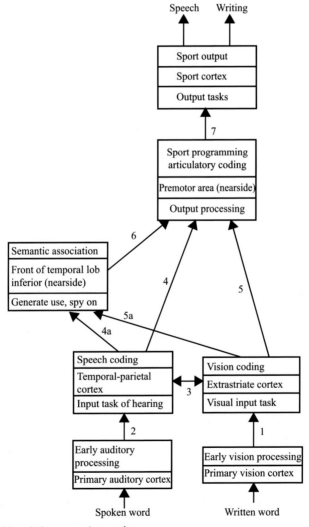

Figure 6.8 Linguistic processing pathway.

Some of the existing evidence supports the basic ideas of the Wernicke-Lichtheim-Geschwind model, but cognitive and brain imaging studies show that the model is too simple. Language function involves a complex interaction between multiple brain regions and these regions, not by the Wernicke area to the Broca area, and the links can be summarized. There are still some obvious defects in the model:

1. Prior to the advent of computer tomography, magnetic resonance imaging (MRI), and neural imaging technology, damage localization was very rough, and sometimes we had to rely on autopsy information, which is difficult to obtain or based on other, better definitions of concurrent symptoms.
2. Determining the differences in the injury site from the autopsy studies and neuroimaging data can be difficult.
3. The damage itself makes a big difference; for example, brain damage can sometimes lead to Wernicke aphasia.
4. The patient is often classified as being in more than one diagnostic category in the classification. For example, there are a number of components of Broca aphasia.

6.8.3 Memory-integration-control model

The neural network model of the new generation is different from the classical Wernicke-Geschwind model. The new model connects a variety of psychological language findings and neural circuits in the brain. In these models, the neural circuits of language are still considered to be determined by the Broca and Wernicke traditional language processing areas, but these areas are no longer considered the classical model that is language specific, and they not only appear in language processing. In addition, some other areas of the brain have become a part of the language processing circuit but not necessarily a specific language processing.

In 2005 Hagoort proposed a new language model [29], which is the result of brain and language research. He points out the three functional components of language processing and the possible representation of them in the brain:

1. *Memory*: Lexical information is stored in and extracted from the mental lexicon or long-term memory.
2. *Integration*: The extracted speech and semantic and syntactic information are integrated into a global output characterization. In language understanding, the processing of speech and semantic and syntactic

information can be performed in parallel and simultaneously. In addition, all kinds of information can be interactive. The integration process allows the Hagoort model to become a model of interaction based on constraints. Friedrich gives a more modular language processing neural model example [30].

3. *Control*: Language is associated with actions, as in a bilingual translation.

The processing of speech, lexical semantics, and syntactic information is involved in many areas, including the Broca area or the left inferior frontal gyrus. But, as the Hagoort neural model has revealed, Broca is certainly neither a language generating module nor the location of syntactic parsing. Moreover, the Broca area is not likely to perform a certain function as defined in the first place.

When people carry out the actual exchange, such as alternative talking during a conversation, the model of the control is particularly important. There are a few studies on cognitive control in language understanding, but in other tasks involving cognitive control of the brain, such as the cingulate gyrus and the back of the prefrontal cortex (i.e., 46/9 Brodmann area) in the language understanding, cognitive control also plays a role.

The human language system is very complex, so how to achieve such a wealth of language and language understanding in the biological mechanism of the brain? There are too many problems that need to be studied. And the combination of the mental language model, neural science, and psychological calculation can clarify the language of the human spirit of encoding. Future language research is full of hope.

6.8.4 Bilingual brain functional areas

Do different regions in the human brain represent different languages? The study of this problem is a hot topic in language functional imaging. Many scholars have bilingual or multilingual individuals as subjects to observe different language activation performances. Although the results vary from person to person, most scholars believe that the bilingual language and the second language have a lot of overlap in the brain activation area, including the Wernicke and Broca areas. For example, the visual stimuli in the brain regions activated by both Chinese and English bilingual brain regions are in the left frontal lobe and left temporal regions. When Spanish and Catalan bilinguals are listening to stories, the left temporal lobe and hippocampus overlap. A wide range of overlap between the left, temporal, and parietal lobes were also found in Spanish and English.

There are many overlapping brain activation areas between the native language and the second language area. The second language area is often found to be activated with broad extension and intensity compared with the mother tongue. This phenomenon usually occurs in less fluent bilingual subjects and rarely appears in bilingual subjects. It is not related to when the subject begins to learn the second language but is associated with the use frequency of the second language.

References

[1] N. Chomsky, Syntactic Structures, Mouton, The Hague, 1957.
[2] W.A. Woods, Transition network grammars for natural language analysis, Comm. ACM 13 (10) (1970).
[3] T. Winograd, Understanding Natural Language, Academic Press, 1972.
[4] R.Q. Lu, Formal Semantics of Computer Language, Science Press, 1992.
[5] Z.Z. Shi, Knowledge Engineering (In Chinese), Tsinghua University Press, 1988.
[6] S.W. Yu, H.M. Duan, X.F. Zhu, B. Sun, Basic processing specification of modern Chinese corpus of Peking University (in Chinese), J. Chin. Inf. Process. 16 (5) (2002) 49−64. 16(6)
[7] D. Jurafsky, J.H. Martin, Speech and Language Processing, Pearson, 2008.
[8] J.C. Yang, Y.Y. Yang, The rhythm generation in speech production, Psychol Sci. 12 (4) (2004) 481−488.
[9] J. Shen, Structure and types of Chinese intonation, Dialects (1994) 221−228. No. 4.
[10] W.J.M. Levelt, Speaking: From Intention to Articulation, The MIT Press, Cambridge, 1989.
[11] W.J.M. Levelt, A.P.A. Roelofs, A.S. Meyer, A theory of lexical access in speech production [target paper], Behav. Brain Sci. 22 (1) (1999) 1−37.
[12] J. Mayer, D. Wildgruber, A. Riecker, et al., Prosody production and perception: converging evidence from fMRI studies, in: Proceedings of Speech Prosody 2002, Aix-en-Provence, France, April, 11−13, pp. 487−490.
[13] D.L. Peng (Ed.), Cognitive Study of Chinese (in Chinese), Shandong Education Press, China, 1997.
[14] G.S. Dell, A spreading activation theory of retrieval in language production, Psychol. Rev. 93 (1986) 226−234.
[15] T. Harley, Language production, The Psychology of Language, Psychology Press Ltd, 2001, pp. 349−390.
[16] A. Roelofs, The WEAVER model of word-form encoding in speech production, Cognition 64 (3) (1997) 249−284.
[17] O.G. Selfridge, Pandemonium: a paradigm for learning, in: Proceedings of a Symposium on the Mechanization of Thought Processes, London: H. M. Stationery Office, (1959) pp. 511−526.
[18] J.L. McClelland, D.E. Rumelhart, An interactive activation model of context effects in letter perception: Part 1. An account of basic findings, Psychol. Rev. 88 (1981) 375−407.
[19] J.A. Fodor, The Modularity of Mind, MIT Press, Cambridge, MA, 1983.

[20] M. Coltheart, B. Curtis, P. Atkins, M. Haller, Models of reading aloud: dual-route and parallel-distributed-processing approaches, Psychol Rev. 100 (1993) 589—608.

[21] M.S. Seidenberg, J.L. McClelland, Visual word recognition and pronunciation: a computational model of acquisition, skilled performance, and dyslexia, in: A. Galaburda (Ed.), From Neurons to Reading, MIT Press, Cambridge, MA, 1989, pp. 255—305.

[22] Z.W. Feng, Formal Model of Natural Language Processing (in Chinese), China University of Science and Technology Press, China, 2010.

[23] R.C. Schank, Conceptual dependency: {A} theory of natural language understanding, Cognit. Psychol. 3 (4) (1972) 532—631.

[24] Y.X. Zhong, Principles of Advanced Artificial Intelligence: Concepts, Methods, Models and Theories (in Chinese), Science Press, China, Beijing, 2014.

[25] R. D. Brown, Example-Based Machine Translation in the Pangloss System. In COLING 1996, Proceedings of the Sixteenth International Conference on Computation Linguistics, Center for Sprogteknologi, Copenhagen, Denmark, August 5—9, (1996) pp.169_174.

[26] E.E. Smith, E.J. Shoben, L.J. Rips, Structure and process in semantic memory: a featural model for semantic decisions, Psychol Rev. 81 (1974) 214—241.

[27] N. Geschwind, Brain mechanisms suggested by studies of hemispheric connections, in: C.H. MiUiken, F.L. Darley (Eds.), Brain Mechanisms Underlying Speech and Language, Gruen and Stratton, New York, 1967.

[28] R. Mayeux, E.R. Kandel, Disorders of language: the aphasias, in: E.R. Kandel, J.H. Schwartz, T.M. Jessell (Eds.), Principles of Neural Science, third ed., Elsevier, 1991, pp. 840—851.

[29] P. Hagoort, On broca, brain, and binding: a new framework, Trends Cognit. Sci. 9 (9) (2005) 416—423.

[30] A.D. Friederici, K. Steinhauer, E. Pfeifer, Brain signatures of artificial language processing: evidence challenging the critical period hypothesis, Proc. Natl Acad. Sci. USA 99 (2002) 529—534.

CHAPTER 7

Learning

Learning ability is a fundamental characteristic of human intelligence [1]. People learn from the objective environment constantly over their whole life span. A person's cognitive ability, wisdom, and lifelong learning is subject to the gradual formation, development, and improvement.

Human learning and machine learning are two different ways of learning. Human learning mainly relies on induction and logical reasoning. Machine learning is mainly statistical analysis, relying on big data and intelligent algorithm.

7.1 Basic principle of learning

Learning and training have always been the main research content of psychology. The definition of learning is being developed constantly too. In 1983 Simon [2] gave a better definition of learning: a certain long-term change that the system produces in order to adapt to the environment, so that the system can finish the same or similar work more effectively the next time [3]. Learning is the change taking place in a system; it can be either permanent improvement of the systematic work or permanent change in the behavior of the organism. In a complicated system, a change in learning is due to many reasons; that is to say, there are many forms of the learning process in the same system, and its different parts will undergo different improvements. People can set new production rules and set up new behaviors.

The principle of learning is that the learner must know the last result, i.e. whether the behavior can be improved. It's better for learner to get information about which parts of the behavior are satisfied and which parts are not. The knowledge and acceptance of the learning results is a kind of remuneration or encouragement, and this knowledge can produce or strengthen learning motivation. The interaction of the information gained and the motivation to achieve the learning result is called reinforcement in psychology, and their relationship is as follows:

$$\text{Reinforcement} = \underset{\text{(information)}}{\text{Resulting knowledge}} + \underset{\text{(motivation)}}{\text{Reward}}$$

Intelligence Science
DOI: https://doi.org/10.1016/B978-0-323-85380-4.00007-5

Reinforcement is possibly extrinsic as well as internal. It can be positive and can be passive. There must be a positive learning motivation when learning, and reinforcement can support learning motivation. The teacher should pay attention to the choice of the learning material in education in order to attract students' attention and encourage them. If the learning material is too simple, it might not attract students, and students grow easily tired of them; if the learning material is too complicated, it might be difficult for students to understand, and students grow disinterested. Therefore, factors influencing learning motivation are various, including the property and composition of learning material, etc.

The author has proposed a kind of learning system framework (see Fig. 7.1) [4], where the ellipse denotes the information unit, the rectangle denotes the processing unit, and the arrow denotes the main direction of data flow in the learning system.

The most important factor influencing the learning system is the environment that provides the system with information, especially its level and quality. The environment provides the learning unit with information; the learning unit uses this information to improve the knowledge base; the execution unit then utilizes the knowledge base to carry out its task; finally, the information obtained can be fed back to the learning unit. For the human being to learn, utility information is produced through the internal learning machine to be fed back to the learning unit.

Learning theory is about learning the essence of the learning process, learning the rules and constraints, in order to study the various conditions and to explore the theory and explanation. Learning theory must provide knowledge in the field, analyze and explore learning methods and means; it must make it clear which aspects of learning are the most worth

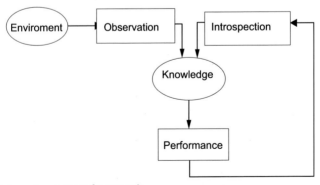

Figure 7.1 Learning system framework.

learning, which independent variables should be controlled, which dependent variables should be analyzed, which methods and techniques can be used, and what kind of terms should be used to describe the results of the learning, so as to provide educators with a framework for research and learning. From this sense, learning theory consists of the guidelines and resources that people learn to conduct scientific research and thinking. It is summarizing a large amount of knowledge about learning the rules and systematizing and standardizing them. However, any theory in the abstract and generally any large amount of specific knowledge about the process will inevitably lose a certain degree of specificity and accuracy, precisely because of theories are general guides. Learning theory should explain how learning works, why some learning methods are effective, and some are invalid. The learning rules tells us "how to learn," and learning theory then tells us "why to learn like this."

Learning is a kind of process, where individuals can produce lasting changes in behavior by training. What does the change denote? How does an individual's behavior change? So far, psychologists have not come to an agreement on these the answers to these questions. Therefore, there are various learning theories. For over 100 years, psychologists have provided all kinds of learning theory schools according to differences in their philosophical foundations, theory backgrounds, research means. These theory schools mainly include the behavioral school, cognitive school, and humanist school.

7.2 The learning theory of the behavioral school

Behavioral psychologists interpret learning as the formation of habit by using the relationship between stimulus and response by training. In their options, an unprecedented relation can be established between a certain stimulus and the related response, and such an establishing process is called learning. This kind of learning theory is therefore called stimuli—response theory, or the behavioral school. The learning theory of the behavioral school emphasizes the kind of behavior that can be observed. According to this theory, numerous happy or painful consequences of behavior can change an individual's behavior. Pavlov's classical conditioned reflex theory, Watson's behaviorism view, Thorndike's connection doctrine, Skinner's operation conditioned reflex theory, etc. all classically belong to the behavioral school.

Other psychologists do not agree that learning is the process of habit formation. In their options, learning is a cognitive process of individual cognizing relation among the things in its environment. So this kind of theory is known as cognitive theory.

7.2.1 Learning theory of conditioned reflex

Russian physiologist Ivan Pavlov is the founder of the classical conditioning reflex theory (Pavlov Website). Pavlov was studying a dog's digestive physiology phenomenon. The food was placed in front of the dog, and its effect on saliva secretion was measured. Usually the dog salivated when the food was about to be eaten. However, Pavlov accidentally discovered that the dog did not have to eat the food; just hearing the food breeder's footsteps, they started to salivate. Pavlov did not ignore this phenomenon. He began to do an experiment. He tried making the dog listen to a ring, but the dog did not respond. But when the dog heard a ring immediately after the food was delivered, after many repetitions, with just a separate ring without the food, the dog "learned" to secrete saliva. The combination of the bell and the unconditional stimulus (food) changed from a neutral stimulus to a conditional stimulus, which caused the conditioned response of saliva secretion. Pavlov called this phenomenon conditioned reflex, that is, classical conditioned reflex. In the Pavlovian conditioned reflex, the physiological mechanism of the formation of the neural connection is temporary and learning is a temporary formation of neural connection.

The impact of Pavlov's classical conditioning theory has been enormous. In Russia, the theory based on Pavlov's classical conditioned reflex theory dominated the circle of psychology for a long time. In the United States, behavioral psychologists Watson, Skinner, and others were all impacted by Pavlov's conditioned reflex theory.

7.2.2 Learning theory of behaviorism

Behaviorism was founded by America psychologist J. B. Watson in 1913 [5]. The characteristics of the theory are as follows:
1. It emphasizes that psychology is a science, so we should pay attention to experiment and observation in method and only observe and record the explicit behavior in the research subject.
2. The basis of explaining constitutive behavior is the individual's external reaction, and the formation and change of the reaction is the course of restriction.

3. Paying attention to the influence of environment on individual behavior and not recognizing the importance of individual free will are regarded as determinism.
4. In education, it advocates both reward and punishment, neglects internal motivation, and emphasizes the training value of external control.

Behaviorism became popular in the United States and extended to the whole world in the 20th century, until nearly all of psychology was dominated by behaviorism, which is also known as behavioral psychology. Behavioralism changed later, due to different points of view in explaining behavior, to radical behaviorism and the new behaviorism (neo-behaviorism).

Watson is the first American psychologist who regarded Pavlov's classical conditioned reflex theory as the theoretical foundation of learning. He believes that learning is the process of establishing conditioned reflex by replacing one stimulus with another. Except for the concentrated conditioned reflex (such as sneezing and knee jerk reflex) at birth, all human behaviors are formed by establishing a new stimulus response connection (S-R connection) through conditioned reflex.

Watson used the principle of conditioned reflex to create fear in a baby in order to prove his point. The experimental objects were an original pair of rabbits and a human baby without any fear. In the experiment, whenever the rabbits appeared in front of the baby, there was at the same time a terrible voice. After many repetitions, the baby felt fear once he saw a rabbit, even just the hair.

7.2.3 Association learning theory

From the end of 19th century to the beginning of 20th century, Thorndike's learning theory had occupied the leadership in American psychological circles for nearly 50 years. Thorndike is the pioneer of animal psychology at Harvard University. Since 1896, he systematically studied animal behaviors by using a chicken, cat, dog, fish, etc., thus first putting forward the most intact learning theory in learning psychology. Through the scientific experiment method, he found that individual learning is via a kind of "try to be successful accidentally by mistake." In this way, a kind of connection or combination between stimulus and response is established through repeated responses to a stimulus. In Thorndike's view, the essence of learning lay in forming the association between situation and response. So this kind of learning theory is known as association theory.

The situation, denoted by S, is sometimes called the stimulus, which includes the cerebral internal situation, the external situation, thought, and emotion. Response, denoted by R, includes internal response, such as "the activities of muscles and glands," and internal response, such as idea, will, emotion, and attitude. The so-called connection includes association, relation, inclination, meaning that a certain situation can only arouse a certain response and cannot arouse other responses. By the symbol "→" we mean "arouse." The formula of association is expressed by $S \rightarrow R$.

The relation between situation and response is the causality. The relation is a directed association without any intermediary. Thorndike thought that association is an instinctive combination. He applied such association to human being's learning. In his terms, all the thoughts, behaviors, and activities of human beings can be resolved into the connection of the basic unit of stimulus with response. The difference between the learning of human being and that of an animal is that "the learning process of the animal is blindfolded" and "does not need the idea as a medium," while the human being's learning needs the idea as a medium and is conscious. But the essential distinction lies in suppleness and complexity as well as in the number of associations. The law of an animal's learning is still suitable for human learning [6].

The association between stimulus and response is subject to three principles:

1. The number of the practices
2. The individual's own preparation state
3. The result after the response

These three principles are known as Thorndike's famous three laws: practice law, prepare law, result law. Practice law means that the more often an individual responds to a certain stimulus, the stronger the association is. Prepare law is in fact a motivation principle. Motivation is an inherent process that causes individual activity and maintains this activity. Result law, the core of association theory, mainly emphasizes that the power of association is determined by the result of the response. If an individual obtains a satisfactory result, the association is strengthened after the response; otherwise is weakened.

After 1930, Thorndike had modified the practice law and result law. He thought that practice cannot strengthen the association between situation and response unconditionally. Practice is helpful only when accompanied by a sense of satisfaction. For result law, an unsatisfactory sense cannot directly weaken the association but just admits that satisfaction can strengthen the association. In Thorndike's terms, association is built by trial and error. Learning is a gradual and blindfolded process. In this process, with the gradual increase of the right response and the gradual reduction of error response, the firm association between stimulus and response is finally formed. Thorndike carried on the experiment with different animals, and the results were quite consistent. Therefore, he thought that the forming of association followed a certain law. Thorndike still proposed accessional laws of learning, including (1) selection response law, (2) multiple response law, (3) fixed response law, (4) apperception response law, and (5) associative transference law.

Thorndike's learning theory is the first comparatively intact learning theory in the history of educational psychology. It was great progress that he used experimentation instead of the argument method to study learning. His theory has caused the academic controversy about learning theory, promoting the development of learning theory. Association theory has helped to establish the key position in the theoretical system and has helped accordingly to set up the discipline system of educational psychology, promoting the development of educational psychology.

Association theory is based on instinct, and the association between situation and response is interpreted as the supreme principle of learning. It is the determinism of heredity and instinct doctrine [6]. But it obliterates the sociality, consciousness, and dynamic role of human beings and fails to open up the essence of the human being and the essential distinction between an animal's learning and a human being's learning. It is a mechanical doctrine. It ignores the roles of cognition, idea, and understanding in the learning process and does not accord with the reality of learning. But test-error theory is still regarded as a kind of the form of learning until today, especially playing an important role in the learning of motor skill and social behavior. Thorndike's learning theory seems a bit simple and cannot explain the essential law of learning. But there are some corrections too. Even today, some of the laws are still of directive significance.

7.2.4 Operational learning theory

Operational learning theory was proposed by the US new behaviorist psychologist B. F. Skinner in *Verbal Behavior* [7]. This theory is based on the operate conditioning reflex experiment that is carried on with an animal. During this experiment, the organism encounters a special kind of stimulus, called a reinforcing stimulus or simply a reinforcer. This special stimulus has the effect of increasing the operant, that is, the behavior occurring just before the reinforcer. This is operant conditioning: The behavior is followed by a consequence, and the nature of the consequence modifies the organism's tendency to repeat the behavior in the future. By this theory, the power of child's ability to speaking is owing to acquired learning. Like studying other behaviors, it is acquired by operational conditioned reflex.

Skinner thought that there are two kinds of conditioning: Pavlov's classical conditioning and operational conditioning. Pavlov's classical conditioned reflex is a responsive (or irritant) conditioned reflex process. It is a reaction first caused by a known stimulus and a process of combining reinforcement and stimulus. Reinforcement strengthens the stimulus. Skinner's operant conditioning is a process of reactive conditioning. There is no known stimulus. It is a spontaneous response by the organism itself. It is a process of combining reinforcement and response. Reinforcement enhances the response.

Skinner thought that all behaviors were made up of reflection. There are two kinds of behaviors and then two kinds of behaviors: responsive behavior and operational behavior. Therefore, there are two kinds of learning: responsive learning and operational learning. Skinner paid more attention to operational learning. He thought that operational behavior could better reflect a human being's learning, which is all operational learning. Therefore, the most effective method to study behavioral science is to investigate the forming of operational behavior and its law.

In Skinner's terms, reinforcement is an important means by which operational behavior is formed. Reinforcement plays an extremely important role in Skinner's theory. It is the foundation and core of Skinner's theory and is also called reinforcement theory or reinforcement doctrine. Its basic law is as follows: If reinforcement stimulus appears after an operation happens, the strength (the probability of reacting) of this operation is increased. The change of learning and behavior is an intensive result, and behavior can be controlled by controlling enhancing. Reinforcement is the key to molding behavior and keeping up behavioral intensity. The process of molding behavior is a learning process; education is the molding of behavior. As long as we can control the intensity of behavior, it is possible to optionally mold people's and animal's behaviors.

In 1954 in his paper "The Art of Teaching Science and Learning," Skinner criticized traditional teaching according to his reinforcement theory [7]. Hence Skinner strongly maintained that class teaching should be reformed by performing procedure teaching and machine teaching. The learning content should be programmed as a procedure and installed in a machine, according to the operate conditioning reflex principle. Students could complete their learning by using the installed procedure. The process of procedure learning is to divide a big problem into several small questions and addressing them in a certain order and asking students to answer each question. In this way, students can receive related feedback information. The question is equivalent to "stimulus" in the forming process of the conditioned reflex, while the student's answer is then equivalent to the "response," and feedback information is equivalent to "reinforcement." The key to procedure learning is to program good procedure. For this reason, Skinner proposed five basic principles in establishing a procedure:

1. Small step principle: Divide total learning content into teaching materials that consist of pieces of knowledge, which are sorted in ascending order by the knowledge's difficulty, thus enabling students to learn step by step.
2. Positive reaction principle: We should make students react positively to what they have learned and deny the view that "although they have not shown any reaction, they really understand."
3. Reinforcement in time (feedback) principle: The response to students should be reinforced in time, so that they can get feedback information.
4. Making the step by oneself principle: Students determine their learning progress by themselves according to their own learning situations.
5. Low wrong rate: Students must make the correct response each time, and the wrong rate must be minimized as much as possible.

Skinner thinks that procedural teaching has the following advantages: step by step learning; learning speed and learning capacity of the same; correcting student's mistakes in time, speeding up learning; conducive to improving student learning initiatives; students' self-learning abilities and habits. Procedural teaching is not perfect. Since it makes the acquisition of knowledge the main goal of individualized learning styles, three aspects of it have been criticized: It makes students acquire more rigid knowledge; collective classes lack interpersonal contacts and are not conducive to the socialization of children; it neglects the role of teachers.

7.2.5 Contiguity theory of learning

Edwin R. Guthrie largely agreed with the view of behaviorism in psychology. In 1921, he explained behaviors mainly in terms of the association between stimulus and response. In his view, there are two forms of learning. The first one is active adaptation, that is to say, the organism will react constantly in order to adapt to the environment. But this is just the reprint of Watson's theory. The second one is the condition function. This is similar to Pavlov's learning theory. Guthrie thought that all responses were initially caused by a certain unconditioned stimulus. Such stimulus also may be an existing neutral stimulus. The essence of the condition function is to replace unconditioned stimulus with neutral stimulus in order to cause response. In a sense, this formula is suitable for all learning. So conditional function has become synonymous of learning in fact. This was the creed of nearly all theoreticians at that time.

In 1935 Guthery published his book "Psychology of Learning" [8]. In this book, he had proposed the learning theory with his own characteristics. Guthrie's contiguity theory specifies that a combination of stimuli which has accompanied a movement will on its recurrence tend to be followed by that movement. According to Guthrie, all learning was a consequence of association between a particular stimulus and response. Furthermore, Guthrie argued that stimuli and responses affect specific sensory motor patterns; movements are learned, not behaviors.

In contiguity theory, rewards or punishment play no significant role in learning since they occur after the association between stimulus and response has been made. Learning takes place in a single trial (all or none). However, since each stimulus pattern is slightly different, many trials may be necessary to produce a general response. One interesting principle that arises from this position is called postremity, which specifies that we always learn the last thing we do in response to a specific stimulus situation. Contiguity theory suggests that forgetting is due to interference rather than the passage of time; stimuli become associated with new responses. Previous conditioning can also be changed by being associated with inhibiting responses such as fear or fatigue. The role of motivation is to create a state of arousal and activity that produces responses that can be conditioned. Contiguity theory is intended to be a general theory of learning, although most of the research supporting the theory was done with animals. Guthrie did apply his framework to personality disorders [9].

7.2.6 Need reduction theory

American psychologist and behaviorist Clark Leonard Hull conducted research demonstrating that his theories could predict and control behavior. His most significant works were the *Mathematico-Deductive Theory of Rote Learning* (1940) and *Principles of Behavior* (1943), which established his analysis of animal learning and conditioning as the dominant learning theory of its time. Hull created the "hypothetic-deductive" systematic method, after the observation and elaboration of hypotheses [10]. This method brought him precise definitions and conceptualized axioms that helped him develop his theories. He believed that behavior was a set of interactions between an individual and the environment. He analyzed behavior from a perspective of biological adaptation, which is an optimization of living conditions through need reduction.

Hull's need reduction theory emphasizes that the learning process consists of four elements: motivation, tips, response, and reward. Motivation is a driving action of the internal stimulus produced in an individual. Some incentives are biological in nature—not academic—such as pain, thirst, hunger, etc., and some have to do with learning to manage, such as fear, social needs. Motivation is the basis of behavior; without incentives, individuals do not act, there would be no learning.

Tips lead to individual responses and determine when, where, and what kind of reaction an individual will have. The value of a hint lies in its characteristics. A hint can be the goal of an individual action and the inspiration to achieve that goal, and it can also have the preceding two functions.

Incentives to promote the individual's reaction are in the form of the reward paid after reaction. The same reaction will continue to be generated if the individual continues to receive remuneration, and habits can be formed. If the reaction is not to be paid, the reaction is reduced, along with the tendency to repeat. Therefore, reducing the incentive reward for repeating the reaction constitutes learning. The incentive for reduction is the individual's need for satisfaction; that is, the individual seeks to meet the needs of his or her needs. This theory is therefore known as the need reduction theory.

Hull's theory system is presented in three main works: "Behavioral Principle," "Behavioral Foundation," and "Behavioral System." There are 17 formulas and 17 inferences in the most basic form of this system. These forms are used for the symbol units, which expound the following issues [11]:

1. The association between stimulus and response and the feeling of ability that organism takes to learning situation
2. The process of motivation and the state of inner drive that can effectively strengthen behaviors

3. The law of forming habit
4. The elements that influence no–association caused by response
5. The reverse condition inhibition that response trends toward
6. The elements causing both habit strength and response trend to be complicated
7. When more than one stimulus appears at the same time, the elements causing the excitability of stimulus to be complicated is greater than the constant alterations in formulas caused by individual differences. Enhancing principle is the foundation of this system.

The strengthening principle is the cornerstone of this system. In its initial form, Hull strengthened the hypothesis that a response to basic needs or driving force is due to a tendency to be met and enhanced.

7.3 Cognitive learning theory

An opposition school to behaviorism theory was derived from the Gestalt school of cognitive learning theory After a period of silence, the mid-1950s saw the appearance of much creative work by many cognitive psychologists, such as Bruner or Ausubel, and learning theory entered the most brilliant period since Thorndike. They believed that learning is at the heart of the problems of the day and that organizations needed to make active efforts to form and develop the process of cognitive structure, emphasizing that the link between stimulus and response is mediated consciousness and asserting the importance of cognitive processes. Cognitivism learning theory began to dominate in the study of learning theory.

Cognitive refers to the process of cognition and cognitive process analysis. American psychologist G. A. Gilbert thought that a person's cognitive understanding of the objective world is generally experienced by means of several processes, including perception, understanding, reasoning, and several relatively unique processes, leading to awareness of the meaning. Cognitive structure has become a modern educational psychology trying to understand the core issue of students' psychology. Learning is the cognitive school of thought within cognitive changes; learning is an S-R association that is a much more complex process. The cognitive school focuses on explaining the intermediate process of learning behavior, that is, purpose, meaning, and so on, and believes that these processes are the variable factors controlling learning. The main contributions of cognitive school's learning theory are as follows:

1. Pay attention to people's subject value in learning activities and affirm fully the learner's conscious dynamic role.

2. Emphasize the important position and function of consciousness activity in learning, such as cognition, understanding, thinking independently.

3. Paid attention to people's preparation state in learning activities. This means that the result of a person's learning depends not only on outside stimuli and the individual's subjective efforts but on a person's existing knowledge level, cognitive structure, noncognitive factor. Preparation is the precondition of any meaningful learning.

4. Emphasize the function of reinforcement. Cognitive learning theory pays much attention to the inherent reinforcement function caused by inner motive and learning itself.

5. Advocate the creativity of people's learning. Bruner's discovery in learning theory emphasizes the flexibility, initiative, and findings of student learning. It requires students to observe, explore, and experiment. Students should develop the spirit of creation, think independently, reorganize materials, find knowledge, and grasp the principle by themselves. Bruner recommend an exploratory learning method. He insisted that student's intelligence potentially should be developed through discovery learning theory and that the learning motive should be regulated and enhanced to grasp knowledge and then develop the ability of innovation.

The weak point in the cognitive learning theory is that it cannot reveal the mental structure of the learning process. In our view, learning psychology consists of the mental structure of the learning process, including intelligence factors and no-intelligence factors. The intelligence factor is a psychological foundation of the learning process, which plays an important role in learning. The no-intelligence factor is the psychological condition of the learning process, which plays an indirect role in learning. Only closely combining intelligence factors with no-intelligence factors can enable learning to achieve the purpose desired. But the cognitive learning theory pays little attention to the research on the no-intelligence factors.

The Gestalt school's learning theory, Tolman's cognitive purpose theory, Piaget's diagrammatic theory, Bruner's discovery learning theory, Ausubel's meaningful learning theory, Gagné's information processing learning theory and the learning theory of constructivism are all considered the representative theory of the cognitive school. This school's representative persons are Piaget, Newell, among others.

7.3.1 Learning theory of Gestalt school

Early 20th-century theorists, such as Kurt Koffka, Max Wertheimer, and Wolfgang Köhler from Germany, established the Gestalt school [12]. The school's learning theory is to study the perception issue in Thorndike's learning theory. They stressed the integrity of experience and behavior against the behavior theory of stimulus-response formula and redesigned the learning experiments with animals.

Gestalt theory is well-known for its concept of insight learning. They think that learning is not a gradual test-error process but the reorganization of perceptual experience and insight in relation to the current situation. The basic standpoints of the Gestalt school are as follows:

1. Learning is a kind of whole form organization. Gestalt views learning as a kind of whole form organization that refers to the style of things and relationships awareness. The learning process to resolve the problem is due to the situation in understanding the relationship of things and constitutes a kind of whole form to achieve. A chimpanzee can find the relationship that the pole can be a tool for it to grasp the banana, thus filling the gap and constituting a whole form. According to the Gestalt school, motor learning, sensory learning, and perceptual learning all lie in generating a whole form organization, not a link between the various parts.

2. Learning is achieved through insight. The Gestalt school holds that learning success and achievement are entirely due to "insight" result, that is, sudden understanding rather than "test-error" or "trial and error." Insight is the overall perception of situations and understanding the relationship of things in the problem situation, that is, the process of whole form organization.

Gestalt justifies the learning process as insight rather than trial and error mainly using the following evidence: (1) sudden transformation from "no" to "yes" and (2) that learning can be maintained so as not to duplicate the error. They point out that, as set out by the Thorndike problem, the situation is not clear, resulting in blind trial-and-error learning.

The evaluations of the Gestalt school's theory are as follows:

1. Gestalt theory has a dialectical study of reasoning factors, mainly in that it confirmed the role of consciousness, emphasizing the cognitive factors (Gestalt organization) in the learning role. This makes up for the learning theory of Thorndike defects that the relationship between stimulus and response is indirect, not direct, and takes consciousness as

the intermediary. Gestalt school criticized test-error and promoted the development of the theory of learning.

2. Gestalt insight was affirmed; at the same time, denying the role of test-error is one-sided. Test-error and the insight occur at different stages of the learning process or different types of learning. Test-error is often a prelude to insight, and insight is often the inevitable result of test-error. The two are not mutually exclusive opposites but should be complementary. The Gestalt theory of learning was not complete and systemic enough. Its impact was far less than that of Thorndike's association theory at that time.

7.3.2 Cognitive purposive theory

Edward Chace Tolman regards himself as a behaviorist. He amalgamated each school's theory and is famous for learning widely from others' strong points. He appreciated not only the link to objectivity and the simple method of measuring behavior but also the Gestalt view of the impact of overall study. His learning theory has many names, such as symbol learning, purpose learning, latent learning, and expecting learning. He insisted that theory should be a completely objective method of testing. However, many people think his is a study of animal learning behavior of the most influential cognitive activists. Affected by the Gestalt school, he stressed the integrity of behavior. He considered that the overall behavior points to a definite purpose, while the organism achieves awareness of the environment's means to an end. He did not agree with a direct link between the situation (stimulus) and response, or S-R. He put forward the "intervening variable" concept that there are intermediary between experimental variables and behavior variables to link the two factors. In particular, the intermediate variable is the psychological process that links stimulus and response. Therefore the formula S-R of the formula should be S-O-R, where O represents an intermediary variable. His learning theory takes this point of view, throughout the whole process of animal learning behavior study.

Tolman is best known for his studies of learning in rats using mazes, and he published many experimental articles, of which his paper with Ritchie and Kalish in 1946 was probably the most influential. His major theoretical contributions came in his 1932 book, *Purposive Behavior in Animals and Men* [13]. The main viewpoints of Tolman's cognitive purposive theory are as follows:

1. Learning is purposeful. In Tolman's terms, the learning of animals is purposeful, which is to get food. He disagreed with Thorndike's viewpoint that learning is blind. The "test-error" animal behaviors are guided by the goal (food) in the labyrinth, and they will not give up without reaching the purpose. He believed that learning was to acquire expectation. The expectation is the individual's idea about the goal. Through the observation of the current stimulus situation and past experience, the individual builds up the expectation of the goal.

2. Awareness of the environmental conditions is a means or way to achieve the goal. Tolman thought that the organism would encounter all kinds of the environmental condition during the process of achieving the goal. Only with an understanding of the condition can the difficulty be overcome and the goal achieved. Therefore, the cognition of the environmental condition is a means or way to achieve the goal. Tolman used symbol to denote the cognition of the environmental condition of the organism. Learning is not a simple, mechanical reflection of the formation of movement but is intended to learn to achieve the purpose of symbols, form a "cognitive map." The so-called cognitive map is formed in the minds of animals in a comprehensive representation of the environment, including the route, direction, distance, even time, and more. This is a relatively vague concept.

In a word, purpose and cognition are two important intermediary variables in Tolman's theory, which is then referred to as cognitive purposive theory.

Tolman's cognitive purposive learning theory pays attention to behavioral integrity and purpose and puts forward the concept of an intermediary variable, emphasizing the psychological processes between stimulus and response and emphasizing the awareness, purpose, and expectations of those involved in the study is progress and should be affirmed. In Tolman theory, some of the terminology, such as "cognitive map," is not clearly defined; it does not distinguish between human learning and animal learning; therefore the attention is mechanical, which makes his theory unable to be a complete rational system.

7.3.3 Cognitive discovery theory

T. S. Bruner is a prominent contemporary American cognitive psychologist. In 1960 he, together with George Miller, established the cognitive research center of Harvard University. He is the main representative of the United States' cognitive theory.

Bruner's cognitive learning theory is influenced by Gestalt theory, Tolman's ideas, and Piaget's epistemology. He thought that learning is a cognitive process, where the learner forwardly forms the cognitive structure. But Bruner's cognitive learning theory is different from Gestalt theory and Tolman's theory. The major difference is that the Gestalt and Tolman's theories are based on research on animal learning, and the related cognition is conscious cognition. Bruner's cognitive learning theory, then, is based on human learning, and related cognition is an abstract thought cognition.

Bruner's discovery learning model states that learning occurs through exploration, in which students discover the unknown or gain interchangeable knowledge. Students develop processes for the attainment of information from their experience. Bruner believed that the student's first growth is through stimulus, which represents how the knowledge is gained though related experiences. This enables the student to attain information that has been stored for later recall. Bruner also discusses how the mental process of the person's mind projects stimulus–response through discovery learning. Discovery learning can be defined as an independent practice on the learner's part to maintain information, without memory and with much self-confidence. Students who complete individual discovery learning tend to recognize the connections within themselves, and what was learned with this type of discovery is placed in high value. In discovery learning, Bruner makes note that students become individual thinkers and encourages youth to adopt the attitude of wanting to discover new ideas and the unknown [14]. Its basic viewpoint is discussed next.

7.3.3.1 Learning is active in the process of the formation of cognitive structures

The cognitive structure refers to an internal cognitive system that reflects the relationship between things or that is all the contents and organizations of a learner's idea. People's understanding activity is organized by a certain order. In Bruner's terms, human beings initiatively acquire knowledge and initiatively select, change, store, and employ the sensory information. That is to say, human beings initiatively select knowledge and are the learners who remember knowledge and transform it instead of being passive recipients of it. In Bruner's views, learning is generated on the basis of the original cognitive structure. No matter what form is taken, individual learning is always to connect the newly acquired information with existing cognitive structure and to actively establish new cognitive structure.

Bruner points out that people represent knowledge in three ways that emerge in developmental sequence: enactive, iconic, and symbolic [15]. Enactive representation includes the use of motor skills. In this representation, people manipulate objects. They learn to do things like drive a car or use a computer. Babies learn that a bottle is something that they suck on to get milk. Iconic representation has to do with images and things that can be altered. For example, we can imagine a bus station that is empty or a station that is crowded with many people. We think about the differences in these two situations separately. Symbolic representation implies using symbols to change knowledge into a code.

7.3.3.2 Emphasize the learning of the basic structure of discipline

Bruner paid much attention to curriculum setting and teaching material construction. He believed that no matter what discipline teachers elects to teach, they do not fail to make students understand the basic structure of discipline, that is, the basic principle or thought summarized. That is to say, students should understand the structure of the things with a meaningful connection method. Influenced by the knowledge concept and the cognitive concept, Bruner paid attention to the learning of the basic structure of discipline. In his terms, all knowledge constitutes a kind of structure with level. The knowledge with such structure can be shown through a code system or a structural system (cognitive structure). The connection of the cognitive structure of the human brain with the basic structure of teaching material will produce a strong learning benefit. Once students have a good grasp of the basic principle of a discipline, it is not difficult to understand the special subjects about the discipline.

In teaching, the teacher's task is to offer the best coding system of the student, so as to ensure that teaching materials have the greatest generality. Bruner thought that it is impossible for teachers to teach students everything. So teachers should ensure that the students acquire the generalized basic thoughts and principles to a certain extent. These basic thoughts and principles constitute the best knowledge structure for students. The higher the generalization level of knowledge, the easier it will be understood and transferred.

7.3.3.3 The formation of cognitive structures through active discovery

Bruner found that teaching on the one hand has to consider people's knowledge structure and the structure of the teaching materials, and on the other, it should pay attention to people's initiative and intrinsic motivation to learn. In his view, the best motivation to learn is what they have learned about material interests rather than external incentives to stimulate competition and the like. Therefore, he advocated to the discovery learning method in order to make students more interested and to engage them in more active learning with confidence.

The feature of discovery learning is that the learning process is better than caring about learning outcomes. Specific knowledge, principles, laws, etc. enable learners themselves to explore, to discover, so that they actively participate in the learning process and undertake independent thinking and the restructuring of the teaching materials. "Learning by discovery does affect students, making it 'constructivist'." Learning is a cognitive structure of organization and reorganization. Bruner emphasized that it involves both the knowledge and experience of the role but also stressed learning materials for their intrinsic logical structure.

Bruner thought that discovery learning has several functions: (1) increasing intellectual potential, (2) enabling external motivation to become intrinsic motivation, (3) being good at discovery, and (4) helping to maintain memory of the learning materials.

Therefore, cognitive discovery is worthy of special attention as a learning theory. Cognitive discovery emphasizes learning initiative, that it has cognitive structure, the structure of learning content, and that students have the important role of independent thinking. The right to cultivate modern talent is a positive.

7.3.4 Cognitive assimilation theory

D. P. Ausubel is a psychology professor in the Academy of New York State University. He is one of proponents of the cognitive school. He has developed the learning and maintenance of the meaningful speech materials since the middle period of 1950. His theory was put forward in the 1960s and was well accepted by the teachers in primary and middle schools. In 1976 he got the Thorndike Award of the American Psychological Association.

Ausubel describes two orthogonal dimensions of learning: meaningful versus rote and reception versus discovery. Assimilation theory seeks to describe how rote learning occurs and the pitfalls of learning material by rote. The theory also explains how concepts might be acquired and organized within a learner's cognitive structure in a meaningful fashion through a broad range of teaching/learning strategies on the recepti-ve—discovery dimension [16].

Ausubel believed that student learning is mainly accepting learning instead of discovery learning. Accepting learning means that teacher directly presents students with learning content in the form of conclu-sions. Traditionally in classroom education, accepting learning has been the main form of classroom learning. But this kind of learning has been misunderstood as mechanical learning. In Ausubel's terms, accepting learning is both meaningful and mechanical. Because some teachers make his students carry on mechanical learning while they themselves apply accepting learning, accepting learning is considered mechanical learning. Likewise, discovery learning can be considered meaningful learning and mechanical learning. Just discovery learning that can find a few facts but cannot understand them is mechanical discovery learning. In Ausubel's terms, learning in the school should be meaningful accepting learning and meaningful discovery learning. But he paid more attention to meaningful accepting learning and believed that it could make students obtain a large amount of systematic knowledge in a short time, which is exactly the pri-mary goal of teaching.

Ausubel thought that the essence of meaningful learning is the process of establishing nonhuman and substantive association through the new idea symbol as its representation and the intrinsic proper idea in the lear-ner's cognitive structure. The cognitive structure defined by Ausubel is all the content of one's idea and organization or partial content of one's idea in a certain field. Intrinsic knowledge in cognitive structure is idea's frame, or the idea with a fixed role. Meaningful learning is intended to assimilate the idea with a fixed role in cognitive structure, and the intrinsic idea changes at the same time, and new knowledge is brought into the intrin-sic cognitive structure, thus obtaining the meaning.

Meaningful learning is to assimilate the new idea with the old one. Ausubel called his own learning theory assimilating theory. The original idea assimilates the new one through three ways: subsumptive learning, superordinate learning, combinational learning. Subsumptive learning is intended to properly combine the new idea with the original idea in the cognitive structure and make them associate with each other.

In subsumptive learning, the original idea is the total idea, while the new idea is the subordinate one. Thus it is also called subsumptive learn-ing. This learning has two forms: derived subsumptive learning and rele-vant subsumptive learning. In derived subsumptive learning, the new idea just makes the original total idea expand but does not change the original total idea in essence. In relevant subsumptive learning, the new idea can deepen, decorate, and limit the original total idea, thus leading to the fundamental changes of the original total idea through assimilation.

Superordinate learning is intended to induce a total idea based on several existing subsumptive ideas. For instance, after grasping the concepts of pencil (a_1), rubber (a_2), and notebook (a_3), the original superordinate idea a_n may serve the total idea A if learning the more advanced total idea "stationery" A. The formed total idea in superordinate learning is higher than already existing ideas in summarizing and forgiving intensity. So this learning is called superordinate learning.

Combinational learning refers to the general connection between the new idea and the whole content in original cognitive structure but not the subsumptive relationship between and the superordinate relationship. For example, suppose that the new idea is the "relation between quality and energy" (A), the original idea is the relation between "heat and the volume "(B), "heredity and variation" (C), "demand and price" (D). Under this condition, the new idea neither belongs to a special relation nor totally generalizes an original relationship. But they possess a certain common attribute. As a result, the new idea can be assimilated by already existing knowledge.

7.3.5 Learning theory of information processing

R. M. Gagne is an education psychology professor at Florida State university. His learning theory is based on behaviorism and cognitive learning [17]. It was established by using modern information theory and a lot of experimental research in the 1970s. In his terms, the learning process receives the message and uses the information. Learning is the result of the interaction of objects with the environment. The learner's internal state and external condition are an interdependent, inalienable entity.

Gagne thought that learning is the complex of different courses taking place in the learner's nervous system. Learning is not a simple association between stimulus and response. The stimulus is dealt within the central nervous system through different methods, so understanding learning is to point out how information processing plays a role. According to Gagne's theory, learning is also regarded as the relationship between stimulus and response. Stimulus reacts on events of the learner's sense organ while the response appears with sense input and its subsequent conversion. Response can be described by way of operating changes. But there are some basic elements such as "learner" and "memory" between stimulus and response. The learner is a real person. They have sense organs and receive stimuli through the sense organs; they have brains and receive information from the sense organs. The information is transferred in various complicated ways; they have muscles, by which the learned contents are showed. The learner is accepting various stimuli constantly, which are input into the neural activities with different forms. Some are stored in memory. When reacting, the content in the memory can be directly transferred into external behaviors. Gagne regarded learning as a process of processing information. In 1974 he depicted a typical structural mode of learning (see Fig. 7.2) [18].

In the figure, Gagne's learning structural mode is divided into two parts: One is the structure on the right, called operative memory; the other is an information flow. The stimulus originating from the external environment reacts on the sensor and then related information is generated and put into sense recorder. Here information undergoes a preliminary choice. After staying no more than 1 second, the information then enters short-term memory. Here the information stays only a few seconds and then arrives at long-term memory. Later if it needs remembering, the information is drawn out and returns to short-term memory and then is put into the generator. Here the information is processed and turned into behaviors,

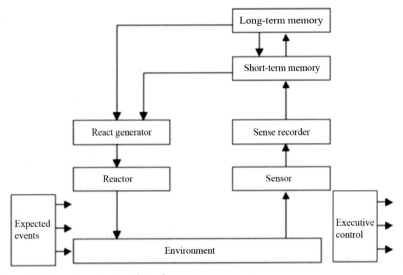

Figure 7.2 Learning structural mode.

which react on the environment. Learning is generated in this way. The second part is the structure on the left. It includes expected events and executive control. The expected link plays a directional role such that learning activities go on along a certain direction. The executive link plays a regulating, controlling role such that learning activities can be realized. The function of the second part causes learners to learn, changes learning, strengthens learning, and promotes learning, and information flow is activated, weakened, and changed in direction at the same time.

Gagne had put forward basic model of learning according to information processing theory. He believed that learning is a process of information processing. Learner cognitively processes the information from the environment, and he had concretely described the typical information processing mode. In his terms, learning can differ in the external condition from the internal condition. The learning process is in fact the learner's internal activities in the mind. Accordingly, the learning process is divided into eight stages: motive stage, understanding stage, obtaining stage, keeping stage, remembering stage, summarizing stage, operating stage, and feedback stage.

Gagne's learning theory pays attention to the internal condition and hierarchy of learning and emphasizes the systematic teaching of systematic knowledge and teacher's progressive instructing function. It has offered a certain basis for controlling teaching. His theory directly involves the classroom instruction. Therefore, there are a positive meaning and certain reference value to actual teaching. Gagne used the viewpoint and method of information theory and cybernetics to explore the learning problems. He has attempted to draw on viewpoints in both the behaviorism and cognitive school's theories to establish his own learning theory. This has reflected a development trend of the west learning theory. In his learning theory, the ability (energy) comes down to a large amount of organized knowledge. This is unilateral and has ignored the function of thinking and intellectual skill and its cultivation.

7.3.6 Learning theory of constructivism

Constructivism is the outcome of the further development of behaviorism and cognitivism. The key to constructivism is, first, that understanding is not a simple, passive response to objective being but an active course of construction, that is, all knowledge is obtained through construction. Second, in the process of construction, the already existing cognitive structure of the subject has played a very important role during the process of construction, and the cognitive structure of subject is also in constant development. Piaget and Vygotsky are the pioneers in constructivism. Though Piaget highly emphasized each individual's innovation and Vygotsky paid more attention to the transition of knowledge's tool, that is, culture and language, they were both constructivist in terms of their basic orientations.

Modern constructivism can be divided into extreme constructivism and society constructivism. The extreme constructivism has two essential features. First, put emphasis on the constructive property of understanding activity and the belief that all knowledge is the construction of subject. We cannot directly sense the outside world. Understanding activity is in fact a process of sense making; that is, the subject uses its own already existing knowledge and experience to make sense of the outside world. Second, absolutely affirm "individual properties" of understanding the activity and belief that each subject has a different knowledge background and experience (or different cognitive structure). Hence even for understanding the same subject, corresponding understanding activity cannot be totally identical but has indubitable individual particularities. For extreme constructivism, individual construction has its abundant independence, i.e. a kind of highly independent activity. That is to say, "there are 100 subjects and 100 different constructions if there are 100 persons." Just in this sense, extreme constructivism is usually also called individual constructivism. The core of society constructivism lies in the definite affirmation of society property of the understanding activity. Social environment and social community play important roles in understanding activity; the individual's understanding activity can be realized in certain social environments. The so-called sense making implies the meaning of "culture inheriting." That is to say, the "individual meanings" generated through individual constructive activity implies the inheritance and understanding of corresponding "social cultural meaning" in fact.

By constructivism, the learner uses personal experience to construct significant understanding but not to understand the already organized knowledge that is passed to him or her. The learner's understanding of the outside world is his or her own positively constructing result, but not something that is passively acceptable. Constructivist believes that knowledge is formed through the individual's constructing the real world. According to this kind of view, learning appears by constantly constructing rule and assumption, in order to explain the observed phenomenon. When consistency appears between the original idea and the new observation, the original idea loses it balance, and then constructing a new rule and assumption is needed.

Obviously, learning activity is a creative understanding process. For general understanding activity, it is mainly an "acclimation" process, that is, constant change and the recombination of cognitive structure, which is just a direct result of interaction of the new learning activity and cognitive structure.

According to constructivism, "acclimation" or change and the recombination of cognitive structure is the subject's main constructive activity. Constructivism emphasizes the initiative of learners, the connection between new knowledge and learners' original knowledge, and the application of knowledge in real situations to obtain understanding. The American psychologist M. C. Wittrock has presented a production process of student's learning, which well explains such a constructive process of learning. In Wittrock's terms, the production process is the process of interaction of the original cognitive structure and sense information (new knowledge) and the process of forwardly choosing information and constructing information.

The theory of constructivism is a somewhat newly developing theory [19]. This theory emphasizes the positive initiative and the understanding of construction of meaning of new knowledge and originality. The theory emphasizes that learning is of societal properties and pays attention to the influence of interactions between teacher and student and among students for learning. By this theory, learning is divided into elementary and advanced learning, with an emphasis on a student's constructing network knowledge structure through advanced learning. A set of novel and creative opinions are put forward in teaching goals, teacher's functions, and teaching methods and design, etc. These opinions have some positive significance in relation to further realizing learning's essence, revealing learning's law, and deepening teaching reform.

The theory of constructivism flourished based on absorbing all kinds of learning theories. However, there are some contradictions in this theory, which reveal its shortcomings, so it needs to be further developed and improved.

7.4 Humanistic learning theory

Humanistic psychology is a psychological thought risen in the fifties or sixties of the 20th century in the United States. Its main representatives are A. Maslow and C. R. Rogers. The humanistic view of learning and teaching profoundly affected worldwide education reform, along with the programmed instruction movement and the subject structure movement in the 20th century—the three major education campaigns.

Humanistic psychologists thought that, to understand human behavior, one must understand the sense world of a person's behavior. When understanding human behavior, of importance is not the external fact but the meaning of the behavior. If we want to change a person's behavior, we should change her faith and perception at first. When the ways that she looks at a problem are different, her behaviors are also different. In other words, the humanistic psychologist attempts to explain and understand the behavior from the person herself instead of from the observer. Here we will introduce the learning theory of Rogers, who is a representative of humanistic learning theory.

C. R. Rogers thought that learning could be divided into two kinds. One kind of learning is similar to the learning of meaningless syllables in psychology. In Rogers's terms, this kind of learning involves only the mind and is the learning that takes place "above the cervix." It does not involve emotional or personal meaning and has nothing to do with the whole person. The other is meaning learning. Meaning learning refers to the learning of individual behavior and attitude, that is, individual change in choosing courses of action but not involving just the accumulation of fact. This is not only a learning of growth knowledge but also a kind of learning merging with every part of individual experience.

Rogers thought that meaning learning mainly includes the following four elements:

1. Learning is of the property of personal involvement, that is, the whole person, including emotion and cognition, is engaged in the learning activities.
2. Learning is self-initiated, even if the stimulus or driving force comes from the external world, but the acquired sensation must come from the internal world.
3. Learning develops in an all-round way; that is, it ensures the all-round development of the student's behavior, attitude, personality, etc.
4. Learning is evaluated by the learner because students know whether this kind of learning meets their own needs, whether it facilitates causing them to know what they want to know.

Rogers thought that the key to promote learning does not lie in the teacher's teaching skill, professional knowledge, course project, guidance material of seeing and hearing, demonstrating and explaining, abundant books, etc. but in the particular psychological atmosphere between teacher and student [20]. Then what does a good psychological atmosphere factor include? Rogers provided his own explanation:

1. Sincerity and reality: As a promoter, the teacher displays his real self and has no namby-pamby, sham, and recovery.
2. Respect, attention and admission: The teacher respects the learner's opinion and emotion, cares about the learner's every aspect, and admits each individual's values and emotional expression.
3. Empathy—key to understanding: The teacher can understand the learner's inherent response and learning process.

The learning that is carried on under such a psychological atmosphere regards the student as the center and the teacher as the promoter, cooperator, or partner. Students are the key to the learning, and the course of learning is the purpose of learning.

In a word, humanistic psychologists such as Rogers, proceeding from their human nature and self-actualization theory, advocate student-centered "meaningful freedom learning" in teaching practice. This has assaulted the traditional education theory and has promoted the development of educational reform. This kind of impact and promotion is manifested in the following ways: stress the position and function of emotion in teaching; form a new teaching model that uses emotion as the basic motive forces of teaching activity; emphasize the importance of interpersonal relationship in teaching with the student's self-perfection at the core; the emphasis of teaching activity is transferred from teacher to student and the student's thought, emotion, experience, and behavior are regarded as the body of teaching, thus promoting the growth of individualized teaching.

Therefore, a lot of viewpoints in humanistic theory are worth our using for reference. For example, the teacher should respect students and deal honestly with students; let students discover the joy of learning and actively participate in teaching; the teacher should understand the learner's inherent response and find out the student's learning process; the teacher is the promoter, cooperator, partner, etc. However, we also can find that Rogers denies the teacher's function vigorously, which is not very correct. In teaching, we stress the subject position of student, while not ignoring the leading role of teacher.

7.5 Observational learning

The remarkable contribution to psychology of Albert Bandura lies in that he had explored the ignored learning form, observational learning, and provided observational learning with a related position and attention. Observational learning is much more complex than simple imitation.

Bandura's theory is often referred to as social learning theory as it emphasizes the role of the vicarious experience (observation) of people impacting
people (models) [21]. The proposed model of observational learning,
together with the classic conditioned and operating reflex, are the three
major tools of observational learning. Observational learning is sometimes
called societal learning theory. Bandura's learning theory does not avoid
behavioral internal reason. On the contrary, it pays attention to the function of the symbol, substitute, self-regulation function. Hence Bandura's
theory is also called cognitive behaviorism.

In Bandura's research, he pays attention to the influence of social factors,
changes the trend that the tradition learning theory to emphasize the individual but despise society, and combines the research of learning psychology
with that of social psychology. Hence he has made great contributions to
the development of learning theory. Bandura has absorbed the research
results of cognitive psychology and has organically combined enhancing
theory with information processing theory and then changes the inclination
of emphasizing "stimulus and response" and despising intermediate process.

Because he emphasizes social factors in the learning process and the
function of the cognitive process in learning, Bandura must pay attention
to the experiment with the person as the measurand in methodology. His
theory has changed the method that the animal is used as the measurand
and has corrected the wrong inclination of extending the results obtained
from animal experimentation to human learning. Bandura thought that
by observing the behaviors of important people in their lives, children can
learn societal behaviors. These observations are expressed in the form of
mental imagery or other symbol and are stored in the mind. This theory
has accepted most of the principles of behavioralist theoreticians but pays
more attention to the function of the clue on behavior, the inherent
mental process. The theory emphasizes the interaction of thought and
behavior. His viewpoint has provided the bridge between the behavioral
school and the cognitive school and has made an enormous contribution
to the treatment of cognition-behavior.

The concept and theory of Bandura are built on solid and rich experiment data. His experimental method is more rigorous, and the conclusions are more convincing. His opening theory frame adheres to the
behavioristic position as well as actively absorbing the research results and
methods of modern cognitive psychology. At the same time, under the
enlightenment of some of the ideas of humanism learning theory, his theory involves some important subjects such as observational learning,

interaction, self-regulation, self-efficiency, etc. It stresses initiative and sociality and is met with general acceptance. Social learning theory explains human behavior in terms of continuous reciprocal interaction between cognitive, behavioral, and environmental influences.

Necessary conditions for effective modeling are as follows:

1. Attention: Various factors increase or decrease the amount of attention paid, including distinctiveness, affective valence, prevalence, complexity, functional value. One's characteristics (e.g., sensory capacities, arousal level, perceptual set, past reinforcement) affect attention.

2. Retention: Remembering what you paid attention to includes symbolic coding, mental images, cognitive organization, symbolic rehearsal, motor rehearsal.

3. Reproduction: Reproducing the image, including physical capabilities, and self-observation of reproduction.

4. Motivation: Having a good reason to imitate includes motives such as past (i.e., traditional behaviorism), promised (imagined incentives), and vicarious (seeing and recalling the reinforced model).

By this theory, individual, environment and behavior are all linked and influenced together. The size of influence of the three is determined by the environment and behavioral property at that time. The theory has often been called a bridge between behaviorist and cognitive learning theories because it encompasses attention, memory, and motivation.

Besides this kind of direct reinforcement, Bandura also proposed other two kinds of reinforcements: alterative reinforcement and self-reinforcement. Alterative reinforcement refers to reinforcement that is tasted because the observer is tasting a reinforcement. For instance, when a teacher enhances a student's act of giving aid, the other students in the class will spend a certain amount of time helping one another too. In addition, the other function of alterative reinforcement is the arousing of emotional response. For example, a star shows a charming way of wearing a kind of clothes or using a kind of shampoo in a TV advertisement; at this time, if you feel or experience the happiness because the star enacts it, this is a kind of alterative reinforcement for you. The self-reinforcement depends on the result that is transmitted through society. When the society transmits a certain behavioral standard to an individual and the individual behavior even exceeds this standard, he will reward himself with his own behavior. In addition, Bandura also provided the concept of self-regulation. Bandura supposed that people can observe their own behaviors and make a judgment according to their own standards, such as reinforcement or punishing themselves.

7.6 Introspective learning

Introspection refers to investigating a person's own thought or emotion, that is, self-observation; it also refers to observing the sensation and perception experience under the control of the experimental condition. Introspection is the opposite of appearance. Appearance is investigating and observing the situation of the exclusion of oneself. The introspection method is an early psychological research approach. It investigates psychological phenomena and process according to the report of the tested person or the experience described by her. Introspection learning is introducing the introspection concept into machine learning. That is to say, by checking and caring about the knowledge processing and reasoning method of the intelligence system itself and finding out problems from failure or poor efficiency, introspection learning forms its own learning goal and then improves the method to solving problems.

Mankind often improves through self-observation. People may conscientiously and unconsciously carry on introspection learning. For example, a long-distance runner, who participates in a match of 10,000 m, may encounter the problem of improperly distributing physical strength. It is possible to influence the outcome of the race if physical endurance is greatly depleted, and he is too spent to dash at the end. After several unsuccessful experiences, he will find out the reason for is lack of success and avoid the same problem in future matches. So he rationally adjusts physical power and tactics, and therefore each match is better than the last. From such instances we find that introspection learning is a good way to improve our ability to solve a problem; from repeated psychological results, we can verify that the human is capable of introspection learning.

A learning system with the ability of introspection learning will improve learning efficiency too. In a complicated world, it is difficult to tell all possible relevant information and deduce a method for the system to advance. A very difficult question is to predict situations that the system will face, what information will be important, and what response condition will be needed. Hence greater flexibly and adaptability are required for the system, so as to appropriately deal with various situations. The system should be have the ability to improve its knowledge and know how to operate. But most learning systems do not possess the ability to change their knowledge processing reasoning method. In a multi-policy learning system, a central issue is to choose and arrange the learning algorithms for the particular situation. It requires the intelligence system to automatically choose and arrange the appropriate algorithm from the algorithm storehouse. By using introspection learning, the learning system can determine its goal based on analyzing the successes and failures of the executed task. In other words, its goal is not the one that the designer of the system or user provides. The system can determine clearly what is needed and what should be learned. In other words, the introspection learning system can understand the causes of the failure and related reasoning and the knowledge in the process of operating system. The system has its own knowledge and ability to check its reasoning. In this way, the system can effectively learn, and the learning would be less effective without such introspection. Therefore introspection is necessary for effective learning.

Introspection learning involves four subproblems:

1. There are standards that determine when the reasoning process should be checked, that is, the monitoring reasoning process.
2. Determine whether failure reasoning takes place according to the standards.
3. Confirm the final reason that led to the failure.
4. Change the reasoning process in order to avoid similar failures in the future.

To be able to find and explain the failure, introspection learning system is required to be able to visit the knowledge about its reasoning process up to the present moment. It needs a rough or clear expectation about the field result and its internal reasoning process. It is able to discovery the failure of expectation in the reasoning process and problem solving. In addition, it also can use reasoning failure to explain expectation failure and to determine how to change the reasoning process and then to correct the error hereafter. The introspection learning process includes three steps:

1. Judge a failure: Determine whether the disappointed expectation should be generated.
2. Explain the failure: The introspection learning system can find out the cause of error of the reasoning line before the failure and give the explanation for the reasoning failure. The system provides the definite goal of introspection learning so as to change its knowledge and reasoning process.
3. Correct the failure: The system carries out the tactics of introspection learning according to the goal of introspection learning.

Given all this, an introspection learning system must itself possess an intact learning structure, such as a knowledge base, algorithm base, inference engine, etc. In addition, it requires a set of meta-reasoning representation in order to track and confirm the realized process of reasoning; the system also requires a set of evaluation standards of reasoning, including explanation, efficiency analysis, mistake, failure, etc.; it requires an introspection mechanism that is used to check the reasoning, to form goals, and to execute policy.

M. T. Cox applied the explanation pattern (XP) to explain anomaly and then created an accident understanding system [22]. It is a goal-driven learning system. The system chooses algorithms from an algorithm toolbox and combines them with a multilearning method, so as to repair the erroneous part that leads to the failure of the system. The input of the system is the data flow of the incident concept entity; the executing task is to generate an interaction model of person and incident. As a system prophesies that a certain explanation is tenable in an incident but a different explanation appears after the incident, a failure will happen. The system will explain why the system fails and form a knowledge learning tactic that can change the failure. Thus the system can learn through failures.

When Meta-AQUA does not succeed in understanding a story passage, it then uses the introspective Meta-XPs (IMXPs) to repair its reasoning process. An IMXP describes the tactics that are related to reasoning failure and repairing reasoning. An IMXP can be consider the template matched with the description of a real reasoning process. It determines whether the reasoning will fail. But the real reasoning process is expressed by Trace Meta-XPs (TMXPs). For different reasoning failures, Meta-AQUA has summed up a failure's symptom category, reason type, and goal type. The symptom of reasoning failure can be used to confirm the reason of the failure, and the reason of the failure also can be used to confirm the related learning goal.

ROBBIE is a route planning system proposed by S. Fox [23]. Its task is to produce a route plan from one place to another under the conditions of several streets, limited map knowledge, and a small amount of initial samples. It examines the quality of planning by carrying out the planning in a simulation world. ROBBIE is a case-based system. Its knowledge can accrue from increasing cases: As the cases increase, it understands the map better. ROBBIE's introspective unit monitors the reasoning of the planning device and compares the expected performance of the real reasoning process with that of case-based reasoning process. When expectation failure takes place, the introspective unit will stay the planning task, attempt to explain the failure, and correct the system. If there is enough information to prove that failure may be generated, the system will continue carrying out the task. When the necessary information is ready, explanation and modification resume from the suspended place. The feature of ROBBIE's system is to apply introspection learning in a case-based retrieval reasoning module and to refine the case index. When retrieval fails, the reason for failure can be found through the introspective unit, and the retrieval process is corrected. In addition, the system has provided the frame for applying introspection learning to the intact process of case-based reasoning.

7.6.1 Basic principles of introspection learning

The general introspection course is divided into three parts: judge the failure, explain the failure, and correct the failure [3].

1. *Judge the failure*: Based on the establishment of definite and finite expectations of the reasoning process, compare the expectations with the real executing process of the system, and then find out the difference. The difference between expected behavior and real behavior is the explanation of the failure. To determine whether the failure takes place means that there is a group of definite expected values about the reasoning state of the system. Expectation failure is monitored in the process of reasoning. When going on every step of the reasoning process, compare the related result with the related expectation. If the expectation is found, then failure will take place.

2. *Explain the failure*: According to the standard of expectation failure and the trace of reasoning, explain the failure. After finding out the reason, a definite correcting suggestion related to the reasoning process should be presented, in order to avoid the same failure again.

3. *Correct the failure*: The related corrective action of the reasoning process can be appended to a particular expectation. So, when an expectation failure takes place, the appended method also can be presented at the same time. The description of corrective method is not able to be detailed enough. So the system should also include forming the mechanism of the revision tactics. The revision module carries out the real revision tactics and the real modification according to the description of failure and the suggestion of revision.

The block diagram of the introspection learning system is shown in Fig. 7.3. Besides judging the failure, explaining the failure, and correcting the failure, the model also includes knowledge base, reasoning trace, reasoning expectation model, monitor protocol, etc. The monitor protocol is

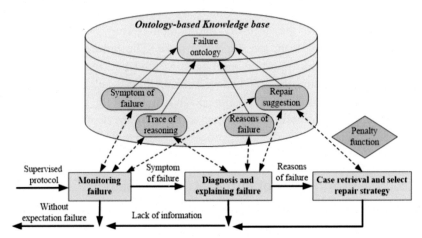

Figure 7.3 Block diagram of introspection learning system.

used to standardize the monitor of the reasoning process. It prescribes where and how the reasoning process should be monitored and the control of the system should be transferred. The knowledge base includes the knowledge relevant to reasoning. It is not only the foundation of reasoning but also the grounds for judging and explaining the failure at the same time. The reasoning trace has recorded the reasoning process. It is specially used in introspection learning and is the important grounds for judging, explaining, and correcting the failure. The reasoning expectation model is an ideal model of a system's reasoning process. It has provided the standard for reasoning expectation and therefore is the main grounds for judging the failure. The introspective learning unit of the system uses a monitor protocol, already existing background, reasoning expectation, and reasoning trace to check whether the current state appears to be expectation failure.

The emergence of expectation failure includes two cases: One is that when a model expectation about the current ideal state of reasoning process does not fit the current real reasoning process, expectation failure will take place. The other is that, when the system cannot continue because of disastrous failure, expectation failure takes place certainly. If there is no expectation failure in the reasoning unit, then all the expectations fit the real process, the system is informed that everything is all right, and then the system regains control again. If a failure is found, the reasoning will use background, reasoning trace, and the ideal expectation model to look for the initial reason for the failure and explain the failure. It is possible that the obtained information possible is not enough to diagnose and correct the failure when a failure is found. At this time, the introspection learning unit can suspend its explanation and revision tasks until there is abundant information. When the necessary information is already obtained, the explanation and revision tasks will resume from the suspended place. The explanation of the failure can provide clues for correcting the failure. After the explanation, the learning goal of correcting the failure is generated, and the revision method is also formed according to the learning goal. After revision, the system will regain control power.

7.6.2 Meta-reasoning of introspection learning

Meta-reasoning originates from the concept of meta-cognition in cognitive process. It is also called self-monitor cognition. Meta-cognition is viewed as the cognition of cognition. It refers to a cognitive process about oneself and the knowledge of all the related things. It includes two kinds of ability of awareness and control. The former refers to knowing one's own ability of limiting, concept, knowledge, and cognitive strategy. The latter refers to appropriately controlling and applying one's own knowledge and strategy. Past learning systems paid more attention to knowledge acquisition and processing. They emphasized the exactness of knowledge as well as that of the reasoning process. This creates a demand of reasonably expressing the reasoning process based on knowledge representation. Like the meta-data of warehouse, i.e. data about the data, meta-reasoning is used in the introspection learning system. By using meta-reasoning, the learning system can acquire the cognition of knowledge and knowledge processing and further finish the proper control and usage of its own knowledge and tactics.

Meta-reasoning involves reasoning about the reasoning. Because one of the main goals of introspection learning is to revise the reasoning process according to reasoning failure or execution, expressing the reasoning process through the basic level is a basic condition of introspection learning. The introduction of meta-reasoning requires reaching two goals. The first goal is to record the reasoning process of the system and to form the reasoning trace. The second one is to explain the reasoning process and provide a causal chain for reasoning failure. And the final goal is to provide the representation for monitoring the reasoning process and the necessary information for explaining and correcting the reasoning failure.

The expression of meta-reasoning can be realized by both external and internal methods. The external way is to establish one ideal model for the reasoning process and design different evaluation standards at different stages. The internal way is to use the expression with the meta–explanation to internally record the reasoning process and explain the anomaly. For instance, the Meta–AQUQ system applies XP theory to express the transition of mind state and names this kind of expression structure as the meta–XP. Its meaning is an XP of one about another explanation mode. Because the standard explanation mode is the expression method of a cause-and-effect structure, the meta–XP can explain its own explanation process. According to the difference of functions, there are two kinds of meta–XPs. One is used for tracking the explanation process and is called TMXP. Another one is to use an introspective explanation and is called IMXP.

7.6.3 Failure classification

Another important problem of the introspection learning system is failure classification. Meta–AQUA system has listed the types of symptom, reason for the failure, and related learning goal. The failure symptom is classified according to whether the actual value (A) and the expected value (E) exist and are the same or not, including contradictory, unexpected, deadlock, strange affair, false proposition, expect proposition, degradation, etc. Each symptom is expressed by the associations of various failure marks. The system has proposed two kinds of wrong marks—inference expectations failure and amalgamation failure—and four kinds of omission marks—overdue prophecy, search failure, structure failure, and input failure. The ROBBIE system classifies the abnormity according to different modules in the model and is combined with related assertion, which is the main grounds for explaining the failure. The failure is divided by the reasoning process. The reasoning process is divided into several stages, such as index example, search case, adjusting case, second retrieval case, executing case, keeping case. The failure is also divided into several stages.

The failure classification is a key element of introspection learning. It is the grounds for judging failure and provides an important clue for explaining the failure and forming a corrected leaning goal at the same time. The failure classification also determines the ability of introspection learning to a certain extent. So it is necessary to set up a rational failure classification for the introspection learning system. Failure classification requires considering two important factors. One is the granularity of the failure classification; the other is the association among the failure classification, the failure explanation, and the goal of introspection learning. The failure classification with granularity can settle the contradiction of classification which is too thin or too thick. For failure of big classification, we can abstractly describe the failure and finish thickly classifying according to the different stages of the reasoning process. In this way, we not only can include some unpredictable situations and increase the adaptability of the systematic introspection but also can accelerate the contrasting process according to the different stages. The thin classification can describe the failure in detail. This way can provide valuable clues for failure explanation. Appropriately dealing with association between failure classification and failure explanation also raises systematic introspection ability. The system not only requires finding out the failure reason through failure symptom and forming introspective learning goal but also has the ability (adaptability) to deal with all kinds of different problems. The failure explanation also can be divided into different levels. The granularity of failure classification facilitates forming a reasonable relationship between failure symptom and failure explanation.

The method of failure classification includes the failure common approach and the reasoning process module approach. The failure common approach proceeds with the common characteristic of failure and finishes the classification. For instance, the lack of input information can come down to input failure; the inference machine's failing to induce or create a solution to a problem comes down to creation failure; knowledge failure is regarded as knowledge contradiction, and so on. The common approach considers the failure classification with respect the whole system. This approach is suitable for introspection learning in the distributed environment. The module approach is to classify reasoning process into several modules and create a partition according to the module. For example, case-based reasoning can be divided into several modules, such as retrieval, adjustment, evaluation, storage. Retrieval failure refers to the anomaly appearing in the retrieval process. The module approach is suitable for the reasoning in a modular system. In some cases, the two kinds of approaches can be combined.

7.6.4 Case-based reasoning in the introspective process

Case-based reasoning is intended to obtain the source case in memory through the suggestion of the goal case and then to guide the goal case by using the source case [24]. In this reasoning, the problems and situations encountered are called the goal case, and the question or situation in memory is called the source case. Its advantage lies in simplifying knowledge acquisition, improving the efficiency and quality of problem solving. The process of case-based reasoning is to form the case's retrieval characteristics according to the current goal and then search related cases in the memory case base by using the retrieval feature. Then it selects a case that is the most similar to the current situation, judges the case in order to suit the current situation, forms a new case, and evaluates the new case. Finally, it stores the new case to the base for further usage. Case-based reasoning and model-based reasoning are important ways to realize introspection learning. On the contrary, introspection learning also can improve the process of case-based reasoning. A key link in the introspection learning process is to find out the reason for the failure according to the failure features. Introspection not only concerns executing failure or reasoning failure but also should contain a less effective execution or reasoning process. Besides finding the error, the system needs to evaluate reasoning.

From the perspective of expectation, the failure judgment is also called supervision and evaluation. The expectation value is considered the criterion of supervision and evaluation. At the same time, the evaluation factor can be used for quantitative evaluation. Supervision is oriented to the reasoning process while evaluation is oriented to the reasoning result. A series of processes, such as case-based reasoning retrieval, adjustment, evaluation, and storage, intended to finish judgment failure and explanation failure, may increase the effectiveness of judgment and explanation. So case-based reasoning is effective. In the Meta-AQUA system, the process of checking error to the forming learning goal is a case-based reasoning process. The system can find the reason for the failure and then form the learning goal by the failure symptom. On the other hand, the usage of introspection learning in different modules of case-based reasoning, such as retrieval and evaluation, has improved the adaptability and accuracy of the system. The evaluation of case is an important step in the case-based reasoning system. Quantitative case evaluation enables the case to automatically modify case weight, so as to improve the effectiveness of case retrieval.

7.7 Reinforcement learning

Reinforcement learning (RL) is defined by the action in the environment and the responding environment instead of special learning methods. Whatever methods are used to implement it, interactive learning can be viewed as an acceptable RL method.

7.7.1 Reinforcement learning model

RL is not supervised learning, which can be gotten from the chapter machine learning. In supervised learning, the "teacher" directly conducts or trains the learning program by the instance. In RL, the learning agent learns the optimal strategy for the objective achieved in the environment through training error and feedback by itself [25].

RL technology is developed from control theory, statistics, psychology, and other related fields, and the event can be traced back to the Pavlov conditioning experiment. Until the late 1980s and early 1990s, RL technology was widely researched and applied in artificial intelligence, machine learning, automatic control, etc. and is considered one of the core technologies in designing intelligent systems. Especially with the breakthrough of the mathematical foundational research in RL, the research and application of RL are gradually developing and have become one of focal points of research in machine learning.

The model of RL in Fig. 7.4 is based on the interactions between agent and environment, which include action, reward, and state. The interactions can be represented as, in each step, the agent selects and executes an action according to the strategy selection, then perceives the state and the real-time reward in the next step and amends the strategy by its experiences. The objective of agent is to maximize the long-time reward.

The RL accepts the state input s from environment and outputs the corresponding actions a in terms of the internal reasoning mechanism. The environment changes to a new state s' under the system action a. The system accepts the new state input from the environment, meanwhile getting the instantaneous rewards and punishments feedback r that the environment responds to the system. The aim of the RL system is to learn a behavioral strategy $\pi:S \rightarrow A$, which make the system action obtain a cumulative largest value of environment reward. In other words, the system maximizes

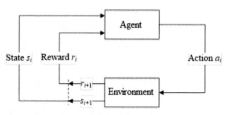

Figure 7.4 Reinforcement learning model.

Eq. (7.1), where γ is a discount factor. In the process of learning, the fundamental of RL technology is that the tendency for the system to produce the action will be increased if an action of the system results in a positive reward, whereas the tendency for the system to produce the action will be decreased. This is similar to the conditional reflex principle in physiology.

$$\sum_{i=0}^{\infty} \gamma^i r_{t+i} \quad 0 < \gamma \leq 1 \tag{7.1}$$

If the environment is a Markov model, the order type of RL problems can be modeled through the Markov decision process. The formal definition of the Markov decision process is described next.

The Markov decision process is defined by a 4-tuple $<S, A, R, P>$, which includes the environment state set S, system action set A, reward function $R:S \times A \to R$, and state transition function $P:S \times A \to PD(S)$. $R(s, a, s')$ indicates the instantaneous reward that the system adopts the action a to change the environment state from s to s'. $P(s, a, s')$ denotes the probability that the system adopts the action a to change the environment state from s to s'.

The essence of the Markov decision process is that the probability and reward of the state transition from the current moment to the next moment are decided by the current state and selected action and have nothing to do with the history state and action. Therefore the dynamics programming technology can be used to solve the optimal strategy when the state transition function P and reward function R have to be known. However, the research of RL focuses on how to learn an optimal strategy when P and R are not known.

To solve this problem, Fig. 7.5 shows the relationships of four essential factors of RL: strategy π, state value mapping V, reward function r, and environment model (common cases). The relationships among four essential factors is the pyramid structure from bottom up. Strategy is defined as the agent's selection and the methods of action at any given time. Thus the strategy can be represented through a group of production rules or a simple query. As just mentioned, the strategy under the special situation may be to widely search and query a result of a model or planning process. The strategy is a stochastic and is an important component of learning because it can produce such actions.

The reward function R_t defines the relation of state/object of the problem at time t. It maps each action or elaborate state−response pair into a reward value to indicate the size that the state accomplishes the

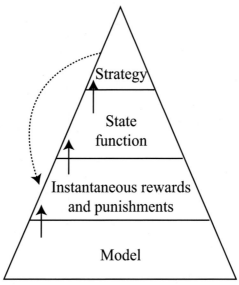

Figure 7.5 Four essential factors of reinforcement learning.

objective desired. The agent in RL has the task of maximizing the total reward that it gets after accomplishing the task.

The assignment function V is an attribute of each state in the environment, which indicates the expected reward of the system when the state continues. The reward function evaluates the instant expected value of the state−response pair, while the assignment indicates the long-time expected value of a state in the environment. The value of a state is computed through its inner quality and the following quality; the value is the reward under these states. For example, a state/action may have a small instant reward and a bigger reward, because a bigger reward is usually produced after its state. A small reward may mean that the state is not related to the successful solution path.

There is no reward value if there is no reward function, and the only aim of the evaluation value is to obtain more reward. But we are most interested in the value when we make the decision because the value indicates the highest reward state and state fusion. The determined value is more difficult to obtain than the determined reward. The reward can be gotten from the environment, while the value is gotten by evaluating, and it needs to freshly evaluate according to success and failure as time goes by. In fact, it is most difficult and important to build an effective method to evaluate the value in RL.

The model of RL is a mechanism for obtaining environment behavior. We need to evaluate future actions without any practical experiments. The plan based on the model is a new supplement of the RL case because the early system tended to be a pure agent's example and error to reward and value parameters.

The environment the system faces is defined by the environment model. Because of the unknown P and R in the model, the system only can select the strategy in terms of the instantaneous reward obtained in each experiment. In the process of selecting the behavioral strategy, the uncertainty of the environment model and the chronicity of objective ought to be considered. So the value function (the utility function of state) constructed by the strategy and instantaneous reward will be used to select strategy.

$$R_t = r_{t+1} + \gamma r_{t+2} + \gamma^2 r_{t+3} + \cdots = r_{t+1} + \gamma R_{t+1} \tag{7.2}$$

$$\begin{aligned} V^\pi(s) &= E_\pi\{R_t|s_t = s\} = E_\pi\{r_{t+1} + \gamma V(s_{t+1})|s_t = s\} \\ &= \sum_a \pi(s, a) \sum_{s'} P^a_{ss'} [R^a_{ss'} + \gamma V^\pi(s')] \end{aligned} \tag{7.3}$$

A reward function R_t is constructed through Eq. (7.2), which denotes the accumulative discount of all rewards of the system after the state s_t in a learning cycle conducted by a strategy π. Because of the uncertainty of the system, the R_t obtained by the system in each learning cycle conducted by a strategy π may be different. The value function under the state s ought to consider the expected value of all reward functions in different learning cycles. So under the strategy π, the value function of the system with state s is defined by the Eq. (7.3), which can give the expected accumulative reward discount if the system adopts the strategy π.

According to the Bellman optimal strategy formula, under the optimal strategy π^*, the value function of the system with state s is defined by Eq. (7.4):

$$\begin{aligned} V^*(s) &= \max_{a \in A(s)} E\{r_{t+1} + \gamma V^*(s_{t+1})|s_t = s, a_t = a\} \\ &= \max_{a \in A(s)} \sum_{s'} P^a_{ss'} [R^a_{ss'} + \gamma V^*(s')] \end{aligned} \tag{7.4}$$

In the dynamic programming technique, when the environment model knowledge, the state transition probability function P, and the reward function R have be known, the system starting from the strategy

π_0 can adopt the strategy iteration to approximate the optimal V^* and π^*. k in Eq. (7.5) and Eq. (7.6) indicates the number of iterations:

$$\pi_k(s) = \arg\max_a \sum_{s'} P_{ss'}^a \left[R_{ss'}^a + \gamma V^{\pi_{k-1}}(s') \right] \tag{7.5}$$

$$V^{\pi_k}(s) \leftarrow \sum_a \pi_{k-1}(s, a) \sum_{s'} P_{ss'}^a \left[R_{ss'}^a + \gamma V^{\pi_{k-1}}(s') \right] \tag{7.6}$$

Due to the unknown P and R functions in RL, the system cannot directly compute the value function through Eqs. (7.5) and (7.6). So the approximation is typically used to evaluate the value function, and Monte Carlo sampling is one of the main methods. In Eq. (7.7), R_t denotes the actual accumulative discount reward value that the system, starting from the state s_t, adopts the strategy π to obtain. Keeping the strategy π invariant, Eq. (7.7) is repeatedly used in each learning cycle. Eq. (7.7) will approximate Eq. (7.3):

$$V(s_t) \leftarrow V(s_t) + \alpha[R_t - V(s_t)] \tag{7.7}$$

Combined with the Monte Carlo method and dynamic programming technique, Eq. (7.8) shows the value function iteration formula of temporal difference (TD) learning in RL:

$$V(s_t) \leftarrow V(s_t) + \alpha[r_{t+1} + \gamma V(s_{t+1}) - V(s_t)] \tag{7.8}$$

7.7.2 Q Learning

In Q learning, Q is a function that the state−action pair maps to a learned value [26]. For all states and actions:

$$Q:(\text{state } x \text{ action}) \rightarrow \text{Value}$$

The first step of Q learning:

$$Q(s_t, a_t) \leftarrow (1 - c) \times Q(s_t, a_t) + c \times \left[r_{t+1} + \gamma \underset{a}{\text{MAX}}\, Q(s_{t+1}, a) - Q(s_t, a_t) \right] \tag{7.9}$$

where $c, \gamma \leq 1$, r_{t+1} is the reward of the state s_{t+1}.

In Q learning, backtracking starts from the action node, and maximizes all possible actions and rewards of the next state. In the completely recursive definition of Q learning, the bottom node of the backtracking tree starts from the action of the root node, and the sequence of reward of following actions of the root node can reach all end nodes. Online Q learning extends forward according to the possible actions and does not need to build a complete world model. Q learning can work offline. We can know that Q learning is a temporal difference method.

The Monte Carlo method approximates the actual value function throughout the reward functions obtained by a learning cycle. RL evaluates the current state value function through the next state value function (the bootstrapping method) and the current instant rewards. Obviously, RL needs repeated learning cycles to approximate the actual value function. Therefore we can make a new λ-reward function R'_t as in Eq. (7.10) through modifying Eq. (7.8), where the system reaches the terminal state after T steps in a learning cycle. The physical interpretation of the λ-reward function R'_t is shown in Fig. 7.6. The value function iteration obeys Eq. (7.11):

$$R'_t = r_{t+1} + \lambda r_{t+2} + \lambda^2 r_{t+3} + \cdots + \lambda^{T-1} r_{t+T} \tag{7.10}$$

$$V(s_t) \leftarrow V(s_t) + \alpha \left[R'_t - V(s_t) \right] \tag{7.11}$$

The value function update of RL performs in each learning step (namely, the updating operation occurs after obtaining the $<s, a, r, s';>$ experience). The new TD(λ) algorithm needs to be designed in order that the value function of the learning algorithm in a learning cycle can satisfy Eq. (7.11). In the TD(λ) algorithm, the $e(s)$ function is constructed to support the value function updates in terms of Eq. (7.11).

Algorithm 7.1: TD(λ) algorithm
Initialize $V(s)$ arbitrarily and $e(s) = 0$ for all $s \in S$.
Repeat (for each episode).
Initialize s.
Repeat (for each step of episode).
$a \leftarrow$ action given by π for s(e.g., ε-greedy).
    Take action a, observer r, s'.

$\delta \leftarrow r + \gamma V(s') - V(s)$
$e(s) \leftarrow e(s) + 1$

for all s:

$V(s) \leftarrow V(s) + \alpha \delta e(s)$
$e(s) \leftarrow \gamma \lambda e(s)$

$s \leftarrow s'$
    until s is terminal.

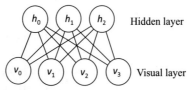

Figure 7.6 Architecture of restricted Boltzmann machine.

The evaluation of the value function and the strategy evaluation can be merged into one operation step. The state–action pair value function, Q function, is constructed in the algorithm. The definition of the Q function is shown in Eq. (7.12). Theory suggests that the Q learning algorithm will converge to the optimal state–action pair value function when the learning rate α satisfies a definite condition. The Q learning algorithm is one of the most popular RL algorithms.

$$Q^{\pi}(s, a) = \sum_{s'} P_{ss'}^{a} \left[R_{ss'}^{a} + \gamma V^{\pi}(s') \right] \qquad (7.12)$$

Algorithm 7.2: Q learning algorithm
  Initialize $Q(s,a)$ arbitrarily.
  Repeat (for each episode).
  Initialize s.
  Repeat (for each step of episode).
  Choose a from s using policy derived from Q (e.g., ε-greedy).
    Take action a, observer r, s'.

$Q(s, a) \leftarrow Q(s, a) + \alpha[r + \gamma \max_{a'} Q(s', a') - Q(s, a)]$
$s \leftarrow s'$

until s is terminal.

7.8 Deep learning

Deep learning is a new field in machine learning, its core idea is to simulate the hierarchy abstraction structure of the human brain, analyze the large-scale data by the unsupervised methods, and reveal the valuable information contained in big data. Deep learning was designed to research big data and provide a deep-thinking brain for big data.

7.8.1 Introduction

In June 2012, the Google Brain project attracted public attention in *The New York Times*. This project is headed by Andrew Ng and Jeff Dean at Stanford University. The parallel computation platform with 16,000 CPU cores serves to train the deep neural networks with 10 billion nodes. The mass data is directly loaded into the algorithm, and the data is left to speak. The system automatically learns from the data.

In November 2012, Microsoft publicly demonstrated a fully automatic simultaneous interpretation system in Tianjin, China. The speaker made a speech in English, and the backend computer automatically accomplished the speech recognition, the machine translated from English to Chinese, and the Chinese speech was synthesized. The key technology supporting the backstage is also the deep learning.

On April 24, 2014, Baidu held the fourth technology Open Day in Beijing. During the Open Day, Baidu announced that it had officially launched a large data engine, including core big data capability with three major components: Open Cloud, Data Factory, Baidu Brain. Baidu provides the big data storage, analysis, and mining techniques to the public through the large data engine. This is the first open big data engine in the world. Andrew Ng took part in the Baidu Institute and carried out the deep learning research.

Suppose that there exists a system S with n layers $(S_1, \ldots, S_n)$. The system with the input I and the output O can be visually represented as $I => S_1 => S_2 => \cdots => S_n => O$. If the output O is equal to the input I, namely the information of the input I is not lost after the system transformation. To maintain this, the input I after each layer S_i does not lose any information; that is, in any layer S_i, the representation of original information is the other kind (that is, input I).

The idea of Deep Learning is to stack multiple layers, and the output in the current layer is served as the input of the next layer. In this way, the layer-wise representation of the input information can be realized. Deep learning is an algorithm based on the representation learning of data in machine learning. So far, several deep learning frameworks, such as the convolutional neural network (CNN), deep belief network (DBN), and recurrent neural network, have been applied in computer vision, speech recognition, natural language processing, audio recognition, and bioinformatics and have achieved excellent results [27].

In 1981 the Nobel Prize in medicine was awarded to David Hubel, Torsten Wiesel, and Roger Sperry. The main contribution of the first two people was in determining the information processing of the vision system. The low-level V1 extracts the edge features, V2 extracts the shape or object parts, etc. The higher-level regions extract the entire object, the behavior of the object, etc.

7.8.2 Autoencoder

Autoencoder is a single hidden layer neural network with the same number of nodes in the input layer and the output layer. The aim of designing Autoencoder is to reconstruct the input signal of the neural network as far as possible. Which means that we need to solve the function $h_{W,b}(X) \approx x$; that is, the output of the neural network is expected to be equal to the input.

Suppose that there exists a sample set $\{(x^{(1)}, y^{(1)}), \ldots, (x^{(m)}, y^{(m)})\}$ containing m samples. The batch gradient descent method can be used to solve the neural networks. In particular, for a single sample (x, y), the cost function is:

$$J(W, b; x, y) = \frac{1}{2} \left\| h_{w,b}(x) - y \right\|^2 \tag{7.13}$$

Eq. (7.13) is a variance cost function. Given a data set containing m samples, we can define the entire cost function:

$$
\begin{aligned}
J(W, b) &= \left[\frac{1}{m} \sum_{i=1}^{m} J(W, b; x^{(i)}, y^{(i)}) \right] + \frac{\lambda}{2} \sum_{l=1}^{n_l-1} \sum_{i=1}^{s_l} \sum_{j=1}^{s_l+1} (W_{ji}^{(l)})^2 \\
&= \left[\frac{1}{m} \sum_{i=1}^{m} \left(\frac{1}{2} \left\| h_{w,b}(x^{(i)}) - y^{(i)} \right\|^2 \right) \right] + \frac{\lambda}{2} \sum_{l=1}^{n_l-1} \sum_{i=1}^{s_l} \sum_{j=1}^{s_l+1} (W_{ji}^{(l)})^2
\end{aligned}
\tag{7.14}
$$

The first item $J(W, b)$ in Eq. (7.14) is a mean square error. The second item is a weight decay. Its aim is to reduce the scope of weight to prevent overfitting.

In Eq. (7.15), $a_j^{(2)}(x)$ indicates the activation value of the input vector x on the hidden unit j. The average activation value of the hidden unit j is:

$$\hat{\rho}_j = \frac{1}{m} \sum_{i=1}^{m} \left[a_j^{(2)}(x^{(i)}) \right] \tag{7.15}$$

In order to reach a sparsity, the least (most sparse) hidden units are used to represent the feature of the input layer. When the average activation value of all hidden units is closed to 0, the KL distance is adopted:

$$\sum_{j=1}^{s_2} \rho \log \frac{\rho}{\hat{\rho}_j} + (1 - \rho)\log \frac{1 - \rho}{1 - \hat{\rho}_j} \qquad (7.16)$$

For ease in writing:

$$KL(\rho||\hat{\rho}_j) = \rho \log \frac{\rho}{\hat{\rho}_j} + (1 - \rho)\log \frac{1 - \rho}{1 - \hat{\rho}_j} \qquad (7.17)$$

So the entire cost function of neural networks can be represented as:

$$J_{sparse}(W, b) = J(W, b) + \beta \sum_{j=1}^{s_2} KL(\rho||\hat{\rho}_j), \qquad (7.18)$$

The error computation formula $\delta_i^{(2)} = (\sum_{j=1}^{s_2} W_{ji}^{(2)} \delta_j^{(3)}) f'(z_i^{(2)})$, in back-propagation (BP) is modified as:

$$\delta_i^{(2)} = \left(\left(\sum_{j=1}^{s_2} W_{ji}^{(2)} \delta_j^{(3)} \right) + \beta \left(-\frac{\rho}{\hat{\rho}_i} + \frac{1 - \rho}{1 - \hat{\rho}_i} \right) \right) f'(z_i^{(2)}). \qquad (7.19)$$

Therefore the dimension of data can be reduced greatly. Only a few useful hidden units can represent the original data.

7.8.3 Restricted Boltzmann machine

In 2002 G. E. Hinton at the University of Toronto proposed a machine learning algorithm called contrastive divergence (CD) [28]. CD can efficiently train some Markov random models with simple architecture, including a restricted Boltzmann machine (RBM). This lays the foundation for the birth of deep learning.

RBM is a single-layer random neural network (generally the input layer is not included in the layer number of neural networks), as in Fig. 7.6. RBM is essentially a probability graph model. The input layer is fully connected to the output layer, while there aren't connections between the neurons in the same layer. Each neuron either is activated (the value is 1) or is not activated (the value is 0). The activation probability satisfies the sigmoid function. The advantage of RBM is that, given a layer, the other layer is independent. So it is convenient to randomly sample a layer when the other layer is fixed. Then this process is carried out alternately. Each update of the weights in theory needs all neurons to be sampled infinitely times; this is called CD. Because CD works too slowly, Hinton proposed an approximation method called the CD-n algorithm, in which the weights are updated once after sampling n times [28].

If RBM has n visual units and m hidden units, the vectors v and h are respectively used to represent the sates of the visual layer and the hidden layer. Where v_i indicates the state of the ith visual unit, and h_j indicates the state of the jth hidden unit. So given a set of states v, h, the system energy of RBM can be defined:

$$E(v, h) = -\sum_{i=1}^{n}\sum_{j=1}^{m} v_i W_{ij} h_j - \sum_{i=1}^{n} v_i b_i - \sum_{j=1}^{m} h_j c_j \qquad (7.20)$$

In Eq. (7.20), W_{ij}, b_i, c_j are the parameters of RBM. They are real numbers. W_{ij} indicates the connection intension between the visual unit i and the hidden layer j. b_i indicates the bias of the visual unit i. c_j indicates the bias of the hidden unit j. The task of RBM is to solve the value of parameters to fit the given training data.

The states of RBM satisfy the form of the canonical distribution. That is to say, when the parameter is confirmed, the probability of the state v, h is:

$$P(v, h) = \frac{1}{Z}\exp(-E(v, h))$$
$$Z = \sum_{v,h}\exp(-E(v, h)) \qquad (7.21)$$

Suppose RBM is in the normal temperature $T = 1$; the temperature variable T is omitted. Based on this definition, when the states for a layer of units is given, the conditional distribution of the states for another layer of units is:

$$P(v_i | h) = S\left(\sum_{j=1}^{m} W_{ij} h_j + b_i\right)$$
$$P(h_j | v) = S\left(\sum_{i=1}^{n} v_i W_{ij} + c_j\right) \qquad (7.22)$$

In Eq. (7.22), $\sigma(\cdot)$ is the sigmoid function, and $\sigma(x) = 1/(1 + \exp(-x))$. Because the units in the same layer in RBM have not connected each other, when the states for a layer of units is given, the conditional distribution of the state for another layer of units is independent:

$$P(v|h) = \prod_{i=1}^{n} P(v_i|h)$$

$$P(h|v) = \prod_{j=1}^{m} P(h_j|v)$$

(7.23)

This means that if we make a Markov chain Monte Carlo (MCMC) sampling on the distribution of RBM [29], block Gibbs sampling can be adopted. The block Gibbs sampling starts with an initial state v, h, then $P(.|h)$ and $P(.|v)$ are alternatively used to compute the state transform of all visual units and hidden units. This shows the efficiency advantage of RBM in the sampling.

The unsupervised learning method can be served to RBM through the maximum likelihood principle [30]. Suppose there are training data $v^{(1)}$, $v^{(2)}$, ..., $v^{(d)}$, training RBM is equal to maximize the following objective function, where the biases b and c are omitted:

$$L(W) = \sum_{k-1}^{d} \log P(v^{(k)}; W) \equiv \sum_{k-1}^{d} \log \sum_{h} P(v^{(k)}, h; W)$$

(7.24)

In order to use the gradient ascent algorithm in the training process, we need to solve the partial derivatives of the objective function about all parameters. After the algebraic transformation, the final results are:

$$\frac{\partial L(W)}{\partial W_{ij}} \propto \frac{1}{d} \sum_{k-1}^{d} v_i^{(k)} P(h_j|v^{(k)}) - \langle v_i h_j \rangle_{p(v,h;W)}$$

(7.25)

Eq. (7.25) can be split into two parts: positive phase and negative phase. The positive phase can be computed by Eq. (7.22) based on the entire training data set. For the negative phase, $\langle f(x) \rangle_{P(x)}$ is defined as the average value of the function $f(x)$ on the distribution $P(.)$. In RBM, this average value cannot be directly represented as a mathematic expression. That is why training RBM is very difficult.

Obviously, the simplest method, MCMC, is used to solve the average value of the negative phase. In each MCMC sampling, MCMC needs to make a large number of samples to ensure that the samples conform to the objective distribution. So we need to get a large number of samples to accurately approximate the average value. These requirements greatly increase the computational complexity of training RBM. Therefore, MCMC sampling is feasible in theory, but it is not a good choice in efficiency.

Hinton proposed the CD algorithm through considering that the state of MCMC starts with the training data [28]. In CD algorithm, the computing process of the average value in the negative phase can be represented as follows. First, each training data is respectively used for the initial states. After a few repetitions of Gibbs sampling on the state transformations, the transformed state serves as the sample to evaluate the average value. Hinton found that just a few repetitions of state transformation can ensure a good learning effect in practical applications.

The CD algorithm greatly improves the training process of RBM and makes a great contribution for the application of RBM and the rise of the deep neural network. General maximum likelihood learning is like minimizing the KL-divergence between the RBM distribution and the training data distribution. In the CD algorithm, this principle is inadmissible. Therefore, essentially the CD algorithm does not offer a maximum likelihood of learning; the model learned by the CD algorithm has a bad model generation capability.

7.8.4 Deep belief networks

In 2006 Hinton proposed a DBN [31] as shown in Fig. 7.7. A deep neural network can be viewed as a stack of multiple RBMs. The training process can be carried out by layer-wise training from the lower layer to the higher layer because the CD algorithm can serve to quickly train RBM. So DBN can avoid the high complexity of directly training neural networks through splitting the entire network into multiple RBMs. Hinton suggested that the traditional global training algorithm can be used to fine-tune the whole network after this training method. Then the model will converge to a local optimal point. This training algorithm is similar to the method initializing the model parameters to a better value by the layer-wise training method and then further training the model through the traditional algorithm. Thus the problem that the speed of training model is slow can be solved. On the other hand, a lot of experiments have proven that this method can produce very good parameter initialization values and improve the quality of the final parameters.

In 2008 Tieleman proposed a training algorithm called as persistent contrastive divergence (PCD) [32], which improves on the imperfection of CD

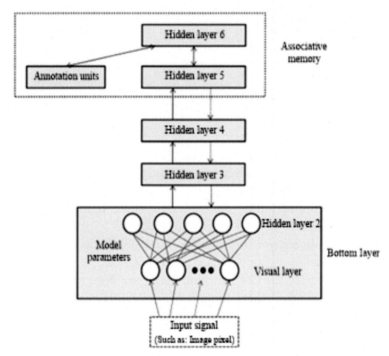

Figure 7.7 Deep belief networks.

algorithm of being unable to maximize the likelihood degree. The efficiency of PCD is the same as that of CD, and it doesn't destroy the training algorithm of the original objective function (maximum likelihood learning). In Tieleman's paper, many an experiment proved that RBMs trained by PCD have stronger model generation capability compared with CD. In 2009 Tieleman further improved PCD and proposed a method employing additional parameters to increase the effect of the training PCD [33]. He revealed the effect of MCMC sampling on training RBM. This lays the foundations for improving the subsequent learning algorithm about RBM. From 2009 to 2010, there existed a series of tempered MCMC RBM training algorithms based on Tieleman's research results [34,35].

7.8.5 Convolutional neural networks

CNNs are multiple stages of globally trainable artificial neural networks [36]. CNN can learn abstract, essential, and advanced features from the data with a little preprocessing or even original data. CNN has been widely applied in License Plate Detection, Face Detection, Handwriting Recognition, Target Tracking, and other fields.

CNN has a better performance in two-dimensional pattern recognition problems than multilayer perceptron because the topology of the two-dimensional model is added into the CNN structure, and CNN employs three important structural features—local accepted field, shared weights, subsampling—ensuring the invariance of the target translation, shrinkage, and distortion of the input signal. CNN mainly consists of the feature extraction and the classifier. The feature extraction contains the multiple convolutional layers and subsampling layers. The classifier consists of one layer or two layers of fully connected neural networks. For the convolutional layer with the local accepted field and the subsampling layer with subsampling structure, they all have the character of sharing the weights. CNN architecture is shown in Fig. 7.8.

In Fig. 7.8, CNN has seven layers: one input layer, two convolutional layers, two subsampling layers, and two fully connected layers. Each input sample in the input layer has $32 \times 32 = 1024$ pixels. C1 is a convolutional layer with six feature maps, and each feature map contains $28 \times 28 = 784$ neurons. Each neuron in C1 is connected to the corresponding local accepted field of size 5×5 in the input layer through the convolutional core of size 5×5 and the convolutional step of length 1. So C1 has $6 \times 784 \times (5 \times 5 + 1) = 122,304$ connections. Each feature map contains the 5×5 weights and biases. Therefore, C1 has $6 \times (5 \times 5 + 1) = 156$ trainable parameters.

S1 is the subsampling layer containing six feature maps, and each feature map consists of $14 \times 14 = 196$ neurons. There is a one-to-one correspondence between the feature maps in S1 and the feature maps in C1. The window of subsampling S1 is a matrix of size 2×2, and the step size

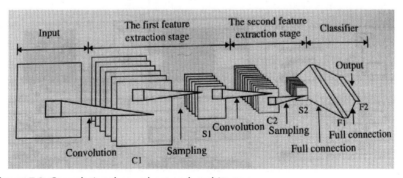

Figure 7.8 Convolutional neural network architecture.

of the subsampling defaults to 1. So there are $6 \times 196 \times (2 \times 2 + 1) = 5880$ connections in the S2 layer. Each feature map in S1 contains a weight and a bias. This means there are 12 trainable parameters.

C2 is the convolutional layer containing 16 feature maps, and each feature map consists of $10 \times 10 = 100$ neurons. Each neuron in C2 is connected to the local accepted field of size 5×5 in the k feature maps in S1 through the k convolutional core of size 5×5, where $k = 6$ if the full connection method is adopted. So there are 41,600 connections in C2 layer. Each feature map in C2 contains $6 \times 5 \times 5 = 150$ weights and biases. This means there are $16 \times (150 + 1) = 2416$ trainable parameters.

S2 is the subsampling layer containing 16 feature maps, and each feature map consists of 5×5 neurons. S2 contains 400 neurons. There is a one-to-one correspondence between the feature maps in S2 and the feature maps in C2. The window of subsampling S2 is a matrix of size 2×2. So there are $16 \times 25 \times (2 \times 2 + 1) = 2000$ connections in S2 layer. Each feature map in S2 contains a weight and a bias. This means there are 32 trainable parameters in S2 layer.

F1 is a full connection layer containing 120 neurons. Each neuron in F1 is connected to the 400 neurons in S2. So the number of the connections or the trainable parameters are $120 \times (400 + 1) = 48,120$. F2 is a full connection layer and the output layer, which contains 10 neurons, 1210 connections, and 1210 trainable parameters.

In Fig. 7.8, the number of the feature maps in the convolutional layer increases layer by layer. This can supplement the loss caused by sampling. On the other hand, the convolutional cores cause the convolutional operation on the feature maps of the former layer to produce the current convolutional feature maps. The produced different features expand the feature space and make the feature extraction more comprehensive.

The error BP algorithm is mostly used to train CNN in a supervised way. In the gradient descent method, the error is back-propagated to constantly adjust the weights and biases. This allows the global sum of squared error on the training samples to reach a minimum value. The BP algorithm consists of the four processes: network initialization, information flow feed-forward propagation, error BP, update of the weights and biases. In error BP, we need to compute the local variation value of the gradient on the weights and biases.

In the initial process of training CNN, the neurons in each layer need to be initialized randomly. The initialization of the weights has a great influence on the convergence rate of the network. So the process of how to initialize the weights is very important. There exists a strong relationship between the initialization of the weights and the selection of the activation function. The weights should be assigned by the fastest changing parts of the activation function. The big weights or the small weights in the initialization process will lead to a small change on the weights.

In the feed-forward propagation of the information flow, the convolutional layer extracts the primary basic features of the input to make up several feature maps. Then the subsampling layer reduces the resolution of the feature maps. After the convolution layer and subsampling alternatively complete feature extraction, the network obtains the high-order invariance features of the input. These high-order invariance features will be transmitted to the full connected neural network and used for classification. After information transformation and computing in the hidden layer and output layer of the fully connected neural network, the network finishes the forward propagation process of the learning. The final results are output by the output layer.

The network starts the error BP process when the actual output is not equal to the expected output. The errors are propagated from the output layer to the hidden layer and then propagated from the hidden layer to the subsampling layer and convolutional layer in the feature extraction stage. The neurons in each layer start to compute the local changed value of the weights and biases when they get their output errors. Finally, the network enters the weights update process.

7.8.5.1 Feed-forward propagation of the convolutional layer

Each neuron in the convolutional layer extracts the features in the local accepted field of the same location of all feature maps in the former layer. The neurons in the same feature map share the same weight matrix. The convolutional process can be viewed as the convolutional neurons seamlessly scan the former feature maps line by line through the weight matrix. The output, $O_{(x,y)}^{(l,k)}$, of the neuron located in line $x-$column y in the kth feature map of the lth convolutional layer can be computed by Eq. (7.26), where $\tanh(\cdot)$ is the activation function:

$$O_{(x,y)}^{(l,k)} = \tanh\left(\sum_{t=0}^{f-1}\sum_{r=0}^{kh}\sum_{c=0}^{kw} W_{(r,c)}^{(k,t)} o_{(x+r,y+c)}^{(l-1,t)} + \text{Bias}^{(l,k)}\right) \qquad (7.26)$$

From Eq. (7.26), we need to traverse all neurons of the convolutional window in all feature maps of the former layer to compute the output of a neuron in the convolutional layer. The feed-forward propagation of the full connection layer is similar to the convolutional layer. This can be viewed as a convolutional operation on the convolutional weight matrix and the input with the same size.

7.8.5.2 Feed-forward propagation of subsampling

The number of feature maps of the subsampling layer is the same as that of the convolution layer of the previous layer, and they correspond to each other one to one. Each neuron in the subsampling layer is connected to the subareas of the same size but are nonoverlapping through the subsampling window. The output, $O_{(x,y)}^{(l,k)}$, of the neuron located in line $x-$column y in the kth feature map of the lth subsampling layer can be computed by Eq. (7.27).

$$O_{(x,y)}^{(l,k)} = \tanh\left(W^{(k)} \sum_{r=0}^{sh} \sum_{c=0}^{sw} O_{(x_{sh}+r,y_{sw}+c)}^{(l-1,t)} + \text{Bias}^{(l,k)} \right) \qquad (7.27)$$

7.8.5.3 Error back-propagation of the subsampling layer

Error BP starts from the output layer and enters the subsampling layer through the hidden layer. The error BP of the output layer needs to first compute the partial derivative of the error about the neurons in the output layer. Suppose the output of the kth neuron is o_k for the training sample d. The expected output of the kth neuron is t_k for the sample d. The error of the output layer for sample d can be represented as $E = 1/2\sum_{k}(o_k - t_k)^{21}$. The partial derivative of the error E about the output o_k is $\partial E/\partial o_k = o_k - t_k$. Similarly, we can solve the partial derivatives of the error about all neurons in the output layer. Then we solve the partial derivatives of the error about the input in the output layer. Set $d(o_k)$ as the partial derivative of the error about the input of the kth neuron in the output layer. $d(o_k)$ can be computed by Eq. (7.28). Where $(1 + o_k)(1-o_k)$ is the partial derivative of the activation function $\tanh(\cdot)$ about the input of the neuron. Then we start to compute the partial derivatives of the error about all neurons in the hidden layer. Suppose the neuron j in the hidden layer is connected to the output neuron through the weight w_{kj}. The partial derivative $d(o_j)$ of the error about the output of the neuron j can be computed by Eq. (7.29). When we obtain the partial derivative of the error about the output of the hidden layer, the error is back-propagated to the hidden layer. Through a similar process, the error will be back-propagated to the subsampling layer. For convenience of expression, the partial derivatives of the error about the outputs of the neuron are called the output error of the neuron. The partial derivatives of the error about the inputs of the neuron are called the input error of the neuron.

$$d(o_k) = (o_k - t_k)(1 + o_k)(1 - o_k) \tag{7.28}$$

$$d(o_j) = \sum d(o_k)w_{kj} \tag{7.29}$$

The numbers of the subsampling layer and the convolution layer are the same and have a one-to-one correspondence, so the error propagation from the subsampling layer to the convolution layer is more intuitive. Eq. (7.28) is used to compute the input errors of all neurons in the subsampling layer. Then the preceding input errors are propagated to the former layer of the subsampling layer. The subsampling layer is set to the lth layer, and then the output error of the neuron located in line x−column y in the kth feature map of the $(l-1)$th layer is computed by Eq. (7.30).

$$d\left(O_{(x,y)}^{(l-1,k)}\right) = d\left(O_{(\lfloor x/sh \rfloor, \lfloor y/sw \rfloor)}^{(l,k)}\right) W^{(k)} \tag{7.30}$$

All neurons in a feature map of the subsampling layer share a weight and a bias. So the local gradient variations of all weights and biases are related to all neurons in the subsampling layer. The weight variation $\Delta W^{(k)}$ and the bias variation $\Delta \text{Bias}^{(l,k)}$ for the kth feature map in the lth subsampling layer can be computed by Eqs. (7.31) and (7.32). In Eq. (7.32), f_h and f_w, respectively, indicate the height and width of the feature map in the lth subsampling layer:

$$\Delta W^{(k)} = \sum_{x=0}^{f_h}\sum_{y=0}^{f_w}\sum_{t=0}^{sh}\sum_{c=0}^{sw} O_{(x,y)}^{(l-1,k)} d\left(O_{(\lfloor x/sh \rfloor, \lfloor y/sw \rfloor)}^{(l,t)}\right) \tag{7.31}$$

$$\Delta \text{Bias}^{(l,k)} = \sum_{x=0}^{f_h}\sum_{y=0}^{f_w} d\left(O_{(x,y)}^{(l,k)}\right) \tag{7.32}$$

7.8.5.4 Error back-propagation of the convolutional layer

There exist two error BP methods in the convolutional layer: push and pull. In the push method (the left figure in Fig. 7.9), the neurons in the lth layer actively propagate the errors to the neurons in the $(l-1)$th layer.

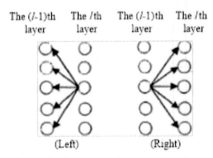

The (*l*-1)th layer   The *l*th layer   The (*l*-1)th layer   The *l*th layer

(Left)   (Right)

Figure 7.9 Two ways of error back-propagation.

This is suitable for serial implementation. There is the write conflict problem in the parallel implementation. In the pull method (the right figure in Fig. 7.9) the neurons in the ($l-1$)th layer actively obtain the errors from the neurons in the *l*th layer. It is difficult to implement the pull method. Due to the border effect of the convolutional operation, we need to confirm which neurons in the feature map of the former layer are connected to the neurons in the current layer.

Here the pull method is used to describe the error BP process of the convolutional layer. Eq. (7.28) is employed to compute the input error of each neuron in the convolutional layer. Then the input error is propagated to the neurons in the former layer of the convolutional layer, as in Eq. (7.33):

$$d\left(O_{(x,y)}^{(l-1,k)}\right) = \sum_{t=0}^{m-1} \sum_{(p,q)\in A} d\left(O_{(p,q)}^{(l,t)}\right) w \qquad (7.33)$$

where *A* is the coordinate set of the neuron located in line *x*—column *y* in the *k*th feature map of the *l*th layer and the neurons in the *l*th layer. *w* indicates the connected weight between the two neurons. The serial computational process by which the error in the convolutional layer is back-propagated to the former subsampling layer is described as follows:

for each neuron *i* in the former layer of the convolutional layer
    Confirm which neurons in the convolutional layer are connected to the neuron *i*
    'Pull' the error from the relevant neurons in the convolutional layer using Eq. (7.33)
end for

The local gradient variation of line r and column y of the weight matrix describing the connection between the kth feature map in the convolutional layer and the tth feature map in the former layer can be computed by Eq. (7.34):

$$\Delta W_{(r,c)}^{(k,t)} = \sum_{x=r}^{f_h - k_h + r} \sum_{y=c}^{f_w - k_w + c} d\left(O_{(x,y)}^{(l,k)}\right) O_{(r+x,c+y)}^{(l-1,t)} \qquad (7.34)$$

All neurons in a feature map of the convolutional layer share a bias. The computational method is same as with the subsampling layer.

With the complication of solving problems and the higher performance requirement for the CNN, training data needs to be more complete and larger. So we need to train the network with stronger capability. This means the network will have more trainable parameters than the famous ImageNet data set containing 14,197,122 labeled images [37]. The CNN, containing 650,000 neurons in the library, [38] is used to classify the ImageNet data set. There are 60,000,000 trainable neurons in the preceding CNN. A large amount of the training data and training parameters significantly increases the computational time; serial computation, in particular, will take a few months of computational time [39]. Therefore researchers have started to research the parallel CNN. There exist at least five parallel ways: the parallelism of the samples, the parallelism between the former back layers, the parallelism between the feature maps in the same layer, the parallelism between the neurons in the feature map, and the parallelism of the neuron weights [40].

7.9 Cognitive machine learning

In March 2016, AlphaGo's Go program, which combines deep RL with a Monte Carlo tree search algorithm, beat Li Shishi, a world champion of Go in Korea, with a score of 4—1, marking great progress in artificial intelligence research, especially in machine learning. But there is still a big difference in intelligence compared to the human level. For machines to have human intelligence, it is necessary to combine machine learning with brain cognition and carry out cognitive machine learning.

As an example of cognitive machine learning, we can combine machine learning with the mind model CAM to carry out the following research [41].

7.9.1 The emergence of learning

The essence of emergence is from small to big, from simple to complex. The first step in the process of cognition is contact with the objects of the external world, which belongs to the stage of perception. The second step is to synthesize the data of perception by sorting out and reconstructing them, which belongs to the stage conception, judgment, and inference. It is only when the data of perception is very rich and correspond to reality that it can be the basis for forming correct concepts and theories.

ImageNet is an image database organized according to the WordNet hierarchy (currently only the nouns), in which each node of the hierarchy is depicted by hundreds and thousands of images. The goal of the ImageNet challenge is to segment and parse an image into different image regions associated with semantic categories, such as sky, road, person, and bed. The data for this challenge comes from the ADE20K Dataset (the full data set will be released after the challenge), which contains more than 20K scene-centric images exhaustively annotated with objects and object parts.

Krizhevsky et al. have been involved in the ImageNet LSVRC-2010 contest and the applied deep CNN to classify the 1.2 million high-resolution images into the 1000 different classes. They achieved top-1 and top-5 error rates of 37.5% and 17.0%, respectively, which is considerably better than the previous state of the art. The neural network, which has 60 million parameters and 650,000 neurons, consists of five convolutional layers, some of which are followed by max-pooling layers, and three fully connected layers with a final 1000-way softmax [42].

In 2012 the deep neural network AlexNet made amazing achievements in an ImageNet large-scale image recognition challenge competition. At that time, AlexNet, which uses eight layers of neurons, dramatically reduced the error rate of image recognition from 25% to 15%. Since then, only 3 years later, people have learned how to train up to 100 layers of neurons in the deep neural network ResNet, which reduces the error rate of image recognition to 3.6%. This level is already above the human level (5%). By June 2020, AlexNet's papers have been cited more than 64,000 times. This is the amazing debut of deep learning technology.

7.9.2 Procedural knowledge learning

In December 2015, "Science" published the paper "Human-level Concept Learning through Probabilistic Program Induction," written by Lake et al. [43]. The paper shows that the learning system can quickly learn the essence from a strange text system. They analyzed three core principles in their paper. These principles are universal and can be applied to characters as well as to other concepts:

1. Compositionality: Representations are constructed from simpler primitives.
2. Causality: The model represents the abstract causal structure of character generation.
3. Learning to learn: Knowledge of past concepts helps in learning new concepts.

The method adopted by the three researchers is Bayesian program learning, which enables a computer system to well simulate human cognition. Traditional machine learning methods need a lot of data to train, but this method needs only a rough model and then uses a reasoning algorithm to analyze the case and supplement the details of the model.

One of the purposes of human perception is to perform operational tasks, and sometimes human beings only need to have a general understanding of the environment when performing operational tasks. Taking visual perception as an example, the differences among perceptual task samples are huge, so a large number of labeled samples are needed. In contrast, the complexity of operating the truth value of tasks is much smaller. For example, no matter what the environment is, the way humans walk is roughly unchanged. If we can directly start from the input and directly fit the function of the operation task to the basis of obtaining a certain degree of perceptual skills, it is possible to reduce the demand for perceptual task data.

7.9.3 Learning evolution

One of the most important mechanisms in the world is to change its own structure to adapt to the outside world. Evolution, learning, and then the development of advanced evolution and learning produce purposefulness, which is actually key; a random purposeless machine can explore its own purpose through learning. In the mid-19th century, Darwin founded the theory of biological evolution. Through heredity, variation, and natural selection, organisms have evolved and developed from low level to high level, from simple to complex, and from few to many.

For intelligence, "evolution" refers to the learning of learning. This learning is different from software, and its structure changes with it. This is a very important one. The structural change records the learning results and improves the learning method. Moreover, its storage and operation are integrated, which is difficult for the computer at present. This area is probably a new topic to study the evolution model of computer learning, and it is a subject worthy of attention.

The study of ancient human skulls reveals the development of the human brain. In the course of 2 million years of evolution, the volume of the human brain has tripled. Due to the joint action of various factors such as human food, culture, skills, groups, and genes, the modern human brain evolved successfully 200,000 years ago. The capacity of the modern human brain is about 1200−1400 mL. In the stage of apes, the development of intelligence is slow. In the stage of *Homo sapiens*, early *Homo sapiens*, and late *Homo sapiens*, the evolution of human intelligence has rapidly improved. Many unique cortical centers of human beings were produced in this period, such as the motor language center, writing center, auditory language center, and so on. At the same time, the cerebral cortex also appeared to enjoy music and painting centers, these centers have obvious positioning characteristics. Especially with the development of human abstract thinking, the frontal lobe of the human brain expands rapidly. It can be seen that the modern human brain is constantly evolving.

In order to endow machines with intelligence at the human level and break through the limitation of learning by computer, we must let the machine have the function of learning and evolution. Learning not only increases knowledge but also changes the memory structure of the machine.

References

[1] Z.Z. Shi, Principles of Machine Learning, International Academic Publishers, 1992.
[2] H.A. Simon, Why should machines learn? in: R.S. Michalski, J.G. Carbonell, T.M. Mitchell (Eds.), Machine Learning, an Artificial Intelligence Approach (Chap. 2), Tioga Publishing, Palo Alto, CA, 1983.
[3] Z.Z. Shi, S.L. Zhang, Case-based introspective learning. IEEE ICCI'05 (2005).
[4] Z.Z. Shi, Intelligence Science (In Chinese), Tsinghua University Press, Beijing, 2006.
[5] J.B. Watson, Psychology as the behaviorist views it, Psychol Rev. 20 (1913) 158−177. Available from: http://psychclassics.yorku.ca/Watson/views.htm.
[6] E.L. Thorndike, Human Learning, Century, New York, 1931.
[7] B.F. Skinner, The science of learning and the art of teaching, Harv. Educ. Rev. 24 (2) (1954) 86−97.
[8] E.R. Guthrie, The Psychology of Learning, Harper, New York, 1935.
[9] E.R. Guthrie, The Psychology of Human Conflict, Harper, New York, 1938.
[10] C.L. Hull, C.I. Hovland, R.T. Ross, et al., Mathematico-Deductive Theory of Rote Learning, Yale University Press, New Haven, 1940.
[11] C.L. Hull, Principles of Behavior, D. Appleton-Century Co., Inc, New York, 1943.

[12] M. Wertheimer, Undersuchungen zur Lehre der Gestalt II, Psycologische Forschung, 4, 301-350. (1923). Translation published as Laws of organization in perceptual forms, in W. Ellis, A Source Book of Gestalt Psychology, pp. 71−88, Routledge & Kegan Paul, London (1938).

[13] E.C. Tolman, Purposive Behavior in Animals and Men, Century, New York, 1932.

[14] J. Bruner, Toward a Theory of Instruction, Harvard University Press, Cambridge, MA, 1966.

[15] J.S. Bruner, The course of cognitive growth, Am. Psychol 19 (1964) 1−15.

[16] D.P. Ausubel, J.D. Novak, H. Hanesian, Educational Psychology: A Cognitive View, second edition, Holt, Rinehart and Winston, Inc, New York, 1978.

[17] R. Gagne, The Conditions of Learning, fourth ed., Holt, Rinehart & Winston, New York, 1985.

[18] R. Gagne, L. Briggs, W. Wager, Principles of Instructional Design, fourth ed., HBJ College Publishers, Fort Worth, TX, 1992.

[19] M.C. Wittrock, A Constractive Review of Research on Learning Strategies, Academic Press, Inc, 1988.

[20] C.R. Rogers, A Theory of Therapy, Personality, and Interpersonal Relationships: As Developed in the Client-Centered Framework, vol. 3, McGraw-Hill, New York, 1959, pp. 184−256.

[21] A. Bandura, Social Learning Theory, General Learning Press, New York, 1977.

[22] M.T. Cox, A. Ram, Introspective multistrategy learning on the construction of learning strategies, Artif. Intell. 112 (1999) 1−55.

[23] S. Fox, Introspective multistrategy learning: constructing a learning strategy under reasoning failure, PhD Thesis, Technical Report No. GIT-CC-96-06, Georgia Institute of Technology, College of Computing, Atlanta, GA, 1996.

[24] Q. Dong, Z. Shi, A research on introspective learning based on CBR, Int. J. Adv. Intell. 3 (1) (2011) 147−157.

[25] R.S. Sutton, A.G. Barto, Reinforcement Learning: An Introduction, MIT Press, Cambridge, MA, 1998.

[26] C.J.C.H. Watkins, P. Dayan, Technical note: Q-learning, Mach. Learn. 8 (3−4) (1992) 279−292.

[27] Y. LeCun, Y. Bengio, G. Hinton, Deep learning, Nature 521 (7553) (2015) 436−444.

[28] G.E. Hinton, Training products of experts by minimizing contrastive divergence, Neural Comput 14 (2002) 1771−1800.

[29] C. Andrieu, N. De Freitas, A. Doucet, et al., An introduction to MCMC for machine learning, Mach. Learn. 50 (1) (2003) 5−43.

[30] G.E. Hinton, A practical guide to training restricted Boltzmann machines. UTML TR 2010−003, 2010.

[31] G.E. Hinton, R. Salakhutdinov, Reducing the dimensionality of data with neural networks, Science 313 (5786) (2006) 504−507.

[32] T. Tieleman, Training restricted Boltzmann machines using approximations to the likelihood gradient, in: Proceedings of the 25th International Conference on Machine Learning, pp. 1064−1071, 2008.

[33] T. Tieleman, G. Hinton, Using fast weights to improve persistent contrastive divergence, in: Proceedings of the 26th Annual International Conference on Machine Learning, New York, NY, 2009.

[34] G. Desjardins, A. Courville, Y. Bengio, et al., Tempered Markov chain monte carlo for training of restricted Boltzmann machine, in: Proceedings of AISTATS., pp. 145−152, 2010.

[35] R. Salakhutdinov, Learning Deep Boltzmann Machines using Adaptive MCMC, in: Proceedings of the 27th International Conference on Machine Learning, 2010.

[36] Y. LeCun, B. Boser, J.S. Denker, et al., Handwritten digit recognition with a back-propagation network, Advances in Neural Information Processing Systems, Morgan Kaufmann, Denver, 1989, pp. 396−404.

[37] ImageNet, <http://www.image-net.org/>, Stanford Vision Lab, Stanford University, (2014).

[38] A. Krizhevsky, I. Sutskever, G.E. Hinton, ImageNet classification with deep convolufional neural networks, in: Annual Conference on Neural Information Processing Systems Lake Tahoe, pp. 1106−1114, 2012.

[39] D.C. Ciresan, U. Meier, L.M. Gambardella, et al., Deep big simple neural nets excel on handwritten digit recognition, Neural Comput-NECO, vol. abs/1003.0, 22 (12) (2010) 3207−3220.

[40] J. Schmidhuber, Deep learning in neural networks: an overview, Neural Netw. 61 (2015) 85−117.

[41] Z.Z. Shi, What are the limitations of learning by machines? Chin. Sci. Bull. 61 (33) (2016) 3548−3556.

[42] A. Krizhevsky, I. Sutskever, G.E. Hinton, ImageNet classification with deep convolutional neural networks, CACM 60 (6) (2017) 84−90.

[43] B.M. Lake, R. Salakhutdinov, J.B. Tenenbaum, Human-level concept learning through probabilistic program induction, Science 350 (6266) (2015) 1332−1338.

CHAPTER 8

Memory

Memory is the human brain's recollection, maintenance, reappearance, or recognition of experience. It is the basis of thinking, imagination, and other advanced psychological activities. Because of the existence of memory, people can keep past reflections, make current reflections based on the previous reflections, and make the reflections more comprehensive and in-depth. With memory, people can accumulate experience and expand it. Memory is mental continuity in time. With memory, successive experiences can be connected, making psychological activities become a developing process, making a person's psychological activities become a unified process, and forming a person's psychological characteristics. Memory is an important aspect of mind ability.

8.1 Overview

Memory is the psychological process that contains the accumulation, preservation, and extraction of individual experience in the brain. In information processing terms, the human brain enters information from the outside world for the coding, storage, and retrieval process. Perceptions of the things people have to think about, the questions raised, and experiences of emotional engagement in activities all leave impressions in people's minds to varying degrees. This is the process in the mind; under certain conditions, according to an individual's needs, the impressions can be aroused, the person can participate in the ongoing activities once again. This is the process of memory. From storage in the brain to extracting the application again, the integrated process is referred to as memory.

Memory consists of three basic processes: entering the information into the memory systems (coding), storing information in memory (storing), extracting the information from memory (extraction). Memory encoding is the first fundamental process by which information from the sensory memory system becomes able to be received and in usable form. In general, we obtain information through a variety of external sensory systems; it is then necessary to convert it into a variety of memory code, that is, the formation of an objective mental representation of physical

Intelligence Science
DOI: https://doi.org/10.1016/B978-0-323-85380-4.00008-7

stimulation. The coding process requires the participation of the attention: attention to the processing of different coding standards or to different forms. For example, looking at characters, you can pay attention to their shape, structure, word pronunciation, or the meaning of the word to form a visual code, sound code, or semantic code. Encoding has a direct impact on the endurance of memory. Of course, a strong emotional experience also enhances the memory effect. In short, how the information is encoded has direct impact on memory storage and on subsequent extraction. Under normal circumstances, information is encoded using a variety of memory effects.

The information that has been encoded must be preserved in the mind and, after a certain period, may be extracted. However, in most cases, the preservation of information for future application is not always automatic; we must strive to find ways to preserve information. Information that has been stored may also be undermined and then forgotten. For psychologists studying memory, the main concern is with the factors that affect memory storage and that fight against oblivion.

Information saved in memory, only to be extracted for application is meaningless. There are two ways to extract information: recall and recognition. Day to day, "remembering" refers to memories. Recognition is easier because the original stimulus is front of us. We have a variety of clues that can be used merely to determine our familiarity with it. Some materials studied cannot be recalled or reidentified. Have they completely disappeared in our minds? No. Memory traces will not completely disappear; further study can serve as good examples of this. Let the subjects learn the same material twice and reach the same proficiency level each time. The number of exercises or time needed for the second study must be less than that of the first study. The difference in the time or times used for the second study indicates the amount in preservation.

According to its content, memory can be divided into the following four types:

1. **Image memory:** Memory with the content of the perceived image of things is called image memory. These specific images can be visual, auditory, olfactory, tactile, or taste images. For example, the memory of a picture that people have seen and a piece of music that they have heard is image memory. The remarkable feature of this kind of memory is that it preserves the perceptual feature of things, which is typically intuitive.

2. **Emotional memory:** This is the memory of emotions or emotions experienced in the past, such as the memory of students' happy mood when

they receive the admission notice. In the process of knowing things or communicating with people, people always have a certain amount of emotional color or emotional content, which is also stored in the brain as the content of memory and becomes a part of human psychological content. Emotional memory is often formed once and never forgotten, which has a great influence on people's behavior. The impression of emotional memory is sometimes more lasting than other forms of memory impression. Even though people have forgotten the fact that caused the emotional experience, the emotional experience remains.

3. Logical memory: This is memory in the form of ideas, concepts, or propositions, such as the memory of a mathematical theorem, formula, philosophical proposition, etc. This kind of memory is based on abstract logical thinking and has the characteristics of generality, understanding, and logicality.

4. Action memory: This is memory based on people's past operational behavior. All the actions and patterns that people keep in their minds belong to action memory. This kind of memory is of great significance to the coherence and accuracy of people's movements, and it is the basis of the formation of movement skills.

These four memory forms are not only different but also closely linked. For example, action memory has a distinct image. If there is no emotional memory in logical memory, its content is difficult to keep for a long time.

American neuroscientist E. R. Kandel devoted his whole life to exploring the mystery of memory. His outstanding contribution to memory research won him the 2000 Nobel Prize in physiology or medicine [1]. There are a lot of deep questions about memory. Although we have a good foundation now, we are only beginning to fully understand the complexity of memory, persistence, and recall. In 2009 E. R. Kandel proposed 11 unsolved problems in memory research [2].

1. How does synaptic growth occur, and how is signaling across the synapse coordinated to induce and maintain growth?

2. What trans-synaptic signals coordinate the conversion of short- to intermediate- to long-term plasticity?

3. What can computational models contribute to understanding synaptic plasticity?

4. Will characterization of the molecular components of the presynaptic and postsynaptic cell compartments revolutionize our understanding of synaptic plasticity and growth?

5. What firing patterns do neurons actually use to initiate LTP at various synapses?
6. What is the function of neurogenesis in the hippocampus?
7. How does memory become stabilized outside the hippocampus?
8. How is memory recalled?
9. What is the role of small RNAs in synaptic plasticity and memory storage?
10. What is the molecular nature of the cognitive deficits in depression, schizophrenia, and non-Alzheimer's age-related memory loss?
11. Does working memory in the prefrontal cortex involve reverberatory self-reexcitatory circuits or intrinsically sustained firing patterns?

If a breakthrough can be made in these important open problems, it will be of great value to the development of intelligence science, especially the study of memory.

8.2 Memory system

According to the temporal length of memory operation, there are three types of human memory: sensory memory, short-term memory, and long-term memory (LTM). The relationship among these three is illustrated in Fig. 8.1. First, the information from the environment reaches the sensory memory. If the information is attentional, it is entered into short-term memory. In the short-term memory of the individual, the information can be restructured, used, and responded to. The information in short-term memory may be analyzed, and the resultant knowledge stored in LTM storage. At the same time, the short-term memory preservation

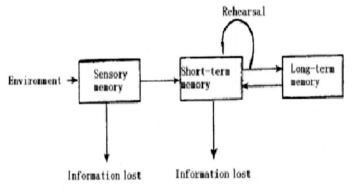

Figure 8.1 Memory system.

of information, if necessary, can also be redeposited after forwarding to LTM. In Fig. 8.1, the arrows indicate the flow of information storage in three runs in the direction of the model.

R. Atkinson and R. M. Shiffrin carried out their expanded memory system model in 1968 [3], that is, sensory memory (register), short-term memory, and LTM of three parts. The difference is that they joined the contents of the control process, and the control of the course of the process is stored in the three works. The model also has a point of concern regarding its LTM of information. In their model of LTM, the information does not disappear; the information does not dissipate from the library of self-addresses.

8.2.1 Sensory memory

Information impinging on the senses initially goes into what is called sensory storage. Sensory storage is the direct impression, the sensory infor-mation, that comes from the sense organ. The sensory register can keep information from each sense organ for only between some dozens to several hundreds of milliseconds. In the sensory register, information can be noticed, the meaning can be encoded, and then it can enter the next step in processing. If it cannot be noticed or encoded, it will disappear automatically.

All kinds of sensory information continue keeping up for some time and working in its characterized form in the sensory register. These forms are called iconic store and echoic store. Representation can be said to be the most direct, most primitive memory. Mental image can only exist for a short time, if the most distinct video lasts only dozens of seconds. Sensory memory possesses the following characteristics:

1. Memory is very transient.
2. Have the ability to deal with as much material incentive energy as in anatomy and physiology.
3. Information encoding in a quietly direct way.

George Sperling's research verified the concept of sensory memory [4]. In this research, Sperling flashed an array of letters and numbers on a screen for a mere 50 ms. Participants were asked to report the identity and location of as many of the symbols as they could recall. Sperling could be sure that participants got only one glance because previous research had shown that 0.05 s is long enough for only a single glance at the pre-sented stimulus.

Sperling found that when participants were asked to report on what they saw, they remembered only about four symbols. The number of symbols recalled was pretty much the same, without regard to how many symbols had been in the visual display. Some of Sperling's participants mentioned that they had seen all the stimuli clearly, but while reporting what they saw, they forgot the other stimuli. The procedure used initially by Sperling is a whole-report procedure. Sperling then introduced a partial-report procedure, in which participants needed to report only part of what they saw.

Sperling found a way to obtain a sample of his participants' knowledge and then extrapolated from this sample to estimate their total knowledge of course material. Sperling presented symbols in three rows of four symbols each. Sperling informed participates that they would have to recall only a single row of the display. The row to be recalled was signaled by a tone of either high, medium, or low pitch, corresponding to the need to recall the top, middle, or bottom row, respectively. Participants had to recall one-third of the information presented but did not know beforehand which of the three lines they would be asked to report.

Using this partial-report procedure, Sperling found that participants had available roughly 9 of the 12 symbols if they were cued immediately before or immediately after the appearance of the display. However, when they were cured 1 s later, their recall was down to four or five of the 12 items, about the same as was obtained through the whole report procedure. These data suggest that the iconic store can hold about nine items, and that it decays very rapidly. Indeed, the advantage of the partial-report procedure is drastically reduced by 0.3 s of delay and is essentially obliterated by 1 s of delay from onset of the tone.

Sperling's results suggest that information fades rapidly from iconic storage. Why are we subjectively unaware of such a fading phenomenon? First, we are rarely subjected to stimuli that appear for only 50 ms and then disappear, for which we need to report. Second and more important, however, we are unable to distinguish what we see in iconic memory from what we actually see in the environment. What we see in iconic memory is what we take to be in the environment. Participants in Sperling's experiment generally reported that they could still see the display up to 150 ms after it had been terminated.

In 1986 Professor Xinbi Fan et al. proposed a visual associative device, auditory associative device, and tactile associative device [5]. Furthermore, an advanced intelligent system with reasoning and decision can be constructed by using various associative devices. The parallel search of associative devices provides the possibility of high-speed data processing. In short, associative devices can be used as components of new computers.

8.2.2 Short-term memory

Information encoded in sensory memory enters short-term memory, through further processing, and then enters into the LTM in which information can be kept for a long time. Information generally is kept in short-term memory only for 20−30 s, but if repeated, it can continue there. Repeating guarantees the delay of disappearance of the information stored in short-term memory—an important function in psychological activity. First, short-term memory is acting as part of consciousness, enabling us to know what we are receiving and what is being done. Second, short-term memory can combine some sensory messages into an intact picture. Third, short-term memory functions as a register temporarily while the individual is thinking and solving a problem. For example, before making the next step in a calculation question, people will temporarily deposit the latest results of the calculation for eventual utilization. Finally, short-term memory keeps present tactics and will. All of these enable us to adopt various complicated behaviors until reaching the final goal. Even though we find these important functions in short-term memory, most present research renames it working memory. Compared with sensory memory, which has much of the information to be used, the ability of short-term memory is quite limited. Participants were given a piece of figure bunch, such as 6-8-3-5-9, which they should be able to recite immediately. If it is more than seven figures, people cannot recite them completely. In 1956 George A. Miller, an American psychologist proposed clearly that our immediate memory capacity for a wide range of items appears to be about seven items, plus or minus 2. To chunk means to combine several little units into a familiar and heavy unit of information processing; it also means the unit that is made up like this. Chunk is a course and a unit. As for that knowledge experience and the chunk, the function of the chunk is to reduce the unit in short-term memory and to increase information in each unit. The more knowledge that people have, the more messages that can be in each chunk. At the same time, the chunk is not divided by meaning; that is, there is no meaning connection between the elements of the composition. So to remember a long figure, we can divide it into several groups. It is an effective method is to reduce the quantity of independent elements in the figures. This kind of organization, called a chunk, plays a great role in LTM.

It has been pointed out that information was stored in short-term memory according to its acoustic characteristic. In other words, even if a message is received by vision, it would be encoded according to the characteristics of acoustics. For example, when you see a group of letters B-C-D, you are according them their pronunciation [bī:]-[sī:]-[dī:] but not according them their shape to encode.

Fig. 8.2 provides the short-term memory buffer. Short-term memory encoding in humans may have a strong acoustical attribute but cannot be rid of the code of other properties. Many who cannot speak can do the work of short-term memory. For example, after seeing a figure, they will select one of two colorful geometric figures, consisting of several slots. Every slot is equivalent to an information canal. The informational unit coming from sensory memory enters different slots separately. The repeated process of the buffer selectively repeats the information in the slot. The information repeated in the slots is entered into LTM. Information that is not repeated is cleared from short-term memory and disappears.

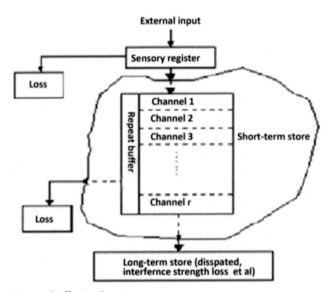

Figure 8.2 Repeat buffer in short-term memory.

The times for information in every slot differ. The longer the time information is kept in the slot, the greater the chance that it will enter LTM, and the greater the chance that it may be washed and squeezed out by a new message coming from sensory memory. Comparatively, LTM is the real storehouse of information, but information can be forgotten by subsidizing, interference, and intensity.

Retrieving the course of short-term memory is quite complicated. It involves a lot of questions and gives rise to different hypotheses. There is no consensus so far.

8.2.2.1 Classic research of Sternberg

Saul Sternberg's research indicates that information retrieval in short-term memory occurs by way of series scanning that is exhaustive to effect. We can interpret it as the model of scanning [6].

Sternberg's experiment is a classic research paradigm. The supposition of the experiment is that until participants scan all items into short-term memory, they will judge the items of the test as "yes" or "no," so that the reaction time of participants' correct judgements should not change with the size of memory. The experimental results show that the reaction time is lengthened with the size of memory. It means that the scanning of short-term memory does not carry on parallel scanning but rather serial scanning.

Sternberg's theory must solve another problem: If information retrieval in short-term memory is serial scanning instead of parallel scanning, then where does the scanning begins, and how does it expire? According to Sternberg, information retrieval takes place via serial scanning even though participants are busy with their own affairs. Meanwhile, the course of judgment includes the comparing and decision-making process. So while participants are judging, they are not self-terminating.

8.2.2.2 Direct an access model

W. A. Wickelgren does not think that retrieving items in short-term memory is done through comparing. People can get to the positions of items in short-term memory directly and retrieve them directly.

The direct access model asserts that the retrieval of information does not occur by scanning in short-term memory [7]. The brain can directly access the positions where items are stored to draw on them directly. According to this model, each item in short-term memory has a certain familiar value or trace intensity. So, according to these standards, people can make a judgement. There is a judgment standard within the brain: If the familiarity is higher than this standard, then the response if "yes"; if it is lower, then "no." The more between familiarity there is with the standard, the faster people can give a "yes" or "no" response.

The direct access model can explain serial position effect (primacy and recency effect). But how does short-term memory know the positions of items? If the retrieval of information is by direct access, why does the reaction time increase linearly when the number of items increases?

8.2.2.3 Double model

R. Atkinson and J. Juola think the retrieval of information already includes scanning and direct access during short-term memory. In brief, both ends are direct, and the middle is scanning, as shown in Fig. 8.3.

The search model and direct access model both have their favorable aspects, but there is a deficiency. The double model attempts to combine the two. Atkinson and Juola put forward the notion of information retrieval in the double model in short-term memory [8]. They imagine that each of the words is input that can be encoded according to its sensorial dimensionality, called sensory code; words has a meaning, called its concept code. Sensory code and concept code form a concept node. Each concept node has a different level of activation or familiarity value.

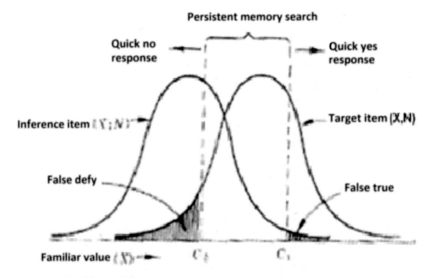

Figure 8.3 Double model.

There are two standards of judging within the brain. One is high-standard (C1): If the familiarity value of a certain word is equal to or higher than this standard, people can make a rapid "yes" response. The other one is the low standard (C0): If the familiarity value of a certain word is equal to or lower than this standard, people can make a rapid "deny" response. Atkinson and Juola state that this is a direct access course. However, if a survey word with a familiarity value lower than the high-standard but higher than the low standard, it will carry on a serial search and make a reaction. So the reaction times are greater.

The research on short-term memory finds that processing speed and material properties or information type of information have relationships. The speed of processing rises with increasing memory capacity; the bigger the capacity of the material, the faster it will scan.

Experimental results indicate that processing speed in short-term memory has a relationship with material properties or information type. In 1972 Cavanaugh, through calculating the average experimental results with materials in different research works, obtained the average time taken for scanning one item and contrasted the corresponding capacity of short-term memory. An interesting phenomenon was found: The processing speed rises with an increase in the memory capacity. The greater the capacity of the material, the faster of scanning is. It is difficult to explain this phenomenon clearly. One imagining is that in short-term memory, information is signified with characteristics. But the storage space of short-term memory is limited; so the larger that each average characteristic is in quantity, then the smaller the quantity will be of free short-term memory. Cavanaugh then thinks that each stimulus's processing time is directly proportional to its average characteristic quantity. If the average characteristic quantity is heavy, then it will need more time to process; otherwise less time is needed. Also, there are many doubtful areas in this explanation, even though it connects the information retrieval of short-term memory, memory capacity, and information representation. This is really an important problem. The processing speed reflects the characteristic of the processing course. Behind the processing speed difference of different materials, the cause may be that memory capacity, information representation, etc. have different courses of information retrieval.

Through the Peterson-Peterson method, the information that was forgotten in short-term memory is discovered [9].

1. Information can keep 15–30 s in short-term memory.
2. If cannot be repeated; so the information in short-term memory will be forgotten rapidly.
3. So long as the quantity in short-term memory does not change, the change of material property has no influence on short-term memory.

E. R. Kandel found through his research that cAMP plays a very important role in repairing brain cells, activating brain cells, and regulating the function of brain cells, turning short-term memory into LTM [1].

8.2.3 Long-term memory

Information maintained for more than a minute is referred to as LTM. The capacity of LTM is the greatest of all memory systems. Experiments are needed to illustrate the capacity, storage, restoration, and duration of LTM. The result measuring how long one thing can be memorized is not definite. Memory cannot last for long time because attention is unstable; if accompanied by repetitions, however, memory will be retained for long time. The capacity of LTM is infinite. Some 8 s are needed to retain one chunk. Before being recovered and applied, information stored in LTM needs to be transferred into short-term memory. During the phase of LTM recovery, the first number needs 2 s; then every following number needs 200–300 s. Different figure numbers, such as 34, 597, 743218, can be used for the experiment to measure how long each number needs to be recovered. The result indicates that a two-figure number needs 2200 ms, a three-figure number needs 2400 ms, and six-figure number needs 3000 ms.

The Bluma Zeigarnik effect results from instructing a subject to complete some tasks [10] while leaving other tasks unfinished. Afterward, the subjects can remember unfinished work better than the finished work when they are asked to remember what they had done. It was revealed that, if a task is stopped before being finished, the task continues activity in another space. Some things are easier to retrieve than others in LTM because their threshold is lower. Other things with high thresholds need more clues to retrieve. The unfinished task's threshold is low and can be activated and spread easily. Activation spreads along the net until the location stores information, and then the information is retrieved.

A lot of psychologists agree that sensory memory and short-term memory will disappear fast and become passive, but few psychologists agree there is the same simple decline mechanism in LTM because it is

Table 8.1 Comparison of three kinds of memory systems.

Memory system	Time interval	Capacity	Type of organization or encode	Mechanism of forgotten
Sensory memory	Less than 1 s	Depend on capacity of receptor	Direct outcome of stimulation	Passive decline
Short-term memory	Less than a minute	Only several items (five to nine)	Indirect encode include a lot of auditory organization	Passive decline
Long-term memory	1 min to several years	Almost infinite	Complicate encode	Interference and forgotten, constrain, productive forgotten

difficult to explain why some materials are forgotten slightly faster than others? Does the completion intensity of the original study material relate to forgetting? Is being forgotten affected by something that happens during the time between studying and remembering? Many psychologists in this area believe that LTM disappears because of interference. This is a passive point. There are some points about being forgotten as an active process as a supplement or substitution for interference. Floyd thinks being forgotten results from constraining. The material will be difficult to remember if it is extremely painful and threatening to the mind. Another standpoint is the "productive forgotten" proposed by Bartlett. If you have not received accurate memory, you will create something like the memory, and then you will get to the real memory. The characteristics of these three kinds of memory systems are provided in Table 8.1.

The human memory system is very much like that of computer. Computer memory layers consist of cache, main memory, and auxiliary memory, whose speed runs from fast to slow and whose capacity runs from small to large, with the optimum control deployment algorithm and reasonable cost composing an acceptable memory system.

8.3 Long-term memory

Information maintained for more than a minute is referred to as LTM. The capacity of LTM is the greatest among all memory systems. Experiments are needed to illustrate the capacity, storage, restoration, and duration of LTM.

The result determined that how long something can be memorized is not definite. Memory cannot last for long time because attention is unstable; if accompanied by repetitions, however, memory can be retained for long time. The capacity of LTM is infinite. Eight seconds are needed to retain one chunk. Before recovered and applied, information stored in LTM needs to be transferred into short-term memory.

LTM can be divided into procedural memory and declarative memory. Procedural memory keeps the skill about operating something, which mainly consists of perceptive-motor skills and cognitive skills. Declarative memory stores the knowledge represented by symbols to reflect the essences of things. Procedural memory and declarative memory are the same memories reflecting someone's experience and action influenced by previous experience and action.

The differences between procedural memory and declarative memory are as follows:

1. There is only one way for representation in procedural memory, which needs skills research. The representations of declarative information can vary and are different from action completely.
2. With respect to true-or-false questions of knowledge, there is no difference between true and false for skilled procedures. Only the knowledge of cognition of the world and the relationship between the world and us has the problem of true or false.
3. The study forms of these two kinds of information are different. Procedural information must be taken through certain exercise, and declarative information needs only chance practice.
4. Skilled action works automatically, but the reparation of declarative information needs attention.

Declarative memory can be further divided into episodic memory and semantic memory. Episodic memory is a person's personal and biographical memory. Semantic memory stores the essential knowledge of the incident that an individual understands or, in other words, world knowledge. Table 8.2 shows the differences between these two kinds of memories.

LTM is divided into two systems in terms of information encoding: the image system and verbal system. The image system stores information on specific objects and events by image code. The verbal system uses verbal code to store verbal information. The theory is called two kinds of coding or dual coding because these two systems are independent while related to each other.

Table 8.2 Comparison of episodic memory and semantic memory.

Characteristics of distinction	Episodic memory	Semantic memory
Information domain		
Input source	Sensory	Understanding
Unit	Event, episodic	Truth, concept
System	Time	Conceptive
Reference	Oneself	World
Facticity	Personal belief	Consistent of society
Operation domain		
Content of memory	Experiential	Symbol
Symbolization of time	Yes, direct	No, indirect
Feeling	İmportant	Not very important
Reasoning ability	Low	High
Context dependent	High	Low
Susceptible	High	Low
Store and read	Depend on intention	Automatically
Retrieval method	According to time or place	According to object
Result of retrieval	Memory structure changed	Memory structure unchanged
Retrieval principle	Concerted	Open
Content recalled	Past memory	Knowledge represented
Retrieval report	Feel	Know
Order of develop	Slow	Fast
Children amnesia	Hindered	No hindered
Application domain		
Education	İndependent	Dependent
Generality	Low	High
Artificial intelligence	Unclear	Very good
Human intelligence	Independent	Dependent
Experience proven	Forgotten	Semantic analyze
Lab topic	Given scene	Generic knowledge
Legal evidence	Yes, witness	No, surveyor
Memory loss	Dependent	Independent
Bicameral men	No	Yes

8.3.1 Semantic memory

Semantic memory was proposed by M. Ross Quillian in 1968 [11]. It is the first model of semantic memory in cognitive psychology. Anderson and Bower, Rumelhart, and Norman all had proposed various memory models

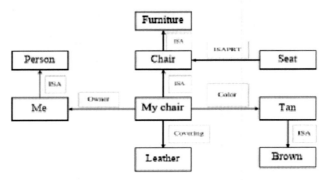

Figure 8.4 Semantic network.

based on the semantic network in cognitive psychology. In this model, the basic unit of semantic memory is the concept that has certain characteristics that are also concept in fact, but they are used to explain other concepts. In the semantic network, information is represented as a set of nodes that are connected with each other by an arc with a mark that represents the relationship between nodes. Fig. 8.4 is a typical semantic network. The is a link is used to represent the layer relationship of the concept node and to link the node-represented specific object with a relevant concept is part links the concepts of global and partial. For example, in Fig. 8.4, Chair is a part of Seat.

8.3.1.1 Hierarchical network model

The hierarchical network model for semantic memory was proposed by Quillian et al. In this model, the primary unit of LTM is concept. Concepts are related to one another and then form a hierarchical structure. As shown in Fig. 8.5, the block is a node representing concept, and the line with an arrow point expresses the dependence between the concepts. For instance, the higher hierarchical concept of bird is animal, while its lower hierarchical concept is ostrich. The lines represent the relationships between concept and attribute to designate the attribute of each hierarchical, for example, has wing, can fly, and has feathers are features of bird. Nodes represent the respective hierarchical concepts, and concept and feature are connected with lines to construct a complicated hierarchical network in which lines are association with a certain significance in fact. This hierarchical network model stores features of concept in a corresponding hierarchy that only stores the concepts within same hierarchy, while the common attributes of concepts in the same hierarchy are stored in at a higher hierarchical level.

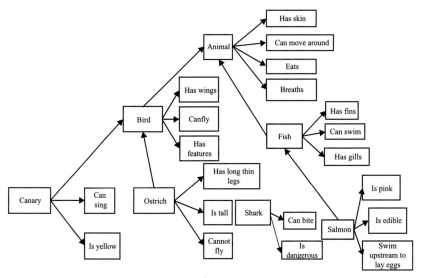

Figure 8.5 Hierarchical network model of semantic memory.

Fig. 8.5 is a fragment of a concept structure from the literature [12]. Concepts such as "canary" and "shark," which are located at the bottom, are called level-0 concepts. Concepts "bird", "fish," and so on are called level-1 concepts. Concept "Animal" is called a level-2 concept. The higher the level is, the more abstract the concepts are, and correspondingly the longer the processing time is. At each level, this level only stores the unique concept characteristics. Thus the meaning of a concept is associated with other characteristics determined by the concept.

8.3.1.2 Spreading activation model

The spreading activation model was proposed by Collins et al. [13]. It is also a network model. Different from the hierarchical network model, this model organizes concepts by semantic connection or semantic similarity instead of hierarchical structure of concept. Fig. 8.6 reveals a fragment of the spreading activation model. Those squares are nodes of network representing concepts. The length of lines means a compact degree of relation—for example, a shorter length indicates that the relationship is close and that there are more common features between two concepts—or if more lines between two nodes with common features mean their relationship is compact, the connected concepts denote their relationship.

As a concept is stimulated or processed, the network node that this concept belongs to is active, and activation will spread all around along

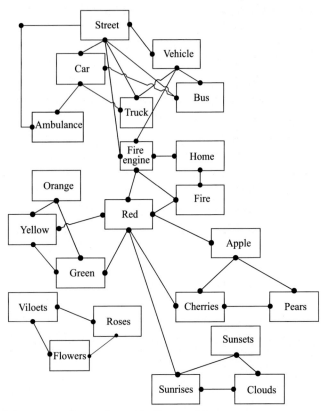

Figure 8.6 Fragment of spreading activation model.

lines. The amount of this kind of activation is finite, so if a concept is processed for a long time, the time of spread activation will increase and the familiarity effect may be formed; on the other hand, activation also follows the rule that energy decreases progressively. This model is a modification of the hierarchical network model, which considers that attributes of every concept may have the same or different hierarchies. The relation of the concept-length of lines illustrates the category size effect and other effects and is the form of spreading activation. This model may be a humanized hierarchical network model.

8.3.1.3 Human association memory

The greatest advantage of the human associative memory (HAM) model is that this model can represent semantic memory as well as episodic memory; it can process semantic information and nonverbal information. What is more, this model can offer a proper explanation of the practice effect and imitate it through the computer very well. But it cannot explain the phenomenon of familiarity effect. The comparison process is composed of several stages and asserts that the basic unit of semantic memory is proposition rather than concept.

A proposition is made up of a small set of associations, and each association combines two concepts. There are four different kinds of association. (1) Context—fact association: The context and fact are combined into associations, in which facts refer to events that happened in the past, and context means the location and exact time of the event. (2) Subject-predicate association: The subject is the principal part of a sentence, and the predicate is intended to describe the specialties of the subject. (3) Relation—object association: This construction served as predicate. Relation means the connection between some special actions of the subject and other things, while the object is the target of actions. (4) Concept—example association: For instance, furniture-desk is a concept-example construction.

Proper combination of these constructions can make up a proposition. The structures and processes of HAM can be described by the propositional tree. When a sentence is received, for example, "The professor ask Bill in classroom," it could be described by a propositional tree (see Fig. 8.7). The figure is composed of nodes and labeled arrows. The nodes are represented by

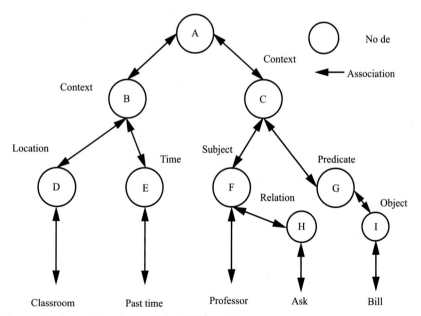

Figure 8.7 Propositional tree of the HAM model.

lower-case letters and the labels on the arrows by upper-case letters, while the arrows represented various kinds of association. Node A represents the idea of proposition, which is composed by facts and associations between contexts. Node B represents the idea of the context, which could be further subdivided into a location node D and a time code E (past time, for the professor had asked). Node C represents the idea of fact, and it leads by arrows to the subject node F and a predicate node G, which could in turn be subdivided into a relation node H and an object node I. At the bottom of the propositional tree are the general nodes that represent our ideas of each concept in the LTM, such as classroom, in the past, professor, ask, Bill. They are terminal node for their indivisibility. The propositional tree is meaningless without these terminal nodes. Those concepts are organized in a propositional tree according to the propositional structure, rather than their own properties or semantic distance. Such an organization approach possesses a network quality. The LTM could be regarded as a network of propositional trees, which also demonstrate the advantage of the HAM model in that it can represent both semantic memory and episodic memory and combine them together. This propositional tree can comprise all kinds of personal events as long as the episodic memory information is represented with a proposition, which is absent in those memory models previously mentioned. HAM propositional structure enables one proposition implanted into another and combined into a more complicated proposition. For example, the two propositions that "The professor asked Bill in classroom," and "it makes the examination over on time" could be combined into a new proposition. In this situation, these two original propositions become the subject and predicate of the new proposition, respectively. This complicated proposition could also be represented with a propositional tree.

According to the HAM model, four stages are needed to accomplish the process of information retrieval to answer a question or understand a sentence:
1. Input a sentence.
2. Analyze the sentence and generate a propositional tree.
3. Search from each related node in long-term memory, until a propositional tree that matches the input proposition is found.
4. Match the input propositional tree with that found in long-term memory.

8.3.2 Episodic memory

Episodic memory was proposed by Canadian psychologist Tulving. In his book *Elements of Episodic Memory* published in 1983, Tulving discussed the principle of episodic memory [14].

The base unit of episodic memory is personal recall behavior. Personal recall behavior begins with an event or a subjective reproducing (remembering experience) of an experience produced by a scene, or a change to other forms that keep information, or a combination of them. There are a lot of composition elements and the relations among the elements about recall. The composition elements that are elements of episodic memory can be divided into two kinds: one observes the possible incident, and the other made up of composition concepts of the hypothesis. The elements of episodic memory consist of encoding and retrieval. Encoding is about the information of the incident of the experience in a certain situation at some given time; it points out the process of transforming to the traces of memory. Retrieval is mainly about the form and technique of retrieval. The elements of episodic memory and their relations are demonstrated in Fig. 8.8.

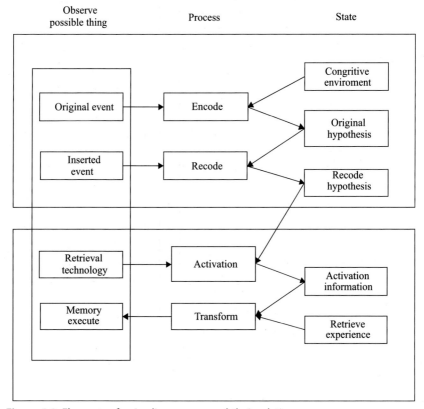

Figure 8.8 Elements of episodic memory and their relations.

Nuxoll and Laird first introduced scene memory into Soar episodic memory in such a way that a scene memory can support a variety of cognitive functions agents [15]. In CAM, the plot fragment is stored in the basic module scenario memory. Plot segment is divided into two levels: the logical level of abstraction and the original level, shown in Fig. 8.9. The abstraction level is described by logic symbols. In the original stage, it includes a description of the related object abstraction—level perceptual information. In order to effectively represent and organize the plot fragments, we use dynamic description logic (DDL) for representation in the abstract level and make use of ontology in the original level. Furthermore, we use an object data map to describe plot fragments.

Fig. 8.10 depicts the structure of the object data graph for the film Waterloo Bridge, in which the plot is associated with other objects by

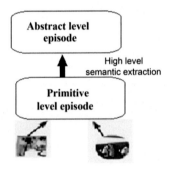

Figure 8.9 Fragments of two level stages.

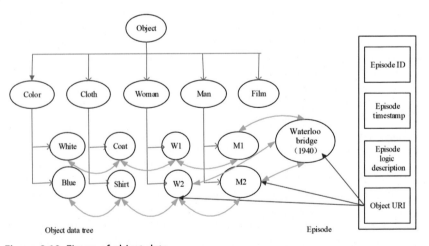

Figure 8.10 Figure of object data.

URI fragments. Fig. 8.10 shows the three objects: M_2, W_2, and the movie Waterloo Bridge. In addition, there is object W_2 wearing a blue skirt. The film also associated with the two main characters M_1, W_1, and W_1 in a white coat.

In Soar, the plot is the case retrieval model—based reasoning, based on past experience, to find solutions to problems [16]. According to the clues in back episodes, we follow this idea to build a case-based system. To simplify the system, we restrict the plot to be like a change sequence. Then the plot retrieval model is aimed at solving the most relevant search event question. In the abstract level plot, it can accurately represent the contents of the event, thus matching the level of abstraction between the tips and the plot. In CAM, the conversion sequence is formally defined as a possible sequence of the world, and the plot clues suggest a tableau by DDL inference algorithm [17,18]. One possible sequence of the world is a directed acyclic graph $Seq = (W_p, E_p)$, where each $w_i \in W_p$ represents a possible world, and each edge $e_i = (w_i, w_j)$ indicates that the action α_i is executed in w_i and consequently causes the translation from the world w_i to the world w_j.

With DDL, a plot e_p implicitly indicates c if the formula $e_p \rightarrow c$ is valid. Therefore, we can check whether $e_p \rightarrow c$ is about the implication relations of effective process between plot and clues. The inference procedure is described in Algorithm 8.1.

Algorithm 8.1 CueMatch(e,c)

Input: episode e, cue c

Output: whether $c \preccurlyeq_p e$ hold

(1) if $length(e) < length(c)$ then
(2) return false;
(3) end
(4) n_e := first_node(e);
(5) n_c := first_node(c);
(6) if MatchPossibleWorld$(n_e; n_c)$ then
(7) α_e := Null;
(8) α_c := action(n_c);
(9) if $\neg$ (Pre(α_e) $\rightarrow$ Pre(α_c)) unsatisfiable according DDL tableaualgorithm then
(10) n_{tmp} := n_e;
(11) while next_node(n_{tmp}) $\neq$ Null do
(12) α_e := $(\alpha_e;$ action$(n_{tmp}))$;
(13) if MatchAction$(\alpha_e; \alpha_c)$ then

(14) Let sub_e be the subsequence by removing α_e from e;
(15) Let sub_c be the subsequence by removing α_c from c;
(16) if CueMatching(sub_e; sub_c) then
(17) return true;
(18) end
(19) end
(20) n_{tmp}: = next node(n_{tmp});
(21) end
(22) end
(23) end
(24) Remove n_e from e;
(25) return *CueMatching(e; c)*;
Function: MatchPossibleWorld(w_i,w_j)
Input: possible worlds w_i, w_j
Output: whether$w_i \vDash w_j$hold
(1) f_w: = Conj(w_i) $\rightarrow$ Conj(w_j);
(2) if $\neg f_w$ is unsatisfiable according to DDL tableau algorithm then
(3) *return* true;
(4) else
(5) *return* false;
(6) end
Function: MatchAction(α_i,α_j)
Input: actionα_i, α_j
Output: whether $\alpha_i \vDash \alpha j$ hold
(1) if $\alpha_i ==$ *null or* $\alpha_j ==$ *null* then
(2) *return* false
(3) end
(4) f_{pre}:=Conj(Pre(α_i)) $\rightarrow$ Conj(Pre(α_j));
(5) f_{eff}:=Conj(Eff(α_i)) $\rightarrow$ Conj(Eff(α_j));
(6) if $\neg f_{pre}$ and $\neg f_{eff}$ are unsatisfiable according to DDL Algorithm then
(7) *return* true;
(8) else
(9) *return* false;
(10) end

In Algorithm 8.1, the function length returns the length of a possible sequence of the world. The length of a possible world sequence is determined by the number contained in the sequence of nodes. Function returns (n), and the implementation of the action is done in a possible world order N inside. Function next node return n' next node in the possible world's sequence. Next node n, by performing the operation of operation (n), reaches the possible sequences of the world. Algorithm 8.1, step 14, through the sequence of actions constructors ";", produce a combined action, connecting the two movements α and action (n_{tmp}). To simplify the algorithm, we assume that the action (NULL;) $==\alpha$. In Algorithm 8.1, MatchPossibleWorld() and MatchAction() are also functions. We use the DDL tableau algorithm to decide whether the negation of the formula is satisfiable or not.

8.3.3 Procedural memory

Procedural memory refers to the memory of how to do things, including perception skills, cognitive skills, motor skills, and memory. Procedural memory is memory of inertia; also known as memory skills, it is often difficult to use language to describe such memories, and often several attempts are needed to gradually get it right.

Procedural memory is the memory of procedural knowledge; that is, "know-why" is about the skills of knowledge and understanding of "how-to" memories. Individuals achieve a degree of automation and refinement via much practice then you can do two things at the same time without feeling labored, such as using a mobile phone while driving or driving when the program remains natural and smooth, that is, when the a call does not affect driving.

Procedural knowledge presumes knowledge of its existence only by means of some form of indirect jobs. It includes inspiration, methods, planning, practices, procedures, practices, strategies, techniques, and tricks to explain "what" and "how." It is about how to do something or knowledge about the link between stimulus and response but also about the behavior of the program or basic skills learning. For example, people know how to drive a car, how to use the ATM, how to use the Internet to search for target information.

Procedural knowledge representation in ACT-R, Soar, and other systems using production systems, that is, a "condition−action" rule. An action procedure takes place when certain conditions are met. Output refers to the coupling condition and action, resulting in an action under the rules of a condition; it consists of the condition items "if" (if) and the action item "then" (then).

We adopt the DDL for describing the procedural knowledge of CAM. To be compatible with the action formalism proposed by Baader et al. [19], we extend the atomic action definition of DDL to support occlusion and conditional postconditions. With respect to a TBox T, the extended atomic action of DDL is a triple $\alpha \equiv (P, O, E)$ [20], where:

- $\alpha \in N_A$.
- P is a finite set of ABox assertions for describing preconditions.
- O is a finite set of occlusions, where each occlusion is of the form $A(p)$ or $R(p, q)$, with A a primitive concept name, R a role name, and $p, q \in N_I$.
- E is a finite set of conditional postconditions, where each postcondition is of the form φ/ψ, with φ an ABox assertion and ψ a primitive literal. In this definition, the set of preconditions describes the conditions under which the action is executable. For each postcondition φ/ψ, if φ holds before the execution of the action, then the formula ψ will hold after the execution. Occlusions describe the formulas that cannot be determined during the execution of the action.

As an example, an action named BuyBookNotified(Tom, Kin) is specified as follows:

BuyBookNotified(Tom,Kin)$\equiv$
  ({customer(Tom), book(*KingLear*)}, { },
  {instore(KingLear)/bought(Tom, *KingLear*),
  instore(*KingLear*)/¬instore(*KingLear*),
  instore(*KingLear*)/notify(Tom, NotifyOrderSucceed),
  ¬instore(*KingLear*)/notify(Tom, NotifyBookOutOf Stock)})

According to this description, if the book *KingLear* is at the store before the execution of the action, then after the execution of the action, the formulas bought(Tom, *KingLear*), ¬instore(*KingLear*) and notify(Tom, NotifyOrderSucceed) will hold; otherwise the formula notify(Tom, NotifyBookOutOfStock) will be true, which indicates that Tom is notified that the book is out of stock.

The difference between declarative memory and procedural memory is that declarative memory works for the description of things, such as "self-introduction," which is an explicit memory, while procedural memory works for technical actions, such as "cycling," which is an implicit memory. The organs for procedural memory are the cerebellum and striatum, and the most essential part is the deep cerebellar nuclei.

8.3.4 Information retrieval from long-term memory

There are two ways of information retrieval from long-term memory (LTM): recognition and recall.

8.3.4.1 Recognition

Recognition is the knowledge of feeling that someone or something had been a perception, thinking, or experiencing before. There is no essential difference between the recognition and recall processes, though recognition is easier than recall. In personal development, recognition appears prior to recall. Infants have the ability of recognition in the first half year after their birth, while they do not acquire the ability of recall until a later stage. Shimizu, a Japanese scholar, had investigated the development of recognition and recall among child in primary school by using pictures. The result indicated that the performance of recognition was better than recall for children in nursery or primary school. This recognition advantage, however, would diminish, and children in the fifth-year class and later had similar recognition and recall performance. There are two kinds of recognition, perceived and cognitive, in the form of compact and opening, respectively. Recognition at the perceived level always happens directly in the compact form. For instance, you could recognize a familiar band just through several melodies. On the contrary, recognition at the cognitive level depends on some special hints, including some other cognitive activities, such as recalling, comparison, deduction, and so on. The recognition process probably causes mistakes, such as failing to recognize a familiar item or making a wrong recognition. Different reasons could be responsible for the mistakes, such as incorrect received information, failure to separate similar objects, or nervousness and sickness.

Several aspects determine whether the recognition process is fast and correct. The most important factors are as follows:

1. Quantity and property of the material: Similar material or items can confound and cause difficulty in the recognition process. The quantity of the items may also affect recognition. It has been found that 38% additional time is needed if a new English word is introduced during the recognition process.

2. Retention interval: Recognition depends on the retention interval. The longer the interval is, the worse the recognition will be.

3. Initiative of the cognitive process: Active cognition helps in comparison, deduction, and memory enhancement when recognizing strange material. For instance, it might be difficult to recognize an old friend immediately whom you had not met for a long time. Then the recall of the living scene in the past makes the recognition easier.

4. Personal expectation: Besides retrieval stimuli information, the subject's experience, mental set, and expectations also affect recognition.
5. Personality: Witkinet and his colleagues divided people into two kinds: field-independent and field-dependent. It was demonstrated that field-independent people are less affected by surrounding circumstances than field-dependent people. These two kinds of people showed significant differences in recognizing the embedded picture, namely, recognizing simple figures to form a complex picture. Generally speaking, field-independent people always have better recognition than field-dependent people.

8.3.4.2 Recall

Recall refers to a process of the reappearance of past things or definitions in the human brain. For instance, people recalled what they have learned according to the content of an examination; the mood of a festival leads to recalling relatives or best friends who are at a distance.

Different approach used in the recalling process would lead to difference memory output.

1. Based on associations: Everything in the outside word is not isolated but dependent on one another. Experiences and memories kept in the human brain are not independent; rather, they are connected with one another. The rise of one thing in the brain can also be a cue to recalling other related things. A cloudy day might remind us rain, and a familiar name might remind us of the voice and appearance of a friend. Such mind activity is called association, which means the recalling of the first thing induces the recalling of another thing. Association has certain characteristics: Proximity is one such characteristics. Elements that are temporally or spatially close to one another tend to be constructed together. For instance, the phrase "Summer palace" might remind people of "Kunming Lake," "Wanshou Mountain," or "The 17-Arch Bridge." A word can be associated with its pronunciation and meaning, and the coming of New Year's Day might remind us of the Spring Festival. Similarly, items that are similar in form or property might be associated. For example, the mention of "Spring" would lead to recalling the revival and burgeoning of life. In contrast, the opposite characteristic of items can form associations. People might think of black from white, short from tall. The cause and effect, another characteristic, between elements form construction.

A cloudy day might be associated with raining; snow and ice might be associated with cold.

2. Mental set and interest: These can influence the recalling process directly. Due to differences in the prepared state, the mental set may have great effect on recalling. Despite same stimuli, people have different memories and associations. Additionally, interest and emotional state might also prefer some specific memories.

3. Double retrieval: Finding useful information is an important strategy. During the recalling process, representation and semantics would improve integrity and accuracy. For instance, when answering the question, "How many windows are there in your home?" the representation of windows and the retrieval of the number would help the recalling effect. Recalling the key point of the material would facilitate information retrieval. When asked what letter comes after "B" in the alphabet, most people would know it is "C." But it would be difficult if the question is, "What letter comes after 'J' in the alphabet?" Some people recall the alphabet from "A" and then know "K" is after "J," while most people go from "G" or "H," because "G" has an distinctive image in the whole alphabet and thus could become a key point for memory.

4. Hint and recognition: When recalling unfamiliar and complex material, the presentation of a context hint is helpful. Another useful approach is the presentation of hints related to the memory content.

5. Disturbance: A common problem during the recalling process was the difficulty of information retrieval resulting from interference. For instance, in an examination, you may fail to recall the answer of some item due to tension, although you know the answer in fact. Such a phenomenon is called the "tip of the tongue" effect; namely you could not say the answer even though you know it. One way to overcome this effect is to give up the recall and try to recall later, and then the memory might come to mind.

8.4 Working memory

In 1974 A. D. Baddeley and Hitch put forward the concept of working memories based on experiments that imitated short-term memory deficit [21]. In the traditional Baddeley model, working memory is composed of a central executive system and two subsidiary systems, including the phonological loop and visuospatial sketch pad [21]. The phonological loop is responsible for information storage and control on the foundation of voice.

It consists of the phonological storage and articulatory control process, which can hold information through subvocal articulation to prevent the disappearance of spoken representation and also switch from the written language to the spoken code. The visuospatial scratch pad is mainly responsible for storing and processing the information in visual or spatial form, possibly including the two subsystems of vision and space. The central executive system is the core of working memory and is responsible for the subsystems and their connection with LTM, the coordination of attention resources, strategy choice and the plan, etc. A large number of behavioral researches and a lot of evidence in neural psychology have shown the existence of three subcompositions; the understanding of the structure of working memory and the function form is enriched and perfected constantly.

8.4.1 Working memory model

All working memory models can be roughly divided into two big classes: One is the European traditional working memory model, among which the representative one is the multicomposition model brought forward by Baddeley, which divided the working memory model into many subsidiary systems with independent resources, stress modality-specific processing, and storage. The other is the North American traditional working memory model, which is represented by the ACT-R model, emphasizing the globality of working memory, general resource allocation, and activation. The investigation of the former mainly focuses on the storage component of the working memory model, that is, phonological loop and visuospatial sketchpad. Baddeley pointed out that short-term storage should be clarified first for it to be operated easily before answering more complicated questions of processing, whereas the North American class emphasizes the working memory's role in complicated cognitive tasks, such as reading and speech comprehension. So the North American working memory model is like the European general central executive system. Now two lines of research are coming up with more and more findings and are exerting a mutual influence with respect to theory construction. For example, the concept of the episodic buffer is like the proposition representation of Barnard's interacting cognitive model. So the two classes have already demonstrated certain integrated and unified trends.

Baddeley developed his working memory theory in recent years based on the traditional model in which a new subsystem-episodic buffer is increased [21]. Baddeley has suggested that the traditional model does not notice how the different kinds of information are combined and how the combined results are maintained, so it cannot explain how subjects could only recall about 5 words in the memory task in *random word* lists, but they could recall about 16 words in the memory task according to prose content. The episodic buffer represents a separate storage system that adopts a multimodal code; it offers a platform where information is combined temporarily in a phonological loop, visuospatial sketchpad, and LTM and integrates information from multiple resources into an intact and consistent form through the central executive system. The episodic buffer, phonological loop, and visuospatial sketchpad are equally controlled by the central executive system, which, though the integration of different kinds of information, maintains and supports the subsequent integration by the episodic buffer. The episodic buffer is independent of LTM, but it is a necessary stage in long-term episodic learning. The episodic buffer can explain questions such as the interference effect of serial position recall, the mutual influence question among speech and visuospatial processing, the memory trunk and unified consciousness experience, etc. The four-component model of working memory, including the newly increased episodic buffer, is shown in Fig. 8.11 [21].

The ACT-R model from Lovett and his colleagues can explain a large number of data with individual difference [22]. This model regards working memory resources as one kind of attention activation, named source activation. Source activation spreads from the present focus-of-attention to the memory node related to the present task and conserves those accessible nodes. ACT-R is a production system that processes information according to the activation production regularity. It emphasizes that the processing

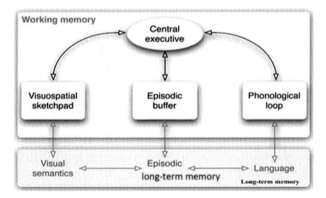

Figure 8.11 Four-component model of working memory.

activities depend on goal information: The stronger the present goal is, the higher the activation level of relevant information will be, and the more rapid and accurate information processing is. This model suggests that the individual difference of the working memory capacity reflects total amount of "source activation" expressed with the parameter W. And it is field–universal and field–unitary. This source activation in phonological and visuo-spatial information is based on the same mechanism.

The obvious deficiency of this model lies in the fact that it explains only a parameter of the individual difference in a complicated cognitive task and neglects that the individual difference of working memory might be related to processing speed, cognitive strategy, and past knowledge skill. But the ACT-R model emphasizes the singleness of working memory, in order to primarily elucidate the common structure in detail; it thereby can remedy the deficiency of the model emphasizing the diversity of working memory.

8.4.2 Working memory and reasoning

Working memory is closely related to reasoning and has two functions: maintaining information and forming the preliminary psychological characteristics. The representation form of the central executive system is more abstract than the two subsystems. Working memory is the core of reasoning, and reasoning is the sum of working memory ability.

According to the concept of the working memory system, a *dual-task* paradigm is adopted to study the relationship between the components of work memory and reasoning. The dual-task paradigm means that two kinds of tasks are carried out at the same time: One is the reasoning task; the other is the secondary task used to interfere with every component of working memory. The tasks to interfere with the central executive system are to demand subjects to randomly produce the letter or figure or to utilize sound to attract subjects' attention and ask them to make corresponding responses. The task to interfere with the phonological loop cycle is to ask subjects to pronounce constantly such as "the, the ..." or to count numbers in a certain order, such as 1, 3, 6, 8. The task to interfere with the visuospatial sketchpad is a lasting space activity, for example typewriting blindly in certain order. All secondary tasks should guarantee certain speed and correct rate and conduct the reasoning task at the same time. The principle of the *dual* task is that two tasks compete for the limited resources at the same time. For example, interference in the phonological loop is to make the reasoning task and the secondary task take up the limited resources of the subsystem in the phonological loop of working memory, both at the same time. If the correct rate of reasoning is decreased and the response time is increased in this condition, then we can confirm that the phonological loop is involved in reasoning process. A series of research works indicate that the secondary task could effectively interfere in the components of working memory.

K. J. Gilhooly studied the relationship between reasoning and working memory. In the first experiment, it was found that the way of presenting the sentence influenced the correct rate of the reasoning: The correct rate was higher in visual presentations than in hearing presentations, the reason for which is that the load of memory in visual presentations was lower than in hearing presentations. In the second experiment, it was found that the deductive reasoning task presented visually was most prone to be damaged by the dual-task paradigm (memory load) used to interfere with the executive system, next by the phonological loop, and least by the visuospatial processing system. This indicates that representation in deductive reasoning is a more abstract form, which is in accordance with the psychological model theory of reasoning and has caused the central executive system to be involved in reasoning activities. Probably, the phonological loop played a role too because the concurrent phonological activities with the reasoning activity slowed down, indicating that two kinds of tasks may compete for the limited resource. In this experiment, Gilhooly and his colleagues found that the subjects may adopt a series of strategies in deductive reasoning and that the kind of strategy adopted can be inferred according to the results of reasoning. Different secondary tasks force the subjects to adopt different strategies, so their memory load is different too. Vice versa. Increasing the memory load will also change the strategy because the changing strategy causes the decreased memory load.

In 1998, Gilhooly and his colleagues explored the relationship between the components of working memory and deductive reasoning in presenting the serial sentence visually using the dual-task paradigm. Sentences presented serially require more storage space than those presented in simultaneously. The result showed that the visuospatial processing system and phonological loop all participated in deductive reasoning and that the central executive system still plays an important role among them. The conclusion can be drawn that the central executive systems all participate in deductive reasoning whether in serial or simultaneous presentation. When memory load increases, the visuospatial processing system and phonological loop may participate in the reasoning process.

8.4.3 Neural mechanism of working memory

The development of brain sciences over nearly a decade has already found that two kinds of working memory are involved in the thinking process: One is used for storing the speech material (concept) with speech coding; the other is used for storing the visual or spatial material (imagery) with figure coding. Further research indicates that not only do concept and imagery have their own working memory, but also imagery itself has two kinds of working memory. There are two kinds of imagery of things: One represents basic attributes of the things used for recognizing them, generally called attribute imagery or object image. The other is used for reflecting the relationship of the spatial and structural aspects of the things (related to visual localization), generally called spatial image or relation image. Spatial image does not include the content information of the object but the characteristic information used to define the required spatial position information and structural relation of the objects. In this way, there are three kinds of working memory:

1. working memory of storing speech material (abbreviated as the speech working memory): suitable for time logical thinking
2. working memory of storing the object image (attribute image) (abbreviated as the object working memory): suitable for the spatial structural thinking that regarded the object image (attribute image) as the processing target, usually named idiographic thinking
3. working memory of storing the spatial image (related image) (abbreviated as the spatial working memory): suitable for the spatial structural thinking that regarded the spatial image (relation image) as the processing target, usually named intuitive thinking

Contemporary neuroscientific research shows that these three kinds of working memory and the corresponding thinking processing mechanisms have their corresponding areas of the cerebral cortex, though the localization of some working memory is not very accurate at present. According to the new development of brain science research, S. E. Blumstein in Brown University has pointed out [23] that the speech function is not localized in a narrow area (according to the traditional idea, the speech function only involves Broca's area and Wernicke's area of the left hemisphere) but is widely distributed in the areas around the *lateral fissure* of the left brain and extend toward the anterior and posterior regions of the frontal lobe, including Broca's area, inferior frontal lobe close to the face *movement cortex* and left precentral gyrus (exclude the frontal and occipital pole). Among them, damage to Broca's area will harm the speech expression function, and damage to Wernicke's area will harm the speech comprehension function. But the brain mechanism related with the speech expression and comprehension functions are not limited to these two areas. The working memory used for maintaining speech materials temporarily is regarded as generally relating to the left prefrontal lobe, but the specific position is still not accurate at present.

Compared with the speech working memory, the localization of object working memory and the spatial working memory are much more accurate. In 1993, J. Jonides and his colleagues in Michigan University investigated the object image and the spatial image with positron emission tomography (PET) and obtained some clarification about their localization and mechanism [24]. PET detected pairs of gamma rays emitted indirectly by a positron-emitting radionuclide (tracer), which was introduced into the body on a biologically active molecule. Images of tracer concentration in three-dimensional space within the body are then reconstructed by computer analysis. Because of its accurate localization and noninvasiveness, this technique is suitable for human subject studies.

8.5 Implicit memory

The psychological study on memory was launched along two lines: One is traditional research—paying attention to explicit, conscious memory research; the other is on implicit memory, the focus and latest tendency of present memory studies.

In 1960s Warrington and Weiskrantz found that some amnesia patients cannot recall their learned task consciously but showed facilitated memory performance through an implicit memory test. This phenomenon was called the priming effect by Cofer. Afterward, it was found through many studies that the priming effect is ubiquitous in normal subjects. It is a kind of automatic, unconscious memory phenomenon. The priming effect was called implicit memory by P. Graf and D. L. Schacter [25], whereas the traditional and conscious memory phenomenon was called explicit memory.

In 1987 Schacter pointed out that implicit memory was a type of memory in which previous experiences are beneficial for the performance of a task without consciousness of those previous experiences. In 2000 K. B. McDermott defined implicit memory as "manifestations of *memory* that occurred in the absence of intentions to re-collect" [26]. In recent years, there have been great improvements in the explanation and modeling of the implicit memory. The most prominent one is that the past model of implicit memory is descriptive and qualitative and that its efficiency depends on their qualitative predictability based on the results of experiments, whereas the recent model is computable and the fitting between the model and experimental data can be quantified. Here we introduce two quantitative models of implicit memory: REMI and ROUSE.

The full name of REMI is Retrieving Effectively from Memory, Implicit. This model's supposition is that people represent the items in the study in vector form of characteristic value and that two characteristics are represented: content information and environmental information. In the task of perceptive recognition, without the priming item, people represent the environmental information of the goal item the same as the interfering item. So people's responses depend on the basis of the content characteristic, and their decision is optimized according to Bayesian inference. REMI further supposes that this kind of optimization inference is based on the diagnostic characteristic or the difference among the alternative items. First, calculating each item separately to judge whether it is in accordance with the diagnosis characteristic of the perception content, then searching which item has more matching characteristic, the winner item will be the response of the perception recognition.

But with the priming item joined, the goal items have the representation of environmental information additionally to the representation of content information in the recognition task (if the priming item is an alternative one in the recognition task). The additional environmental characteristic information can match the environmental information of the testing condition, so the amount of the diagnostic characteristic of the priming item will increase to match the recognition response bias to the priming item.

REMI can predict how the long-term priming changes along with the similar extent between the goal item and interference item. This model predicts that the less similarity there is among the items, the more diagnostic the characteristics are. As a result, the amount of deviation of the diagnostic characteristics matched successfully in two optional items have a larger possible range. If the abscissa is the amount of deviation of the matched diagnose characteristics and the ordinate is incidence, then high-similarity item will produce one high and narrow distribution, and the low similarity task will produce a flat distribution. So REMI predicts that a similar item will influence by the priming effect, and this prediction has been validated by real experimental results.

ROUSE means Responding Optimally with Unknown Sources of Evidence and explains the mechanism of short-term priming. This model includes three parameters: The priming stimulus activates each correlated diagnostic characteristic in the goal item and the interference item by α-probability (each characteristic value is 0 or 1, the initial value is 0); the perception discrimination of the stimulus activates each characteristic of the goal item by the β-probability; and the neural system and environmental noise activate the characteristic of the goal item and the interference item by the γ-probability. ROUSE's supposes that:

1. The activation by the priming stimulus will be confused with the activation by the flash of goal stimulus, that is, the so-called unknown origin's evidence;
2. On the premise of this confusion, the subject will estimate subjectively the size of α-probability in order to give an optimal reaction and will remove the priming stimulus's influence from the comparison of diagnostic characteristic according to this revision.

By analogy, if α-probability is overestimated, then the subjects' reaction will choose the nonpriming item; if it is underestimated, the subjects will choose the priming item.

Then what will happen when the goal item and interference item are all primed or not all primed? According to the prediction of ROUSE, because the goal item is in the equal position with interference one, the subject doesn't continue to estimate α-probability and optimize judgment but judges directly. In this way, in the all-primed condition, α-probability is added simultaneously to the goal item, and the interference item by the priming stimulus is not different from the noise of the γ-probability, whereas the strengthened noise will decrease the correct rate of the goal recognition.

In the experiment to examine the model of D. E. Huber and his colleagues, in the passive priming group, two priming words were presented 500 ms; subsequently a goal word was flashed briefly, then the forced-choice discrimination task between the alternative words was asked to be completed. In the active priming group, the subjects maintained priming stimulus until they gave a "is there a life" judgment on the priming word, subsequently completing the perception discrimination program. The result is very close to ROUSE's prediction: More processing causes overestimation of the priming word, so the subjects prefer the primed item in the passive condition and prefer the nonprimed word in the active condition. In the two conditions, the decreased correct rate was found when the predicted goal and the interference item were both primed.

In the overall direction of implicit memory studies, the constructing quantitative model is an important way to investigate implicit memory, even in generalized perception, learning, and memory.

8.6 Forgetting curve

Hermann Ebbinghaus broke through Wundt's assumption that memory and other advanced mental process cannot be studied with experimental methods. Observing results and strictly controlling the reasoning and carrying on quantitative analysis to the memory course, he specially created the pointless syllable and saving law for the study of memory. His research production *Memory* was issued in 1885. His experimental results can be plotted in a curve, which is called the forgetting curve [27].

Ebbinghaus's results that the course of forgetting is unbalanced see obvious: Within the first hour, information kept in long-time memory is reduced rapidly; thereafter, the forgetting speed slackens gradually [27]. In Ebbinghaus's research, even after 31 days, there is still a certain intensity of saving; the information is still kept to some degree. Ebbinghaus's original work initiated two important discoveries. One is to describe the forgetting process as the forgetting curve. The psychologist replaced the pointless syllable with various materials such as word, sentence even story later on and finally found that, no matter what the material to be remembered was, the developing trend of the forgetting curve was the same as his results. Ebbinghaus's second important discovery was how long the information in long-time memory can be kept. Research found that information can be kept in LTM for decades. Therefore, even things learned in childhood that have not been used for many years, given an opportunity to be learned again, will resume their original level very shortly. If things that are not used any longer, which might be considered total forgotten, in fact are not totally and thoroughly gone.

Amnesia and retention are the two respects of memory contradiction. Amnesia is that memory content cannot be retained or is difficult to retrieve. Take things once remembered, for example; they cannot be recognized and recalled in certain circumstances, or mistakes happen while things are being recognized and recalled. There are various types of amnesia: incomplete amnesia is that you can recognize things but cannot retrieve them; complete amnesia is that you cannot recognize things and cannot retrieve them. Temporarily being unable to recognize things or recollect them is called temporary amnesia. Otherwise amnesia is considered perdurable.

As for the reason for amnesia, there are many viewpoints, and they are summing up here:

1. **Decline theory:** In the decline theory of amnesia, memory traces cannot be strengthened but are gradually weakened, so the information ultimately disappears. This statement is easy for us to accept because some physical and chemical traces do tend to decline and even disappear. In the case of sensory memory and short-term memory, the learned material that is not paid attention to or rehearsed may be forgotten because of a decline in trace. But the decline theory is difficult to verify with experiment because the decline in retention quantity, over an extended time, may be due to the interference of other materials and thus not due to the decline in memory traces. It has already been proved that even in case of short-term memory, interference is also an important cause of amnesia.

2. **Interference theory:** Interference theory holds that LTM of the forgotten information is mainly due to learning and that memory is subject to interference by other stimuli. Once the disturbance is removed, the memory can be resumed. Interference can be divided into proactive and retroactive interference and two interferences. Proactive interference refers to the inhibition of learning new information by learning old information, and retroactive interference refers to the inhibition of learning new information by learning old information. A series of studies have showed that, in LTM, forgetting information despite the spontaneous regression of factors is mainly due to mutual interference between old and new information. Two types of learning materials have become similar in the role of greater interference. Learning how to make reasonable arrangements to reduce the mutual interference effects in the consolidation of learning is worth considering.

3. **Suppression theory:** In suppression theory, things may be forgotten as a result of a depressed mood or the role of motivation. If this suppression can be lifted, memory may be able to resume. Freud first found this phenomenon in clinical practice. He found that, under hypnosis, many people can recall the early years of life in many things, but these things usually are not memories. In his view, these experiences cannot be recalled because they are memories of when patients were suffering, not happy but sad, so he refused to enter their consciousness, where the memories are stored and which is suppressed by unconscious motives. Only when the mood weakens can what has been forgotten be recalled. In daily life, emotional tension in a given situation can

often cause forgetting. For example, at an examination, a student might feel excessive emotional tension, with the result that some of the content learned will not be remembered. To suppress that, the effects of individual needs, desires, motivations, and emotions need to be considered in the role of memory, which is not involved in the previous two theories. Thus, while suppression theory does not have the support of experimental materials, it is still a theory worthy of attention.

4. Retrieval failure: Some researchers believe that the LTM stored in the message is never lost. We cannot remember things because when we attempt to extract the relevant information, at the time of extraction we do not have the right clues. For example, we often have the experience that we are obviously aware of each other's names but cannot remember what they are. The phenomenon of extraction failure suggests that LTM of the extracted information is a complex process rather than a simple all-or-none issue. If we do not know anything about a memory, even though we seek to the extract the memory, we have no idea of where it is. We cannot properly extract the memory if we cannot remember the appropriate information. It's like being in a library to find a book; we do not know its title, author, or retrieval code. Even though the book is there, we cannot find it. Likewise, with a word in memory, we try to remember the words of the other clues, such as word shape, word sound, phrase, the context, and so on, will help us to place the word in a sentence.

In normal reading, information extraction is a very rapid, almost automatic process. But sometimes, the need to extract information through special clues. Extraction via clues enables us to recall what has been forgotten or to reidentify what is stored in the memory of things. When memories cannot be had, we can search for clues. A clue to the effectiveness of extraction depends on the following conditions:

1. The degree of tightness with encoded information: In LTM, information is often organized semantically and is therefore linked with the information significance of the clues, which are often very conducive to the extraction of information. For example, the sight of plants stirs up our feelings, because we have returned to the imagination; because plants are intricately linked with our past, they arouse memories of the past.

2. The degree of dependence on situations and status: Generally speaking, when the efforts of memories are made in a learning environment,

people tend to remember more things. In fact, we learn not only what will be coded in our minds, but also what occurred in many of the environmental characteristics at the same time will pass into LTM. An environmental characteristic of these memories in the future is becoming an effective clue for retrieval. The similarity of the environment that facilitates or hinders the phenomenon of memory is called context dependent memory.

With the external environment, the study of the internal mental state is incorporated into LTM; an extract clues memory is called a state of interdependence. For example, if a person who has had alcohol learns new material, such as under alcohol test conditions, the results are usually recalled better. A good mood often leads to more beautiful memories of the past; on the other hand, poor people are often more likely to remember their troubles.

3. The effects of emotions: Emotional state and learning the contents of the match also affect memory. In one study, a group of subjects were told to read a variety of exciting and sad stories of an incident, under different conditions of their being happy or sad. The results showed that when people are happy, their memory of the story is happy, and for sad people, the opposite is true. Research has shown that the effects of the existing state of mind is consistency in the coding of information for extraction. The emotional intensity of the impact of memory depends on the mood of the person, intensity, and the information content. In general, a positive mood is more conducive to memory than negative mood, and a strong sense of the emotional experience can lead to abnormally vivid, detailed, lifelike, lasting memory. In addition, emotion plays the most important role in long-term memory when the material to be memorized has little connection with the information kept in long-term memory. This may be due to the fact that emotion is the only available extraction cue in this case. This may be due to the emotions in such circumstances being the only clues available for extraction.

8.7 Complementary learning and memory

It is generally believed that the physiological basis of memory is related to the neocortex and hippocampus.

8.7.1 Neocortex

As a result of evolution, the cerebral cortex can be divided into three parts: archeocortex, paleocortex, and neocortex. The archeocortex and the paleocortex are related to olfaction and are collectively known as the olfactory brain. The neocortex is highly developed in humans, accounting for 96% of the total cortex [28].

The neocortex stores structured knowledge in the connections between the neocortex neurons. When the multilayered neural network is trained, it gradually learns to extract structure. By adjusting the connection weight, the output error of the network is minimized and becomes a relatively stable LTM.

8.7.2 Hippocampus

The hippocampus is a large nerve tissue in the brain, which is located at the junction of the medial cortex and brain stem. The hippocampus is a forebrain structure located within the medial temporal lobe that consists of the subiculum, CA1, CA2, CA3, and dentate gyrus regions shown in Fig. 8.12.

The hippocampus plays an important role in the process of information storage. Short-term memory is stored in the hippocampus [29]. If a memory segment, such as a phone number or a person's name, is repeatedly mentioned in a short period of time, the hippocampus will transfer it to the cerebral cortex, and it becomes LTM. If the information stored in the hippocampus is not used for a period, it is "deleted," that is to say, forgotten. The information stored in the cerebral cortex is not completely permanent. When you do not use the information for a long time, the cerebral cortex may "delete" the information. Some people lose some or

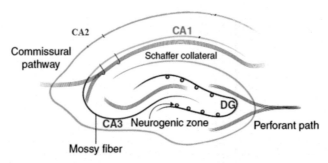

Figure 8.12 Structure of hippocampus.

all their memories when their hippocampus is injured. The process of memory transfer between hippocampus and cerebral cortex lasts for several weeks, and this transfer may occur during sleep.

8.7.3 Complementary learning system

According to his early ideas, James L. McClelland, a psychology professor at Stanford University, put forward the theory of complementary learning systems (CLS) in 1995 [30]. According to his theory, human brain learning is a comprehensive product of two CLS. One is the neocortex learning system, which slowly learns knowledge and skills through experience. The other is the hippocampus learning system, which memorizes specific experiences and enables them to be replayed so as to effectively integrate with the neocortex learning system. In 2016, Dharshan Kumaran and Demis Hassabis of Google's deep thinking and James L. McClelland of Stanford University published an article on cognitive science trends [31], expanding the theory of CLS. The neocortical learning system is a structured knowledge representation, while the hippocampal learning system quickly learns the details of individual experience. This paper extended the role of memory replay in the hippocampus and points out that memory replay can measure the target's dependence on experience statistics. By periodically displaying the traces of the hippocampus and supporting partial generalization, the neocortex can learn the knowledge of known structures very quickly. Finally, the paper points out the correlation between the theory and design of an artificial intelligence agent and highlights the relationship between neuroscience and machine learning.

8.8 Hierarchical temporal memory

Jeff Hawkins believed that intelligence is the behavior of many clusters of neurons, with a series of predictions of future events based on the world model of memory. In 2004, he published the book *On Intelligence* and proposed a theory of cortical operation that he called the memory prediction framework [32]. This framework mainly expounds some principles of cortical operation, such as that the neocortex is to establish a model of space and time, with the purpose of prediction, that it has hierarchical structure, and that it can be modeled by memory mode and sequence. The information between different levels is transmitted to each other. This is the core idea of later hierarchical temporal memory (HTM).

On March 24, 2005, Jeff Hawkins and Donna Dubinsky, Dileep George, et al. founded Numenta, a machine intelligence company, and put the idea of the framework into practice, becoming the main position for the development of the cortical learning algorithm.

8.8.1 Memory prediction framework

HTM is a kind of artificial simulation algorithm for the structure and function operation of a new cortical layer. Its design is based on the memory prediction framework. In HTM algorithm, the following contents are very core and key: hierarchy, invariant representations of spatial patterns and temporal patterns, and sequence memory.

Four visual cortical areas of the object are denoted as V1, V2, V4, and IT. V1 indicates the region of the striped visual cortex, which is rarely a pretreated image but contains much detail image information. V2 indicates visual mapping, whose visual mapping information is less than that of V1. Visual input with the arrow indicates upward; beginning in the retina, the transmission starts from the bottom to the V1 area. The input represents the time-varying model; visual neural transmission consists of about 1 million axons.

In the four different levels of regions from area VI to area IT, the cells change from rapidly changed and spatially correlated ones that are capable of identifying subtle features, to stable and space-independent ones that are capable of identifying objects. Take, for example, the so-called Face cells of IT cells; as long as there is a human face, the cell will be activated, regardless of whether the face is tilted, rotating, or partially obscured. It is a constant representation of the face.

The feedback connection is especially important when considering prediction; the brain needs to send the input information back to the original input area. Predictions need to compare what is real and what is expected to happen. Information about what really happens will flow from bottom to top, and the information that is expected to happen will flow from top to bottom.

The density and shape of cells in the cerebral cortex are different, and this difference results in stratification. The first layer is unique among all the six layers. It contains only a small number of cells and is mainly composed of a layer of nerve axons that are parallel to the cortical surface. The second and third layers are similar, mainly in their many close-together pyramidal cells. The fourth layer is composed of astrocytes. The fifth layer has pyramid-shaped cells in general and particularly large pyramid-shaped cells. The sixth layer also has several unique neuronal cells.

Fig. 8.13 shows the level of the brain area and the vertical column of the longitudinal cell unit that work together. Different layers of each vertical column are connected with one another by axons extending vertically and forming synapses. The vertical columns in the V1 region are some of the inclined line segments (/) in that direction, while others react to a line segment (\) in the other direction. Cells in each vertical column are closely interconnected, and they respond to the same stimulus as a whole. The activated cells in the fourth layer will activate the third and second layers. And then it will activate the fifth and sixth layers. Information is transmitted up and down in a cell of the same vertical column. Hawkins believes that the vertical column is a basic unit of prediction.

There is a direct link between the fifth layer of cells in the motor cortex (M1) and movement in the muscle and spinal cord. These cells are highly coordinated to continuously activate and inhibit, so that muscle contraction, drive motion. In each region of the cerebral cortex, fifth cells are spread all over and play a role in all kinds of sports.

Axons of the fifth layer of cells get into the thalamus, and make connections to a class of non-specific cells. These non-specific cells will then project these axons back into the first layer of cerebral cortex in different regions. This loop is just like the delayed feedback sequence that can learn from associative memory. The first layer carries a lot of information, including the name of the sequence and the position in the sequence.

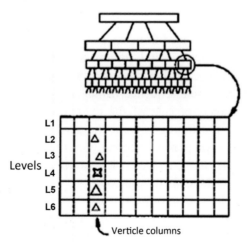

Figure 8.13 Levels and vertical columns of the brain.

Using these two kinds of information of the first layers, a cortical area is able to learn and recall patterns of sequence.

There are three kinds of circuits in the cerebral cortex: convergence along the cortical system with an approach from bottom to top, divergence along the cortical system with an approach from top to bottom, and the delayed feedback of the thalamus, which is very important for the function of the cerebral cortex. These functions are as follows:

1. How does the brain cortex classify the input pattern?
2. How to learn the pattern sequence?
3. How to form a sequence's constant pattern or name?
4. How to make a concrete forecast?

In the vertical column of the cerebral cortex, the input information from the lower region activates the fourth layer of cells, leading to the cell's excitement. Then the fourth layer of cells activates the third and second layers of cells and then the fifth layer, which leads to the sixth layer of cells being activated. So the whole vertical column is activated by the input information of the low-level area. When some of synapses are activated by the second, third, and fifth layers, they are enhanced. If this happens often enough, the first layer of these synapses become strong enough to allow the second, third, and fifth layers of cells to be also activated; the fourth layer of cells is not activated. In this way, the second, third, and fifth layers of the cell can predict when they should be activated by the first layer mode. After this study, the vertical column cells can be partly activated by memory. When the vertical column is activated by synapses of first layer, it is predicting the input information from the lower region; this is the forecast.

Some information received from the first layer is derived from the fifth layer cells of the adjacent vertical column and the adjacent area, which represents the event that has just occurred. Another part comes from the sixth cell, which are stable sequence names. As shown in Fig. 8.14, the second and third layers of cells of the axon usually form a synapse in the fifth layer, and the fourth layer of the axon forms a synapse in the sixth layer. The two synapses intersecting with the sixth layer receive two kinds of input information, and then it is activated and makes a specific forecast according to the constant memory.

As a general rule, the information low along the cerebral cortex is transmitted through the synapses near the cell body. Thus the upward flow of information is increasingly identified in the transmission process. Similarly, as a general rule, the feedback information flowing along the

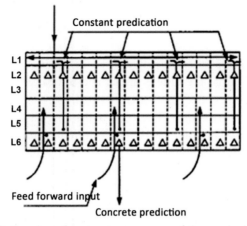

Figure 8.14 Predictions based on constant memory of the cerebral cortex.

cerebral cortex is transmitted through the synapses away from the cell body. Synapses on the long range of thin dendrites can play an active and highly specific role in cell activation. In general, the axon fiber of the feedback is more than the feed forward; the feedback information can quickly and accurately activate many cells in the second layers of the cerebral cortex.

8.8.2 Cortical learning algorithm

There are four basic functions of HTM: learning, recognition, prediction, and behavior (response). Each of these areas performs the first three functions: learning, recognition, and prediction. But behavior is different. The cortical learning algorithm is a kind of artificial simulation algorithm for the structure and function operation of the new cortical layer. The cortical learning algorithm contains the following contents: hierarchy, invariant representations of spatial patterns and temporal patterns, and sequence memory.

- Hierarchical structure: Anatomical studies have shown that the function of the new cortex layer is (possibly) realized by connecting a region with another region. In the cortical learning algorithm, the hierarchical structure between regions is also simulated.
- Invariant representation of spatial and temporal patterns: Many deep models have explored the invariant representation of patterns, but most of them stay on the invariant representation of spatial patterns. However, when there is intersection of spatial pattern sets (subspaces)

representing two objects, these models are not easy to use for spatial recognition and classification. Therefore, time is introduced into the cortical learning algorithm. By looking for the time relationship between patterns, different patterns can be distinguished better under the assumption that the time is similar and the patterns are close.

- Sequence memory: Sequence memory is the key to the representation of time pattern invariance. The cortical learning algorithm can achieve the pre- and post-transfer probability of different patterns by establishing the Markov chain inside each node or training synaptic weights between cells horizontally, so as to memorize the changes of sequence.

In the HTM cortical learning algorithm used to establish the connection of each column area of the input subset and to determine the input level of each column area, the use of suppression to filter a sparse set of active column areas is called spatial sedimentation pool. A time deposition pool is used to represent the two steps of adding context environment and prediction. By building a slowly changing output of pattern sequences, we deposit different patterns in time. The study of the time and space sedimentation pool is similar. Both types of learning involve building connections, or synapses, between cells. The time sedimentation pool is responsible for the connection between cells in the same area. The spatial sedimentation pool is responsible for the feedforward connection between the input and the columnar areas.

The learning process involves an increase and decrease in the connectivity of potential synapses in the dendrite region. The rule of increasing or decreasing synaptic connectivity is similar to that of Hebbian rule. The main function of the spatial sedimentation pool is to convert the input of a key area into a sparse mode.

Time deposition is much more complex than space deposition. How to learn sequence and make predictions in a time sedimentation pool? The basic way is that, when a cell becomes active, it establishes a connection with the cells that are active before it. Cells can then predict when they will be activated by focusing on their connections. If all cells do that, they can store and recall sequences, and they can predict what might happen next.

References

[1] E.R. Kandel, In Search of Memory: The Emergence of a New Science of Mind, W. W. Norton & Company, 2006.
[2] E.R. Kandel, The biology of memory: a forty-year perspective, J. Neurosci. 29 (41) (2009) 12748–12756.

[3] R.C. Atkinson, R.M. Shiffrin, Human memory: a proposed system and its control processes, in: K.W. Spence, J.T. Spence (Eds.), The Psychology of Learning and Motivation: Advances in Research and Theory, vol. 2, Academic Press, New York, 1968.

[4] G. Sperling, The information available in brief visual presentations, Psychol. Monogr Gen. Appl. 74 (11) (1960) 1−30.

[5] X.B. Fan, P.Z. Zhao, A design of associative processing memory, J. Comput Res. Dev. 23 (1) (1986) 1−10.

[6] S. Sternberg, High-speed scanning in human memory, Science 153 (1966) 652−654.

[7] W.A. Wickelgren, Short-term memory for phonemically similar lists, Am. J. Psychol. 78 (1965) 567−574. 1965.

[8] R.C. Atkinson, J.F. Juola, Factors influencing the speed and accuracy of word recognition, in: S. Kornblum (Ed.), Attention and Performance IV, Academic Press, New York, 1973, pp. 583−612.

[9] L.R. Peterson, M.J. Peterson, Short-term retention of individual verbal items, J. Exp. Psychol. 58 (1959) 193−198.

[10] A.V. Zeigarnik, Bluma Zeigarnik: a memoir, Gestalt. Theory 3 (2007) 256−268.

[11] M.R. Quillian, Semantic memory, in: M. Minsky (Ed.), Semantic Information Processing, MIT Press, Cambridge, MA, 1968, pp. 227−270.

[12] A.M. Collins, M.R. Quillian, Retrieval time from semantic memory, J. Verbal Learn. Verbal Behav. 8 (1969) 240−247.

[13] A.M. Collins, E.F. Loftus, A spreading activation theory of semantic memory, Psychol Rev. 82 (1975) 407−428.

[14] E. Tulving, Elements of Episodic Memory, Oxford Clarendon Press, London, 1983. UK.

[15] A. Nuxoll, J.E. Larid, Extending cognitive architecture with episodic memory, in: Proceedings of the 22nd AAAI Conference on Artificial Intelligence, (2007) pp. 1560−1564.

[16] J.E. Laird, The Soar Cognitive Architecture, MIT Press, Cambridge, MA, 2012.

[17] Z.Z. Shi, M.K. Dong, Y.C. Jiang, H.J. Zhang, A logic foundation for the semantic web, Sci. China, Ser. F, Inf. Sci. 48 (2) (2005) 161−178.

[18] L. Chang, F. Lin, Z.Z. Shi, A dynamic description logic for representation and reasoning about actions, Knowledge Science, Engineering and Management, Springer, 2007, pp. 115−127.

[19] F. Baader, C. Lutz, M. Milicic, U. Sattler, F. Wolter. Integrating description logics and action formalisms: first results, In: Proceedings of the 12th National Conference on Artificial Intelligence (AAAI'05), (AAAI Press/MIT Press) (2005) pp. 572−577.

[20] L. Chang, Z.Z. Shi, T.L. Gu, L.Z. Zhao, A family of dynamic description logics for representing and reasoning about actions, J. Autom. Reasoning 49 (1) (2012) 1−52.

[21] A.D. Baddeley, The episodic buffer: a new component of working memory? Trends Cogn. Sci. 4 (2000) 417−423.

[22] A. Miyake, P. Shan, Models of Working Memory: Mechanisms of Active Maintenance and Executive Control, Cambridge University Press, New York, 1999.

[23] S.E. Blumstein, W.P. Milberg, Language deficits in Broca's and Wernicke's aphasia: a singular impairment, in: Y. Grodzinsky, L. Shapiro, D. Swinney (Eds.), Language and the Brain: Representation and Processing, Academic Press, 2000.

[24] J. Jonides, E.E. Smith, R.A. Koeppe, E. Awh, S. Minoshima, M.A. Mintun, Spatial working memory in humans as revealed by PET, Nature 363 (1993) 623−625.

[25] P. Graf, D.L. Schacter, Implicit and explicit memory for new associations in normal and amnesic subjects, J. Exp. Psychol Learn Memory, Cogn 11 (1985) 501−518.

[26] K.B. McDermott, in: V.S. Ramachandran (Ed.), Explicit and Implicit Memory. Encyclopedia of the Human Brain, vol. 2, Academic Press, 2002, pp. 773−781.

[27] H. Ebbinghaus, Memory. A Contribution to Experimental Psychology, Teachers College, Columbia University, New York, 1913.

[28] D.S. Modha, R. Ananthanarayanan, S.K. Esser, et al., Cognitive computing, Commun. ACM 54 (8) (2011) 62–71.

[29] C. Pittenger, R.S. Duman, Stress, depression, and neuroplasticity: a convergence of mechanisms, Neuropsychopharmacol Rev. 33 (2008) 88–109.

[30] J.L. McClelland, et al., Why there are complementary learning systems in the hippocampus and neocortex: insights from the successes and failures of connectionist models of learning and memory, Psychol. Rev. 102 (1995) 419–457.

[31] D. Kumaran, D. Hassabis, J.L. McClelland, What learning systems do intelligent agents need? Complementary learning systems theory updated, Trends Cogn. Sci. 20 (7) (2016) 512–534.

[32] J. Hawkins, S. Blakeslee, On Intelligence, Times Books, Henry Holt and Company, New York, 2004.

CHAPTER 9

Thought

Thought is the reflection process of objective reality, which constitutes the advanced stage of human cognition. Thought provides knowledge about the characteristics, connections, and relations of the essence of objective reality and realizes the transformation from phenomenon to essence in the process of cognition. Different from feeling and perception, that is, from the direct perceptual reflection process, thought is the indirect reflection of reality through complex intermediary. Thought takes sensation and perception as its only sources, but it goes beyond the boundary of direct perceptual knowledge and enables people to get knowledge about the characteristics, processes, connections, and relationships of reality that its sense organs cannot perceive.

9.1 Introduction

Thought is the conscious, indirect, and general reflection of the human brain on the essential attribute and internal regularity of objective reality. The essence of thinking is the reflection of conscious mind of the object. Conscious mind means a mind with knowledge and the habit of consciously absorbing knowledge. The reflection of the object is the reflection of the internal connection and essential attribute of the object, not the reflection of the surface phenomenon.

The most remarkable characteristic of thought is generality. The reason that thinking can reveal the relationship between the essence and the internal regularity of things mainly comes from the process of abstraction and generalization; that is, thinking is the reflection of generalization. The so-called general reflection means that what it reflects is not individual things or their individual characteristics but the common essential characteristics of a kind of things. The generality of thinking not only reflects the essential characteristics of objective things but also reflects the essential relations and laws between things.

The so-called indirect reflection means not directly but through the media of other things to reflect objective things. First, by virtue of knowledge and experience, thought can reflect things and their attributes or connections that do not directly affect the sensory organs. For example, experts in traditional

Intelligence Science
DOI: https://doi.org/10.1016/B978-0-323-85380-4.00009-9

Chinese medicine can determine the symptoms and signs of patients by looking, smelling, asking and by culling the information from four clinics to reveal the relationship between the essence of things and the internal regularity through the phenomenon.

In the history of psychology, the first one to literally study thought as a subject of psychology was O. Kulpe, who was a student of Wundt. He and his students heavily studied thought psychology in Wurzburg University and formed the Wurzburg School, also known as the thought psychology school. Under the direction of Kulpe, his students conducted much research on thought.

Gestalt psychologists studied thought particularly and started the study of children's thought. They proposed a view on the effect of the subject in thought activities. They insisted thought is a progression, which is generated by nervousness in a problem situation. Whether the nervousness can be generated or not, that is, whether the subject of the thought progress can be constructed, acts as a key role in thought activities. Insight theory is one of the important theories of learning. Gestalt psychology insistence on thought progress, from nervous to not nervous, is eventually solved by the constant reorganization of problem situations. In their terms, the constant reorganization of the Gestalt does not stop until the internal relations among the problems are mastered, which leads to "insight."

Behaviorism looked on thought as an inaudible language. Watson believed thought is self-talking. B. F. Skinner insisted that thought is just a behavior, words or nonwords, open or concealed. Behaviorism does not admit thought as a function of the brain. Instead, it takes thought as the implicit behaviors of body muscles, especially throat muscles. On methods used in studies on children's thought and learning, behaviorism opposed self-observation and encouraged experiments. Behaviorism used conditioned reflex to study the development of children's reproductive thought, leading to the conclusion that thought, learning, etc. were learned by conditioned reflex.

Jean Piaget, the founder of the School of Geneva, Switzerland, is one of the most important contemporary child psychologists and experts of genetic epistemology. Piaget spent his whole life on the research of children's thought activities. He published more than 30 books and more than 100 works. He regards cognition, intelligence, thinking, and psychology as synonyms. He integrated the research of biology, mathematical logic, psychology, and philosophy and established his own structuralist child psychology or genetic epistemology. In 1955, he gathered famous psychologists, logicians, linguists, cybernetics scholars, mathematicians, physicists and other scholars from all over the world to study the occurrence and development of children's cognition, and he established the international research center of occurrence epistemology in Geneva.

Lev Vygotsky is the founder of the Social-Cultural-Historical School of the Soviet Union (USSR). His book *Thought and Language* was a directional work in what was then the USSR. In this book, he pointed out the constraints of life on thought and the decisive effect of objective reality on thought. He also pointed out that thought is using experience from the past to solve emerging new problems. The brain does that by means of analysis and synthesis in the form of language. Again, in his book, he provided some opinions on children's, especially preschool children's, formation of thought. He believed children's brains have the possibility of a natural development of thought whose progress is realized constantly guided by adults and interactions with the surroundings.

In 1984 Xuesen Qian put forward the research of noetic science [1] to study the rules and forms of thinking activities and divided the noetic science into three levels: the foundation of noetic science, the technical science of noetic science, and the engineering technology of noetic science. The basic science of noetic science studies is the basic forms of thinking activities—logical thought, image thought, and inspiration thought—and reveals the general and specific laws of thought through the study of these basic forms of thinking activities. Therefore, the basic science of noetic science can have several branches, such as logical thought, image thought, and so on. The accumulation and collection of individual thought constitute the collective thought of social groups. Social thought is the study of the collective thought of social groups.

In 1995 Nina Robin and others from the Department of Psychology of the University of California published a paper entitled "The Complexity of the Function and Relationship of the Prefrontal Cortex" [2]. Starting from the prefrontal cortex is the neurophysiological basis controlling the highest thought form of human beings, they tried to explore the relationship between the highest thought model of human beings and the brain nerve mechanism. The so-called theoretical framework of relationship complexity is a system of knowledge representation based on predicate logic, which is specially used to represent "clear relationship knowledge."

The advanced thinking model of Robin and others is based on their theoretical framework of relational complexity. The so-called relationship complexity is determined by the number of independent variable dimensions

n in the relationship, so the complexity level of different relationships can be given according to the value of n.

Level 1: One-dimensional functional relationship, which describes that things have certain attributes (which are called attribution schema by Robin)

Level 2: Two-dimensional functional relationship, which describes the binary relationship between two things (called relational schema by Robin)

Level 3: Three-dimensional functional relationship, which describes the ternary relationship between three things (called system schema by Robin)

Level 4: n-dimensional functional relationship ($n > 3$), describing the n-ary relationship between N kinds of things (which is called a multisystem schema by Robin)

By using this system, we can easily determine the complexity level of the current processed knowledge from the simplest to the most complex.

9.2 Hierarchical model of thought

Human thought mainly involves perceptual thought, imagery thought, abstract thought, and inspirational thought. Perceptual thought is the primary level of thought. When people begin to understand the world, perceptual materials are simply organized to form self-consistent information; thus only phenomena are understood. The form of thought based on this process is perceptual thought. Perceptual thought about the surface phenomena of all kinds of things can be obtained in practice via direct contact with the objective environment through sensory organs such as eyes, ears, noses, tongues, and bodies; thus its sources and contents are objective and substantial.

Imagery thought mainly relies on generalization through methods of typification and the introduction of imagery materials in thinking. It is common to all higher organisms. Imagery thought corresponds to the connection theories of neural mechanisms. AI topics related to imagery thought include pattern recognition, image processing, visual information processing, etc.

Abstract thought is a form of thought based on abstract concepts, through thinking with symbol information processing. Only with the emergence of language is abstract thought possible: Language and thought boost each other and promote each other. Thus a physical symbol system can be viewed as the basis of abstract thought.

Little research has been done on inspirational thought. Some researchers hold that inspirational thought is the extension of imagery thought to subconsciousness, during which person do not realize that part of their brain is processing information. Others argue that inspirational thought is sudden enlightenment. Despite all these disagreements, inspirational thought is particularly important to creative thinking and needs further research.

In the process of human thinking, attention plays an important role. Attention sets a certain orientation and concentration for noetic activities to ensure that one can promptly respond to the changes of the objective realities and be better accustomed to the environment. Attention limits the number of parallel thinking. Thus for most conscious activities, the brain works serially, with an exception of parallel looking and listening.

Based on this analysis, we propose a hierarchical model of human thought, as shown in Fig. 9.1 [3]. In the figure, perceptual thought is the simplest form of thought, which is constructed from the surface phenomena through sensories such as eyes, ears, noses, tongues, and bodies. Imagery thought is based on the connection theories of neural networks for highly parallel processing. Abstract thought is based on the theory of the physical symbol system in which abstract concepts are represented with languages. With the effect of attention, different forms of thought are processed serially most of the time.

The model of thought studies the interrelationships among these three forms of thought, as well as the microprocesses of transformation from one form to other. Presently, much progress has been made. For example, attractors of neural networks can be used to represent problems such as associative memory and image recognition. Yet there is still a long way to go for a thorough understanding and application of the whole model.

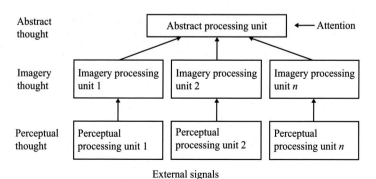

Figure 9.1 Hierarchical model of thought.

9.2.1 Abstract thought

Abstract thought reflects the essence of things and the far-reaching process of the development of the objective world with the help of scientific abstract concepts, which enables people to acquire knowledge far beyond the direct perception of sensory organs through cognitive activities. Abstract of science is the thought that reflects the internal essence of the natural or social material process in the concept. It is based on the analysis, synthesis, and comparison of the essential attributes of things, taking out the essential attributes of things, leaving aside their nonessential attributes, so that knowledge can enter the abstract provisions from the perceptual entities and form the concept. Empty, fabricated, and unpredictable abstractions are unscientific abstractions. Scientific and logical abstract thought is formed based on social practice.

Abstract thought deeply reflects the external world, enables people to foresee the development trend of things and phenomena scientifically on the basis of understanding the objective laws, and predicts the natural phenomena and characteristics that are not directly provided by "vivid intuition" but that exist outside consciousness. It is of great significance to scientific research.

Based on perceptual knowledge, the process of reflecting the essence of things and revealing the internal relations of things through concepts, judgments, and reasoning is abstract thinking. Concept is a thinking form reflecting the essence and internal connection of things. Concept is not only the product of practice but also the result of abstract thought. Based on the analysis, synthesis, and comparison of the attributes of things, the essential attributes of things are extracted and the nonessential attributes are left out, so as to form the concept of something. For example, on the basis of analyzing, synthesizing, and comparing different people, the concept of "human" draws out their essential attributes (skin color, language, country, gender, age, occupation, etc.) regardless of their nonessential attributes. They are all animals that can carry out high-level thinking activities and can make and use tools for a certain purpose. This is abstraction. Generalization refers to the extension of the essential attributes extracted from some things with the same attributes to all things with the same attributes, so as to form a general concept of such things. Any scientific concept, category, and general principle are formed through abstraction and generalization. All correct and scientific abstractions and generalizations form concepts and thoughts that reflect the essence of objective things more profoundly, comprehensively, and correctly.

Judgment is a form of thinking that affirms or negates the situation of things. Judgment is an expanded concept, which represents a certain connection and relationship between concepts. Objective things are always concrete. Therefore, to make a proper judgment, we must pay attention to the time, place, and conditions of things. People's practice and understanding are constantly developing. To adapt to this, the form of judgment is constantly changing, from low level to high level, that is, from single judgment to special judgment, and then to general judgment.

From judgment to reasoning is the process of deepening cognition. Judgment is the unfolding of contradiction between concepts; thus it reveals the essence of concepts more profoundly. Reasoning is the unfolding of the contradiction between judgments. It exposes the inevitable connection between judgments, that is, to logically infer new judgments (conclusions) from the existing judgments (premises). Judgment constitutes reasoning, which develops continuously. This shows that reasoning, concept, and judgment are interrelated and promote each other.

9.2.2 Imagery thought

Imagery thought is the thought activity that uses the images stored in the brain. Such thought activities occur in the right sphere of the brain because this sphere is responsible for the direct, generalized, geometric and drawing thought, cognition, and behavior. Imagery thought uses typification to achieve generalization and applies image materials to thought. Images are the cells of imagery thought. Imagery thought has four characteristics:

1. Imagery: It's the key characteristic of imagery materials, that is, the specific nature of intuitive. This is obviously different from the concepts, theories, numbers, etc. used by abstract thought.
2. Generality: This means mastering the common characteristics owned by a group of similar objects through corresponding typical or general images. Techniques such as sampling, analysis of typical cases, scientific modeling, etc., which are used widely in scientific research, all have the generality feature.
3. Creativity: The materials used by creative thought and its products are mostly the processed, reformed, and recreated images. The personae created in literature or the new products designed have this characteristic. Since all creativity and remake show in the imagery reformation, designers must create or reform the images in their thought when

making a design. The creation of something new works in this way, and so does the cognition of something by visual thought. When physician Ernest Rutherford was studying the internal structure of atoms in the particle scattering experiment, he imaged the interior of the atom as a microcosmic solar system: The nucleus was the center, with electrons circling in various orbits around it. This is the origin of the famous planetary model of the atom.

4. Mobility: As a rational cognition, related thought materials are not still, isolated, and invariant. They provide a lot of imagination, association, and creativity, to promote the motion of thought, analyze profoundly the images, and acquire needed knowledge.

These characteristics make imagery thought expand from perceptive cognition into the scope of rational cognition. However, it's still different from abstract thought, just another kind of rational cognition. Pattern recognition is typical imagery thought. It uses computers to process the information about the patterns, classifying, describing, analyzing, and interpreting of the texts, sounds, images, and objects. Currently pattern recognition has been applied directly or indirectly in some areas, and many systems of the pattern information have been proposed, like optical character recognition, cell or blood corpuscle recognition, voice recognition, etc. The research on the analysis of sequence images, computer vision, speech or image understanding systems, with their implementations, has acquired widespread interest.

Pattern recognition methods are generally divided into statistical (decision theory) pattern recognition and syntactic (structural) pattern recognition. Statistical pattern recognition focuses on finding a set of features that can reflect the characteristics of patterns. First, the data of patterns is compressed to extract features, taking into account that the selected features are invariant or at least insensitive to the interference and distortion usually encountered. If extracting N features can basically describe the original pattern, then a vector composed of N features is used to represent the original pattern. Therefore the statistical method of pattern recognition is based on high-dimensional random vector analysis. Pattern classification is equivalent to dividing the feature space into several parts, each part corresponding to a pattern class. When a new pattern appears, it is judged according to which part of the feature space the vector describing the pattern belongs to. The syntactic pattern recognition method, which solves the problem of pattern recognition completely from different ways, focuses on the analogy between the composition of pattern and the generation of language, and draws lessons from the methods and results of mathematical linguistics. In this way, the recognition method is based on mathematical language. The phrasal structure grammar introduced earlier can be used to describe the pattern of phase recognition image with a little modification, as long as we focus on how an image is composed of simpler subimages and how subimages are composed of simpler subimages, etc. Just as an English clause is made up of clauses and clauses are made up of phrases, an image is equivalent to a clause produced by some grammar rule. The expression form of a pattern can be a chain composed of some features or basic units, or a tree structure, or a graph form, just like a language chain composed of symbols. The recognition pattern can be embodied in that the feature chain of the description pattern is accepted by a certain type of automata, or the feature chain (sentence) of the description pattern is syntactically analyzed to determine whether a sentence is syntactically correct for a certain grammar, so as to decide which type of pattern described by the sentence it belongs to, which not only determines the type of pattern but also gives a description. The research of syntactic pattern recognition is not as thorough as that of statistical pattern recognition. It developed gradually in the 1980s. In 1974 Professor Jingsun Fu of Purdue University published the second monograph *Syntactic Methods in Pattern Recognition*, which laid the foundation of syntactic pattern recognition [4]. Syntactic methods grasp the structural commonness between image pattern and language, communicate with each other, and open a new situation for pattern recognition.

9.2.3 Perceptual thought

Perceptual thought, that is, intuitive thought, is a kind of quick recognition, keen and deep insight, a direct essential understanding and comprehensive overall judgment by human brain for the things, new phenomena, new problems, and their relations that suddenly appear in front of us. In short, intuition is direct awareness.

Intuitive thought refers to the quick judgment, conjecture, and assumption of an answer to a question based on the perception of internal cause without step-by-step analysis or the sudden "inspiration" and "epiphany" in response to a question, even "premonition" and "prediction" of the result of future things in the process of being unable to solve the problem.

Intuitive thought is characterized by freedom, flexibility, spontaneity, contingency, and unreliability. From the perspective of the importance of intuitive thought, there are mainly three points:

1. Simplicity: Intuitive thought is a sharp and rapid assumption, conjecture, or judgment made through rich imagination by investigating the

thinking object as a whole and mobilizing all knowledge and experience of oneself. It omits the intermediate link of step-by-step analysis and reasoning and takes the form of "jumping." It is a flash of thinking spark, a sublimation of long-term accumulation, an inspiration and insight of the thinker, a highly simplified thinking process, but it clearly touches the "essence" of things.

2. Creativity: Intuitive thought is based on the overall grasp of the research object, not focused on the details of the scrutiny; it is a big hand in thinking. It is because of the unconsciousness of thinking that its imagination is rich and divergent, which makes people's cognitive structure expand infinitely outward, so it has the originality of abnormal laws.

3. Self-confidence: Success can cultivate one's self-confidence. Intuition discovery is accompanied by strong "self-confidence." Compared with other material rewards and emotional incentives, this kind of self-confidence is more stable and lasting. When a problem does not take the form of logical proof but goes through one's own intuition, the shock brought by success is huge, and a strong motivation for study and research is generated in one's heart, so as to believe in one's own ability more.

Inspirational thought is also known as insight. It is intuitive for people with a sudden burst of inspiration as a form of thinking, insight, or understanding. The "magic stroke" of poets and writers, the "surprise victory" of military commanders, the "sudden breakthrough" of ideological strategists, and the "sudden opening" of scientists and inventors etc.,. All of them illustrate this characteristic of inspiration. It is a way of thinking when, after a long period of thinking, the problem is not resolved, but suddenly, inspired by a certain thing, the problem is immediately resolved. "Everything takes its time to ripen, giving a birth in one day" is a figurative description of this approach. It is inspired by information from the induced accumulation of experience, the advance of association, and the boost of motivation.

In general, abstract thought occurs during significant awareness, by means of the concept of strict logical reasoning; from a premise, step-by-step reasoning continues toward the conclusion. The performance of the whole reasoning process is linear, one-dimensional. Imagery thought mainly occurs amid significant awareness and is unconscious from time to time while engaged in activities. Thinking in images is to use images to think and express. The image of the place of thinking processes not only cannot do without sensitivity, intuition, imagination, and other nonlogical thinking, inspiration and ultimately similarity to laws in accordance with the control law and other methods of inference. Place thinking is a more complicated process than abstract thinking and is two-dimensional. Inspiration occurs mainly in the subconscious mind, which is a remarkable blend of results from conscious and unconscious processes. The process of inspiration breeds performance information for perceptual experience and fresh information on a given subject. High-level nervous system "construction" activities conducted in these three aspects are integrated with the structure formed by topology. Inspirational thought is nonlinear and three-dimensional. Thus inspiration thought has different characteristics from abstract thought or imagery thought. Here is a list of the characteristics of inspiration thought:

1. Abruptness: Abruptness is the situation in which a long pondered problem is suddenly solved by a str0ke of something else, such as walking, chatting, flowers, tourism, and so on. This is the inspiration thought of the performances from the time and place of the state. The abruptness of inspiration means that regarding time, it happens all of a sudden; regarding the effect, it is unexpected and unpredictable. However, all this is related to the subconscious inference, which is an integrated reasoning of information isomorphism and the functional constructing of the neurological system. The result of this kind of reasoning goes from implicit to explicit. The essence of this thought activity is the precise isomorphism that occurs between the source and sink of information, which is to say, that two things share some rare but precise intercommunity deep inside (in the information essence) and information essence transits from this basis to a higher level. It is accompanied by the transition of EEG power that occurs in the mutual effect between the conscious and the subconscious mind.

2. Occasionality: From a space point of view, inspiration is suddenly evoked by something else, and this inspiration lasts so briefly that it is difficult to trace. That is what occasionality means. Engels pointed out that inevitability has occasionality as its supplement and manifestation. This kind of occasionality must comply with the law of causation. Although the subconsciousness cannot be realized by us, inspiration, from start to end, occurs with the participation of the conscious mind. Regarding the pondered subject, it provides information related to the subject in a divergent manner. It is possible that some information will lead to the inspiration. Therefore, the inspiring information has some kind of occasionality

regarding the time, location, conditions, and chances. But this occasionality has some kind of inevitability hidden inside.

3. Originality: Originality is the essential characteristic of inspirational thought that differs from other forms of thought. Inspiration appears in every important invention or discovery in the whole history of humankind. From literature to poetry, from military actions to scientific creation, inspiration exists everywhere.

4. Vagueness: An inspiration thought comprehensive survey, produced by new clues, new results, new conclusions, will find that inspiration ideas often come with a certain degree of ambiguity. From fuzzy to clear, with precise description of the vague, it is the world's diversity and complexity of performance. The development of modern science and the overall trend show that the deepening of science requires more precision. However, the deepening of science itself implies that the problem is more complicated, but complicated and difficult to make precise. Thus the complexity of things just does not accompany the accuracy of that ambiguity.

According to human experience, the mechanism to produce inspiration has roughly five stages: conditions, enlightenment, transition, insight and validation:

1. Conditions refer to the necessary and sufficient conditions that can lead to the burst of inspiration.

2. Enlightenment refers to the random information encountered by chance that intrigues the occurrence of inspiration. Epistemologically speaking, enlightenment is a universal form to intrigue inspiration, connecting different information of thoughts. It is the "golden key" to the new discovery.

3. Transition is that the nonlogical way of the qualitative change at the moment inspiration occurs. When the conscious and subconscious minds mutually affect each other, different thoughts appear in the brain, and this is the result of the thought transition. This kind of transition is a characteristic of subthought and a noncontiguous way of the qualitative change that is beyond reasoning procedures.

4. Insight means the manifestation at the moment when the matured but not yet shown inspiration communicates with the conscious mind. Ancient Chinese philosopher Zhu Xi described enlightenment as "to see everything suddenly in a clear light" or as when the scales fall from one's eyes. This proves that, at that moment, inspiration can be realized by humans.

5. Validation is the scientific analysis and evaluation of the product of inspirational thought. Along with the advance of inspiration, new concepts, theories, and views start to emerge. However, intuition may be vague, so it is possible that there are flaws in the insight. Therefore, not every conclusion is valid, and proper validation is needed.

The human brain is a complex system. Complex systems are often taken to constitute a hierarchical structure. Hierarchical structure is composed of interrelated subsystems, and each subsystem is hierarchical in structure type, until we reach a certain minimum level of basic subsystems. In the human central nervous system where there are many levels, the inspiration may be more than self. The problem is solved when the different parts of the brain suddenly connect at work.

9.3 Deductive inference

Deductive inference is reasoning on the implication relation between the premises and conclusions or, rather, the reasoning on the necessary connection between the premises and conclusions, from the general to the specific.

A is the logical inference of Γ (i.e., formula in Γ), which is recorded as $\Gamma \vDash A$. if and only if any assignment φ in any nonempty field, if $\varphi(\Gamma) = 1$, then $\varphi(A) = 1$.

Given the nonempty field S, any assignment φ in S makes:

$$\varphi(I) = 1 \Rightarrow (A) = 1$$

When it was established, we said that A in S was a logical inference of Γ and that it was recorded as $\Gamma \vDash A$ in S.

In mathematical logic, reasoning is studied, and deductive reasoning is studied through formal reasoning system. It can be proved that the relationship between the premise and conclusion reflected by formal reasoning is tenable in deductive reasoning, so formal reasoning does not go beyond the scope of deductive reasoning, and formal reasoning reliably reflects deductive reasoning; the relationship between the premise and conclusion established in deductive reasonin12g can be reflected by formal reasoning, so formal reasoning reflects deductive reasoning The formal reasoning is complete for the reflection of deductive reasoning.

One form of reasoning that is often used is syllogism. Aristotle's theory of the syllogism plays an important role. It consists of only three judgments, two of which are premise and the other is conclusion. As far as the subject and predicate are concerned, it contains only three different concepts, each of which appears once in each of the two judgments. These three different concepts are the major term, minor term, and middle term. The concept of large term is the predicate term of conclusion, which is represented by P. A small term is the concept of the main term of a conclusion, denoted by S. The middle term is the concept that appears in both premises, expressed in M. Different forms of syllogism formed by different positions of the major, middle, and minor terms in the premise are called syllogism lattices. Syllogism has the following four lattices:

$$\text{First grid:} \quad \begin{array}{c} M - P \\ S - M \\ \hline S - P \end{array}$$

$$\text{Second grid:} \quad \begin{array}{c} P - M \\ S - M \\ \hline S - P \end{array}$$

$$\text{Third grid:} \quad \begin{array}{c} M - P \\ M - S \\ \hline S - P \end{array}$$

$$\text{Fourth grid:} \quad \begin{array}{c} P - M \\ M - S \\ \hline S - P \end{array}$$

Rule-based deductive systems are often classified as forward, backward, and two-way integrated systems. In the rule-based forward deductive systems, implications used as rule F keep operating the factual database until a terminal condition of the goal formulations is produced. In the rule-based backward deductive system, implications used as rule B keep operating the goal database until a terminal condition of the facts is produced. In the rule-based two-way integrated systems, implications should use different rules (Rule F or B) to operate from both directions. This type of system is a direct proof system, not a resolution refutation system.

9.4 Inductive inference

Inductive inference is the reasoning that starts from particular objects or phenomena and eventually concludes the general principles of these. This type of reasoning indicates the necessary connections between premises and conclusions. It is a specific-to-general thought progress. In recent decades, studies on inductive logic from overseas are mainly carried in two directions. One is based on the classical meaning of Francis Bacon's inductive logic, trying to find out the logic route to produce the universal principles from related experiences and facts. The other deploys the probability theory and other formal and reasonable methods from the limited experiences and facts available in order to explore the "support" and "validation" of a universal proposition about certain fields. The latter is actually logic of theoretical evaluation.

The main points of Bacon's inductive methods are as follows:

1. Senses must be guided to overcome the partiality and superficiality of the perceptual cognition.
2. Proper inductive procedures are needed when forming the concept.
3. Escalation must be used for the construction of axioms.
4. In the inductive progress, the importance of the inversion method and exclusion method must be emphasized.

These points are also the basis of the four rules of the inductive method, proposed by John S. Mill. Mill also introduced the method of agreement, difference, concomitant variation, and residues in his book *A System of Logic, Ratiocinative and Inductive*. He asserted that "induction can be defined as the operation of discovering and proving the general propositions."

Probabilistic logic bloomed in the 1930s. Hans Reichenbach used probability theory to calculate the frequency limit of a certain proposition from relative frequency and used this to predict future events. During the 1940s and 1950s, Rudolf Carnap founded probabilistic logic based on rational belief. Using the same standpoint as Bayesianism, he described the rational belief as a probability function and took probability as the logic relation between two evidential statements. Bayes' theorem can be written as:

$$p(h/e) = P(e/h)\frac{P(h)}{P(e)} \tag{9.1}$$

where P is the probability, h is a hypothesis, and e is the evidence. This formula stated that the probability of h to e equals the likelihood value of h to e or, rather, the probability of h when e is true multiplying the prior probability of h, then divided by the prior probability of e. Here the prior probability refers to the probability known before the current experiment. For example, A_1, $A_2, \ldots$, are the "causes" of test results, and $P(A_i)$ is called a prior probability. But if the experiment leads to the event B, and this information is useful to the discussion about the "cause" of the event, conditional probability $P(A_i|B)$ is called the posterior probability. Therefore, Carnap needed to make a reasonable explanation of prior probability, since he used the same standpoint as Bayes. However, Carnap did not agree on the interpretation of prior probability being a personal and subjective degree of belief and tried to explain rational belief objectively.

Carnap interpreted his logic concepts of probability as the degree of "confidence" [5]. He used C to present his own interpretation of probability, as $C(h, e)$ stands for "the degree of confidence of the hypothesis h to the evidence e", and further introduced credit function item Cred and belief function item Cr to apply inductive logic to the reasonable decision. Degree of confidence C is defined as

$$C(h, e_1, e_2, \ldots, e_n) = r \tag{9.2}$$

This means the joint probability of statements (inductive premises) e_1, $e_2, \ldots, e_n$ contributes the logic probability r to the statement (inductive conclusion) h. In this way, Carnap defined the belief function item and other items by the expectation an observer x gives to the value of a conditional probability at the time h. C_r, which is the belief item for hypothesis H to evidence E, is defined as:

$$C_{rx,t}(H/E) = \frac{Crx, t(EIH)}{C_{rx,t}(E)} \tag{9.3}$$

Further, he introduced the credit function item Cred. It definition is, if A is all knowledge known by an observer x at the time T, his degree of credit to H at the time T is Cred(H/A). The belief function item is based on the credit function item:

$$C_{rT}(H_1) = \text{Cred}\left(H_1/A_1\right) \tag{9.4}$$

Carnap believed that with these two concepts, the transition of the regulated decision theory to inductive logic can be achieved. He also thought the belief function item and credit function item could correspond to the pure logic concepts. What C_r corresponded to was called the m-function item, that is, the inductive measurement function item, while the C-function item, that is, the inductive validation function item, corresponded to Cred. In this way, the axioms for probability calculation can also be used as the axioms for inductive logic. He pointed out: In inductive logic, the C-function item is more important than the m-function because C stands for the degree of reasonableness of the belief, and it helps to in making a reasonable decision. The m-function item is more of a tool for the definition and evaluation of the C-function item. In the sense of the axiomatic probability calculation, the m-function item is a universal (absolute) function item, while the C-function item is conditional (relative). He stated if we used C as the initial item, the axioms for C could be described as [6]:

1. The axiom of the lower limit: $C(H/E) \geq 0$ (9.5)

2. The axiom of self-validation: $C(H/E) = 1$ (9.6)

3. The axiom of complementation: $C(H/E) + C(-H/E) = 1$ (9.7)

4. The axiom of general multiplication: If $E \cap H$ is possible.

Then:

$$C(H \cap H'/E) = C(H/E) * C(H'/E \cap H)$$ (9.8)

These axioms are the basis of Carnap's formal system of inductive logic.

The reasonableness of logic has always been controversial in the history of philosophy. David Hume raised his problem of induction with the key point that the future could not be inducted from the past and that the general could not be inducted from the specific. Hume insisted "every induction from experiences are the result of habits, instead of results of ration." So, he concluded that the reasonableness of inductive method was improvable and that there is no reasonable agnostic conclusion in the related empirical science.

K. R. Popper described the problem of induction in his book *Objective Knowledge: An Evolutionary Approach*:
1. Is induction provable?
2. Is the principle of induction provable?
3. Are some inductive theories like "the future is the same as the past," that is, "the uniformity of nature's laws" provable?

9.5 Abductive inference

In abductive inference, we give out the rule of $p \Rightarrow q$ and the rational belief of q. Then we hope to obtain that predicate p is true with some explanations.

The method based on logic is set up on the more advanced concept of explanations. Levesque defined the phenomenon set O, which could not be explained earlier in 1989 as the minimal set of items in H and background knowledge set K. Hypothesis H together with background knowledge K must be able to entail O. A more formal description is abduce $(K,O) = H$ if and only if:

1. K is unable to entail O.
2. $H \cup K$ is able to entail O.
3. $H \cup K$ is consistent.
4. No subsets of H exist with properties (1), (2), and (3).

It is necessary to point out that, generally speaking, there could be many hypothesis sets, which means there could be many potential explanation sets for a given phenomenon.

The definition of abductive explanation based on logic suggests that explanations of the content in the discovery knowledge base system have corresponding mechanisms. If an explainable hypothesis must be able to entail phenomena O, the way to set up a complete explanation is reasoning backward from O.

9.6 Analogical inference

According to a similar relationship between two objects, the reasoning process that one object has a certain property and another object has a corresponding property is called analogical reasoning [7]. The mode of analogical reasoning can be described as:

If A has attributes of a, b, c, and d
and B has attributes of a, b, and c
Then B has the attribute of d

Therefore, analogical reasoning is a method using the information of one system to speculate the information of another, similar system. The objective basis of analogical reasoning lies in the universal relation among the objects, progressions, and elements in different systems, as well as their comparability.

Object S_1:	premises $\beta_1, \ldots, \beta_n \rightarrow$ conclusion α
	Similarity φ
Object S_2:	premises $\beta'_1, \ldots, \beta'_n \rightarrow$ conclusion α'?

Figure 9.2 Principle of analogical reasoning.

How the theory of analogical works is shown in Fig. 9.2. Here β_i and α are the established facts in S_1. β'_i is the established fact in S_2. φ is the relation similarity between the objects. The analogical inference is that, when $\beta_i \varphi \beta'_i$ $(1 \leq i \leq n)$ exists, $\alpha \varphi \alpha'$ in S_2 leads to α'. To achieve this, the conditions given here are necessary:

1. The definition of similarity φ
2. The procedure to produce φ from given objects S_1 and S_2
3. The procedure to produce α' in $\alpha \varphi \alpha'$

Firstly, the definition of similarity φ shall be relevant to the form of the object and its meaning. Here the object of analogy is the finite set of judgment clauses S_i. Define clause A, β_i as literal constants to form the if-then rule. Item t_i does not include any variables from S_i, and it presents the individual object. Predicate symbol P presents the relation among the individuals, for example, the atom logical expression P $(t_i, \ldots, t_n)$ stands for the relation among t_i. (From now on, atom logical expression will be called "atom" for short) The set that consists of all the atoms is denoted as β_i. The minimum model M_i is the set of atoms logically deducted from S_i.

$$M_i = \{\alpha \in \beta_i : S_i \cong \alpha\} \qquad (9.9)$$

where $\cong$ stands for logical reasoning in predicate logic. Moreover, the individual of M_i is called the fact of S_i.

To determine the analogy between M_i, it is necessary to consider the corresponding relationship of M_i. For this reason, the corresponding definitions of S_i are as follows:

1. $U(S_i)$ is a set of S_i without arguments. In this case, the finite $\varphi \subseteq U(S_1) \times U(S_2)$ is called φ pairing, and $\times$ represents the direct product of the set.

   Because the term represents an individual of the object S_i, pairing can be interpreted as representing a certain correspondence between individuals. S_i is not a constant in general but has a function sign, so the corresponding pair φ can be extended to the corresponding relationship φ^+ between $U(S_i)$.

2. The relation φ^+ of the item generated by φ is defined as the minimum relation if the following relations are met:

$$(a)\ \varphi \subseteq \varphi^+ \tag{9.10}$$

$$(b)\ < t_i, t_i' > E\varphi^+ (1 \le i \le n) \Rightarrow\ < f(t_1, \ldots, t_n), f(t_1', \ldots t_n') \in \varphi^+ \tag{9.11}$$

where f is the function symbol jointly represented by S_1 and S_2.

However, for the given S_1 and S_2, there are usually multiple possible pairings. Each pair φ relationship is the same, that is, the analogy with the same predicate symbol can be determined as follows:

3. Let $t_j \in U(S_i)$, φ be pairing, and α, α' be S_1 and S_2, respectively. In this case, α and α' are regarded as the same by φ and refer to the predicate symbol P written as:

$$a = P(t_1, \ldots, t_n)$$

$$a' = P(t'_1, \ldots, t'_n)$$

and $< t_j, t'_j > \in \varphi^+$. According to φ, α, and α' are regarded as the same and are written as $\alpha \varphi \alpha'$. According to analogy, in order to find the atom α, the rule:

$$\boldsymbol{R'}: \alpha' \leftarrow \beta'_1, \ldots, \beta'_n$$

is made using φ by rule:

$$\boldsymbol{R}: \alpha \leftarrow \beta_1, \ldots, \beta_n$$

From $\alpha \leftarrow \beta_1, \ldots, \beta_n$ and the known facts $\beta_1, \ldots, \beta_n$, by using syllogism, we can deduce α. Based on φ, R is constructed by R, which is called the rule transformation. The process of solving α can be expressed as the basic schema of Fig. 9.2.

Analogical inference is widely used, such as case-based reasoning, transfer learning, machine translation, and so on.

9.7 Causal inference

Causal inference is a kind of logical inference. According to the reasons and conditions of things, we can judge through logical thinking and derive the results. This inference method is called causal inference.

In 2018 Judea Pearl and Dana Mackenzie published a book entitled *The Book of Why: The New Science of Cause and Effect* [8]. The core question the authors answer in this book is how to make intelligent machines think like people. In other words, can artificial general intelligence be realized? With the help of three levels of the ladder of causality, the essence of causal inference is gradually revealed, and the corresponding automatic processing tools and mathematical analysis paradigms are constructed accordingly. The authors give a positive answer. The authors believe that most of the machine learning technologies we are familiar with today are based on correlation rather than on causality. In order to realize strong artificial intelligence and even transform an intelligent machine into an organism with moral consciousness, we must let the machine learn to ask why, that is to say, let the machine learn causal inference and understand causal relationship. Perhaps this is the most meaningful work we can do for intelligent machines that are ready to take over our future lives.

Judea Pearl points out that a causal learner must master at least three distinct levels of cognitive ability: seeing, doing, and imagining. The first is the bottom layer, which refers to the general observation of the phenomena of things and, according to the observed phenomenon, find the relevance. According to Pearl, the current machine learning model can only stay in the first stage. This is because the statistical machine learning model can only observe phenomena (data) and fit a possible probability distribution. The result of this fitting is that the model can only find the correlation between two variables rather than the real causality.

The middle layer is intervention, that is, through the change of variables, in order to study the impact of this variable on the results, including whether to change the nature of the results and the intensity of the change. Finally, it is counterfactual, that is, controlling other variables through simulation, only turning over the studied variables and exploring the possible development. In a sense, counterfactual is about a fictional world or unrealized possibility because its antecedent is the opposite of the fact: It is about what might happen, but not. Therefore, on the surface, it is to be beyond the scope of normal scientific research. Counterfactual is so closely related to causality that it is impossible to think with causality instead of counterfactual reasoning. No matter how large the data set is, the causal conclusion is drawn not only from the observed statistical laws. Instead, we must use all our clues and imagination to create reasonable causal hypotheses and then analyze these hypotheses to see whether they are reasonable and how to test them through data. Just piling up more numbers is not a shortcut to gain causal insight.

Causal inference is a logical way to deduce a certain positive result from the cause of things. Through causal inference, human beings can solve the problems in life and science. To express causality in language in mathematical form, Pearl proposed the causality diagram, a graphic simulation that represents the causal relationship between variables. A point represents a variable, and an edge with a point represents the causal effect of the variable. This kind of point—edge graph is called a causality graph. Pearl thinks that the cause-and-effect diagram can well show the cause-and-effect relationship. If each edge has a weight, it can represent the influence intensity of different factors on this result.

9.8 Commonsense reasoning

Commonsense reasoning is a field of artificial intelligence, which aims to help computers understand and interact with people more naturally by collecting all background assumptions and teaching them to computers. The representative system of commonsense reasoning is the Cyc system of the Cycrop company, which operates a commonsense knowledge-based logic.

Cyc system was developed by Doug Lenat in 1984. The initial goal of the project was to encode millions of pieces of knowledge into machine-usable forms to represent human common sense. Cycl is a Cyc project-specific knowledge representation language that is based on first-order relations. In 1986 Lennart predicted that it would take 350 person-years to complete a huge commonsense knowledge system like Cyc, which would involve 250,000 rules. In 1994 the Cyc project was independent from the company, and based on this, Cycrop was established in Austin, Texas.

In July 2009, OpenCyc version 2.0 was released, which covers the complete Cyc ontology, including 47,000 concepts and 306,000 facts, mainly classification assertion, and does not contain complex rules in Cyc. These resources are described in CycL language, which takes predicate algebra description, and its syntax is similar to the LISP programming language. CycL and SubL interpreters (which allow users to browse and edit the knowledge base and have reasoning function) are freely distributed to users but contain only binary files, not source code.

OpenCyc has distributions for the Linux operating system and Microsoft Windows operating system. The open source Texai Project released the RDF version of the OpenCyc repository.

The Cyc knowledge base is composed of many MicroTheories (MT) [9]. The concept set and fact set are generally associated with specific MTs. Different from the overall knowledge base, each MT does not contradict others. Each MT has a constant name, and the MT constant convention ends with the string "MT." For example: #$MathMt represents MT containing mathematical knowledge, which can be inherited from one another and organized into a hierarchical structure. For example, #$MathMt at a more refined level, it contains the MT of geometry.

The Cyc reasoning engine is a computer program that can get the answer from the knowledge base by reasoning. The Cyc reasoning engine supports general logical deductive reasoning, including positive antecedent hypothetical reasoning, negative posterior hypothetical reasoning, universal quantification, and existential quantification.

On February 14, 2011, IBM's Watson supercomputer competed with Ken Jennings and Brad Rutter on *Jeopardy*. On February 16, Watson won a $1 million prize on the Q&A show on *Jeopardy* after three rounds of competition. The intelligent computer Watson has successfully adopted the Cyc system of commonsense reasoning.

9.9 Mathematics mechanization

As two mainstreams in mathematics, mathematics axiomatization and mechanization have played an important role in the development of mathematics. After a deep study of ancient Chinese mathematics and decades of research in mathematics, Wenjun Wu finally formulated his idea of mathematics mechanization, well-known as Wu's method [10].

Wu's method, also known as the mechanized method of geometry, consists of mainly two steps. The first step is to express the premises and conclusions of the theorem to be proved in algebraic equations by introducing coordinates. This is applicable only to theorems whose algebraic relations can be encoded in polynomial equations, such as parallel, perpendicular, intersection, distance, etc. This step may be called the algebra of geometry. The second step is the resolution of coordinates in the equations encoding conclusions with the help of the polynomial relationships in the equations' encoding premises. The theorem is proved if all coordinates in the condition equations can be eliminated and should be checked further. This step is entirely algebraic. These two steps can be carried out in mechanically and rigidly. There are no significant difficulties in realizing this method in computers. Its principle runs as follows [10]:

Assume a supply of variables $x_1, \ldots, x_n$, and a domain k with the characteristic O. The following polynomials are from $k[x_1, \ldots, x_n]$. A group $TPS = (f_1, \ldots, f_n)$ of polynomials is a triangle, if $x_1, \ldots, x_n$ can be divided into two parts, that is, $u_1, \ldots, u_s$ and $y_1, \ldots, y_r$ $(r + s = n)$, such that f_i has the following forms:

$$f_1 = I_1 y_1^{m_1} + o(y_1^{m_1})$$
$$f_2 = I_2 y_2^{m_2} + o(y_2^{m_2})$$
$$\cdots\cdots\cdots$$
$$f_n = I_n y_n^{m_n} + o(y_n^{m_n})$$

subject to the following conditions:
1. The coefficient of each y_i in f_i is a polynomial in $k[u, y_1, \ldots, y_{i-1}]$.
2. The exponent of each y_i $(j < i)$ in I_i is less than m_j.

For any polynomial G, we can identify the following equation:

$$I_1^{S_1} \Lambda I_n^{S_n} G = \sum Q_i f_i + R$$

where $s_i \geq 0$, $Q_i \in k[x_1, \ldots, x_n]$, $R \in k[x_1, \ldots, x_n] = k[u, y_1, \ldots, y_n]$, and the exponent of each y_i in R is less than m_i. R is referred to as the remainder of G w.r.t. TPS, in symbols, $R = \text{Remdr}(G/TPS)$.

The polynomial triangular group TPS is irresolutionable, if each f_i is irresolutionable w.r.t. y_i in the expansion domain of $k = [u, y_1, \ldots, y_{i-1}]$. The number of u is the dimension n of TPS; in symbols, $\dim TPS$.

For any polynomial group PS and another polynomial H, we denote by Zero (PS/H) the set of elements in k's expansion domain such that $PS = 0$ and $H \neq 0$. Wu's mechanized method is based on the following two theorems:
1. Ritt's principle: For any polynomial group PS, we can mechanically produce a polynomial triangular group TPS (not unique), called the characteristic set of PS, such that:
   a. $\text{Zero}(TPS/J) \subset \text{Zero}(PS) \subset \text{Zero}(TPS)$;
   b. $\text{Zero}(PS) = \text{Zero}(TPS/J) + \Sigma \text{Zero}(PS_i)$.
   where J refers to the product of all I_i of TPS, and PS_i is the resulting polynomial group by adding I_i to PS.

2. Zero decomposition theorem: For any polynomial group PS and another polynomial H, we can mechanically compute a decomposition (not unique) such that:

$$\text{Zero}(PS/H) = \Sigma \text{Zero}(IRR_i/R_i),$$

where each IRR_i is an irresolutionable polynomial triangular group with Remdr $(R_i/IRR_i) \neq 0$.

These two theorems can be naturally generalized to the case of differential polynomial groups. The mechanization method based on these two theorems can be applied in solving but not limited to the following problems:

1. The machine proof of theorems in elementary geometry
2. The machine proof of theorems in differential geometry
3. The mechanical derivation of unknown relationships
4. The solution to high exponent algebraic equations
5. The factorization problems

The basic idea of the Wu method is simple: The geometric propositions are treated in algebraic form. The Wu method is used in many high-tech fields, including surface modeling, position analysis of robot structure, intelligent computer-aided design, image compression in information transmission, etc.

References

[1] X.S. Qian, Developing the research of noetic science, in: X.S. Qian (Ed.), About Noetic Science, Shanghai: Shanghai People's Publishing House, 1986.

[2] R. Nina, J. Holyoak, Relational complexity and the functions of prefrontal cortex, in: M.S. Gazzaniga (Ed.), The Cognitive Neurosciences, VIII Thought and Imagery, The MIT Press, London, 1995.

[3] Z.Z. Shi, Hierarchical model of mind, Invited Speaker, Chinese Joint Conference on Artificial Intelligence (1990).

[4] K.S. Fu, Syntactic Method in Pattern Recognition, Academic Press, New York, 1974.

[5] R. Carnap, Logical Foundations of Probability, University of Chicago Press, Chicago, 1950.

[6] R. Carnap, The Continuum of Inductive Methods, University of Chicago Press, Chicago, 1952.

[7] J.G. Carbonell, Learning and problem solving by analogy, Preprints of the CMU Machine Learning Workshop-Symposium, (1980).

[8] J. Pearl, D. Mackenzie, The Book of Why: The New Science of Causal and Effect, Basic Books, 2018.

[9] D.B. Lenat, R.V. Guha, Building large knowledge-based systems: representation and inference in the cyc project, Artif. Intell. 61 (1) (1993) 95−104.

[10] W. Wu, Wu Wenjun on Mathematical Mechanization, Shandong Education Press, Jinan, 1996.

CHAPTER 10

Intelligence development

Intelligence development refers to the regular change of individual intelligence with the increase in age under the influence of social living conditions and education. Intelligence development is an important part of overall psychological development. From birth to maturity, the development of children's intelligence is a continuous process in a certain order. The order of development is certain, but the development speed of each development stage is not exactly the same, and the development speed of each stage of different individuals is not the same.

In this chapter, we will mainly explain intelligence development based on operation and intelligence development based on the morphism-category theory.

10.1 Intelligence

What is intelligence? Psychologist could not put forward a clear definition until now. Some think that intelligence is the ability of abstract thinking. And some others define it as adaptive capacity, learning ability, and the integrated ability of perceive activities. What is more, some of the pioneers of intelligence test think: "Intelligence is that thing of the intelligence test." The definition of intelligence according to psychologists can be roughly divided into three categories:

1. Intelligence is the individual's ability of adaptability. A person who adapts to the living environment more easily, especially a changing environment, will have a higher level of intelligence.
2. Intelligence is the individual's capability of learning. The faster and easier someone can learn new things and can solve problems by using experience, the higher level of intelligence that person will have.
3. Intelligence is the individual's ability of abstract thinking. People who obtain new conceptions from concrete things and do logical reasoning through those conceptions show their relatively high intelligence.

The contemporary well-known American psychologist David Weissler integrated these three kinds of views: Intelligence is the individual

Intelligence Science
DOI: https://doi.org/10.1016/B978-0-323-85380-4.00010-5

intentional action, rational thinking, and effective comprehensive ability to adapt to the environment.

All of these definitions, although some stress a certain aspect and some emphasize the whole, but there are two aspects in common:

1. Intelligence is an ability and belongs to potential capability.
2. This capability develops through behavior. Expression, or adapting to the environment, learning, abstract thinking—such are the acts of individual performance or behavior of the resulting three kinds of overall performance. In other words, intelligence can be seen as individual performance in response to things, objects, and scene features; such functions are performed by behaviors.

In 1938 American psychologist L. L. Thurstone engaged students of the University of Chicago in research on his 56 abilities. And he found that seven of the 56 abilities are highly related and seem to have less of a relation to others. These seven abilities are coherence and comprehension of words and phrases, sense of space, speed of consciousness, ability of counting, reasoning, and memory. Thurstone proposed that any group formed by seven or more kinds of individual mental abilities would be marked as a multifactor intelligence case. With this foundation, Thurstone set up the framework for general mental ability testing. The research results show that there are different degrees of positive correlation among the seven basic abilities, and it seems that higher psychological factors, that is, g factors, can still be abstracted.

The theory of multiple intelligence was proposed by American psychologist H. Gardner [1]. In his view, the connotation of intelligence is diverse and relatively independent from the seven kinds of intelligence components of the composition. Each element is a separate mental functional system, and these systems can interact to produce explicit intelligent behavior. The seven kinds of intelligence are as follows:

1. Speech intelligence infiltrates all of the ability of speech, including reading, writing, and daily communication.
2. Logic-mathematical intelligence involves mathematical operations and logical thinking ability, such as doing proof questions of mathematics and reasoning from logic.
3. Space intelligence, including navigation, is the understanding of environment, such as reading maps and painting.
4. Music intelligence, including distinguishing sound and expressing a melody, such as playing the violin or writing melodies.
5. Body mobility intelligence, including governing your body to accurately accomplish tasks, such as playing basketball or dancing.

6. Interpersonal intelligence, including the ability to affiliate with friendly people, such as knowing other people's feeling, motivation, and mood.

7. Introspection intelligence means the condition of one's inside world and the ability to possess a high level of sensitivity, including contemplation of oneself and the ability of choosing one's own way of life.

With the deepening of research, more types of intelligence will be identified, and the original intelligence classification will be modified. For example, Gardner put forward the eighth kind of intelligence in 1996—the intelligence to understand nature.

10.2 Intelligence test

From the viewpoint of intelligence tests, intelligence displayed through behavior is an important view. Therefore some psychologists simplified the definition of intelligence as follows: Intelligence is the object of an intelligence test. Questioning this further: what is the object of the test? Although it's not so easy to answer that question, one point is certain: Instead of measuring intelligence itself, the object is measured by an individual's external actions. Indirect measurement of individual behavior characteristics acted externally is then quantified in order to estimate the level of intelligence, which is the basic principle of the intelligence test. Intelligence is an abstract concept and cannot be directly measured, which is like the case of "energy" in physics since it must be measured by the work generated by the movement of objects.

In the early 20th century, the French psychologist A. Binet was entrusted by the education authorities of Paris to produce a set of tests to identify students with mental deficiency, so that they can enter schools that did not teach the standard curriculum. Since then, the intelligence test is used to predict the ability of children and students and the benefit of "intellectual" training. Now there is an increasing tendency to establish and apply intelligence tests to measure different aspects of a person's capabilities. The main purpose of intelligence test is to categorize people according to their level of capacity, which also depends on the studies of intelligence theory and the establishment of new intelligence tests.

We can categorize intelligence tests into many sorts. For instance, they can be divided into individual tests and group tests according to the number of people tested. The speed test is scored on the basis of the number of correct reactions in a limited time, and in the capacity test, the score is determined by the difficulty of the mission completed successfully. The verbal test requires testee's response verbally, and, on the contrary, the tasking test requires nonverbal reactions. No matter what type of intelligence test it is, generally speaking, a large number of test items or assignments have different contents. The score is decided by the number of assignments completed successfully.

Each item of intelligence tests can provide the level of age that fits it. When a child is tested, the score is based on the items the child passed. So the score can be indicated by age. For example, Terman-Merrill's test requires defining each word, and 60% of 13-year-old children can do so, so it is given to the 13-year-old child.

Given this, a child has to pass not only all the items of the 10-year-old child tests but also the items of the 11-year-old and 12-year-old children tests. The child is first given the scores of the items for age 10, then half the items of the 11-year-old tests and a quarter of the items of the 12-year-old test. The scores should therefore be plus six months (11-year-old) and three months (12-year-old), so the final score is 10 years and 9 months. This is the Month Age (MA). Therefore, MA is based on the scores derived from the intelligence test, it is determined by the difficulty levels of the tests.

Intelligence quotient (IQ) is defined as MA divided by the chronological age, then multiplied it by 100. The formula is as follows:

$$IQ = \frac{MA}{CA} * 100 \tag{10.1}$$

Multiplying the formula by 100 eliminates decimals, so that the IQ is obtained as an integrated and shows the level of intelligence. To determine IQ, this approach assumes that mental age grows together with actual age. On the contrary, sometime intellectual age no longer grows at the pace of actual age. After people reach a certain actual age, the development of intellectual age stays at a relatively stable level. Because intelligence no longer grows in direct proportion to actual age after the age of 15, the formula used to test the intelligence of a 15-year-old and older is as follows:

$$IQ = \frac{MA}{15} * 100 \tag{10.2}$$

But we cannot get satisfactory results using this approach. D. Wechsler proposes the Adult Intelligence Scale, the main component of which are as follows:

1. Property and content: In property, items of the test are divided into language and assignment. The former contains 84 questions and can be divided into six subtests: common sense, comprehension, arithmetic, analogy, memory span, and vocabulary. The latter contains 44 questions, including allocation of object and its form, chart filling, lining up a picture series, building blocks according to the designed picture, and symbol substitution. The 128 questions cover a wide range of people's general abilities.

2. Sphere of application: At the age of 16-plus.

3. Implementation of procedure: Implemented individually, all of the tests consume about an hour.

4. Score and criterion: The original scores of each subtest are processed into a weighted score through conversion. The weighted score of the first six subtests is the total scale of verbal. The sum of the latter five weighted scores of the subtests is the total scores of assignments. Check the total sum of the two scale scores against the standard table, and then get the standard scores of IQ.

    The criterion of this test is based on the standardized sample made up of 700 representational persons. There are appropriate considerations about many aspects, such as gender, age, district, race, occupation, and educational background; in this sample, it is of high representativeness.

5. Reliability and related coefficient: The multiple coefficient obtained by midpoint subdivision is as follows: the scale of verbal is 0.96, the scale of assignment is 0.93, and the total scale is 0.97. The research of the related coefficient is based on the Stanford–Binet scale. The related coefficient is: the scale of verbal is 0.83, the scale of assignment is 0.93, and the total scale is 0.85.

In the 1920s, American psychologist L. M. Terman conducted a large-scale research experiment to study the talent development of gifted children by using the method of tracking observation. He chose 1528 children whose IQs were above 130: 857 boys, 671 girls. He made a visit to the schools and families, got detailed appraisements of the teachers and parents, and made personality inspections of a third part of those people. He visited the schools and families of those people to inquire about development and the change of their intelligence when they were adolescent. In 1936 those people had grown up and got different jobs. Termen went on doing a random survey by letters, getting the information of the development of their ability. In 1940 he invited them to Stanford University and made a psychological test. From then on, he took a letter survey every five years, until 1960.

After Terman's death, American psychologist Hills continued his research. In 1960 the average age of those research subjects was 49 years old. Hills did a letter survey of the number of the remaining people (80% of those who started). He made a survey again in 1972, of the 67% of the people originally investigated. To that point, the average of them was more than 60 years old.

This research lasted about a half century and accumulated a great deal of valuable materials. The research indicates that superior intelligence in early age does not guarantee outstanding ability in adult life. The ability of a person over a lifetime does not have much to do with intelligence at early age; the capable and intelligence person is not always the "smart" child in the eyes of teacher and parents, but the persistent person who seeks greater perfection. The researcher received a Distinguished Contribution Award in 1999 for his groundbreaking achievements in psychology.

10.3 Cognitive structure

Cognitive structure refers to the organizational form and operational mode of cognitive activities, including a series of operational processes such as the components of cognitive activities and the interaction between components, namely the mechanism of psychological activities. Cognitive structure theory takes cognitive structure as the research core, emphasizing the nature of cognitive structure construction, the interaction between cognitive structure and learning.

Throughout the theoretical development of cognitive structure, there are mainly Piaget's schema theory, Gestalt's insight theory, Tolman's cognitive map theory, Bruner's classification theory, Ausubel's cognitive assimilation theory, and so on.

10.3.1 Piaget's schema theory

Piaget thinks that schema is the cognitive structure of the subject, and the process of schema construction is completed in the two roles of assimilation and adaptation. Piaget starts from the relationship between subject and object and thinks that the cognitive structure of the subject originates from the internal construction based on the action of the subject. Action is the root of cognitive structure. Cognitive structure has experienced development from perceptual movement schema → representation schema → intuitive thinking schema → operational thinking schema.

10.3.2 Gestalt's insight theory

Wertheime believes that learning is the reorganization of perception and the construction of Gestalt. In the process of learning, problem solving is realized by a kind of "Gestalt" formed by understanding the relationship between things in the environment. Success and the realization of learning are completely determined by insight [2].

10.3.3 Tolman's cognitive map theory

Tolman insists on the symbol Gestalt model of learning. What the organism acquires is knowledge about the surrounding environment, the target location, and the means and ways to achieve the target, that is, the process of forming the cognitive map, rather than a simple and mechanical response. The so-called cognitive map is a comprehensive representation of a local environment, which includes not only the simple sequence of events but also the direction, distance, and even time relationship. In the process of the continuous transformation and reorganization of cognitive map, organisms constantly acquire knowledge about the environment, form a comprehensive image, and achieve the target symbols.

10.3.4 Bruner's theory of classification

Bruner believes that cognitive structure is a coding system of classified categories (concepts, knowledge, experience, etc.) according to the level of hierarchy. The essence of learning lies in the active formation of cognitive structure. Bruner proposed three stages of the development of cognitive structure: action representation, image representation, and symbol representation. The initial cognitive structure of children is movement representation. They "recognize from movement," that is, most of their cognition is generated through behavior.

10.3.5 Ausubel's theory of cognitive assimilation

According to Ausubel, the so-called cognitive structure refers to the quantity, clarity, and organization of knowledge, which is composed of facts, concepts, propositions, and theories. It is a way for individuals to perceive, understand, and think about the world. As for the content of cognitive structure, Ausubel makes a creative analysis, which is called the cognitive structure variable, which means that the concept in individual cognitive structure has its organizational characteristics.

According to the theory of cognitive structure, the cognitive structure existing in the human brain is always in the process of change and construction. The learning process is the process of continuous change and the reorganization of cognitive structure, in which the environment and the individual characteristics of learners are the decisive factors. Piaget used assimilation, adaptation, balance, and other processes to represent the mechanism of cognitive structure construction and emphasized the importance of the external overall environment. He believed that the rich and good multiple stimuli provided by the environment for learners were the basic conditions for the improvement and change of cognitive structure. According to Nathar, a modern cognitive psychologist, the cognitive process has a constructive nature, which consists of two processes: the process in which individuals react to external stimuli and the process in which learners consciously control, transform, and construct ideas and images. Cognitive structure is a process of gradual self-construction under the condition of the combination of external stimulation and the individual characteristics of learners.

10.4 Intelligence development based on operation

Jean Piaget, a psychologist, had his distinctive view on psychology in both experiment and theory. The Piaget school made great efforts to explore children's language, judgment, deduction, cause-and-effect view, world outlook, moral concept, symbol, time, space, number, quantity, geometry, probability, conservation, and logic. Adherents of the school put forward a brand-new theory for child psychology, cognitive psychology, or thinking psychology, which has had a broad and deep influence on contemporary child psychology.

For intelligence development, Piaget's formal work can be divided into two stages: the early period of structuralism and the later period of poststructuralism. The former is also called classical theory, and the latter is called the new theory stage. Piaget's new formalization theory basically gave up the theory of operational structure and replaced it with the theory of morphism category. So the development series of traditional preoperation—concrete operation—formal operation has become the development series of intramorphic-intermorphic-extramorphic.

10.4.1 Schema

Jean Piaget thinks intelligence has a structural foundation, and schema is what he used to describe the cognitive structure [3]. He defined schema as an organized and repeatable behavior or way of thinking, or as things that are repeatable and summarizing. In short, schema is the structure or framework of any action. Also it is a part of cognitive structure as we can divide one's cognitive structure into many schemas. As newborn babies have the innate abilities of sucking, crying, looking, hearing, and grasping that helped them to survive. Those are inborn genetic schemas. The synthesis of all genetic schemas composes a baby's intelligence structure. Genetic schema is formed with the long period evolution of schema. Based on those inborn genetic schema, with the increase in age and the maturity of ingenuity, young children' s schemas and cognitive structure develop constantly through assimilation, adaptation, and balance with interaction with the environment. There are different schemas in different stages of the development of children's intelligence. For example, the schema is called the perceptive activity schema in the stage of perceptive activity and operation thinking schema in the stage of thinking.

As a psychological structure of intelligence, schema is a biological structure based on the physical condition of the nerve system. Current studies can hardly explain physical and chemical quality. On the contrary, the existence of those schemas in people's brains can be speculated from people's behaviors. Actually, Piaget analyzed the intelligence structure based on a large number of clinical cases using biology, psychology, philosophy and logic, and mathematical concepts (group, throng, and grid). Since this intellectual structure accords with the principles of logic and epistemology, it is not only a biological structure but more importantly is a logical structure (computing schema). The neurophysiological basis of the predescribed visual prehension action is nerve pathway myelin sheath, which seems to be a product of genetic development. Natural maturity, which includes genetic factors, really plays an indispensable role in the sequence that the development of children's intelligence consistently follows. However, maturity does not play a decisive role in the schema development from infant to adult. The evolution of wisdom as a functional structure is the outcome of many factors. The whole development of intelligence structure during children's growth is not decided by the inherited program. The factor of inheritance mainly provides the probability for the development or approach for structure, and nothing will be evolved in structure until the probabilities are provided. However, between probability and reality, some other factors play a crucial role in changing the structure, such as practice, experience, and society.

We still need to point out that the structure of intelligence proposed by Piaget has three factors: integrity, conversion, and automatic adjustment. Integrity of structure refers to internal coherence while every part interacts with others by inherent laws in which every schema has its own law, and the sum of it all is not the children's intelligence structure. The conversion of structure shows that structure is not static but is developing with the effects of assimilating, adapting, and balance. Automatic adjustment of structure means self-adjustment based on the discipline of structure. It also means that the change of one component in the structure will result in changes of other components. Therefore a self-adjusting system must be viewed as a whole, then as a structure.

Assimilation and acclimation are terms Piaget used to describe the basic process of the development of children's intellectual schema. He believes that assimilation is a forming or formed structure that integrates external factors. In another words, taking the environment into consideration is aimed at enriching the main action, or, say, to obtaining new knowledge using existing knowledge. For example, an infant, who knows how to grab, will try to get a toy by grabbing repeatedly when he sees the toy on his bed. When he is alone and the toy is too far to get, this baby still tries to get it by grabbing. This action is acclimatization. In this case, the infant uses his old experience to meet the new situation (a toy far away from him). So we can see that acclimatization applies not only to an organism's life but also to actions from the explanations previously talked about. Acclimation is "the format and structure of assimilability [that] will change according to the influence of assimilated elements," that is, change the action of subject to adapt to objective changes or to improve the cognitive structure to deal with new problems. And let us suppose that that the baby accidentally gets that toy by drawing the sheet or something like that. This action is acclimation.

Piaget used assimilation and adaptation to explain the relationship between the main cognitive structure and the environmental stimulation. Acclimation makes the stimulation a part of the cognitive structure. A main body will respond to certain environment stimulations only when those stimulations are assimilated in its cognitive structure (schema). In other words, the assimilation structure makes the main body respond to stimulation. The story in acclimatization is quite different because the cognitive structure is changing rather than staying the same. Simply, the filter or change of input simulation is called assimilation, and the change of internal structure to adapt to reality is called adaptation. The balance between assimilation and acclimatization is the understanding of adaptation and the essence of human wisdom.

Assimilation does not change or improve the schema, but acclimation does. Piaget thinks assimilation plays an important role in the formation of intelligence structure. Structural changes due to adaptation, however, are formed during the procedure of assimilation through repeating and abstraction.

Mental operation, which is one of the main concepts of Piaget's theory, is internalized, reversible, conservational, and logical. So we can see four characteristics of operation or mental operation:

1. Psychological operation is a sort of psychological and internalized action. For example, pouring water out of a thermos bottle into a cup, we can see in this action a series of characteristics, which are explicit and can appeal directly to sense. However, as for adults and children of a certain age, there is no need to carry out this action but just imagine finishing it and predicting its result in the mind. This process of pouring water in psychology is the so-called "internalized action" or one of the factors in such actions that can be called operation. It is observed that this kind of operation is an internalized thought caused by external actions or an action directed by thoughts. The actions of a newborn baby, such as crying, sipping, gripping, and so on, are non-thought reflex that should not be treated as operation. In fact, because operation is based on some other conditions, the actions by children will never have such so-called operational actions until they reach a certain age.

2. Mental computing is an internal reversible action. This leads to the concept of reversibility, which can be explained by the process of pouring water. We can imagine pouring water into a glass from a thermos bottle. In fact, we can also imagine water in the glass returning to the thermos bottle, and this is the concept of reversibility, which is another factor that makes actions become operation. If a child has a reversible way of thinking, it can be considered that his wisdom of action has reached the level of computing.

3. Computing is an action that has the prerequisite of conservation. An action is not only internalized and reversible but also has the premise of conservation once it has the meaning of thinking. So-called conservation means that amounts, length, area, volume, weight, quality, etc. stay unchanged, although they present in different ways or different forms. For example, 100 ml water in big glass is still 100 ml after it is poured into a smaller glass. And weight does not change when a whole apple is chopped into four parts. Conservation of energy,

momentum conservation, and charge conservation in nature are concrete examples. When children can recognize conservation, that means their intelligence has developed and reached the level of computing. Conservation and reversibility are interrelated; they are two forms of expression of the same process. Reversibility means that the turn of a process can be forward direction or negative direction, while conservation means that the quantity in a process stays unchanged. If children's thoughts have the feature of reversibility or conservation, we can almost say that their thoughts have the quality of conservation or reversibility. Otherwise, neither of them would exist.

4. Operation is an action of logical structure. As previously mentioned, intelligence has its structurally named foundation-schema. As long as children's intelligence has developed into the level of computing, or, say, their intelligence structures have already been equipped with internalization, reversibility, and conservation, the structure begins to become the computing schema. Computing schema or computing exists in an organized operation system that is not separated. A single internalized action does not mean computing but just a simple instinctive representation. However, action is not separated and alone but, in fact, coordinated and organized. For example, in order to reach a certain goal, an ordinary person needs organic coordination of goal and action, and the structure is formed during the procedure of goal attainment. In the introduction of schema, we have mentioned that computing schema is a logical structure not just because the biologic basis of computing is not clear and is reasoned by people. The most important reason is that the view of structure conforms to the principle of logic and epistemology. Computing is a logical structure; therefore psychological computing is an action with logical structure.

Marked by operation, children's intelligence development stage can be divided into the preoperational stage and operational stage. The former includes the sensor motor stage and representative stage; the latter distinguishes the concrete operation stage and formal operation stage.

10.4.2 Stages of children's intelligence development

Jean Piaget proposes four distinct, increasingly sophisticated stages of mental representation that children pass through on their way to an adult level of intelligence [4]. These four stages have been found to have the following characteristics:

1. Even if the timing may vary, the sequence of the stages does not. The development of stages is universal to every child who experiences them in an unalterable order. The appearance of each specific stage depends on the level of intelligence rather than age. In order to show the various stages of the age range that may arise, Piaget used the approximate age in the concrete description of each stage. The average ages appearing in the stages are quite different because of the dissimilarities of social culture or education.

2. The unique cognitive structure of each stage determines the common characteristics of child behavior. When intelligence is developed to a certain stage, children can engage in various kinds of activities at the same level.

3. The development of cognitive structure is a process of continuous construction. Every stage is an extension of the previous stage, and it forms a new system after reorganizing the previous stage. So the structure of the former stage is the prerequisite of the latter one and is replaced by it.

10.4.2.1 Sensorimotor period (0−2 years old)

From birth to 2 years old is the sensorimotor stage. Not much reflective action can be found in children by this stage. In this stage, infants construct an understanding of the world by coordinating sensory experiences (such as seeing and hearing) with physical, motoric actions. And the cognitive structure of the action format is formed. Piaget divided the sensorimotor stage into six substages, from actions by newborn babies, such as crying, sucking, hearing, and seeing, to more organized and meaningful actions with the maturing of the brain and organisms at the end of this stage.

The first substage (practice of reflexive behaviors, birth−1 month): The newborn baby adapts to the new environment with innate unconditional reflexes, including the reflexes of sucking, swallowing, grasping, embracing, crying, seeing, and hearing. The development and coordination of these inherent reflexes lie in repeated practices and imply the functions of assimilation and accommodation. By observing how an infant sucks, Piaget discovered the development of and change in the sucking reflex. For example, if we give a breast-feeding infant a feeding bottle, the movement of the mouth between the sucking of the breast and the bottle is quite different. Since it is easier to suck the feeding bottle than the breast, sometimes the infant may refuse to suck the breast or become

upset once given the chance to suck the bottle. From this we can generalize the development of children's intelligence, that is, she is willing to
suck the labor-saving feeding bottle rather than the breast.

The second substage (formation of habits and perception, 1—4 months):
Based on the first substage, children connect their actions and make them
into new behavior through the integration of the organisms. As long as an
infant learns a new action, she will try to repeat it again and again, for
example, sucking the finger, grasping and opening up the hand constantly,
finding a sound source, and gazing at the movement of an object or a person. The repeating and modeling of behavior indicate its assimilation and
then forming behavior structure; what's more, the reflex is transformed to
intelligence. We don't call these activities intelligence because they are
aimless and determined only by perceptual stimulus. Accommodation,
however, has taken place in this phase, for all these actions are not as simple as reflex actions.

The third substage (formation of formation of, 4—9 months): From the
fourth month, infants begin to form a good coordination between the
movements of seeing and grasping. Then the infants become more object
oriented, moving beyond self-preoccupation and the influenced objects
leads to more subjective movements in turn. So a relation between action
and the outcome of it circulates, and then polarization between the
schemes and intentionality of actions emerges, and eventually the movements exerted for a special purpose come forth. For example, the shaking
of a rattle can attract the children's attention by its special sound.
Repeating this attraction, we find that infants will try to grasp or kick the
rattle once hung on the cradle. Obviously, children grow wisdom at this
stage as they begin to act purposefully rather than accidentally. But the
polarization of schemes and intentionality appearing in this phase are neither complete nor clear.

The forth substage (coordination of schemes and intentionality, 9—12
months): This stage can also be called the coordination of schemas. In this
phase, the schemes and intentionality of the infants begin to polarize, and
intelligence activities show up. This means that some of the schemas are
used as purpose and the rest as means, such as a child who pulls the adult's
hand to the toy that is out of his reach or demanding the adult to uncover
the cloth with the toy under it. This indicates that before the conducting
of these actions, the children already have intentions. The more practice
they get, the more flexible they are in operations of all kinds of action
models. Just as we use concepts to understand the world, infants use grasp,

push, pull, and other actions to get acquainted with their new world. With accommodation to the new environment, children are acting to become wiser. But, in this phase, creativity and innovative thinking have never been found.

The fifth substage (perceptual intelligence period, 12−18 months): According to Piaget, infants in this phase can manage to achieve their purposes by way of testing. When a child accidentally finds an interesting movement, he tries to make some change in repeating the previous action or to resolve a new problem for the first time through experiencing mistakes. For example, an infant who wants to catch the toy on the pillow out of his reach, without a parent around, has been trying but has failed. Accidentally, he grabs the pillow and eventually catches the toy with the movement of the pillow. Thereafter, he easily gets the toy on the pillow by way of pulling the pillow first. It is a big step in the development of the child's intelligence. However, it is not a way thought out by him but found accidentally.

The sixth substage (intelligence synthetic phase, 18−24 months): In this phase, an infant can not only find out but also "think out" some new ways with her body and external movements. What we describe as "thinking out" is resolving new problems by way of "inner connections"; for example, a child tries to get the strip in a matchbox even if it isn't opened big enough for him to take the strip out. She looks at the box over and over again or tries to put her finger into the open slit; if it is not useful, she stops the action and then gazes at it with her mouth open and shut. Suddenly, she opens the draw of the box and takes out the strip. In this process, the opening and shutting of her mouth is an indication of the internalized movement of the opening of the box because a child is not good at representation ability. The action can be "thought out" by the child if she sees the similar action conducted by a parent before. Infants develop the ability to use primitive symbols and form enduring mental representations, indicating that intelligence development is running toward a new stage.

The sensorimotor period marks the development of intelligence in three functions: First, with the development of infant language and memory, the consciousness of conservation gradually comes into being. The concrete manifestation of this is that, when there is something (parents or toys) in front of him, the child is conscious of it; vice versa, the child is still convinced of its existence even if it is not visible. Parents leave, and the child believes that they will appear again; toys disappear, and they should be found again somewhere in the drawer or under the sheet. These cases indicate that the format of the stable cognitive object is made up. According to recent studies, the permanent consciousness of the mother is related to the maternal and child attachment, so it appears earlier than any other consciousness. Second, with the construction of the permanent cognitive schema of the stable object, the spatiotemporal structure also attains a certain level. Before the child looks for an object, he must locate the object in space; then the continuity of time is constructed because the space location occurs following a certain sequence. Thirdly, the emergence of cause-and-effect cognition, the construction of permanent cognitive schema, and the level of spatiotemporal structure are inextricable linked. The original cause-and-effect cognition is the outcome of children's movements, the polarization of movements, and the relations among the objects caused by the movements. If a child can realize a special purpose (such as taking a toy by pulling the pillow) with a series of coordinated actions, that predicts the formation of cause-and-effect cognition.

10.4.2.2 Preoperational stage (2–7 years)

Compared with the sensorimotor stage, the preoperation stage undergoes a big qualitative change. In the sensorimotor stage, children only think of matters they can currently feel. In the middle and late phases of the stage, permanent awareness and early internalization have been formed. Until the preoperational stage, the awareness of permanence has been consolidated; moreover, the actions have become more internalized. With the rapid development and improvement of the linguistic ability, more and more symbolic expressions are used for external objects. In this stage, children are gradually liberated from concrete actions, paying attention to external activities, and processing "presensitive thought" by means of symbolic format. That's why it is called the presensitive thought stage. Internalization is of great significance in this new stage. To describe internalization, Piaget told us his personal experiences: Once, he took his 3-year-old daughter to visit one of his friends who had a 1-year-old little boy. As the boy played in the playpen, he fell to the ground and consequently cried aloud with anger. Piaget's daughter saw that with a surprise and muttered to herself. More importantly, three days later, his daughter mimicked the scene she saw three days prior. She tried to fall repeatedly and cackled since she was just experiencing the fun of the "game" that she had seen and never experienced. Piaget pointed out that the action of the little boy has been internalized into his daughter's mind.

In the process of presensitive thinking, children mainly use the symbolic function and vicarious function to internalize the objects and actions. Not as easy as accepting everything like photography or transcript, this internalization means the reconstruction of experienced sensual activities in the mind, neglecting some unrelated details (Piaget's daughter did not cry when she fell), and then the presentation comes into being. The internalized action is in the mind but is not carried out concretely. This nonphysical action boosts the development of children's intelligence.

The preoperational stage can be further broken down into the preconceptual stage and the intuitive stage.

10.4.2.2.1 Preconceptual stage (2–4 years)

The symbol of this stage is that children begin to use symbols. In games, for example, a wooden bench is treated as a car, a bamboo pole is considered a horse; so the wooden bench and bamboo pole are the symbols of the car and horse, respectively. In addition, there must be something in their mind that we call differentiation, connecting the objects with symbols. Piaget thinks it is the occurrence of cognition and the symbolic system.

Language is also a symbol produced by social activities and widely used in society. Children's symbolic thinking develops by creating presensitive symbols and mastering linguistic symbols. In this stage, the children's words are only the combination of linguistic symbols and words that are lack general conception. As a result, they can only conduct a special-special deduction, not a special-general one. It can be concluded by the mistakes often made by kids. For example, when they see a cow for the first time, they know that a cow is an animal with four legs. Or a child might say, "It is my hat" upon seeing someone wearing the same hat as hers. Also she will think there are two moons, since she saw it from the window of her room and then saw it outside when she walked on the road.

10.4.2.2.2 Intuitive stage (4–7 years)

The intuitive stage is a transition of children's intelligence from the preconceptual stage to the operational stage, and its typical characteristics are still the lacking of conservation and reversibility; however, it begins to transit from single-dimensional focus to two-dimensional focus.

Conservation is about to form, followed by mental operation, which can be proved by the following example: A father who took two bottles (of same size) of cola (same quantity) and was ready to give them to his 6- and 8-year-old children. At first, both kids knew that the quantities of cola in the two bottles are the same. Then the father poured the cola into three glasses (one bottle into a bigger glass and another into two smaller ones), and let the kids choose.

The 6-year-old kid first picked the bigger glass, hesitated, and then took the two smaller glasses. Not decided yet, he took the bigger glass at last and muttered, "This glass contains more." The kid made the last choice with hesitation. When waiting for the younger brother's decision, the older brother looked impatient and cried with a scorn voice, "Ah, dummy! They're the same amount. You'll find this if you try to pour them back." Then he demonstrated it. From this case, we can see the improvements and limitations of children's intelligence in this stage. Sometime in the past, he would have chosen the bigger glass without hesitation, which explains the lack of conservation and reversibility. He judges the quantity by the size of container. Now, however, his hesitation indicates that he starts to take notice both of the size and number of the glasses. His last choice reveals that conservation and reversibility are still not formed, while intuitive thinking is transiting from a single-dimensional focus to a two-dimensional focus. The hesitation shown in the process of picking a glass is the contradiction (or imbalance) of the children's inner world, that is, an imbalance of assimilation and accommodation. The present problem cannot be resolved by the existing cognitive schema (assimilative cognitive structure) when the new one does not exist. The situation of imbalance cannot last for long when the equalization factor takes effect and will develop toward balance, which is decided by the accommodation function. As a result, the preoperational cognitive structure is evolved to mental operation ones, which is symbolized by conservation and reversibility. The 8-year-old boy's cry and demonstration prove that.

To summarize, the characteristics of children's cognitive activities are as follows: (1) relative concreteness, that is, thinking lies in presentation, not operation; (2) lack of reversibility and conservation structure; (3) self-centeredness, that is, children have no realization of the thinking process and understanding the world occurs by reference of themselves, the specific one; the topic of their conversation is mostly on themselves; (4) stereotyping, which means, when thinking out a current problem, their attention can be neither distracted nor distributed, and they have no concept of rank when generalizing the nature of things.

Thinking at this stage is called semilogical thinking by Piaget, which shows great progress compared with that in the sensorimotor stage without logical and thinking.

10.4.2.3 Concrete operational stage (7–11 years)

This stage, which follows the preoperational stage, occurs between the ages of 7 and 11 years and is characterized by the appropriate use of internalized, reversible, conservative, and logical actions.

We say this operation is a concrete one because children begin thinking logically about concrete events but have difficulty understanding abstract or hypothetical concepts. For example, Edith's hair color is lighter than Susan's but darker than Liza's. When the question "Whose hair is the darkest" is asked, it is a difficult one for children in the concrete operational stage. However, we can take three dolls with black hair to different degrees, make a comparison between two of them, then raise the same question. This time, there is no difficulty for the children to give the answer: Susan's hair is the darkest.

The most important manifestation of children's intelligence development in this stage is the acquisition of the concepts of conservation and reversibility. The concept of conservation consists of the conservation of quality, weight, corresponding quantity, area, volume, and length. Children do not acquire these conservations at one time but gradually with the growth of age. In the years 7–8, the quality of conservation is acquired, then quantity in the years 9–10, followed volume conservation in the years 11–12. Piaget believes that the beginning of the concrete operational stage is the obtaining of quality conservation and is ended by the volume conservation, which is the beginning of the following stage.

The achievements of children's intelligence in this stage are as follows:

1. On the basis of the formation of reversibility, with the help of transitivity, children can sort objects in order according to size, shape, or any other characteristic. For example, if given sticks of different lengths, say, from the longest one to the shortest one in the order of A, B, C, D. Children will put them together and pick out the longest one and then the less longer one and so on. By doing this, they can sort out the length order (that is $A > B > C > D \ldots$) of the four sticks, even if they don't use algebraic signs to express their ideas.

2. The ability to name and identify sets of objects according to appearance, size, or other characteristic, including the idea that one set of

objects can include another. For example, they know the quantity of sparrows (A) is less than that of birds (B) and that birds are fewer than animals (C) and that animals are fewer than creatures (D). The ability to classify belongs to mental operation.

3. The ability to make correspondence (complementary or noncomplementary) of objects in different categories. The simple correspondence is one to one. For example, if the students are given a series of numbers, each student matches a number and vice versa. There are also some more complicated correspondences, such as duplicate correspondence and multiple ones. For example, a group of people can be divided by either complexion or nationality, and everyone in the group is duplicated correspondingly.

4. The weakening of egoism. In the stages of sensorimotor and preoperational, children are self-centered and take themselves as the reference when looking at the external world. The idea of taking their own inner world as the only existing psychological world that impedes them from looking at external things objectively. With the interactions of the external world, children's self-centeredness gradually fades away in this stage. There is a case studied by a scholar: two boys, one is 6-year old (preoperation stage) and another is 8-year old (specific operation stage), sit together against the wall in a room with four walls. The four sides of the wall are hung with different pictures (A, B, C, and D) with obvious differences. The pictures are photographed, and four photos (a、 b、 c、 d) are made. The two kids are required to look at the pictures first and then are presented the four photos. After that, they are asked which photo is the one hung on the wall they are leaning against. Both of them give the right answer after some hard thinking. Then, the two kids are asked, "If you lean against that wall, which picture will be the one opposite to that wall?" The answer of the 6-year-old boy is still the same (photo a), while the 8-year-old boy correctly gives the answer (photo c). To make the 6-year-old boy understand that correctly, the 8-year-old boy was asked to sit down opposite him. Then the researcher asked the younger boy, "What's the picture on his opposite wall?" However, the answer is the same (photo a) as before.

To generalize, children acquire the abilities of systematic logical thinking, which includes reversibility and conservation, categorization, seriation, and corresponding, grasping the concept of numbers in operational level, and the fading of self-centeredness.

10.4.2.4 Formal operational stage (12 ~ 15 years)

In the previous part, we have discussed that children have acquired the ability of thinking or operation with concrete objects but not those described in words. Children are incapable of making a correct judgment with only words, such as in the example of the hair color. However, when entering the stage of formal operation, children can resolve a problem only with words by reconstructing the object and its process through thinking and imagination. That is why children can give the answer without reference to dolls. The child who needs to draw a picture or use objects is still in the concrete operational stage, whereas children who can reason the answer in their heads are using formal operational thinking. And the ability to resolve problems with reconstructing objects and its process is what we call formal operation.

Besides words, children in this stage can also take conception or hypothesis as a premise and then deducing and drawing a conclusion. Therefore, formal operation is also called hypothetical priori operation. Hypothetical priori thinking is the basis of all formal operations including logic, math, and natural and social science, so it is an important measurement of children's IQ.

According to Piaget, children in the formal operational stage are able to do not only hypothetical priori thinking but also the "basic operations" needed in the fields of technology. Besides the operations in the concrete operational stage, "basic operations" also include the consideration of all possibilities, separated and controlling variables, eliminating outlying factors, observing the functional relations of variables, and organizing the related elements into an organic one.

Formal operational stage is the last period of children's intelligence development. Here we want to give a further explanation: (1) Not all children gain the ability of formal operation at the age of 12-plus. It was found by recent studies that in the United States, nearly half or more college students' IQs are still in the stage of concrete operation or between concrete operation and formal operation. (2) People's intelligence is still developing at the age of 15-plus. Overall, this is the stage in which formal operation can be substaged. Piaget thinks that the development of intelligence is influenced by many factors and that there is no inevitable relation between age and intelligence. So children who enter a stage (divided by age) but who are quite different in the development of their intelligence do not contradict Piaget's theory.

From these discussions, we can generalize that operational thinking structure of Piaget's genetic epistemology is the main one in cognitive or intellectual activities. Piaget indicates that operational structure is not only a biological one but also a logical structure. The basic character of operational thinking is conservation, meaning internalized and reversible actions, and it is realized by the realization of reversibility and reciprocity.

At present, the development of thinking of children and adolescents at home and abroad is generally divided into three stages: (1) intuitive action thinking, (2) concrete imaginable thinking, and (3) abstract logical thinking. It can be subdivided into primary logic thinking, practical logic thinking, and theoretical logic thinking.

The topic of cognition is complicated since each cognitive subject lives in a complex social relationship, which unavoidably restricts the appearance and development of cognition. So the limitation of Piaget's genetic epistemology is the failure of taking the study of children's intellectual development into social relations.

10.5 Intelligence development based on morphism category theory

In his later years, Jean Piaget tried to formalize intelligence development with new logical mathematical tools, so as to better explain the transition and transformation from one stage of intelligence development to the next, that is, the constructive characteristics of intelligence development. In *Morphism et Categories: Comparer et transformer* [5], Piaget points out that his theory is based on two coordinated mathematical tools: morphism and category. Morphism is a structure based on the relationship system between two sets, which have one or several common compensation rules just like the mathematical cluster. Category is a part of topological algebra.

10.5.1 Category theory

Category theory is a kind of mathematical theory dealing with the relationship between mathematical structure and structure in an abstract way [6]. It deals with mathematical concepts in an abstract way and forms them into a group of objects and morphisms. In 1945 S. Eilenberg and S. Maclane introduced category, functor, and natural transformation. These concepts first appeared in topology, especially in algebra topology, and played an important role in the process of homomorphism (with geometric intuition) into homology (axiomatic method). Category itself is also a mathematical structure. Functor connects every object of one category with the object of another category and connects every morphism of the first category with the morphism of the second category. A category C consists of two parts: object and morphism.

Morphism is a process abstraction that keeps the structure between two mathematical structures. In set theory, morphisms are functions; in group theory, they are group homomorphisms; in topology, they are continuous functions; in the scope of universal algebra, morphisms are usually homomorphisms.

Category C is defined as follows:

1. A family of objects $\text{ob}C$
2. Any pair of objects A, B corresponds to a set $C(A, B)$, whose elements are called morphisms, so that when $A \neq A'$ or $B \neq B'$, $C(A, B)$ and $C(A', B')$ do not intersect.

Composition meets the following conditions:

1. Compound law: If A, B, C, $\in \text{ob}C$, $f \in C(A, B)$, $g \in C(B, C)$, there is a unique $gf \in C(A, C)$, which is called the compound of f and g.
2. Law of union: If A, B, C, $D \in \text{ob}C$, $f \in C(A, B)$, $g \in C(B, C)$.
3. $h \in C(C, D)$, then $h(gf) = (hg)f$.
4. Unit morphism: For each object A, there is a morphism $1_A \in C(A, A)$, so that for any $f \in C(A, B)$ and $g \in C(C, A)$ there is $f1_A = f$, $1_A g = g$.

The definition of category has different expression forms in some documents. The definition of category in some documents does not require that all the morphisms between any two objects are a set. In category theory, the notation is as follows: The category is represented by fancy letters such as $\mathcal{D}$, $\mathcal{C}$, etc., the object in category is represented by capital English letters, and the morphism is represented by lowercase English letters or lowercase Greek letters. Let $\mathcal{C}$ be a category, and the whole morphism of $\mathcal{C}$ be recorded as Mor $\mathcal{C}$.

In the following list of category examples, only objects and morphisms are given:

- Set category: Set (in a given set theory model), whose object is set and morphism is mapping.
- Group category: Gp, whose object is group and morphism are group homomorphism. Similarly, there are the *Abel* group category $AbGp$, the ring category Rng, and the R module category Mod_R.
- Topological space category: Top, whose object is topological space, and morphism is continuous mapping. Similarly, there is the category of topological group $TopGp$, whose object is topological group, and morphism is the continuous group homomorphism.

The differentiable manifold is a category *Diff* whose object is smooth and mapped to morphism.

- Homotopy category: *Htop* of topological space, whose object is topological space, and morphism is the homotopy equivalent class of continuous mapping.
- The category of point topological space: *Top**, whose object is an ordered pair(X, x), where X is a nonempty topological space, $x \in X$, and morphism is a point preserving continuous mapping f: $(X, x) \rightarrow (Y, y)$ is called a point preserving continuous mapping if and only if (f: $X \rightarrow Y$ is a continuous mapping and satisfies $f(x) = y$).

10.5.2 Topos

In the early 1960s, Grothendieck used the Greek word *topos* to express the general framework of mathematical objects. He proposed the category sh(x), which is made up of all the sets of the valued sheaf in the topological space X, as a generalized topological space X, to study the cohomology in space X. He extended the concept of topology to a small category C, called a site (or Grothendieck topology).

Francis W. Lawvere studied the categories composed of Grothendieck Topos and the Boolean model, and finds that they all have the truth object D. In the summer of 1969, Lowell and Tierney decided to study the axiomatization of the sheaf theory. In the early 1970s, they found that a class wider than sheaf can be described by first-order logic, which is also a generalized set theory. They proposed the concept of elementary Topos [7]. In this way, the categories of Sh(X), Sh(C, J) and the Boolean model are primary Topos, but the latter includes other categories besides sheaf. Primary Topos has both geometric and logical properties. The core idea of Topos is to replace the traditional constant set with the continuous changing set, which provides a more effective basis for the study of variable structure.

Topos and primary Topos are categories that satisfy one of the following equivalent conditions:

1. Complete category with index and subobject classification
2. Subobject classification and its power object complete category
3. Cartesian closed category with equivalence class and subobject classification

10.5.3 Morphisms and categories

Piaget's new formalization theory basically gave up the theory of operation structure and replaced it with the theory of morphisms and categories. So the development series of traditional preoperation—concrete operation—formal operation has become the development series of intra-morphic—intermorphic-extramorphic [5].

The first stage is called the intramorphic level. Psychologically, it is just a simple correspondence, no combination. Common characteristics are based on correct or incorrect observation, especially on visible prediction. This is only a comparison of experience, depending on a simple state transition.

The second stage is called the intermorphic level, which marks the beginning of systematic combinatorial construction. The combinatorial construction of the intermorphic level is only local and gradual and, in the end, does not constitute a closed general system.

The last stage is the extramorphic level. The main body compares morphisms with the help of operation tools. And the operation tools are just to explain and summarize the content of the previous morphism.

10.6 Psychological logic

Mathematical logic originated from G. W. Leibniz. It diverged between Boolean and Frege, forming the so-called algebraic tradition of logic and the linguistic tradition of logic. In Turing machine theory, the Turing core expounds the two concepts of Automata and instruction table language, which fit Leibniz's conception of rational calculus and universal language. In the process of his research on the generation and development of children's thinking, Piaget discovered the structure of psychological operation, reformed classic mathematical logic, and created a new type of logic, psycological logic, which was used to describe the cognitive structure of children's different intelligence levels [8]. This logic includes two systems: concrete operation and formal operation. Concrete operations mainly include eight clusters of classes and relations, while formal operations include 16 propositional opera-tions and the INRC group structure. Piaget's psychological logic system updates our concept of logic and becomes the basis of solving the problem of logical epistemology. It uses logical structure to describe cognitive structure. In his later years, Piaget revised and developed his theory in a new way in a series of new works, such as logic toward meaning, morphism and category, possibility and necessity, and called it Piaget's new theory.

10.6.1 Combined system

Piaget thinks that when children's thinking can be separated from concrete things, the first result is to liberate the "relationship" and "classification"

Table 10.1 Sixteen types of truth value of binary compound.

(P,Q)	f₁	f₂	f₃	f₄	f₅	f₆	f₇	f₈	f₉	f₁₀	f₁₁	f₁₂	f₁₃	f₁₄	f₁₅	f₁₆
(1,1)	1	1	1	1	1	1	1	1	0	0	0	0	0	0	0	0
(1,0)	1	1	1	1	0	0	0	0	1	1	1	1	0	0	0	0
(0,1)	1	1	0	0	1	1	0	0	1	1	0	0	1	1	0	0
(0,0)	1	0	1	0	1	0	1	0	1	0	1	0	1	0	1	0

between things from their concrete or intuitive constraints, and the combination system enables children's to expand and strengthen. The so-called 16 kinds of binary propositions are generally called 16 types of truth value function terms that a compound proposition with two supporting propositions may have. Table 10.1 gives 16 types of truth value function terms of the binary compound proposition.

In general mathematical logic books, the four most basic binary true value forms of $p \vee q$, $p \rightarrow q$, $p \leftrightarrow q$, and $p \wedge q$, namely disjunction, implication, equivalence, and conjunction, are respectively used to express the four true value terms, f_2, f_5, f_7, f_8. Piaget also named the rest of the propositional functions: f_1 is $p \bullet q$ (completely positive), f_3 is $p \leftarrow q$ (anti-implication), f_4 is $p(q)$ (P's positive), f_9 is p/q $[\bar{p} \vee \bar{q}]$ (incompatible), f_{10} is PW (mutual anti exclusion), f_{11} is q $[\bar{p}]$ (q's negative), f_{12} is $p \cdot \bar{q}$ (nonimplication), f_{13} is $\bar{p}$ $[q]$ (P's negative), f_{10} is $q \cdot \bar{p}$ (non-anti-implication), f_{15} is (joint negation); non–disjunctive), and f_{16} are (0) completely negative. Piaget believes that they are embodied in the actual thinking of teenagers and constitute their cognitive structure.

10.6.2 INRC quaternion group structure

The INRC transformation group is another cognitive structure of formal thinking, which is closely related to proposition operation. Piaget takes two kinds of reversibility, inversion and mutual inversion, as axes, and forms four kinds of INRC transformation groups. Piaget tried to use it as a tool to clarify the thinking mechanism of reality, especially its reversible nature. It is one of the characteristics of Piaget's theory that the concept of reversibility runs through the development process of the analytical subject's wisdom.

The meaning of the INRC quaternion group is that any proposition has four corresponding transformation propositions, or it can be transformed into four different propositions. One of the transformations is to repeat the original proposition (I), which is called identity transformation. The other three transformations are the inversion transformation (N) based on inversion reversibility, the inversion transformation (R) based on mutual reversibility, and the mapping transformation (C) based on these two reversibilities. The four propositions generated by these four transformations (one of which is the original proposition) constitute a group about "transformation." Although there are only four propositions, that is, four elements, the relationship between them conforms to the four basic conditions of group structure. The synthesis of the two reversibilities in the quaternion transformation group is reflected in the transformation of the injectivity because injectivity is the inversion or inversion of the reciprocal, that is, $C = NR$ or $C = RN$.

Therefore, the essence of the quaternion transformation group is a kind of whole organization formed by the internal relations among operators (such as conjunction, disjunction, implication, etc.). Therefore, it is necessary to analyze the structure of the quaternion group from proposition. According to Piaget, the 16 binary propositions constitute four types of quaternion transformation groups:

Type A: Disjunction, conjunction negation, incompatibility, and conjunction constitute a type a quaternion group.

Type B: Implication, nonimplication, anti-implication, and non-anti-implication form a type B quaternion group.

Type C and type D are two special types. In type C, the original operation is the same as the reciprocal operation, and the inversion operation is the same as the opposite operation. Complete affirmation and complete negation, equivalence and mutual exclusion constitute two subtypes of type C. In the type D, the original operation is the same as the mapping operation, and the inversion operation is the same as the reciprocal operation. P's affirmation and P's negation, Q's affirmation and Q's negation constitute two subtypes of the type D.

The set of INRC has the following properties:

1. The combination of two elements in a set is still one element in the set (closeness).
2. Combination is combination.
3. Each element has an inverse operation.
4. There is a neutral element (I).
5. The combination is exchangeable.

10.7 Artificial system of intelligence development

With the development of computer science and technology, people try to make a further understanding of the biologic mechanism by the computer or other artificial systems and the use computer to replicate the phenomenon and behavior of nature and natural lives. In 1987 the new subject, artificial life, was established [9]. Artificial life is a simulation system or model system, which is constructed by the computer and precise machinery, shows natural life behavior, and reflects the process of organization and behavior. Its behavior characteristics and dynamics principle present as some basic properties, such as self-organize, self-repair, and self-replicate, which are formed by chaotic dynamics, environmental adaptability, and evolution [10].

Researching artificial life intelligence development will shed more and more light on human self-learning. The essential or the most intrinsic problem is that an artificial life system possesses the ability of learning like a human. This problem has proven difficult. Over the past several decades, scientists have taken four approaches.

1. Knowledge-based approach: An intelligent machine is directly programmed to perform a given task.
2. Behavior-based approach: The world model is replaced by the behavior model, and the intelligent programmers compile programming according to different layers of behavioral status and desired behavior. This is a hand-modeling and hand-programming method.
3. Genetic search approach: Robots have evolved through generations by the principle of survival of the fittest, mostly in a computer-simulated virtual world. Although notable, none of these is powerful enough to lead to machines having the complex, diverse, and highly integrated capabilities of an adult brain.
4. Learning-based approach: A computer is "spoon-fed" human-edited sensory data while the machine is controlled by a task-specific learning program. However, the process is nonautomatic, and the cost is high for training the system.

The traditional manual development paradigm can be described as follows: starting with a problem or task that is understood by a human engineer, then designing a task-specific representation, programming for the specific task using the representation, and finally running the "intelligent" program on the machine. If, during program execution, sensory data are used to modify the parameters of the predesigned task-specific representation, we say that this is machine learning. In this traditional paradigm, a machine cannot do anything beyond the predesigned representation. In fact, it does not even "know" what it is doing. All it does is ruled by the program.

The autonomous development paradigm is different from the traditional manual development paradigm [11], and it is described as follows: First, design a body according to the robot's ecological working conditions (e.g., on land or under water), then design a developmental program, and, finally, at "birth," the robot starts to run the developmental program. To develop its mind, humans mentally "raise" the developmental robot by interacting with it in real time. According to this paradigm, robots should be designed to go through a long period of autonomous mental development (AMD), and the essence of mental development is to enable robots to autonomously "live" in the world and to become smart on their own. In 2007 Juyang Weng proposed a biologically inspired system that is capable of AMD. The AMD is an agent, natural or artificial, that improves its mental capabilities through autonomous interactions with its environment. Six types of architecture are presented, beginning with the observation-driven Markov decision process as Type 1. From Type 1 to Type 6, the architecture progressively becomes more complete toward the necessary function of AMD.

Juyang Weng proposed the developmental network (DN) in 2018. Learning the DN can enable the accomplishment of grounded, emergent, natural, incremental, skulled, attentive, motivated, and abstractive tasks, so that a universal Turing machine GENISAMA is constructed [12]. Its learning from a teacher TM is one transition observation at a time, immediate, and error-free until all its neurons have been initialized by early observed teacher transitions.

For the agent to own the ability of self-learning, we introduced the self-learning mechanism, and Fig. 10.1 shows its structure [13], where AMD is the agent root, and the knowledge database, communication mechanism, inductor, and effecter are an absolutely necessary subassembly. Then the control main center is similar to the neural center of the brain, which can control and coordinate others and also displays the agent function. AMD is an intelligence agent's self-learning system, which embodies an ability of self-learning. The communication mechanism interacts with the agent's environment, which is a special inductor or effecter. The inductor is a sensory organ like the eye and ear and senses the environment around it. The effecter is another organ like the hand, feet, and mouth and finishes the tasks required by the agent. The agent enriches knowledge and improves itself by an automated animal-like learning algorithm and is reflected in the increasing module quantity and function. The knowledge database is a part of the memory of brain and stores the

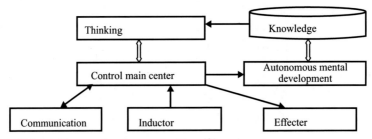

Figure 10.1 Intelligence development with self-learning.

information. How to store automatically is important for the intelligence developmental artificial system, and the key of AMS is to organize effectively and store automatically all kinds of information, for example, image, voice, text, and so on.

References

[1] H. Gardner, Frames of Mind: The Theory of Multiple Intelligences, Basic Books, 1983.
[2] M. Wertheimer, Laws of organization in perceptual forms. First published as Untersuchungen zur Lehre von der Gestalt II, in Psycologische Forschung, 4, 301-350. Translation published in Ellis, W. (1938), A Source Book of Gestalt Psychology, Routledge & Kegan Paul, London, 1923, pp. 71−88.
[3] J. Piaget, Structuralism, Harper & Row, New York, 1970.
[4] J. Piaget, Genetic Epistemology, Columbia UP, New York, 1968.
[5] J. Piaget, E. Ackerman-Valladao, G. Henriques, et al., Morphismes et Categories: Comparer et Transformer, Delachaux et Niestlé, Neuchatel, Suisse, 1990.
[6] M. Barr, C. Wells, Category Theory for Computing Science, Prentice-Hall, Inc, 1990.
[7] P.T. Johnstone, Topos Theory, Academic Press, London, 1977.
[8] J. Piaget, Logic and Psychology, Manchester University Press, Manchester, 1953.
[9] C. Langton (Ed.), Artificial Life, vol 1., Addison-Wesley, MA, 1987.
[10] Z.Z. Shi, C.H. Mo, Artificial life, J. Comput Res. Dev. 32 (12) (1995) 1−9.
[11] J.Y. Weng, Autonomous mental development by robots and animals, Science 291 (5504) (2001) 599−600. Issue of 26 Jan.
[12] J.Y. Weng, A model for auto-programming for general purposes, (2018) arXiv:1810.05764 [cs. AI].
[13] Z.Z. Shi, Jun Shi, J.H. Zheng, Study on intelligence in artificial life, in: Xuyan Tu, Yixin Yin (Eds.), Artificial Life and Applications, Beijing University of Posts and Telecommunications Press, 2004, pp. 27−32.

CHAPTER 11

Emotion intelligence

People's live in society. People's cognition is the result not only from cognitive ability but also from the integrated effect of multiple factors, such as affect, emotion, will, personality, etc. So in the research of artificial intelligence, should human advanced ability be simulated to the utmost extent, it must also take account of the effect of affect. Machine intelligence will be able to recognize human emotion and express effect itself only if it has affective ability. In this way we can make human−computer interaction more effective. Emotion is a multielement combinational, multidimensional, structured, multilevel, integrated mental activity process, and a psychological motive power that interacts with cognition in order to adapt the organism's survival and effective human communication.

11.1 Introduction

Subjective experience, such as joy or sadness, happiness or pain, love or hate, will occur when mankind cognizes external things. The attitude experience and corresponding reaction toward objective things is defined as emotion and affect.

In general, emotion is considered to contain three aspects, and most emotion researchers give the definition of emotion according to those three aspects: subjective experience on the cognitional aspect, physiological arousal on the physiological aspect, and external behavior on the expressional aspect. These three aspects interact when emotion occurs and thus form a complete emotional experience course.

The subjective experience is a person's self-awareness, that is, a kind of feeling state of the brain. People have many kinds of subjective experience, such as joy, anger, sadness, happiness, love, fear, hate, etc. Attitudes toward different things will produce different feelings. Certain attitudes occur toward certain things that may be oneself, other people, or objective things. These attitudes could be sympathy for the misfortune of a friend, hate for the fierceness of the enemy, happiness for success in undertaking or sadness for failing on an examination. This subjective experience could be felt just by one's own

Intelligence Science
DOI: https://doi.org/10.1016/B978-0-323-85380-4.00011-7

heart; for instance, that I know, "I am very happy," I feel, "I am very sad," I realize, "I am very guilty," and so on.

Physiological arousal is a kind of physiological reaction arising from emotion and affect. It relates to many neural elements, such as brainstem, central gray, thalamus, amygdala, hypothalamus, locus coeruleus, pineal, and prefrontal cortex, which are in central nervous system and also include the peripheral nervous system, endocrine gland, and exocrine gland. Physiological arousal is a physiological activation level. The physiological reaction model aroused by different emotions and affections is different too. Cardiac rhythm is regular when people are satisfied or happy. But cardiac rhythm accelerates and blood pressure becomes elevated when people are in a mood of fear or fury; at the same time, respiratory rate increases and even becomes intermittent or paused. In a similar way, vascular volume is reduced when people are in pain. Physiological indexes such as pause rate, muscle tensility, blood pressure, and blood velocity are representative of inner physiological reactions. They always change with emotion.

External behavior appears when people are in a mood. This is emotional expression cause. For example, one will cry bitter tears when sad, flourish when excited, laugh a hearty laugh when happy, etc. These body gestures and facial expressions are emotional external behaviors. People always judge and deduce one's emotion by these indexes. But sometimes external behavior and subjective experience are inconsistent because of the complexity of people's psychology. For instance, a person who is very nervous when addressing big audiences must pretend to be perfectly calm and collected.

Subjective experience, physiological arousal, and external behavior are the three necessary aspects of emotion. None of them can be dispensed with when estimating one's emotion. An emotional process is complete only if these three parts exist and at play at the same time. For example, when someone pretends to be angry, only external behavior is presented, but the authentic subjective experience and physiological arousal are lost, so it is not a complete emotional process. So any emotion must have these three aspects, and these aspects must be consistent; if not, the emotion cannot be identified. When we research and give the definition of emotion, that is the rub.

In real life, emotion and affect are well connected, but there are some differences between them.

11.1.1 Difference lies in requirement

Emotion refers chiefly to the attitude experience, which relates to material requirement and spirit requirement. For example, one is happy when his requirement of thirst is satisfied, one is scared when her safety is under threat; these are both emotional reactions, whereas affect relates mainly to people's spirit or social demand. For instance, a sense of friendship is due to the meeting of our communication demand, the sense of achievement comes from one's success. The sense of friendship and sense of achievement are both affect.

11.1.2 Difference lies in occurrence time

In terms of development, emotion happens before affect. One could have an emotional reaction at birth but cannot have affect. Emotion belongs to both humans and animals, but affect is characteristic only of humans. Affect develops with one's growth. One could not have a sense of moral, a sense of achievement, and a sense of beauty at birth. These affect reactions are forming along with children's socialization process.

11.1.3 Difference lies in reaction characteristics

Emotion and affect are different in reaction characteristics. Emotion has the trait of irritability, temporality, superficiality, and explicitness. We are very fearful when we encounter danger. But the feeling disappears when the danger is past, whereas affect has the trait of stability, persistence, profundity, and implicitness. For example, most people do not change their national self-respect whatever the frustration they meet. Elders' warm expectations and deep love for their next generation reflect the trait of profundity and implicitness of affect.

Emotion and affect are different, but they are relevant to each other. They are always interdependent and blend with each other. Stable affect is form based on emotion and is expressed by emotional reaction. So there will be no affect without emotion. The change of emotion reflects the deepness of affect. The changing process of emotion is filled with affect.

Humans have four basic emotions: joy, anger, fear, and sadness. Joy is a satisfied experience when people pursue and achieve the goal. It is a positive emotion with hedonic tone. It has high hedonic dimension and certain dimension. It can make one have a sense of transcendence, freedom, and acceptance. Anger is a kind of disturbed experience that occurs when one cannot achieve a goal. One gets angry suddenly when realizing that something is unreasonable or vicious. Fear is a kind of experience that occurs when one tries to escape from danger. Lack of the ability and the means to deal with danger are the main cause for anger arousal. Sadness is a kind of experience that occurs when one has lost love or has failed to satisfy a desire and expectation. The degree of experience depends on the importance and value of object, desire, or wish.

Many complex emotions such as disgust, shame, regret, envy, favor, compassion, etc., can derive from the four basic emotions.

11.2 Emotion theory

11.2.1 James-Lange's theory of emotion

The 19th-century American psychologist William James and the Danish physiologist Carl Lange respectively put forward a similar theory of emotion in 1884 and 1885. The theory is based on the direct connection of emotional state and physiological changes and proposed that emotion is the perception that is the sum of the feeling of a variety of body organs in the body. James thinks that when we perceive the object that we moved, our physical immediately changes. When these changes occur, we feel emotional changes. Langer thinks that any role in a wide range of blood vessels can cause nerve system changes, and then there will be emotional expression. The James—Lange's theory of emotions emphasizes physiological changes in the role of emotions. This theory has historical significance, but it is one-sided and exaggerates the impact role of external environment change and neglects the leading role of the central nervous system in emotions.

11.2.2 Cognitive theory of emotion

The cognitive theory of emotion is a theory in psychology claiming that emotion comes from the evaluation of stimulus situations or things. The attribution theory of emotion proposed by U.S. psychologists S. Schachter and J. E. Singer holds that emotion is determined by two main factors, physiological arousal and cognitive factors. In 1962 Schachter and Singer's experiment studied the cognitive and physiological determinants of the emotional state [1]. Experimental results support Schachter and Singer's implicit assumptions (1) that the anger and euphoria conditions are not inherently emotional and (2) that the confederate's mood is perceived by subjects in the intended manner.

In 1970, S. Schachter proposed three factors of emotion [2]. He asserted that emotion is not simply a decision in reaction to external stimulus and the body's internal physiological changes and that the attributes of the emerging emotion stimulate the factors: physiological factors and cognitive factors. In his view, cognitive factors play an important role in the context of current estimates and past experience in the formation of emotional memories. For example, a person once faced a dangerous situation but safely got past it; when he experiences such a danger again, the memories from the past experience makes him at ease. In other words, when the real-life experience is the same with the model established in the past, he believes it can be deal with; there is no obvious emotional reaction; when real-life is inconsistent with expectations and people feel unable to cope, tension results. This theory emphasizes human's regulation in the process of cognitive.

11.2.3 Basic emotions theory

Basic emotions theory thinks that there are a number of basic prototype forms of pan-human emotions and that each type has its own unique characteristics of experience, physical wake-up mode, and explicit mode, the combination of different forms compose all human emotions. At this point in individual development, the emergence of the basic emotional maturity is the result of natural organisms rather than learned. In biological evolution, the prototype of emotion is a product of adaptation and evolution but also a means of adaptation and evolution; from ape to human, from the ancient cortex cortical to the new cortex cortical, the division of facial muscle system and distribution of facial blood vessels, as well as the occurrence and differentiation of emotional are simultaneously carried out. The most mentioned is aversion, anger, happiness, sadness, fear, and so on, which are the basic emotions for different views.

The most famous study that supports the basic theory of emotion is the response to facial expressions and movement carried out by Ekman [3] and Izard [4]. Ekman requested students to consider themselves characters in some story and, as much as possible, to show the facial expressions of the characters. At the same time, researchers video-recorded their facial expressions. Finally, they required students to look at their faces and asked to identify the states. As a result, American students identified four types of expression (happiness, anger, disgust, sadness) from the six. Meng Shaoran's experiment also proved that the standardized basic emotional expressions of Chinese infants and md of the Western model is the same; Similarly, Chinese adults and Chinese infants are the same in emotional expression of the basic model, and the socialization of the adult face retains the basic expression model. Levenson and other young people, in a test west of Sumatra, guided people to move their facial muscles in order to be outside the marked basic emotions and took a series of physiological measurements; finally, they compared the results of the measurements with U.S. college students' results and found that the autonomic nervous physiological responses of the system model associated with the underlying sentiment had great cross-cultural consistency. Such results tend to confirm that the basic emotions exist specifically in a pan-human physical wake-up mode.

The main objections to basic emotions theory are:

1. Notwithstanding that these experiments confirmed the pancultural patterns of emotion, the study has also shown some cross-cultural differences.
2. Studies in psychology and linguistics have found that the basic meaning of emotional words has a significant difference between different languages.
3. There is not sufficient evidence to prove that the basic emotions have different neurophysiologic mechanisms.
4. The basis of recognition of facial expression may not be the basic type of emotions but may be the location of bipolar dimensions of facial expressions in the emotional experience, or acts in preparatory mode induced by facial expression.

11.2.4 Dimension theory

Dimension theory thinks that several dimensions can construct all human emotions; the distance in dimensionality space presents the similarities and dissimilarities among the different emotions. They take emotion as a gradual and calm change. In the last two decades, dimension approach has been favored by many researchers, but there is also a lot of debate about which dimensions to adopt. The most widely accepted model consists of the following dimensions composed of two-dimensional space:

1. Valence, or hedonic tone: Its theory is based on the separation of positive and negative emotional activation.
2. Arousal or activation: This refers to the degree of activation energy associated with emotional states, and the function of wake-up is a call to mobilize the body's functions, so as to prepare for action.

At present we have a tendency to make the activate dimensions linking with the integrated wake-up call or the intensity of the emotional experience. In the early 1970s, because of the impact of information processing theory, Mandle put forward that the autonomic wake-up of perception decides the intensity of emotional experience and that cognitive evaluation decides the nature of emotional, which, when integrated, rises to awareness, resulting in emotional experience. The International Affective Picture System reflects two-dimensional space. In two-dimensional-coordinate space with pleasant and wake-up degrees, the average assessed value of tested objects for emotional pictures showed a regular distribution. The different views of the dimension approach areas follow:

1. The evaluation of emotional has individual differences, with some people reporting and experiencing emotion in the way of dimension and others experiencing and reporting emotion more in accord with the theory of basic emotions.
2. Although some research has shown hemispheric differences in positive and negative emotions, there are also some studies that did not come up with similar results. Tor D. Wager comprehensively analyzed 65 different brain imaging studies from 1992 to February 2002, and the conclusion was that there is no adequate and consistent experimental evidence to support the positive and negative emotional differences in the hemispheres; the analysis also thinks that hemispheric differences in emotional activities are very complex and largely have regional specificity.
3. There is evidence that activation dimension and strength of experience are not completely related.

11.2.5 Emotional semantic network theory

The main characteristics of the semantic network theory proposed by Bauer and his assistants are shown in Fig. 11.1, which can be summarized in the following six hypotheses:

1. Emotion is a unit or node in the semantic network, which has many connections with related concepts, physiological systems, events, muscles, and expression patterns.
2. Emotional materials are stored in semantic networks in the form of propositions or propositions.
3. Thinking is generated by activating nodes in semantic networks.
4. Nodes can be activated by external or internal stimuli.
5. The activated node spreads activation to other nodes connected with it. This assumption is quite critical because it means that the activation of an emotional node (such as sadness) causes the activation of

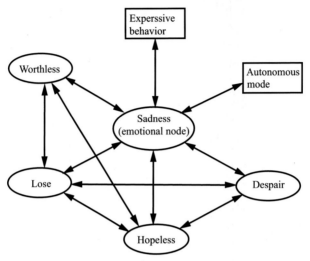

Figure 11.1 Emotional semantic network.

emotion-related nodes or concepts (such as loss and despair) in the semantic network.

6. Consciousness means that the total activation amount of all activated nodes in the network exceeds a certain threshold value.

Bauer's semantic network theory is too simple. In this theory, emotions or mood and cognitive concepts are represented as nodes in semantic networks. However, mood and cognition are actually quite different. For example, mood changes slowly in terms of intensity, while cognition is often all or nothing, often changing rapidly from one cognitive process to another.

11.2.6 Beck's schema theory

A. T. Beck put forward a schema theory [5], whose core content is that some people have higher vulnerability than others and that they are prone to develop depression or anxiety disorders. This predisposition depends on some schemata or organized knowledge structure formed by individuals in their early life experience. A. T. Beck and D. A. Clark's hypothesis schema can affect most cognitive processes, such as attention, perception, learning, and information extraction. Schemata can cause processing bias, that is, the processing of schema-consistent or emotionally consistent information is more popular. Thus individuals with anxiety-related schemata should choose to process threatening information, while those with depression-related schemata choose to process negative emotional information. Although A. T. Beck and D. A. Clark emphasized the effect of schemata on processing bias, they believed that schemata can be activated and affect processing only when individuals are in a state of anxiety or depression.

Beck's schema theory was originally designed to provide a theoretical framework for understanding clinical anxiety and depression. However, the theory can also be applied to personality research. Some individuals have schemata that make them show clinical symptoms of anxiety or depression. This point of view is valuable. However, it is difficult to prove that the schema is the cause of anxiety disorder or depression. There are some defects in this method:

1. The core theoretical framework of schema is vague, which is often just a belief.
2. The evidence of the existence of a particular schema is often based on a circular argument. In anxiety patients, behavioral data about cognitive biases are used to deduce the existence of schemata, and then these schemata are used to explain the observed cognitive biases. In other words, there is usually no direct or independent evidence to prove the existence of schema.

11.3 Emotional model

With the introduction of emotion computing technology, machines can observe, understand, and express all kinds of emotional characteristics like human beings and can have emotional communication with human beings in interaction, so that human beings can communicate with machines more naturally, cordially, and vividly, and people can have a sense of dependence. Therefore emotion computing and its application in human—computer interaction will be an important research direction in the field of artificial intelligence.

Emotion modeling is an important process of emotion computing, which is the key of emotion recognition, emotion expression, and human—computer Emotion interaction. Its significance lies in that it can describe and understand the connotation of emotion more intuitively by establishing the mathematical model of emotion state.

11.3.1 Mathematical model

A mathematical model is a kind of simulation, which is an abstract and concise depiction of the essential attributes of the actual subject using mathematical symbols, mathematical formulas, programs, graphs, etc. It can explain some objective phenomena, predict a future developmental law, or provide the best or good enough strategy for controlling the development of a phenomenon.

The philosophical nature of emotion is a subjective reflection of the value relationship of things. The relationship between emotion and value is essentially the relationship between subjective and objective. It can also be said that the logical process of human emotional activities is basically the same as that of general cognitive activities, the main difference being that they reflect different objects. The objects reflected by general cognitive activities are the fact relations of things, while the objects reflected by emotional activities are the value relations of things.

The objective purpose of values is to identify the value rate of things, which is the subjective reflection of the value rate of things. Under the guidance of values, people can choose different things differently.

According to the value rate of all activities of the subject and the corresponding scale of action, we can find a weighted average value rate, which is called the median value rate or average value rate of the subject, expressed by P_o.

The difference between the value rate P of the thing and the median value rate P_o of the subject is called the high difference between the value rate of the thing, expressed by ΔP:

$$\Delta P = P - P_o \qquad (11.1)$$

The high difference of the value rate of things is a very important value characteristic parameter, which fundamentally determines people's basic "position, attitude, principle and behavior orientation" to things and which determines people's value investment way and scale to the things. So it will inevitably reflect people's minds and form a specific subjective consciousness emotion.

The subjective reflection value produced by the high difference ΔP of the value rate of people to things is defined as the emotion of people to the things, expressed in μ.

The logical process of emotion occurrence is as follows: When the height difference of the value rate of things is greater than zero, people usually produce positive emotions, such as satisfaction, happiness, trust, etc. When the height difference of the value rate of things is less than zero, people usually have negative emotions, such as disappointment, pain, concern, etc. When the high difference of the value rate of things is equal to zero, people usually do not produce emotions, thus maintaining the original scale of action of things. The intensity of emotion is not in direct proportion to the difference of value rate of things but is in exponential function:

$$\mu = Km \log(1 + \Delta P) \qquad (11.2)$$

where Km is the emotional intensity coefficient. The objective purpose of the biological or physiological laws is that, when the emotional intensity is small, the emotional intensity is directly proportional to the high difference of the value rate, and people's emotion can accurately and small-scale perceive the change information of the price value rate; when the emotional intensity is large, the emotional intensity is logarithmic to the high difference of the value rate In direct proportion, people can get the change information of the value rate of things in a rough and wide range.

The mathematical vector of human emotion for all things is called the emotion vector, which is expressed by M:

$$M = \{\mu_1, \mu_2, \ldots, \mu_n\} \qquad (11.3)$$

where μ_i refers to people's feelings for the thing i. Some abstract things are composed of many concrete things; then the emotion of abstract things can be described by the emotion vector composed of the emotion of many concrete things.

At this time, the emotion of abstract things can be described by a two-dimensional emotion matrix:

$$M = \{\mu_{i \times j}\}_{m \times n} \qquad (11.4)$$

Similarly, the n-dimensional emotion matrix can be defined.

11.3.2 Cognitive model

In 1988 A. Ortony, G. L. Clore, and A. Collins constructed a cognitive model of emotion OCC [6], which is shown in Fig. 11.2. OCC is the first model developed for the purpose of computer implementation. They hypothesized that emotions are the result of a cognitive process called evaluation. Evaluation depends on three components: event, subject, and object. Events in the objective world are evaluated as satisfied or dissatisfied according to the objective of the subject; the behaviors of the subject or other subjects are evaluated as approved or disapproved according to a set of criteria; the objects are evaluated as liked or disliked according to the attitude of the subject.

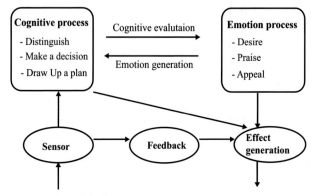

Figure 11.2 Cognitive model of emotion.

The OCC model does not use the basic emotion set or a clear multi-dimensional space to express emotion but to express emotion with consistently cognitive-derived conditions. Especially, in this model, it is assumed that emotion is a (positive or negative) response to events (happy or not), agents (satisfied or not), and objects (liked or not). Through the deduction and induction of different cognitive conditions, about 22 kinds of emotion types are standardized, including the basic construction rules used to produce these emotion types. It should be said that OCC is the first cognitive emotion generation model that is easy to be realized by computer.

11.3.3 Emotion model based on Markov decision process

The Markov decision process (MDP) is a mathematical model of sequential decisions and a dynamic optimization method. A MDP consists of the following five elements:

$$\{T, S, A, p, r\}$$

where
1. T is all decision time sets.
2. S is a set of countable nonempty states, which is a set of all possible states of the system.
3. A is a set of all possible decision-making behaviors when the system is in a given state.
4. p indicates the probability of moving to state j when the system is in state $i \in S$ and the decision-making behavior $a \in A(i)$ is taken.

$$\sum_{j \in S} p(j|i, a) = 1 \qquad (11.5)$$

5. $r = r \, (i, \, a)$ is called a reward function, which represents the expected reward obtained when the system is in a state $i \in S$ at any time and adopts a decision-making behavior $a \in A(i)$.

The strategy π expresses that, in every state, we should adopt a certain action. In the Markov decision-making process, the transition probability and reward only depend on the current state and the action chosen by the decision maker but have nothing to do with past situations.

11.4 Emotional quotient

Emotional quotient (EQ) mainly refers to people's qualities in emotion, will, tolerance of setbacks, etc. It is a concept that psychologists put forward in recent years, corresponding to IQ. Defined at the simplest level, the foundation for improving EQ is to cultivate self-awareness, so as to enhance the ability to understand and express oneself.

In 1988 Rcufen Bar-0n, an Israeli psychologist, was the first to use the term EQ and developed the world's first standardized emotional intelligence scale. In 1990 American psychologists Peter Saloway and John Mayer reinterpreted the concept of EQ. In 1995 psychologist Daniel Goleman of Harvard University published the book Emotional Quotient, which was ranked as the best-selling book in the world, setting off a wave of EQ craze in the world and taking EQ out of the academic circles of psychology and into people's daily lives.

Daniel Goleman accepted P. Saloway's view that EQ consists of five main aspects:

1. Know yourself: Monitor the changes of emotions all the time, be able to detect the emergence of certain emotions, and observe and examine your own inner world experience, which is the core of emotional intelligence. Only by knowing yourself can you become the master of your life.

2. Self-management: Regulate your own emotions so that they can be properly expressed, that is to say, regulate oneself.

3. Self-motivation: Mobilize and command emotions according to certain goals of activities, which can make people walk out of the low tides of life and start anew.

4. Recognize others' emotions: Feel others' needs and desires sensitively through subtle social signals; this is the basis of recognizing others' emotions, which is normal communication with others and realizing smooth communication.

5. Dealing with interpersonal relationships: Regulate emotional reactions between yourself and others.

The relationship between EQ and IQ is as follows:

1. EQ is an independent concept compared with IQ.
2. EQ mainly refers to people's ability in emotion cognition, emotion management, frustration tolerance, interpersonal communication, and the like.
3. EQ and IQ complement each other and influence each other.
4. EQ is a kind of ability, mainly acquired, that can be greatly improved under the guidance of people.
5. EQ team power can be used to promote and achieve significant results in practice.

The concept and theory of EQ play a positive role. It should be noted that the problem of intelligence is extraordinarily complex. The concept of EQ analyzes the essence of intelligence from emotional process, which provides a new perspective and analytical approach for people to find or approach the essence of intelligence. It provides a theoretical basis for the reform of intelligence theory from a new angle. In the analysis of EQ, the theory highlights the role of emotion monitoring and management and regulation in intellectual activities. In the elaboration of interpersonal relationships, a large number of humanistic psychological views are incorporated, which is conducive to children's emotional development and emotional education. It began to involve the influence of social and cultural factors on intelligence, beyond the scope of traditional intelligence theory but also beyond the scope of intelligence theory based on cognitive process analysis, greatly enriching the connotation of intelligence. However, when we accept this new view, it is necessary to clearly see its limitations and have a correct view of the concept and of the concept of emotional intelligence.

11.5 Affective computing

Scientific research shows that affect is a part of intelligence rather than a separation between affect and intelligence, and therefore the field of artificial intelligence may be the next breakthrough in empowering the affective capacity of computers. Affective capacity is essentially important for natural interaction between humans and computers. Traditional human—computer interaction has been primarily through the keyboard, mouse, screen, etc. and only in the pursuit of convenience and accuracy. All of that cannot understand or adapt to one's mood or state of mind. But how can the machine realize intelligence without affect? It is difficult to count on the same computer engaging with similarly intelligent people, and we can hardly expect the human–computer interaction to realize harmony with nature. Because human communication and exchange are natural and full of feelings, so in the course of human–computer interaction, it is natural to expect the same affective capacity from computers. Affective computing endows the computer with the ability to observe, understand, and generate various emotional features that are similar to those of human beings, so that the computer can interact naturally, cordially, and vividly like human beings.

The in-depth study of human affect has been going on since as early as the late 19th century. However, aside from science fiction, in the past, very few people linked "feelings" with the machine. So if the computer from the MIT University in the United States has affective ability, as Minsky put forward in 1985, the question is not whether intelligent machines have any "feelings" but rather how intelligent machines cannot be affective Minsky [7]. Since then, giving affective capacity to the computer and letting the computer understand and express feelings has cause great interest in the computer industry. The MIT Media Lab Professor Picard defined affective computing as being about the feelings, emotions, and impact of emotions arising from the calculation of a million surfaces [8]. Letting the machine (the computer) also have "feelings" in order to extract the signal from perceived emotional characteristics and the analysis of a variety of emotional and perceptual signals related to the international community, in recent years, is just emerging as a research direction.

Affective computing is the focus of study through a variety of sensors to obtain a person's feelings caused by physiological and behavioral characteristics of a signal in order to establish a "model of affect" and to create the capacity of awareness, recognition, and understanding of human affect and feelings that personal computing systems can do for a smart, sensitive, and friendly response to users, thus shortening the distance between the machine and creating a truly harmonious man-machine environment.

Affective computing is a highly integrated technology-based field [9], whose main research contents include:

1. Mechanism of affection: This is about affective determinate and the relationship between physiology and behavior, which is related to psychology, physiology, cognitive science, etc., in order to provide a theoretical basis for affective computing. Research on human affection is a very old topic; psychologists and physiologists have been doing a lot of work in this regard. Any kind of affective state may be accompanied

by several physiological or behavioral characteristics of the change, and some affective or behavioral characteristics may also be due to a number of emotional states. Therefore, determining the state of affective and physiological or behavioral characteristics is a fundamental premise of the theories of affective computing. This relationship is not very clear and needs further exploration and research.

2. Affective signals acquisition: This research develops various kinds of effective sensors. It is most important in affective computing because, if there are no effective sensors, there can be no study of affective computing because all the studies are based on signals received from sensors. Various types of sensors should have the following basic features: The use of the process should not affect the user (such as weight, volume, pressure, etc.); they should be subject to medical tests without injury to the user; data privacy, security, and reliability; low cost; and easy to manufacture. MIT Media Lab developed the first such sensor and has developed a variety of sensors, such as the pulse pressure sensor, current sensor skin, and sweat and muscle current sensors. Skin current sensors can do real-time measurement of the conductivity coefficient of the skin, through measurable changes in the electrical conductivity coefficient of the user's level of tension. The time monitoring of the pulse pressure sensor can be changed by the cardiac pulse pressure caused by changes. The sweat sensor is a band that can be scalable through the time monitoring of changes in the relationship between respiration and sweat. The muscle current sensor can measure voltage value along with the time of the week.

3. Affective signal analysis, modeling, and recognition: After the sensors respond from all kinds of effective access to the emotional signals, the next task is the gather the affective signals and aspects of the mechanism of corresponding counterparts and then to construct the signal modeling and identification. Because the affective state is an unobservable quantity hidden in multiple physiological and behavioral characteristics, it is not easy to model. Some can use a mathematical model, such as the hidden Markov model or Bayesian network model. The MIT Media Lab uses a hidden Markov model based on changes in the probability of human affection in order to draw the appropriate inferences for the affection; how to measure the depth of artificial affection and intensity, the qualitative and quantitative measures of the theoretical model of affection, the indicator system, the calculation methods, and measurement techniques.

4. Affective understanding: Through affective acquisition, analysis, and identification, the computer is able to understand the affective state. The ultimate goal of affective computing is to have an appropriate response, then adapt to changing user affection on the basis of users' understanding the emotional states. Therefore this part of the main study is about how the identification of affective information is in accordance with the results of changes in the user's emotional response in the most appropriate way. Within the affective understanding and application of the model, we should note the following: Affective signal tracking should be real-time and keep a certain time record; affective expression is based on the current affective state and is timely. The affective model is for personal life and can be edited in a specific state; The recognition pattern is adjusted by understanding the situation feedback.

5. Affective expression: Previous research infers affective states from physiological or behavioral characteristics. Affective expression is to study its anti-process; that is, given a particular affective state, research on how to make this affective state is reflected in one or more physical or behavioral characteristics—for example, how to reflect the speech synthesis and synthesis of facial expressions—gives the machinery emotion, and users can exchange feelings. The expression of affective feelings provides the possibility of interaction and exchange; for a single user, affective exchanges include man and man, man and machine, man and nature, and human interaction in their own exchange.

6. Affect generation: On the basis of affective expression, further study might be on how the computer or robot can simulate or generate emotional patterns, how to develop a virtual or physical or affective robot with artificial affection, and applications of computer equipment to generate emotion theory, methods, and techniques.

So far, research has made progress in facial expression, gesture analysis, speech recognition, and expression of emotion. Next we give examples to illustrate.

11.5.1 Facial expressions

In life, it is difficult to maintain a rigid facial expression. Facial expressions reflect common sentiments in a natural way. The affective performance of the region includes the mouth, cheeks, eyes, eyebrows, forehead, and so on. In the expression of affection, just a slight change of local facial features (e.g., wrinkled eyebrows) can reflect a state of mind. In 1972 the well-known scholar Paul Ekman proposed a method of facial expression of affection (facial movement coding system, or FACS) [10]. This involved coding and movement through different combinations of modules that can be formed in the face for complex changes in expression, such as happiness, anger, sadness, and so on. The results have been accepted by most researchers, and the facial expressions have been used in automatic recognition and synthesis.

With the rapid development of computer technology, in order to meet the needs of communication, the work of face recognition and synthesis will be merged into the communications code. The most typical is the MPEG4 V2 visual standards, which define the parameters of three major sets: definition of parameters for facial recognition, the related interpolation transforms, and facial animation parameter. The expression of specific parameter values representative of the degree of emotion and facial expressions can be combined to simulate a variety of mixed expressions.

11.5.2 Gesture change

The general gestures of people accompanied by changes in the interactive process express some information. For example, a gesture usually reflects a mood or mentality, perhaps nervousness, that causes a certain part of the body to move. Compared with changes in vocal and facial expressions, gestures are more difficult to obtain in the discipline, but because changes in people's gestures make for more vivid expression, people express a strong concern for gesturing. Scientists researching physical movement have captured a series of sports and physical information with capture devices, such as motion capture devices, data gloves, seats, and the like. Some well-known foreign universities and multinational companies, such as the Massachusetts Institute of Technology and IBM, collaborating to develop equipment to build a smart space. At the same time, an intelligent vehicle driving seat monitors a driver's emotional state dynamically and dispatches a timely warning. Some scientists in Italy are performing automatic sentiment analysis for office staff through a series of posture analyses in order to design a more comfortable office environment.

11.5.3 Speech understanding

In the course of human interaction, voice is the most direct channel of communication; it is clear that through voice people feel one another's emotional changes, such as through special word tone, the tone changed, and so on.

On the phone, although people do not see each other, from the tone they can feel the other's emotional changes. For example, the same phrase, "For you", can express appreciation, irony, or jealousy depending on tone.

At present, the international research on affective speech has focused mainly on the affective characteristics of acoustic analysis in this area. Generally speaking, the affective characteristics of voice are often manifested through changes in rhythm. For example, when a person is angry, the rate of speech becomes faster, the volume goes up, the pitch becomes higher, and a number of phonemic features (formant, channel cross-section function, etc.) can also reflect the affective changes. Experts from the Chinese Academy of Sciences State Key Laboratory, Pattern Recognition Institute of Automation, first put forward the affective focus generation model for the phenomenon of language. Speech synthesis for the affective state of the automatic forecast provides a basis, combined with a high-quality acoustic model, for emotional speech synthesis and identification to reach the level of practical application.

11.5.4 Multimodal affective computing

Although the human face, gesture, voice, etc. can, to a certain degree, independently express sentiment, in the process of exchange, the overall performance occurs through the preceding information. Therefore, only the realization of a multichannel interface will be satisfactory, and the computer is the most natural means of interaction, with its focus on natural language, voice, sign language, face, lip reading, the first potential and multiple potential channels. These channels of information employ coding, compression, and integration to focus on image, audio, video, text, and other multimedia information. At present, multimodal technology itself is becoming a hot research topic in human—computer interaction. With affective computing and multimodal integration processing technology, you can achieve more than just the characteristics of emotional integration; you can effectively increase the depth of affective computing research and promote high quality, making human—computer interaction more harmonious.

11.5.5 Affective computing and personalized service

Research on affective computing has been more than satisfactory with its application on a simple human—computer interaction platform, but the development of a wide range of interface designs, psychological analyses, and all aspects of behavior investigation are needed to improve the quality of services and to increase the content of personalized services. Toward this end, to the view of the affective agent study is to adopt the behavior patterns of affective interaction and build an affection identification and generating type of life. This model could replace the traditional calculation of this model in some applications (for example, the role of computer games, etc.), so that the application of computers may become more "alive" and people can produce a number of similar acts or thinking. The research will have a great promoting role in the overall study of artificial intelligence.

11.5.6 The influence of affective understanding

The affection state of recognition and understanding, given to the computer to understand affection and make appropriate responses, is the key step. The steps usually require people to extract the information used to identify the affective characteristics—for example, to distinguish between the eyebrows on a smiley face—and then allow the computer to learn about these characteristics in order to be able to accurately identify feelings.

In order to better accomplish computer tasks of affection recognition, scientists have been clear on a reasonable classification of the states of human affection and have proposed basic affection categories. At present, the methods of affective recognition and understanding use a large number of research results of pattern recognition, artificial intelligence, and voice and image technology. For example, based on acoustic analysis of voice affection, they use linear statistical methods and neural network models of emotion based on a voice recognition prototype; through facial movement coded regions, using different models such as Hidden Markov Model (HMM), they establish the characteristics of facial affection identification methods; through human posture and movement analysis, they explore the affective types of motor movement and so on.

However, despite the impact of technology on the capture of information on affection and the lack of large-scale data resources on affection, a multifeature integration model of affective understanding has yet to be thoroughly explored. With future technological advances, a more effective mechanism for machine learning may emerge.

Affective computing and intelligent interaction attempt to establish the precise nature of the interaction between the computer and humans, which will be an important means for computer technology to infiltrate human society comprehensively. With future breakthroughs in technology, the application of the affective computing is imperative, and it will impact all aspects of daily life in the future. Here are some things we can expect:

1. Affective computing will effectively change the past mechanical computer interactive services to enhance human—computer interaction in terms of accuracy and kind. A computer with affective capacity is able to carry out human affection in the acquisition, classification, identification, and response in order to help users feel warm and efficient and effectively reduce computer frustration, making it even easier to help people understand themselves and the emotional world of others.

2. It can also help us increase the use of safety equipment (e.g., when using such technologies, it can detect a driver who cannot focus and change the status and response of the vehicle), make the experience become human-like, enable the computer to function as a mediator for learning at its best, and collect feedback from us. For example, a research project uses a computer in the car to measure the level of perceived pressure that drivers exert in order to help resolve the so-called road rage disorder problem.

3. Affective computing and related research are also able to benefit the field of enterprise e-commerce. Some studies have shown that different images can arouse different emotions in a human. For example, a picture of snakes, spiders, and guns can cause fear, and a large number of dollars in cash and gold bullion make human have a very strong positive response. If shopping sites and sites in the design of stock research were to consider the significance of these factors, the increase in traffic should have a positive impact.

4. In information appliances and smart devices, with the capability of auto-perceiving people's emotional states, can provide better service. In information retrieval applications, through the analysis of the concept of emotional analytic functions, intelligent information retrieval can increase accuracy and efficiency. In the distance education platform, the application of affective computing technology can increase the effectiveness of teaching.

5. Multimodal affective interactive technology can be more involved in people's lives by building a smart space, virtual scene, and on the like. Also used in affective computing, robotics, intelligent toys and games, and other related technologies can bring about a more anthropomorphic style and more realistic scenes.

11.6 Neural basis of emotion

Emotion is people's attitude experience and corresponding behavior response to objective things. In terms of the neural basis of emotion, scientists first focused on the subcortical structure and its related circuits. For example, in 1928, Bard proposed that the hypothalamus plays a key role in emotion; in 1937, Papez proposed a more complex emotional neural mechanism, namely, the Papez circuit, and MacLean (1949) further proposed the concept of the limbic system. It is believed that the limbic system, including the amygdala, is the neural basis of emotion in Fig. 11.3.

11.6.1 Emotion pathway

The amygdala, attached to the end of the hippocampus, is almond shaped and part of the limbic system. It is the brain tissue that produces emotions, recognizes and regulates emotions, and controls learning and memory. Moreover, research has found that autism in young children seems to be related to the enlarged amygdala.

The amygdala is divided into two parts: the basolateral nucleus group and the medial cortex group. The medial cortical nuclei form the dorsomedial part of the amygdala. The medial cortical nucleus group includes: (1) anterior amygdala, (2) lateral olfactory tract nucleus, (3) medial amygdala, (4) cortical amygdala, (5) central amygdala. The lateral olfactory tract nucleus of the human is the most developed.

The basolateral nucleus group, the largest and best differentiated part of the human brain, includes: (1) lateral amygdala, (2) basal amygdala, (3) parabasal amygdala, whose medial side is related to the olfactory function area and whose lateral side is related to the plate-like nucleus. One part of

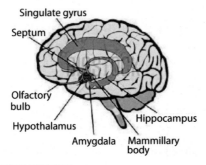

Figure 11.3 Limbic system structure.

its dorsal side is covered by the lenticular nucleus and connected to the caudate nucleus.

The basolateral nucleus group is the nonolfactory functional area of the amygdala. It receives the reticular structure of the brainstem and the fibers from the piriform cortex. It may also receive some fibers from the inferior gyrus: fibers from the amygdala, most of which form the final stria: fibers from the ventral side of the amygdala; and finally fibers from the ventral side of the lenticular nucleus to the medial side, the medial preoptic nucleus, the anterior hypothalamic nucleus, the supraoptic nucleus, and the ventromedial nucleus. The fibers from the spinal side of the amygdala pass through the ventral side of the lenticular nucleus to the medial side and finally to the innominate substance, preoptic lateral nucleus, hypothalamic area, septum, diagonal nucleus, and olfactory tubercle. There are also some fibers across the preoptic area and finally the thalamus.

As for the mechanism of emotional response, there are two reflex pathways.

1. Long pathway: stimulation → thalamus → cingulate → gyrus → corresponding cortex of brain
2. Short pathway: stimulation → thalamus → amygdala

The stimulation information of the long pathway goes through the fine processing of the cortex, which is conducive to the control of emotions and the adoption of appropriate coping styles. The stimulation information of the short pathway does not go through the fine processing of the cortex, which is faster and ensures the rapid response to fear stimulation, which is very important for the survival of all creatures including human beings. It can be seen that the main function of the amygdala is to produce emotions that are compatible with various external information introduced into the neocortex of the brain.

11.6.2 Papez loop

In 1878 P. Broca noticed that a circle of tissues—the inferior part of the corpus callosum, cingulate gyrus, uncinate gyrus, ventral hippocampus, and other structures—were anatomically related to one another and formed a circle, which he called the limbic lobe. In 1937 James Papez, a comparative anatomist at Cornell University, put forward the hypothesis of emotional cognition and brain circuits [11]. He observed that rabies patients have strong emotional performance, especially fear and aggressive behavior. Anatomy found that the brain lesions mainly in the limbic system, so that the limbic system plays a very important role in emotion. Papez's theory of emotion opens the door for exploration from the perspective of brain science.

In autopsies after the death of patients with emotional disorders, the neuroanatomist Papez found that most of the brain structures damaged by these patients contain many cross-linked channels in the limbic system, such as the hypothalamus, papillary body, anterior part of the thalamus, the cingulate cortex, and so on. Later, it was found that the amygdala, phrenic region, and dome were also included in the loop, so the term Papez loop was proposed.

J. W. Papez postulated that emotional experience is generated as follows: The hippocampus is stimulated, and the impulses pass through the white fibers under the corpus callosum, are relayed to the papillary body of the hypothalamus, and then from the hypothalamus to the anterior nucleus of the thalamus, back to the cingulate gyrus. The excitement of the cingulate gyrus affects the cerebral cortex, and the subject produces emotional experience.

The prefrontal lobe is a brain area closely related to emotion. Patients with prefrontal lobe injury can show personality changes, and their emotions are prone to fluctuation, euphoria or irritability, and lack of appropriate regulation of emotional activities. The anterior cingulate cortex adjacent to the prefrontal cortex was damaged, and the patient developed apathy, lack of emotion, and akinetic mutism. Upon stimulation of the anterior cingulate gyrus of conscious animals, the animals became extremely excited and have angry reactions such as roaring. When the cingulate gyrus was damaged on both sides, the animal's mood became cold, the reaction of "fear" and "anger" was reduced, and the reaction to the surrounding environment was indifferent. Clinically, the cingulate gyrus was removed for the treatment of patients with excitable and aggressive behaviors.

11.6.3 Cognitive neuroscience

Through the study of animal emotions, Panksepp believed that primary emotions appear earlier than complex cognition in the evolutionary process, and the processing process that appears earlier must become the basis of the later process. Therefore, our great cognitive ability is likely to be built on the shared emotion system of all mammals.

In the scientific research on emotion, basic emotion theory is always the most important and accepted theory. Because of the complexity of emotions, basic emotions are not a unified theory. There are many controversies in the study of basic emotions. Because of different perspectives, researchers cannot reach an agreement on the types and criteria of basic emotions [12].

Panksepp believed that emotions have independent psychological and brain mechanisms, while basic emotions only involve primary processes. How to judge whether an emotion is a basic emotion? Under the influence of cognitive neuroscience, Panksepp believed that basic emotions should have seven properties that conform to neuropsychological standards [13]:

1. Basic emotions can be triggered by specific nonconditional environmental stimuli.
2. Basic emotions should bring about a series of behaviors and corresponding physiological changes.
3. Basic emotions should be able to choose the environmental information input from the outside world.
4. Basic emotions can be activated for a period of time after being stimulated.
5. Emotional response can be caused by cognitive activation.
6. Basic emotions can activate or adjust various complex cognitive strategies.
7. Mental illness—related emotional experience must come from this brain structure, and emotion must reflect the dynamic operation of this complex brain structure.

After research, Panksepp found that there are seven basic emotions in human and animal coexistence. He named them as seeking, rage, fear, lust, care, panic grief, and play. These seven basic emotions can be distinguished by local electrical stimulation.

Panksepp described a small set of "hard-wired" emotion systems found in mammalian brains [14]. The first four emotion systems appear shortly after birth in mammals:

1. Seeking: This remarkable system mediates all appetitive desire to find and harvest the fruits of the world. The underlying system is the one that mediates our intense appetitive motivation to obtain resources from the environment and promotes goal-directed stimulus-bound appetitive behavior and self-stimulation.

   The concept of the seeking system includes a classic reward pathway in the brainstem as well as other subcortical areas. The primary reward pathways in mammals include the mesolimbic dopamine pathway and the mesocortical dopamine pathway. The mesolimbic dopamine pathway consists of dopaminergic neurons that originate in the ventral tegmental area (VTA) of the brainstem and terminate at the nucleus accumbens in the forebrain. The mesocortical dopamine pathway consists of dopaminergic neurons that project from the VTA to the orbitofrontal cortex.

2. Rage: This system mediates anger and is aroused by restraint, frustration, and various other irritations, as well as directly by brain stimulation. The associated mammalian brain areas include medial amygdala to the bed nucleus of the stria terminalis (BNST) and perifornical hypothalamic to the periaqueductal gray matter (PAG).

3. Fear: The world has abundant dangers, some of which can arouse the major fear system of the brain. The system that responds to pain and the threat of destruction and that leads to the well-known flight, fight, or freeze behavior. It is based primarily in the central and lateral nuclei of the amygdala with connections to the medial hypothalamus and dorsal PAG of the midbrain.

4. Lust: This system coordinates sexual behavior and feeling. Associated brain areas include the cortico-medial amygdala, BNST, as well as the preoptic area, VTA, and PAG.

In addition to the four basic emotion systems, three other special-purpose systems come online at different stages of mammalian development. We briefly describe them here:

1. Care: The caregiving system promotes social bonding and the nurturing of each other. The associated mammalian brain areas include the anterior cingulate, BNST, as well as the preoptic area, VTA, and PAG.

2. Panic grief: This system responds to cries and calls caused by sadness or shyness. The associated mammalian brain areas include the anterior cingulate, BNST, and preoptic area, as well as the dorsomedial thalamus and PAG.

3. Play: The system supports laughter and joy. Associated brain areas include the dorsomedial hypothalamus, as well as the parafascicular area and PAG.

Since each of these emotional systems has its own wiring diagram, emotion in the brain is a quite complex system. Primary emotion appears earlier than complex cognition in the evolutionary process, and the processing process that appears earlier must become the basis of the later process. It is of great significance to explore the nature of emotion.

References

[1] S. Schachter, J.E. Singer, Cognitive, social and physiological determinants of emotional state, Psychol Rev. (1962) 379–399.

[2] S. Schachter, Emotion, Obesity and Crime, Academic Press, New York, 1971.

[3] P. Ekman, Facial expressions of emotion: new findings, new questions, Psychol Sci. 3 (1992) 34–38.

[4] C.E. Izard, The Face of Emotion, vol. 23, Appleton-Century-Crofts, New York, NY, 1971.

[5] A.T. Beck, Cognitive Therapy and Emotional Disorders, International Universities Press, New York, 1976.

[6] A. Ortony, G.L. Clore, A. Collins, The Cognitive Structure of Emotions, Cambridge University Press, Cambridge, 1988.

[7] M. Minsky, The Society of Mind, Simon & Schuster, New York, 1985.

[8] R.W. Picard, Affective Computing, MIT Press, London, England, 1997.

[9] M. Minsky, The Emotion Machine, Simon & Schuster, New York, 2006.

[10] P. Ekman, W.V. Friesen, Facial action coding system, ISBN 9993626619, 1978.

[11] J.W. Papez, A proposed mechanism of emotion, Arch. Neurol. Psychiatry 38 (4) (1937) 725–743.

[12] J. Panksepp, D. Watt, What is basic about basic emotions? Lasting lessons from affective neuroscience, Emot. Rev. 3 (4) (2011) 387–396.

[13] J. Panksepp, Criteria for basic emotions: is DISGUST a primary "emotion"? Cognition Emot. 21 (8) (2007) 1819–1828.

[14] J. Panksepp, Affective Neuroscience, Oxford University Press, New York, 1998.

CHAPTER 12

Consciousness

The origin and essence of consciousness are among the most important scientific problems. Consciousness is a challenging issue in intelligence science. It is not only a theme studied by philosophy but also an important subject of contemporary natural scientific research about determining consciousness and how the objective world is reflected in the subjective world. Consciousness involves such advanced cognitive processes as perception, attention, memory, representation, signifying, thinking, language, etc.; its core is awareness. In recent years, because of the development of cognitive science, neural science, and computer science, especially the appearance of the intact experimental technique, research on consciousness has once again become the common focus of numerous subjects. In the 21st century, consciousness will be one of the issues that intelligence science is trying hard to solve.

12.1 Overview

Consciousness is a complex biological phenomenon, and the philosopher, physician, and psychologist have no common concept of consciousness. There is no final conclusion about consciousness so far. Contemporary famous thinker Dennett believes [1] that human consciousness is probably the last difficult mystery to resolve. To this day, we puzzle about consciousness, yet it remains a unique topic that baffles wise and farsighted thinkers, who still cannot adequately understand it.

In philosophy, consciousness is a highly developed and highly organized special function of the human brain; it is the reflection of objective reality that is owned by humankind only. Consciousness is also a synonym of thinking, but the range of consciousness is relatively wide, including the cognition of the emotional and rational stages, whereas thinking only means the cognition of rational stage. Dialectical materialism believes that consciousness is the result of the high development of material and the reflection of existing. There is also at play a huge activism role in existing.

In medical science, the understanding of consciousness differs according to discipline. In the field of clinical medicine, consciousness refers to a patient's understanding and ability to react to surroundings and oneself; it is

Intelligence Science
DOI: https://doi.org/10.1016/B978-0-323-85380-4.00012-9
Copyright © 2021 Tsinghua University Press.
465

divided into different consciousness levels such as consciousness clearing, consciousness fuzzy, lethargy, coma. In spiritual medical science, consciousness distinguishes between ego consciousness and environmental awareness. Consciousness is sometimes hampered by clouding of consciousness, somnolence, stupor, coma, delirium, twilight state, dream-like state, and confusion.

The view on consciousness in psychology is awareness or experience of objective things in the external environment and one's psychological activity, such as feeling, consciousness, attention, memory, thought. The evolutionary biologist and theoretical scientist Calvin lists some of the definitions of consciousness in the book *How Brains Think* [2].

From the viewpoint of intelligence science, consciousness is the experiential integration with the external world, one's own body, and the mental process. Consciousness is "instinct" or "function"; the brain is inherently a "state," and it consists of many biological "combinations" in the brain structure. Generalized consciousness is the life phenomenon that all higher organisms and lower organisms have. With continuous biological evolution, the organ that processes consciousness, the brain has become the organ of human consciousness activity. In order to reveal the scientific law of consciousness, to build a brain model of consciousness, is there a need to study not only the conscious cognitive process but also the unconscious cognitive process, that is, the automatic information processing of brain, and the transformation mechanisms of two processes in the brain. Consciousness research is the indispensable content in cognitive neuroscience; the research on consciousness and brain mechanism is an important content of the natural science. Philosophy involves problems such as the origin of consciousness, the authenticity of consciousness, etc. A key problem in the intellectual scientific research of consciousness is the brain's mechanism for producing consciousness—how consciousness comes about.

The first one in history to use the word consciousness was Francis Bacon. His definition of consciousness is a person's understanding of what has happened in his thought. Thereafter the consciousness problem became a subject of philosophical research. German psychologist Wundt established the first psychology laboratory in 1879. He clearly proposed that consciousness research is the major study in psychology, using physiological methods to study consciousness, reporting the consciousness state while sitting quietly, working, and sleeping. Psychology entered a new historical period with the advent of the scientific experiment. From then on, research on a series of psychological phenomena developed rapidly, but progress in consciousness study is slow because it lacks nonconscious direct objective indicators. James proposed the concept of the stream of consciousness in 1902 and pointed out that consciousness rises and falls and that its origin is constant, just like flowing water. Freud believes that a person's feeling and behavior are influenced by conscious needs, hopes, and conflicts. According to Freud's view, the stream of consciousness has depth; it has different levels of understanding between the process of consciousness and the process of nonconsciousness. It is an all or none phenomenon. However, because science was not developed enough at the time, introspection method was used, but it lacked objective indicators and remained primarily descriptive and was unable to advance. Since Watson declared that psychology is a behavior science, the consciousness problem has been shelved. So, for a very long time, no one studied neuroscience because it was too complex, and psychology was unwilling to become a forgotten science.

In the 1950s—1960s scientists understood the neurophysiological foundation of the state of consciousness by anatomical and physiological experimentation. For example, Moruzzi and Magoun found the reticular activation system of awareness in 1949; Aserinsky and Kleitman observed the consciousness state of rapid eye movement sleep in 1953; in the 1960s—1970s they studied a split-brain patient and reported that there are independent consciousness systems in the two hemispheres of the brain. The result of this study opened up and established the foundation for cognitive neuroscience research on consciousness.

Modern cognitive psychology started in the 1960s. For cognitive psychologists, it is always a long-term challenge to explain the neural mechanism of objective consciousness. Direct research about consciousness of objective experience and its relation to neural activity is still very rare. In recent years, with the rapid development of science and technology, using modern electrophysiological techniques (electroencephalography, event-related potential) and radiation imaging technology (positron emission tomography scan, functional magnetic resonance imaging), consciousness study has become the newborn focus of life sciences and intelligence science.

Research on the brain mechanism of consciousness is very complex, and the task is arduous, but the effect is of great significance and has caused great interest among scholars all over the world and in many domains, such as cognitive science, neuroscience (neural physiology, neural imaging and neural biochemistry), social science, computer science. The Association for the Scientific Studies of Consciousness was founded in 1997, and international conferences on consciousness have been held continuously. The conference themes are the relation of latent cognitive and consciousness (1997); neural relevance of consciousness (1998); consciousness and self-perception and self-representation (1999); consciousness joint (2000); the content of consciousness: consciousness, attention, and phenomenon (2001); consciousness and language (2002); the model and mechanism of consciousness (2003); empirical and theoretical problems in consciousness research (2004).

Scientists who study the problem of consciousness have a wide variety of views. From having enough of an understanding to finally solve the problem of consciousness, there is a sense of mystery and reductionism. People who hold the mysticist's view assert that we will never be able to understand. The famous contemporary philosopher Fodor in *Towards to Science of Consciousness* suspected publicly at the time of the meeting: How could any kind of physical system have a consciousness state? In the study of consciousness, the very active American philosopher Chalmers thought that consciousness should be divided into an easy problem and a hard problem [3]. His total view of the consciousness is "without any rigorous theoretical physics (quantum mechanics or neural mechanisms) to understand the problem of the consciousness."

Crick declared publicly his reductionist view on consciousness in his book *The Astonishing Hypothesis* [4]. He and his young follower Koch stated this view in many articles. They "reduced" the complex consciousness problem to the collective behavior of neural cells and related molecules. The view held by the famous American neuroscientist Sejnowski and the American philosopher Dennett is generally like that of Crick.

While studying consciousness, considered from the philosophical point of view, there has always been two opposite points of view. One kind is monism, that spirit (including consciousness) is produced by the material (brain) and that the mental phenomena of the brain can be studied and explained. Another kind is a dualism, i.e., the spiritual world is independent of the human body (human brain), and there is no direct link between the two. Descartes was a typical dualist, and he believes that everyone has a body and a soul (mind). Man's body and mind are usually held together, but the mind's activity is not bound by the laws of the machine. After the body dies, the soul will continue to exist and play a role. The activities of a person's mind cannot be observed by others, so that only I can directly perceive the state and process of my own heart. If the body is compared to the "machine," in accordance with the laws of physics, then the mind is "the soul of the machine." Descartes was a great mathematician, so he had to face up to the reality in science that clearly and explicitly proposed "people are machines." But he was also deeply influenced by ancient philosophy and the contemporary social environment, so he made the product of the brain (mind) as completely separate from the human body.

Many contemporary scientists engaged in natural science research believe in dualism. The Nobel Prize laureate John Carew Eccles was keen to study the issue of consciousness. He himself is a scientist who studies the structure and function of synapses and has made great achievements in the structure and function of nerve cells. He does not deny his consciousness is dualism. He and his collaborators have published seven books on brain functions. The book written by him and philosopher Popper put forward the theory of *Three Worlds*, in which the first world is the physical world, including the structure and function of the brain; the second world is all subjective spirit and experience; and the social, scientific, and cultural activities are the third world. In his later works, according to the structure and function of the nervous system, he presented the hypothesis of the dendron. The dendron is the basic structure and functional unit of the nervous system and is composed of about 100 top dendrites. It is estimated that there are 400,000 dendrons in the human brain. He then put forward the hypothesis of the psychon; the second world's psychon corresponds to the first world of the dendron. Quantum physics is likely to be used in the sense of consciousness because the microstructure of the dendrites is similar to that of the quantum scale.

In 2003 Z. Z. Shi proposed a model of the consciousness system based on awareness and attention [5]. In 2007 X. W. Tang presented the four-ingredient theory of consciousness [6]. The four ingredients consciousness are awareness, content, intentionality, and affection of consciousness. Consciousness activity is the result of the interaction and cooperation of many brain regions related to the four functional systems of the brain.

12.1.1 Base elements of consciousness

I. B. Farber and P. S. Churchland discussed the consciousness concept at three levels in the article "Consciousness and the Neurosciences: Philosophical and Theoretical Issues" [7]. The first level is sense of awareness, including feeling awareness (by sensory channel with external stimulate), generality awareness (referring to a feeling that without any connection to a channel, the internal state of the body awareness, such as fatigue, dizziness, anxiety, comfort, hunger, etc.), metacognitive consciousness (referring to awareness of all things within one's cognitive range, including thinking activity in the present and the past), conscious remembering (being aware of something that happened in the past), etc. Here, we can be aware of some signs of things and report these things in language. This method is convenient to measure; at the same time it excludes animal who cannot speak. The second level is the high-level ability; it is advanced functions that not only passively perceive and awareness of information but also has the activity of function or control. These functions include attention, reasoning, and self-control (for example, physiological impulse is inhibited by reason or morals). The third level is the consciousness state; it can be interpreted as a person's ongoing psychological activity, including links to the most difficult and the most commonsense things in the consciousness concept. This state can be divided into different levels: consciousness and unconsciousness, comprehensive regulation, rough feeling, etc. The definitions of the first two levels of consciousness by Farber are enlightening, but the third level lacks substantive content.

In 1977 R. E. Ornstein put forth two modes in which consciousness exists: active-verbal-rational mode and receptive-spatial-intuitive-holistic mode [8], referred to as the active mode and perception mode, respectively. He believes that the two modes are controlled on one side of the brain. The evaluation of the active mode is automatic, and human limits to the automation of awareness block experiences, events, and stimuli that are not directly related to their viability. When people need to strengthen induction and judgment, they increase their normal awareness through the perception mode. According to the view of R. E. Ornstein, sitting quietly, biofeedback, hypnosis, and specific drugs can also help in learning, using a perceptual model to balance the active mode. Intellection activity is active and has an advantage in the left hemisphere, while receptivity with behavioral intuition is dominant in the right hemisphere. The integration of the two modes forms the basis of the high-level functions of human beings.

Which key elements form the consciousness function? In response to this question, F. Crick thinks consciousness includes two basic functions [4]: one is attention, and the second is short-term memory (STM). Attention has been the main function of consciousness, which has been recognized by everyone. B. J. Baars offers the "theater" metaphor, the metaphor of consciousness as a stage, on which different scenes take turns playing [9]. On the stage, the spotlight can be likened to the attention mechanism, which is a popular metaphor. F. Crick also recognized this metaphor. For people who have no memory, there can be no "self-consciousness." People or machines without memory can forget when they have seen something or when they have heard it and can't talk about consciousness and responsibility. The length of time the memory lasts is subject to discussion; long-term memory (LTM) is important, but F. Crick believes that STM is more necessary.

American philosopher and psychologist William James thought that the characteristics of consciousness are:
1. Consciousness is personal and cannot be shared with others;
2. Consciousness is always changing and will not stay in a state for long;
3. Consciousness is continuous, one content contains another content;
4. Consciousness is selective.

In short, James does not think consciousness is a thing but a process, or a kind of "flow," a kind of process can be changed in a fraction of a second. This concept of "stream of consciousness," which is valued in psychology, vividly depicts some of his characteristics of consciousness.

G. M. Edelman stressed the integration and differentiation of consciousness [10]. On the basis of the physiological pathology and anatomy of the brain, Edelman believes the thalamus-cortex system plays a key role in the production of consciousness.

P. S. Churchland, the American philosopher of mind, lists a characteristic table for the consciousness problem [7]:
- working memory related;
- not reliant on sensory input (that is, we can think of something that does not exist and that is not true);
- showing control of attention;
- ability to interpret complex or ambiguous materials; disappears in deep sleep
- reemergence in a dream;
- a single unified experience can be inclusive of the contents of a number of sensory modalities.

In 2012 B. J. Baars and D. E. Edelman explained their natural view about consciousness [11], listing 17 characteristics of the state of consciousness:
1. EEG signature of conscious states: The electrophysiological activities of the brain are irregular, of low amplitude and fast electrical activity, and the frequency is from 0.5 to 400 Hz. The EEG of consciousness and of no state of consciousness (similar to the sleeping condition)

were significantly different; epilepsy patients and general anesthesia state of consciousness present rules, high amplitude, and slowly changing voltage.

2. Cortex and thalamus: Consciousness depends on the complexity of the hypothalamus, which is modulated by the brain stem and has no interaction with the subcortical area, so it does not directly support the experience of consciousness.

3. Widespread brain activity: The report of the event is related to a wide range of specific brain activities. Unconscious stimulation evokes only local brain activity. Conscious moments also have a wide range of effects on the content of outside attention, such as implicit learning, episodic memory, biofeedback training, and so on.

4. Wide range of reportable contents: Consciousness has a very wide range of different contents: the perception of a variety of sensations, the appearance of an endogenous image, emotional feelings, inner speech, concepts, action-related ideas, and the experience of the familiar.

5. Informativeness: Consciousness can disappear when the signal becomes superfluous; loss of information can lead to loss of consciousness. Selective attention studies also show a strong preference for information on more abundant conscious stimuli.

6. The adaptive and fleeting nature of conscious events: Immediately experienced sensory input can be maintained for a few seconds; we have a brief knowledge of the duration of less than half a minute. On the contrary, the vast unconscious knowledge can reside in LTM.

7. Internal consistency: Consciousness is characterized by uniform constraint. In general, two stimuli at the same time are not consistent; only one can be sensed. When a word is ambiguous, there is only one meaning at any time.

8. Limited capacity and seriality: The ability of consciousness in any prescribed moment seems to be limited to only one consistent picture. The flow of such conscious scenes is serial, in contrast to the massive parallel processing of the brain when it is observed directly at the same time.

9. Sensory binding: The sensory brain is functionally divided into blocks, so that different cortical areas are specialized to respond to different features, such as shape, color, or object motion. One fundamental problem is how to coordinate the activities of the brain regions that are separated by their functional roles to generate the integrated gestalts of ordinary conscious perception.

10. Self-attribution: Conscious experience is always characterized by self-experience, what William James called the "observing ego." Self-function seems to related to central brain areas, including the brainstem, precuneus, and orbitofrontal cortex in humans.

11. Accurate reportability: The most used behavioral index of consciousness is accurate reportability. The full range of conscious contents are reportable by a wide range of voluntary responses, often with very high accuracy. The report does not require a complete explicit vocabulary because the subject can automatically compare, contrast, point to, and play a role in the event of consciousness.

12. Subjectivity: Consciousness is marked by a private flow of events available only to the experiencing subject. Such privacy is not in violation of legislation. This shows that self—object synthesis is the key to conscious cognition.

13. Focus-fringe structure: Consciousness is thought to be inclined to focus on clear content; "fringe conscious" events, such as feelings of familiarity, the tip-of-the-tongue experience, intuition, and so on, are equally important.

14. Facilitation of learning: There is little evidence to show that learning takes place without consciousness. In contrast, the evidence for the conscious experience to promote learning is overwhelming. Even implicit (indirect) learning also requires conscious attention.

15. Stability of contents: Conscious contents are impressively stable. Changes in input and task production are required, such as the eye movements that readers constantly use to scan sentences. Even its own beliefs, concepts, and topics of the same abstract content may be very stable over decades.

16. Allocentric attribution: The scenes and objects of consciousness, in general, are concerned with external sources, although their formation is heavily dependent on unconscious frameworks.

17. Conscious knowing and decision making: Consciousness is useful for us to know about the world around us, as well as some of our internal processes. Conscious representation, including percepts, concepts, judgments, and beliefs, may be particularly well suited to decision making. However, not all conscious events involve a wide range of unconscious facilities. In this way, the content of the consciousness report is by no means the only feature that needs to be interpreted.

12.1.2 The attribute of consciousness

P. Johnson-Laird, a professor of the Psychology Department at Princeton University, is a distinguished British cognitive psychologist. His main interest is to study language, especially words, sentences, and paragraphs. P. Johnson-Laird was convinced that any computer, especially a highly parallel computer, must have an operating system used to control (even if not to completely control) the rest of the work. He thought there exists a close relationship between the operating system and the consciousness in the brain's higher parts [12].

R. Jackendoff, a professor of linguistics and cognition at Brandeis University, is a famous American cognitive scientist. He has a special interest in language and music. Like most cognitive scientists, he thinks it's better to think of the brain as an information processing system [13]. But unlike most scientists, he regards "how to produce consciousness" as a most fundamental problem of psychology. His middle-level theory of consciousness is that consciousness is neither from the processing of perceptual units nor from the top of the thoughts but from the representtaive layers between the lowest surroundings (similar to feeling) and the highest central (similar to thought). He highlighted this very new point of view, also believing that there is a close connection between consciousness and STM. He said consciousness needs the content of STM for support, which reflects such a point of view. But it should be added that STM is involved in the rapid process and that the slow change process has no direct phenomenological effect. When it comes to attention, he thinks, paying attention to the calculation effect causes attention to the material experience to involve more in-depth and detailed processing. He thinks this can explain why the attention capacity is so limited.

In 1988, B. J. Baars at the Wright's Institute, Berkeley, California, wrote the book *A Cognitive Theory of Consciousness* [14]. Although Baars is a cognitive scientist, he is more concerned about the human brain than Jackendoff or Johnson-Laird. He called his basic thought the global working space. He believes that information in this workspace at any given moment is the content of consciousness. As the working space of the central information exchange, it relates to many of the unconscious receiving processors. These specialized processors have high efficiency only in their own areas. In addition, they can also get into the working space through cooperation and competition. B. J. Baars improved the model in several ways. For example, the receiving processor can reduce uncertainty by interacting until the input conforms to a unique valid explanation. In a broad sense, he thinks that consciousness is highly active and that the attention control mechanism can enter the consciousness. We are aware of some of the projects in the STM but not all.

These three cognitive theoreticians have roughly reached three common understandings to the attribute of consciousness. They agree that not all the activities of the brain are directly and consciously related and that consciousness is an initiative course. They believe that the process of consciousness is involved in attention and some form of STM. They may also agree that the information in consciousness can enter into long-term episodic memory and can enter into the high-level planning level of the motor nervous system in order to control voluntary movement. In other ways, their ideas are very different.

Next, we will introduce important theories of consciousness, including the global workspace theory, reductionism theory, neuron group selection theory, quantum theory of consciousness, integrated information theory, machine consciousness system, etc.

12.2 Global workspace theory

12.2.1 The theater of consciousness

The most classical assumption in the consciousness problem is a metaphor of the "bright spot in dramaturgy." In this metaphor, we aggregate into a conscious experience from a lot of input of feelings, and a spotlight beams a light somewhere in dark theater and then spreads to a large number of unconscious audiences. In cognitive science, most of the assumptions about consciousness and selective attention come from this basic metaphor. B. J. Baars is the most important person to inherit and carry forward the "dramaturgical assumption" [9].

B. J. Baars closely combined psychology with brain science and cognitive neuroscience, The theater metaphor has been used to understand consciousness from the time of Plato and Aristotle and has been transformed into the theater model of consciousness. A number of noticeable neuroimaging advanced research results describe the complexity of the human spiritual world (see Fig. 12.1) [9].

The basic idea of this model is that man's consciousness is a limited stage and that it needs a central cognitive working space, which is very similar to the stage of a theater. Consciousness, as a kind of psychological state of a great epistemological phenomenon, basically has five kinds of activities:

1. Working memory is like a theater stage and mainly includes two components: inner language and visual imagination.

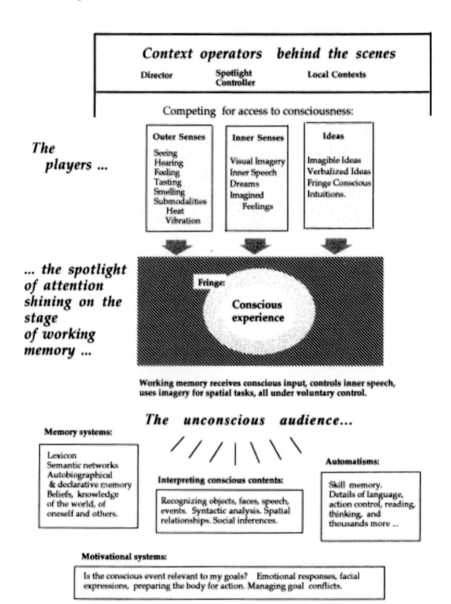

Figure 12.1 Theater model of consciousness.

2. The content of the conscious experience is like the onstage actor, showing the relationship between competition and cooperation in different contexts of the consciousness experience.

3. Attention is like a spotlight, which shines on the actor on the stage of working memory, making the content of consciousness appear.

4. The background operation of the backstage is carried out by the postern background operator's system of the setting, among them "oneself" similar to the director operating behind the scenes. A lot of ubiquitous unconscious activities form the stage like background effects; the background operator is the execution and control system of the cerebral cortex.

5. The unconscious automatic activity procedure and knowledge resources form the "audience" in the theater.

According to his point of view, although people's consciousness is limited, the advantage is that it can access a lot of information and has a certain amount of computing power. These abilities include multisensory input, memory, innate and acquired skills, etc. B. J. Baars also put forward that consciousness in the work of the brain is widely distributed, like the many roles in theater. There is a total of four brain structure spatial dimensions, four types of brain function module systems to support. They are also projected on the time axis, forming a super integration of three-dimensional space and time dimensions like the mind model of the theater stage. The four dimensions of the structure of the brain simultaneously project on the time axis:

1. Cortical dimensions from the deep to cortex of the brain

2. Front side development dimension from the back of the head forward to the front head

3. The two hemispheres of the brain function of left and right-side development dimension

4. Cerebral dorsal and ventral development dimension to form the space—time dimension of a super cube
Brain function system is composed of four modules:

1. Instinct-related function modules—with clear functional orientation

2. Human species-specific instinct behavior module—the function orientation of automation

3. Individual acquisition of habitual behavior module—positioning semi-automation system

4. High-level conscious activity—there is no clear positioning system. The contents of consciousness seem to spread to all over the brain's neural networks, so as to form a distributed structure of the system. The human consciousness experience is a unity, the self is the "director" of the unity.

Based on the "theater model of consciousness," B. J. Baars proposed a "conscious and unconsciousness interaction model," a simple metaphor for the dynamic process of mutual transformation between the conscious and unconscious, namely diversified forms of consciousness activities and unconscious active reciprocal transformation, conscious information processing of the whole job, conscious content and rich and colorful experience to restrain oneself subjectively in a complicated brain. According to Baars's point of view, there is a special processor, which is unified or modular. It needs to be emphasized that processor of the unconsciousness is very effective and fast and makes few errors; at the same time, such a processor may be in operation together with other systems. the dedicated processor is separate and independent but can deal with the main information dynamically. The characteristics of this special processor are very similar to those "modules" of cognitive psychology.

Is the formation of consciousness caused by a specific brain process? Can such a complex system be used to establish a model for the formation of brain processes? These are the problems of consciousness research. The exploration of the active neural mechanism of consciousness finds that the sober state of consciousness is the primary condition in which psychological activity can be carried on and that the sober states of consciousness are closely linked with net structure, thalamus of the brain stem, etc. and neural pathways in the limbic system. Generally speaking, the excitability of the netted structural system of the brain stem relates to the intensity of attention. Sensory input of a large amount of information need to go through the network structure system for primary analysis and integration, where much unrelated or secondary information is selectively filtered out, and attention is paid to only relevant information and passed on to the network structure system. Therefore, some scholars have suggested that consciousness activity mainly is reflected in an attention mechanism based on the net structure as the neural basis, paying attention only to the stimulus causing our consciousness. Much irrelevant or secondary information is selectively filtered out, and only information that attracts attention can reach the reticular system. Therefore some scholars have proposed that conscious activity is mainly reflected in the attention mechanism based on the reticular structure. Only a noticed stimulus can arouse our consciousness, while many nonnoticed stimuli can not be realized if they fail to reach the level of consciousness. The activity of consciousness depends on a certain mental function of attention intervention. Of course, consciousness and unconsciousness have different physiological bases and operating mechanisms. Many unconscious activities involve parallel processing, and the conscious activity is the process of serial processing. Different states of consciousness can entail fast conversion within a short time; the opening of the consciousness refers to the transformation of the unconscious state to the state of consciousness.

The model accurately describes the relations and differences between the conscious and unconscious, attention, working memory, self-consciousness, etc. With the support of much neurobiological evidence, its influence is growing in academia. The famous scholar Simon has said that Barrs has offered an exciting explanation about consciousness that frees us from the philosophical yoke and places studies firmly in the experimental arena. Some scholars think that the consciousness theater model proposed by B. J. Barrs has offered a kind of core assumption for the current study of consciousness. He compares the differences between the unconscious and the conscious mind, and the core idea is that there are two different processes of consciousness and nonconsciousness. In this analytical foundation, B. J. Baars view of conscious and unconscious events can be recognized in the nervous system as a variety of construction processes. The research of Crick et al. shows that visual consciousness evolves from the cortex area on the brain's occipital lobe, so it is possible think of it as a the "theater stage" spotlight, which is activated and lighted by attention, thus showing the coherent information of consciousness [15]. "Audience" means an unconscious brain area, such as the cortex, hippocampus, basal nucleus, or amygdala, and a motor execution system and interpretation system. The "theater assumption" of the consciousness implies that there are a lot of roles on the stage at the same time to perform, as the human brain accepts many kinds of stimuli of internal and external receptors at the same time, but only a small number of roles get the spotlight, and the beam does not stay on a place or role but flows with time.

The theater metaphor of consciousness is also opposed by some scholars. Dennett believes that this assumption must have a "stage" to have a sense of "performance," that is, there is a special place in the brain as a stage of consciousness. This assumption is very easy to conflate with Descartes's 17th century theory about the psychological soul in the pineal body. Opponents believe that the brain does not have a special place to concentrate all input stimuli.

12.2.2 Global workspace model

The purpose of the global workspace method is to elaborate role of the brain's consciousness in cognitive activities. Fig. 12.2 shows the global

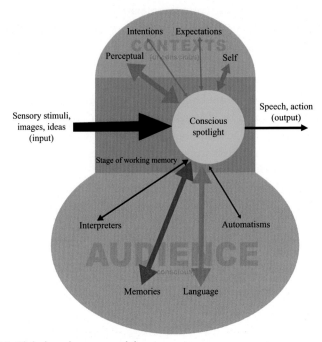

Figure 12.2 Global workspace model.

workspace model [16]. It is the most appropriate way to use theater as a metaphor for the global workspace. As the unconscious processor in the theater, the audience receives the broadcast of the conscious focus on the stage. Control of this focus is equivalent to selective attention. In the background, the unconscious connection system forms and guides the conscious content. The global work interval method is a strict set of testable hypotheses, which are used to illustrate some of its basic characteristics.

The global workspace method is based on the strong evidence of conscious processing. Conscious processing combines the concept of the "blackboard structure," which combines different cognitive sources to identify a sound signal in a complex noisy and ambiguous environment. It is common for people to observe, think, plan, and control such noisy and ambiguous signals. Based on many experiments comparing conscious and unconscious activities, people put forward an empirical summary. This shows that conscious activities are strongly related to limited capacity processing, showing the internal compatibility of conscious content and low computational efficiency.

The global workspace approach assumes that human cognitive processes are performed by quite a few specialized processes that are almost all unconscious. Although it seems like a cliché today, the concept of specialized processing widely distributed in the brain was controversial when it was first proposed. Different processes need to compete for channels that use the global workspace. This limited capacity global workspace method is used to transfer information from the competitive processing components to all the unconscious processing components. The purpose is to engage more resources to deal with abnormal and high-priority input and to solve existing problems. From this point of view, consciousness allows us to deal with exceptions or challenging situations that cannot be effectively handled by conventional unconscious processing. Conscious cognition can solve the "association problem" in artificial intelligence and robotics by giving access to unpredictable but necessary knowledge sources.

By default, consciousness provides a search function to find potential dangers and opportunities, so there is an especially close relationship between the content of consciousness and important perceptual input. The external feeling can be simulated through visual representation, inner language, and inner feeling behavior. These endogenous "sensations" have been shown to activate cortical and subcutaneous areas that are activated by similar external activities.

Consciousness content is always guided and constrained by unconscious content: target content, perceived content, conceptual content, and shared environment content. Each content itself is a combination of processing. Although the content itself is unconscious, they form a conscious processing process. For example, unconscious spatial cognition is required to indicate the direction of the conscious observation target. In the global workspace approach, learning activities are generally caused by the conscious parts. When the unconscious processor is required to execute the conscious content, and the hard-to-report rule generation problem is solved, implicit learning occurs. Tasks like language learning are largely implicit, but they are mainly caused by consciousness input.

12.3 Reductionism

The Nobel laureate and author of the DNA double helix structure, F. Crick, is a typical representative in this respect. He believes that the consciousness problem is a key problem in the whole advanced function of the nervous system; he published an advanced popular science book in 1994 called *The Astonishing Hypothesis,* with the subtitle *The Scientific Search for the Soul* [4]. He boldly proposed "the astonishing hypothesis" based on "reductionism." He believes, "People's spiritual activity is completely determined by the behaviors of nerve cells and glial cells and the property of compositions and affects from their atoms, ions and molecules." He believes that the difficult psychological problem of consciousness can be solved using the scientific method. He believes that the consciousness problem relates to STM and the shift of attention. He also believes that the consciousness problem involves people's many feelings, but he prefers to work with the visual sense because human are visual animals, visual attention is easy to study in psychophysical experiments, and neural science has accumulated a lot of materials in research of the visual system. At the end of the 20th century, in the 1980s and early 1990s, there was a great discovery in visual physiological studies: the phenomenon of synchronous oscillations recorded in different neurons. Approximately 40 Hz synchronous oscillations are considered the neural signal between different picture characteristics. Crick proposed the 40 Hz oscillation model of visual attention and inferred that the 40 Hz synchronous oscillations of neurons may be a form of "bundling" of different visual characteristics. As for the "free will," Crick believes it relates to consciousness; it involves the execution of behavior and plan. Crick analyzed the situations of some persons who lose their "will" and believes that a part of the brain for free will lies in the anterior cingulate gyrus, close to Brodmanm area (area 24).

Crick and C. Koch think that the most difficult problem is studying the sense of the problem, that is, how you feel the red color, the feeling of pain, and so on. This is determined by subjectivity and nonexpression of consciousness. Thus they turn to the study of the neural correlates of consciousness (NCC), that is, to understand the general nature of neural activity in certain aspects of consciousness. Crick and Koch listed ten frames of neural correlates in the study of consciousness [17].

1. The (unconscious?) homunculus: First, consider the overall work of the brain. The front of the brain is largely the sensory system, but the main task of the sensory system is in the back of the brain. People do not know their thoughts directly but only know the sense of the image in the image. Currently, the neural activity in the forebrain is unconscious. There is a "hypothesis of homunculus" in the brain, and it is no longer fashionable now, but how can people imagine themselves?

2. Zombie modes and consciousness: For sensory stimuli, many responses are rapid, transient, stereotyped, and unintentional, while conscious processing is slower, more extensive, and requires more time to determine the right ideas and appropriate responses. These two strategies evolved to complement each other, and the visual system of the dorsal channel (the large cell system) was performing a rigid fast response to the ventral system (small cells).

3. Coalitions of neurons: This alliance is the Hebb cluster and the competition between them. The neurons in the coalition are not fixed but dynamic. The alliance to gain an advantage in the competition will remain dominant for some time, and that is when we realize something. This process is like a country's election: The election victory of the party will be in power for a period of time, until the impact of the next stage of the political situation. The role of the attention mechanism is equivalent to public opinion and election forecasters, trying to influence the election situation. Large pyramidal cells in layer V of the cortex seem to be on the ballot. But the time interval between each election is not regular. Of course, this is just a metaphor.

   There are changes in the size and characteristics of the alliance. The consciousness of alliance and dreaming awake when the eyes are not the same, imagination and open my eyes to watch is not the same. Awareness of cerebral anterior part of the union may reflect the "pleasure", "rule," free will, and posterior cerebral alliance may produce in different ways, and before and after brain alliance may be more than one, will influence and interaction each other.

4. Explicit representations: An explicit representation of a part of the field of view implies that a group of neurons, which correspond to the properties of this part, can react as a detector, without the need for a complex process. In some cases, the lack of some dominant neurons causes a loss, for example, color agnosia, prosopagnosia, movement agnosia. Other visual features of these patients remain normal.

   In monkeys, a small portion of the motor cortex (MT/VS) is impaired, resulting in loss of motion perception. Less damaged parts can be recovered within a few days, if the damage is caused by a large range of permanent loss. It must be noted that the dominant representation is a necessary condition for the NCC, not a sufficient condition.

5. The higher levels first: After coming to a new visual input, neural activity first quickly unconsciously uplinks to the high-level visual system, maybe the forebrain. Then the signals are fed back to the

low level and so reach consciousness in the first stage at a high level. Then the sense signal is sent to the frontal cortex and to the lower level causing the corresponding activities. Of course, this is too simple a description. There are many cross-links in the whole system.

6. Driving and modulating connections: It is important to understand the nature of neural connections, which cannot be considered the same type of excitatory connections. Cortical neurons can be roughly divided into two categories: One is the driving, and the other is the modulation. In cortical pyramidal cells, the driving links are mostly derived from the basal dendrites and modulated by the transmission of human derived from the dendrites, which include reverse projection, dispersion-like projection, especially the nucleus of the thalamus. The link from the side of the knee to the V1 region is the driving. From the back of the brain to the front of the link is the driving. And the reverse link is mostly modulated. The cells on the fifth layer of the cortex, which project to the thalamus, are driving, while the sixth layer is modulated.

7. Snapshots: Neurons may be in some way beyond the threshold of consciousness or to maintain a high firing rate or a type of synchronous oscillation or a cluster firing. These neurons may be pyramidal cells, which project to the forebrain. Maintaining a higher threshold of neural activity involves the internal dynamics of neurons, such as the accumulation of chemical substances Ca^{2+}, or the role of reentry circuits in the cortical system. It is also possible that the function of the positive and negative feedback loop can increase the activity of the neuron, reach the threshold, and maintain a high activity for some time. There may also be some sort of complexity in the threshold problem, which may depend on the rate at which the threshold is reached or how long it will be maintained.

   The visual awareness process consists of a series of static snapshots, which is a perception that occurs in discrete time. The constant firing rate of the relevant neurons in the visual cortex, representing a certain motion occurting, motion takes place between snapshots, so the duration of each snapshot is not fixed. The snapshot times of shapes and colors may happen to be the same, and their residence times are related to an α rhythm or even a δ rhythm. The residence time of the snapshot depends on the opening signal, closing signal, competition, and adaptation.

8. Attention and binding: It is useful to divide attention into two classes: One class is fast, significant, and bottom-up; the other is slow,

self-controlled, and top-down. Attention plays a role in those active alliances in competition: attention from bottom to top, the fifth layer of neurons in the cortex, and projection to the thalamus and the epithalamus. Attention from top to bottom proceeds from the forebrain, to the dispersion of the back projection to the cortex I, II, and III neurons in the apical dendrite, and to the possible pathway of the hypothalamic nucleus. It is commonly believed that the thalamus is the organ of attention. The function of the reticular nucleus of the thalamus is to make choices from a wide range of objects. The role of attention is to select a tendency in a group of competitive alliances, so as to feel the object and the event, and objects that are not paid attention to immediately disappear.

The binding is the different aspects of the object or event, such as the shape, color, motion, etc. There may be several types of binding. If the binding is acquired or learned from experience, it may be embodied in one or several nodes and does not require a special binding mechanism. If the binding is new, the activities of the dispersed basic nodes need to be combined.

9. Styles of firing: Synchronous oscillation can increase the efficiency of a neuron without affecting the average firing rate. The significance and extent of synchronization are still controversial. Computational studies show that the effect is dependent on the degree of input. We no longer have sufficient conditions for the simultaneous oscillation (e.g. 40 Hz) as a neural correlate. The purpose of synchronous distribution may be to support a new alliance in the competition. If visual stimulation is simple, such as strip matters on the vacant auditoria, then there is no meaningful competition, and synchronous firing may not occur. In the same vein, a successful alliance is in a state of consciousness, and this firing may not be necessary. As you get a permanent job, you may relax for a while. On a basic node, an earlier arrival of the spike may have the advantage of being greater than the subsequent spike. In other words, the exact timing of the spike can affect the result of competition.

10. Penumbra and meaning: In a small group of neurons, some may react to the certain aspects of the human face. We know about the visual properties of the small group of cells, but how does the brain know what is represented by these firings? That is the question of meaning. Neural correlates are only directly related to the part of all pyramidal

cells, but it can affect many other neurons, which is the penumbra. The penumbra is composed of two parts: One is the synaptic effect, the second is the firing rate. The penumbra is not the sum of the basic nodal effects but the result of the whole of the neural correlates. This penumbra includes neural correlates of the neuronal past, neural correlates of the desired outcome, and motor-related neuronal correlates. By definition, the penumbra itself cannot be realized, and apparently part of it may be a part of the neural correlates. The penumbra of some members of the neuron may be feedback to part of the members of the neural correlates, supporting the activities of the neural correlates. The penumbra neurons may be the site of the unconscious priming.

The idea of Crick and Koch is that the framework of the consciousness weaves the idea of the neural correlates with the philosophical, psychological, and neural perspectives and that the key idea is a competitive alliance. Guessing a node with a minimum number of neurons may be a cortical function column. This bold hypothesis indicates that the study of consciousness has pointed out a path; that is, through the study of neural networks, cells, molecules, and other levels of the material foundation, we eventually will find the answer to the consciousness question. But this hypothesis is faced with a central question: Who has "consciousness" in the end? If it is the nerve cell, so who is the "I"?

12.4 Theory of neuronal group selection

Nobel laureate G. M. Edelman, based on the physiological pathology and anatomy of the brain, emphasized the conformability and division of consciousness [18]. He believes that a thalamus—cortex system plays a key role in the generation of consciousness. The thalamus here refers in particular to the thalamus interlaminar nucleus, the bottom of the reticular nucleus, and forebrain, collectively referred to as the reticular activating system. This part of neurons disseminate a projection to the thalamus and cerebral cortex; its function is to stimulate a thalamus—cortex system, putting the whole cortex in the waking state. In recent years, brain damage experiments have shown that multiple brain areas of the cortex simultaneously stimulate rather than a single brain region alone.

In 2003 Edelman published a paper [10] at the American Academy of Sciences series, he argues that we should abandon dualism. After analyzing the characteristics of consciousness, he pointed out that the study of consciousness must consider:

1. The contrast between the diversity and changeability of conscious states and the unitary appearance to the conscious individual of each conscious state: This unity requires the binding together of diverse sensory modalities that show constructive features such as those seen in Gestalt phenomena.

2. The property of intentionality: This term refers to the fact that consciousness is generally but not always about objects or events. At the same time, consciousness is modulated by attention and has wide access to memory and imagery.

3. Subjective feelings or qualia: For example, the experiencing of the redness of red, the warmness of warmth.

Neuroscience shows that consciousness is not the nature of a single brain region or some type of neuron but the result of the dynamic interaction of a widely distributed group of neurons. A major system that is essential for conscious activity is the thalamocortical system. The integrative dynamics of conscious experience suggest that the thalamocortical system behaves as a functional cluster; that is, it interacts mainly with itself. Of course, it also interacts with other brain systems. For example, interactions between the basal ganglia and the thalamocortical system are likely to influence the modulation of consciousness by attention as well as the development of automaticity through learning. The threshold of activity in these neural structures is governed by diffuse ascending value systems, such as the mesencephalic reticular activating system interacting with the intralaminar nuclei of the thalamus, as well as noradrenergic, serotonergic, cholinergic, and dopaminergic nuclei.

Edelman believes that the brain is a selective system. In this selection system, different roads of the structure may carry out the same function or produce the same output. Inasmuch as the theory of neuronal group selection (TNGS) abandons the basic computational notions of logic and a clock, a means for spatiotemporal coordination must be put in place. This is provided by a process called reentry, the operation of which is central to the emergence of consciousness. Reentry is an ongoing process of recursive signaling among neuronal groups taking place across massively parallel reciprocal fibers that link mapped regions such as those found in the cortex. Reentry is a selection process occurring in parallel; it differs from feedback, which is instructional and involves an error function that is serially transmitted over a single pathway. The interaction between competitive neuronal groups and reentry, in a wide range of synchronous activities in the brain areas, will be decided by the choice of the orientation of reentry. This provides a solution to the so-called binding problem: How do functionally segregated areas of the brain correlate their activities in the absence of an executive program or superordinate map? Binding of the activity of functionally segregated cortical areas for each sensory modality is essential for perceptual categorization, the selective discrimination of different objects or events for adaptive purposes.

According to the TNGS, selectional events in the brain are necessarily constrained by the activity of diffuse ascending value systems. The activity of these systems affects the selectional process by modulating or altering synaptic thresholds. These systems, which include the locus coeruleus, the raphe nucleus, and the cholinergic, dopaminergic, and histaminergic nuclei, are necessary to bias selective events and thereby favor certain species-specific behaviors during evolution. Value systems also affect systems of learning and memory. The dynamic synaptic changes in individual neuronal groups that are based on past perceptual categorizations are positively and negatively influenced by limbic and brainstem value systems. This system, based largely on the activity of frontal, parietal, and temporal cortices, is critical to the emergence of consciousness.

Edelman proposed that the theory of the neuronal group selection (or neural Darwinism) is the center of the theoretical framework of his consciousness, which is mainly reflected in the following two points: (1) By its nature, a selection neural system has huge diversity, a property that is a necessary basis for the differentiated complexity of conscious brain events. (2) Reentry is a key role to provide the critical means by which the activities of distributed multiple brain areas are linked, bound, and then dynamically altered in time during perceptual categorization. Both diversity and reentry are necessary to account for the fundamental properties of conscious experience. Therefore, both diversity and reentry are the basic properties of the conscious experience.

Edelman divides consciousness into two categories: the primary consciousness and the higher-order consciousness. The primary consciousness only considers the events of the present. Animals with primary consciousness can integrate perceptual and motor events with memory to construct a multimodal scene in the present. Higher-order consciousness emerges later in evolution and is seen in animals with semantic capabilities such as chimpanzees. It is present in its richest form in the human species, which is unique in possessing true language made up of syntax and semantics. Edelman believes that, with the divergence of reptiles into mammals and then into birds, the embryological development of large numbers of new reciprocal connections allowed rich reentrant activity to take place between the more posterior brain systems carrying out perceptual categorization and the more frontally located systems responsible for value-category memory. At much later evolutionary epochs, further reentrant circuits appeared that linked semantic and linguistic performance to categorical and conceptual memory systems. This development enabled the emergence of higher-order consciousness.

On this basis, Edelman introduced the reentry dynamic core concept. In a complex system, it is composed of a number of small areas, which are semi-independent activities and then forms a large cluster through interaction to produce the integrated functions. The critical reentrant events within an integrated circuit of this system are metastable and, in time periods of 500 MS or less, give way to a new set of integrated circuits. This process occurs in an ongoing manner over successive time periods within the thalamocortical system, which, as a functional cluster, interacts mainly with itself. This functional cluster has been called the reentrant dynamic core to emphasize its central properties as a complex system capable of yielding differentiated yet unitary states, which has much in common with Crick's "competitive alliance," and their coalitions correspond roughly to core states.

12.5 Quantum theories

Quantum theory reveals the basic laws of the microscopic physical world, which is the basis of all physical processes, biological processes, and physiological processes. The quantum system goes beyond the particle and wave or the interaction with the material, which is integrated with integral parallel and distributed processing. Nonlocal and long-distance correlations are quantum properties, which may be closely related to consciousness.

Quantum wave function collapse is a change and refers to the amount of wavelet function from numerous quantum eigenstates as a linear combination of the description state to the transition of an intrinsic pure state; simply put, the schema of many quantum superpositions of a wave is transformed into a single quantum schema. The collapse of the wave function means selective projection from a subconscious memory to an explicit memory awareness representation. There are two possible theories of memory and recall: the quantum theory previously mentioned, or the classical (neural) theory. Memory may be a parallel distribution schema of the synaptic connection system, but it may also be a more refined structure, such as the parallel world of quantum theory and Bohm's implicit order proposed by H. Everett [19].

Philosopher D. J. Chalmers proposed a variety of quantum mechanics to explain consciousness [3]. He believes that the dynamic mechanism of the collapse provides an open space for the interpretation of the interpretation of the interaction. Chalmers thinks the problem is how we explain it. What we want to know is not just the association, we want to explain how consciousness emerges in the brain course: Why does consciousness emerge? This is the mystery. The most likely explanation is that the state of consciousness is not likely to be superimposed on the state of consciousness and the overall quantum state of the system. The brain as a physical system of consciousness; in the quantum state that is not superposed, the physical state and the spiritual phenomenon of this system are interrelated.

American mathematician and physicist R. Penrose developed his own theory from the Gödel theorem, that the human brain can exceed axioms and a formal system. Proposed [20] in his first book about consciousness, *The Emperor's New Mind*, the brain has additional features that do not depend on the rules of calculation. It is a noncomputational process and is not computational rule driven. The basic properties of the algorithm is for most of the physics, the computer must be driven by computation rules. For the noncomputation process, the collapse of the quantum wave at a certain location determines the location of random selection. The random nature of the collapse of the wave function is not restricted by the algorithm. The fundamental difference between the human brain and the computer may be caused by the uncertainty of quantum mechanics and the chaos of the complex nonlinear system. The human brain contains the nondeterministic nature of the neural network system, an "intuition" that the computer does not have—a system of "fuzzy" processing ability and the efficiency of high performance. And conventional Turing machines are deterministic serial processing systems; although it is possible to simulate such fuzzy processing, the efficiency is too low. The quantum computer and neural network computer are being involved in the study to solve such problems in order to achieve the ability of the human brain.

R. Penrose also proposed a wave function collapse theory, which is suitable for the quantum system and which does not interact with the environment. He believes that each quantum superposition has its own space−time curvature; when they are away from each other by more than Planck length (10^{-35} m), they will collapse. This is called the objective reduction. Penrose believes that objective reduction represents neither a random nor an algorithmic process that most physics relies on but is noncomputational, influenced by the basic level of space—time geometry, on which computation and consciousness are generated.

In 1989 Penrose wrote the first book on consciousness, specifically on the lack of a detailed description of the role of quantum processes in the brain. S. R. Hameroff, who is engaged in cancer research and anesthesiology, read Penrose's book and presented the microtubule structure as support to the quantum of the brain.

Cooperation between Penrose and Hameroff in the early 1990s established a controversial "harmonious and objective reduction model (Orch-OR model)." After operation in accordance with the Orch-OR provisions of the quantum superposition state, Hameroff's team announced a new quantum annealing coherent time scales and requiring greater than a 7 order obtained by Tegmark. But this result is still less than the time required for the 25 ms, if you want to achieve the quantum process as described by Orch-OR, and can be associated with the 40 Hz gamma synchronization. In order to make up for this link, Hameroff made a series of assumptions and proposals. First, he assumes that the liquid and gel can be converted to each other in the microtube. In the gel state, he further assumes, the water dipoles along the periphery of the tubulin microtubules are arranged in the same direction. Hameroff thought that the orderly arrangement of water would shield any quantum annealing process in tubulin. Each tubulin also extends a negatively charged "tail" from the microtubule to attract positively charged ions. This can further screen the quantum coherent process. In addition, there is speculation that the microtubule can be driven by the biological energy into the coherent state.

M. Perus proposed an imagination of the combination of neural computing and quantum consciousness [21]. In the neural network theory, the state of the neuron system is described by a vector, which exactly reflects the activity distribution of the time of the neuron system. Particular neuron schemata represent certain information. In the quantum theory, the state of the quantum system can be described by the wave function changes over time. In this way, the neuron state is a kind of superposition of the neuron schema, which can be changed into a superposition of the quantum eigen wave function; the intrinsic wave function of quantum superposed usually has orthogonality and is regular. In the linear combination of the eigen states, each of the eigen states has a corresponding coefficient, which describes the probability of expression of a specific meaning in the actual state of the system. The integrated space—time neuronal signal can be described by the Schrodinger equation in the form of Feynman. The consciousness transformation from the subconscious in the nervous system corresponds to the "collapse of the wave function" with the change from implicit order to explicit order [22].

The neural system model expresses the spatial information encoding of the nervous system in an explicit way, and, for the time, information encoding is to be more indirect. However, through the Fourier transform, we also can easily establish a model with explicit time structure information. If we say that the neural activation pattern represents the description of the object of consciousness, then the Fourier transform of the neural activation spectrum, which represents the frequency distribution of the activation of neurons, is associated with consciousness itself. These are the two aspects of the complementarity of the consciousness activities, with the globality space—time coding of consciousness course together.

12.6 Information integration theory

G. Tononi and Edelman published a series of papers to clarify their comprehensive information theory on consciousness [23]. The literature [24,25] has proposed that the amount of consciousness is related to the quality of the integrated information generated by the complex elements and the quality of the experience stipulated by the information that it produces and that is provided by the complex elements. G. Tononi put forward two measures of integrated information [26].

1. **Measure Φ_1**: Tononi's first measure, Φ_1, is a measure of a static property of a neural system. If Tononi is right, it would measure something like the potential for consciousness in a system. It cannot be a measure of the current consciousness level of the system, for it is a fixed value for a fixed neural architecture, regardless of the system's current firing rates. Tononi's first measure works by considering all the various bipartitions of a neural system. The capacity to integrate information is called Φ and is given by the minimum amount of effective information (EI) that can be exchanged across a bipartition of a subset. Tononi's approach requires examining every subset of the system under consideration. And then, for each subset, every bipartition is considered. Given a subset, S, and a bipartition into A and B, G, Tononi defines a measure called EI. EI uses the standard information theoretic measure of mutual information (MI):

$$MI(A:B) = H(A) + H(B) - H(AB)$$

where H(...) is a entropy, a measure of uncertainty. If there is no interaction between A and B, the MI is zero; otherwise it is positive.

But rather than the standard MI measure that quantifies the information gain from taking account of the connectedness between A and B, Tononi's EI is a measure of the information gain that would accrue if one considered the effect on B when the outputs of A vary randomly across all possible values.

2. **Measure Φ_2:** In more recent work, Tononi and collaborators proposed a revised measure of Φ, that is, Φ_2. This revised measure has some advantages over the previous measure, in that it can deal with a time-varying system, providing a varying, moment-to-moment measure of Φ_2.

   Φ_2 is also defined in terms of EI, though EI is now defined quite differently from the version in Φ_1. In this case, EI is defined by considering a system that evolves in discrete time steps, with a known causal architecture. Take the system at time t_1 and state x_1. Given the architecture of the system, only certain states could possibly lead to x_1. Tononi calls this set of states, with their associated probabilities, a posteriori repertoire. Tononi also requires a measure of the possible states of the system (and their probabilities), in that situation where we do not know the state at time t_1. This he called the a priori repertoire. The a priori repertoire is calculated by treating the system as if we knew nothing at all about its causal architecture, in which case we must treat all possible activation values of each neuron as equally probable. The a priori and a posteriori repertoires each have a corresponding entropy value, for instance, if the a priori repertoire consists of four equally probable states, and the a posteriori repertoire has two equally probable states, then the entropy values will be two bits and one bits, respectively. This means that, in finding out that the state of the system is x_1 at time t_1, we gain information about the state of the system one time step earlier.

   Tononi argues that this is a measure of how much information the system generates in moving into state x_1. Having defined this measure of how much information the system generates, Tononi once again required a measure of how integrated this information is. In the case where the system does not decompose into totally independent parts, we can once again look for the decomposition that gives the lowest additional information from the whole as opposed to the parts. G. Tononi calls this the minimum information partition. The EI for the minimum information partition is then the Φ_2 value for the system.

We can do an exhaustive search across all subsystems and all partitions, and once again we can define complexes. A complex is a system with a given Φ_2 value, which is not contained within any larger system of higher Φ. Similarly, the main complex is the complex with highest Φ_2 in the whole system—and the true measure of Φ_2 (or consciousness) for the system is the Φ_2 of the main complex.

In examining Φ_2, we note that many of the problems with Φ_1 still apply. First, EI and Φ_2 itself are defined in ways that are closely tied to the particular type of system being examined. Although Φ_1, Φ_2, and EI are intended as general-purpose concepts, current mathematics has nothing like the broad range of applicability of standard information theoretic measures. For a further discussion of the shortcomings of information integration theories, refer to Aleksander and Beaton [26].

Tononi recognizes that the integrated information theory is used to study the ability of the maintenance state of the system, which can be regarded as "intelligence." In the literature [23], he described the state quality method and the careful deliberation of qualia with Balduzzi. The qualia were originally used by philosophers to indicate the quality of the internal experience, such as the redness of the rose.

Tononi announced finding a sense of information mechanism of qualia and faced the related controversy with courage. Tononi adopted the geometric manner, the introduction of shape, reflecting the system generated by the interaction of a set of information on the relationship, as the concept of qualia. The literature [25] has canvased the qualia involved in the characteristics of the bottom layer system and essential feature of experience and has offered a geometric neurophysiology and geometrical original mathematics dictionary of phenomenology on qualia.

The qualia space (Q) is the axis space of each possible state (active mode). In Q, each submechanism provides a point of correspondence to the system state. The arrows within the Q project define the information relationship. In short, these arrows define the shape of the qualia, reflecting the quality of the conscious experience with complete and clear features. The height W of the shape is the amount of consciousness associated with the experience.

12.7 Consciousness system in CAM

Consciousness in machines is commonly understood to be the knowledge of a situation or a fact. It is this functionality, the ability to know about

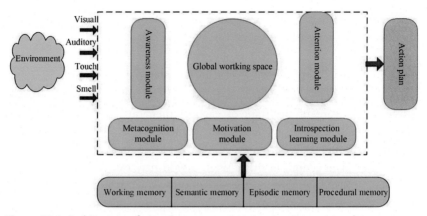

Figure 12.3 Architecture of consciousness system in consciousness and memory.

one's inner knowledge and external surroundings, that makes machines functional, intelligent, aware, and conscious [27].

Fig. 12.3 shows the architecture of consciousness system in consciousness and memory (CAM). It consists of global workspace, awareness, attention, motivation, metacognition, and introspective learning modules [28].

12.7.1 Awareness module

Awareness begins with the input of external stimuli, when the primary features of the sensing system are activated. The output signal is sent to the sensory memory, where a higher level of functional detectors are used for more abstract entities, such as objects, categories, actions, events, etc. The resulting perception is sent to the workspace, where local connections the short episodic memory and declarative memory will mark the thread. These local associations are combined with perception to produce the current situation model, which is used to represent the understanding of the current events that are happening.

In CAM, awareness is basically a perception combination of detecting sensation. Agents work effectively in complex environments, and a subset of these combinations must be selected as the value of perception. The awareness function is the sensed state of $S_{(t)}$ mapped to a subset of the $A_{S(t)}$.

Definition 12.1: (*awareness function*) Awareness function is defined as a perceptual combination of further processing of the sensory state, containing less sensory information that will affect the attention of the agent; the subset of the state space is limited. Among them, the typical awareness function $A_{S(t)}$ can be expressed as:

$$A_{S(t)} = \left\{ \left(a_{1(t)}, a_{2(t)}, \ldots, a_{L(t)}, \ldots \right) \mid a_{L(t)} = s_{L(t)}(\forall L) \right\} \qquad (12.1)$$

Eq. (12.1) defines the awareness function $A_{S(t)}$, which means that each awareness is aware of the state of each element at the time t. L is the length of the element that is felt; it is variable.

Events are introduced to model the transitions between sensed states. Events differ from actions in that a single action may cause a number of different transitions, depending on the situation in which it is performed, while an event describes a specific transition. Events enable attention to be focused on the actual transition that results from an action by modeling the difference between successive sensed states. Events are represented in terms of the difference between two sensed states. The difference between two sensed states, $S_{(t')} = (s_{1(t')}, s_{2(t')}, \ldots s_{L(t')} \ldots)$ and $S_{(t)} = (s_{1(t)}, s_{2(t)}, \ldots s_{L(t)} \ldots)$, where $t' < t$, as a vector of difference variables is calculated using a difference function Δ.

Definition 12.2: (*difference function*) Difference function is assigned a value that represents the difference between the two senses $S_{L(t)}$ and $S_{L(t')}$ in the sense state $S_{(t)}$ and $S_{(t')}$ as follows:

$$\Delta\left(S_{L(t)}, S_{L(t')} \right) = \begin{cases} S_{L(t)} & \text{if } \neg\exists \, S_{L(t')} \\ -S_{L(t')} & \text{if } \neg\exists \, S_{L(t)} \\ S_{L(t)} - S_{L(t')} & \text{if } S_{L(t)} - S_{L(t')} \neq 0 \\ \text{null} & \text{otherwise} \end{cases} \qquad (12.2)$$

The information provided by the differential function reflects the change of the state of one after another.

Definition 12.3: (*event function*) Event function is defined as the combination of the different variables of the agent identification event, and each event contains only one nonzero difference variable. The event function can be defined:

$$E_{S(t)} = \left\{ E_{L(t)} = \left(e_{1(t)}, e_{2(t)}, \ldots, e_{L(t)}, \ldots \right) \mid e_{e(t)} \right\} \qquad (12.3)$$

where

$$e_{e(t)} = \begin{cases} \Delta\left(s_{e(t)}, s_{e(t')} \right), & e = L \\ 0, & \text{otherwise} \end{cases} \qquad (12.4)$$

Events may be of varying length or even empty, depending on the number of sensations to change.

12.7.2 Attention module

Detection of new events is an important feature of any signal classification method. Because we are not able to train all the data that may be encountered in the machine learning system, it becomes very important to distinguish known and unknown object information in the test. Novelty detection is a particularly challenging task, which can be found in a complex, dynamic environment of novel, interesting events. Novelty detection is an essential requirement for a good classification or recognition system because sometimes the information contained in the test data is not known when the training model information is included. The novelty of awareness is related to cognition, and the novelty of cognition is related to knowledge. Based on a fixed set of training samples from a fixed number of categories, novelty detection is a dual decision task for each test sample to determine whether it belongs to a known classification or not.

Definition 12.4: (*novelty detection function*) Novelty detection function N, using the concept of the intelligent body state, $c \in C$, and compare with the memory of a previous experience, $m \in M$, by long memory construction produces a new state $n \in N$:

$$N : C \times M \to N \qquad (12.5)$$

In CAM, the detection of novelty is implemented by a self-organizing map neural network proposed by Kohonen [29]. This neural network is an unsupervised and competitive learning clustering network. Kohonen thinks that a neural network to accept input from the outside world will be divided into different areas, with different regions of different modes having different response characteristics, namely different neurons to best respond depending on the nature of the excitation signal, resulting in the formation of a topologically ordered map. The ordered map is also called a feature map; it is actually a nonlinear mapping relation, and the topological relation of each mode in the signal space is almost invariably reflected in the picture, that is, the output response of neurons. Since this kind of mapping is completed by the unsupervised adaptive process, it is also called a self-organizing feature map.

Interestingness is defined as novelty and surprise, which depends on awareness of the current knowledge and computing power. The degree of interestingness can be objective or subjective: The objective degree of interestingness in the use of relationships is completely considered to be interesting in the object, while the subjective interest is compared with the belief that the attributes of the object are determined by the interests of the user. The interestingness of situation is the measure of the importance of the existing knowledge of the agent. It is interesting that the previous experience is not very similar or may be even very different.

Definition 12.5: (*interestingness function*) The interestingness function determines the interesting value of scenarios, $i \in I$, based on novelty detection, $n \in N$:

$$I.N. \rightarrow I \tag{12.6}$$

Attention is to concentrate on a certain aspect of the environment and ignore other behavior and the cognitive process of thing selectively. According to the interestingness, the threshold selection mechanism [30] is a threshold–filtering algorithm. Assuming that we get a threshold value, T, if the interestingness is greater than T, then the event is selected to create an incentive to attract attention; conversely, if the value is less than T, the event is omitted.

Definition 12.6: (*attention selective*) Attention is a complex cognitive function, which is the nature of human behavior. Attention is an external selection process (sound, image, smell ...); internal (thought) events must be kept at a certain level of awareness. In the given context, selective attention should be given priority processing in the information. Selective attention allows you to focus on a project and to identify and distinguish the irrelevant information wisely. CAM uses the interestingness rate to realize the attention choice.

What we have been discussing is the awareness stage or the attention to the context of the outside world, which plays an important role in the generation of consciousness. After the formation of consciousness, the other type of attention plays a role in arousing and coordinating all the parts of brain functions, finish the task in collaboration, and reach the desired goal.

12.7.3 Global workspace module

The global workspace module is in the working memory area, in which different systems can perform their activities. Global means that the symbols in this memory are distributed and have passed through a large number of processors. Of course, each processor may have a number of local variables and run. But it is very sensitive to the symbol of the overall situation, and the information can be made in a timely manner. When faced with new, different, unusual things, our senses will produce an orienting reaction. At the same time, all kinds of intelligent processors will display their new things on the cognitive analysis scheme by way of cooperation or competition in the global workspace, until you get the best results. It is in this process that we have a sense of new things. The global working space is a blackboard system of information sharing; through the use of the blackboard, each processor tries to spread the information of the global situation and the joint establishment of the problem-solving approach.

The internal structure of the work area is a variety of input buffer and three main modules: the current scenario mode, the register, and the queue of awareness contents. The current scenario model is a structure that stores the current internal and external events that represent the reality. The construction encoder is responsible for creating the structure of the elements in each seed model using the work area. Registered in the auxiliary space, the construction encoder can construct a possible structure and then transfer it to the scenario mode. The queue of the consciousness content stores the contents of the continuous broadcast, which makes the CAM model understandable and which operates the concepts related to time.

The competition of the global working space selects the most outstanding, the most relevant, the most important, and the most urgent affairs; their content becomes the content of consciousness. Then the contents of the consciousness are broadcast to the whole space, and the action selection phase is initiated.

12.7.4 Motivation module

Motivation is defined by psychologists as an internal process that activates, guides, and maintains behavior over time. Motivation learning aims to create abstract motivations and related goals [31]. Based on motivation learning, the motivation module is designed and developed.

1. *Motivation model*: Motivation could be represented as a three-tuple $\{N, G, I\}$, where N means needs, G is goal, and I means the motivation intensity. A motivation is activated by motivational rules whose structure has following format:

$$R = (P, D, \text{Strength}(P|D)) \tag{12.7}$$

where P indicates the conditions of rule activation, D is a set of actions for the motivation, and $\text{Strength}(P|D)$ is a value within interval $[0,1]$.

At present, CAM is going to apply to the animal robot which is a brain—computer integration system. All behaviors of brain—computer integration stem from a fixed and finite number of needs. According to characteristics and requirements of brain—computer integration, there are three types of needs: perception, adaptation, and cooperation:

1. *Perception needs*: Acquire environment information through vision, audition, touch, taste, smell.
2. *Adaptation needs*: Adapt environment condition and optimize impaction of action.
3. *Cooperation needs*: Promise to reward a cooperation action between brain and machine.

2. *Architecture of motivation module*: The architecture of motivation system is shown in Fig. 12.4. The architecture consists of seven components: environment, internal context, motivation, motivation base, goal, action selection, and action composition. Their main functions are explained as follows:

1. *Environment* provides the external information through sensory devices or other agents.
2. *Internal context* represents the homeostatic internal state of the agent and evolves according to the effects of actions.
3. *Motivation* is an abstraction corresponding to the tendency to behave in particular ways according to environmental information. Motivations set goals for the agent in order to satisfy internal context.

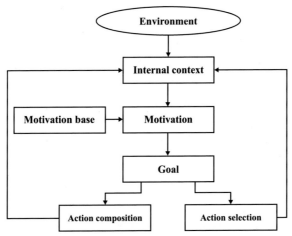

Figure 12.4 Architecture of motivation system.

4. *Motivation base* contains a set of motivations and motivation knowledge with defined format.

5. *Goal* is a desired result for a person or an organization. It used to define a sequence of actions to reach specific goals.

6. *Actions selection* is used to perform motivated action that can satisfy one or several motivations.

7. *Action composition* is the process of constructing a complex composite action from atomic actions to achieve a specific task.

   The action composition is composed of overlapping hierarchical decision loops running in parallel. The number of motivations is not limited. Action composition of the most activated node is not carried out for each cycle, as in a classical hierarchy but only at the end in the action layer, as in a free flow hierarchy. In the end, the selected action is activated.

3. *Motivation execution flow.* In mind model CAM, the realization of the motivation system is through the short-time memory system. In the CAM system, the current belief of the belief memory storage contains the agent motivation knowledge. A desire is a goal or a desired final state. Intention is the need for the smart body to choose the current implementation of the goal. The goal/intention memory module stores the current goal and intention information. In CAM, the goal is a directed acyclic graph by the subgoal composition and is realized step by step. According to a directed acyclic graph, a subgoal is represented by a path to complete, and the total goal finishes when all subgoals are completed.

For an execution system of motivation, the most critical is the internal planning part of the agent. Through planning, each subgoal will complete, through a series of the actions, to achieve what we want to see. Planning mainly deals with the internal information and the new motivation generated by the system.

Motivation execution flow is shown in Fig. 12.5. The receiver gets information from the environment and places it into the queue of motivation. The distributor selects events from the list of events and provides the corresponding planning for the event. When the goal arrives, detect the conditions of the existing environment to see whether they satisfy the goal. The distributor chooses the corresponding plan to accomplish the desired goal, which requires the cooperation of the reasoning machine. This means that the system will find one or more of schemes that were made in the past. It is possible to find a solution that is not the only solution when it is used to reason about an existing object. At this time, the inference engine

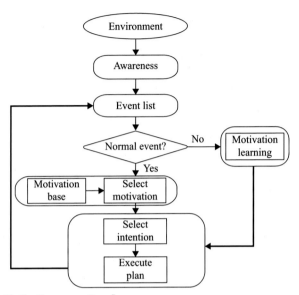

Figure 12.5 Motivation execution flow.

needs to select according to its internal rules. The selection criteria needs to be specified beforehand. Different selection criteria will lead to the agent different behavioral responses in decision making.

After choosing a good plan, the system will need to link up the goal and the plan in advance. This will enable the planning of a detailed understanding of the objectives, and there is sufficient information for use in planning the goal.

The scheduler selects the goal that needs to be executed in the goal list. In the execution of the goal, each goal cannot be interrupted, that is, the execution of the goal cannot be interrupted to execute another goal when a goal is executed.

12.7.5 Metacognition module

In mind model CAM, metacognition module provides agents with cognition and monitoring of their own thinking and learning activities, and its core is cognition to cognition. The metacognitive module has the function of metacognitive knowledge, metacognitive self- regulation control, and metacognitive experience. Metacognitive knowledge includes knowledge about the subject, knowledge of the task, and knowledge of the strategy. Metacognitive experience refers to the experience of their own cognitive process. The cognitive process, through the metacognitive self-regulation control, selects the appropriate strategy to realize the use of strategy, the comparison of process and goal, the adjustment of the strategy, and so on.

12.7.6 Introspective learning module

The introspective learning module is a knowledge-based construction using ontology technology based on the general introspective learning model [32]. The classification problem of failure is an important problem in introspective learning. The classification of failure is the basis of the diagnostic task, and it provides important clues to explain the failure and to construct correct learning objectives. Two important factors of failure classification should be considered: One is the granularity of failure classification, and the other is the relationship between failure classification, failure explanation, and introspective learning goals. The ontology-based knowledge base is the combination of ontology-based knowledge representation and the expert system knowledge base, which has the advantages of conceptual, formal, semantic, and sharing. By using the method of an ontology-based knowledge base to solve the failure classification problem of introspective learning, failure classification will be clearer, and the retrieval process more effective. On the key contents of introspective learning please refer to Chapter 7, Learning.

12.8 Conscious Turing machine

The Turing machine is an abstract machine; it has an infinite length of paper tape, the paper tape is divided into small squares, and each square has a different color. A machine head moves around on the paper tape and has a set of internal states and some fixed programs. The machine head reads a grid information from the current paper tape, combines that with its own internal-state search program table according to the program output information to the paper tape grid, changes its internal state, and then moves on.

Based on the theory of global workspace consciousness proposed by B. J. Baars, Manuel Blum et al. presented a conscious Turing machine (CTM) [33]. In Baars's theory of global workspace consciousness, LTM is compared to the "audience," while STM is compared to "actor," which vividly explains the relationship between LTM and STM. The architecture of CTM is shown in Fig. 12.6.

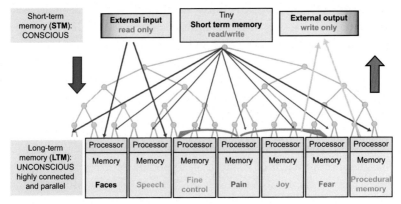

Figure 12.6 Architecture of the conscious Turing machine.

Fig. 12.6 shows that the CTM can be described in a seven-tuple where

STM: short-term memory;

LTM: long-term memory;

Down-tree: top-down tree;

Up-tree: bottom-up tree;

Links: link between the processors of long-term memory;

Input: sense from external environment;

Output: effect to external environment;

Consciousness in CTM is defined as the awareness by all long-term processors. All LTM processors know what is in the short-term memory. Both inner and outer sensations are broadcast from STM.

References

[1] D.C. Dennett, Consciousness Explained, Little Brown and Company, Boston, MA, 1991.
[2] W.H. Calvin, How Brains Think: Evolving Intelligence, Then and Now, Basic Books, 1997.
[3] D.J. Chalmers, The Conscious Mind: In Search of a Fundamental Theory, Oxford University Press, UK, 1996.
[4] F. Crick, The Astonishing Hypothesis, Scribner, 1994.
[5] Z.Z. Shi, Model of consciousness system (in Chinese), in: Y.J. Wang, Y.F. Yang, et al. (Eds.), Consciousness and Brain, People's Publishing House, 2003, pp. 226—231.
[6] X.W. Tang, Four ingredients theory of consciousness, Brain and Mind (in Chinese), Zhejiang University Press, 2007, pp. 91—98.
[7] I.B. Farber, P.S. Churchland, Consciousness and the neurosciences: philosophical and theoretical issues, in: M.S. Gazzaniga (Ed.), The Cognitive Neurosciences, MIT Press, Cambridge, MA, 1995, pp. 1295—1306.

[8] R.E. Ornstein, The Psychology of Consciousness, second ed., Harcount Brace Jovaovich, New Work, 1977.

[9] B. Baars, In the Theater of Consciousness: The Workspace of the Mind, Oxford University Press, NY, 1997.

[10] G.M. Edelman, Naturalizing consciousness: a theoretical framework, Proc. Natl Acad. Sci. USA 100 (9) (2003) 5520−5524.

[11] B.J. Baars, D.E. Edelman, Consciousness, biology and quantum hypotheses, Phys. Life Rev. 9 (2012) 285−294.

[12] P.N. Johnson-Laird, Mental models and human reasoning, Proc. Natl Acad. Sci. USA 107 (2010) 18243−18250.

[13] R. Jackendoff, Language, Consciousness, Culture: Essays on Mental Structure, MIT Press, 2007.

[14] B.J. Baars, A Cognitive Theory of Consciousness, Cambridge University Press, New York, 1988.

[15] F. Crick, C. Koch, Consciousness and neuroscience, Cereb. Cortex 8 (1998) 97−107.

[16] B.J. Baars, S. Franklin, An architectural model of conscious and unconscious brain functions: global workspace theory and IDA, Neural Netw. 20 (9) (2007) 955−961.

[17] F. Crick, C. Koch, A framework for consciousness, Nat. Neurosci. 6 (2003) 119−126.

[18] G.M. Edelman, Biochemistry and the sciences of recognition, J. Biol. Chem. 279 (2004) 7361−7369.

[19] H. Everett, On the foundations of quantum mechanics, Ph.D. thesis, Princeton University, Department of Physics (1957).

[20] R. Penrose, The Emperor's New Mind, Oxford University Press, UK, 1989.

[21] M. Perus, Neuro-Quantum parallelism in brain-mind and computers, Informatica 20 (1996) 173−184.

[22] D. Bohm, B.J. Hiley, The Undivided Universe: An ontological Interpretation of Quantum Theory, Routledge, London, 1993.

[23] G. Tononi, Consciousness as integrated information: a provisional manifesto, Biol. Bull. 215 (2008) 216−242.

[24] G.M. Edelman, G. Tononi, A Universe of Consciousness: How Matter Becomes Imagination, Basic Books, New York, NY, 2000.

[25] D. Balduzzi, G.Q. Tononi, The geometry of integrated information, PLoS Comput. Biol. 5 (8) (2009) 1−224.

[26] M. Beaton, I. Aleksander, World-related integrated information: enactivist and phenomenal perspectives, Int. J. Mach. Conscious. 4 (02) (2012) 439−455.

[27] J. Pandya, Are machine consious? (2019) https://www.forbes.com/sites/cognitive-world/, (accessed 03.13.19.).

[28] Z.Z. Shi, G. Ma, J.Q. Li, Machine consciousness of mind model CAM, in: The 12th International Conference on Knowledge Management in Organizations, Beijing, (2017) 16−26, Heidelberg, London: Springer.

[29] T. Kohonen, Self-organized formation of topologically correct feature maps, Biol. Cybern. 43 (1982) 59−69.

[30] Q.Y. Li, J. Shi, Z.Z. Shi, A model of attention-guided visual sparse coding. ICCI2005, (2005) 120−125.

[31] Z.Z. Shi, G. Ma, X. Yang, C.X. Lu, Motivation learning in mind model CAM, Int. J. Intell. Sci. 5 (2) (2015) 63−71.

[32] Q. Dong, Z.Z. Shi, A research on introspective learning based on CBR, Int. J. Adv. Intell. 3 (1) (2011) 147−157.

[33] M. Blum, L. Blum, A. Blum, Towards a conscious AI: a computer architecture inspired by cognitive neuroscience, Lecture Notes, in: 2020 BAAI Conference, Beijing, (2020) 21−24 June.

CHAPTER 13

Brain−computer integration

Brain−computer interface (BCI) is a direct communication pathway between the brain and an external device. Brain−computer integration is a new kind of intelligent system based on BCI, which aims to combine living beings' intelligence and machines' intelligence. It has a great potential in many applications, such as clinical rehabilitation, entertainment, and military surveillance.

The integration of biological intelligence (brain) and computer intelligence (machine), the perfect combination of brain's perception and cognitive ability and machine's computing ability, is expected to produce a stronger intelligent form that extends beyond the existing biological intelligence system and machine intelligence system.

13.1 Overview

The brain−computer interface (BCI) is the interface that connects the human brain or animal brain with the outside world. However, this connection is done not in a normal and regular way but in a special way to connect with the outside world, for example, stimulating the artificial cochlea, the external signal commanding mice to walk in the maze, the monkey taking bananas with the machine hand, and the brain wave controlling the computer. Some think the essence of the life is information. Since the essence of both the artificial brain and the biological brain is information and they have the same mechanism of information processing, they should be able to exchange with the help of the interface. Information is uniform in essence, which will make a great development in computer techniques, artificial brain, and the combination of the human brain and the computer.

In 1973 Vidal published the first paper related to the BCI [1]. The BCI does not depend on the brain's normal output path, namely nervous peripherals and muscular tissue; the system can realize human brain communication directly with the external world (computer or other peripheral devices). The failure of setting up the first brain−machine interface system was the partial start in the run program of IBM360/91

Intelligence Science
DOI: https://doi.org/10.1016/B978-0-323-85380-4.00013-0

computer. This kind of machine is a batch processing machine, which cannot meet the needs of real-time processing of the brain—computer interface system. The progress of recent computer and signal processing technology has opened up a new era of electroencephalography (EEG) signal analysis and BCI research; computer speeds now can meet the needs of BCI signal processing. So why can't the real-time detection of thought be achieved? Placement in neurons in the vicinity of the microelectrodes to record cell excitatory signals with the idea of controlling a BCI has many problems. First is using a large number of brain electrodes to control the individual's thinking, because each individual has a million neurons. In addition, scientists do not understand the relationship between cell excitability and thinking.

The scientists at MIT, Bell Labs, and Neural Information Science Research Institute have developed successfully a microcomputer chip that can simulate the human nervous system, successfully implanted in the brain, and repair human nerves using the principle of bionics. It cooperates with the brain and sends out complicated orders for the electronic device, monitoring the activity of the brain to achieve very good results. People will be able to put microchips in the brain to increase memory, so that people have a "spare brain" in the near future.

American researchers in the field of biological computer—bonded cells taken from animal brain tissue with computer hardware, such a developed machine is called a biological electronic robot or cyborg. If the chip is in good agreement with the nerve endings, the chip can be connected to the nerve fibers and the body's brain nervous system. This improves the human brain function through the computer.

In 1999 Liaw and Burger of the University of Southern California proposed a dynamic synapse neural circuit model [2] and in 2003 developed a brain chip, which can replace the function of the hippocampus. The brain chip was successfully demonstrated in vivo mouse, which was consistent with the information processing in the brain of in vivo rat. This project is a part of the mind-machine merger, which has made breakthrough progress, and has been ranked as one of the top ten scientific and technological advances in the world in 2003 by the Chinese scientific community.

In July 2016 Elon Musk founded a company, Neuralink, which studies BCI technology. Their research focuses on creating brain—computer interaction devices that can be implanted in the human brain, allowing the human brain to connect directly to computing devices.

On July 16, 2019 Elon Musk, CEO of Neuralink, a BCI company, held a press conference. Neuralink said that it had found an efficient way to implement BCI. According to Neuralink's method, thin threads, which are only a quarter the width of a human hair, are passed through special surgical robots and "stitched" into the brain. A "wire harness" of 1024 wires is attached to a small chip, ten of which are implanted into the skin, each of which can be wirelessly connected to a wearable, detachable, and upgraded device behind the ear, which can communicate wirelessly with a mobile phone.

To implement such a system, three core technologies are involved: the implanted "wire" of the brain, the neurosurgical robot for implantation, and the chip for reading brain signals. The first major improvement of this BCI is the "wire." which is $4-6$ μm wide, which is equivalent to 1/10 of human hair. Compared with the materials currently used, it is not likely to damage the brain and can transmit more data. These wires are distributed in 96 threads with up to 3072 electrodes per array.

Another major advance is the neurosurgical robots used for implant lines. The robot is vividly named the "sewing machine" because its working principle is similar to that of a sewing machine: Thread is inserted into the brain needle by needle. The robot can implant six wires per minute and can precisely avoid other tissues such as blood vessels.

The third breakthrough is the development of a chip that can better read, clean up, and amplify signals from the brain. The chip is connected to the brain through the wiring harness, and each harness is composed of 1024 wires. Each wire harness attached to the chip can be wirelessly connected to a wearable, detachable, scalable "pod" device behind the ear, and the device can communicate wirelessly with a mobile phone. Now, the chip can only transmit data over a wired connection (it uses USB-C), but the ultimate goal is to create a wireless working system. To do this, Neuralink plans to implant four of these sensors, three in the motion area and one in the somatosensory area. It will wirelessly connect to an external device mounted behind the ear, which will contain a unique battery.

13.2 Modules of the brain—computer interface

The BCI is an effective as well as a powerful tool for user—system communication [3]. It can be defined as a hardware and software communications strategy that empowers humans to interact with their surroundings with no inclusion of peripheral nerves or muscles by utilizing control signals produced from electroencephalographic activity. Every BCI system essentially consists of three function modules: signal acquisition, signal analysis, and controller (see Fig. 13.1).

1. Signal acquisition: The experimenter header wears an electrode cap, gathers an EEG signal, and conveys to the amplifier; the signal generally needs to be amplified about 10,000 times. Through preprocessing, including signal filtering and A/D conversion, the signal is finally transformed into digital form and stored in the computer.

2. Signal analysis: Utilizing algorithms such as fast fourier transformation (FFT), wavelet analysis, etc., from the preprocessed EEG signals are drawn from the particular features correlated to the experimenter's intention. After drawing, the features are classified by the classifier. The output of the classifier is regarded as the input of the controller.

3. Controller: The classified signal is converted to the actual action, such as the cursor on the display movement, mechanical hand movement, the letter input, control of the wheelchair, open the television, etc. Some of the BCI system is also provided with a feedback loop, as shown in Fig. 13.1; it can not only let experimenters clear think about their control results but can also help them adjust the brain's electric signal according to the results in order to reach the desired objectives.

This chapter [4] introduces EEG-based BCI, particularly to investigate its methodological advantages and disadvantages and the essential contributions required in this field of research. In spite of the many outstanding

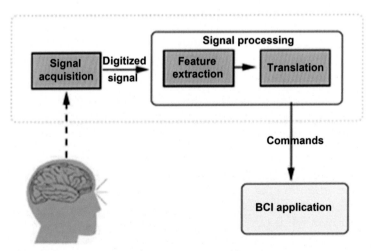

Figure 13.1 Basic structure of brain−computer interface system.

breakthroughs that have been achieved in BCI research, some issues still need to be resolved. Firstly, a general BCI standard is currently the main issue. The BCI community should declare a general BCI standard that must be adhered to by BCI researchers. Second, the existing BCIs offer a somewhat poor information transfer rate (ITR) for any type of effectual BCI application. Hence, future research should concentrate on increasing the ITR of BCI systems. Moreover, matching the most relevant EEG control signal with the intended BCI application is another important issue in EEG-based BCI research.

13.3 Electroencephalography signal analysis

13.3.1 Electroencephalography signal sorting

The electroencephalogram is divided into spontaneous EEG and evoked potentials (EP). Spontaneous EEG is the spontaneous generation of neural cells in the human brain without specific external stimuli. Here, the so-called spontaneity is relative, referring to nothing in particular outside to stimulate. The spontaneous electroencephalogram is a nonstationary random signal; not only its rhythm with changes in mental state but also the basic rhythm of the background will occur from time to time, such as rapid eye movement, etc. Evoked potential means something that exerts and stimulates the sense organ (photic, acoustic, or electric) and artificially changes the brain electric potential. Evocations by stimulation patterns can be divided into auditory-evoked potentials; visual-evoked potentials (VEP); a body feeling—evoked potentials (somatosensorily evoked potential), and the use of a variety of psychological factors as expected; preparation; a variety of voluntary activities evoked event-related potentials (ERP). ERP fusion up the psychology of the cerebral cortex of neurophysiology and cognitive process. It includes P300 (reflecting the objective indicator of the cognitive function of the human brain), N400 (language comprehension and expression of related potentials), and endogenous components. ERP and a number of cognitive processes, such as psychological judgment, understanding, identification, attention, selection, making decisions, directional response, some language functions, etc. are closely related.

Spontaneous EEG signals reflect the electrical activity of the human brain and the functional state of the brain, and its essential features include cycle, amplitude, phase, and so on. Regarding the classification of electroencephalography (EEG) according to the frequency band and amplitude, EEG is generally divided into the following waves:

1. δ *wave*: Frequency band range 0.5~3 Hz, the amplitude is generally about 100 μV. In sober, normal people's electroencephalogram, we cannot generally record the δ wave. In a lethargic adult, an infant or preschool child, or mature adult of developed intelligence, we can record this kind of wave. When influenced by some medicines, the brain will create a δ wave with organic disease.

2. θ *wave*: in the frequency band range 4~7 Hz, the amplitude is generally 20~40 μV. This wave appears in the frontal lobe, terminal leaf, and is relatively obvious, generally in sleepy subjects. It is the manifestation of the inhibitory state of the central nervous system.

3. α *wave*: In the frequency band range 8~13 Hz, the amplitude of the rhythm is generally 10~ 0 μV; this is the amplitude and space distribution of the normal person's α wave, with some individual differences. Of the activities of an α wave, the most prominent by carrying the pillow department, and bilateral symmetry, appear the greatest when the subject is quiet and has eyes close. The amplitude is also the highest with open eyes, except other while irritating at the question of thinking, α wave disappears and presents another fast wave.

4. β *wave*: In the frequency band range 14~30 Hz, the amplitude is generally less than 30 μV, distributed over the central area and center front temple; it is easiest to present in the frontal lobe. The α rhythm disappears and presents a β rhythm at the time of the physiological reaction. The β rhythm relates nervousness and excitement. So usually the β rhythm is related to activity, or desynchronizing typologically.

5. γ *wave*: In the frequency band range 30~45 Hz, the amplitude is generally less than 30 μV. The frontal area and central areas exhibit this wave the most. This and the β wave are fast waves, which increase with excitement, manifesting an increased amplitude in the nerve cell.

It is generally believed that normal brain wave frequency range is in generally4~45 Hz. A cortex pathological change will cause an unusual frequency component in some brain waves.

ERP fusion up the psychology of the cerebral cortex of neurophysiolog0cal and cognitive process. Many cognitive processes, such as psychological judgment, understanding, recognition, attention, selection, making decisions, orienting response, some language functions etc., are closely associated. Typical ERP are as follows:

1. P300: P300 is a kind of ERP, and its peak value is about 300 ms after the event occurs. The smaller the probability of occurrence of relevant events, the more prominent is the P300 caused.

2. VEP: The VEP changes specific parts of the brain, called VEP.

3. Event-related synchronization (ERS) or desynchronization electric potential (ERD): Given unilateral limb movements or imagined movements, the contralateral brain areas produce events related to the synchronous potential; the same side of the brain region generates ERS.

4. Slow cortical electric potentials (SCP): SCP consists of changes of the cortical potentials, for the duration of a few hundred milliseconds to a few seconds. Through feedback training, autonomous control SCP amplitude positive or negative deviation can be achieved.

These several kinds of brain electric signals, as BCI input signals, have their own characteristics and limitations. P300 and VEP belong to the evoked potential category, do not need training, and signal detection is simpler and more accurate with the processing method. The drawbacks are that a special device is needed for stimulation, and results depend on a certain level of consciousness of people (such as vision). Other kinds signals do not require outside stimulation, but they do require a large amount of special training.

13.3.2 Electroencephalography signal analytical method

In 1932 Dietch first used the Fourier transform for EEG feature analysis, introducing classic methods such as frequency-domain analysis, time domain analysis, etc. in the EEG research field. In recent years, methods such as wavelet analysis, nonlinear dynamics analysis, neural network analysis, chaos analysis, statistics, etc. and the organic combination of analytical methods effectively promoted the development of the EEG signal analysis method. With the development of research work, the analysis of EEG patterns with time and spatial information has also become an effective way to study EEG signals. EEG signal analysis technology is widely used at present:

1. Time domain analysis: The extraction of features directly from the time domain is the first developed method because it is very intuitive and has clear physical meaning. Time domain analysis is mainly used to directly extract waveform features, such as zero crossing point analysis, histogram analysis, analysis of variance, correlation analysis, peak detection and waveform parameter analysis, coherent average,

waveform recognition, and so on. In addition, using the parameter model (such as the AR model, etc.) is an important means to analyze the signal in the 1 time domain, and the feature parameters can be classified, identified, and tracked by EEG. However, because the waveform of EEG signal is very complex, there is no particularly effective method of EEG waveform analysis.

2. Frequency-domain analysis: Because many of the main features of the EEG signal are reflected in the frequency domain, power spectrum estimation is an important means of frequency-domain analysis, and spectrum analysis technology plays an especially important position in EEG signal processing. Its significance lies in the change of amplitude with time in the brain wave transform to EEG power with frequency changes in the spectrum, which can be directly observed in the distribution and transformation of EEG frequency. Spectral estimation methods can generally be divided into classic methods and modern methods. The classic spectrum estimation method, by definition, uses finite—length data to estimate, namely short-period data of the Fourier transform—based cycle method, mainly in two ways: the indirect method to estimate the correlation function, after Fourier transform, to obtain the power spectrum estimation (according to the Wiener Khintchine theorem); the direct method and random data direct Fourier transform, taking the amplitude square to get the corresponding power spectrum estimation, also known as a periodogram. The common problem of the two methods is that the variance of the estimation is not good, and the estimated value along the frequency axis of the fluctuation is more severe; the longer the data, the more serious the phenomenon. In order to improve the resolution of spectral estimation, a set of modern spectral estimation theory is formed based on the parameter model. The parametric model estimation method can obtain high-resolution spectrum analysis result, which provides an effective method for the extraction of the EEG signal in the frequency domain. However, the power spectrum estimation cannot reflect the time variability of the EEG spectrum. Therefore, the power spectrum of the time-varying nonstationary process of EEG can be lost when the power spectrum of the single frequency domain is lost.

3. Time frequency analysis: Time frequency analysis technology is different from traditional time domain or frequency-domain analysis. It is simultaneous in the time and frequency domains of signal analysis technology, mainly divided into two types of linear and nonlinear transform. Linear transformation mainly includes short-time Fourier

transform, Gabor transform, and wavelet transform technology. Nonlinear transformations mainly include Wigner-Ville distribution, Cohen class distribution, etc. The main idea behind time frequency analysis is to spread the time domain signal in the time frequency plane. In time, the independent variable signal is expressed by two parameters: time and frequency as a function of the independent variables, thus showing the frequency components of the signal at different time points. Compared with the traditional Fourier transform, time frequency analysis is more advantageous due to the characteristic of having nonstationary and time-varying signals. In the EEG signal analysis, the main application of time frequency analysis technology is to EEG feature waveform recognition and feature extraction. At present, the most widely used method is the wavelet transform. Wavelet analysis uses a short window at high frequency and a wide window at low frequency, which fully embodies the idea of relative bandwidth frequency analysis and adaptive variable resolution analysis, thus providing a possible means for real-time signal analysis. At present, the time frequency analysis of EEG has led to a lot of valuable research results.

4. Space—time analysis: Considering the spatial distribution of the EEG on the scalp and merging the analytic intersection of space—time and analytical methods is helpful to reveal and enhance the implicit characteristics of the multisignal. For example, motor, sensory, and cognitive activities in space for performance parts have obvious differences; therefore, temporal and spatial information for identifying, analyzing, and fusion may get more in-depth research results. The analytical methods of spatial and temporal patterns are greater, such as the micro state, spatial spectrum estimation, classical statistical methods (correlation function), spatial filter, and so on. Combining the multidimensional statistical analysis methods of spatial filtering methods, such as principal component analysis (PCA), independent component analysis (ICA), public space model (common spatial pattern, CSP), in the EEG signal analysis processing fields has been a very important application. Specifically, PCA is a linear transform; processing is the signal to do singular value decomposition, before determining the signals in the main composition as a basis for judgment. Based on higher-order statistics, the ICA represents the latest development theories of modern statistical signal analysis. Studies have shown that ICA is very suitable for multichannel EEG signal analysis and has yielded very good results in EEG noise elimination

and feature extraction. Calculating the spatial filter to detect the event related to the phenomenon of the CSP (ERD) algorithm is the most successful in the EEG feature extraction algorithm and has been widely used in BCI. The time and space analysis method can provide more information, and it has been an important research direction in EEG signal analysis in recent years.

13.4 Brain−computer interface technology

In the past ten years, BCI technology has been developed rapidly in the following research directions of information technology.

13.4.1 Visual-evoked potential

A plurality of options is displayed on the display device, and the user is looking at a desired option. Processing the display mode can enable users to produce different EEG signals when looking at different options. A more direct way to get a look at the target is to track people's attention. But this method requires the head to remain motionless, it is difficult to achieve practical applications. And the BCI based on EEG does not restrict the movement of the head. In 1992 Sutter developed a real-time BCI system called brain response system [5]. Displaying an 8*8 matrix notation in accordance with a pseudo-random binary sequence (known as the *m*-sequence) red/green alternately, while the user is watching the symbol you want selected and comparing the measured EEG signal with a prerecorded template, you can determine whether the user is watching the goal. Users can use the system to operate word processing software.

13.4.2 Event-related potential

13.4.2.1 P300 potential

P300 is a kind of ERP, and its peak value appears about 300 ms after the dependent event happens. Event-related probability is small, is caused by P300, is significant, and is the most significant in the parietal region (middle part in head or posterior). When one is exerted in several different ways while subjected to the constituent stimulus, the range of P300 that each kind of stimulus causes can be measured; the P300 range that those stimuli cause should be larger. This kind of stimulus is what experimenters count, that is, the stimulus that the user wants to choose. In 1988 Farwell et al. developed a virtual typewriter using P300 [6]. A 6 × 6 character matrix is flashed by row or column, and the order was is random;

then the row or column flicker is in related events, showings the character the user wants to enter. Seeking to detect the P300 amplitude of the largest row and column, the line and the column intersection for the character, the character is printed.

13.4.2.2 Event-related desynchronization

Pfunscheller and his colleagues developed a system [7] whose method is similar with the literature [8]. They concentrated on the central area of the scalp, that is, multielectrodes on the sensory motor cortex, and observed the μ rhythm produced (under the awake state). When people were not processing sensory input or generating output motion, the sensory and motor cortical areas often showed EEG activity of 8−12 Hz. When they concentrated on the sensory or motor cortex, the slow wave was a μ rhythm. Focusing on the visual cortex produced an amplitude change of the visual μ rhythm and other rhythms. The amplitude of this particular frequency band is associated with increased motor activity and decreases with ERS and ERD.

Training a neural network to recognize the ERS/ERD patterns caused by particular sports (for example, right- or left-hand movement or holding the game card T in one hand to the right or left) and to discern finally the pattern produced by the action, then the Hibert transform is adopted to extract the key features of these pattern. Learning vector quantization or the Kohonen neural network is used to classify them. When the neural network is trained 100 ∼ 200 times, the system will be able to identify the EEG pattern caused by specific movement with very high accuracy, which can control the cursor movement or other external devices. For example, the EEG data for one second can be predicted with the left- or right-hand movement, and the accuracy rate is as high as 89%. Now, researchers are studying the stability of the pattern that corresponds to the continuous motion and the method of improving the rate and accuracy of the pattern recognition.

13.4.3 Spontaneous electroencephalography for action training

Wolpaw et al. found that people can learn to use spontaneous EEG activity [9] that is not caused by special evoked stimulation activities to control an external instrument. They focused on training the obtained μ rhythm and the related EEG component. The obtained μ rhythm is generated by the sensorimotor cortex, recorded in the center of the head of the electrical activity. Experimenters learn to use the selected μ rhythm and/or other EEG components. Move a cursor located in the center of the display screen to the surrounding target. Move the cursor as the output because it is objective, easy to implement and quantify, can be used as a prototype of a variety of rehabilitation equipment, and can be used to operate the mouse driver. In one dimensional model, the target is located at the top or bottom of the screen edge, and the cursor moves vertically.

In a two-dimensional mode, the target may be located anywhere (e.g., one of the four corners), and the cursor has both vertical movement and horizontal movement. The EEG in a specific frequency range is obtained by online spectral analysis and is converted to the cursor movement. For example, in one dimension, high-amplitude rhythms ($8-12$ Hz μ rhythm) recorded in the sensorimotor cortex of one cerebral hemisphere were used to move the cursor. Low amplitude was used to move the cursor down. A function that transforms the magnitude to the cursor movement is a linear equation. The parameters are derived from the evaluation of the previous performance of the user. In a two-dimensional model, an equation controls the vertical movement, and another equation controls the level of movement. Most users can get obvious control ability after $5 \sim 10$ stages. After more training, they will be able to reach the top or bottom of the target in $1-2$ seconds with accuracy higher than or equal to 90%. For two-dimensional control, although it is very significant, it cannot achieve such a high accuracy rate. Efforts are being made to improve the accuracy and speed of the cursor movement, depending on the definition of alternatives, to increase the training of the EEG component, or to improve the EEG control in the cursor moving algorithm. The ultimate goal of this work is a mouse cursor movement, so as to enable brain, based on the EEG and via the human−computer interface, to operate a commercial mouse driver.

13.4.4 Self-regulation of steady-state visual-evoked professional

By a movement training method, McMillan et al. trained some volunteers to control the steady-state VEP amplitude caused by fluorescent tubes with a flash frequency of 13.25 Hz [10]. The electrode is placed in the occipital cortex to measure the change of the magnitude, with a horizontal strip and/or feedback auditory sound to the experimenter. The change of magnitude is transformed into the input of control through real-time analysis. If the VEPI amplitude is above or below the specified threshold, a discrete control output is generated. These outputs can be used to control many kinds of instruments. After training for about 6 hours, the experimenters basically could command a flight simulator to make left or right turns with an accuracy rate higher than 80%. After $3 \sim 5$ stages of flight simulation training, the experimenter were able to control a neuromuscular controller to execute the knee extension with 95% accuracy.

At present, in BCI area the leading laboratories around the world and their BCI research directions are as follows.

1. Graz University of Technology, Austria

    Pfunscheller et al. apply ERS/desynchronization potential as the BCI signal input. In this system, experimenters can control the movement of the cursor [7].

2. Wadsworth Center, USA

    Wolpaw et al. trained experimenters to adjust the μ rhythm by themselves and, through changes of μ rhythms, to achieve cursor movement, spelling letters, and prosthetic control and other functions [9]. Due to its flexible control of one's own μ rhythm, it is more difficult to use, so not every experimenter can learn to use this device.

3. Tübingen University, Germany

    Birbaumer et al. designed a thought translation device (TTD), through changes of the slow cortical potentials to achieve control of the outside world, using visual feedback, to realize the function of spelling letters [11].

4. University of Illinois, USA

    Farwell et al. adopted a P300-evoked potential as the BCI signal input [6]. On a computer screen, 36 letters were shown in a 6×6 lattice. The experimenter is required to select a particular letter. Each line and each column flickers with a frequency of 10 Hz; calculated for each row and each column is the scintillation average reaction, measuring P300 amplitude. The greatest response to rows and columns for a particular letter can be "found" from the P300-evoked potential.

5. Department of Biomedical Engineering, Tsinghua University, China

    Shangkai Gao et al. developed a noninvasive BCI system with a high transmission rate based on steady-state visual-evoked potentials (SSVEP) [12], which can be used for motion control, environmental control equipment, and other purposes, after they study in-depth the characteristics analysis and extraction method of SSVEP.

13.5 P300 brain—computer interface system

P300-ERP is a kind of ERP that is induced by a small probability event (visual, auditory, tactile, and other sensory) and gains its name due to a positive potential waveform in the EEG that happens about 300 ms after the incident corresponding to it. Based on the P300 potential of the BCI, an specific event stimulus sequence is used to evoke the user's P300 potential and, through the occurrence of P300, to determine the user's awareness activities. This type of BCI is particularly suitable for selecting a target from multiple options. In recent years there have been new P300–BCI systems that use nonalphabetic symbols and objects as input options, a combination of evoked potential P300 and virtual reality applications, and so on

13.5.1 Architecture

Take the P300 Chinese input BCI system as an example to explain the architecture of the P300–BCI system [13]. The system consists of a user interface, an EEG acquisition system, and an EEG analysis program; the composition of the system is shown in Fig. 13.2. The user interface induces the P300 potentials of the user by visual stimulation and to transmit amplified marking flashing moment event code. The EEG acquisition system consists

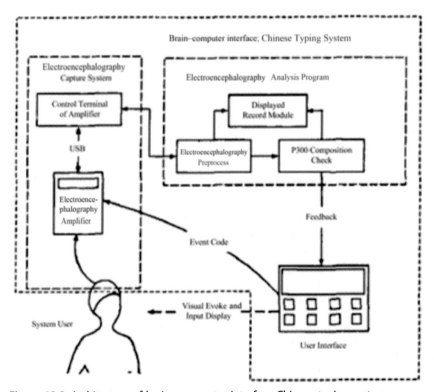

Figure 13.2 Architecture of brain–computer interface Chinese typing system.

of the P300 EEG signal, amplification, filtering, digitalization, merging with the event code, and transfer to the EEG analysis program. The analysis program is responsible for the EEG online processing, converting the acquisition of P300 information into the selection of instructions, and then real-time feedback to the user interface for the input of Chinese characters.

The EEG analysis program and user interface program run on different PC machines. The user interface appears through the computer display. The EEG acquisition system use a neuroscan with a 40 EEG amplifier and multichannel electrode cap. The EEG analysis program processes the EEG signal data and preservation of intermediate data of EEG for later experimental analysis. As shown in Fig. 13.2, if the user is regarded as a constituent element of the system, then the flow of information of the overall system forms a closed loop.

In the course of typing, the user interface sends a flickering message to the EEG processing program to indicate it is finished and then enters the wait state, after the end of each selection phase. After receiving this message, the processing program reads the EEG data from the buffer and sends the corresponding P300 command to the interface after analyzing and judging. If the program thinks that the P300 cannot be reliably identified, the command is sent out empty. If an effective command is received by the interface, it will be sent to the input of the Chinese character spelling module; if an empty command is received, the system does not carry out any action and starts a new round of selection of flashing.

13.5.2 Visual elicitor subsystem

A visual-evoked signal is the core module of P300 brain—computer interface system and the most flexible part in the entire system, and it has a certain decisive role in the configuration modes of other modules. The visual elicitor subsystem includes three parts: layout management, experimental parameter configuration, and maintenance of experimental scheme. The layout management module supports different types of control calls and the location, distance, and other parameters of the adjustment function, and it is very user-friendly to operate and control. The parameter configuration interface involves a variety of experimental parameters. In the configuration of the appearance parameters of the control, there is very high configuration flexibility to meet the needs of the general P300 experiment parameters control. The maintenance module maintains the experimental evoking design scheme, including the storage, reading, and other functions of the experimental scheme.

13.5.3 Electroencephalography acquisition subsystem

The EEG acquisition subsystem contains P300 EEG signal amalgamates with incident code after amplification, filtering, digitization, and transfer to the EEG analysis program to improve the reliability of P300 detection. The preprocessing program processes the EEG signal corresponding to each option as a unit.

1. Removing the direct current drift of signals: Deduct the mean value of the original signal first, then remove the general direct component. This signal still contains a frequency of less than 0.5 Hz of the DC drift, the performance of the baseline of the ups and downs. Regard 1 second as the sampling interval to fetch the sample equally. The sampling points generate three spline curves, as the baseline of signal. The signal is subtracted from the spline curve, and the baseline drift is eliminated.

2. Eliminating the electric disturbance of eyes: The blinking movements of experimental subjects will alias the relevant electric potential of the eye in the EEG. Because of its large peak amplitude, it will seriously interfere with the identification of P300 potential. A regression algorithm can be used to eliminate the interference of the eye. In addition to the EEG, the simultaneous acquisition of electrical signals of eye (EOG) is needed. By calculating whether the slope of the EOG baseline exceeds a certain threshold to judge the occurrence time of the blink, the EEG signal is corrected for this time period.

3. Filter: The signal to the cutoff frequency of low-pass filtering 15 Hz, eliminates the high-frequency interference. A fifth-order Butterworth filter is used as filter algorithm.

4. Signal segmentation: The selected signal is divided into n segments corresponding to the round. Each round signal is subdivided into seven flash sections. The time span of each flash is 600 ms, which is calculated from the time when the corresponding event code appears. The flash segment contains a possible P300 potential.

13.5.4 Electroencephalography analysis subsystem

EEG analysis subsystem is responsible for the EEG online processing. The P300 information is converted into the choice instruction and then sends real-time feedback to the user interface for the input of Chinese characters. The system has the functions of superposition average, template matching, discriminant recognition, and so on.

1. **Superimposed average:** The different rounds of flash data corresponding to the same event code is classified as one kind, so we get total of seven categories, each class containing n flashing sections. The flashing sections of each class are superimposed on Eq. (13.1):

$$mEEG_i = \frac{1}{n \sum\limits_{k=1}^{n} EEG_{i,k}} \quad (13.1)$$

where $EEG_{i,k}$ is the value of the k flashing segment at the time point i, and $mEEG_i$ is represented by the value of the superimposed signal at the time point i. After overlay, each choice gets the seven flashing data segment, respectively representing the EEG data after different option box flashing.

2. **Template matching:** The template is a prepared P300 data in advance, which is a typical P300 potential waveform signal for each pathway of the user. The time span of the template signal is 400 ms, corresponding to the $200 \sim 600$ ms of the scintillation (flash) segment.

   Template matching is performed by the degree of the difference between a metric to characterize both the measured scintillation (flash) signal segment and the template signal. The random signal correlation number s as the matching metric and pathway c and its template s value expressions can be shown in the Eq. (13.2):

$$S_c = \frac{\sum x_{c,i} m_{c,i}}{\sqrt{\sum x_{c,i}^2 \sum m_{c,i}^2}} \quad (13.2)$$

where x_i and m_i are the flashing signal and template values in the moment i, respectively, and the subscript c indicates the c pathway. Because the flash and template mean is all set to 0, there is no need to subtract the mean value of the signal from each x_i or m_i. The greater S value shows that the signal is closer to the template.

3. **Discrimination:** The EEG signal of M pathways is collected by the system. By template matching, every choice gets $7 \times m$ matching value. The average s' of m matching values of each option represents the average similarity between the EEG collected by each electrode and the template. The flash segment with the largest s' is most likely to be the P300 potential. On the basis of improving reliability, the gap between maximum s' and other flash s' values should reach a certain level in order to assure the validity of results. For this reason, the

system presumes that the discriminant procedure sends the corresponding option as the P300 command to the user interface only when the difference between maximum s' and the second largest s' is greater than 0.2; otherwise the program outputs an empty instruction.

13.6 ABGP agent

In intelligence science and artificial intelligence, an agent can be viewed as perceiving its environment information through sensors and as acting with the environment through effectors. As an internal mental model of agent, the BDI (belief, desire, intention) model has been well recognized in the philosophical and artificial intelligence areas. Bratman's philosophical theory was formalized by Cohen and Levesque [14]. In their formalism, intentions are defined in terms of the temporal sequences of the agent's beliefs and goals. Rao and Georgeff have proposed a possible-worlds formalism for BDI architecture [15]. The abstract architecture they proposed comprises three dynamic data structures representing the agent's beliefs, desires, and intentions, together with an input queue of events. The update operations on beliefs, desires, and intentions are subject to respective compatibility requirements. These functions are critical in enforcing the formalized constraints upon the agent's mental attitudes. The events that the system can recognize include both external events and internal events.

A cognitive model for multiagent collaboration should consider the external perception and internal mental state of agents. A 4-tuple framework (Awareness, Belief, Goal, Plan) is proposed for the agent, whose architecture is shown in Fig. 13.3. Awareness is an information pathway connecting to the world (including natural scenes and other agents in the multiagent system). M. Endsley pointed out awareness has four basic characteristics [16]:

1. Awareness is knowledge about the state of a particular environment.
2. Environments change over time, so awareness must be kept up-to-date.
3. People maintain their awareness by interacting with the environment.
4. Awareness is usually a secondary goal—that is, the overall goal is not simply.

Beliefs can be viewed as the agent's knowledge about its setting and itself. Goals make up the agent's wishes and drive the course of its actions. Plans represent the agent's means to achieve its goals.

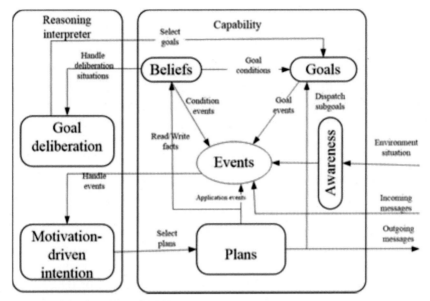

Figure 13.3 Architecture of ABGP agent.

The Awareness, Belief, Goal, Plan (ABGP) agent considers not only the internal mental state of the agent but also the cognition and interaction of the external scene, which plays an important role in the decision-making of the agent. ABGP agent is the core component of brain—computer collaborative simulation environment.

13.7 Key technologies of brain—computer integration

Brain—computer integration is a new intelligent system based on brain—computer interface technology, which is integrated with biological intelligence and machine intelligence [17,18]. Brain—computer integration is an inevitable trend in the development of brain—computer interface technology. In the brain—computer integration system, not only must the brain and the machine be interoperable on the signal level, but the brain's cognitive ability must be integrated with the computer's computing ability. But the cognitive unit of the brain has different relationships from those of the intelligent unit of the machine. Therefore, one of the key scientific issues of brain—computer integration is how to establish the cognitive computing model of brain—computer integration.

At present brain—computer integration is an active research area in intelligent science. In 2009 DiGiovanna developed the mutually adaptive

BCI system based on reinforcement learning [19], which regulates brain activity by the reward and punishment mechanism. The machine adopts the reinforcement learning algorithm to adapt the motion control of a mechanical arm and has the optimized performance of the manipulator motion control. In 2010 Fukayarna et al. controlled a mechanical car by extraction and analysis of mouse motor nerve signals [20]. In 2011 the Nicolelis team developed a new brain−computer−brain information channel with a bidirectional closed-loop system. As reported in *Nature* [21], it turned a monkey's touch information into an electric stimulus signal to feed back to the brain while decoding the nerve information of monkey's brain in order to effect the brain−computer cooperation.

The brain−computer integration system has three remarkable characteristics: (1) more comprehensive perception of organisms, including understanding behavior and decoding neural signals; (2) organisms are a system of sensing, a computation body, and an executive body, with a bidirectional information exchange channel with the rest of the system; (3) comprehensive utilization of the organism and machine on multilevels and with multigranularity greatly enhances system intelligence.

In 2013 the Zhaohui Wu team of Zhejiang University developed a visual enhanced rat robot [22]. Compared with the general robot, the rat robot has the advantage in the aspects of flexibility, stability, and environmental adaptability. In this project, rats were the main carriers; through the camera combined with the computer vision technology, the visual recognition ability of the rat was strengthened. The visual enhancement of the rat robot system mainly consisted of three parts: the implanted electrode, the rat pack, and the calculation module. A pinhole camera was installed on the mouse carrying the backpack. The camera was capable of the real-time capture of the video image of the rat, the video transmission was analyzed by the computer through the wireless module in the backpack. According to the analysis results, the backpack on the stimulation circuit produced an electrical stimulation signal that was transferred to the related brain regions of the rat, and the rat robot could produce different behaviors (turn left, turn right, go) and explore unknown environments. In the computing system of brain−computer integration, the spatial decision-making ability and execution ability of the rats are combined with the decision ability of the machine (closed-loop control) and the perceptual ability (camera perception).

The core of brain−computer integration is the cognitive computing model of brain−computer collaboration. The cognitive process of the brain—machine collaboration is composed of environment perception, motivation analysis, intention, understanding, action planning, and so on, in support of the perception memory, episodic memory, semantic memory, and working memory to complete the brain—computer group awareness and coordinated action.

13.7.1 Cognitive model of brain—computer integration

Brain—computer integration is a new form of intelligence, which is different from both human intelligence and artificial intelligence. It is a new generation of intelligence science system that combines physics and biology. The brain—computer integration intelligence is different from human intelligence and artificial intelligence in the following three aspects: (1) At the intelligent input, the idea of brain—computer integration intelligence not only depends on the objective data collected by hardware sensors or the subjective information sensed by human facial features but also combines the two effectively, forming a new input mode with the prior knowledge of person. (2) In the stage of information processing, which is also an important stage of intelligence generation, a new way of understanding is constructed by integrating the cognitive mode of human beings with the computing ability of the computer. (3) At the output end of intelligence, the value effect of human beings in decision-making is added to the algorithm of gradual iteration of the computer to match each other, forming an organic and probabilistic coordination optimized judgment. In the continuous adaptation of human—computer integration, people will consciously think about commonsense behavior, and machines will find the difference of the value weight from the decision-making of people under different conditions.

Brain—computer integration adopts a hierarchical architecture. Human beings analyze and perceive the external environment through their acquired perfect cognitive ability. The cognitive process can be divided into perception and behavior layer, a decision-making layer, and a memory and intention layer, forming mental thinking. The machine perceives and analyzes the external environment through detecting data, and the cognitive process can be divided into an awareness and actuator layer, a planning layer, and a belief and motivation layer, forming formal thinking. The same architecture indicates that humans and machines can merge at the same level and that cause-and-effect relationships can be generated at different levels. Fig. 13.4 is the cognitive model of brain—computer

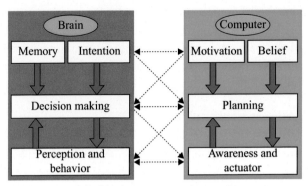

Figure 13.4 Cognitive model of brain–computer integration.

integration [23]. In this model, the left part is a simulated human brain in terms of consciousness and memory mind model; the right part is the computer based on an ABGP agent.

13.7.2 Environment awareness

Environmental awareness refers to the process of individually processing environmental information. It is the process in which an individual feels various stimuli in the environment and organizes them into a higher-level psychological model on the basis of previous experience. It processes not only the current sensory information but also the environmental information stored in memory according to the individual's current needs and environmental characteristics. The former is structural while the latter is functional.

In a certain time and space the components of the environment are perceived and understood, and then a prediction is made concerning the subsequent changes of these components. In 1988 M. Endsley gave the general framework of situation awareness shown in Fig. 13.5 [16].

In the Intelligence Science Laboratory, several methods have been developed for environment awareness. Here we describe how convolutional neural networks (CNNs) are used for visual awareness [23]. CNNs are multiple-stage, globally trainable artificial neural networks. CNNs have better performance in two-dimensional pattern recognition problems than the multilayer perceptron, because the topology of the two-dimensional model is added into the CNN structure, and the CNN employs three important structure features—local accepted field, shared weights, and subsampling—ensuring the invariance of target translation, shrinkage, and distortion for the input signal. CNN mainly consists of the feature extraction

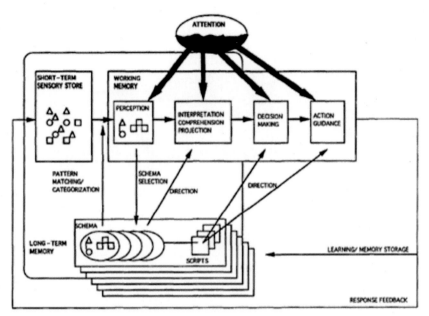

Figure 13.5 Mechanism of environment awareness.

and the classifier [24]. The feature extraction contains multiple convolutional layers and subsampling layers. The classifier consists of one or two layers of fully connected neural networks. Both the convolutional layer with the local accepted field and the subsampling layer with the subsampling structure have the character of sharing the weights. The awareness module has been changed into a convolutional generative stochastic model (CGSM) compared with the original ABGP model with the single preestablished rules, and the parameters of CGSM will be a part of the knowledge in the belief base accessed through the dotted line path in Fig. 13.6.

A major attraction of ABGP-CGSM is the intrinsic properties of CGSM, such as the nonlinearity, the hierarchic feature representation, and especially the robustness for the noisy natural scenes. Those properties can be directly adopted to make up one of the abilities and knowledge of a cognitive agent and enable the agent such as a human to recognize the true world. Because of the introduction of CGSM in the awareness module, an agent based on the ABGP-CGSM model needs also to undergo a good learning process before cognizing the natural scenes.

Multiagent awareness should consider basic elements and relationship in a multiagent system [25]. Multiagent awareness model is defined as a

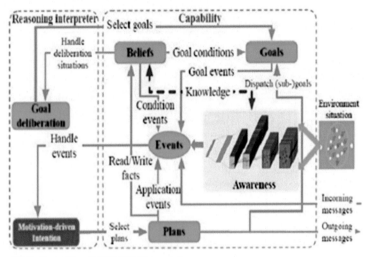

Figure 13.6 Cognitive ABGP-CGSM model.

2-tuple MA = {ElementÿRelation}, where Elements of awareness are as follows:

- Identity(Role): Who is participating?
- Location: Where are they?
- Intentions: What are they going to do?
- Actions: What are they doing?
- Abilities: What can they do?
- Objects: What objects are they using?
- Time point: When does the action execute?

Basic relationships contain task relationships, role relationships, operation relationships, activity relationships, and cooperation relationships.

1. Task relationships define task decomposition and composition relationships. Task involves activities with a clear and unique role attribute
2. Role relationships describe the role relationship of agents in the multiagent activities.
3. Operation relationships describe the operation set of agents.
4. Activity relationships describe activity of the role at a time.
5. Cooperation relationships describe the interactions between agents.

A partnership can be investigated through cooperation activities relevance among agents to ensure the transmission of information between different perception of the role and tasks for maintenance of the entire multiagent perception.

13.7.3 Autonomous reasoning

Motivation is the internal driving force of subjective reasoning, which directly drives individual activities to initiate and maintain a mental state to achieve a specific purpose. The automatic reasoning is realized by the motive driven planning. In the brain—computer fusion system, there are two types of motivation: demand-based motivation and curiosity-based motivation.

Demand-based motivation is represented as a 3-tuple $\{n, G, I\}$, where n represents need, G is the target, and I represents motivation strength. In the brain—computer integration system, there are three kinds of requirements: perception needs, adaptation needs, and cooperation needs. Motivation is activated by incentive rules.

The motivation based on curiosity is to build a new motivation through a motivation learning algorithm [26]. The agent creates the observed perceptual input as an internal expression and associates this expression with the learned behavior that is conducive to operation. If the action result of an agent is not related to its current goal, motivation learning will not be carried out, which is very useful for the selection of learning content. But even when learning is not triggered by other motivations, novel learning can still occur in such a situation.

The learning process of motivation is to acquire the perceptual state through observation, and then the perceptual state is transformed from event to event. Discovering novel events arouses the interest of agents. Once the interest is aroused, the agent's attention can be selected and focused on one aspect of the environment. In the motivation learning algorithm based on novelty, the observation function is used to focus attention on the subset of the perception state. Then the difference degree on the subset is calculated by the difference function, and the event is formed by the event function. The event drives the introspective search, and the most interesting event is selected by the novelty and interest degree, so that the agent can focus on the event item. Finally, based on the focus on the event of maximum interest, a new motivation is created.

13.7.4 Collaborative decision-making

The collaborative decision-making of the brain—computer integration is based on the theory of joint intention, which can effectively support the description and analysis of joint social behaviors among agents [27]. In the brain—computer integration, brain and computer are defined as agents with common goals and mental states. With the support of short-term memory, distributed dynamic description logic (D^3L) is used to describe the joint intention [28]. The distributed dynamic description logic fully considers the characteristics of dynamic description logic in the distributed environment, uses the bridge rules to form the chain, realizes the joint intention through distributed reasoning, and enables the agents in the brain—computer integration to make a collaborative decision.

Since the brain—computer integration system is a distributed and heterogeneous system, a chain-supported bridge rule distributed dynamic description logic (CD^3L) is proposed by us [29]. The CD^3L consists of five basic components: the distributed dynamic description logic D^3L, the distributed TBox, the distributed ABox, the distributed ActBox, and the reasoning mechanism. The CD^3L distributed dynamic description logic introduces the combination of consistency semantics, through the bridge rules for knowledge dissemination, provides a theoretical basis for the integration and sharing of heterogeneous information, and supports the collaborative cognition of distributed heterogeneous brain—computer integration.

13.7.5 Simulation experiment

Here, we present a detailed implementation of ABGP-CNN for the conceptual framework of brain—machine integration. To significantly demonstrate the feasibility of the conceptual framework of brain—machine integration based on the ABGP-CNN agent model, we give a simulated application. The following will mainly represent the actual design of the rat agent based on ABGP-CNN supported by the conceptual framework of brain—machine integration.

Under belief knowledge conditions, the goals (here mainly visual information) constantly trigger the awareness module to capture environmental visual information, and the event module converts the visual information into the unified internal motivation signal events that are transferred to action plan module. Then the action plan module selects proper actions to respond the environment.

In simulation application, we construct a maze and design a rat agent based on ABGP-CNN to move in the maze depending on the guidepost of the maze path in Fig. 13.7 [23]. The task of the rat agent is to start moving at the maze entrance (top left of maze), and finally reach the maze exit (bottom right) following the guideposts.

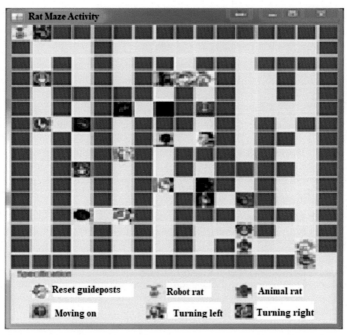

Figure 13.7 Rat agent activities in maze.

(A) Moving on   (B) Turning left   (C) Turning right

Figure 13.8 Traffic guideposts in maze.

In order to fulfill the maze activity shown in Fig. 13.7, the rat agent is implemented in all the three basic modules: <Awareness>, <Motivation>, <Action Plan>. In the rat maze activity experiment, the rat agent is designed to have three basic behaviors: moving on, turning left, and turning right in the maze. In order to guide the rat's behaviors, we construct a true traffic guidepost dataset of the three different signals: moving on, turning left, and turning right. The different signals correspond to the different guidepost images, as shown in Fig. 13.8.

When the rat agent moves on the path, its goals constantly drive the awareness module to capture environmental visual information (here, the guideposts in the maze) and generate the motivation signal events to drive its behaviors' plan selection. In the experiment, given the three motivation signals (moving on, turning left, and turning right) and the guideposts in the maze path, the agent can respond with three types of action plans to finish the maze activities.

References

[1] J.J. Vidal, Toward direct brain—computer communication, Annu. Rev. Biophv (1973) 157—180.

[2] J. Liaw, T. Berger, Dynamic synapse: harnessing the computing power of synaptic dynamics, Neurocomputing 26—27 (1999) 199—206.

[3] F.N. Ozkan, E. Kahya, An experiment in use of brain computer interfaces for cognitive researches, Int. J. Intell. Sci. 5 (2015) 80—88. Available from: https://doi.org/10.4236/ijis.2015.52008.

[4] M. Rashid, N. Sulaiman, et al., Current status, challenges, and possible solutions of EEG-based brain-computer interface: a comprehensive review, Front. Neurorobotics 14 (2020) 1—35.

[5] E.E. Sutter, The brain response interface: communication through electrical brain response, Microcomput Appl. 15 (1992) 31—45.

[6] L.A. Farwell, E. Donchin, Talking off the top of your head: toward a mental prosthesis utilizing event-related brain potentials, Electroencephalogr Clin. Neurophysiol. 70 (6) (1988) 510—523.

[7] G. Pfurtscheller, et al., Prediction of the side of hand movements from single trial multichannel EEG data using neural networks, Electroencephalogr Ctin Neurophysiol. 82 (1992) 313—315.

[8] W.A. Woods, Transition network grammars for natural language analysis, Commun. ACM 13((10)) (1970).

[9] J.R. Wolpaw, et al., An EEG-based brain-computer interface for cursor control, Electroenceph Clin. Neurophysiol. 78 (1991) 252—259.

[10] G.R. McMillan, et al., Direct brain interface utilizing self-regulation of steady—atate visual evoked response (ssver), Proc. RESNA (1995) 693—695.

[11] N. Birbaumer, T. Hinterberger, A. Kubler, N. Neumann, The thought-translation device (TTD): neurobehavioral mechanisms and clinical outcome, IEEE Trans. Neural Syst. Rehabil Eng. 11 (2) (2003) 120—123.

[12] S.K. Gao, Neural engineering and brain-computer interface (in Chinese), Chin. Bull. Life Sci. 21 (2) (2009) 177—180.

[13] B. Wu, Y. Su, J. Zhang, X. Li, J. Zhang, W. Chen, et al., BCI Chinese input virtual keyboard system Based on P300 (in Chinese), Chin. J. Electron. 37 (8) (2009) 1733—1738. 1745.

[14] P.R. Cohen, H.J. Levesque, Intention is choice with commitment, Artif. Intell. 42 (2—3) (1990) 213—361.

[15] A.S. Rao, M.P. Georgeff, Modeling rational agents within a BDI-architecture, in: J. Al-Len, R. Fikes, E. Sandewall (Eds.), Proceedings of the Second International Conference on Principles of Knowledge Representation and Reasoning, (1991) Morgan Kaufmann Publishers, San Mateo, CA.

[16] M.R. Endsley, Toward a theory of situation awareness in dynamic systems, Hum. Factors 37 (1) (1995) 32—64.

[17] Z.H. Wu, G. Pan, J.C. Principe, et al., Cyborg intelligence: towards bio-machine intelligent systems, IEEE Intell. Syst. 29 (6) (2014) 2—4.

[18] Z.H. Wu, Y.D. Zhou, Z.Z. Shi, et al., Cyborg intelligence: recent progress and future directions, IEEE Intell. Syst. 31 (6) (2016) 44—50.

[19] J. DiGiovanna, B. Mahmoudi, J. Fortes, et al., Coadaptive brain-machine interface via reinforcement learning, IEEE Trans. Biomed. Eng. 56 (1) (2009) 54−64.
[20] O. Fukuyama, T. Suzuki, K. Mabuchi, RatCar: a vehicular neuro-robotic platform for a rat with a sustaining structure of the rat body under the vehicle, in: Annual International Conference of the IEEE Engineering in Medicine and Biology Society, IEEE, Buenos Aires, (2010).
[21] J.E. O'Doherty, M.A. Lebedev, P.J. Ifft, et al., Active tactile exploration using a brain-machine-brain interface, Nature 479 (7372) (2011) 228−231.
[22] Y.M. Wang, M.L. Lu, Z.H. Wu, et al., Ratbot: a rat "understanding" what humans see, in: International Workshop on Intelligence Science, Beijing, in conjunction with IJCAI-2013, (2013) pp. 63−68.
[23] Z.Z. Shi, Z.Q. Huang, Cognitive model of brain-machine integration, in: AGI-19 Proceedings, Springer, (2019) pp. 168−177.
[24] Y. LeCun, L. Bottou, Y. Bengio, P. Haffner, Gradient-based learning applied to document recognition, Proc. IEEE 1998 (1998) 2278−2324.
[25] Z.Z. Shi, J.H. Zhang, J.P. Yue, X. Yang, A cognitive model for multi-agent collaboration, Int. J. Intell. Sci. 4 (1) (2014) 1−6.
[26] Z.Z. Shi, G. Ma, X. Yang, C.X. Lu, Motivation learning in mind model CAM, Int. J. Intell. Sci. 5 (2) (2015) 63−71.
[27] Z.Z. Shi, J.H. Zhang, X. Yang, et al., Computational cognitive models for brain-machine collaborations, IEEE Intell. Syst. 11/12 (2014) (2014) 24−31.
[28] X.F. Zhao, D.P. Tian, Y.H. Shi, Z.Z. Shi, Knowledge propagation and reasoning induced by bridge rule chains in D3L, Chin. J. Comput 37 (12) (2014) 2419−2425.
[29] J.H. Zhang, Z.Z. Shi, J.P. Yue, et al., Chain supported bridge rule distributed dynamic description logic, High. Tech. Commun. 24 (5) (2014) 452−457.

CHAPTER 14

Brain-like intelligence

Brain-like intelligence is the simulation of the human brain to process information by using neuromorphic computing, which is the current research hotspot in intelligence science. Through the cross-research of brain science, cognitive science, and artificial intelligence (AI), we strive to strengthen the basic and original research in the cross-field of intelligence science, solve the major basic theoretical problems in the development of cognitive science and information science, and perform research in the frontier field of innovative brain-like intelligence.

14.1 Introduction

The 21st century is the century of the intelligence revolution. Advanced technology with intelligence science at the core and life science in the lead will set off a new high-tech revolution—the intelligent technology revolution. In particular, the combination of intelligent technology, biotechnology and nanotechnology, and the development of the intelligent machine with biological characteristics will be the breakthrough of the high-tech revolution in the 21st century.

The intelligence revolution will create the history of human postcivilization. Different from the energy revolution which realized the conversion and utilization of energy, the intelligence revolution has the potential to realize the conversion and utilization of intelligence, that is, people give their own intelligence to machines, and intelligent machines transform human intelligence into machine intelligence and release human intelligence; people may also transform machine intelligence into human intelligence and make use of it. If the steam engine magically created the industrial society, then the intelligent machine can likewise miraculously create the intelligent society.

In 1936 Turing put forward the great idea of the Turing machine, which is based on the prototype of the human brain's information process and laid the theoretical foundation of the modern computer [1]. Turing tried to build "a brain" and first raised the notion that putting programs into a machine can make a single machine perform multiple functions.

Intelligence Science
DOI: https://doi.org/10.1016/B978-0-323-85380-4.00014-2

Intelligence Science

Since the 1960s, von Neumann architecture had been the mainstream of computer architecture. The following problems exist in classical computer technologies:

1. Moore's law shows that devices will reach the limit of physical miniaturization in the coming 10-15 years.
2. Limited by the structure of the data bus, programming is hard and causes high energy consumption when we process large-scale and complex problems.
3. There is no advantage in analyses that are complex, varied, real-time, and dynamic.
4. The technology cannot meet the demand of processing the huge amount of information of the "digital world." In the data sea produced every day, 80% of the data is original without any processing, whereas a lot of original data's half-life is only three hours.
5. In a long-term endeavor, the calculating speed of a computer is up to one quadrillion times that of humans, but the level of intelligence is low.

We study the human brain, researching the methods and algorithms of the brain's process, and developing brain-like intelligence has now become an urgent requirement [2]. Now, much attention has been paid to the research of brain science and intelligence science in the world. On January 28, 2013, the EU launched the Human Brain Project (HBP), investing €1 billion to fund research and development in the next decade. The goal is to use supercomputers to completely multistage- and multilayer-simulate the human brain and to help people understand the function of human brain. Previous American President Obama announced an important project on April 2, 2013, which would cost about 10 years and a total amount of $1 billion. This project is called Brain Research through Advancing Innovative Neuro Technologies (BRAIN), in order to study the functions of the billions of neurons, to explore human perception, behavior, and consciousness, and to find the method to cure diseases related to the brain, such as Alzheimer's disease.

IBM has promised to devote $1 billion used in the commercial application of its cognitive computing platform Watson. Google has purchased nine robot companies and one machine learning company, including Boston Dynamics. The father of high-throughput sequencing J. Rothberg and Yale university professor Xu Tian established a new bio-tech company, combining deep learning with biomedical-tech in research and development for new medicines and diagnostic technology.

Among several major frontier science and technology projects, China's Brain Project (CBP) on Brain Science and Brain-like Intelligence Technology has attracted much attention and was initiated by the Chinese government in 2018. On March 22, 2018, Beijing's brain science and brain-like research center was established. On May, 2018, the Shanghai brain science and brain-like research center was established in Zhangjiang laboratory. The establishment of these two centers marks the beginning of the China Brain Project. "Intelligence + " helps China's high-quality economic development and will comprehensively promote the arrival of the intelligence revolution.

14.2 Blue Brain Project

14.2.1 Brain neural network

The Blue Brain Project is intended to use the IBM blue gene supercomputer to simulate the various functions of the human brain, such as cognition, perception, memory, and so on. The Blue Brain Project is the first comprehensive attempt by detailed simulations to understand brain function and dynamic function with reverse engineering methods to research the mammalian brain.

The brain size of a human is only 1400 cm^3, and it has only 20 W of power, but its computing power is far beyond today's supercomputers. The 20 billion neurons of the cerebral cortex and the millions of kilometers of axons, which connect the cerebral white matter, provide the most advanced human brain functions, like emotions, planning, thinking, and the main memory. Recent continuing research has produced much scientific data on neurons, but the interaction of neurons, the structure of the neocortex, the information processing mechanisms are still unclear. Neuroscience research has shown that the brain's neural network (NN) is a multiscale, sparsely directed graph. Local short-distance connections can be regulated through repeated statistical changes to descriptions and global remote connection. Brain behavior is entirely formed by individual functional units of nonrandom and associated interactions, and this is a key factor about organized complexity.

Markram, director of the Swiss Federal Institute of Technology in Lausanne, and his experimental group have spent more than a decade building a database of nerve centers and have the largest single nerve cell database around the world.

In July, 2005, the Swiss Federal Institute of Technology in Lausanne and IBM announced their intention to develop research for the Blue Brain Project [3], to make progress in understanding the function of the brain and functional disorders, and to provide a way to solve mental health and intractable problems involving neuropathy. At the end of 2006, the Blue Brain Project created a basic unit model of the cortical function column. In 2008 IBM used the blue gene supercomputer to simulate 55 million neurons and 500 billion synapses of a rat brain. IBM gained $4.9 million from DARPA (Defense Advanced Research Projects Agency) to study neuromorphic computing. The IBM Almaden Research Center and IBM TJ Watson Research Center, along with Stanford University, University of Wisconsin—Madison University, Cornell University, Columbia University Medical Center, and the University of California Merced have participated in the program study.

14.2.2 Cerebral cortex model

One of the earliest discoveries was that cortical structures include six different levels of cortical thickness. Researchers had found a leathery and special network of connections within the cortex and obtained patterns with different characteristics [4]. For the purpose of simulation, IBM translated this typical layered gray matter in the cortico–hypothalamic structure into a prototype of the gray matter network [5].

Connections between layers are primarily vertical, with only a small amount of lateral spread in the diameter of the cylindrical structure called the cortical function column. In many cortical regions, the functional neurons in the column share the same features, which show that features include not only the structural entities but also functions. Cylinder range measurements of collected information will help us to build a scale model, as shown in Fig. 14.1.

The cortical function column usually occupies only a few millimeters and seems to be responsible for specific functions, including motor control, vision, and planning. According to the change of cell density in the six cortex, the brain is divided into cortical areas. Each function corresponds to a special possibility of cortical circuits [6]. For example, the Brodmann area 17 is clearly associated with the core vision processing functions. Over the decades, hundreds of scientists have focused on understanding how each cortical region of the brain plays a corresponding function and how it carries out structure functions.

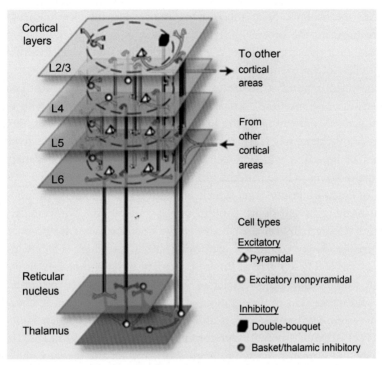

Figure 14.1 Hierarchical structure of the thalamocortical system.

In the 20th century, much research showed overwhelming evidence in support of cortical areas being associated with a view of specific function and that the brain demonstrates an alarming degree of plasticity. At present, research has proved that, in the process of ferret brain development, visual pathways in the white matter connect to the auditory cortex and that auditory pathways simultaneously connect to the visual cortex. They are specialized for the corresponding auditory area and can also be modified for the corresponding visual area, and vice versa. This amazing natural reconstruction allows us to expect that the core algorithm of neural computation may not depend on the morphology of specific sensory organs or motor neurons, while the observed changes in the cortical structure of the regions may indicate the fine of typical neural circuits. We expect these typical circuits to carry out reverse engineering. The existence of such a typical microloop is an important hypothesis. Although many local cortical circuit layouts have been estimated, the exact form of the microloop is still unknown, and its role in neural computing has not been confirmed. Even if we could find a basis for typical circuits, in order to unlock its potential mechanism, we must identify and implement them with plasticity mechanisms. Such mechanisms ensure that the development and mature stages in the process of a typical circuit of tailoring and refinement complete their specific functions. We will later further study plasticity problems and possible local synaptic mechanisms.

The organizational structure of the nervous system in the most coarse-grained scale and multiple cortical areas form a network to deal with complex functions. For example, the brain performs a series of intricate dexterity eye movements when we read. We look in between the lines to select a series of lines and edges, which combine to form complex spatial and temporal patterns. These patterns can be seen as a key to opening a masterpiece of linguistic knowledge, which bathes the brain in the corresponding word meaning of the sights, sounds, smells, and objects. Surprisingly, this complex feature relies on a small area of the brain network. Regions of the structure are closely connected with one another, and there is a certain distance in space. These made us think of a variety of brain function supported by the whole brain characteristics of subnets. These subnets promote the flows and integration of information, at the same time promoting cooperation between existing differences and distribution. The Almaden Research Center of IBM Corporation performed research in 2009 and 2010 on macaque and human brain white matter structure for the measurement and analysis process and achieved two important breakthroughs [7,8]. This result can be used as a way to further understand the network of brain regions.

Different connections of the six layers of the cerebral cortex indicate their different functions. For example, the input connection is usually sent to the fourth layer, the second or third layer. According to the document [9] of the rat cortex model, the model of the cerebral cortex is presented in Fig. 14.2 [10,11].

Fig. 14.2A represents the geometric distribution about a plane of the cortex. The plane includes 100 super functional columns, each column is distinguished by color, and each super functional column is formed by the 100 small feature column. Fig. 14.2B represents the connectivity of the model. Each small functional column contains 30 conical cells activated by a short distance to neighboring cells. Cone cells project onto the local cell belonging to the same cluster of another small feature column of core cells and other clusters of conventional spikes of noncone cells. Basket cells keep active in the local super functional column, and regular spiking nonpyramidal (RSNP) provide partial inhibition of cone cells.

Long-range projection between small function columns constitutes the memory of the attractor matrix and defines the cell clusters. Only the

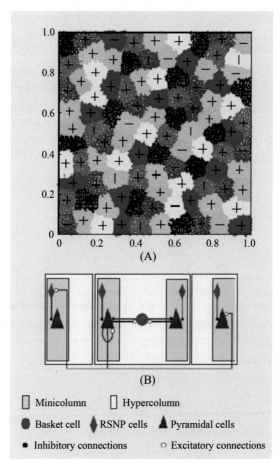

Figure 14.2 System structure of cerebral cortex model. (A) the geometric layout of 100 hypercolumns consisting of 100 minicolumns each; (B) schematic connectivity of the model. *RSNP*, Regular spiking nonpyramidal.

small function columns that have collective memory mode or cell clusters can have mutual encouragement.

Each super function column also contains approximately 100 basket cells activated by cone cells. Basket cells make the connection routine by inhibiting the conical cells. Such an ultrafunctional column is like the model of winner-take-all. Each small column also includes two partial RSNP cells that connect conical cells and have an inhibiting function. The abstract NN based on the current long-distance connection model indicates that the cell cluster competition has an additive property. The competition of cell clusters is implemented through the cone cells and the other RSNP cells in small feature columns.

Because RSNP cells would inhibit cone cells located in the local small columns, the activities of cell clusters are affected. Although such connections are not confirmed in anatomy and physiology, the experiment data of connectivity is in an acceptable range. For simplicity, the small features of the column model and ultrafunctional column are more obvious, which is contrary to the experimental observations of the local Gauss model [12]. The model consists of a single cell set, in which the fourth layer of the cortex provides the input of the cone cells, while the external input of the memory of synaptic events is simulated by these cells.

The cells in the model are established according to the Hodgkin-Huxley formula [13,14], and the cell membrane potential of the nerve is expressed as a differential equation:

$$C_m \frac{dV}{dt} = I_{comp} + I_{cond} + I_{syn} \tag{14.1}$$

where C_m denotes membrane capacitance, I_{comp} denotes the total current adjacent compartments, I_{cond} denotes the total ion current in the cell membrane channel, and I_{syn} represents the sum of synaptic currents. The electrical behavior of cells is described by the activation and inactive variables of the ion current. For example, the delay of potassium ions carrying plastic electric current can be expressed as:

$$I_{Kr} = (E_{Kr} - V(t))G_{Kr}n^4 \tag{14.2}$$

where n is an activation variable and can be expressed as:

$$\frac{dn}{dt} = \alpha_n(1 - n) - \beta_n n \tag{14.3}$$

where α_n and β_n are nonlinearly dependent with $V(t)$. A cone cell in the model is composed of six compartments. Each compartment has a state variable corresponding to cell membrane potential and one or two state variables representing ion current (each compartment at most has five ion currents). Some booths with a flow of intracellular calcium ion flow will have more than one state variable. In addition, some synapses carry other calcium ion flows and want to add other variables. In general, the synapse is determined by three state variables: one represents the degree of opening, and the other two represent synaptic strength (facilitation and inhibition) of short-range change.

In order to achieve the simulation, a project team at IBM created a mode collection about nonoverlapping vertical memory: picking a small column to form a pattern in each column with super function. Two long distances in the same pattern of small function columns are randomly and remotely connected. In this way, each cone cell only receives a pattern of remote activation. Similarly, each RSNP cell receives conical cell excitation of the small functional column from the external model.

14.2.3 Super computational simulation

Basic elements of the simulator include the neurons used to display a large number of behaviors like the presentation model, the communication of peak potential, dynamic channel of synapses, synaptic plasticity, structure in plastic, and stratification, microfunction column, ultrafunctional column, and cortical network consisting of regional and multiregional network architecture, as shown in Fig. 14.2. Each of these elements is modular and can be configured individually, so we have the flexibility to test a large number of brain structures and dynamics of biological thought-provoking hypotheses. Correspondingly, its possible combination is a great space, and this requires that the simulator runs at a certain rate so as to achieve rapid user-driven exploration.

The history of neural simulation can be traced to 1950. Since then, studies on cortical simulation have been developed along two lines: the detail and scale. Several publicly available simulators, including NEURON and GENESIS, are applied to the detail simulation of a small number of neurons [15]. Unfortunately, the biophysics of the fine details can lead to the nearly real-time simulation of mammals, and the size of this task is computationally impossible. Regrettably, such fine details in biophysics will lead to mammalian scale, and the calculations needed for near real-time simulation tasks cannot be achieved. On the other hand, other studies have used compact imaging neurons, which demonstrate the simulation for millions of neurons and billions of synapses. The research goal is close to real-time simulation speed, at the same time, in the direction of a model scale and neuroanatomical detail in the direction of expanding the boundaries of cutting-edge research.

A simulation meets the requirements of size, speed, and detail at the same time, corresponding to the three resources of the computing system: storage, computation, and communication. Obviously, it is a serious challenge. For example, cats' cerebral cortex has nearly 1 billion neurons, and more than 6 trillion synapses. Since the number of synapses is more than 10,000 times that of neurons, the required memory must support the number of state representations required by the simulation scale which is proportional to the number of synapses. Therefore, even if we can use 1 byte of storage space to describe the state of a synapse, a cat simulation will need at least 6 TB memory space. Each synapse's efficient synaptic data structure requires about 16 bytes of storage space. In addition, each neuron is assumed to be updated frequently, and the dynamic differential equation describing the evolution of the neuron state is 1 trillion times per second. The biological neurons excite at an average rate of once per second, and most synapses will receive one spike per second, so there will be 6 trillion peak message deliveries in a NN. In order to meet this demand, we will accelerate the development of supercomputing, algorithms, and software architecture, which are critical for the pace of innovation.

From the aspects of hardware, the blue gene supercomputer system offers many computing processors and a large number of distributed memory and high-bandwidth communication subsystems. From the software aspect, the IBM project team has developed a cerebral cortex called the C2 simulator. The simulator adopts the distributed storage multiprocessor architecture. The analog scale continues to expand, and the simulation of neurophysiology and neuroanatomy constraint continues to increase.

Since 2007, the early work was performed on the cerebral cortex of rats and mice. The simulations of the IBM project team have maintained a steady growth. In May 2009 the team used the Dawn Blue Gene/P supercomputer system in cooperation with the Lawrence Berkeley National Laboratory and got the latest research results. The research results make full use of the storage capacity of the supercomputer system, and they are a valuable milestone about cat-scale cortical simulation (roughly equivalent to 4.5% of the size of the human brain) [16,17]. These analog networks show neurons forming a reproducible and lock-feature-asynchronous packet by self-organization [16].

Analog to the frequency of α (8−12 HZ) and γ ($>$ 30 HZ), mammals' neural activity shows frequent vibration in large areas of the cerebral cortex NN. In a similar visual stimulation paradigm, the analog network displays that a specific population response delay is consistent with observations in the mammalian cerebral cortex [17]. Simulator allows us to analyze thousands of nerve tissues, but animal memory is limited and can record only dozens in a nerve group. With this advantage, we can construct a stimulus-evoked detailed picture of events in network communication.

The C2 Simulator provides a key integrated workbench for detecting brain algorithms. So far, the simulation of the IBM project team, including the key feature of a lot of nerve structure and dynamics, is only scratching the surface of neuroscience data. For example, the IBM project team introduced long-distance white matter project, involving other important subcortical structures (such as basal ganglia) and structural plasticity mechanisms. The IBM project team has always adopted an open attitude to deal with emerging technologies that bring new measuring methods for cortical circuits in detail.

It is unrealistic to expect that cognitive function can be automatically generated from the biological neural simulations. The IBM project team expected that a simulator could be consistent with brain background and that thus it can be formed and performed by means of neural computing theory. Through studying behavioral simulation, a complete mathematical theory could provide clues for the mind of brain and developing intelligent business machines. On this point, the structures being built are not the answer but rather the tools used to find the answers, like linear accelerators (used to explore the structure of matter). It will lay a foundation for future in-depth understanding of the brain calculation and neuromorphic engineering innovation.

Cognitive brain research to promote the arrival of large data is accompanied by the cognitive computing era. On March 6, 2014, IBM announced that its big data analytics platform was renamed by the Watson foundations. "Watson" as a synonym for "cognitive computing" has become IBM's future strategic direction in big data. Cognitive computing systems, through assistance, understanding, decision, insight, and discovery, can help companies to quickly discover new problems, new opportunities, and new value and to achieve customer-centric wisdom transformation.

14.3 Human Brain Project

On January 28, 2013, the European Commission announced that the HBP has won and has been approved to receive €1 billion in research funding in the next 10 years [18]. The HBP hopes to create an integrated research platform, which aims to develop the most detailed model of the human brain based on information communication. Under the coordination of Markram, who is in École Polytechnique Fédérale (EPF) Lausanne, 87 organizations, including universities from 23 countries (including 16 EU countries), research institutions, and industry organizations will collaborate using computer simulation methods to study the human brain. The study is expected to promote the development of AI, robots, and neuromorphic computing systems to lay the foundations for medical advances in science and technology and to contribute to knowledge of the nervous system and related diagnosis and treatment and drug tests.

On June 29, 2020, the HBP announced the start of its final phase as an EU-funded future and emerging technology (FET) Flagship [19]. The European Commission has signed a grant agreement to fund the HBP with €150 million from now until 2023. Over the next three years, the project will narrow its focus to advance three core scientific areas—brain networks, their role in consciousness, and artificial neural nets—while expanding its innovative EBRAINS infrastructure. EBRAINS offers the most comprehensive atlas and database on the human brain, directly coupled with powerful computing and simulation tools, to research communities in neuroscience, medicine, and technology. Currently transitioning into a sustainable infrastructure, EBRAINS will remain available to the scientific community, as a lasting contribution of the HBP to global scientific progress.

14.3.1 Research contents of the project

HBP aims to explore and understand the human brain's running processes; to study the human brain's low-power, high-efficiency mode of operation and its learning function, the association function, innovative features etc.; to simulate the human brain through information processing, modeling, and supercomputing technologies; and to develop human brain energy-efficient supercomputers through supercomputing technology for the diagnosis and treatment of the human brain, human interface, and the human brain—controlled robot research [20].

The HBP is divided into five areas, and each area is based on existing work for further research [18].

14.3.1.1 Data

It is necessary to collect and filter out the necessary strategic data to draw the human brain atlas, to design the human brain model, and, at the same time, to attract research institutions to contribute data outside the project. Nowadays, neural cognitive science has accumulated massive experimental data, and a large amount of original research brings new discoveries. Even so, the vast majority of core knowledge, which constructs a multilevel brain atlas and a unified brain model, is still needed. So the primary task of the human brain plan is to collect and describe strategic data that is filtered and valuable. The HBP points three key points about the research of data:

1. The multilevel data of rats' brain: Earlier studies have shown that the results of the research about rat brain also apply to all mammals. So it will provide a key reference for the system research about the relationships between different levels of rats' brain tissue.

2. The multilevel data of human brain: The research data of rats' brain can provide an important reference in the study of the human brain to a certain extent, although there is fundamental difference between them. In order to define and explain the difference, the plan of the human brain research team includes a strategy for the human brain and the accumulation of as much of the existing rat's brain data as possible.

3. The structure of human cognitive systems: It is one of the important goals for HBP to make clear the association between the structure of the human brain and its function. HBP will focus on the structure of neuron about specific cognitive and behavioral skills, from other non-human species' simple behavior to human-specific advanced skills, like language.

14.3.1.2 Theory

As the mathematical and theoretical basis of human brain research, it is necessary to define a mathematical model, which tries to explain internal relations between different brain tissue levels among the acquisition of information, the description of information, and the storage function of information. If the research lacks a uniform and reliable theoretical basis, it will be difficult to solve the problem about the data of neuroscience and the problem of fragmentation in the research. So HBP should have a coordinating institution studying the mathematical theory and models to explain the inner relationships in different brain levels to achieve information acquirement, description, and the information storage function. As a part of this coordinating institution, the human brain plan should establish an open "European Institute for Theoretical Neuroscience" to attract more outstanding scientists, who will become involved in this project, and to act as an incubator for innovative research.

14.3.1.3 The technology platform of information and communication

In order to improve research efficiency in providing services for neuroscientists, clinical researchers, and technology developers, it is necessary to establish comprehensive information and communications platforms, including six big platforms: a neural information system, human brain simulation system, medical information system, high-performance computing system, neuromorphic computing system, and neural robotics system.

1. Neural information system: The neural information platform of the HBP provides an effective technical method for neuroscientists, analyzes the structure of the brain and the data of function more easily, and indicates the direction for multilevel of the human brain mapping. These platforms also include many tools for neural predictive information. These tools help to analyze the data of different brain levels that describe brain tissue and to evaluate some parameter values, which cannot be gotten from natural experiment. Before this study, the lack of data and knowledge was an important obstacle blocking systematically understanding brain. With such tools, these problems are solved.

2. The simulation system of human brain: The HBP can establish a sufficiently scaled human simulation platform, aiming to establish and simulate the human multilevel and multidimension model to tackle many kinds of specific issues. This platform plays a key role in the whole project. It provides modeling tools, workflows, and simulators for researchers and helps them get abundant and diverse data to process dynamic simulation from the brain's models of rats and humans. It makes model of "computer simulation experiment" possible. With all kinds of tools in the platform, we can generate a variety of input values, which are essential for medical research (disease models and drug effects model), neuromorphic computing, neural robot research.

3. High-performance computing system: The high-performance computing platform of the HBP provides sufficient computing power to establish and simulate the human brain model. It has not only advanced supercomputer technology but also new interactive computing and visual performance.

4. Medical information system: The medical information system of the HBP gathers clinical data from hospital archives and private databases (to strictly protect patient information security as a precondition). These functions can help researchers define diseases' "biological signatures" in each stage in order to find a key breakthrough. Once researchers have detection and classification methods for this biological basis, they can easily find the original disease and study related effective treatment.

5. Neuromorphic computing system: Neuromorphic computing platform of HBP provides researchers and application developers with hardware; at the same time it also provides a variety of equipment and software prototypes for modeling the brain. Using the platform, developers can develop compact low-power equipment and systems that are closer to human intelligence.

6. Neural robotics platform: The neural robot of the HBP provides tools and workflow for researchers. So they can use a sophisticated brain model to connect to the virtual environment in physical simulation. But they have previously had to rely on human and animal studies in natural for similar conclusions. The system provides a brand-new research strategy for neurocognitive scientists, helps them to discern many kinds of principles of human behaviors. From the technical standpoint, the platform will provide developers with the necessary development tools and help them develop robots that have human potential. This goal was not achieved in past studies due to the lack of central controller "type of brain."

14.3.1.4 Applications

The fourth major goal of the HBP is that HBP can reflect a variety of practical value for cognitive science research, clinical research, and technology development.

1. Principle of unified knowledge system: "Simulation system of the human brain" and "neural robot platform" are detailed explanations for the neural circuits of specific behavior, which researchers can use to implement specific applications, such as the effect of genetic defects, analyzing the result of different levels of tissue cells, and setting up a drug effect evaluation model. A human brain model can be used to distinguish human from animal in nature. For example, the model can show the human language skill. This model will allow us to change our minds about the knowledge of the brain, and it also can be applied in the field of specific medical and technical development.

2. The awareness, diagnosis, and treatment of brain diseases: Researchers can make full use of the medical information system, neuromorphic computing system, and brain simulation system to find the biological signatures in the evolution of various diseases, in-depth analysis and simulation of these processes, and finally new disease prevention and treatment options. This project will fully embody the practical value of HBP. New diagnostic techniques, which can predict diseases before

they cause irreversible harm, can advance its diagnosis and achieve "customized medicament," so it will ultimately benefit patients and reduce health care costs. To better understand disease and diagnosis will optimize the drug development process and will be beneficial in improving the success rate of experiments and reducing the cost of new drug research.

3. The future computing technology: Researchers can use high-performance computing systems, neuromorphic computing systems, and neural robots in the human brain plan to develop new computing technology and applications. High-performance computing platforms will be equipped with supercomputing resources for them and integrated with the technologies of a mix of multiple neural morphological tools. With the help of neuromorphic computing systems and neural robot platforms, researchers can make a software prototype that has great market potential. These prototypes include house robots and service robots; these robots are inconspicuous but have a strong technical capability, including data mining, motor control, video processing, imaging, and information communications.

14.3.1.5 Social ethics

Considering the huge impact of research and technique of human brain plan, HBP will set up an important social ethics group to finance the research on the potential social and economic impacts. This group affects the human brain plan researcher in ethics and improves the level of ethics and social responsibility. Its primary task is to engage in a positive dialog between stakeholders and community groups, which have different methodology and values.

The roadmap of the HBP is shown in Fig. 14.3 [21].

14.3.2 Timing plasticity of peak potential

Learning and memory in the brain are core issues in neuroscience. Nowadays, brain synaptic plasticity is the key in studying the information storage of the brain. The concept is affected by the Hebb's hypothesis, which Hebb described as follows: Repeated and continuous active cells act together to store a memory trace, also called memory imprinting, which is able to increase the bonding strength among the groups of interconnected neurons [22]. In recent years, a new concept in the study of cells has emerged, and it emphasizes timing rather than frequency. This kind of new learning paradigm is called spike-timing-dependent plasticity.

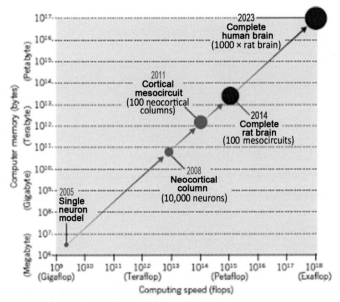

Figure 14.3 Roadmap of Human Brain Project.

This paradigm has aroused great interest because of its simplicity, its rationale of biological and computing capacity.

Hebb's principle is essentially a causal selection principle which is based on an award synapse so as to drive the postsynaptic neuron successfully. It is also a natural neural mechanism that is a simultaneous associated and sequential perception event. During 1850−1867, Hebb's thought inspired a number of researchers, who tried to explain how synaptic plasticity explains Pavlov and Watson's classical conditioning and Skinner's operational conditions.

The discovery of hippocampal plasticity caused excitement among researchers. Douglas and Goddard show that repeated high frequency is a more effective burst in long-term potentiation (LTP) than a single long ankylosing training. It is an important milestone in the history of synaptic plasticity. LTP became a popular protocol induced by repeated short bursts, and it confirms the importance of simulating the induction of LTP and persistent time. Hebb predicted and elaborated this conclusion in the 20th century. Douglas and Goddard named LTP under the recommendation of Per Andersen. A great number of experimental and theoretical studies based on the Hebb assumption have involved combined potential cells, synapses, and network mechanisms. The debate changes as presynaptic or postsynaptic trajectories become the focus of competition, Synapse can be changed in many ways, including presynaptic, postsynaptic, and both.

In the Sakmann laboratory, Stuart won a landmark discovery that records information from the somatic cells of the same neurons and dendrites by patch–clamp recording. The experiment clearly confirms that the action potential spreads back to the dendrites [23]. Markram of the Sakmann laboratory suggested that single subthreshold synaptic potential energy causes a calcium increment of low–level influx [24], leaves a large single–action potential, and lets the 100 ms long trail of calcium reverse back to dendritic [25]. Markram isolated single synaptic connections between conical neurons in the cortex and developed a matching pair with the patch–clamp recording technique.

In the annual meeting of 1995 Neuroscience, Markram has presented the first experimental study, which is about single synaptic connections between neurons in the cerebral cortex, demonstrating the importance of accurate timing of the launch of presynaptic and postsynaptic neuron peak potentials [25]. Single–pulse peak potential marked a turning point in the relative time of the launch millisecond timescale. It is the opposite of the decision on the direction and the size of relative time of the competition type, general depolarization, or simulation sequence [26]. Back-propagation peak potential can be viewed as the sum of all synaptic input; therefore the ideal correlation between individual synaptic inputs is generated along dendrites. The postsynaptic timing of potential peaks is spread by direct current injection, so these changes are not heterogeneous. The postsynaptic timing of potential peaks can play along an associated diaphragm, and it has identical discovery with the previous polarized synaptic input diaphragm. The study reveals that the LTP is a causal relationship of presynaptic preceding postsynaptic timing of peak potential, instead of 10 ms instantaneous time. However, long–term depression is inspired by the presynaptic of the noncausal relationship of postsynaptic timing. In other words, because of time, the cells that release together are not always connected and electrified together. The bigger time of 100 ms will not cause any plasticity, named STDP (spiking timing dependent plasticity). These experiments also showed that the block of postsynaptic peak potential destroys LTP, as the resistance of NMDA receptors.

Two theories about STDP were published in 1996. Gerstner [27] extended his old theory, which is based on the timing of the peak potential of Herb's potential difference, to the potential difference of causality peak potential timing and suppression of noncausation. Although there is still a 1 ms window of time to explain how the barn owl auditory system in the receptive field generates very detailed transient accuracy. The article builds on the peak potential timing level, including drawing the STDP function. Abbott and Blum published a model about plastic temporal correlation and applied it to the model of hippocampus to explain the rodents' navigation experiment [28]. Based on their study, Blum and Abbott [29] proposed a possible method to reduce the transmission efficiency in the condition of the presynaptic electric pulse after the postsynaptic electrical pulse. According to the speed of the construction, it is also very simple to re-explain the study of Blum and Abbott in the STDP framework.

Markram and Tsodyks developed a widely used synaptic stimulation test, beyond the single shock test, revealed the connection with short-term plasticity, and reported that Hebb's pairing is not necessary to change the effect of synapses and their short-term dynamics. This revived Eccles's test about high-frequency stimulation in the synaptic transmission path. Long-term plasticity can be increased to a new research level; namely, short-term plasticity can be changed into long-term plasticity, in what is called the redistribution of synapse effect or redistribution of synaptic efficacy (RSE) [30]. Tsodyks and Markram have also developed a dynamic model of synaptic transmission, demonstrating how simple changes in various synaptic parameters change the transmission of the synaptic, introduce the possibility of release and synaptic inhibition, and encourage using these concepts to determine transmission signal coding [31]. Markram and his colleagues studied the STDP in 1997 [26].

In 1999, Guoqiang Bi and Muming Pu made a large number of time series to verify the causal STDP window in detail [32]. For example, using paired recordings of split neurons, they recovered the long-time window with 40 ms at a very alarming speed between LTP and LTD and reached almost perfect consistency between presynaptic and postsynaptic activity. This rapid variation between LTP and LTD is called an instantaneous effect in biology and is resurrected in the cerebral cortex [33], regarded as one feature of STDP.

Some of the recent studies on STDP are clustered in STDP factors such as speed, high-order peak potential sequence motif, and parametric aspects of dendritic location. Another important area for future experimental study is the relationship between STDP and short-term plasticity. To a great extent, the model of STDP and dependency rate change only the strength of synaptic. This change in transient sensitivity is still completely unknown—how the STDP recombines activity patterns in a recurrent local loop.

Future research is needed to clarify the relationship between synaptic learning rules and internal equilibrium plasticity. Paying attention to the nature of Hebb's plasticity algorithm is not stable: Persistent relevant release among connect neurons can cause synaptic enhancement, which in turn can leads to the increase of the degree of the relevant release, cause a positive feedback, and result in the uncontrolled growth of synapses. Although some form of STDP remains at the issuance rate of postsynaptic in a stable state, the stability of the inherent characteristics in a highly connected network may not be fast enough to track the rate of rapid increase.

Future studies need to clarify the network topology of Hebb's collection. This problem seems to need the methods of graph theory. An important question is whether the topology is uniquely determined by the experience, or is the experience mechanism independent of experience. After Hebb's hypothesis was published, theorists pointed out that, if the synapse is saturated, these collections for storing a plurality of memory are not very helpful. Therefore, synaptic inhibition must also exist, taking into account better storage.

14.3.3 Unified brain model

The HBP is aim to set up a uniform brain model that can simulate a supercomputer, covering all the current understanding of the human brain. A prototype of the HBP is the blue brain project [21], which starts from a neuron model to the establishment of the cortex of simulation area from bottom to top.

In the HBP, Markram wants to put all the points together for a unified modeling and completes their countless ion channels. He is modeling not only a neural circuit for the related sense of smell but also the whole brain. We understand how these levels are combined and make clear how the brain controls behavior and cognition, including the genetic level, the molecular level, the neuron, and the chromosomes, the principle of the microcircuit, the big loop, the middle loop, and the brain region.

It was a fable in the 1980s to research a compete unified theory of brain, which needed a computer performing 10^{18} calculations per second. But Markram is not afraid of difficulties and goes up, doubling the computing power of computers every 18 months or so, which means there will be megabytes computer by 2020. At the same time, he also believes that neuroscientists should be ready for it.

Since the 1980s, Markram and his students collect data from the perspective of the cerebral cortex of rats, including the results obtained in different laboratories from some 20,000 experiments. The information includes morphology, three-dimensional restructuring, electrical properties, the communication of synapses, the location neuron synapses, the behavior of synapses, and even the genes involved in gene expression data. By the end of 2005, Markram's team integrated part of the related information into a single neuron model. By 2008, researchers have done about 10,000 models, composed of tubular model cortex known as the cortical function column. Currently, they have simulated 100 units of connection using a more advanced blue gene computer.

The unified model can be used to preserve data about cortical structure and function. In fact, the majority of the team's efforts is intended to set up "basic framework and software for large-scale ecosystem," so that the blue brain is useful for all scientists. The system will contain tools that autoconvert the data into simulation and a tool of information.

14.4 Brain research in the United States

In April 2, 2013, the White House announced the BRAIN program, referred to as the Brain Project. The program is comparable to the human genome project, and it will explore mechanisms of the human brain, draw the whole brain activity map, and develop new therapies for incurable brain disease.

After the BRAIN Project of the United States was released, the National Institutes of Health immediately set up a Brain Project working group. The BRAIN Project working group proposed nine funding areas: statistical brain cell types; the establishment of brain structure diagram; the development of large-scale NN recording technology; the development of neural circuits operations tools; understanding the contact between nerve cells and individual behavior; integrating the neuroscience experiments and theory, models, statistics; describing the mechanism of the human brain imaging techniques; the establishment of mechanisms to collect human data for scientific research; and knowledge dissemination and training.

The United States carried out in-depth research in brain science and brain-like computing and has made progress.

14.4.1 Human connectome project

The Human Brain Atlas is the great challenge of the 21st-century science. The human linker project (Human Connectome Project [HCP]) will clarify the neural pathways underlying brain function and behavior, which is a key factor to face up to this challenge. Decrypting this amazing complex connection diagram will reveal what makes us unique and makes everyone different.

The research project (HCP consortium WU-Minn) was led by the University of Washington, University of Minnesota, and University of Oxford, and its goal is to use noninvasive imaging of cutting-edge technology to create an integrated human brain circuits atlas of 1200 healthy adults (twins and their nontwin siblings). This research will produce valuable information on brain connectivity and reveal the relationship between behavior and the contribution of genetic and environmental factors to the individual difference of brain behavior. The Van Essen (Essen Van) laboratory of the University of Washington developed the connection group workbench, which will provide a flexible user-convenient access, provided mass data stored in ConnectomeDB database for free, and played a leading role in the development of other brain atlas analysis method. The beta version of the connection group workbench has been published on the website www.humanconnectome.org.

14.4.2 MoNETA

The school of cognition and the nervous system of Boston University carried out the long-term studies of the brain neural model in the United States. As early as 1976, Grossberg proposed an adaptive resonance theory (ART) [34,35]. The top-down mechanism is expecting to control the forecasting of encoding and matching and triggers effectively the rapid learning resisting total oblivion. Achieving the goal of rapid and stable study but not total oblivion is usually attributed to the stability/plasticity dilemma. The stability/plasticity dilemma is that each brain system requires fast and stable learning. If brain system design is too economical then we should expect to find a similar principle to run in all brain systems. The principle can be based on the whole life process of changing conditions to make different responses to learn the growing knowledge stably. ART presets some basic features of humans' and animals' perception and cognition, which is part of the answer to the brain stability/plasticity dilemma. In particular, the human being is a conscious creature, who can learn about expectations for the world and make inferences for what is going to happen. Human beings are a kind of attention-type creature as well. The data processing resources are concentrated on a limited amount of available information at any given time. Why are human beings conscious and attention-type creatures? The stability/plasticity dilemma and the solution of making use of the resonance state provide a unified framework for understanding this problem.

ART assumes that there is a close connection between the processing mechanism that makes us learn quickly and steadily for the changing world and the other processing mechanisms that focus on the information we are interested in. Only the resonance state can drive rapid new learning processes in order to solve the stability/plasticity dilemma, which is the origin of the name of this theory.

The recent ART model, known as LAMINART, shows that ART predictions may be specific [36] in the thalamus cortical circuit. The LAMINART model integrates visual development, learning, perception, attention, and 3D vision. However, it does not include the control mechanisms of the dynamics of peak potential on learning, higher-order-specific thalamic nuclei, nonspecific thalamic nuclei, regularity resonance and reset, and the pharmacological modulation.

In 2008 Grossberg put forward the SMART (synchronous matching ART) model [37], in which the brain coordinates a multistage thalamus and cortex learning process and stabilizes important information out of memory. The SMART model shows bottom-up and top-down paths that work together and through coordinating the several processes of learning expectations, focus, resonance and synchronize to complete these objectives. In particular, the SMART model explains how to achieve needs about concentrating on learning through the brain's subtle loop, especially the cell hierarchical organization in the new cortex loop.

The SMART model explains how to naturally coexist in the LAMINART structure, so it is beyond the ART and the LAMINART models. In particular, the SMART model explains and simulates: Shallow cortical circuits may interact with the specific primary and higher thalamic nuclei and nonspecific thalamic nuclei, in order to control the process of matching nonspecific thalamic nuclei used to control cognitive learning and resisted complete forgetting. Based on the process of acetylcholine, it is possible to crystallize the nature of the predicted alertness control, which only makes use of the local computation signal control via learning from continuous environment data.

The SMART model is the first work to link the cognitive and brain vibrations, especially in the frequency domains γ and β, which are obtained from a series of cortical and subcortical structures. The SMART model shows why β vibrations can become a modulated top-down feed-back and a resetting symbol. The SMART model developed earlier simu-lation work and explained how the gamma vibration is generated when the modulated top-down expectation is matched with the consistent bottom-up input. Such a match makes cells more efficient across their incentive threshold in stimulating action potentials, leading to the overall enhancement of the local gamma frequency synchronization in the shared top-down modulation.

The SMART model associated different vibration frequencies with STDP. If the average incentive of presynaptic and postsynaptic cells is $10 \sim 20$ ms; in other words, in the STDP learning window, learning sce-narios will be more easily restricted to matching conditions. This model predicts that STDP will further enhance the synchronous excitability of related cortical and subcortical regions, and the effect of spurious synchro-nization on long-term memory weights in fast learning can be prevented or reversed by synchronous resonance in matching state. In the matched condition, the amplified γ vibration compressed the presynaptic excite-ment into a narrow time domain window, which will help excitement to spread over the cortex hierarchical structure. The prediction is consistent with the rapid reduction of effects of postsynaptic excitation of the observed lateral geniculate nucleus.

Different oscillation frequencies and matching/resonances (γ fre-quency) or mismatches/reset (β frequency) are associated with these fre-quencies, not only for the selection of learning but also for discovering the active search process of the cortical mechanisms supporting new learn-ing. No match can predict the expressed fact in the components of ERP N200, which pointed out that new experimentation can be used to com-bine ERP and oscillation frequency as a cognitive process index for dynamic regularity learning.

Funded by the US National Science Foundation, the Institute of Cognitive and Neural Systems, Boston University, set up the Center of Excellence for Learning in Education, Science and Technology (CELEST). In CELEST, the designers of the calculation model, neuroscientists, psychologists, engineers, and researchers from the cognitive and neurological department of Harvard University, Massachusetts Institute of Technology, Brandeis University, and Boston University carried out communication and collaboration. They research the basic principles of planning, organizing, communicating, memory, especially the brain model of application learning and memory, and they want to construct a low-power-consumption, high-density neural chip and to achieve more and more complex large-scale brain circuits, to solve the problem of challenging pattern recognition.

The Institute of Cognitive and Neural Systems, Boston University, has designed software called MoNETA (modular neural exploring traveling agent) [38], which is the brain of a chip. MoNETA will run on the brain-inspired microprocessor, which was developed by the US California HP Labs. Its basic idea is the principle that distinguishes us from a high-speed machine with no Intelligence quotient (IQ). MoNETA happens to be a name in Roman mythology for the goddess of memory. "Moneta" will do what other computers have never done before. It will perceive the surrounding environment and decide what information is useful; then this information will be added to the structure of reality taking shape in some application. It will develop a plan to ensure its own survival. In other words, MoNETA will have the motivation of cockroaches, cats, and people. The place of MoNETA is distinguished from other AI in that it does not need to be explicitly programmed like the mammalian brain, and MoNETA can act in a variety of environments for dynamic learning.

14.4.3 Neurocore chip

Stanford University's Boahen and his research team developed 16 custom Neurogrid chips. Each chip can simulate 65,536 neurons. These chips can simulate 1 million neurons and billions of synaptic connections. In design, the Neurocore chip has a very high energy efficiency. A strategy taken by Bergen et al. is to make the assured synaptic share the hardware circuit. The size of the Neurogrid is comparable to an iPad the number of neurons and synapses that can be simulated is far greater than that of other brain simulations performed on a tablet computer under the same conditions of energy consumption. The Neurogrid development has funding from the US National Institutes of Health.

The operating speed of the circuit board is 9000 times faster than the average personal computer, while the power consumption is far lower than that of the PC. It is used for humanoid robots and artificial limb control and other purposes. Neurogrid, named Neurocore, used 16 dedicated integrated chips (ICs). With these ICs, it can reproduce the action of about 1,050,000 neurons in the brain and billions of synapses. Stanford University said the Neurocore made use of semiconductor technology in its manufacture about 15 years ago. The Neurogrid development cost is $40,000. Bergen said that if we can use the latest manufacturing process, the manufacturing cost can be reduced to only $400 for the current 1/100. Stanford University said that, because the strategy is making use of a small number of circuits to reproduce a large number of synaptic action has been a success, they used the older process technology in the IC package. This strategy is particularly significant in the low-power consumption of the IC.

14.5 China Brain Project

Brain science and brain-like intelligence technology are two important cutting-edge scientific and technological fields. These two areas learn from each other and develop in combination. It is a new trend emerging in the international scientific community in recent years. The understanding of brain science research on the cognitive neural principle of the brain has promoted human beings' understanding of self and of the level of diagnosis and treatment for major brain diseases; it is also conducive to the development of brain-like computing systems and devices, breaking through the shackles of traditional computer architecture. In the face of fierce international competition and urgent social needs, the implementation of the project "brain science and brain-like research" will help China make significant breakthroughs in the frontiers of the brain's cognitive principles, brain-like AI, and brain disease diagnosis and treatment, play a leading role in the world.

14.5.1 Brain map and connectome

Compared with the other projects, CBP is more comprehensive in nature; it covers basic research on the neural basis of cognitive functions, applied research in developing methods for diagnosis and intervention of brain disorders, as well as brain-inspired computing methods and devices. The goal of CBP is to promote major advances in the basic understanding of the brain and, at the same time, address some urgent societal needs by applying basic neuroscience knowledge to improve human health and to develop new technology.

To understand how the brain works, we need to have three types of maps: first, a "cell type map," that is, to identify the diverse types of cells (neurons and glia) and their distributions in all brain regions, as well as the molecular expression pattern in each cell type. Using molecules specifically expressed in different cell types as markers, we can then draw the second type of map—"connectivity map" (the so-called connectome), which is the wiring diagram of nerve connections among all neurons in the brain. Mapping the connectome is often compared to mapping the genome—the complete sequence of all nucleotides and genes encoded along the entire DNA of an organism. The third type, the activity map, refers to the mapping of the firing (spiking) pattern of all neurons in the brain associated with a particular state of the brain [39]. Connectome alone without cell type and activity information has very limited usefulness for understanding the neural circuit basis of brain functions.

The brain is the most complex organ of the human body. The brain atlas is the cornerstone of understanding the structure and function of brain. It provides a means of "navigation" for exploring complex brain structures and abnormal changes. Therefore, brain mapping has always been a common frontier of neuroscience, cognitive science, psychology, and brain disease research. Many current human brain atlases cover only specific structures, lack fine-grained parcellations, and fail to provide functionally important connectivity information. Using noninvasive multimodal neuroimaging techniques, Tianzi Jiang et al. designed a connectivity-based parcellation framework that identifies the subdivisions of the entire human brain, revealing the in vivo connectivity architecture [40]. The resulting human Brainnetome Atlas, with 210 cortical and 36 subcortical subregions, provides a fine-grained, cross-validated atlas and contains information on both anatomical and functional connections.

14.5.2 General intelligent platform

After more than 60 years of ups and downs, AI has been reborn under the collision of three development forces: deep learning, big data, and computing power. According to the different stages of AI problem solving, it can be roughly divided into three stages: perceptual intelligence, cognitive intelligence, and decision-making intelligence.

The first stage is perceptual intelligence, with speech recognition, image understanding, character recognition as the main task, which is manifested as "being able to listen, speak, see and recognize," and the single task has approached or surpassed the human level. As far as the speech recognition field with the greatest progress in AI is concerned, on the basis of tens of thousands or even hundreds of thousands of hours of labeled speech data, deep learning can reach or even exceed our human dictation level. At present, the technology of AI in the perceptual intelligence layer has entered a mature stage.

The second stage is cognitive intelligence, with reasoning, decision making, and learning as the main tasks, which is manifested as "being able to understand, think and have cognition." Let the machine answer, "Will this weather condition cause flight delays tomorrow?" For example, the machine needs to know not only what the current weather conditions are and what kind of weather will cause flight delays and other common knowledge but also needs the basic departure criteria specific to an airline or airport aircraft. Behind language understanding are common sense and reasoning, while words are only the tip of the iceberg of human cognitive space. The research of cognitive intelligence has just started, and the cognitive level of AI is still very low.

With the increasing level of machine cognition, its "autonomy" is further enhanced, and it has the ability to deal with more situations and functions. Human beings will inevitably present more and more problems to machine decision making. But must the decisions of machine be more correct than those of human? Therefore, it is necessary to enhance the research of human–computer trust, the intelligence of interaction, and cooperation between humans and intelligent systems, that is, decision-making intelligence.

As the engine of social development, intelligence science must be deeply combined with various industries, and the intelligence platform is therefore particularly important. Like the steam engine of the human industrial civilization, the platform can adapt to different application fields, form different intelligence science communities to help solve medical auxiliary diagnosis, improve production and management processes, provide climate change reports, and change human teaching methods. In the era of intelligence science, we need new thinking logic, data and algorithms have become the bottom of the world and also the key to our understanding of the future. But constrained by intelligent technology and business push, the change is only in its infancy.

CogDL, developed by Tsinghua University, is a graph representation learning toolkit that allows researchers and developers to easily train and compare baseline or custom models for node classification, link prediction, and other tasks on graphs. Pytorch is the underlying architecture, and Python is used as the programming language. It provides implementations of many popular models, including nonGNN Baselines like Deepwalk, GNN Baselines like GCN, GraphSAGE. CogDL allows researchers and developers to train baseline in pipeline fashion or custom models for node classification, link prediction, and other tasks on graphs. CogDL also has many advanced features such as arbitrary graph support and a distributed computation, extensible framework.

14.5.3 Artificial intelligence chip

In 2012 Yunji Chen, Tianshi Chen et al. from the Institute of Computing Technology, Chinese Academy of Sciences, proposed the first international benchmark set of artificial NN hardware, benchnn. This work improves the processing speed of artificial NNs and effectively accelerates general computing. A series of special processors for the Cambrian NN have been launched successively: DianNao (prototype processor structure for a variety of artificial NNs) [41], DaDianNao (for a large-scale artificial NN) [42] and PuDianNao (for a variety of machine learning algorithms) [43]. At the 2015 ACM/IEEE International Conference on Computer Architecture, ShiDianNao, a convolutional NN-oriented architecture, was released. In March 2016 Zhongke Cambrian Technology Co., Ltd was founded by Tianshi Chen and Yunji Chen.

DianNao, proposed by Tianshi Chen et al., is the first prototype processor structure of the Cambrian series [41], including a processor core with a main frequency of 0.98 GHz and peak performance of 452 billion basic NN operations per second (such as addition, multiplication, etc.). The accelerator processor has a power consumption of 0.485 W and an area of 3.02 mm^2 under 65 nm, shown in Fig. 14.4. The experimental results on several representative NNs show that the average performance of DianNao is 100 times higher than that of the mainstream CPU core, the area and power consumption are only $1/30 \sim 1/5$ of the CPU core, and the efficiency is improved to three orders of magnitude; the average performance of DianNao is equivalent to that of the mainstream general graphics processor (NVIDIAK20M), but the area and power consumption are only 1% of the latter.

DianNao wants to solve the core problem is how to make the limited memory bandwidth meet the needs of the computing functional components, so as to achieve a balance between the computing and memory

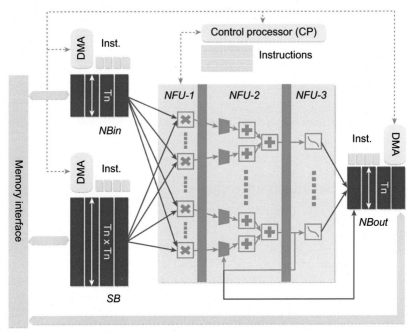

Figure 14.4 DianNao accelerator. *DMA*, Direct memory access; *SB*, synaptic weights buffer.

access and achieve high efficiency. For this purpose, a set of performance modeling methods based on machine learning are proposed. Finally, all design parameters are selected for DianNao based on the model. The balance between operation and memory access is achieved, which significantly improves the efficiency of executing the NN algorithm.

On June 20, 2019, Cambrian announced the launch of the cloud AI chip Siyuan. Siyuan 270 adopts the MLUv02 instruction set independently developed by Cambrian. The theoretical peak performance reaches 128 trillion basic AI operations (int8) per second, while compatible with int4 and int16 operations, the theoretical peak performance reaches 256 trillion and 64 trillion times per second, respectively. The Siyuan chip can support highly diversified AI applications such as vision, voice, natural language processing, and traditional machine learning. It also integrates video and image encoding and decoding hardware units for vision applications.

A general platform that could support the prevailing computer-science-based artificial NNs as well as neuroscience-inspired models and algorithms is highly desirable. Luping Shi and his colleagues developed the Tianjic chip, which integrates the two approaches to provide a hybrid, synergistic platform [44]. The Tianjic chip adopts a many-core architecture, reconfigurable building blocks and a streamlined dataflow with hybrid coding schemes, and can not only accommodate computer-science-based machine-learning algorithms, but also easily implement brain-inspired circuits and several coding schemes. Using just one chip, they demonstrated the simultaneous processing of versatile algorithms and models in an unmanned bicycle system, realizing real-time object detection, tracking, voice control, obstacle avoidance, and balance control.

14.5.4 Tianjic chip

There are two general approaches to developing an AI chip: computer-science oriented and neuroscience oriented. The Tianjic chip integrated the two approaches to provide a hybrid, synergistic platform [44]. The unified functional core (FCore) combines the axon, synapse, dendrite, and soma blocks together. To achieve deep fusion, nearly the whole of the FCore is reconfigurable for high utilization in different modes. The dendrite and soma are divided into multiple groups during operation. The computation within each group is parallelized, while the intergroup execution is serialized.

To support the parallel processing of large networks or multiple networks concurrently, the Tianjic chip adopts a many-core architecture with scattered localized memory for timely and seamless communication. The FCores on this chip are arranged in a two-dimensional (2-D) mesh manner. A reconfigurable routing table in the router of each FCore allows an arbitrary connection topology. By configuring the routing table, we can connect a neuron to any other neuron inside or outside an FCore or even outside the chip, which helps to build multigranular network topologies. The Tianjic chip consists of 156 FCores, containing approximately 40,000 neurons and 10 million synapses. Fabricated using 28 nm processing technology, Tianjic occupies a die area of 3.8×3.8 mm^2.

Fig. 14.5 shows the structure of the large-scale spiking neural networks (SNN) with artificial neural networks (ANN) dendritic relay (left). With the help of ANN relays to transfer intermediate membrane potentials with high precision (right), a hybrid device was able to achieve higher recognition accuracy than with an SNN alone, with negligible hardware overhead.

In general, Tianjic adopts a non—von Neumann paradigm with hybrid compatibility, many-core architecture, localized memory, and streamlined dataflow, which is able to support cross-paradigm modeling, maximize

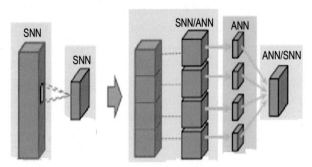

Figure 14.5 Structure of the large-scale SNN with ANN. *ANN*, Artificial neural networks; *SNN*, spiking neural networks.

parallelism, and improved power efficiency. To demonstrate the utility of building a brain-like cross-paradigm system, an unmanned bicycle experiment was designed by deploying multiple specialized networks in parallel within one Tianjic chip. Equipped with versatile algorithms and models, the bicycle was able to perform real-time object detection, tracking, voice command recognition, riding over a speed bump, obstacle avoidance, balance control, and decision making.

14.5.5 Decoupled NEUTRAMS

Recently, very-large-scale integration systems have been widely employed to mimic neurobiological architectures (called neuromorphic engineering). A multicore processor with a Network-on-Chip has emerged as a promising platform for NN simulation, motivating many recent studies of neuromorphic chips. The design of neuromorphic chips is promising for enabling a new computing paradigm. One major issue is that neuromorphic hardware usually places constraints on NN models that it can support, and the hardware types of neurons or activation functions are usually simpler than the software counterparts. One way to avoid the limitation on the connection number is to decouple synaptic weight storage from processing logic and to use software to control the memory I/O and resource reusage, which has been adopted by some custom architectures to accelerate AI algorithms [45].

The team of Professor Zhang Youhui of Tsinghua University and Professor Xie Yuan of University of California, Santa Barbara, completed the joint project and published a paper [46] to introduce NEUTRAMS (neural network transformation, mapping, and simulation). NEUTRAMS includes three key components: a NN transformation algorithm, a

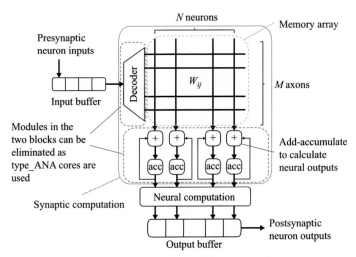

Figure 14.6 Basic core architecture of neural network transformation, mapping, and simulation.

configurable clock-driven simulator of neuromorphic chips, and an optimized run time tool that maps NNs onto the target hardware for better resource utilization. Fig. 14.6 shows the basic core architecture of NEUTRAMS. Each core processes a collection of N neurons, with each neuron having up to M input axons. The synaptic weights ($W_{i,j}$, $0 \leq i < N$ and $0 \leq j < M$) are stored in a memory array. If an output spike is generated, it will be sent to the local router for further processing. Input and output buffers store presynaptic inputs and postsynaptic outputs, respectively. The NEUTRAMS has been used for TIANJI [47] and PRIME [48] architecture design. PRIME is a novel processing-in-memory architecture built upon emerging metal oxide resistive random access memory (ReRAM) for NN applications. It exploits how crossbar-structured ReRAM has both data storage and NN computation capabilities. In the ReRAM-based main memory design, a portion of the ReRAM crossbar arrays in each bank is enabled to work as an accelerator for NN applications with supported peripheral circuit design.

14.6 Neuromorphic chip

The essential difference between von Neumann architecture and Human brain architecture is that the human brain achieves storing and processing information by synapses and there is no obvious boundary between storing and processing. Because of the plasticity of one quadrillion synapses, nerve change after various factors and prevailing conditions actualizes the functions of the human brain.

Imitating the understanding, action, and cognitive ability of the human brain becomes a significant bionic researching goal. The latest achievement of this field is the neuromorphic chip. On April 23, 2014, the *MIT Technology Review* published an article named "10 Breakthrough Technologies 2014," and the neuromorphic chip of Qualcomm was in it.

14.6.1 The development history

In 1990 honored Professor C. Mead of the California Institute of Technology gave the definition of neuromorphic chip: "Simulating chips are different from data chips which only have binary results. It can obtain various results like the real world and simulate the electrical activity of human brain neurons and synapses" [49]. However, Mead did not complete the design of simulating chip.

The chip company in speech signal processing, Audience, studied the characteristics of the nervous system, such as learning and plasticity, fault-tolerance, avoiding programming, and low energy consumption. Audience has researched and developed a neuromorphic chip based on human cochlea. The chip simulates human ears that can suppress noise and be applied to smartphone. Thus Audience has become the top company in the field of speech signal processing.

Qualcomm's neural-net processor is different from the usual processors in working principal. In essence, it is a typical computer chip made up of silicon crystal materials, but it can complete "qualitative" functions not "quantitative." The software tool developed by Qualcomm can simulate the brain's activities, and the "neural-network" on the processors is designed according to how information is passed by the human NN. The tool can permit developers to write programs based on biological excitation. Qualcomm assumed that its neural-net processor can accomplish the cognitive tasks of classification and prediction.

Qualcomm gave his neural-network processor the name Zeroth, which derives from Zeroth Law. The law rules that a robot should not harm humanity or allow humanity to come to harm by inaction. The R&D team of Qualcomm is working to develop a new computing architecture that breaks from the traditional model. They hope to build a new computing processor that simulates the human brain and nervous system and lets terminal own the embedded cognition. There are three goals of Zeroth: bionic learning, enabling the terminal to observe and know the world like a human, and creating a definite neural processing unit. According to Qualcomm, the company completed bionic learning based on studying dopamine, the neurotransmitter substance, rather than coding.

Since IBM created the first human brain simulator in 1956, it has been working on the study of the brain-like computer. Developing a neuromorphic chip based on large nervous system—like group became part of its vision, after the chip imitated synaptic transmission lines. Among them, IBM developed the first generation of neurosynaptic chips used in the development of a cognitive computer. Although a cognitive computer cannot be coded like traditional computers, it can learn by accumulating experience, finding relationships between things, and simulating brain structure and the plasticity of synapses.

In 2008 with funding from DARPA, IBM developed the second phase of the Systems of Neuromorphic Adaptive Plastic Scalable Electronics (SyNAPSE) project working on creating the system that can both simultaneously process multisource information and update constantly by itself according to the environment, achieving the characteristics of a nervous system—like learning and plasticity, fault tolerance, avoiding programming, and low energy consumption. The project leader Modha thought that the neuromorphic chip would be another milestone in the evolutionary history of computer.

At the beginning of August 2013, IBM announced the brain-like system TrueNorth and hoped it would replace today's computer in some application scenarios. Deep Blue and Watson of IBM actually defeated a human at chess, but it depended on speed and memory space rather than intelligence. Watson stored a 4 TB text database, including the whole Wikipedia and Internet database like WordNet, when it took part in the contest. Deep Blue is capable of examining 200 million moves per second and chooses the fittest one at the contest of the international chess game. Nevertheless, it only won by the advantage of one round when confronting Kasparov. The efficiency of computers is not high, for example, Watson, formed by 90 servers, consumed 85,000 W, while an adult's brain consumes about 20 W.

On August 8, 2014, IBM published the chip that could simulate the human brain in the journal "Science." The chip can simulate the functions of the human brain's neurons and synapses and other brain functions, so that it can complete computing functions. This was great progress in the field of chip brain simulation. IBM said that this microchip named TrueNorth was good at completing the missions of pattern recognition and object classification and so on and that its power consumption was very much lower than that of traditional hardware.

In 2003 British ARM began to develop the hardware of a brain-like NN, called SpiNNaker. In 2011 the company officially launched the SpiNNaker chip containing 18 ARM cores. In 2013 ARM began to develop a spiking interface based on UDP that can be used in the communication of heterogeneous neuromorphic systems. In 2014 the company joined hands with Waterloo University, supporting hardware calculation of the Spaun model.

In 2011 Germany's Heidelberg University launched a four-year program, BrainScales, on the basis of FACTS and under the funding of Proactive FP7 [50]. In 2013 they joined the EU Human Brain Plan. At the international supercomputer meeting held in Leipzig ending on June 20, 2013, Professor Meier, one of the human brain research program's coordinators in Heidelberg University, introduced the research progress gained by German science. Meier announced a neuromorphic system that would appear on silicon chips or wafer. This is not only a kind of chip but also a complete silicon wafer. There are 200,000 neurons and 5 million synapses integrated on the chip. The size of this silicon wafer is like a bigger plate. These silicon wafers are the cornerstone of the new type of brain-like computer architecture that will be developed by the Brain Research Project of the EU in the next 10 years.

14.6.2 IBM's TrueNorth neuromorphic system

DARPA began a plan named SyNAPSE in 2008. IBM was the first to launch the chip prototype of single core containing 256 neurons, 256 times 256 synapses, and 256 axons in 2011. The prototype had already processed complex missions like playing Pong at that time. But it was relatively simple, and the brain capacity of such a single core was equal to that of an insect in terms of scale.

After a three-year endeavor, IBM had made a breakthrough in complexity and usability and launched the TrueNorth chip [51]. This chip can simulate the functions of neurons and synapses to execute computing. The Samsung Electronic was responsible for the production of the chip, which has 5.4 billion transistors; that is four times as many as traditional

PC processors. Its core area is packed with 4096 processing cores, and the effect is equal to 1 million neurons and 256 million synapses. At present, IBM has already used 16 chips to develop a supercomputer of synapses.

The structure of TrueNorth is similar to the human brain, and each kernel includes about 1.2 million transistors. Among the transistors, the part of data processing and dispatching is little, but the majority of transistors are used for data storage and other aspects of kernel communication. Among the 4096 kernels, each kernel owns its own native memory, and they can quickly communicate with other kernels through a special communication mode. Their working method is very similar to the synergy between human brain neurons and synapses, but only the chemical signals turn into current pulses on this occasion. IBM calls the structure Synapses Kernel Architecture.

IBM used a software ecosystem to add well-known algorithms, including convolutional network, liquid machine, restricted Boltzmann machine, hidden Markov model, support vector machine, optical flow, and multimodality classification, into architecture by offline learning. Now these algorithms in TrueNorth need not be changed.

The biggest selling point of this chip is the extremely high efficiency of communication and thus greatly reducing power consumption. Each TrueNorth's kernel has 256 neurons, and each nerve is connected by 256 neurons that are distributed at the nerve's inner and outer sides, respectively.

By comparison, the human brain has over 100 billion neurons, and each neuron has thousands of synapses; such a NN cannot be imagined. The final goal of IBM is to build a computer containing 10 billion neurons and 100 trillion synapses. The functions of such a computer are 10 times stronger than that of the human brain, while power consumption is only 1000 W.

In March 29, 2016, the Lawrence Livermore National Laboratory announced that it has purchased the first brain-like supercomputing platform developed by IBM based on TrueNorth neuromorphic chips. The platform contains 16 chips and only needs to consume the power required by a tablet computer, 2.5 W, the processing amount of calculation can be equivalent to about 16 million neurons and 40 million synapses.

14.6.3 British SpiNNaker

SpiNNaker is the program launched jointly by many universities in Manchester, Southampton, Cambridge, and Sheffield, as well as enterprises, and it has investment from Engineering and Physical Sciences Research Council (EPSRC). The leader is Professor Furber of

Manchester University, who has worked on the study of human brain functions and structure for many years. He is one of the union designers for Acorn RISC Machine, the antecedent of the ARM processor. After the project received permission, ARM supported it strongly and offered processors and physical IP to the scientific team.

There are about 100 billion neurons and up to 1 quadrillion connections in the human brain, so even 1 million processors can only simulate 1% of the human brain. Neurons transmit information by the way of simulating electron peak's electronic pulse, while SpiNNaker uses the method of describing data package for simulation. In 2011 the company formally published the chip including 18 ARM cores [52].

A single SpiNNaker multiprocessor chip contains 18 low-power-consumption advanced RISC machine (ARM) 986 kernels, and each kernel can simulate 1000 neurons. Each chip also has a 128 MB synchronous dynamic random-access memory (SDRAM), with low-power-consumption, to store the information of the connecting weight of synapses between neurons and the time delay of synapses. A single chip's power consumption is lower than 1 W, taking the method of partial synchronization in the chip and using the measure of global asynchronous between chips.

These is no central timer in the SpiNNaker system; that means the send and receive of signals will not be synchronous, and these signals will interfere each other. And the output will change by the millions of random microchanges. It sounds disorderly, and it actually needs high precision for some missions, like mathematical calculations. But this system can calmly deal with fuzzy operating calculations. For example, when you should use your hands in order to throw a ball easily, or which word comes at the end of a sentence. After all, brains need not calculate results to 10 decimal places; the human brain is more like a disorderly system. A large number of SpiNNaker processors may be asynchronously interconnected by Ethernet. Each SpiNNaker contains a specially made router, which is used to achieve the communication of inner neurons and the chip neurons of SpiNNaker.

In 2013 Manchester University developed an interface of spike potential based on user datagram protocol (UDP), which can be used in the communication of heterogeneous neuromorphic systems. This interface shows the mixed communication of the SpiNNaker and BrainScale system, developing a large-scale neuromorphic network.

The number of connections is the main limiting factor in the upscaling of NN implementations. It dominates the required chip area and power consumption in special-purpose hardware, as well as the required memory and computation time. Deep Rewiring is a training algorithm that continuously rewires the network while preserving very sparse connectivity all along the training procedure. Technische Universität Dresden in Germany and University of Manchester in the United Kingdom jointly developed a prototype chip of the second generation SpiNNaker system in 2018 [53]. The local memory of a single core on this chip is limited to 64 KB, and a deep network architecture is trained entirely within this constraint without the use of external memory. Throughout training, the proportion of active connections is limited to 1.3%. On the handwritten digits dataset MNIST, this extremely sparse network achieves 96.6% classification accuracy at convergence. When compared to an X86 CPU implementation, NN training on the SpiNNaker 2 prototype improves power and energy consumption by two orders of magnitude.

14.7 Memristor

Memristor is a new passive nano information device. With the advantages of high integration density, high read—write speed, low-power consumption, and multivalue computing potential, it is on the research frontier and focuses in current international academic and industrial circles.

14.7.1 Overview

In 1971 Professor Leon Chua of the University of California, Berkeley, found that the direct relationship between magnetic flux and charge is absent in the pairwise relationship between basic circuit variables. From the perspective of symmetry and completeness of circuit variable relationship, Chua deduced the missing relation, defined the fourth basic passive circuit element, and named it memory resistor (memristor) [54,55]. The resistance state memristor M represents the state-dependent relationship between magnetic flux and charge:

Charge controlled

$$M = \frac{d\phi}{dq}$$

or
Flux controlled

$$M = \frac{dq}{d\phi}$$

The main difference between memristor and other passive devices is that its current voltage characteristic curve is a self-crossing hysteresis

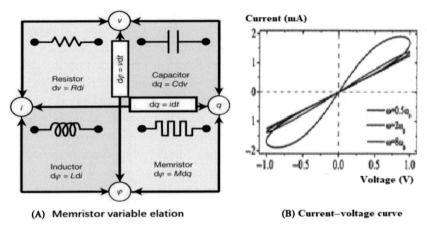

(A) Memristor variable elation   (B) Current–voltage curve

Figure 14.7 Memristor.

curve, and the curve will gradually shrink into a straight line with the increase of frequency is shown in Fig. 14.7.

In 1976 Chua extended the definition of the memristor to the state-dependent relationship between current and voltage, so as to cover all terminal, passive, and nonvolatile memory devices. This generalized memristor is also called a memristor system. In 2009 Pershin et al. further proposed the concepts of the memcapactive system and the meminductive system, thus establishing a complete theoretical system of memristor devices [56].

In the past 40 years after Chua proposed the memristor theory, due to processing technology, related research on the memristor physical realization has been stagnant. In 2008 HP's laboratory published a paper that announced that it had found the "disappeared" memristor [57]. When the HP team led by HP Senior Fellow Williams researched silica, they accidentally discovered the silica had a latch crossbar function, which can be used for memristor. Memristor is a piece of thin TiO_2 sandwiched between two electrodes (above platinum) with an intermediate. The titanium piece is divided into two parts: One half is normal TiO_2, and the other half is slightly "hypoxia" with a few less oxygen atoms. The hypoxia half is positively charged, so the current through the resistor is relatively small, when the current leads from the hypoxia side to the normal side. The hypoxia "hole" will gradually vacillate to the normal side under the influence of an electric field. To the piece of material, the part of gas shortage will be relatively a high proportion, but the resistor of the system will be reduced. When the current flows from the normal side to the anoxic side, the electric field will push the oxygen hole back, and the resistor will increase. The state of the resistor is the state of being frozen after the power is cut off.

It is a challenge to integrate memory and computation to construct a brain-inspired structure. Memristor is the best technology to achieve this task because it has enough energy consumption efficiency and storage density and can equal biological memory. With this device, the AI system, which is close in size and energy consumption to that of the mammalian brain, can be constructed.

DARPA began a program in 2008 called SyNAPSE. HP has generated a more complex memristor under the auspices of the United States Department of DARPA. The architecture of the brain-inspired microprocessor developed by HP labs can be considered a multicore chip based on the memristor. Today, high-end microprocessors have multiple cores, or processing units. But unlike the typical microprocessor with about eight cores, HP hardware includes hundreds of simple, ordinary silicon processing cores, and each core has its own high-density jungle-like memristor lattice array. Each silicon core is directly connected to their megabyte cache accessed instantaneously; the cache consists of millions of memristor, which means each core has its own dedicated huge memory pool. Even by today's semiconductor standards, memristor volume is very small. Williams claimed that it will be possible to build a 1,000,000,000,000,000 bits per square centimeter of nonvolatile memristor memory. Hewlett-Packard completed the design and implementation of the hardware platforms, and the Nerve morphology lab at Boston University did the work on software.

Memristor as a biological system snugly combines calculation and data, using very little energy to store information like the brain. We need to abandon the idea of software and hardware separation because the brain does not function in that way. There is just wetware in the brain. If you really want to copy a mammal's brain, software and hardware need to merge with each other. Although memristor is intensive, cheap, tiny its failure rate is high, and it is similar to the characteristics of brain synapses. This means that the architecture must allow single circuit defects, just like the brain. When the synapse loss, it cannot cause system failure but can reduce the quality in a fault-tolerance way.

The research of the HP laboratory has triggered a worldwide upsurge of memristor research, and the international academic and industrial circles have invested a lot of research effort. At present, the related research of memristor is mainly divided into three directions: device preparation, characterization and testing, and the application of new computing systems based on memristor.

The fabrication of memristor devices has been studied in domestic academia. The Institute of Microelectronics, Chinese Academy of Sciences, and the University of Defense Science and Technology have carried out cooperative research on the memristor of ZrO_x, HfO_x, and WO_x. A number of research results have been achieved in device design and fabrication, such as the switching resistance ratio of a Pt/hf02: Cu/Cu device is more than 100, the closing speed is less than 40 ns, the number of cycles is more than 108, and the holding time is more than ten years (85°C).

Professor Yichun Liu and Professor Haiyang Xu of Northeast Normal University cooperated with Milan Polytechnic University in Italy and published a paper "Toward a Generalized Bienenstock Cooper Munro Rule for Spatiotemporal Learning via Triplet STDP in Memorial" on nature communications [58]. In this paper, they first report that the generalized BCM learning rules are successfully simulated on memristor by using the STDP. Furthermore, the space-time learning function with frequency characteristics is realized by designing the memristor double-layer neural feedforward network.

At present, memristors have shown broad application prospects in nonvolatile storage, logic operation, new computing/storage fusion architecture computing, and new neural morphology computing, which will provide a new physical basis for the development of IT technology.

14.7.2 In-memory computing

With the development of big data technology and the rise of deep learning technology with a NN as the core, the computing power of traditional mainstream hardware platform has heightened requirements. Because the deep learning algorithm needs to deal with the streaming data, a lot of data will flow between the computing unit and the storage unit when the hardware platform based on von Neumann computing architecture deals with the related tasks. The reading and writing speed of the latter is much slower than that of the former, and the operation process of accessing memory accounts for most of the total energy consumption and delay, which limits the processing speed of data, which is called von Neumann bottleneck or memory bottleneck. The memory bottleneck makes the computing system show high power consumption, slow speed, and other shortcomings. In the computing task centered on large amounts of data, the problem brought on by the separation of storage and computation is more prominent.

At present, people use a graphics processing unit that can process data in a parallel or special acceleration chip designed for data flow, such as TPU (tensor processing unit) and other hardware to accelerate to meet the demand of computing power. Generally, this kind of acceleration hardware has strong parallel processing ability and large data bandwidth, but the storage and computing units are still separated in space. Unlike the von Neumann computing platform, in the human brain with large-scale parallel, adaptive, and self-learning characteristics, there is no clear boundary between information storage and computing, which are all completed by neurons and synapses. People began to study new nano devices, hoping to simulate the characteristics of neurons and synapses. In this kind of nano device, memristors are very similar to synapses and have great potential. By using this new type of memristor, the data can be stored and the in-situ computing can be realized so that the storage and computing can be integrated, and the memory bottleneck can be fundamentally eliminated. These new types of memristors include magnetic range access memory, phase change range access memory, and resistive range access memory.

There are two kinds of in-memory computing based on memristor: logic operation with two value memristors, simulation computing with analog memristor. The Boolean operations based on memristor can be divided into three types according to the different input, output types, and operation modes: R-R logic operation, V-R logic operation, and V-V logic operation. In the R-R logic operation, the input and output represent logic 0 and 1, respectively by the high- and low-resistance states of the memristor, and the operation process is completed in the memristor. In V-R logic, input is applied to a single memory. The voltage amplitudes X_1 and X_2 at both ends of the resistor are represented, while the logic output Y is represented by high- and low-resistance states (representing logic 0 and 1, respectively). The operation requires that the memristor is bipolar, and applying positive and negative polarity voltage will make the device transfer to high- and low-resistance states, respectively. In V-V logic operation, both input and output are through voltage low- and high-amplitudes representing logic 0 and 1, respectively.

In 2019 the Yang research group reported on the use of the analog memristor array to achieve the reinforcement learning in Nature Electronics [59]. The hybrid (analog and digital) reinforcement learning architecture is proposed in the report, which allocates the computing of matrix vector multiplication to the operation of analog memristor array, thus combining the advantages of the analog operation of memristor array with the advantages of the logic operation of complementary metal oxide semiconductor (CMOS).

At present, in-memory computing based on memristor has not developed into a reliable and mature memory bottleneck solution, and there are still challenges in-memory computing based on memristor. First of all, the consistency of memristor is the primary problem. Secondly, the stability of memristor will also have a negative impact on the computing accuracy. Moreover, the integration scale of memristor is also critical to the development of in-memory computing.

14.8 Development roadmap of intelligence science

Through the crossing cooperation of the field of brain science, cognitive science, and AI, we should strengthen our nation's research of basic and originality at the crossing field of intelligence science, solve the significant basic theory problems at the development of cognitive science and information science, drive the development of intelligent information processing key technology relating to the nation's economy, society and national safety, and put forward the theoretical basis for the prevention and treatment of brain disease and brain disorders.

On October 29, 2013, at the summit forum of "Innovation Driven Development — Artificial Intelligence in the Era of Big Data" of Chinese Association of Artificial Intelligence, the author described the roadmap of intelligence science development. In 2025 we achieve the primary class of brain computing, namely Elementary Brain-like Computing, and computers can achieve the goal to complete precise listening, speaking, reading, and writing. In 2035 we enter Advanced Brain-like Computing, and computers have not only IQ but also emotional intelligence. In 2050 we combine intelligence science and nanotechnology and develop a neuromorphic computer, achieving super-brain computing.

14.8.1 Elementary brain-like computing

In recent years, the organic combination and fusion of nanotechnology, information, biology, and cognition become the highlight of the world, called Nanoscience, Biotechnology, Information technology, Cognitive Science (NBIC) converging technologies. Any converging technology of these four fields will accelerate the development of science and society. The development of brain and cognitive science will drive a new breakthrough of information's expressing and processing. Intelligent tech based on brain and cognitive science will drive a new revolution of information technology.

By 2025 in order to achieve elementary brain-like computing and make the machines to hear, speak, read, and write or even easily communicate with humans, we should overcome the difficulty of semantic processing. Semantic meaning is data meaning. There is no meaning for the data itself; there is meaning only when data is given meaning. At this time, data turns into information, and the meaning of data is semantic. Semantic is the interpretation of the data symbol and can be regarded as the meaning of concepts of things standing for what in reality is corresponding data, and the relationship between semantic that is data explanation and logical expressing. Semantics have the characteristic of territoriality, and there is no semantic that does not belong to any domain. For computer science, semantic meaning usually aims at users for the explanation of computer expressions used to depict reality, that is, the method used to connect computer expression with reality by users.

Computer data appears in many forms, such as text, voice, graphics, pictures, videos, and animation. At the elementary phase, if scientists want to make robots understand the context of media like humans, they must break through robotic semantic processing.

14.8.1.1 Natural language processing

Text semantic processing is essentially natural language processing. Natural language processing is not studying natural language as usual but studying a computer system that can efficiently achieve natural language communication, especially soft systems. So it is a part of computer science. Natural language communication between human and computer means that the computer can understand the meaning of natural language text and express the given intention and idea by natural language. The former is called natural language understanding, and the latter is called natural language generation. So natural language processing generally includes natural language understanding and natural language generation.

Natural language processing, that is, natural language communication, or natural language understanding and natural language generation, is very difficult. The root reason is the widespread variable ambiguity in natural language text and dialog. From the format, a Chinese text is a string formed by characters (including punctuation). Characters can form words, words can form sentences, and then some sentences form paragraphs, sections, chapters, and article. Whether it is a variety of levels or a shift from low level to high level, there is the phenomenon of ambiguity. That is, a string with the same format can be understood as different strings under different scenes or context and have different meanings. Under normal circumstances, the majority of these problems can be solved according to the rules of corresponding context and scenes. In other words, there is no overall ambiguity. This is why we do not think natural language is ambiguous, and we can correctly communicate using natural language. On the other hand, as we can see, in order to eliminate it, much knowledge and inference are needed. How to collect and sort out the knowledge completely? How to find a suitable form to save into computer science? How to efficiently use them to eliminate ambiguity? All of them mean very difficult work, and the workload is extremely great. The work cannot be finished by a few people in the short term; it remains a long-term and systematic task.

From recent theory and technology, a universal and high-quality natural language system is also a goal that needs long-term effort. But aiming at certain applications, some practical systems with the ability of natural language processing have emerged. Some of the systems have been commercialized, even industrialized, for example, the natural language interface of database and experts system, all kinds of machine-translation systems, full-text information retrieval systems, automatic abstracting systems, and so on.

14.8.1.2 Image semantics generation

With the development of image processing technology, multimedia technology, and network technology, the amount of image information becomes greater and greater. How to autogenerate image semantic meaning and understand image semantics is a significant scientific problem in image retrieval and pattern recognition.

Because of the inherent characteristics of images, if we want to autogenerate an image's semantic meaning, we must combine the image's feature, research's level, and cultural environment. We can build the semantic meaning mode by studying the image's semantic meaning, then depicting the image in semantic meaning mode, and promoting the improvement of the image semantic meaning research level.

Image semantic meaning is divided into three layers: the bottom features layer, the object layer, and the concept layer. The bottom feature, in essence, is no image semantics information, and its basic idea is to extract the relationship of the image's colors, texture, shape, and space. At present, content-based retrieval is on this layer. The object layer mainly considers the problems about the objects and objects' space in images. Perception feature extraction is based on biological mechanism. The concept layer mainly solves the meaning expressed by images through scene, knowledge, and emotion. Scene semantics refers to the scene of the image. Knowledge semantics combines scene semantics with the knowledge base, ratiocinating the knowledge in images, and focuses on the action expressed in images. Emotion semantics is included by the image from the perspective of people, for example the romantic image and the horror image. Semantics concept layer usually involves abstract attributes of image. It is built on the basis of image recognition and the extraction of bottom features, and what is needed are high-level reasoning to the objects and the meaning and goal of scene, achieving the association of bottom physical features and high-level semantics, building the index of concept semantics layer, and achieving the retrieval of concept semantics layer.

14.8.1.3 Speech recognition

Automatic speech recognition is a high-tech that makes machine turn the speech signal to the corresponding text or command after recognizing and understanding. Automatic speech recognition (ASR) includes the extraction and determination of the acoustic feature, the acoustic model, and the language model. The extraction and determination of the acoustic feature is a significant part of speech recognition. The extraction and determination of the acoustic feature is a procedure of information compression, as well as a procedure of signal deconvolution.

The acoustic model is the calculation from speech to syllable probability. The acoustic model in speech recognition usually uses hidden markov model (HMM) to modeling for element recognition, and a speech element it is a three- to five-status HMM. A word is an HMM formed by a string of speech elements that form this word. While all models of continuous speech recognition is an HMM combined with word and mute.

Language model is the calculation from speech to word probability, mainly divided into a statistical model and a rule model. The statistical language model uses a probability statistic to show the inner statistic regulars, N-gram is simple and efficient and is widely used. Regular model refers to some rules or grammatical structure.

Due to the diversity and complexity of the speech signal, the present speech recognition system can only be satisfied based on performance under certain conditions or used in some specific occasions. The speech recognition system roughly depends on four factors: recognize size of vocabulary and acoustic complexity, the quality of speech signal, single speaker or speakers, and hardware platform. Speech is the most natural communicating media in the present communicating system. With the development of computer and voice processing technology, the voice—voice translation between different languages will become the hot spot of speech research. The research hot spots of speech recognition include design data base of natural language; speech features extraction; use of corpus to processing acoustic model; algorithm of speech recognition research; language translation; and speech synthesis and dialog processing research.

Deng Li, coworking with Xin Dun, found that the deep network can improve the precision of speech recognition. The fruit was further deepened by Microsoft Research Asia. They built a huge NN, which includes 6.6 million neural connections. This is the biggest such model in the research history of speech recognition. This model's recognition error rate was reduced by a third from the lowest error rate in the Switchboard standard data sets. In the field of speech recognition, the lowest error rate in these data sets has already not been updated for many years.

14.8.1.4 Language cognitive

The development of psychological science has already revealed that understanding and generating language is an extremely complex problem. Language offers a unique condition of understanding the relationship between heredity and environment. The study of language not only can make us understand the function of heredity and environment in the understanding and generating of language but also enable us to further understand learning and heredity's role in other various cognitive functions and relative important revelations. This research gives us a great opportunity to reveal the essence of human various cognitive and intelligence procedures.

The characteristic of Chinese is the perfect combination of speech, shape, and meaning. Capturing this characteristic can create a new way of natural language processing.

14.8.2 Advanced brain-like computing

By 2035 the goal of intelligent science is advanced brain-like computing and requires an artificial system with high IQ and high EQ.

IQ refers to the abilities of number, space, logic, vocabulary, and memory, and it is the ability of humans to understand objective things and to apply knowledge to solve practical issues. The discretion of *IQ* is used to mark the development level of intelligence. The test of *IQ* was invented by Alfred Binet and his students. The calculating formula is:

$$IQ = 100 \times \frac{MA}{CA}$$

where *MA* = Mental Age, *CA* = Physical Age.

If someone's *MA* as same as *CA*, the *IQ* is 100, showing that the person's *IQ* is medium. The majority of a person's *IQ* is between 85 and 115.

EQ is the ability of self-knowledge, self-understanding, and emotion-control. EQ was first presented by the two American psychologists Salover and Mayer in 1990. After being put forward in 1990, it didn't arouse attention worldwide. Until 1995, Goleman, who is the scientific journalist of "The New York Times," had published a book named "EQ: Why EQ Is More Important Than IQ," and had aroused global research and discussion of EQ. Goleman Daniel was honored as the father of EQ.

Goleman summarized EQ as the ability in five terms: "self-awareness ability; self-regular ability; self-motivation ability; the ability of know other emotions; the ability of managing interpersonal relationship." The connotations of EQ can be divided into inter and outer: the inner EQ refers to the ability of knowing one's own talent, gift, clearly perceiving one's own emotion, and high tolerance when facing setback; the outer EQ refers to the ability of acute observation to distinguish others' motivation, reading others' emotional effect, knowing how to work with others to achieve the team goals.

From the definition of EQ, the core of EQ includes knowing and managing emotion, self-motivation, dealing with interpersonal relationship correctly. They are embodied in the following respects:

14.8.2.1 The perception, assessment, and presentation of emotion

1. Identify self-mood from one's own physical status, emotional experience and thought.

2. Identify mood from others' art, various designs by language, voice, appearance, and action.
3. Present mood and present the necessity related to this mood.
4. Distinguish authenticity and veracity in mood presenting.

14.8.2.2 Promote mood in the process of thinking
1. The ability of guiding mood and thought
2. Mood imparting the direction of attention to information
3. Positive emotion affecting positive work to the judge related to emotion and memory procedure
4. Prompting individual thinking from multiperspectives through the change of mood, moving the individual from being positive to being negative
5. Emotional status making promotion to certain problem solutions

14.8.2.3 The understanding and feeling of mood
1. Tag on mood, know the relationship between mood and presentation, such as the knowledge of the difference between "love" and "like."
2. Understand the meaning presented by emotion.
3. Know and analyze the reason of emotion generation.
4. Understand complex mood, such as the emotion of love—hate.
5. Know the possibility of emotional transformation; for example, angry can convert to satisfy or shame.

14.8.2.4 Adjust maturely to emotion
1. Accept any mood with open spirit.
2. Maturely immersed in or depart from a certain mood according to the known information and judgment.
3. Maturely supervise the emotion related to self and others.
4. Process the emotion of self and others, mitigate negative emotions, enhance positive emotions, and do not depress or exaggerate.

14.8.2.5 Maintain the harmonious interpersonal relationship
1. Accurately express and properly control self-emotion.
2. Exercise the basic skills of interpersonal communication.
3. Cowork with others.
4. Exhibit the capacity of processing any problems in interpersonal communication.

14.8.2.6 Deal with frustration

1. Objectively know frustration.
2. Rationally reason the frustration.
3. Form the mechanism of frustration defense and regulatory mechanism.

14.8.3 Super-brain computing

By 2050 the goal of intelligent science is to achieve super-brain computing, in which the artificial system has the characteristics of high-intelligence, high-performance, low-power-consumption, high fault-tolerance, and all-consciousness.

14.8.3.1 High intelligence

High intelligence is the intelligence at the human level expressed by artificial systems. On the basis of understanding the biological intelligence mechanism, high intelligence gives an accurate and testable computing model for the working principle of the human brain and makes machines perform the functions that otherwise need human intelligence to achieve it. Researchers should investigate intelligent science and build the mind model and adopt the view of information to study all of human's mental activities, including feeling, perception, appearance, language, learning, memory, thinking, emotion, and consciousness. The brain-like computer, in essence, is a kind of nerve computer that simulates the function of human neural information processing by way of parallel distribution processing and self-organizing, and it is a system connected by a large amount of basic processing units. Such systems build the mental model of the brain system by the reverse program of the brain's structure, dynamics, functions, and actions and then achieve the mental-like intelligent machine in the program. Intelligent science will offer theoretical bases and key technology for brain-like computers, such as building the neural function column, cluster coding model, and mental model of the brain system; exploring the mechanism of learning memory, language cognition, cowork of different brain areas, emotional computing, and intelligent evolution; and achieving intelligent machine as the same level as human brain.

14.8.3.2 High-performance

High-performance mainly refers to running speed. The performance of computer will increase between 10^8 and 10^9 times in 40 years, and the speed will be up to 10^{24} time per second. Traditional information devices have met huge obstacles at the aspects of complexity, cost and power-consumption.

The chip tech based on CMOS has been close to the physical limit, and it's eager to expect subversive new technology. On the other hand, the chip will assemble the multifunction of computing, memory and communication, and satisfy the features of multitype, short-term design.

Silicon microelectronics devices, evolving from micron to nanometer, achieved a huge success according to Moore Law and Scaling Law. Now, 65 nm silicon CMOS technology has already achieved large-scale production, and 45 nm silicon CMOS technology has begun production in which integrating the scale of a single chip is more than 800 million transistors. In 2007 Intel and IBM successfully researched high k–gate dielectric and metal gate technology and has applied it in 45 nm silicon CMOS technology. By combining strained silicon channel technology with SOI (Silicon On Insulator) structure, 32 nm silicon CMOS technology has been put into trial production. Some companies like Intel and Samsung have successfully researched devices whose size are less than 10 nm. Experts predict that, when line width is under 11 nm, silicon CMOS technology will be under the limit at the aspects of speed, power consumption, integration, cost, and reliability. So the solution that continuous innovation in the basic research field of nanometer device physics and new material will become one of the most significant scientific technology problems in the 21st century.

In January 2009 IBM developed the Graphene transistor whose gate is 150 nm, and the cutoff frequency is 26 GHz. Graphene has extremely high mobility, its saturated speed is between six and seven times that of Si, and its coefficient of thermal conductivity is high. Graphene is fit for high speed, low-power consumption, high integration, and low noise in a microwave circuit. At present, the operating frequency of a graphene MOS transistor with 150 nm gate can reach 26 GHz. If the gate goes down to 50 nanometer, the frequency graphene transistor is expected to exceed 1 THz. Around 2020, we can successfully develop the graphene material and transistors with great performance and solve the technological problems of interconnection and integration. Around 2025, graphene system chip can be successfully developed and form scale production.

In addition to electronic computing technology based on CMOS chip, quantum computing, spinning electron computing, molecular computing, DNA computing, and optical computing, the prospective system technology research is developing vigorously as well.

14.8.3.3 Low energy consumption

When the human brain operates, it consumes power similar to lighting a 20 W bulb. Even if we reproduce the function of the brain on an advanced huge computer, it needs a dedicated power plant. Of course, it is not the only difference. The brain owns some effective components that we cannot reproduce. The key is that the brain can run under a voltage of about 100 mV. But the CMOS logic circuit needs higher voltage to make it correctly operate. The higher working voltage means requiring a higher cost of power when wires transmit signals.

For computers today, the consumption on the circuit level is picojoule, while the consumption on the system layer is micro-joule. Both of them are far above the theoretical lower limit given by physics. There is a lot of room to decrease the consumption of system. Technologies of low energy consumption are related to many aspects, such as material, devices, system architecture, system software, and management mode. Technologies breaking through low energy consumption would be the great challenge of chip and system designed in the next decades.

14.8.3.4 High fault-tolerance

When systems have an inner breakdown, the system still can offer correct services to the outer environment. This ability is referred to as fault tolerance. The concept of fault tolerance technology was first put forward by Avizienis in 1967, that is, a program of a system can still be correctly processed in the case of logical problems.

Both the human brain and the NN has the feature of fault tolerance. When units become partly invalid, they still can continue correctly working. So super-brain computing system must have highly reliable performance.

In the future, the probability of manufacturing defects widely expected in adapting nanoscale electronic equipment will increase. The article [60] puts forward a novel and high fault-tolerance crossing switch architecture that can reliably implement based on the architecture of the memristor crossing switch, whose rapid convergence for the single-layer crossing switch adapts the Delta rule to study the Boolean function. The architecture can learn Boolean function, has a manufacturing defects rate as high as 13%, and has reasonable redundancy. Compared with other technology, such as cascaded triple modular redundancy or reusing and reconfiguring von Neumann architecture, it shows the greatest fault tolerance performance.

14.8.3.5 All-consciousness

Consciousness may be one of the biggest secrets and highest achievements of human brains. Consciousness is organisms' perception of the outer world and the objective things of self-psychology and physiological action. The brain mechanism of consciousness is the object studied by all kinds of brain science, and it is also the core problem of psychological research. Brain is the organ that the human conducts conscious activities. In order to reveal regular science and build the brain model of conscious, we need to research not only conscious cognitive processes but also to nonconsciousness cognitive processes. At the same time, self-consciousness and circumstance-consciousness are also problems to which great importance needs to be attached. Self-consciousness is the individual's perceiving to the existence of oneself, and it is the organization system of self-perception and the method by which one treats oneself. It includes three kinds of psychological components: self-cognition, self-experience, and self-control. Circumstance-consciousness is the inner representation of the individual to the continuous changing of the outer environment. In the environment of social information that is complex, dynamic, and changeable, circumstance-consciousness is the key reason that affects people in decisions and performance.

At July 2005 the 125th anniversary of the establishment of the journal *Science*, the journal published the special "Questions: What Don't We Know?" and put forward 125 questions that needed to be answered. The second question was, "What is the biological basis of conscious?" [61]. Descartes, a French philosopher of the 17th century, said, "I think, therefore I am." It is observed that consciousness is the topic discussed by philosophers in the long term. Modern scientists say that consciousness springs from the collaboration of billions of neurons in brain. But that is too ambiguous. How do neurons generate consciousness? Recently, scientists have found the methods and tools that can conduct objective research to the most subjective and the most individual thing and can help patients whose brains are injured. Besides making clear the concrete operating method of consciousness, scientists also want to know the answer to a deeper level question: Why does it exist? How does it originate?

Intelligence science is a cutting-edge interdisciplinary subject. Through the interdisciplinary research of brain science, cognitive science, and AI, there will be new sparks leading to the age of intelligence.

References

[1] A.M. Turing, On computable numbers with an application to the Entscheidungsproblem, Proc. Lond. Maths. Soc. 2 (42) (1936) 230−265. ser.
[2] Z.Z. Shi, Research on Brain-Like Computer, Keynote Speaker, Beijing, 2009. BI-AMT 2009.
[3] H. Markram, The blue brain project, Nat. Rev. Neurosci. 7 (2006) 153−160.

[4] T. Binzegger, R.J. Douglas, K.A. Martin, A quantitative map of the circuit of cat primary visual cortex, J. Neurosci. 24 (39) (2004) 8441−8453.

[5] D.S. Modha, R. Ananthanarayanan, S.K. Esser, et al., Cognitive computing, Commun. ACM 54 (8) (2011) 62−71.

[6] E.R. Kandel, J.H. Schwartz, T.M. Jessell, Principles of Neural Science, fourth ed., McGraw-Hill Medical, New York, 2000.

[7] D.S. Modha, R. Singh, Network architecture of the long-distance pathways in the Macaque brain, Proc. Natl Acad. Sci. USA 107 (2010) 13485−13490.

[8] A.J. Sherbondy, R.F. Dougherty, R. Ananthanaraynan, et al., Think global, act local: projectome estimation with BlueMatter, in: Proceedings of the Medical Image Computing and Computer Assisted Intervention Society, Lecture Notes in Computer Science (London, September 20−24). Springer, Berlin, (2009), pp. 861−868.

[9] M. Lundqvist, M. Rehn, M. Djurfeldt, A. Lansner, Attractor dynamics in a modular network model of the neocortex, Netw. Comput Neural Syst. 17 (2006) 253−276.

[10] M. Djurfeldt, The connection-set algebra-a novel formalism for the representation of connectivity structure in neuronal network models, Neuroinformatic 10 (3) (2012) 287−304.

[11] M. Djurfeldt, M. Lundqvist, C. Johansson, M. Rehn, O. Ekeberg, A. Lansner, Brain-scale simulation of the neocortex on the IBM Blue Gene/L supercomputer, IBM J. Res. Dev. 52 (1/2) (2008) 31−41.

[12] P. Buzas, K. Kovacs, A.S. Ferecsko, J.M.L. Budd, et al., Model-based analysis of excitatory lateral connections in the visual cortex, J. Comp. Neurol. 499 (6) (2006) 861−881.

[13] O. Ekeberg, P. Walle, A. Lansner, H. Traven, L. Brodin, S. Grillner, A computer based model for realistic simulations of neural networks. I: the single neuron and synaptic interaction, Biol. Cybern. 65 (2) (1991) 81−90.

[14] A.L. Hodgkin, A.F. Huxley, A quantitative description of ion currents and its applications to conduction and excitation in nerve membranes, J. Physiol. (Lond.) 117 (1952) 500−544.

[15] R. Brette, et al., Simulation of networks of spiking neurons: a review of tools and strategies, J. Comput Neurosci. 23 (3) (2007) 349−398.

[16] R. Ananthanarayanan, D.S. Modha, Anatomy of a cortical simulator. In Proceedings of the ACM/IEEE Conference on Supercomputing, (Reno, NV, Nov.10−16). ACM, New York, NY, (2007), pp. 3−14.

[17] R. Ananthanarayanan, S.K. Esser, H.D. Simon, D.S. Modha, The cat is out of the bag: cortical simulations with 109 neurons and 1013 synapses. Gordon Bell Prize Winner, in: Proceedings of the ACM/IEEE Conference on Supercomputing, Portland, OR, November 14−20, ACM, New York, NY, (2009) 1−12.

[18] HBP, Sub-subprojects. <https://www.humanbrainproject.eu/discover/the-project/sub-projects>, 2013.

[19] HBP, <https://www.humanbrainproject.eu/en/follow-hbp/news/human-brain-project-announces-new-phase/>, 2020.

[20] H. Markram, K. Meier, T. Lippert, et al., Introducing the Human Brain Project, Proc CS 7 (2011) 39−42.

[21] M.M. Waldrop, Computer modelling: brain in a box, Nature 482 (2012) 456−458.

[22] D.O. Hebb, The Organization of Behavior: A Neuropsychological Theory, Wiley, New York, 1949.

[23] G.J. Stuart, B. Sakmann, Active propagation of somatic action potentials into neocortical pyramidal cell dendrites, Nature 367 (1994) 69−72.

[24] H. Markram, B. Sakmann, Calcium transients in dendrites of neocortical neurons evoked by single subthreshold excitatory postsynaptic potentials via low- voltage-activated calcium channels, Proc. Natl. Acad. Sci. USA 91 (1994) 5207−5521.

[25] H. Markram, B. Sakmann, Action potentials propogating back into dendrites triggers changes in efficacy of single-axon synapses between layer V pyramidal cells, Society of the Neuroscience Abstracts, 2007.

[26] H. Markram, J. Lübke, M. Frotscher, B. Sakmann, Regulation of synaptic efficacy by coincidence of postsynaptic APs and EPSPs, Science 275 (1997) 213−215.

[27] W. Gerstner, R. Kempter, J.L. van Hemmen, H. Wagner, A neuronal learning rule for sub-millisecond temporal coding, Nature 383 (1996) 76−81.

[28] L.F. Abbott, K.I. Blum, Functional significance of long-term potentiation for sequence learning and prediction, Cereb. Cortex 6 (1996) 406−416.

[29] K.I. Blum, L.F. Abbott, A model of spatial map formation in the hippocampus of the rat, Neural. Comput. 8 (1996) 85−93.

[30] H. Markram, M. Tsodyks, Redistribution of synaptic efficacy: a mechanism to generate infinite synaptic input diversity from a homogeneous population of neurons with out changing absolute synaptic efficacies, J. Physiol. Paris. 90 (1996) 229−232.

[31] M. Tsodyks, Spike-timing-dependent synaptic plasticity-the long road towards understanding neuronal mechanisms of learning and memory, Trends Neurosci. 25 (2002) 599−600.

[32] G. Bhumbra, R. Dyball, Measuring spike coding in the supraoptic nucleus, J. Physiol. 555 (2004) 281−296.

[33] T. Celikel, V.A. Szostak, D.E. Feldman, Modulationof spike timing by sensory deprivation during induction of corticalmap plasticity, Nat. Neurosci. 7 (2004) 534−541.

[34] S. Grossberg, Adaptive pattern classification and universal recoding: I. Parallel development and coding of neural detectors, Biol. Cybern. 23 (1976) 121−134.

[35] S. Grossberg, Adaptive pattern classification and universal recoding: II. Feedback, expectation, olfaction, illusions, Biol. Cybern. 23 (1976) 187−202.

[36] S. Grossberg, Laminar cortical dynamics of visual form perception, Neural Netw. 16 (5−6) (2003) 925−931.

[37] S. Grossberg, V. Massimiliano, Spikes, synchrony, and attentive learning by laminar thalamocortical circuits, Brain Res. 1218 (2008) 278−312.

[38] M. Versace, B. Chandler, The brain of a new machine, IEEE Spectr. (2010) 28−35.

[39] L. Wang, Mu-ming Poo: China Brain Project and the future of Chinese neuroscience, Natl Sci. Rev. 4 (2017) 258−263.

[40] L. Fan, H. Li, T. Jiang, The human brainnetome atlas: a new brain atlas based on connectional architecture, Cereb. Cortex 26 (2016) 3508−3526.

[41] T.S. Chen, Z.D. Du, N.H. Sun, et al., DianNao: a small footprint high-throughput accelerator for ubiquitous machine elearning, in: Proceedings of the 19th International Conference on Architectural Support for Programming Languages and Operating Systems-ASPLOS'14, Salt Lake City, UT, 2014, pp. 269−284, ISBN: 9781450323055.

[42] Y.J. Chen, T. Luo, S.L. Liu, et al., DaDianNao: a machine-learning supercomputer, in: International Symposium on Microarchitecture, 2014, pp. 609−622.

[43] D.F. Liu, T.S. Chen, S.L. Liu, et al., PuDianNao: a polyvalent machine learning accelerator, in: Proceedings of the 20th International Conference on Architectural Support for Programming Languages and Operating Systems, 2015, pp. 369−381.

[44] J. Pei, L. Deng, L.P. Shi, et al., Towards artificial general intelligence with hybrid Tianjic chip architecture, Nature 572 (2019) 106−111.

[45] M. Prezioso, F. Merrikh-Bayat, B.D. Hoskins, et al., Training and operation of an integrated neuromorphic network based on metal-oxide memristors, Nature 24 (521) (2015) 61−64.

[46] Y. Ji, Y.H. Zhang, S.C. Li, NEUTRAMS: neural network transformation and co-design under neuromorphic hardware constraints, in: 49th Annual IEEE/ACM International Symposium on Microarchitecture (MICRO), Taipei, 2016, pp. 1−13.

[47] L.P. Shi, J. Pei, N. Deng, et al., Development of a neuromorphic computing system, in: 2015 IEEE International Electron Devices Meeting (IEDM), 2015, pp. 4.3.1—4.3.4.

[48] P. Chi, S. Li, C. Xu et al., Processing-in-memory in reram-based main memory. in: 2016 International Symopsium on Computer Architecture, IEEE, Los Angeles, CA, USA, 2016.

[49] C.A. Mead, Neuromorphic electronic systems, Proc. Inst. Electr. Electron. Eng. 78 (1990) 1629—1636.

[50] J. Schemmel, D. Brüderle, K. Meier, et al., A wafer-scale neuromorphic hardware system for large-scale neural modeling, ISCAS (2010) 1947—1950.

[51] P.A. Merolla, J.V. Arthur, R. Alvarez-Icaza, et al., A million spiking-neuron integrated circuit with a scalable communication network and interface, Science 345 (6197) (2014) 668—672.

[52] E. Painkras, L.A. Plana, et al., SpiNNaker: a 1-W 18-core system-on-chip for massively-parallel neural network simulation, IEEE J. Solid-State Circuits 48 (8) (2013) 1943—1953.

[53] C. Liu, G. Beller, S.B. Furber, et al., Memory-efficient deep learning on a SpiNNaker 2 prototype, Front. Neurosci. 12 (2018) 840. Available from: https://doi.org/10.3389/fnins.2018.00840.

[54] L.O. Chua, Memristor-the missing circuit element, IEEE Trans. Circuit Theory ct-18 (5) (1971) 507—519.

[55] L.O. Chua, M.K. Sung, Memristive devices and systems, Proc. IEEE 64 (2) (1976) 209—223.

[56] D.V. Massimiliano, Y.V. Pershin, L.O. Chua, Circuit elements with memory: memristors, memcapacitors, and meminductors, Proc. IEEE 97 (10) (2009) 1717—1724.

[57] B.S. Dmitri, S.S. Gregory, R.S. Duncan, et al., The missing found, Nature 453 (7191) (2008) 80—83.

[58] Z.Q. Wang, T. Zeng, Y.C. Liu, et al., Toward a generalized Bienenstock-Cooper-Munro rule for spatiotemporal learning via triplet-STDP in memristive devices, Nat. Commun. 11 (2020) 1510. Available from: https://doi.org/10.1038/s41467-020-15158-3.

[59] Z.R. Wang, C. Li, J.J. Yang, et al., Reinforcement learning with analogue memristor arrays, Nat. Electron. 2 (2019) 115—124. Available from: https://doi.org/10.1038/s41928-019-0221-6.

[60] D. Chabi, J. Klein, Hight fault tolerance in neural crossbar, in: 5th International Conference on Design and Technology of Integrated Systems in Nanoscale Era (DTIS), 2010, pp. 1—6.

[61] G. Miller, What is the biological basis of consciousness? Science 309 (2005) 79.

Index

Printed in the United States
by Baker & Taylor Publisher Services